# Buy, Keep or Sell?

Judith Miller
and Mark Hill

The first and second editions are a joint production from
DK and THE PRICE GUIDE COMPANY

**Senior Editor** Amber Tokeley
**Project Editor** Sarah O'Neill
**Senior Art Editors** Stephen Knowlden, Karla Jennings
**Designer** Martin Dieguez
**Managing Editor** Julie Oughton
**Managing Art Editor** Heather McCarry
**Art Director** Carole Ash
**Category Publisher** Jackie Douglas
**DTP Designer** Mike Grigoletti
**Digital Library Manager** Scott Stickland
**Digital Image Co-ordinator** Jonathan Brooks
**Production** Joanna Bull

Produced for Dorling Kindersley by

DUNCAN BAIRD PUBLISHING LTD
Castle House, 75-76 Wells Street, London W1T 3QH

**Managing Art Editor** Dan Sturges
**Managing Editors** Caroline Ball, Theresa Bebbington, Julia Charles
**Designers** Rebecca Johns, Gail Jones, Clare Thorpe
**Editors** Rachel Connolly, James Hodgson, Jill Steed, Yvonne Worth, Ann Yelland
**Assistant Editor** Natasha Lomas

THE PRICE GUIDE COMPANY (UK) LTD
**Editors** Emma Clegg, David Lloyd, Sara Sturgess
**Photographers** Graham Rae, Byron Slater, Dave Pincott, Steve Tanner, Martin Spillane, Andy Johnson, John McKenzie

This work was created in conjunction
with the Reader's Digest Association Ltd

2017 EDITION
**Editors** Nishtha Kapil, Zoe Rutland
**Art Editors** Vikas Chauhan, Renata Latipova
**Managing Editors** Gareth Jones, Rohan Sinha
**Managing Art Editors** Lee Griffiths, Arunesh Talapatra
**DTP Designers** Shanker Prasad, Rajesh Singh
**Picture Researcher** Surya Sarangi
**Picture Research Manager** Taiyaba Khatoon
**Jacket Designers** Mark Cavanagh, Dhirendra Singh
**Managing Jackets Editor** Sreshtha Bhattacharya
**Jacket Design Development Manager** Sophia MTT
**Pre-production Manager** Balwant Singh
**Production Manager** Pankaj Sharma
**Producer, pre-production** Jacqueline Street
**Producer** Mandy Inness
**Associate Publishing Director** Liz Wheeler
**Art Director** Karen Self
**Publishing Director** Jonathan Metcalf

This edition published in 2017
First published in Great Britain in 2004 by
Dorling Kindersley Limited
80 Strand, London, WC2R 0RL



A Penguin Random House Company

10 9 8 7 6 5 4 3 2 1
001–298871–Jul/2017



A CIP catalogue record for this book is available from the British Library

ISBN: 978-0-2412-8443-8

Printed and bound in China

A WORLD OF IDEAS:
**SEE ALL THERE IS TO KNOW**

**www.dk.com**

## Editor-in-Chief
**Judith Miller**

## Chief Consultant
**Mark Hill**

## Specialist Consultants

CERAMICS
Beth Adams (Alfie's Antiques Market, London)
Andrew Casey (Lecturer and author)
Joy McCall (Christies, London) – **Clarice Cliff**
Joy Humphries (Feljoy Antiques, London) – **Chintzware**
Marilyn Gentry (Gentry Antiques, Cornwall) – **Cornishware**
Gillian Neale (Dealer) – **Blue & White**

HISTORICAL MEMORABILIA
John Pym (Hope & Glory, London) – **Commemorative Ceramics**
Bill Harriman (BASC) – **Militaria**
Yasha Beresiner (Intercol, London) – **Coins & Scripophily**
Jean Scott (Collector and author) – **Stanhopes & Sewing tools**
Simon Dunlavey (Collector) – **Stamps**

HOUSEHOLD AND KITCHENALIA
Nigel Wiggin (The Old Hall Club, Stafford) – **Stainless Steel**

GLASS
Alan Blakeman (BBR Auctions, Barnsley) – **Bottles**
Graham Cooley (Dealer) – **20th-Century Glass**
Jeanette Hayhurst (Jeanette Hayhurst Fine Glass, London)
Robert Block (Auctionblocks, Connecticut, USA) – **Marbles**

BEAUTY AND FASHION
Alycen Mitchell (Fashion author)
Graham Wilson (70s-watches.com) – **Watches**
Julie Brooke (Price Guide Company UK Ltd.)
Esther and Kirby Harris (Vintage Eyewear of New York) – **Sunglasses**

TOYS, DOLLS, AND TEDDIES
Leigh Gotch (Bonhams, London) – **Toys**
Glenn Butler (Wallis & Wallis, Lewes, Sussex) – **Toys**
Heather Bond (Victoriana Dolls, London) – **Dolls**
Tracie Vallis (Dealer) – **Dolls**

ENTERTAINMENT AND SPORTS
Miles Barton (Dealer) – **Posters**
Nicolette White (Christies, London) – **Posters**
Ted Owen (Cooper Owen, London) – **Rock 'n' Roll and Entertainment Memorabilia**
Manfred Schotten (Manfred Schotten Antiques, Burford) – **Golf**
Charles Kewley (Bonhams, Honiton) – **Fishing**

THE WRITTEN WORD AND EPHEMERA
Geoff West (The Book Palace, London) – **Comics**
Dave Roberts (Carlton Antiques, Worcesteshire) – **Postcards**
Stephen Poole (Biblion, London) – **Books**

TECHNOLOGY AND TRAVEL
Alexander Crum Ewing (Auctioneer) – **Pens**
Hugo Lee-Jones (Electronic Collectables) – **Computer Games**
Peter Boyd-Smith (Cobwebs, Southampton) – **Marine Memorabilia**
Geoff Weiner (C.A.R.S., Brighton, Sussex) – **Automobilia**
Tony Hoskins (Great Western Railwayana Auctions) – **Railwayana**

MODERN DESIGN
Ian Broughton (Manic Attic, Alfie's Antiques Market, London)

## Contributors

Sally Adams, Jessica Bishop, Julie Brooke, Andrew Casey, Alexander Clement, Tarquin Cooper, Daniel Dunlavey, Catherine Early, Sarah Foster, Philip Hunt, Nicholas King, Frankie Leibe, Alycen Mitchell, Joan Porter, Nick Smurthwaite, John Wainwright, Sally Walton,
With special thanks to Beth & Beverley Adams for their help in preparing this second edition. Thanks also to Dominic Winter and Ian Broughton.

## Disclaimer:

While every care has been taken in the compilation of this guide, neither the authors nor the publishers accept any liability for any financial or other loss incurred by reliance placed on the information contained in *Buy, Keep or Sell?*

# Contents

Half dolls, pp238–9

## Ceramics



## Historical Memorabilia



## Household and Kitchenalia

British medals, pp88–9

# Glass

Snow domes, pp234–5

Studio and factory glass, pp158–65

# Beauty and Fashion



# Toys, Dolls, and Teddies



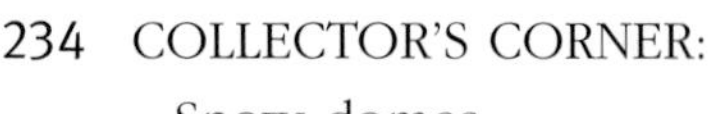

Teddy bears, pp228–31

## Entertainment and Sports

*Doctor Who, pp262-63*



## The Written Word and Ephemera



## Technology and Travel



## Modern Design

*Vintage advertising, pp322–3*

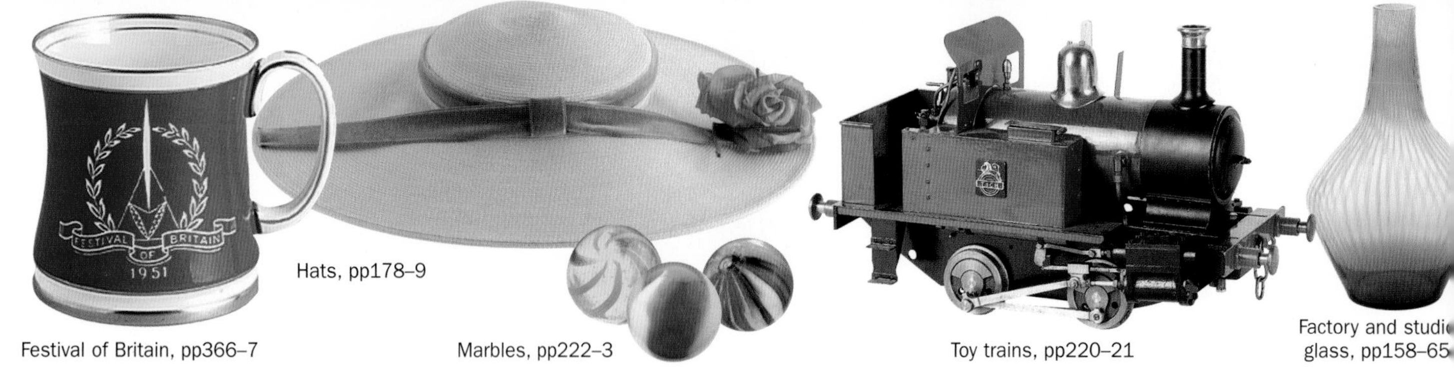

Hats, pp178–9

Festival of Britain, pp366–7

Marbles, pp222–3

Toy trains, pp220–21

Factory and studio glass, pp158–65

# Introduction

I bought my first collectables in the late 1960s, in an Edinburgh junk shop. Those inexpensive blue-and-white plates were just meant to liven up the walls of my student bed-sit. But I soon became intrigued as to who made them, when, where, and whether they were worth more than I'd paid. I was hooked, to the extent that since then much of my working life has been spent collecting, writing about, and broadcasting on antiques and collectables.

## The expanding market

The collectables market has expanded enormously in recent years, fuelled by the publication of annual price guides like mine, TV programmes, collectables fairs, car-boot sales, and Internet auction sites. The latter have created a global market for buyers and sellers.

## Why collect and what's collectable?

People collect for many reasons: the pleasure of displaying beautiful or interesting objects in the home; nostalgia for items associated with childhood or youth, famous people, or events; and financial investment. All are perfectly valid. As the following pages reveal, the range of objects considered collectable is now immense. Traditional areas such as ceramics, glass, and textiles have been augmented with newer, equally sought-after categories as diverse as mobile phones, jelly moulds, sunglasses, and even shoes!

Sunglasses, pp184–5

## Desirability and value

The desirability and value of any collectable is determined by a combination of factors. Fashion plays a major role: the 1950s look has been growing in popularity in recent years and 'Ant' stacking chairs from the period *(see right)* can fetch around £60–100. Quality of design and manufacture are also important: many of Trifari's exquisitely made 'Jelly Belly' brooches of the 1930s have almost doubled in value (from £250 to £500) in the last three years, while their mass-produced, post-war pieces have only risen by around 15 per cent.

The 1950s, pp364–5

Rarity is also highly desirable: a plain blue bud-shaped Whitefriars vase may fetch around £20–30 but a rare two-colour example may fetch up to £1,200. Provenance can be even more compelling: a football

Vintage advertising, pp322–3

Scottie dogs, pp112–13

Computer games, pp272–3

Coca-Cola, pp320–21

Snow domes, pp234–5

### Fakes

*Fakes and forgeries do appear on the market. You can avoid them by buying from reputable dealers or auction houses. Beyond that, the ability to spot fakes comes with experience. Beware of:*

- Incorrect or no maker's marks.
- Wrong proportions or weight (too light or too heavy).
- Unrealistic simulations of natural patination and wear and tear.
- Poorer quality decoration or materials in comparison to an original.

shirt worn by a star player can command a high price, especially if it has a certificate of authenticity to prove it *(see right)*. Apart from the rarest pieces with exceptional provenance, condition is also critical: 'mint and boxed' toys and games can command 30–80 per cent more than slightly damaged equivalents without original packaging. Age, on the other hand, doesn't necessarily confer greater desirability. Many new items become 'instant collectables'. In 2003, a limited-edition model of a *Doctor Who* Dalek, in white rather than ubiquitous grey, was launched at £25. A few weeks later it was changing hands for £50.

A note of caution, however, about limited editions. Some manufacturers advertise runs of 20,000 or more as 'limited edition'. While legitimate, the sheer volume means you won't get your money back in the forseeable future. Remember – for values to rise, demand has to outweigh supply; for this reason, avoid 'limited editions' of more than 1,000 pieces.

Football memorabilia, pp284–7

### State of the market

*The current economic crisis has led to a drop in the values of many collectables, as demand has contracted. However, based on experience of previous recessions, this is likely to be only temporary. The very best dealers and collectors still buy in hard times, as lower prices can mean that something that was previously out of reach is now more affordable. Prices in general should rise again once the recession is over.*

Dr Who, pp262–3

Paperweights, pp148–9

Matchbox and other diecast makers, pp218–9

Plastic dolls, pp242–3

Perfume bottles, pp136–7

Children's books, pp300–1

Radios and TVs, pp336–7

## What to pay

When I started out, deciding what to pay was often a matter of instinct. Nowadays, there is far more specific information available. Publications such as the *DK Collectables Price Guide* give current price trends, as do auction catalogues and internet auction sites such as eBay. You can also keep up with all the latest information by joining a collectors' club *(see Clubs and societies, pp384–87)*, and visiting fairs.

## Where and how to buy

Always look first in your own home, especially the attic. Inherited or previously overlooked pieces provide the starting point for many collectors. Scour 'For Sale' advertisements in local papers and weekly magazines such as *Loot and Exchange & Mart.* Regularly pop into charity shops and junk shops, and go to local jumble sales and car-boot sales. In each case, make up your own mind as to authenticity and

### *Buying at auction*

*Local auction houses are listed in Yellow Pages, while local newspapers often carry notices of forthcoming auctions. The major auction houses usually have their own websites. Alternatively, try sites such as www.invaluable.com or www.antiquestradegazette.com.*

- Buy a sale catalogue through the post or at the auction preview. Mark the lots you are interested in.
- Attend the preview and closely examine the lots, checking especially for condition. For more information, always ask a member of staff.
- Decide the maximum you are prepared to bid. Use the estimated low-to-high price bands in the catalogue as a guide, or ask a member of staff, and factor in the auctioneer's 'buyer's premium' (10–20 per cent plus VAT of the sale price).
- Confirm acceptable methods and timing of payment – the latter is usually within one to three days.
- If required, register your name and contact details in order to bid; you will be given a numbered card or paddle to hold up if your bid is successful. This enables auction staff to note who won the bid.
- If you are unable to go to the sale, leave a written bid (the highest price that you are prepared to pay) with a member of the auction house staff.
- Get to the sale in plenty of time for your first lot. Auctioneers can get through 80–120 lots an hour, sometimes more, so build in a margin of error.
- The auctioneer will start the bidding around the lower catalogue estimate, but will keep lowering it until there is a bid. The bids will then be increased in regular increments, usually of around 10–20 per cent of the bid amount (£10s, £20s, £100s, £1,000s, depending on the lot), until one bidder is left. The auctioneer ends the bidding by banging a gavel on his rostrum.
- Don't worry about coughs or twitches winning you an unwanted lot and a hefty bill. This is a myth. To join the bidding at any stage, catch the auctioneer's attention by holding up your card or paddle, or your catalogue. After acknowledging your first bid, he will accept subsequent bids on the nod of a head – or your withdrawal on a sideways shake of the head.

- Don't get caught up in 'auction fever'. Stick to the price limit you set yourself at the preview.
- Having paid for your lots, you can remove them. Most auction houses request collection within three days, or storage may be added to your bill.

Cornishware, pp104–5 · Salt and pepper shakers, pp122–3 · Jewellery, pp202–3 · Drinking glasses, pp142–3 · Cult TV, pp258–9

value, and politely haggle over the asking price. Always ask for a written receipt, not only for your own records, but also to prove you bought in good faith in case, as very occasionally happens, the object turns out to have been stolen.

Of the various sources dedicated to collectables, auction houses are the most intimidating to new collectors. Don't be put off! Buying at auction is great fun, addictive, and allows you to compete with dealers and other collectors on equal terms. Stick to a few simple rules *(see left, 'Buying at Auction')* and you'll be fine.

Children's books, pp300–1

Professional dealers tend to concentrate on specific collectables, such as those by certain manufacturers or designers. Some dealers trade from shops (names and addresses listed in the Antique Collectors' Club annual *Guide to the Antique Shops of Britain*; some are also listed at the end of this book). Others trade at local, national, or international collectors' fairs (dates and locations flagged on the Internet, in local press, or in leaflets and booklets at many collectables fairs). Some trade from all these places and many also have a website and mail-order service. Establishing friendly relationships with reputable dealers will prove invaluable. They are a great source of information and expertise. If they don't have a particular piece in stock, they can often find it for you through their contacts. After a while they may also offer you first refusal on new acquisitions, and sometimes the more you buy from them, the more generous their discounts.

The newest source of collectables is the Internet. Online auction sites, such as www.ebay.com, have revolutionised the market. You can now bid for Murano glass in Manchester or Staffordshire figures in Salt Lake City: location is no obstacle. Again, don't feel intimidated about stepping into this global shopping

### Cataloguing and insurance

*Since most household contents insurance policies exclude collectables, you should take out an 'All Risks' policy or a special independent policy that covers fire, theft, or accidental loss or damage, and values each piece by the cost of its replacement. To facilitate a claim, catalogue each piece as follows:*

- Photograph it, preferably from several different angles – also showing any damage or identifying features.
- Store photographic prints in a record book; if you use a digital camera, store image files on a disk.
- Keep all receipts, detailing the vendor, purchase date, price paid, and a full description of the piece. If bought at auction, also keep the sale catalogue.

Lamps, pp372-3

Guinness, pp318–19

Studio and factory glass, pp158–65

Keith Murray, pp36–7

### Setting out your stall

*When selling at a car-boot sale or collectables fair, maximise the attractiveness of your wares and encourage buyers to return at a future sale, as follows:*

- Cover your table with neutral, plain-coloured fabric – patterns and vibrant colours won't show off your pieces to best effect.
- Ensure the table is well lit. Augment overhead lighting with desk lamps; an extension cable is invaluable.
- Don't overload the table so that pieces obscure one another.
- Label each piece with an asking price.
- Answer any questions as fully as possible, and in a friendly and enthusiastic manner.
- Be prepared to negotiate over price, but never accept less than your pre-set minimum (and only accept cheques with a cheque guarantee card).
- Present fragile purchases in bubble wrap.

mall; most sellers are keen to help because they want to sell their item. If you ask them questions such as whether they can supply further images of any damage or maker's marks, you should receive a reply. Each site provides user-friendly instructions on how to register, how to contact the seller for additional information, and how to bid. They also give instructions on when and how to pay (including secure electronic systems such as Nochex, Bidpay, or Paypal).

## Care and repair

Collectables that are in good condition not only look better; they also command higher prices than their dirty, worn, or damaged equivalents. Equally, an incorrectly cleaned or badly repaired collectable is invariably worth much less than a slightly shabby or unrestored example. Always entrust any repairs to a professional restorer, and refer to one of the many books on caring for collectables before starting to clean. These give specific do's and don'ts on cleaning the various materials from which collectables are made.

## Where and how to sell

Some of the sources for buying collectables *(see pp10–11)* also apply to selling them. Consider a conventional auction house or an Internet auction site if selling only one or two pieces. The former describes the object for you in a catalogue and markets it to buyers as well as handling the sale for you (for a 'seller's commission' of 10–20 per cent

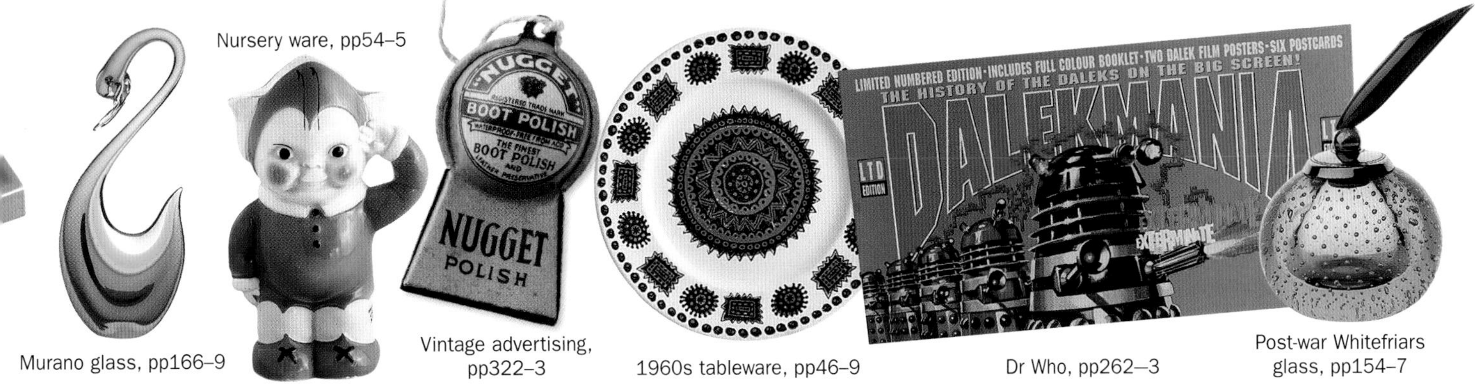


Murano glass, pp166–9

Nursery ware, pp54–5

Vintage advertising, pp322–3

1960s tableware, pp46–9

Dr Who, pp262–3

Post-war Whitefriars glass, pp154–7

Scandinavian glass, pp150–53

plus VAT). The latter (usually for a small fee and commission rate) gives detailed instructions on how to conduct, monitor, and close the sale but you must do all the work yourself, including photography. For both an auction house and an Internet auction site, set a 'reserve' price – the minimum you will accept. A good alternative can be selling direct to dealers: you may be offered as much as you would get at auction, but remember that they will price the object higher when they sell it to cover their overheads and costs.

For larger numbers of collectables under £50 – say, 20 or more – consider paying for a 'pitch' at a car-boot sale (at around £5–30 for the day). For a similar number of more expensive pieces, apply for a stand at a local collectables fair or market. Forthcoming dates, locations, and organisers' details can be found in the *Antiques Trade Gazette*. How well you do depends on the desirability of your pieces, and how realistically they are priced. But basic selling techniques *(see 'Setting out your stall')*, also play an important part.

## Enthusiasm and knowledge

Looking back over the last 30 years, I can conclude that enthusiasm and knowledge maximise pleasure and profit in the world of collectables. The purpose of this book is to inspire that enthusiasm and convey that knowledge. If it does, I'm sure you will derive as much enjoyment from buying, keeping, or selling collectables as I have.

Judith Miller.

# How to use this book

*Buy, Keep or Sell? – The insider's guide to identifying trash, treasure or tomorrow's antiques* is divided into 10 chapters, each devoted to a specific collecting field ranging from ceramics to beauty and fashion. Most of the book is made up of short sections on particular types of collectable: these may focus on the work of a specific designer or manufacturer; on a subject area, such as Scandinavian glass; or on a general collecting field, such as the 1950s. As well as setting the topic in its historic and social context, each section offers an insight into influences, styles, techniques, and market values. Special feature boxes range from *Top Tips* to *A closer look at price comparisons, makers' marks,* or *why a particular piece is special.* Central to the book's theme are the featured *Buy, Keep,* and *Sell* items highlighted at the end of each topic. Scattered through the pages are *Collector's Corner* features which explore specialised collecting themes, such as Barbie dolls or paperweights. At the end of the book there is invaluable information on clubs, societies, specialist dealers, and auction houses.

**The Essentials feature boxes** show either the essential collectables in a featured field, or key designs from a particular designer or manufacturer.

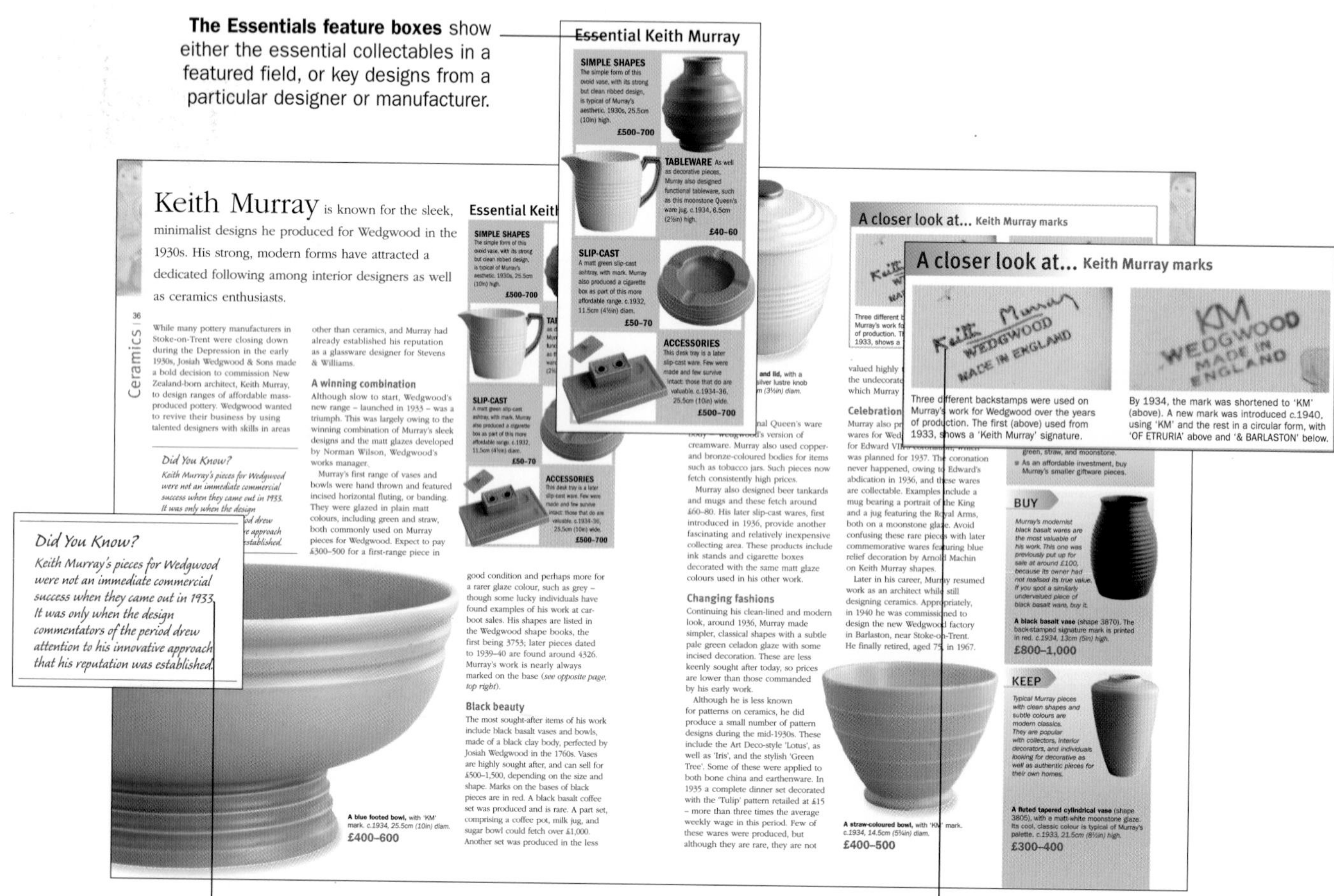

**Did You Know? boxes** are interesting, quirky, or record-beating snippets of information to entertain and enhance your knowledge. *Fact or Fiction?* serves a similar purpose. *Collectors' Tales* are attributed stories from real people about their collecting experiences.

**A closer look** appears in several variations: a closer look at makers' marks (above); at a specific generic item, such as a vase; at an outstanding example of a designer's work; or at price comparisons of two similar yet differently priced items.

**Top Tips** give expert advice on what to look for, care and storage, and how to recognise fakes.

### Top Tips

- Try to buy posters in good condition, without pinholes or tape marks, and don't consider those that have been trimmed or dry-mounted.
- Look for rare variations in poster artwork, which can add to the value.
- Some firms are reproducing original packaging for vintage Bond toys, so pay close attention to copyright notices when considering purchase.

### James Bond

### KEEP

*Toy cars are highly collectable, especially the cars used in the Bond films. As so many were produced, look for those in near mint condition, with the box and any other accessories that came with them.*

**A Corgi James Bond Aston Martin DB5, No 261,** with its original picture box. The Aston Martin DB5 is perhaps the most famous Bond car of all. *1964, 102cm (40in) wide.*

**£80–120**

### Some film posters to look for:

- From Russia With Love
- The Living Daylights

**Some film posters to look for** highlights key examples of the featured subject and gives an overview of relevant information such as styles, inspirations, and techniques.

**Buy, Keep or Sell** identifies a specific type of collectable to buy, keep, or sell and explains why.

COLLECTOR'S CORNER

### Barbie

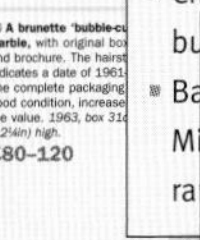

### Collectors' Tips

- Check the Barbie mark, usually on the buttock but occasionally on the shoulder
- Barbie's friends and family – including Ken, Midge, and Scooter – are less valuable but rarer, and their values could rise

**Collector's Corner** is a themed collecting spread that appears regularly throughout the book.

**Captions** give information about the featured collectable and its market value range, based on real prices at auction.

**Collectors' Tips** is a mini-feature giving expert collecting pointers.

# Ceramics

**From the ornate, traditional styles of the 19th century to the colourful, excitingly modern forms of the mid-20th century, ceramic ware offers a huge diversity of styles packed into a relatively short time span.**

Royal Crown Derby vase, p.41

Satsuma vase, p.39

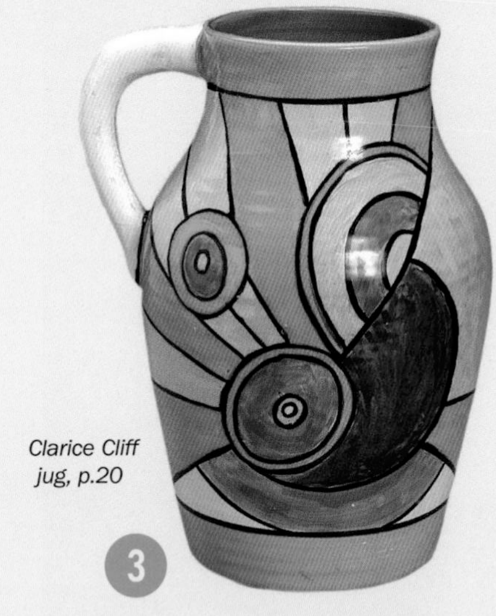

Clarice Cliff jug, p.20

# The evolving styles of....

**Ceramic ware styles are a faithful reflection of the rapidly changing world for which they were created. Industrialisation in the 19th century gave rise to a wealthy middle class with money to spend on household goods, and an insatiable demand for new designs and modern styles.**

Royal Doulton jester figure, p.58

Traditional 19th-century ceramic ware ①, with floral decoration and gilding, was produced by manufacturers such as Royal Worcester and Crown Derby and is as familiar today as it was in its heyday. Consider buying a traditional early 20th-century dinner service instead of a new one; it frequently costs less. Oriental ceramics ② have been exported to the West for centuries. Pieces are sometimes sold at auction as salvage from shipwreck cargoes and there are still some bargains to find, if you're lucky.

## Bold design

But ceramics really started to respond to modernism in the 1920s and 30s, with an explosion of vivid colours and bold, geometric designs. Clarice Cliff ③ and Susie Cooper created pieces that encapsulated the Jazz Age and were the antithesis of traditional styles. Their work is now sought after and expensive. Happily, though, they inspired other manufacturers such as Royal Winton ④, who produced similar, more affordable styles.

Some designers continued to seek inspiration in the past: 1930s chintzware, for

Ceramics really started to respond to modernism in the 1920s and 30s, with an explosion of vivid colours and bold, geometric designs.

Beswick Peter Rabbit figure, p.64

J.H. Cope & Co. wall mask, p.29

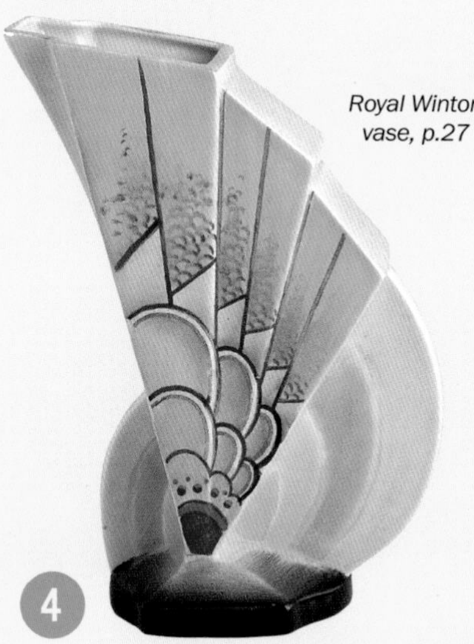


Royal Winton vase, p.27

Keith Murray vase, p.36

Maling bowl, p.31

# ...ceramics

example, was based on the floral fabric designs imported from Asia in the 17th and 18th centuries. The architectural forms, clean lines, and cool, plain colours of Keith Murray's work (5) provide a complete contrast.

Lustre ware (6), with its dazzling, iridescent surfaces, is another example of how traditional elements have been reworked. Carlton Ware produced an outstanding range of Art Deco-style pieces in the 1930s.

## People and animals

Royal Doulton figurines (7), mainly produced from the 1920s onwards, have a strong collectors' following, and animal figurines, including those by SylvaC and others featuring Beatrix Potter characters, (8) can still be found in many homes today.

Other popular ceramics include the cottage ware produced in the 1920s and 30s – pastoral nostalgia in reaction to the upheaval of World War I – ceramic wall masks (9), and nursery ware, which includes the whimsical characters designed by Mabel Lucie Atwell (10).

## What a bargain

Ceramics from the 1950s and 60s by manufacturers such as Midwinter, Beswick, and Portmeirion (11) can often be found at bargain prices. Cylindrical shapes, clean-cut forms, and striking graphic decoration are typical of the period. Many pieces may well rise in value in the future.

Tea set designed by Mabel Lucie Atwell for Shelley, p.54

Portmeirion storage jar, p.47

# Clarice Cliff, the most famous and innovative English designer of Art Deco ceramics, was known as the 'Sunshine Girl', an expression that aptly conjures up the bold patterns and bright colours of her extraordinarily zestful output.

**A Bizarre salt cellar and pepper pot.** The salt cellar is painted with stylised flowers, the pepper pot with yachts under sail. *1930s, salt cellar 8cm (3in) high.*

**£150–200 for the pair**

In their time, Clarice Cliff pieces were outrageous – an exuberant raspberry blown at the drab, boring pottery that she encountered as a student at London's Royal College of Art in 1927. As a result of Cliff's growth in popularity over recent decades, most people are familiar with her extrovert style. Today there is nothing more desirable among ceramic collectables of the 1930s – the demand seems insatiable. While a plate can fetch up to £500 and a jug up to 10 times that amount, small objects such as cruet sets or anything in the 'Crocus' pattern are usually less expensive and make a good starting point for a collection.

## Learning the trade

Born in 1899 in Tunstall, Stoke-on-Trent, Clarice Cliff grew up in a region known for its pottery production. At the age of 13 she began work as an apprentice freehand pottery painter in a local factory. Four years later – at a time when most men were away fighting in World War I, and there was a shortage of workers – she moved to the A.J. Wilkinson Royal Staffordshire Pottery in Burslem. The move proved to be a positive one for Cliff: it was here that she learned the techniques of modelling, gilding, decorating, and designing pottery.

## Brushstrokes

Colley Shorter, the managing director at the factory, soon recognised Cliff's talents. He became her protector, sponsor, lover, and, eventually, her husband. By 1927 Shorter had set up a small studio for Cliff at his own Newport Pottery in Burslem. Inspired by the brilliant colours used by artists such as Pablo Picasso and Henri Matisse, as well as by a visit with Colley to the Paris Exhibition in 1925, Cliff created a range of patterns, which were then copied onto the pottery by a team of assistants. Shorter had supplied Cliff with an old stock of inferior white pottery to work on and, to hide its defects, paint was applied in a thick coating. The design was first outlined in black, then filled in with colour. Brushstrokes were left visible on purpose, to emphasise that these were hand-painted wares. This later

## A closer look at... a Clarice Cliff Lotus jug with 'Sliced Circle' pattern

This jug was made at the height of Bizarre-ware production using the 'Sliced Circle' pattern on a Lotus-shape jug. It is fully marked with Bizarre stamping and signature on the base.

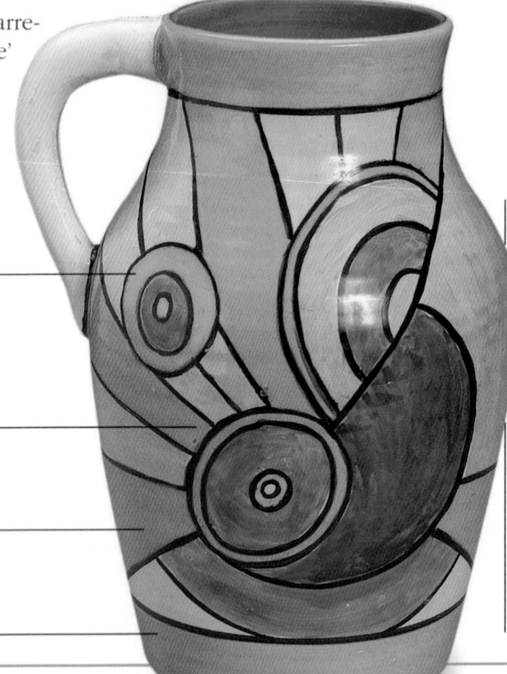


**A 'Sliced Circle' pattern Lotus jug.** *c.1929–30, 29cm (11½in) high.*

**£3,000–5,000**

### Makers' marks

*Rubber-stamped or printed (lithographed) marks were used from 1928 onwards. The stamp sometimes printed unevenly.*

This mark was used around 1929–30. It is a typical printed Fantasque mark. Bizarre replaced the word 'Fantasque' from 1930–36.

became a strong selling point. In 1928 the all-new Bizarre range, which had a distinctive, warm yellow 'honey' glaze, was launched as cheerful, inexpensive domestic pottery. Cliff's designs were shockingly innovative for her era, with their cacophony of bright colours and jazzy geometric shapes.

**An 'Aurea' pattern Bizarre ribbed bowl.** *1930s, 24cm (9½in) diam.*

**£200–300**

## Bizarre tales

Bizarre ware was a phenomenal success, and Cliff's team of lady painters became known as the 'Bizarre Girls' – by late 1928 she had more than 25 painters working for her.

Around 1929 the initial tableware range was expanded to include teapots, bookends, candlesticks, and other decorative 'fancies' (non-essential items) – and the forms and patterns of most of these fulfilled Cliff's love of the extravagant. But she was also practical, creating shapes that 'didn't harbour grease or dust'.

Cliff was appointed art director of the Newport Pottery by 1930, the first woman to achieve such status in the Potteries. Productivity of her Bizarre ware increased dramatically. Within 12 months Clarice Cliff was a household name.

World War II brought with it the decline of hand-painted pottery, with materials in short supply and many of the workers drafted into service.

The year after her husband's death in 1963, Cliff sold both of the factories to W.R. Midwinter Ltd.

## Patterns and shapes

During her long career, Cliff designed more than 2,000 patterns and 500 shapes. Although Bizarre is probably her best-known range, others such as Fantasque (launched in 1928) are also popular, as are her 1930s landscape designs rendered in the Art Deco style and using the same palette of bold, bright colours.

Among Cliff's most sought-after patterns are 'May Avenue', 'Appliqué', 'Inspiration', 'Sunray', 'Mountain', and 'Solitude'. 'Crocus', a bestseller of the time (available 1928–63), is still commonly found. By 1934, it came in

◄ **A 'Crocus' pattern preserve jar and cover,** with printed Bizarre marks. *1930s, 10cm (4in) high.*

**£150–200**

▲ **An 'Autumn' pattern beehive honey pot.** *c.1931, 10cm (4in) high.*

**£250–350**

### *Did You Know?*

*Clarice Cliff's enthusiasm for her designs extended to her home. Her first flat, above a hairdresser's shop in Snow Hill in Hanley, had the 'wow factor'. The lounge walls were covered in bright red paper with large scrolled motifs, the doors were painted in a vivid red, and the chimney breast was decorated with a huge mural of a Bizarre-style scene of giant leaves and lotus flowers painted in orange, red, blue, and black.*

different colour schemes: 'Spring' (with flowers in pale pink, blue, and green), 'Sungleam' (orange and yellow), and 'Autumn' (red, purple, and blue). 'Honolulu', 'Oranges and Lemons', and 'Windbells' – all part of the Bizarre range – are also desirable, as are 'Secrets' and 'Nasturtium'. Particularly collectable shapes include the 1930s Conical range of cone-shaped bowls, vases, and tea ware with triangular handles or feet. Other popular shapes include Bon Jour, Stamford, Biarritz, and Lotus.

## The perfect marriage

The value of a Cliff piece is determined by the combination of its shape and pattern. A circular bowl in the 'May Avenue' pattern is common, so it will not be as valuable as the same pattern on a conical sugar sifter, which is less often seen. The earlier Bizarre pieces are most in demand and consequently fetch the highest prices. But a stunning Bizarre vase will not be worth as much if it is decorated in a pattern that is unfashionable today, such as 'Whisper'.

The appeal of a particular pattern or shape can change according to contemporary tastes. Although the 'Gay Day' pattern has remained consistently popular, the appeal of others, such as 'Latona Red Rose' and 'Inspiration Caprice', has fallen and risen over time, resulting in fluctuating values.

▲ **A 'Delicia Citrus' pattern Athens teacup and saucer.** *1930s, cup 6cm (2½in) high.*

**£200–300**

Clarice Cliff was the first ceramics designer to use fruit and flowers on a large scale and in startling colours – striking images that captured the public's imagination.

▼ **Clarice Cliff painting the Etna charger.**

► **An 'Oranges and Lemons' pattern plate.** *1931–32, 24cm (9½in) wide.*

**£600–800**

## The inside track

Recent prices at auction indicate Cliff's continued popularity, but also demonstrate the importance of condition. An otherwise desirable Bizarre vase, made around 1929, failed to sell at auction because two holes had been drilled into its base to turn it into a lamp.

In general, check spouts and handles for signs of chipping and run a finger around the rims and bases. Make sure a set is complete – a coffee set with a pot and cover, cream jug, sugar bowl, and six cups but only four saucers may fetch about 10 to 20 per cent less than one with all the matching saucers.

Cone-shaped sugar sifters are highly collectable as they are the epitome of Art Deco, but look out for damaged tips and restored holes. Beehive honey pots are also much loved, but check that the lids match the pots and are not replacements.

Most pieces, apart from smaller examples such as salt cellars and pepper pots, carry a printed mark and signature on the base. Look for these when buying a piece.

For those looking for purely decorative pieces there is a strong market in Clarice Cliff reproductions, but these are not a serious collecting area as prices are unlikely to rise.

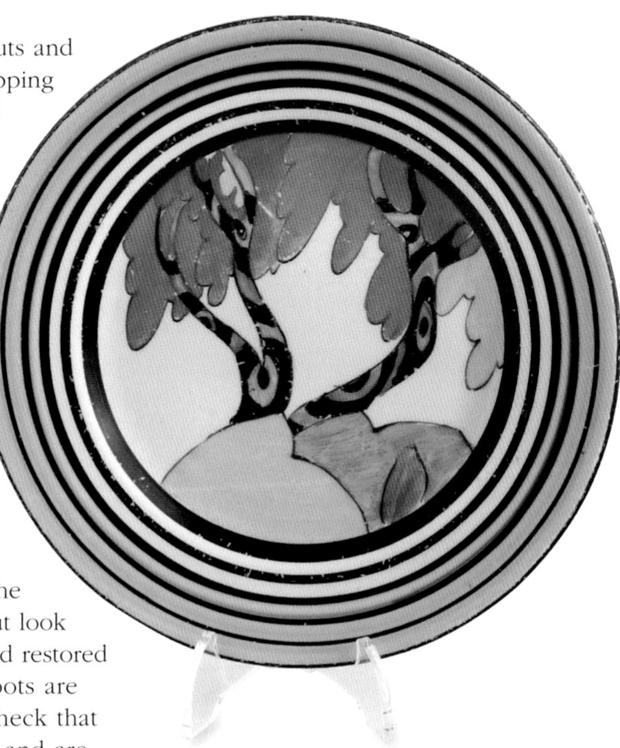

**A 'Honolulu' pattern side plate.** *c.1933, 18cm (7in) diam.*

**£800–900**

**A 'shape 362' vase,** with colourful geometric and triangular design, and blue borders. *c.1930, 19.5cm (7¾in) high.*

**£800–1,200**

### *Did You Know?*

*After 30 years on top of a wardrobe, a never-before-seen c.1932 Clarice Cliff charger in the desirable 'May Avenue' pattern set a new world auction record. After much frantic bidding, it sold for £39,950 at Christie's, South Kensington. Chargers are rare anyway, but the unusual colour, large size of 46cm (18in) diameter, and immaculate condition made collectors the world over long to add it to their collections. The inspiration for the 'May Avenue' design came from an oil painting by the Italian artist Modigliani, and the name of the design was taken from a street near Cliff's Tunstall birthplace.*

### *Top Tips*

- Opt for rarer colour variations such as blue or purple. These can often fetch a higher price than the more common orange-coloured pieces.
- Look for wares that are thickly painted with visible brushstrokes and have designs outlined in black. These typify early Cliff and are much sought after.
- Expand your collection with non-geometric patterns and shapes that show hallmarks of Cliff's typical designs.
- Beware of fakes. Telltale signs include wishy-washy colours, an uneven 'honey' glaze, and artificial crackling in the glaze around the mark to simulate age.
- On a jug handle, look for a blow hole, indicating that it has been hollow cast – a sure sign of a fake, as the handles on Cliff's originals were always solid.
- Check that all the pieces in a set match. Examine lids carefully to make sure that they are original. Patterns should line up exactly, with the design sometimes flowing from the body onto the lid.

### KEEP

*The 'Crocus' pattern is one of Cliff's most popular designs and was a bestseller in its day. Look for shapes that epitomise Art Deco, such as this cone-shaped sugar sifter. Pieces with appealing designs on typical Art Deco shapes are increasingly sought after and should rise in value.*

**A 'Crocus' pattern conical sugar sifter.** The brown band was meant to represent the earth and the yellow band the sun. *1930s, 14.5cm (5¾in) high.*

**£400–600**

### SELL

*Pieces in muted colours, such as this preserve pot, are not as popular with collectors, who want the colourful, stylised, geometric look. Sell this and invest in a piece more typical of Cliff.*

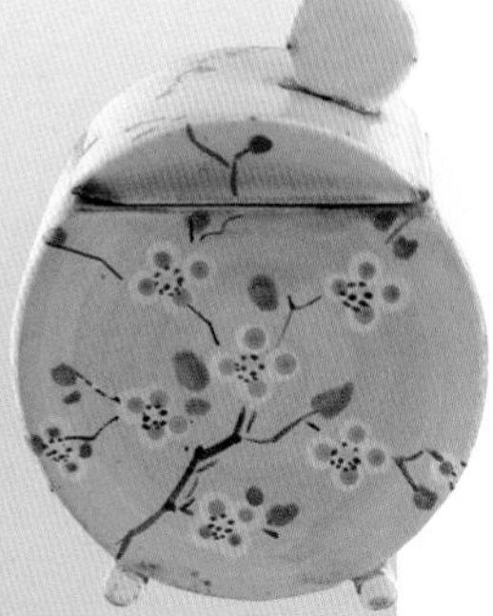

**A 'May Blossom' pattern Bon Jour preserve pot and cover.** The piece is damaged, which reduces its value. *c.1936, 10cm (4in) high.*

**£40–50**

# Susie Cooper, one of the most influential ceramics designers of the 20th century, had a passionate belief that good design should not cost the Earth. Her style is as fresh today as it was in the 1930s.



Born into a middle-class family in the Potteries in 1902, Susie Cooper was hardly a typical factory worker. She joined local pottery A.E. Gray & Co. Ltd to gain the experience of working in the decorative arts that she required to attend London's Royal College of Art. Initially Cooper was a production-line painter, but her talents were soon recognised. Instead of going to study in London, she became a designer at Gray's, working on its Gloria Lustre range, a silver-medal winner at the 1925 Paris Exhibition.

## Bands of colour

Cooper was influenced by other artists, particularly Paul Cézanne and Frank Brangwyn, but her contribution to the company's style – hand-painted floral and abstract patterns with thick bands of colour – was highly personal.

Gray's used a factory mark with the words 'Designed by Susie Cooper' under a steamship – a pictorial designer mark of the type that came into vogue in the 1930s. In response to the new demand for brightly coloured wares, Cooper introduced geometric patterns such as 'Moon and Mountains' and the modern 'Cubist' on a large range of household wares. These daring designs became her trademark and are still favourites among collectors. But seeing these geometric designs as 'crude', she was most proud of her banding – juxtaposed thin and thick bands in muted or bright colours.

## A rising star

Cooper left Gray's in 1929, setting up on her own in premises at the Chelsea Works, Burslem, in 1930. She painted white-ware blanks with simple banded and stylised floral patterns similar to those she had developed at Gray's, marking them 'A Susie Cooper Production'. Business prospered. Wood & Sons, a successful local pottery, approached Cooper with an offer to make earthenware to her own designs and provide her with a larger studio. In 1931, she moved to its Crown Works and began to mark her wares with the leaping deer mark most often associated with her work.

The early 1930s were the most dazzling years for Cooper. She was a rising star in pottery design and she also controlled the production process,

**A Susie Cooper 'Seagull' side plate with printed marks.** *c.1930, 17.5cm (6¾in) diam.*

**£300–350**

designing patterns and shapes together. Her modernist sculptural forms, such as the Kestrel and Falcon ranges, were designed to be both visually interesting and functional.

Cooper's work offered a marriage of elegance and utility. Her artistry was rooted in commercial sense as well as practicability.

## Beautifully practical

Teapots and coffee pots poured perfectly, and tureens had lids that doubled as dishes, stacking neatly to save space. Cooper extended the forms to include ashtrays, vinegar bottles, chamber pots, butter dishes,

## Essential Susie Cooper

**EARLY WORK** This lemonade jug is an example of Cooper's work for A.E. Gray & Co. Ltd in the 1920s, when flowers and chintzware were popular. c.1928, 18.5cm (7¼in) high.

**£250–350**

**TOWARDS ART DECO** The beginnings of Art Deco stylisation can be seen on this floral box's coloured curves and frieze-like decoration. c.1928, 6.5cm (2½in) high.

**£200–250**

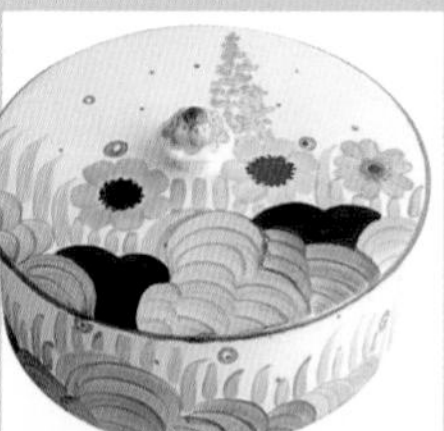

**ART DECO** With a brightly coloured Art Deco pattern this 'Moon and Mountains' jug is simple in form, with clean lines and a modern-style handle. c.1928, 12cm (4¾in) high.

**£200–300**

**NURSERY WARE** By the 1930s, Cooper's nursery ware was whimsical and colourful. This plate carries the rare 'Guardsman' pattern. c.1936–37, 16cm (6¼in) diam.

**£180–220**

**RESTRAINED DESIGN** Such cool colours and restrained classical lines are typical of the 1930s. c.1935, coffee pot 28cm (11in) high.

**£200–300 the set**

**LATE STYLE** The design of the 'Chinese Fern' plate, with its leaflike motif and dark green colour, is characteristic of Cooper's late mass-produced ware. c.1947, 25cm (9¾in) diam.

**£35–45**

lamp stands, and nursery ware. The demand for Cooper's work led her to use lithography at a time when few firms were using mechanical decoration. She worked closely with lithographic printers to create patterns that best suited both the technique and her wares. Borders remained hand painted. One of the most popular patterns was 'Dresden Spray', first used in 1935.

## Modern yet timeless

By the late 1930s, Cooper was producing up to 200 new designs a year, featuring banding, polka dots, and stylised flowers. Patterns that were both modern and timeless, such as 'Patricia Rose' and 'Endon', were key to her success, appealing to a far wider public than the work of many of her contemporaries.

In 1942 a fire destroyed Cooper's factory, but it reopened after the war. Colours became more subdued, and plant forms were introduced. In 1947 several patterns were shown at the first post-war British Industries Fair, including 'Chinese Fern' and 'Tree of Life', mostly on wares exported to South Africa and North America. Cooper purchased the Jason China Co. Ltd in 1950, and by 1952 the same patterns were used on both china and earthenware. Production of earthenware ended in 1964.

**A Susie Cooper for Grays cup and saucer, hand painted with an Art Deco design.** *c.1929, Cup 7cm (2¾in) high.*

**£150–200**

**A hand-painted geometric coffee pot.** *c.1928, 20.5cm (8in) high.*

**£350–450**

*Did You Know?*

*A total of 50 painters were employed at the Susie Cooper Pottery in 1939. The room in which they worked was studiously quiet, and the women talked in whispers. The atmosphere was very different in Clarice Cliff's Bizarre Shop, where there was a radio on all day – apparently to deter the painters from talking.*

Cooper's Kestrel wares, and the bold patterns of early works such as 'Cubist', are likely to retain their current appeal. The restrained quality and detail often found on the litho-printed designs, such as 'Dresden Spray', make these later wares equally sought after, especially among Japanese collectors.

### Top Tips

- Note that an 'A' next to the pattern number on a piece of Gray's pottery dates it after 1933 and shows that it was not designed by Susie Cooper.
- Make sure that lids on tea and coffee pots are in good condition – damage lowers value.
- Look for important early wares such as those with the floral 'Freesia' pattern. They can still be bought reasonably.

### BUY

*Unlike Clarice Cliff, Cooper designed both patterns and shapes. Many collectors consider her the most innovative force in 20th-century ceramic design. Pieces that combine typical Cooper shapes and patterns, such as this coffee set, can sometimes be found at very good prices at car-boot sales.*

**A 'Green Feather' coffee set.** Introduced in 1937, the Falcon shape is decorated here with the delicate 'Green Feather' pattern. *c.1957, coffee pot 19cm (7½in) high.*

**£150–250**

### KEEP

*Cooper's early geometric hand-painted designs are highly sought after. These patterns were popular at the end of the 1920s because they combined originality and affordability. They had a short lifespan, as tastes changed in the early 1930s, and this raises their value.*

**A geometric plate.** The vivid colours and Art Deco design represent the best of Cooper's geometric ware. This example would be worth keeping as demand for her most typical work increases. *c.1929, 22cm (8½in) diam.*

**£300–400**

# 1930s ceramics, like most other areas of the visual arts at the time, were hugely influenced by Art Deco. The vogue for Clarice Cliff and Susie Cooper has stimulated a growing interest in less expensive pieces by smaller manufacturers.

**A Wilkinson 'Memory Lane' jardinière,** with stylised trees and landscape in the manner of Clarice Cliff. *1930s, 21.5cm (8½in) diam.*

**£100–150**

The 1930s were a time of high unemployment, especially in the north of England, yet there were many bright sparks of light amid the gloom. Architecture, the cinema, fashion, and café society flourished. Cocktail parties continued the gaiety of the 1920s, and the arts reflected an interest in exotic cultures. On a more day-to-day level, Britain's new building programme produced stylish, modern homes complete with electric appliances and plumbed-in bathrooms.

## Mix and match

To suit these new homes, 1930s ceramics were bright and bold, often using the colourful geometric patterns pioneered by designers such as Clarice Cliff. Mostly made in earthenware rather than the more costly bone china, Art Deco ceramics were first dismissed as a passing fancy by the more traditional makers. But it soon became clear that the style was here to stay.

## Art Deco on the map

The vogue for hand-painted decoration gave designers a broad palette with which to express new ideas. The influential 1925 Paris Exhibition, often seen as the starting point of Art Deco, featured pieces that imprinted the style on the popular consciousness.

Smaller British makers, such as A.E. Gray & Co. Ltd, Myott, Crown Devon, and Wade Heath, responded quickly to these changing tastes, and developed subjects and patterns that included ladies in crinolines, stylised floral motifs, leaping deer, sun-ray and geometric designs, budgerigars and parrots, and the ever-popular cottage scene.

## Drawing a blank

Many smaller firms could not afford to invest in the production of new shapes, and were forced to use their new jazzy patterns on forms that had been created 30 years earlier. Art Deco decoration on a Victorian teapot created an uncomfortable hybrid, and such pieces do not find as much

## Some makers to look for:

- Wade Heath
- Crown Devon
- Burleigh Ware

**A Wade Heath vase.** Although better known for its nursery ware patterns, this notable pottery introduced several Art Deco lines. *1930s, 18.5cm (7¼in) high.*

**£150–200**

**A Crown Devon 'Matilda' fairy castle vase.** Crown Devon enjoyed great success during the 1930s. This pattern echoed the early designs by Daisy Makeig-Jones for Wedgwood. *1930s, 20.5cm (8in) high.*

**£400–600**

**A Burleigh Ware parrot vase** with its liner. Burleigh Ware produced a wide range of unusual vases featuring various moulded motifs, including birds and soldiers, all with a bold egg-yellow glaze. *1930s, 19cm (7½in) high.*

**£150–200**

favour with collectors. Fortunately, a number of manufacturers, such as Gray's, often bought in blank wares from suppliers of undecorated pottery on which to apply their own patterns. They produced pieces in a style similar to Clarice Cliff's but painted with softer colours. A typical successful example is the Losol ware cheese dish by Gray's, which shows a traditional country cottage scene in bright, bold colours.

## Geometry and relief

Another name to look out for is the Shelley factory. Keep an eye open for items that epitomise Art Deco – those with bright colours and geometric patterns. Charlotte Rhead, another potter of note, was a skilled 'tube-line' decorator, creating designs with a raised outline in liquid clay. Rhead worked on many pottery ranges, including Crown Ducal, using this technique.

The 1930s were a time for fun and frivolity – people wanted exciting colours and patterns to chase away their deeper forebodings.

### *Fact or Fiction?*

*Colourful and typically Art Deco, Myott ware perhaps ought to be more highly valued. But collectors can't find any information on the factory, its production, or its designers, as all the company records and pattern books were destroyed in a factory fire in 1949. However, a keen-eyed member of the Myott Collectors' Club has reported seeing a pattern book in Leeds recently. If it does exist, it would not only shed much-needed light on designers and production: it could also help values to rise.*

### Top Tips

- Resist wares with plain decoration or chintzy patterns – they are less popular. Look instead for examples with angular, unusual shapes.
- Check hand-painted pieces for flaking, as any such damage will reduce value.
- Always look in charity shops and car boot sales: many people still ignore pieces unless they are by 'big' names, such as Clarice Cliff or Susie Cooper.

**An early Crown Devon jug,** hand painted with a geometric design. *1930s, 8.5cm (3½in) high.*

**£150–200**

### BUY

*One notable, yet lesser-known, maker active in the Art Deco period was Myott & Son. It produced a diverse range of unusual shapes decorated with bold and abstract patterns reflecting the influence of ancient cultures, such as the Aztecs. Its most desirable pieces are still affordable and, as interest and knowledge grows, may rise in value (see Fact or Fiction?, left).*

**A Myott Star vase,** hand painted. *1930s, 22cm (8¾in) high.*

**£140–160**

■ Royal Winton ■ Shelley ■

**A Royal Winton vase.** This hand-painted vase is quite different from the popular chintz designs that established Royal Winton's reputation and is testimony to the firm's ability to adapt to changing tastes. *1930s, 23cm (9in) high.*

**£150–200**

**A Shelley Vogue-shape trio set,** 11474, in green. Shelley was a prolific manufacturer, producing work in many different styles. Bright colours and geometric shapes and patterns are typical of its Art Deco ranges. *c.1931, larger plate 16cm (6¼in) diam.*

**£180–220**

### KEEP

*Shelley used bone china, rather than earthenware, for its range of Vogue wares designed by Eric Slater, which borrowed their clean and streamlined shapes from the architecture of the period. This design is likely to become a period classic, so hold on to a complete set if you have one.*

**A Shelley 'Sun Ray' Vogue-shape coffee set,** 11742. The solid triangular handle is as overtly Art Deco as the 'Sun Ray' pattern. *c.1935, jug 18cm (7in) high.*

**£1,000–1,500**

# Ceramic wall masks

## were inspired by the wooden tribal African face masks eagerly collected during the 1930s. Many lovers of kitsch and Art Deco find this unusual form of portraiture irresistible. It makes a striking feature on a staircase wall.



Unlike the tribal masks that inspired them, ceramic wall masks of the 1930s to 50s were given the bold colours and sharp contours of the period. Most masks were female, which allowed for a full exploration of flamboyant fashions in hair, make-up, and dress. The most important makers were the central Europeans Goldscheider, Goebel, and Royal Dux, based in Austria, Bavaria, and Bohemia respectively. In Britain, the outstanding makers were Beswick, which had made its name in tableware and also produced popular animal figurines, and J.H. Cope of Staffordshire, which has a reputation for domestic ceramics. The masks often featured screen goddesses of the day, such as Marlene Dietrich, Dorothy Lamour, and Greta Garbo. Anonymous young women were also shown, modelling fashionable styles such as cropped, boyish hair. Masks were produced in various poses, as well as in groups, and faces often had idealised features such as arched eyebrows and almond eyes.

The 1950s examples displayed much more highly made-up faces, consistent with the post-war return to glamour in women's fashions. Dietrich, for example, was shown with high-arched, plucked eyebrows, almond eyes, yellow hair, and, on some of the Beswick models, a rakish French beret.

▲ **A plaster reproduction face wall mask of Betty Grable,** a favourite pin-up actress during World War II. *1950s, 25.5cm (10in) high.*

**£35–45**

▲ **A miniature Goldscheider wall mask** with short, black hair elaborately coiffed. The butterfly is a delicate feature and should be inspected for damage or repair. *c.1925–28, 11.5cm (4½in) high.*

**£250–350**

▲ **A J.H. Cope & Co. wall mask** featuring a blonde with typically 1930s hair and make-up, wearing a hat with feather trim. *c.1934, 30.5cm (12in) wide.*

**£60–80**

► **A Beswick wall mask** with a high-fashion Art Deco look and a high-gloss glaze typical of a pre-World War II example. *1930s, 30.5cm (12in) high.*

**£200–250**

◄ **A rare Goldscheider wall mask** with finely modelled features and elaborate hair. This manufacturer is known for good modelling and painting, as well as fine materials. *c.1925–28, 21.5cm (8½in) high.*

**£800–900**

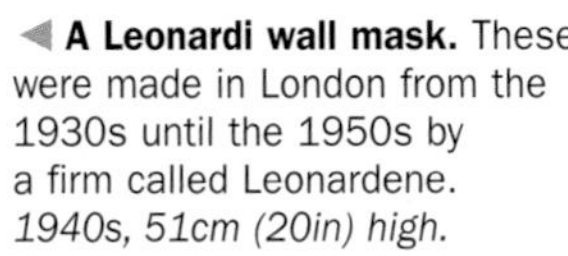

◀ **A Leonardi wall mask.** These were made in London from the 1930s until the 1950s by a firm called Leonardene. *1940s, 51cm (20in) high.*

**£80–120**

◀ **A Goldscheider wall mask** with half-closed eyes and black ringleted 'gypsy' hair. *c.1925–28, 25.5cm (10in) high.*

**£600–700**

▶ **A faithfully painted plaster reproduction of a 1940s face wall mask.** *1980s, 25.5cm (10in) high.*

**£35–45**

▶ **A J.H. Cope & Co. wall mask** featuring a stylish lady in left profile with a hat and lustrous black hair. *c.1934, 16.5cm (6½in) high.*

**£80–120**

◀ **A Goebel wall mask** with superb modelling and hand-painting, further distinguished by the richness of the hair and the coquettish expression. *c.1928–34, 20cm (8in) high.*

**£180–200**

## Collectors' Tips

Look out for these desirable features:

- Good-quality painting and modelling
- Period details including accessories, hair styles, and make-up
- Signs of ageing that suggest a piece is genuine

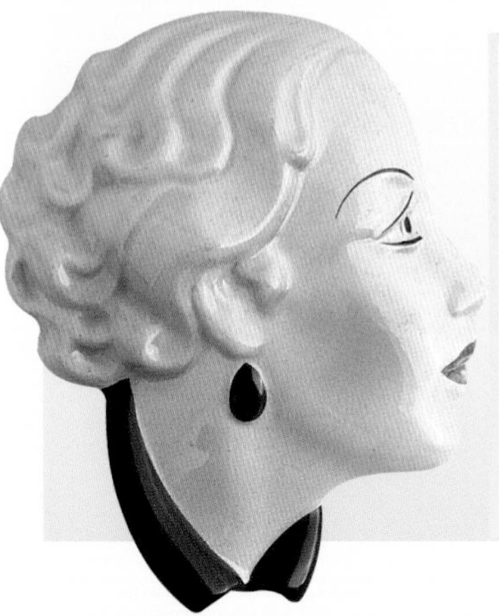

◀ **A J.H. Cope & Co. wall mask** with high-gloss glazing, featuring a fashionable, typically 1930s woman. Cope is a popular manufacturer and this is one of their rarer right-profile masks. *c.1934, 18cm (7in) high.*

**£50–60**

◀ **A miniature Goldscheider wall mask.** Black face masks are less common than white examples. *c.1925–8, 11.5cm (4½in) high.*

**£250–300**

# Lustre ware has a shimmering iridescence of colour, mysterious and fascinating to the eye. This unusual quality, together with the great range of forms and patterns available, underlies its appeal.

**An A.E. Gray & Co. Ltd silver-resist lustre cigarette box and cover,** with wear to lustre. Made in Stoke-on-Trent. *1930s, 10cm (4in) long.*

**£8–12**

Lustre ware is produced by applying a thin metallic paint onto a pottery glaze. The technique can be traced back to Persia in AD 800, and is also associated with Granada in Spain in the 14th century and northern Italy in the 16th. Most lustre pieces on the market today were made from the 19th century onwards, with many reasonably priced examples dating from the 1930s to the 50s. Four different metals are used in lustre ware: silver, gold, copper, and platinum. Only platinum produces a silver tint: silver yields a straw colour, gold creates shades of red from yellowish to ruby, and copper yields a deep copper colour.

**A Wedgwood 'Fairy in a Cage' Fairyland lustre bowl,** designed by Daisy Makeig-Jones, the exterior with the Woodland Elves VII-Toadstool pattern. *23cm (9in) diam.*

**£4,000–5,000**

## Exotic appeal

The popularity of lustre ware in the Victorian era can be traced back to Wedgwood, who were refining ancient lustre techniques in the 1770s for the market of the day. In the early 19th century, Wedgwood mostly used copper lustres, reserving the more costly platinum for a 'silver-resist' effect, and gold for exotic pieces. The appeal of lustre ware for the Victorians was its exoticism, combined with its heavy decoration and colour. The early Victorians also covered whole items in silver-resist lustre to give the impression that a piece was made of silver. The lustre in such pieces can wear thin and become patchy. In this condition, they are not greatly valued.

## The century turns

In the late 19th and early 20th centuries, developments in oxidisation technology improved the purity of lustre liquids. Other manufacturers in Britain – including the Staffordshire, Swansea, Sunderland, and Leeds potteries – adopted the technique, applying it to earthenware and porcelain. They gave their wares a uniquely British style, which met with a good response from their customers.

The 'splatter' technique, in which only a little lustre was applied, was

## Some makers to look for:

- Wedgwood
- Carlton Ware

▲ **A Carlton Ware bowl** with (scratched) mottled glaze and gilt highlights. Carlton's lustre wares typically have dark back-grounds, in blue, red, or black. *c.1930s, 22.5cm (8¾in) diam.*

**£80–120**

used by the Sunderland potteries. Their ranges of pink lustre wares, transfer-printed with pictures and mottoes or rhymes, are highly collectable.

## Shimmering fairytales

Wedgwood continued to produce lustres from around 1917, making a series of Ordinary Lustre pieces decorated with dragons, fish, and butterflies. These were developed by Daisy Makeig-Jones, one of the firm's most respected designers. Ordinary Lustre was followed by her Fairyland range of more intricate and sparkling effects. These were inspired by a mixture of fairytales, exotic landscapes, and mythology – evoked in patterns such as 'Ghostly Wood', 'Candlemas', 'Bubbles', and 'Lahore'. Their brilliant colours and designs gave the company a commercial edge. Expensive when launched, the Fairyland pieces are more sought after than the Ordinary Lustre range and fetch high prices.

## In Wedgwood's wake

The success of the Fairyland lustres influenced other manufacturers including Crown Devon, Royal Winton, and Carlton Ware, although these never achieved the quality of Wedgwood, or the prices that Fairyland pieces command in today's market. Carlton Ware produced an outstanding range of Art Deco pieces in colourful lustres, such as 'Jazz', 'Mikado', and 'Barges', and these can fetch high prices, depending on their size, pattern, and shape.

The smaller manufacturer A.E. Gray & Co. Ltd produced lustre wares from the 1920s to 50s. Some of the earliest, most desirable patterns were designed by Susie Cooper and Gordon Forsyth, and feature dragons and leaping deer. These patterns appeared on plaques and ginger jars, which were probably used in showrooms and on trade stands, but many were also sold commercially. At the cheaper end of the market, in the 1950s Gray's revived the 'Sunderland Splatter' technique for a popular range of giftwares, often incorporating black-and-white prints of shells and ships.

**A Maling lustre bowl,** decorated in pattern 4075, with the Maling castle mark. *1930s, 25.9cm (10in) diam.*

**£50–60**

### Top Tips

- Check the standard of potting and painting on pieces of copper lustre ware. Fine examples of landscape and still-life painting can be found, but quality varies.
- Beware of thin, patchy areas where over-zealous cleaning has removed layers of lustre. Also, clean your own collection with care, using distilled water.
- Look out for silver-resist lustre on a canary yellow or blue ground; this is less common than the more usual white ground.

### KEEP

*The condition of Sunderland lustre ware greatly affects its value, as so much of it was produced. Look out for marine or political themes that tell a story of the time.*

**A Sunderland jug,** with ochre lustre ovals, printed and painted with the ship The Unfortunate London on one side and a verse on the other (both sides are shown). Slightly damaged. *c.1850s, 14.5cm (5¾in) high.*

**£50–80**

## ▪ Royal Winton ▪ Ruskin Pottery ▪

**A Royal Winton lustre floral centrepiece,** decorated with a yellow rose motif. Royal Winton is better known for lustre wares in brighter colours than this. *1930s, 32cm (12½in) wide.*

**£15–20**

► **A Ruskin Pottery vase,** glazed in a mottled mauve lustre, with an impressed date. Ruskin Pottery was renowned for its high-fired glazes in vibrant colours. *1925, 25.5cm (10in) high.*

**£400–600**

### KEEP

*Carlton Ware went into lustre wares after the commercial success of Wedgwood's Fairyland range. Carlton Ware's chinoiserie pattern lustre-style pieces are immensely popular. Look carefully at the condition of this type of ware, as the enamel can easily be rubbed or chipped.*

**A Carlton Ware 'New Mikado' pattern Rouge Royale ginger jar,** decorated with chinoiserie scenes. The shape complements the oriental pattern. *1940s–50s, 23cm (9in) high.*

**£250–350**

# Floral ceramics of the 1930s and 50s encompass a range of styles, from intricate, colourful and complex patterns evocative of the past, to strikingly modern abstract designs that raced headlong into an exciting future.

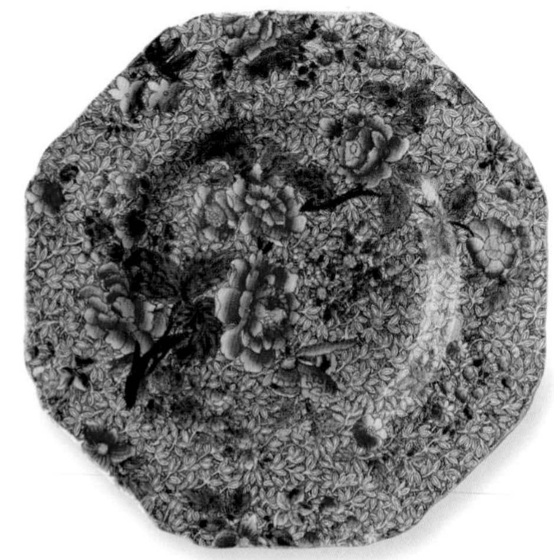

**A Spode 'New Fayence' chintz dessert plate,** with sheet transfer background and large hand-painted flowers. *c.1820, 21.5cm (8½in) wide.*

**£20–30**

Among the most popular examples of floral ceramics are tea, coffee, and other tablewares printed with an all-over pattern. Known as 'chintz' (from the Hindi word *chhintna*, meaning 'to sprinkle with'), these intricate patterns were inspired by floral fabrics imported to the West on East India Company ships in the late 17th century. In the 1820s handpainting was superseded by an underglaze transfer-printing process. Improved multicolour transfer techniques were developed in the late 19th century.

## A festival of flowers

Production of chintzware began in the early 19th century, with dressing-table washing sets (including wash bowl, jug, and candlesticks) and tableware. Most pieces were unmarked and produced in Staffordshire-based factories: those that are marked are usually by Spode. Some of the chintzware produced during this period is characterised by ornate forms, muted colours, and spaces between the flowers. The background is often a transfer, and the flowers may be hand painted – in which case the petals will have slightly uneven brushstrokes, rather than the uniform colour found on a transfer.

◄ **A Royal Winton 'Marguerite' chintz cup and saucer.** *1930s, cup 7.5cm (3in) high.*

**£20–30**

▼ **A Royal Winton 'Summertime' chintz sandwich tray.** *c.1950, 31cm (12¼in) wide.*

**£20–30**

Production of chintzware peaked during the 1930s and 50s. Compared to 19th-century pieces, examples from this period have compact designs, with little space between the flowers, and bright colours. Patterns were given cheerful names evocative of the flowers themselves, such as 'Primula' and 'Sweet Pea'. Simple shapes were adopted to match the taste for clean-lined Art Deco.

## Notable names

Most items are marked with a maker's name, one of the most notable being Royal Winton, owned by the Grimwade brothers, whose chintzware is extremely popular. Royal Winton developed a new lithographic transfer-printing process using flexible paper to transfer the pattern so that complex shapes could be covered without the paper tearing. Royal Winton ceramics always bear the shape name stamped into the base with the pattern name printed nearby. Other notable makers of chintzware include Wade, Crown Ducal, and Shelley.

The popularity of chintzware has grown dramatically over the past decade, especially in North America. As so many pieces were made in the 1930s and 50s, it is still widely available, with smaller, more common pieces in standard patterns such as Royal Winton's 'Summertime' often priced at less than £30. Prices for plates, trays, teapots, and other decorative tablewares are now generally more affordable than over the past few years.

## Radical change

The hand-thrown, hand-painted pottery produced by Carter, Stabler & Adams Ltd, now known as Poole Pottery, started a new movement against conventional style. Along with Clarice Cliff and Susie Cooper, the company offered a new interpretation of floral decoration, with bold, colourful, and often abstract designs in place of more traditional motifs. It swiftly earned a reputation for its bright, exuberant patterns, created chiefly by the designer Truda Carter. Most pieces are in soft yellows, bright blues, and greens on a glazed white body. The flowers are stylised and often combined with geometric motifs typical of Art Deco. Designs featuring birds and animals are much prized.

## Rising prices

An increasing demand for 1930s pieces by Carter, Stabler & Adams Ltd has led to rapidly escalating prices – the highest prices are paid for items with

**A Royal Winton 'Hazel' chintz three-bar toast rack.** *1934, 11.5cm (4½in) long.*

**£30–40**

## A closer look at... a Poole Pottery vase

The designs produced by Carter, Stabler & Adams Ltd in the 1930s are the most sought after of the Poole Pottery products. Prices have risen considerably over the past few years, making examples that show typical decoration and form valuable.

The Art Deco shape and decoration appeal to collectors

The blue, green, brown, and yellow colours are typical of Poole Pottery in this period

The zigzag pattern is highly desirable

**A Carter, Stabler & Adams Ltd earthenware vase** decorated in an Art Deco pattern designed by Truda Carter. *c.1934–37, 24.7cm (9¾in) high.*

**£600–800**

### Makers' marks

*All pieces are clearly marked on the base, bearing an impressed stamp with the factory name, a painted symbol identifying the painter of the piece, and a number-and-letter combination signifying the pattern name and period of production.*

A typical impressed mark found on the base of a Carter, Stabler & Adams Ltd piece from the 1930s.

**A Carter, Stabler & Adams Ltd jug,** with a pattern by Truda Carter, painted by Ruth Pavely. Impressed 'Poole England' and marked '321_ED' alongside the painter's mark. *1930s, 12cm (4¾in) high.*

**£60–80**

### *Top Tips: chintzware*

- Examine chintz patterns closely, as many of them differ only minutely from others.
- Choose chintzware on which the pattern covers as much of the surface as possible, even the inside of handles – such pieces tend to be preferred by collectors, which makes them more valuable.
- Avoid chipped or cracked pieces, as these are worth substantially less. As so much chintzware was produced, it is essential to find pieces that are in good condition.
- Examine pieces for gaps in the pattern (between transfers) – these can devalue a piece, although some collectors like them.

visual impact, such as large bowls, and heavily stylised decoration. Smaller or later pieces, which often lack the tight detail and energy of earlier designs, are less expensive, but may rise in value as demand for top-quality early examples outstrips supply.

**A hand-painted Radford dish.** *1930s, 21.5cm (8½in) diam.*

**£10–20**

## Floral relief

William Moorcroft, a ceramicist working from around 1901 to his death in 1945, had a huge influence on floral Art Nouveau ceramics. He headed the art-pottery department at Staffordshire's MacIntyre & Co., before founding his own factory in 1913. Moorcroft used a tube-lining technique to pick out his patterns – slip, or thin, liquid clay was squeezed through a narrow glass tube onto the surface of the ware. The Moorcroft company, still one of the leading manufacturers working with tube-lining, produced a variety of popular floral designs for long periods, such as 'Orchid', 'Magnolia', and 'Anemone'. The rich colours, subtle shapes, and stylised floral motifs underlie their popularity. Prices have risen considerably over the past decade, and remain high, as demand still exceeds supply. The best pieces (*c.*1905–15) showcasing Moorcroft's exotic designs are worth hundreds or even thousands of pounds, depending on size, period, and condition. His Florian ware is often influenced by Moorish designs or the work of the pioneer designer William Morris. Examples can fetch around £1,000 or more. Today, Moorcroft offers work by designers such as Rachel Bishop and Sally Tuffin. Some of its limited-edition pieces sell for more than their original prices.

## Flowery forms

If Moorcroft is one of the major makers, then Carlton Ware was one of the most prolific. Its less-expensive floral range of ceramics was aimed at the middle market, and many pieces can now be found for less than £100.

This type of Carlton Ware is easily recognised – pieces are shaped like flowers, fruit, or vegetables, or else decorated with raised floral designs. In yellows, greens, and pinks, Carlton Ware was mass-produced until the late 1950s. Cracks and chips are common, as this was pottery for everyday use, so search for undamaged pieces.

A satisfying collection of common patterns can easily be acquired, but anyone looking to invest should concentrate on what is scarce.

**An earthenware A.E. Gray & Co. Ltd jug,** with hand-painted floral pattern. *1930s, 14.5cm (5¾in) high.*

**£40–60**

▼ **The traditional style of floral decoration** remained perennially popular. Here, youngsters enjoy a cup of tea from a floral tea set as they watch dancing at the Casino Dance Room in Birmingham, 1939.

## Essential Moorcroft

**FLORIAN WARE**
Moorcroft's early Florian ware designs are sought after. Good examples, such as this rare miniature vase, fetch high prices. c.1903, 10cm (4in) high.
**£1,000–1,500**

**NATIVE FLOWERS**
Small items in more common patterns, such as this miniature vase, are ideal purchases for the budget buyer. c.1970s, 6cm (2¼in) high.
**£200–300**

**ART NOUVEAU**
The curling lines and stylised flowers of these Florian ware vases show the influential Art Nouveau style associated with Moorcroft's early work. c.1902, 24cm (9½in) high.
**£2,000–3,000**

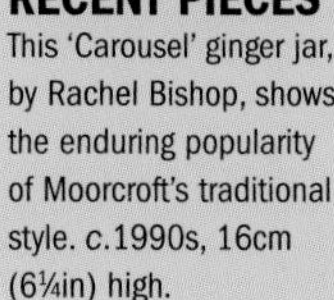

**RECENT PIECES**
This 'Carousel' ginger jar, by Rachel Bishop, shows the enduring popularity of Moorcroft's traditional style. c.1990s, 16cm (6¼in) high.
**£800–1,200**

'Cherries' was produced in smaller numbers than 'Apple Blossom', making it rarer and more sought after. Colours are also important. A pink 'Buttercup' trefoil dish *(see below)* is less common and worth more than one in yellow.

### Not just the giants

Floral ceramics are not solely the province of the giants of chintzware – there is a whole range of smaller factories worth considering, such as A.E. Gray & Co. Ltd (or Gray's Pottery), for whom Susie Cooper worked in the late 1920s. It is possible to find representative and attractive pieces for less than £100, although you should expect to pay up to £200 or more for designs by Susie Cooper. The boldly rendered, hand-painted floral pottery made by E. Radford of Staffordshire generally costs less than £100.

Ceramics by the Scottish firm Wemyss are slightly more expensive but may be a good investment as they achieve consistently high prices and, depending on the condition and rarity, may appreciate in value in the future.

**A Carlton Ware 'Buttercup' trefoil dish.** *1930s, 26.5cm (10½in) wide.*
**£50–60**

### Top Tips: specific makers

- Look out for work by contemporary Moorcroft designers such as Sally Tuffin and Rachel Bishop, as they are becoming increasingly collectable.
- Search for sought-after boxed sets of 1930s floral Carlton Ware. Some collectors even buy the empty boxes to fill later.
- Check the base of Wemyss pieces for the signature of Karel Nekola, the chief painter until 1915, as this adds value – especially as few Wemyss pieces are signed by a painter.

### BUY

*Decorative and functional chintzware pieces that can still be used today should hold their value, if not rise, if in good condition.*

**A Royal Winton chintz 'Cranstone' pattern two-tier cake stand.** Popularity of baking programmes on TV add to its desirability. *1930s, 22cm (8¾in) high.*
**£50–70**

### KEEP

*The Wemyss pig is characteristic of the manufacturer, and animal shapes are desirable generally. Wemyss have a strong following of collectors, including Prince Charles, so prices are unlikely to fall. Larger and earlier pieces will reach much higher values.*

**A Wemyss pig, decorated with roses.** This is a rare piece in perfect condition. *c.1890, 16cm (6¼in) long.*
**£2,000–3,000**

### SELL

*Standard Carlton Ware ranges are commonly found and unlikely to rise much in value in the foreseeable future, so the best option is to sell and invest in rarer pieces instead.*

**A yellow Carlton Ware 'Apple Blossom' bowl.** Although this is jaunty and attractive, such pieces are easy to obtain and consistently fetch comparatively low prices. *c.1930s, 23.5cm (9¼in) wide.*
**£30–40**

# Keith Murray is known for the sleek, minimalist designs he produced for Wedgwood in the 1930s. His strong, modern forms have attracted a dedicated following among interior designers as well as ceramics enthusiasts.



While many pottery manufacturers in Stoke-on-Trent were closing down during the Depression in the early 1930s, Josiah Wedgwood & Sons made a bold decision to commission New Zealand-born architect, Keith Murray, to design ranges of affordable mass-produced pottery. Wedgwood wanted to revive their business by using talented designers with skills in areas other than ceramics, and Murray had already established his reputation as a glassware designer for Stevens & Williams.

## A winning combination

Although slow to start, Wedgwood's new range – launched in 1933 – was a triumph. This was largely owing to the winning combination of Murray's sleek designs and the matt glazes developed by Norman Wilson, Wedgwood's works manager.

Murray's first range of vases and bowls were hand thrown and featured incised horizontal fluting, or banding. They were glazed in plain matt colours, including green and straw, both commonly used on Murray pieces for Wedgwood. Expect to pay £300–500 for a first-range piece in good condition and perhaps more for a rarer glaze colour, such as grey – though some lucky individuals have found examples of his work at car-boot sales. His shapes are listed in the Wedgwood shape books, the first being 3753; later pieces dated to 1939–40 are found around 4326. Murray's work is nearly always marked on the base (*see opposite page, top right*).

### Did You Know?

*Keith Murray's pieces for Wedgwood were not an immediate commercial success when they came out in 1933. It was only when the design commentators of the period drew attention to his innovative approach that his reputation was established.*

## Black beauty

The most sought-after items of his work include black basalt vases and bowls, made of a black clay body, perfected by Josiah Wedgwood in the 1760s. Vases are highly sought after, and can sell for £500–1,500, depending on the size and shape. Marks on the bases of black pieces are in red. A black basalt coffee set was produced and is rare. A part set, comprising a coffee pot, milk jug, and sugar bowl could fetch over £1,000. Another set was produced in the less

**A blue footed bowl,** with 'KM' mark. *c.1934, 25.5cm (10in) diam.*

**£400–600**

## Essential Keith Murray

**SIMPLE SHAPES** The simple form of this ovoid vase, with its strong but clean ribbed design, is typical of Murray's aesthetic. 1930s, 25.5cm (10in) high.

**£500–700**

**TABLEWARE** As well as decorative pieces, Murray also designed functional tableware, such as this moonstone Queen's ware jug. c.1934, 6.5cm (2½in) high.

**£40–60**

**SLIP-CAST** A matt green slip-cast ashtray, with mark. Murray also produced a cigarette box as part of this more affordable range. c.1932, 11.5cm (4½in) diam.

**£50–70**

**ACCESSORIES** This desk tray is a later slip-cast ware. Few were made and few survive intact: those that do are valuable. c.1934–36, 25.5cm (10in) wide.

**£500–700**

**A slip-cast sugar bowl and lid,** with a moonstone glaze and silver lustre knob decoration. *c.1934, 9cm (3½in) diam.*

**£100–150**

expensive, traditional Queen's ware body – Wedgwood's version of creamware. Murray also used copper- and bronze-coloured bodies for items such as tobacco jars. Such pieces now fetch consistently high prices.

Murray also designed beer tankards and mugs and these fetch around £60–80. His later slip-cast wares, first introduced in 1936, provide another fascinating and relatively inexpensive collecting area. These products include ink stands and cigarette boxes decorated with the same matt glaze colours used in his other work.

## Changing fashions

Continuing his clean-lined and modern look, around 1936, Murray made simpler, classical shapes with a subtle pale green celadon glaze with some incised decoration. These are less keenly sought after today, so prices are lower than those commanded by his early work.

Although he is less known for patterns on ceramics, he did produce a small number of pattern designs during the mid-1930s. These include the Art Deco-style 'Lotus', as well as 'Iris', and the stylish 'Green Tree'. Some of these were applied to both bone china and earthenware. In 1935 a complete dinner set decorated with the 'Tulip' pattern retailed at £15 – more than three times the average weekly wage in this period. Few of these wares were produced, but although they are rare, they are not valued highly today. Collectors prefer the undecorated, simple shapes for which Murray is best known.

## Celebrations

Murray also produced commemorative wares for Wedgwood, including some for Edward VIII's coronation, which was planned for 1937. The coronation never happened, owing to Edward's abdication in 1936, and these wares are collectable. Examples include a mug bearing a portrait of the King and a jug featuring the Royal Arms, both on a moonstone glaze. Avoid confusing these rare pieces with later commemorative wares featuring blue relief decoration by Arnold Machin on Keith Murray shapes.

Later in his career, Murray resumed work as an architect while still designing ceramics. Appropriately, in 1940 he was commissioned to design the new Wedgwood factory in Barlaston, near Stoke-on-Trent. He finally retired, aged 75, in 1967.

**A straw-coloured bowl,** with 'KM' mark. *c.1934, 14.5cm (5¾in) diam.*

**£400–500**

## A closer look at... Keith Murray marks

Three different backstamps were used on Murray's work for Wedgwood over the years of production. The first (above) used from 1933, shows a 'Keith Murray' signature.

By 1934, the mark was shortened to 'KM' (above). A new mark was introduced *c.*1940, using 'KM' and the rest in a circular form, with 'OF ETRURIA' above and '& BARLASTON' below.

### *Top Tips*

- Always ensure that Murray ceramics are chip-free. The minimal, glazed quality of his pieces causes chips to show up dramatically.
- Look for the rarer colours on Murray's designs for Wedgwood, such as black or grey, rather than the more common green, straw, and moonstone.
- As an affordable investment, buy Murray's smaller giftware pieces.

### BUY

*Murray's modernist black basalt wares are the most valuable of his work. This one was previously put up for sale at around £100, because its owner had not realised its true value. If you spot a similarly undervalued piece of black basalt ware, buy it.*

**A black basalt vase** (shape 3870). The back-stamped signature mark is printed in red. *c.1934, 13cm (5in) high.*

**£800–1,000**

### KEEP

*Typical Murray pieces with clean shapes and subtle colours are modern classics. They are popular with collectors, interior decorators, and individuals looking for decorative as well as authentic pieces for their own homes.*

**A fluted tapered cylindrical vase** (shape 3805), with a matt-white moonstone glaze. Its cool, classic colour is typical of Murray's palette. *c.1933, 21.5cm (8½in) high.*

**£300–400**

# Oriental ceramics

bring an air of exotic sumptuousness to the home. Many pieces were made for export, with designs created to appeal to Western tastes of the time.

**A 19th-century Chinese famille rose dish,** painted with nine boys, each standing and with various attributes including vases, ruyi sceptres, and flower stems, with a Jiaqing mark. *23cm (9in) diam.*

**£800–900**



Porcelain was first produced in China during the T'ang period (AD 618–906). The best-known pieces used the 'underglaze blue' technique (blue painting under a clear glaze), which became popular during the early Ming dynasty (14th century). The export trade began in earnest in the 16th century and peaked during the 18th and 19th centuries. Much of this later ware can be found for £25 to £100.

## A colourful history

The palette of colours used by Chinese ceramic artists during the 18th century is divided into *famille verte* (mainly green) and *famille rose* (largely pink). The *famille rose* palette took over from about 1718. The colours were mixed with opaque white to allow shading, adding depth and variety. Prices can reach thousands of pounds, but more common, smaller, inferior pieces with simpler designs can be found for less than £100.

## Pretty in pink

In the 19th century, the *famille rose* palette was used for wares known as Rose Medallion, Rose Mandarin, and Rose Canton. These vibrant and detailed pieces often depicted birds, flowers, butterflies, and domestic interiors. Avoid the 20th-century pieces of inferior quality, which have less detail and brasher colours – these often bear square 'seal' marks, or the words 'Made in China' on the base.

## Reclaimed from the sea

Hundreds of years after trade vessels from the Far East were shipwrecked, some of their cargoes have been recovered in superb condition. The Dutch ship *Geldermalsen*, wrecked in 1752, was salvaged in 1985. Its freight, the Nanking Cargo, included a huge quantity of porcelain. Prices start at around £50. Look out for items from the cargoes of *Gotheborg, Diana*, and *Tek Sing*. Prices for these pieces are currently fairly low, but there is a finite supply, so values may increase.

**An Imari bowl,** decorated inside and outside with stylised trees and panels of dragons. *c.1850s–90s, 14.5cm (5¾in) diam.*

**£50–70**

## Essential shipwreck cargoes

**HOI AN HOARD** Heavy pottery decorated in an underglaze blue is typical of this Vietnamese cargo, which yielded the earliest salvaged ceramics. *c.*1450- 1500, 24cm (9½in) diam.

**£150-200**

**HATCHER** Most of the items, such as this vase, were blue and white. They helped experts to understand Chinese ceramics from this era. *c.*1643, 12cm (4¾in) high.

**£250-350**

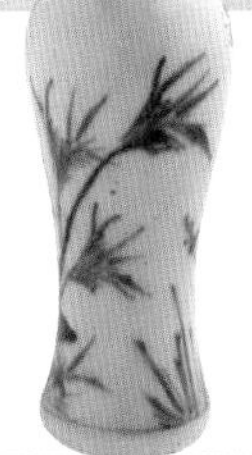

**VUNG TAO** As well as formal Kangxi period blue-and-white ware, plainer, more humble 'provincial' ware, such as this bowl, was also found. *c.*1690-1700, 15cm (6in) diam.

**£40-50**

**NANKING** Utilitarian pieces dominated this cargo. Encrustations caused by salt water have created abstract effects popular among collectors. *c.*1750, 13cm (5in) diam.

**£80-120**

**DIANA** Most of this cargo was made to compete with cheaper European ceramics, so is of lesser quality: for example, these painted porcelain toys. *c.*1817, 5.5cm (2in) high.

**£90-120 each**

**TEK SING** Bowls and dishes with blue designs were found on the *Tek Sing*. The freehand-painted design on this 'Spiral Lotus' dish adds value. *c.*1822, 18.5cm (7¼in) diam.

**£180-220**

### Japanese style in demand

Early Japanese porcelain ranges from the sparsely decorated Kakiemon to the ornate Imari style. These wares were exported by Dutch traders from the mid-17th to the mid-18th centuries, as well as in the late 19th century, when there was fresh demand.

The quality can vary, so look for detail and fine brushwork, and choose examples on which the gilding is intact and follows the blue-and-red design beneath. Pieces from the 20th century have looser, less detailed decoration, and the iron red is less subtle. Large, well-painted 19th-century Imari wall plaques can fetch £80–200, but finely decorated 18th-century Imari costs thousands of pounds.

Japanese Satsuma pottery is known for its distinctive creamy colours and rich palette of iron red, burnt umber, and gold. Medium-quality 19th-century pieces can cost less than £100. Those signed on the base are more valuable.

### Noritake goes West

Among the ceramics made for export were those from the Noritake factory, which was the main supplier of Japanese ware for the American market by 1910. For Western taste, it adopted Art Nouveau and Art Deco styles, and used decorative, raised gilding, and Western-style painted motifs. A good collection of Noritake wares from the first half of the 20th century need not be costly. A decorated cup and saucer may cost £20–40, while a tea set may fetch over £150 at a specialist auction.

### Top Tips

- Examine each object with a magnifying glass and, when buying later Chinese and Japanese export wares, avoid even the tiniest chip or faintest crack.
- Tap each piece, or flick it gently with your fingernail and listen to its 'ring'. A dull sound indicates a crack.
- Be wary of dating Chinese ceramics by emperors' reign marks – earlier reign marks were used on some later pieces as a mark of respect to the past.
- Avoid pieces marked 'Made in China', 'Made In Japan', or 'Foreign'. They are often of a late date and a low quality.

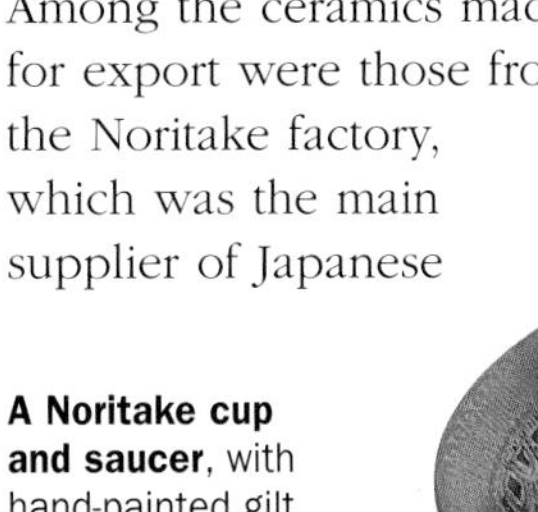

**A Noritake cup and saucer**, with hand-painted gilt decoration and a lakeside scene. *1920s, saucer 12.5cm (5in) diam.*

**£20–30**

### KEEP

*After a period of strong popularity, prices for Satsuma ware have fallen because the heavy, ornate style is now seen as old-fashioned. But high-quality pieces could be worth keeping as an investment, especially if they have fine and intricate detailing – any signs of wear to the gilding or painting will reduce value considerably.*

**A Satsuma vase,** probably from the late Meiji period, with pierced demi 'mon' handles. Warriors, as seen here, or ladies in landscapes are typical themes. *c.1900, 39cm (15¼in) high.*

**£300–400**

### BUY

*Vases and other wares made by Noritake are likely to rise in value if they are representative of the factory's work, are influenced by Western Art Deco styles, and are of fine quality.*

**A Noritake vase,** with hand-painted pink roses and neoclassical motifs. It is Western in style and typical of Noritake production. *1930s, 18.5cm (7¼in) high.*

**£25–35**

# Traditional ceramic ware

of the 19th and early 20th centuries includes some richly painted porcelain and pottery. Their sumptuous decoration makes them objects to covet, yet prices can be surprisingly low.

Decoratively gilded, and with floral, pastoral, and animal motifs, traditional ceramics were often 'kept for best' and passed down through the family. Renowned firms such as Royal Doulton, Royal Worcester, Royal Crown Derby, and Wedgwood began making items in the neoclassical style in the 19th century. If you are lucky enough to have inherited any pieces, it may be well worth keeping them.

## Setting the table

An amazing volume of tableware was made from the 1860s onwards. In fact, these dinner and tea services fetch low prices compared with contemporary wares. A good dinner service from around 1890–1920, with six, eight, or 12 settings, may be worth £80–150; a tea or coffee set, even less. Missing pieces or obvious wear and tear can lower the value considerably.

Dessert services, which were popular until the late 1930s, can be especially ornamental. Examine the painting carefully to ensure that it is not scratched or worn. Look for pieces with plenty of decoration rather than narrow border designs, as these look more attractive when displayed. Late Victorian services featuring landscape paintings may fetch £50–250.

The better potteries employed established artists to paint finely detailed flowers, fruit, landscapes, and animals. Prices vary hugely, depending on the decorator, although the quality of painting might not. Many decorators

**A Royal Worcester plate,** painted by H. Ayrton with fruit and berries, within a gilt rim that is gadrooned (edged in a cablelike design); with a black printed mark. *1951, 22cm (8½in) diam.*

**£500–600**

### *Did You Know?*

*Percy Curnock, the longest-serving artist at Royal Doulton, was famous for painting fine Italian landscapes on cabinet plates (made for display rather than use), but he never set foot in Italy. All his paintings on these now sought-after ceramics were inspired by picture postcards.*

## A closer look at... two Royal Doulton flambé vases

The flambé effect, introduced in 1902, was achieved by using a copper oxide formula. It was designed to mimic the Chinese *sang de boeuf* ('beef's blood') glaze. Flambé was used to decorate vases and won many prizes. Both these vases are valuable, but one is worth almost twice as much as the other.

**A Royal Doulton flambé vase,** covered in purple, red, and yellow flambé glazes by Harry Nixon, with printed marks and painted monogram. *c.1930s, 21cm (8¼in) high.*

**£350–400**

**A Royal Doulton flambé vase,** decorated by Harry Nixon, with rooks on a red and orange flambé ground. Printed marks include his 'HN' monogram. *c.1930s, 18cm (7in) high.*

**£800–1,000**

**A pair of Royal Doulton stoneware vases,** of waisted cylindrical form, with tube-lined decoration of cabbage roses, on a graduated lilac ground, with impressed marks. *c.1920s, 26cm (10¼in) high.*

**£100–200**

specialised in one subject: at Royal Worcester John and Harry Stinton were known for Highland cattle, James Stinton for game birds, Harry Ayrton for fruit, and Harry Davies for landscapes. They often signed their work.

## Popular patterns

Coalport is a favourite factory to collect. Prices can range from less than £100 for a 19th- or early 20th-century jug with a simple floral band to thousands of pounds for earlier and larger, more richly decorated pieces. Royal Crown Derby is known for its imitations of the saturated richness of Japanese Imari porcelain. The pattern numbers on Royal Crown Derby Imari are an indication of rarity: patterns still made, such as 1128 and 2451, are more common and less valuable.

Some Royal Worcester wares feature 'blush ivory': printed or painted sprays of flowers or foliage outlined in gilt against an ivory-coloured background. At present their popularity is on the wane, but this could change. Small pieces may fetch up to £50, while larger, more elaborate items range between £60 and hundreds of pounds.

**A Coalport two-handled sugar bowl and cover,** printed and painted with flowers in cartouches, on a blue ground. *c.1920, 11.5cm (4½in) high.*

**£20–30**

## Painting the lily

Minton & Co., a prominent Victorian Staffordshire porcelain factory, was known for its delicately painted and gilded wares. Look for examples encrusted with flowers which imitate 18th-century Meissen originals – they can fetch £200–1,000. Its later Art Nouveau work is also desirable.

Doulton has a reputation for quality. Its wares are marked on the base with stamps and incised initials to indicate the decorators. Look for designs by Florence and Hannah Barlow, Eliza Simmance, George Tinworth, and Harry Nixon.

Baskets made by Belleek, known for its creamy white china, are popular. Learn to spot valuable early items (1863–90) with the desirable black mark: the name 'Belleek' printed in a rectangle surmounted by a dog, tower, and Irish harp.

**A small Royal Crown Derby vase,** painted with flowers in enamels and gilt on a blue ground, with red mark. *c.1902, 10.7cm (4¼in) high.*

**£30–40**

## Top Tips

- To identify restored porcelain, hold different areas of the piece to your cheek – a restored section will feel slightly warmer than the rest of the piece.
- Hold porcelain up to a light to reveal hidden cracks or restored areas. A narrow-necked vase can be illuminated from the inside with a penlight torch.
- Look out for miniature Royal Crown Derby Imari pieces modelled as flat-irons, milk churns, and other novelty shapes. These are highly collectable.
- Firms such as Minton & Co. and Royal Crown Derby often used ciphers and other codes to indicate the date of manufacture. Refer to a pottery marks book to date items.

## BUY

*Many museum exhibitions are based around particular aesthetic styles, and collecting within one of these areas is now popular with a younger generation. Striking pieces in the Secessionist style, an important strand of Art Nouveau, are an interesting part of Minton's work. Pieces cost around £150–500, so buy now while you still can.*

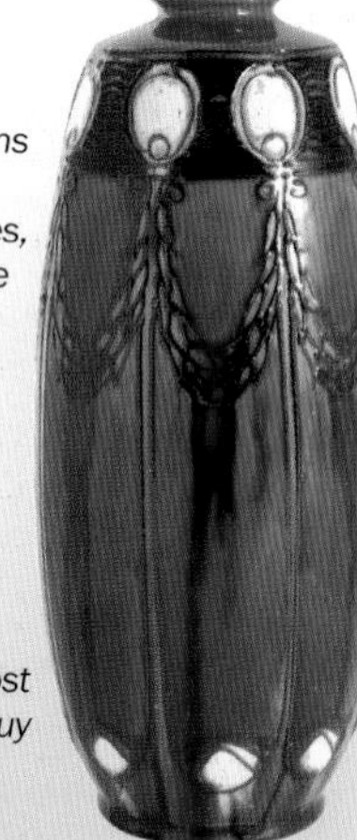

**A Minton Secessionist vase,** with tube-line decoration in the form of stylised plantlife and Minton's maker's marks on the base. *c.1900, 32cm (12½in) high.*

**£200–300**

## KEEP

*Prices for Doulton Lambeth stoneware have dropped over the past five years, but this key maker could soon make a comeback. If your piece is signed by and in the typical style of a sought-after decorator, such as Hannah Barlow, it is likely to become even more desirable.*

**A Doulton Lambeth vase,** with a band of incised decoration of cattle by Hannah Barlow. *1883, 30.5cm (12in) high.*

**£300–400**

# Cups and saucers summon up the elegance of afternoon tea in more leisured times. Sometimes found with a matching plate for dainty sandwiches, they are less expensive to acquire and easier to display than whole tea sets.

Many manufacturers have produced cups and saucers as stand-alone items, which gives them extra cachet for collectors.

In 1784 the tax on tea was reduced, making tea drinking a more popular habit, and the production of British and European tea cups – made with handles from the 1720s onwards – boomed. Anna, the seventh Duchess of Bedford, is said to have invented 'afternoon tea' in the early 19th century by having tea with sandwiches at around four or five o'clock to stave off pre-dinner pangs of hunger.

Fine cups and saucers produced by names such as Worcester, Meissen, and Minton command high prices, but there are many less expensive examples to be found, even from these makers. Check the bases for marks which can help to identify the maker and date. When checking whether a cup and saucer are a genuine pair, bear in mind that popular patterns were often simplified over the years to reduce prices and thus appeal to a wider market.

Modern manufacturers often extend their ranges by copying successful designs from the past.

▲ **A Shelley 'Vogue' trio set.** The set is pure Art Deco, with a solid triangular handle to the cup, and simple decoration in a single, strong colour. *1930s, cup 6.5cm (2½in) high.*

**£40–60**

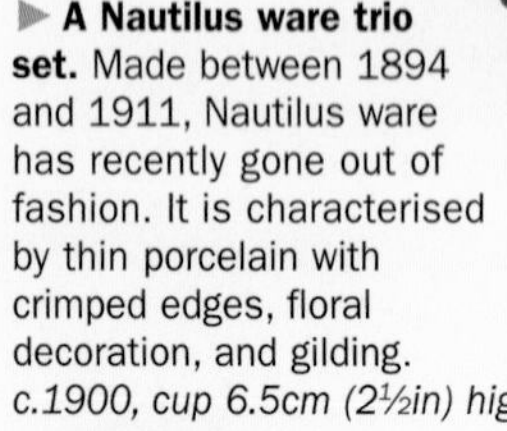

► **A Nautilus ware trio set.** Made between 1894 and 1911, Nautilus ware has recently gone out of fashion. It is characterised by thin porcelain with crimped edges, floral decoration, and gilding. *c.1900, cup 6.5cm (2½in) high.*

**£10–20**

► **A Spode cup and saucer.** Spode invented bone china in the late 18th century, and is also famed for its excellent gilding and hand-painted flowers. *c.1825–6, cup 7cm (2¾in) high.*

**£20–30**

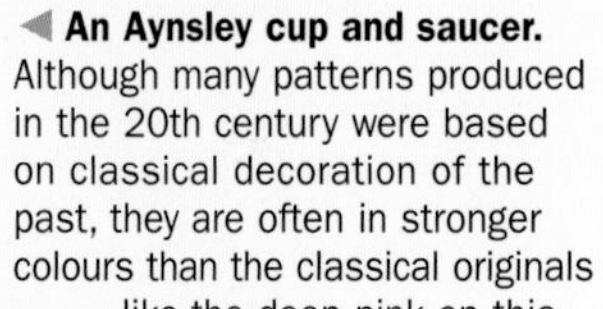

◄ **An Aynsley cup and saucer.** Although many patterns produced in the 20th century were based on classical decoration of the past, they are often in stronger colours than the classical originals – like the deep pink on this cup and saucer. *c.1900, cup 6.5cm (2½in) high.*

**£20–30**

◄ **A royal-blue Coalport cup and saucer.** Coalport is known for its bold, strong background colours, particularly the royal blue on this cup and saucer. Crimped edges and gilding are also typical features. *c.1907, cup 6.5cm (2½in) high.*

**£20–30**

◀ **A Hammersley trio set.** Produced as Europe teetered on the verge of war, traditional floral wares, particularly with gilding, were popular, as they evoked safer, more luxurious times. *c.1939, cup 6.5cm (2½in) high.*

**£20–30**

◀ **A Meyer & Sherratt (Melba China) plate, cup, and saucer.** *c.1935–41, cup 8cm (3in) high.*

**£20–30**

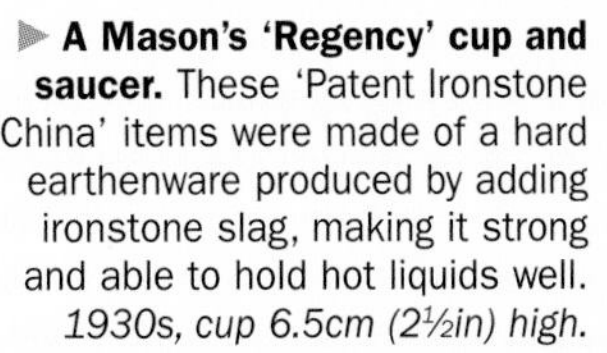

## Collectors' Tips

- Check gilding for signs of wear, cup rims for chips, and handles for evidence of repair
- Where possible, buy cups with their original saucers, or the match may not be perfect

▶ **A Mason's 'Regency' cup and saucer.** These 'Patent Ironstone China' items were made of a hard earthenware produced by adding ironstone slag, making it strong and able to hold hot liquids well. *1930s, cup 6.5cm (2½in) high.*

**£10–15**

◀ **An 'Orange Tree' cup and saucer by A.G. Richardson Ltd,** (pattern no.439), produced from about 1925 onwards. *c.1928, 8cm (3in) high.*

**£25–35**

◀ **An Alfred Meakin 'Cactus' plate, cup, and saucer.** 1950s ceramics often moved right away from traditional flowers and gilt. The potted cacti here were a wry touch aimed at younger householders. *1950s, cup 7cm (2¾in) high.*

**£30–50**

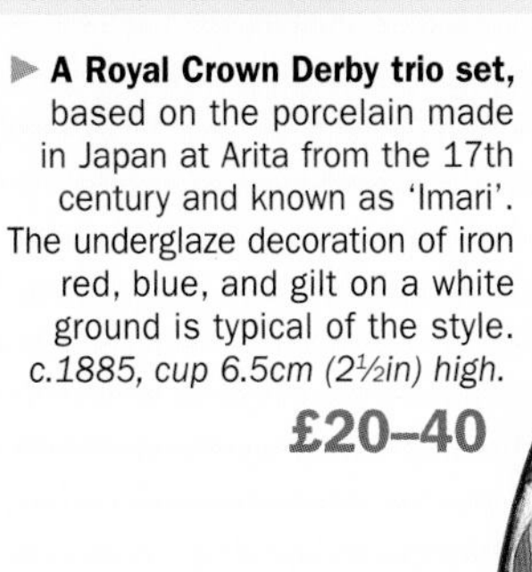

▶ **A Royal Crown Derby trio set,** based on the porcelain made in Japan at Arita from the 17th century and known as 'Imari'. The underglaze decoration of iron red, blue, and gilt on a white ground is typical of the style. *c.1885, cup 6.5cm (2½in) high.*

**£20–40**

▲ **A Coalport cup and saucer.** The delicate floral design and heavy gilding are reminiscent of the popular French designs of the early 19th century. *c.1940, cup 7cm (2¾in) high.*

**£20–30**

# 1950s ceramics are instantly recognisable by their bold, informal, often monochrome or two-colour decoration. The exciting look of these pieces – vital and optimistic – still attracts enthusiasts today.



Following World War II and the restrictions placed on 'non-essential' manufacturing, the pottery industry was slow to restart, and many smaller concerns closed for good. At the same time, the public turned away from the styles of the 1930s and before. Younger people wanted pottery that matched their modern way of life. Restrictions on colour and pattern used for domestic wares were finally lifted in 1952. This change, following the Festival of Britain in 1951, gave British industry an opportunity to present the latest developments in science and industrial design, and offered people renewed hope and a much-needed break from the mood of austerity.

## Atomic age

The pottery industry was quick to capitalise on these developments, and the styles that were introduced set the tone for the next 20 years, drawing on an eccentric and eclectic range of sources. There were patterns incorporating 'atomic' styling – inspired by diagrams showing electrons and neutrons – as well as Parisian street-scenes, circus motifs, shooting stars, and even tableware decorated with contemporary furniture designs.

The most notable producers of this new style were Midwinter, Beswick, and Ridgway, but there are numerous others. Unless you are looking for rare or large ceramics, it is easy to find pieces for much less than £50 each. Designs included Beswick's much sought-after 'Circus' range and Ridgway's popular black-and-white 'Parisienne' print.

**A Ridgway 'Homemaker' transfer-printed trio set,** designed by Enid Seeney. *c.1957–1970s, plate 18cm (7in) diam.*

**£40–50**

## No more flowers

Midwinter pioneered a particularly progressive approach to design. During a sales trip to Canada, Roy Midwinter discovered that his company's traditional floral-patterned ware was not in demand. In contrast to the situation in Britain, American design had not been so seriously held back by World War II restrictions, and by the early 1950s it had moved towards softer, more organic shapes developed by popular American designers such as Eva Ziesel, Raymond Loewy, and Russell Wright. Roy Midwinter was inspired by this new look and developed similar products in Britain. The result was the Stylecraft range,

**A Beswick 'Zebrette' bowl,** marked '1354'. *1950s, 23cm (9in) long.*

**£80–120**

## Essential Jessie Tait for Midwinter

**YOUTH APPEAL**
Bright colours and jaunty designs – as on this rare hand-painted 'Primavera' divided plate – were aimed at the younger buyer. 1954, 32cm (12½in) diam.
**£40–50**

**ATOMIC DESIGN**
An interest in the dawning of the 'atomic age' is reflected in this 'Festival' pattern jug, with its atom-like motifs. 1955, 11cm (4¼in) high.
**£30–40**

**FIFTIES FLOWERS**
The 1950s brought a more stylised treatment of floral motifs, as on this transfer-printed Fashion-shape 'Quite Contrary' plate. 1959, 15.5cm (6in) diam.
**£5–10**

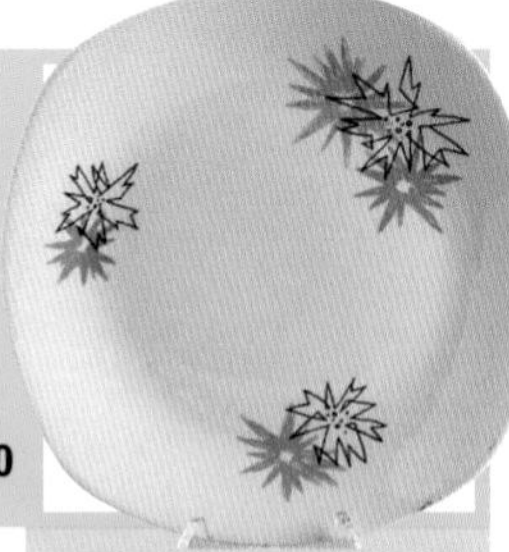

**POLKA DOTS**
Polka dots, as on this hand-painted Stylecraft-shape 'Domino Variant' trio set, are a typical 1950s motif. 1954, plate 15.5cm (6in) diam.
**£30–40**

**BLACK AND WHITE**
Midwinter's black-and-white 'Zambesi' pattern is seen here on a Fashion-shape trio set. c.1956, plate 15.5cm (6in) diam.
**£35–45**

**RARE SHAPES**
Unusual shapes, such as this cake stand in the 'Mosaic' pattern, are rare, so they should rise in value as interest grows. c.1959, 24cm (9¾in) wide.
**£70–100**

launched in 1953, decorated with a mixture of printed and painted contemporary patterns, all on simple, modern shapes, with rounded corners. Plates and bowls were flat and unfussy, often with 'wells', or slight indentations, in the centre.

### The lure of abroad

Pieces by major designers and those that capture the style of the period are well worth looking for. Examples of particularly desirable patterns are 'Primavera', 'Fiesta', and 'Zambesi', all designed by the prolific designer Jessie Tait for Midwinter. 'Zambesi' also inspired many copies, such as Beswick's 'Zebrette' range, which tends to cost less today.

Designs by Terence Conran for Midwinter dating from this era are also worth buying – particularly 'Chequers', his hand-painted 'Salad Ware' pattern, and 'Plant Life', the latter illustrating the increasing use of commonplace household features (in this case, pot plants) as motifs.

Hugh Casson created the highly collectable 'Cannes' pattern, which was later used on Midwinter's Fashion shape and renamed 'Riviera' from 1955. This design shows the public's growing fascination with foreign places, an increasingly common experience for people as air fares became less expensive and foreign holiday destinations began to overtake British ones in popularity.

Hand-painted ceramics are more valuable than those that are solely printed – a hand-painted 'atomic'-inspired 'Festival' dinner plate can cost up to £30. Some pieces combine printing with painting, and these too attract interest.

### Home pride

The striking use of black on white is evident on a number of 1950s patterns. One of the most popular is the 'Homemaker' design created by Enid Seeney for Ridgway around 1957 and sold by Woolworths. The state-of-the-art furniture it showed included a fashionable chair created by the designer Robin Day and a boomerang table alongside plants and lamps. It was used on two different pottery shapes, first Metro and then Cadenza, so when building up a set check that all pieces are from the same range.

It is worth keeping an eye open for classic patterns in unusual shapes, such as divided plates, TV dinner plates, and coffee pots, as well as on larger pieces, as all these are keenly sought after.

### Top Tips

- Look out for hand-painted designs by Jessie Tait and Terence Conran. These are easy to identify as the designer's name was often incorporated into the backstamp.
- Opt for patterns that break away from traditional florals and are more typical of the period, such as black-and-white colour combinations and bright, modern, stylised designs.
- Check the condition of pieces carefully – many were produced in large numbers and were used daily, so only those in the best condition are likely to appreciate in value.

### BUY

*Patterns by well-known designers that are brightly coloured and typical of the age they were produced in are worth buying. Certain tablewares are also rarer today as only one was needed by a family, as opposed to plates, of which many were usually needed.*

**A Midwinter 'Salad Ware' celery vase,** by Sir Terence Conran. The pattern shows vegetables – considered luxurious after wartime rationing. To avoid taxes on decorative wares, this was sold as a celery holder. *1955, 18cm (7in) high.*
**£200–300**

### SELL

*More realistic designs that do not capture the look of the period, and those by less prominent designers, are not popular and are unlikely to increase much in value.*

**A Midwinter Fashion-shape 'Bali H'ai' plate,** by John Russell, with printed and enamelled decoration. The natural pattern would not have appealed as much to younger buyers. *c.1960, 22.5cm (8¾in) diam.*
**£5–10**

# 1960s tableware is often recognisable by its tall, cylindrical shapes, striking patterns, and bold colours. There is still plenty around, but prices are rising as people increasingly appreciate its strong period appeal.

**A Portmeirion 'Talisman' cigarette box,** with transfer-printed design. Boxes are more desirable. *c.1962, 13.5cm (5¼in) wide.*

**£30–50**

Many people will have some 1960s tableware at home without realising its potential interest as a collectable. Anyone who married in the 1960s probably received contemporary tableware, such as Portmeirion, as a wedding gift. If so, it may well have some investment value.

## Wind of change

Although the audacious patterns and striking styles of the 1950s continued into the next decade, 1960s tableware is characterised by bolder colours such as deep browns, purples, and oranges. Changing lifestyles and competition from overseas forced pottery firms to be inventive. At the same time, innovations in manufacturing and printing made production faster and cheaper, so hand-painted decoration became redundant.

The demands of modern living inspired oven-to-table ware, a novel concept embraced by factories such as Midwinter and Poole. The ability to update their production range quickly brought these factories ahead of the market, as they regularly released new patterns, shapes, and speciality lines such as boxed sets intended as gifts for newly-weds.

## Welsh wizardry

One of the key factories in the 1960s was the Portmeirion Pottery. In 1953 Susan Williams-Ellis began creating giftware for a shop in Portmeirion in Wales. Her wares, decorated by A.E. Gray & Co. Ltd in Stoke-on-Trent, proved popular, and she and her husband bought Gray's in 1960. The following year she acquired Kirkhams Pottery, which had made blanks for Gray's, so that she could now design and make shapes as well as decorate them.

Today, Portmeirion is best known for its 'Botanic Garden' range, introduced in the 1970s. But the company's diverse ranges from the 1960s may be worth watching. Prices have fallen, but may rise again. Look out for moulded patterns such as 'Totem', and 'Tivoli' and 'Magic Garden', which are printed patterns. Prices range from a few pounds for a plate, up to £15–20 for a storage jar and £30–50 for a coffee set.

Some patterns from the early 1960s, such as green swirling 'Malachite' and 'Moss Agate' with its gold-coloured disc shapes, were too expensive to make and were quickly withdrawn. Today, these are rare and sought after, with pieces fetching £100–150 or more.

**A Portmeirion 'Variations' storage jar.** *c.1964, 15.5cm (6in) high.*

**£15–20**

### Did You Know?

*The Portmeirion Pottery created a pattern range for the Ikea store during the 1960s called 'What the Butler Saw', drawing on vintage Victorian prints of semi-clad ladies and male wrestlers, with cheeky phrases added by the designer. They were rejected by Ikea as being too risqué.*

## Magic city

Mass-produced, inexpensive shapes and patterns were soon developed to satisfy the market – young professionals with modern tastes. The new tableware was decorated cost-effectively with all-over body transfers. The designs were by Williams-Ellis, who was inspired by a variety of sources. Typical examples include 'Greek Key', 'Magic City', and

'Talisman'. Later, in 1970, 'Magic Garden' was released, but this complex pattern was unpopular and was only produced for a short period. This makes it highly collectable today. Other rare patterns include 'Gold Signs', 'Gold Diamond', and 'Reddington's New Foot Soldiers'. The patterns can fetch £10–50, or more for unusual or large pieces.

## Totem power

Portmeirion created shock waves in the British pottery industry in 1963 when they launched the 'Totem' range, with its tall cylinder-shaped coffee pot. The daring shape of the pot, decorated with stylised abstract motifs moulded on to the ware, was mocked by competitors – until it sold so well that several of them copied it. 'Totem', produced in various colours, put Portmeirion at the forefront of British design.

As so many 'Totem' pieces were made, values vary depending on colour and item. Plain green and amber are the most common, while white is rarer, and cobalt blue the most desirable and valuable. Expect to pay about £5–7 for a green or amber egg cup, and up to £30 for a white coffee pot. The success of 'Totem' inspired several variations, including 'Cypher' and 'Jupiter', the latter featuring rows of indented circles. These fetch similar prices to 'Totem'. The blue version of 'Jupiter' faded when it came into contact with washing-up liquid, so strong blue examples are rare and sought after.

**A Portmeirion Serif-shape 'Jupiter' tureen,** with a lid and in a blue glaze. *c.1964, 23cm (9in) wide.*

**£10–15**

## Monochrome

In addition to bold colours, black and white were also used. But many black-and-white items are less valuable than the better-known colour ranges: a decorative wall plate in 'Sailing Ships' or 'Velocipedes' can usually be found for less than £20. Antiquarian engravings were used for a number of black-and-white patterns, such as 'Chemist Prints' and 'Corsets'.

**A Portmeirion 'Velocipedes' plate.** *c.1968, 18.5cm (7in) diam.*

**£8–10**

## Fine Midwinter

During the 1960s, Midwinter continued to be innovative. In 1962 they launched the Fine shape, which moved away from the organic forms of the 1950s to a purer, cylindrical shape that better reflected 1960s tastes. Most of the printed patterns were colourful semi-abstract designs. Examples include 'Spanish Garden', 'Queensbury', 'Sienna', and 'Cherry Tree'. As with Portmeirion, many people still use Fine pieces in their homes and are unaware that they

# Essential Portmeirion

**TALISMAN** Transfer-printed rectangles and circles make a pattern which came in several colour combinations. This plate is in blue/purple. c.1962, 25.5cm (10in) diam.

**£10–20**

**TOTEM** The opaque glaze appears lighter over the raised motifs of this pattern – as seen on this white, cylinder-shaped coffee pot. 1963, 33cm (13in) high.

**£40–60**

**MAGIC GARDEN** The transfer-printed pattern featured on this coffee set is a Williams-Ellis design, said to have been inspired by the 1969 moon landing. c.1970, pot 33.5cm (13¼in) high.

**£80–120 for the set**

**TIVOLI** The 'Tivoli' pattern was designed by Susan Williams-Ellis after a visit to the Tivoli Gardens in Copenhagen. It is seen here on a storage jar. 1964, 15.5cm (6in) high.

**£20–30**

**MONTE SOL** This storage jar has the 'Monte Sol' pattern – Williams-Ellis is reputed to have designed the range when staying in the Monte Sol Hotel, Ibiza. c.1966, 16cm (6¼in) high.

**£20–30**

**MAGIC CITY** This Serif-shape cup and saucer showcase one of the most successful transfer-printed patterns of the 1960s. c.1966, cup 8.5cm (3½in) high.

**£15–25**

could become more collectable. Most pieces currently sell for up to £30, with plates generally fetching less than £15.

It is worth looking for the less well-known shape ranges including MQ2, which had bowl-shaped cups on a cylindrical base. Launched in 1967, it was soon phased out because it proved unpopular. At present, it fetches slightly less than 1950s shapes and designs. The work of key Midwinter designers, such as Jessie Tait, is always worth searching for. Values range from around £2–3 for a milk jug or plate, and a complete coffee set often fetches over £50.

## Studio start

Having established its reputation in the first half of the 20th century, Poole Pottery continued to produce fresh, high-quality designs in the 1960s. From 1958, a young designer, Robert Jefferson, developed new shapes and patterns. He created the Delphis Studio ware which started life in a craft studio and was mainly confined to large decorative plaques, plates, and vases. These are popular today and fetch around £150–500 or more, depending on size and design. Inspiration came from various sources, including landscapes, fish, and birds; colours are typically brown, deep orange, yellow, and green. Eventually, the range was modified and extended to include utility ware, and given the shorter name, Delphis. This range is more affordable today than the Delphis Studio ware which inspired it. Delphis pieces can fetch from as little as £25 up to £100 for larger or finely decorated examples.

**A Carlton Ware/Lustre Pottery 'Walking Ware' breakfast set.** *c.1960s–70s, teapot 18cm (7in) high.*

**£80–120**

## Another world

Carlton Ware is another name to search out. Its two-tone 'Orbit' range reflected, in both form and name, the fascination with space exploration. Larger pieces, such as teapots, can fetch around £60; smaller items around £20. By the late 1960s, the company's range included pieces such as 'Walking Ware', designed by Roger Michell and Danka Napiorkowska, which featured bowls, teapots, and egg cups with legs. These fetch around £30–50 for single pieces, with teapots or rarer pieces, such as candlesticks, often fetching over £100. Some 'Walking

## Some 1960s designs to look for:

- Whispering Grass
- Cherry Tree

**A Midwinter Fashion-shape 'Whispering Grass' plate,** by Jessie Tait – a naturalistic design. *c.1960, 24.5cm (9½in) diam.*

**£5–10**

**A Midwinter Fine-shape 'Cherry Tree' coffee set.** This pattern, which breaks the cherry tree into vertical bands of colour, was designed by Nigel Wilde. *c.1966, pot 20cm (7¾in) high.*

**£40–60**

Ware' also has a Lustre Pottery mark, as used by the designers' own studio.

Although less well known, tableware produced by J. & G. Meakin Ltd is attracting growing interest, primarily because its designs reflect period tastes so well. In 1968 Meakin bought Midwinter – then in financial trouble after a series of failures, including the launch of the MQ2 shape. Meakin unveiled its cylindrical Studio shape in 1964, with patterns typical of the decade, including 'Impact', which shows a stylised four-petalled flower.

## Stirring up interest

Denby was another notable pottery which successfully responded to contemporary tastes, with patterns such as 'Arabesque', designed by Gill Pemberton in 1964 and now considered a classic. Items from both Denby and Meakin can be found for well under £30, with coffee pots or sets often fetching around £50–100.

## North and south

Although smaller and less well known, the Buchan Pottery, at Crieff, Scotland, produced some interesting, brightly coloured tableware. All its designs were hand painted, so each piece is unique, but look for recurring motifs that can be built up into a set, such as 'Riviera' (fruits encircled in blue). Prices are still relatively low (usually about £10–50).

Also hand decorated are pieces by the Isle of Wight Pottery, now beginning to enjoy a revival. Prices are still low at under £20–30, but interest is rising. Look for colourful pieces designed by the pottery's founder, Jo Lester.

**A Carlton Ware 'Orbit' jam pot and saucer.** Spoon missing. 1960s *13.5cm (5¼in) high.*

**£40–60**

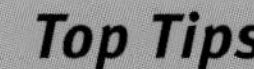

## Top Tips

- Always look for shapes, styles, and colours that typify the period (as illustrated here).
- Check the base of an item for maker's marks. Pieces by leading factories such as Midwinter, Portmeirion, and Poole have broad appeal, which increases value.
- Avoid buying damaged or worn pieces: any damage will greatly affect value as there are still many undamaged pieces on the market.

## BUY

*Although names such as Portmeirion and Midwinter are already collectable, Denby, Hornsea, and J. & G. Meakin are not yet in the same league. Always look for shapes and patterns that represent the tastes and innovations of the 1960s.*

**A J. & G. Meakin Studio 'Cornflower' coffee service.** The cylindrical shape and pattern are typical of 1960s styling. This set would have had a higher value if it had been supplied with more cups and saucers. *1960s, pot 30.5cm (12in) high.*

**£40–50**

## SELL

*Midwinter is already one of the most popular names in mid-20th-century ceramic collecting. Prices for some of its 1950s designs have greatly increased in value recently. Key designs from the 1960s are yet to show similar rises, but are likely to do so, so hold on to any pieces you have already, if they are in excellent condition.*

**A Midwinter Fine-shape 'Sienna' milk jug and sugar pot.** The 'Sienna' pattern, designed by Jessie Tait, suits the typical 1960s cylindrical shape. *1962, 5.5cm (2¼in) high.*

**£5–10**

## ▪ Delphis ▪ Arabesque ▪

**A Poole Delphis spear-shaped dish.** The deep shades of orange, green, and brown used in the 'Delphis' range are typical of 1960s Poole Pottery. *1960s, 26cm (10¼in) diam.*

**£40–70**

**A Denby 'Arabesque' coffee pot.** This design by Gill Pemberton has both a colour scheme and a shape typical of the 1960s. *c.1964, 31cm (12¼in) high.*

**£8–12**

# Cottage ware evokes the nostalgic rustic idyll of rose-clad cottages and half-timbered buildings of 'Shakespeare country'. This is an evocative and currently low-priced collecting area for anyone inspired by 'Olde England'.

Bone china and pottery cottage ware is a familiar sight in many homes around the country. Perfumed pastille burners and nightlights disguised as cottages were produced by manufacturers such as Spode, Coalport, and Worcester from the 1760s and throughout the 1800s. They appealed to a population uprooted from their rural traditions by a mass exodus to the cities.

There was a similar pastoral nostalgia in the late 1920s and early 30s, inspiring pieces that were intended both as stand-alone souvenirs and to serve a particular function.

## A comforting glow

In 1893 Goss introduced a range of seven nightlight cottages that were reproductions of period houses. The open back of each housed a candle-holder: when the candle was lit, smoke came out of the chimney and the extra-thin porcelain windows glowed. These cottages were made until 1929, and were so successful that the range was extended to 35. Prices vary from less than £50 to around £200. Goss cottages dated after 1929, when the factory was sold, are worth much less than earlier models.

## Country teas

Manufacturers also applied the cottage shape to tea and coffee sets, which usually consisted of a tea or coffee pot, hot water jug, milk jug, and sugar bowl. Extra items could be added to the set, such as cruets or biscuit barrels. Prices have fallen recently, making it a great time to buy if you like the look. Individual pieces can now be found from £20-80. Teapots, though, are a popular collecting field in themselves and are usually more valuable, because they are in such high demand. Jugs also command high prices.

**An early Goss nightlight model of a Manx cottage,** coloured and with black-printed Goshawk mark and inscription 'Model of Manx Cottage, Rd.No.273243'. *c.1896, 12cm (4¾in) long.*

**£100–150**

## Essential cottage ware

**COFFEE POTS**
Teapots and coffee pots work well with the cottage shape and hold their value. This is a Price Bros coffee pot. 1945-50, 25.5cm (10in) high.
**£40-60**

**JUGS**
Jugs, such as this finely detailed Price Bros half-timbered creamer, are highly sought after. 1930s, 8cm (3in) high.
**£40-60**

**CHEESE DISHES**
A water mill makes a good cover for a cheese dish. This one, with desirable realistic detail, is by Royal Winton. 1930s, 18.5cm (7¼in) wide.
**£100-150**

**JAM POTS**
A double jam pot is worth more than twice the value of a single one. This one is by Price Bros. c.1930, 20.5cm (8in) wide.
**£40-60**

## A dream of thatch

In 1933 Wade Heath launched its popular 'thatched cottage' tableware, including items such as biscuit barrels and jam pots. As production lasted until 1971, pieces are easily found and prices start at £20. Beswick cottage ware, also produced from the 1930s, is not as collectable as Royal Winton (its decoration is often less fine), but Beswick cottage ware teapots have a following – as do those by Burlington, J.H. Wood, and Price Bros.

## An idyll lives on

Lilliput Lane, established in 1982, is renowned worldwide for its delicately painted, miniature resin cottages. As new models were launched, older ones were 'retired' and have become collectable. Some of the early cottages were produced in small numbers, or the colour was changed, or a chimney or window was added. The original versions can fetch a high price. For

**Lilliput Lane's 'Sweet Pea Cottage',** retired from production in March 1997. *c.1994, 5cm (2in) wide.*

**£15–20**

example, 'Dove Cottage' was produced in two versions between 1983 and 1988. Those produced in the first year have a name-plate and can be worth £300–400; the more numerous models produced until 1988, without a nameplate, often fetch less than £60. Lilliput Lane's limited editions are highly valued: 'Cliburn School', produced in 1983 in an edition of 64, can sell for over £1,000. The most sought-after Lilliput Lane patterns are 'Drapers' (first two versions); 'Crofters Cottage', also known as 'The Croft' (first two versions); 'Dale Farm' (any version); 'Fire House'; 'Holly' (first version); and 'Out of the Storm'. 'Old Mill' and 'Old Mine' are rare.

David Winter is a name to watch, especially for special- or limited-edition cottages or the larger, rarer models. In 1981 Winter produced the bestselling 'Stratford House' model, with rickety roof, wobbly walls, and giant chimneys – the trademarks of his style. 'Fairytale Castle' (1982), 'The Bakehouse' (1983), and 'The Bothy' (1983) are enduring favourites. Also collectable are 'Sabrina's Cottage', 'Double Oast', 'Chichester Cross', 'The Coaching Inn', 'Little Mill' (first mould – others followed), and 'Mill House' (first mould). Many Winter cottages sell for much less than £100; rarer pieces will fetch more.

### Did You Know?

*Most Lilliput Lane cottages are made to a scale of 1:76. The modellers have more than 200 different tools at their disposal (including dentistry tools) to create a wax model, which is then used to make a mould for the cottage. It can take more than two weeks for a modeller to make the basic wax model.*

**David Winter's 'O'Donovan's Castle'.** *1980s, 14cm (5½in) high.*

**£20–30**

**David Winter's 'The Flower Shop',** with its box. *1980s, 14cm (5½in) high.*

**£15–25**

## Top Tips

- Note that a special edition is different from a limited edition: the former is made for a set time, while the latter is limited to a set number of pieces.
- Look for any Royal Winton cottage ware cups, saucers, plates, and table lamp bases, as they are all rare.
- If collecting Lilliput Lane, ensure that all cottages have an authentic stamp and the correct sticker. Also, keep the box and title deeds in good condition.
- When selling, consider using the Internet to reach the American market, where cottage ware is highly popular, and prices may be higher.

## KEEP

*Lilliput Lane cottages are collectors' favourites. Look out for variations from standard designs, short runs, or strictly limited editions. Mint-condition examples with deeds and box are preferable.*

**Lilliput Lane's 'Dove Cottage'.** This version was only made in 1983, so comparatively few exist. *1983, 13cm (5in) wide.*

**£200–300**

## KEEP

*Teapots appeal to both teapot and cottage ware collectors. They should at least hold their value and look promising for future appreciation. This example is valuable as the combination of colours is rare.*

**A Price Bros 'Ye Olde Inn' teapot.** The quality of the detailing, with leaded windows, makes this a desirable piece. *1930s, 21cm (8¼in) high.*

**£60–100**

# Toby and character jugs

bring earthy humour into the home. Their charm stems not only from their subject matter – from bluff ale-drinkers to wartime heroes such as Winston Churchill – but also from their hand-painted individuality.

**A small Royal Doulton 'Mad Hatter' character jug,** complete with dormouse. The backstamp is 'D6602'. *1965–83, 10cm (4in) high.*

**£30–50**

Potters have always had a keen eye for a likeness, sometimes combined with a wicked sense of humour. Many of us have a toby or character jug at home – a caricature version of a well-known political or historical figure or of a popular character from fiction. Such jugs can be colourful, whimsical, and topical within their period – often all three at once. Modern portrait jugs maintain the tradition of affectionate humour, but with a wider cast of characters – today you can find jugs on a range of themes from composers to comedians. In fact, 20th-century character jugs are now more collectable than the original toby jugs which inspired them. But what all these pottery portraits have in common is their gentle satire and their handmade appeal.

## Toby and his tribe

A toby jug takes the form of a full-length portrait, typically seated – often with a jug in one hand. The tradition was established in Britain in the mid-18th century, when the tricorne hat, which forms the classic toby's spout, was the height of fashion. These jugs were still being made in the early 20th century by companies such as Royal Doulton. Examples from the 18th and 19th centuries continue to be readily available, but those with fine moulding, painted detailing, and unusual poses often run into thousands of pounds. More standard types can be found from around £150 upwards. Visit dealers, antiques fairs, and auctions to study the jugs and get to know their range of colours, materials, weights, and forms.

**A toby jug of the kind made by the Staffordshire potter Ralph Wood.** *1780–90, 25cm (9¾in) high.*

**£500–800**

## Full of character

Character jugs are the toby's younger cousins. In the late 1920s, Charles Noke, a Doulton modeller, hit upon the idea of creating jugs featuring only the subject's head and shoulders. This gave more scope for creating faces filled with personality, which in turn made greater variety possible. Noke's first character jug, 'John Barleycorn', was launched in 1934 and produced in various sizes until 1982. Values start at around £20–30 for the smaller sizes, rising to around £100 or more for larger ones in mint condition. Today, some of the early jugs made shortly after 'John Barleycorn' are among the rarest and most desirable. The 'Toothless Granny' can fetch over £250, while others are pricier still. The 'Clown' jug was first issued with red hair, which changed to brown

### A closer look at... a Royal Doulton character jug

Variations in colour and size in some Royal Doulton jugs can lead to dramatically different values. The 'Pearly Boy' was made in three sizes: miniature shown here), small, and large.

Moulded buttons on the hat identify this as the rare 'Pearly Boy' version

This 'Pearly Boy' has a brown coat – the rarer blue variation can be worth up to twice as much

**A miniature Royal Doulton 'Pearly Boy' character jug,** with factory and 'A' marks on the base, designed by the notable modeller Harry Fenton. *c.1950s, 6cm (2¼in) high.*

**£400–500**

during World War II owing to a shortage of suitable paints. In 1951 the clown's hair turned white and remained so until the range was discontinued four years later. White-haired Clowns can fetch up to £400, but the rarer redheads and brunettes may cost over £1,000.

## Copycats

The popularity of character jugs encouraged other potteries to design their own versions during the early to mid-20th century. One such firm was Shaw & Copestake, whose immense range of ornaments was sold under the SylvaC brand. Principally known for its decorative animals, including highly collectable rabbits and dogs, the firm also produced many character jugs during the 1960s and 70s. Its 'Robin Hood' range is a perennial favourite, and Robin himself could carry a price tag of around £30.

### Did You Know?

*Two characters called Toby can lay claim to being the inspiration for the ale jug's name: Toby Fillpot, the subject of the 18th-century song 'The Brown Jug', and Toby Belch, from Shakespeare's play 'Twelfth Night'. They have one trait in common – they were both renowned drinkers.*

## Trend-spotting

Future trends are an important consideration when starting a collection of toby or character jugs. Some subjects, such as royalty, are sure to stand the test of time; military themes have enjoyed a revival recently while jugs connected with hobbies have enduring appeal.

Prototype jugs, made before the main run to experiment with colours and postures, are also sought after by keen collectors within their speciality. Examples, such as Royal Doulton jugs, have been surfacing recently following factory closures; Kevin Francis now sells its prototypes direct to collectors.

**A SylvaC 'Robin Hood' character jug,** stamped '5114'. *1970s, 16cm (6¼in) high.*

**£20–30**

### Top Tips

- Check the backstamp on all Royal Doulton character jugs: this printed number on the base, preceded by a 'D', identifies the character. Use it to find the production dates in a specialist reference book.
- Buy the best jug you can afford: one or two rare jugs make a better investment than 10 ordinary ones.
- Avoid Royal Doulton 'seconds' – the factory brands these as substandard by drilling a hole through the centre of the backstamp.



### BUY

*The Kevin Francis company (formed by Kevin Pearson and Francis Salmon) specialises in limited editions. Its series of toby jugs depicting well-known potters also attracts people who collect pieces by the potters themselves. This cross-market appeal, and the relatively small limited-edition runs of jugs in this series, make them highly desirable.*

**A Kevin Francis 'Susie Cooper' toby jug,** from a limited edition of 350. *1990s, 24cm (9¼in) high.*

**£80–120**

### SELL

*Falstaff is one of the most common Royal Doulton character jugs, made from 1950 until 1995. Unless you have the rarer limited-edition version featuring yellow clothes, this jug is unlikely to gain value for a considerable time.*

**A large Royal Doulton 'Falstaff' character jug,** numbered on the base 'D6287'. *1950–95, 16cm (6¼in) high.*

**£15–20**

# Nursery ware has been a favourite in Britain from the 19th century. Items scaled and designed for a child's use – from mugs to plates and divided dishes – reflect the changing fashions of their era. Many pieces are charming and unusual.

**A Mabel Lucie Attwell elf milk jug,** part of a 'Boo-Boo' nursery tea set. *c.1926, 15cm (6in) high.*

**£150–200**

Illustrations of childhood stories and rhymes on ceramic nursery ware have a nostalgic appeal. The images adopted the style of children's book illustration, which links them indelibly to their era. Victorian pieces often included designs based on nursery rhymes, especially those with a religious or moral message. Some of the earliest patterns, dating from the mid-Victorian period, were printed in single colours, such as black or sepia; others in multiple colours, such as black and green.

## Painting and printing

By the early 20th century, the designs on nursery ware were often hand painted. In 1927 Susie Cooper designed her 'Quadrupeds' range, printed in blue with hand-painted decoration showing animals among apple trees. A 'Quadrupeds' plate might fetch around £150 and a mug around £100. The hand-painted work of Hilda Cowham is also collectable. From 1923 she produced a range of nursery patterns including 'Children at Play' (1927), a rare novelty tea set with the teapot modelled as a tent; a milk jug in the form of a shell decorated with a mermaid (1928); and a milk jug shaped as a bucket (1928).

In the early 1930s Susie Cooper decorated children's mugs, beakers, and porringers (small bowls) with images of lambs, rabbits, and other animals. Some of these hand-painted patterns were so popular that they were printed from 1935 to 1936. Many printed wares had hand-painted borders, to create a crafted look.

Between 1928 and 1939, W.R. Midwinter Ltd produced a range of wares decorated with 12 nursery rhymes by William Heath Robinson. In the early 1980s it produced items featuring the television character Roland Rat; these pieces are now quite rare and may be a good investment.

In the 1930s Eric Ravilious designed patterns for Wedgwood, including his notable 'Alphabet' series of plates, mugs, jugs, and bowls, on which each letter of the alphabet was represented by an illustration.

## Chubby children

Shelley Potteries captured the market for nursery ware after 1926 when they introduced a range of patterns designed by Mabel Lucie Attwell, decorated with cartoons of small children. Today, an Attwell mug can cost up to £200. In 1995 fake Mabel Lucie Attwell plates began to appear. They are not hard to distinguish as the transfers are often badly scratched.

## Collecting themes

Although some collectors only seek early pieces, the popularity of nursery ware has less to do with age and value than with visual appeal, or a link to a certain manufacturer or subject. Many collectors focus on a particular range, such as 'Bunnykins' by Royal Doulton, a designer, or themed items such as egg cups or mugs, regardless of the maker, date, or style.

**A 'Duck' nursery tea set by Mabel Lucie Attwell for Shelley.** *1930s, teapot 20cm (7¾in) high.*

**£800–1,200**

## A closer look at... a Mabel Lucie Attwell nursery bowl

The work of Mabel Lucie Attwell is much prized. Particularly cherished are pieces from the 1930s adorned with painted figures, as well as her brightly coloured novelty tea ware in the shape of children and elves. The value of either of these sets is not seriously affected by the large number produced.

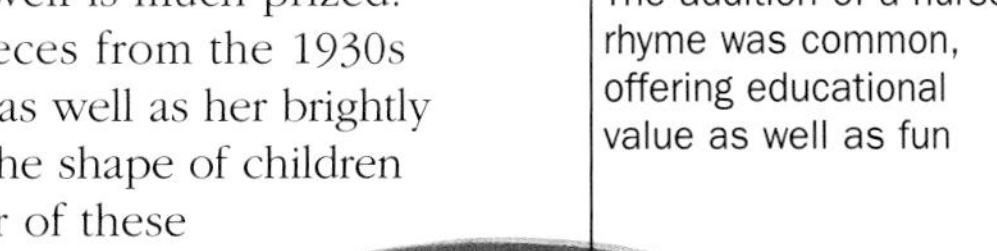

The addition of a nursery rhyme was common, offering educational value as well as fun

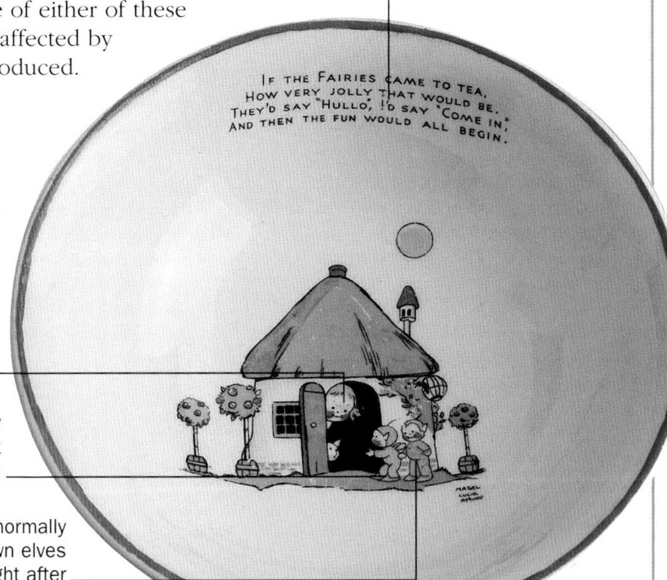


**A Mabel Lucie Attwell nursery bowl,** designed for Shelley. *1930s, 15cm (6in) diam.*

**£80–100**

Her children and elves are usually very rounded

Characters wear brightly coloured clothing that appeals to children

Attwell's elves are normally green. Yellow and brown elves are rarer and more sought after

### Makers' marks

*The leading companies were keen to promote their special ranges (such as nursery ware) by giving them individual backstamps in a different style from the main company mark. The designer's or artist's name was often featured, too. Mabel Lucie Attwell's name was incorporated within the pattern, just like an artist's signature. This gave extra cachet to the item and was a strong selling point.*

**On the base** of a Mabel Lucie Attwell nursery chamber pot the standard Shelley mark was used.

**On the front** of the same chamber pot the designer's name is featured next to a decorative motif.

**Royal Doulton 'Bunnykins' child's breakfast service,** designed by the artist Barbara Vernon Bailey. *c.1934, plate 18cm (7in) diam.*

**£30–50**

### Top Tips

- Be vigilant when buying a Susie Cooper nursery piece. Do not assume that it is hand painted: check for signs of hand painting such as brushstrokes and uneven paintwork.
- Be on your guard against fake Mabel Lucie Attwell plates. The colours are not as bold as on genuine examples and the transfers used are easy to scratch.
- Look out for 19th-century nursery ware that sheds light on the social history of the time: this adds to its interest and value.

### BUY

*Nursery wares from the 19th century are popular with collectors, especially if they show a childhood scene. Not surprisingly, ceramic nursery wares were often damaged. Surviving examples in good condition, especially those from the 19th and early 20th centuries, are often valuable.*

**A child's plate** inscribed with the title 'The Pet Lamb'. Showing a girl playing with a lamb beneath a tree, the plate uses pastoral imagery typical of the period. *c.1830–60, 13.5cm (5¼in) diam.*

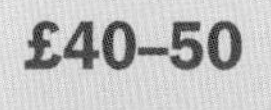

**£40–50**

### KEEP

*The fresh style of Eric Ravilious, who worked for Wedgwood from 1936–40, is much sought after. Official reproductions have been produced and are marked as such. The 'Alphabet' range included a jug, a plate, a porringer, a double egg cup, two sizes of mug, and a lamp base.*

**A Wedgwood 'Alphabet' mug,** designed by Eric Ravilious. It has a transfer print of the alphabet with images relating to the letters. *1938, 8cm (3¼in) high.*

**£200–300**

# Staffordshire and fairings

are two categories of ceramic figures inexpensively produced during the 19th and early 20th centuries. Their 'cheap and cheerful' nature lends them a naïve charm that ensures their continuing popularity.

In response to the popularity of expensive porcelain figurines, the Staffordshire potteries manufactured an enormous number of less costly ceramic figures throughout the 19th century. These brightly painted ornaments were made to stand on mantelpieces, and were sometimes sold as a pair. As well as a base, some had undecorated, flat backs that faced the wall. 'Flat backs' are sought after today and can fetch £100–300 or more, depending on subject matter and size.

Similar to Staffordshire figures, fairings were ceramic figure groups, often humorous in nature, that were sold, or won as prizes, at village fairs during the mid- to late 19th century. They tend to be smaller than Staffordshire figures, less colourful, and also less varied in subject matter. But despite humble origins, fairings are now a thriving collecting field.

## From rural to royal

Early Staffordshire figures tend to be stock characters and groups, such as lovers, children, and pastoral scenes. Many of these rural compositions contain a bush or a tree behind the group, known as 'bocage'. Some have a moral or religious theme. Despite their charm, stock characters are common, so are often less desirable. They usually fetch £80–300 or more, depending on size and quality. Pairs and those with complex 'bocage' can fetch up to £2,000 or more. Figures of the royal family were also made in large numbers. Lesser-quality Staffordshire pieces are unlikely to rise in value, because of the numbers made, their gaudy colours, and a current trend away from ornate Victorian styles. But if fashions change, the best examples may show modest gains.

## Heroes and villains

The most desirable Staffordshire pieces to invest in are identifiable portrait figures from Victorian life, produced from about 1840 onwards. Look for military or naval heroes, especially from the Napoleonic wars, or for infamous and newsworthy characters such as the highwayman Dick Turpin, as they are usually worth more. Values are around £100–500 or even higher, depending on size, modelling,

**'The harvest festival', a Staffordshire group,** with figures standing in front of a 'bocage' tree, on a landscaped base, with wheat sheaves. There are minor chips, without which the piece would be worth up to double the value listed. *c.1850s, 19cm (7½in) wide.*

**£300–400**

**'A long pull and a strong pull': a comic fairing** of a dentist extracting a tooth. *c.1880s, 13cm (5in) long.*

**£80–120**

## A closer look at... two naval Staffordshire figures

Along with Victorian personalities, naval and military figures are among the most popular subjects. Larger and more visually appealing figures will usually make the best investments, especially if they are modelled on well-known personalities such as Admiral Lord Nelson.

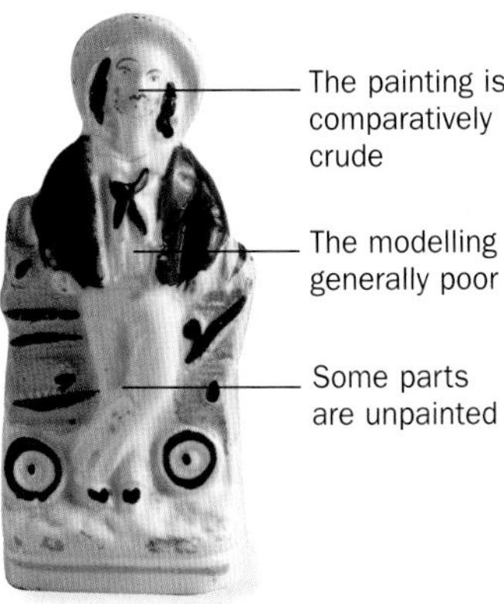

The painting is comparatively crude

The modelling is generally poor

Some parts are unpainted

**A small mid-19th century Staffordshire sailor,** leaning on a gun carriage. This figure would have been inexpensive in its day. *c.1850s, 11cm (4¼in) high.*

**£20–30**

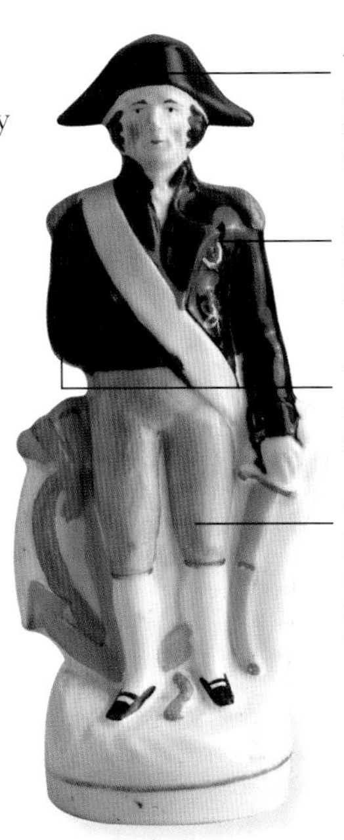

The distinctive cocked hat is characteristic of Nelson

Gilt has been used as a highlighter

The missing right arm is another accurate detail

The painting incorporates more colours and covers more of the piece than on the sailor

**A large Staffordshire figure of Admiral Lord Nelson,** standing before an anchor. The tip of his hat has been restored, which lowers the value. *c.1850s, 20cm (7¾in) high.*

**£150–200**

condition, and the personality in question. Also look out for figures marking key military events: a trio of soldiers under a flag commemorating victory in the Crimean War could fetch more than £500.

### Sporting heroes

Sporting figures are also collectable, but beware of modern reproductions: a lightweight body, poor-quality painting, and clumsily executed details are all tell-tale signs. A pair of cricketers standing beside wickets can fetch around £1,500: pairs are usually worth more and, in this case, the figure will appeal to collectors of sporting memorabilia too.

Many glazed white ceramic fairings were manufactured in Germany – the best by Conta & Boehme. These took the form of bawdy, humorous vignettes, such as hen-pecked husbands. They were set on oblong bases inscribed in gilt with a saucy title. A 'before and after' pair can be worth up to 10 times as much as a single piece.

Conta & Boehme fairings were unmarked until the late 1870s, when an impressed crooked arm holding a dagger within a shield was introduced. Early examples from the 1850s and 60s are of better quality and have sharper detail, as the moulds were fresher. They are always worth more: the best pieces can exceed £150.

Look for pieces that are solid, rather than hollow, and have gilt-painted copperplate titles. Reproductions often have a black printed title on the base and larger 'airholes' underneath.

**'Welsh tea party': a group fairing.** *c.1880s, 12cm (4¾in).*

**£15–20**

### Top Tips

- Examine gold decoration on a Staffordshire figure to help date it: burnished gold was used in the 1850s–70s. A cheaper 'bright gold' was invented in the 1880s.
- Look out for titles or tell-tale signs, such as distinctive clothing or props, to help identify historical characters.
- Avoid fairings that are marked 'Made In Germany' on the underside. These are not Conta & Boehme and will have been made after around 1920.
- When buying, check all the figure's extremities under a magnifying glass for repairs or restoration – the tiniest fault can have a huge impact on value.
- Beware of reproductions, which are generally more crudely painted and modelled than the originals.

### SELL

*Always consider the subject matter of fairings: certain niche subjects, such as bicycling and sporting themes, can cross collecting markets and yield higher prices. Sell to take advantage of the healthy competition between two separate, but equally dedicated, collecting groups.*

**'A dangerous encounter': a cyclist's fairing.** The early style of the bicycles shown, dating from after 1865, would make this piece attractive to collectors of bicycling memorabilia. *c.1870, 8.5cm (3¼in) high.*

**£400–500**

### KEEP

*Undamaged fairings showing typical subject matter (usually vaguely erotic or risqué) will always be of interest – particularly if the colours are bright, as on higher-quality, earlier examples. Prices are rising steadily among a small but dedicated and growing band of collectors.*

**'Kiss me quick': a butler and maid fairing.** The 'seaside peepshow' humour of this piece sums up the spirit of many fairings. *c.1890s, 9cm (3½in) high.*

**£80–120**

# Royal Doulton figures were one of the company's most popular products, and are prized today. At one extreme are the 'fair ladies', with their flounced petticoats and crinolines; at the other, the earthier charms of town criers and fictional characters from Dickens and Tolkien.

**Charles Noke's miniature 'The Jester', orginally one of his 'Vellum' range but remodelled by Robert Tabbenor,** HN3335. Noke was fascinated by entertainers. His original 'Vellum' pieces, made in the 1890s before the HN series began, and named after their parchment colour, can fetch more than £1,000. *1990, 10cm (4in) high.*

**£150–250**

Despite having produced a few decorative figures in the late 19th century, it was not until the 1920s that Royal Doulton began in earnest to release the pieces that have become so popular with collectors today. The range now numbers more than 2,000 different figures.

## Slender and small

Posed in expressive, carefree, or romantic postures, Doulton ladies can be found for less than £50 or as much as several thousand pounds, depending on the model, date, and colour. Some enthusiasts choose to collect by colour, others by modeller – certain modellers being well known for particular themes. As well as the 'fair ladies', other popular topics include children and historical and literary personalities.

Miniature figurines, launched in 1932 and again in 1988, are also popular, especially for those with limited space. Two of the most sought-after series are the miniature Charles Dickens characters and 'fair ladies'. Some of these pieces have a rarity value and can command prices close to or greater than prices for the larger models.

**'Town Crier', designed by Peggy Davies,** HN2119. *1953–76, 20.5cm (8in) high.*

**£50–70**

## Some designers to look for:

- Charles Noke
- Leslie Harradine
- Peggy Davies

**Leslie Harradine's 'Paisley Shawl' figurine, with red shawl and cream dress with painted flowers,** HN1392. Designing at least one figure per month from 1920, Harradine was one of Doulton's best modellers. Stylish, 'fair ladies' in crinoline dresses dominated his work. *1930–49, 21cm (8¼in) high.*

**£50–70**

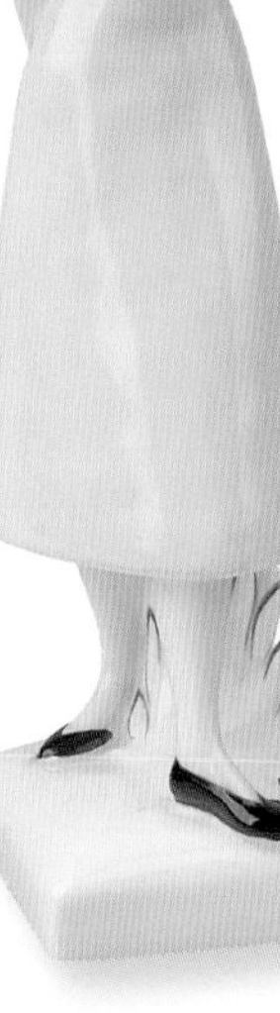

**Peggy Davies's 'Sweet Sixteen', from her 'Teenagers' series,** HN2231. Margaret ('Peggy') Davies created more than 250 figurines from 1946 to 1984. As well as her teenagers, she is known for her 1950s figures in period dress, historical personalities, and children. *1958–65, 18.5cm (7¼in) high.*

**£50–80**

## The numbers game

Values tend to be high for early figures, dating from the 1920s and 30s, and for those produced for limited periods of only a year or so. Every year, Royal Doulton announces a list of figures to be withdrawn from production – a practice that was started just before World War II. When the first withdrawals were announced, many of the designs affected had been made in runs of fewer than 2,000, which makes them valuable today. A good example is Harry Fenton's 'The Newhaven Fishwife', produced from 1931–37.

Prices have fallen for more common figurines, or those that were produced recently. Collectors should focus on earlier or rare examples, and look out for variations, which can be desirable.

A knowledge of colour variations is essential when deciding whether to buy or sell a Royal Doulton figure. A good example is Leslie Harradine's 'Paisley Shawl'. If she is numbered HN1392, she will be wearing a red shawl and may fetch up to £100. If numbered HN1707, she will have a much rarer purple shawl, and can be worth up to one and a half times as much.

**'The Newhaven Fishwife', designed by Harry Fenton,** HN1480. *1931–37, 19.5cm (7¾in) high.*

**£1,000–1,500**

## In Doulton's wake

Other makers produced similar decorative figures. Wade issued a series of Art Deco dancing ladies in flowing gowns. The finish of these pieces was prone to flaking, so it is hard to find them in mint condition. Prices for Wade are generally low, which makes this a good place to look for stylish Art Deco figures for less than £100. Arcadian produced a range of 'fair ladies' along the same lines as Royal Doulton. Slightly less well modelled, but just as colourful, examples can be found for about £50 or less.

### Top Tips

- Know your numbers. Most Royal Doulton figures can be identified from the 'HN' number on the base. Miniatures made between 1932 and 1949 have an 'M' number instead, and sometimes the words 'Doulton England' instead of the standard factory mark.
- Look for unusual colours. Some can fetch a premium, so even if you have one of the more common figures, find out if you have a rare colour.
- Use backstamps for dating. Backstamps that include a printed name refer to the designer of the original figure, and these figures nearly always date from after 1984.
- To prevent damage, do not stand figures too close together.

### SELL

*Although attractive and very popular with the original buyers, figures produced for long periods are unlikely to rise much in value, as so many examples can be found. But look out for unusual variations in colour on a particular figure, as these are the exception to the rule.*

**'Top o' the Hill', designed by Leslie Harradine,** HN1834. This figure was released in 1937 and has been in continuous production ever since. *c.1990s, 19cm (7½in) high.*

**£15–25**

### KEEP

*Many people collect by series. Dickens' miniatures are popular, and collectors are increasingly drawn to the 'Middle Earth' series, inspired by Tolkien's Lord of The Rings, which are becoming scarcer and more valuable. TV programmes have contributed to interest in the Dickens series, while Tolkien has gained fans thanks to the movie blockbusters. Many of these figurines were only produced for a short period. The price rises look set to continue, as demand outstrips the limited supply.*

**'Barliman Butterbur', designed by David Lyttleton, from the Tolkien 'Middle Earth' series,** HN2923. The Tom Bombadil figure from this series is even more scarce and valuable. *1982–84, 13.3cm (5¼in) high.*

**£30–50**

## ▪ Nada Pedley ▪ Pauline Parsons ▪

**Nada Pedley's 'Christine',** HN3767. Pedley's figures usually wear idealised and romantic Victorian and Edwardian clothes. *1996–98, 20cm (7¾in) high.*

**£20–30**

**Pauline Parsons' 'Susan',** HN3050, boxed. Since Peggy Davies's retirement in 1984, Parsons has become the leading modeller of 'fair lady' figures at Royal Doulton. *1986–95, 21.6cm (8½in) high.*

**£20–30**

# Ceramic figures of elegant ladies, beguiling children, and scenes from mythology are collected avidly. Apart from Royal Doulton, there are many makers, such as Hummel, Lladró, Coalport, and Royal Dux, each with their admirers.

**A Royal Copenhagen porcelain figure of a girl with a goose,** no. 528. *1980s–90s, 18.5cm (7¼in) high.*

**£40–60**

Firms that specialise in this highly collectable area of ceramics are found throughout Europe. Central Europe, in particular, has provided many sought-after ranges of figures, including Art Nouveau maidens from Royal Dux in Duchcov, and sophisticated Art Deco ladies from the Austrian factory of Goldscheider.

## Lovable Hummels

The most widely collected figures are the Hummel figures of children, developed from sketches by a Franciscan nun, Berta Hummel, for the Goebel company in Bavaria. Introduced in 1935, the figures were an instant success. By 1946, she had produced around 600 drawings for Goebel.

Hummels from the 1950s and 60s can be bought for £30–100, but larger figures, groups, and earlier pieces can reach £150–250 or more. Hummel is popular in the USA, so selling on the Internet can yield worthwhile results, particularly for rarities.

Factory marks help in dating Hummels. In the 1930s, the firm used a script 'Goebel' mark under a crown. After 1950, a 'V' mark with a small bee was used, and from 1960 the bee became further stylised as a simple dot with triangular wings. The marks can also lead you to other helpful information, such as the name of the figure and the modeller.

In 2008, Goebel announced that they would discontinue the Hummel range, and although it is too early to tell, this may affect values in the future.

## Spanish elegance

The Spanish firm Lladró has produced figures since the 1970s. They can be recognised by their fine detailing, sleek shapes, and muted tones of blue and grey. As a relatively recent collecting area, prices are still reasonable: some of the smaller child figures can be

## Some Hummel figures to look for:

- Puppy Love
- Merry Wanderer
- Mother's Darling
- Weary Wanderer

**'Puppy Love',** with some damage. This is one of the first 46 models issued in 1935. This version, with the head facing right, is rare and valuable. *1950s, 12cm (4¾in) high.*

**£20–30**

**'Merry Wanderer',** standard size. This model has been made in three versions: the largest (24cm/9½in high) can fetch more than £1,000. *1950s, 10cm (4in) high.*

**£20–30**

**'Mother's Darling'.** Older versions, like this one, have light pink and yellow-green bags. Newer versions have blue and red bags. *1945–97, 15cm (6in) high.*

**£20–30**

**'Weary Wanderer'.** This figure was modelled in 1949 and has been made ever since. A rare variation with blue eyes can fetch up to £200. *1940s, 15cm (6in) high.*

**£30–40**

bought for about £30–40 at auction, and mid-sized figures and groups often sell for around £80–150. Large centrepieces can reach £700–1,000.

## Danish blue

Royal Copenhagen figures are finely modelled and usually found in pale colours, often with a blue tone. Subjects tend to be pastoral, domestic, or mythical. A figure of Pan fighting with a bear, from the 1940s, can be worth £300, as can 'Friends', from the same period, showing a girl with a dog. Large and early figures are usually the most valuable.

## Back in England

As well as their many other products, the English firms Royal Worcester and Coalport are renowned for their figures. Among the most collectable Royal Worcester figures are children made by the noted modeller Freda Doughty in the 1930s. Today, Royal Worcester figures can be found for £50–500, or more for early or large figures, works by notable designers, or those in limited editions with low production runs.

Look out for 1960s figures designed by Ronald and Ruth van Ruyckevelt, which can fetch up to £500, and are yet to reach their peak.

Coalport started producing figures of elegant ladies in flowing gowns in the 1970s. They are grouped in series, such as 'High Society' and 'Age of Elegance'. Collecting a full set is not easy, as many figures are discontinued each year. Prices range from about £30 to £200, with higher prices being paid for examples by noted designers, such as David Shilling, or those in limited editions with production runs in the low hundreds.

The SylvaC pottery is better known for its animals, but its figures from the 1920s and 30s are sought after. Those in the Art Deco style are usually worth £30–70. Other, more whimsical subjects including gnomes, sailors, and Welsh ladies, can be found for around £20–50.

### ■ Skier ■

**'Skier',** modelled and introduced in 1936. The ski poles were originally made from wood, but they can also be found in metal and plastic. *1950s, 13cm (5in) high.*

**£100–150**

## Top Tips

- Check the extremities of a Hummel figure carefully for signs of repair – they were made in brittle ceramic. Leave space between them when displaying to avoid damage.
- Choose figures from well-known factories rather than smaller ones, as these were often better made and are more valuable.
- Look for finely detailed modelling and painting whatever the period, although, as a rule, figures from the 1930s tend to be better modelled and painted than later examples.
- Beware of 'limited' editions of many thousands, as these are less likely to rise in value than figures made in a limited run of several hundred.
- Bear in mind that the more recent or common the figure, the more vital its condition in determining value.

## BUY

*SylvaC is highly collectable, but 1930s pieces finished in cellulose paint are often ignored, as they do not look typical of the firm. Go for those in a good condition (watch out for flaking paint). Interest is sure to spread to these early pieces soon.*

**A SylvaC 'Flapper Girl',** stamped '880'. This is a popular subject and style. *1930s, 22cm (8¾in) high.*

**£60–80**

## KEEP

*The Royal Worcester figures produced by Freda Doughty in the 1930s represent a landmark in the factory's history, as they challenged Royal Doulton's supremacy. Popularity remains strong, and prices should rise, especially if a piece is in excellent condition.*

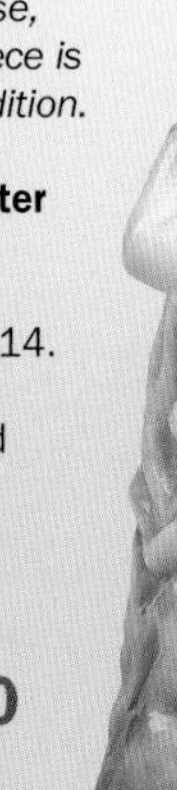

**A Royal Worcester 'My Favourite' figure, by Freda Doughty,** no. 3014. The figure was based on a child from Doughty's neighbourhood. *c.1933, 14cm (5¾in) high.*

**£150–200**

# Ceramic animals are enormously popular, especially among those who enjoy collecting a favourite species. Ranging from realistic models to characters from children's books, they were often made by notable factories such as Royal Doulton.

**A Staffordshire Dalmatian,** standing on an oblong base. *c.1870, 15.5cm (6¼in) high.*

**£120–180**

Dogs are among the most collectable of ceramic animals, perhaps reflecting the loyalty people show their pets. Other creatures collected range from breeds of cattle and sheep to the wild beasts of far-distant lands.

## Spaniels and sheepdogs

Ceramic Staffordshire animals were produced in great numbers from the early 19th century, when these inexpensive figurines were in vogue. They were often produced in facing pairs. Classic Staffordshire spaniels and sheepdogs are plentiful and usually fetch less than £200 for a pair in good condition. Earlier examples (1820s–40s) have longer snouts and more detail in the modelling and painting. Look for earlier, colourful pieces in preference to later, plainer ones, but avoid those with 'bright gold' collars and leads, as these were made after 1880 and are much more common. Single dogs are of less value, as are matched pairs (from similar moulds but not originally sold together). These can fetch less than half the value of a genuine pair.

Greyhounds from the 19th century usually fetch around £100–300 for a pair. Rabbits come in a range of sizes, but owing to their scarcity can sell for very high prices: a large pair can be worth up to £4,000 or more, if in good condition. Cows were often modelled with milkmaids or as holders for spills (strips of wood for lighting hearths, pipes, and candles).

Wild animals are among the more popular Staffordshire figures today. Scarce creatures such as zebras, especially facing pairs, can fetch £100–300 or more. Other wild animals such as lions and tigers are rarer still, and can fetch £400–600 or more. Beware of modern reproductions and 'marrieds' – models from different periods that have been brought together to form a pair.

## Doulton's menagerie

The choice of animal figures made by Royal Doulton is vast – more than 1,000 designs were issued. Like its human figures, Doulton's animals came under the auspices of the 'HN' range,

## Some Beswick animals to look for:

▪ Birds ▪ Cattle ▪ Dogs ▪

**A 'Lesser Spotted Woodpecker',** gloss, 2420, by modeller Graham Tongue. Beswick made wall-mounted mallards as well as freestanding birds. *1972–82, 14cm (5½in) high.*

**£100–150**

**A 'Hereford Bull',** gloss, 1363a. This is the first version: the second version, 1363b, with horns flush with the ears, is worth much less. *c.1960s, 10.8cm (4½in) high.*

**£200–300**

### *Did You Know?*

*The glaze recipe and kiln conditions used to produce Royal Doulton's flambé glaze have remained a closely guarded secret known only to the flambé staff. The secret has been passed down the generations since 1904, when Cuthbert Bailey of Royal Doulton and Bernard Moore of Moore Brothers originally developed the glaze.*

which dates from 1913 until the present day. Heights vary from 15cm (6in) for a parrot to more than 35cm (14in) for an elephant. Penguins were among the first exotic creatures to appear in the HN range, and these can be worth around £150–200. Some rarer figures can fetch more: HN141, an early rhinoceros (made from 1917 to 1946), can fetch up to £1,200.

At Doulton's Burslem factory, some early animal figures were designed by the art director Charles Noke from 1913 into the 1920s. Accurate depictions of pedigree breeds of dogs were modelled by Frederick Daws. Prices usually range from around £30 to £1,000; the highest values are reserved for short production runs or unusual colour variations.

Royal Doulton experimented with glaze techniques, such as 'flambé', which has a rich red colour. Some

**A Royal Doulton flambé figure of a seated cat,** with a printed maker's mark on the base. The figure with a mouse on the cat's tail is worth £300–400. *c.1980s, 12.5cm (5in) high.*

**£75–95**

animal pieces in this style from the early 20th century are rare. The flambé glaze lends itself well to wild animals, enhancing their drama or ferocity. Monkeys, elephants, rhinoceroses, and polar bears are among the more sought-after pieces. Prices for post-1980 figures often range from around £20 to £30 for a small fox up to around £2,500 for a large elephant.

## Beswick bestiary

Since the 1930s, Beswick has produced an extensive range of animals, including exotic species. Their earthenware 'fancies' – decorative, whimsical pieces – are finely modelled and well decorated, although their original retail value was low. Beswick's animal figures are still among the most popular with collectors. Values have risen since the closure of the Beswick factory in 2002, but there are still some bargains to be had. Cattle, birds, fish, and dogs are often found for less than £100. Beswick's extensive wild animal range includes native and foreign species, from foxes, rabbits, and hares to pumas, leopards, and giraffes. Prices start at about £5–10 for a rabbit rising to as much as around £250 for a moose.

One of Beswick's most notable designers, Arthur Gredington, modelled a series of horses, some based on

### *Top Tips*

- Beware of fake Staffordshire animals – usually lighter in weight and paler in colour than originals, and less well modelled and painted.
- Inspect Beswick and Doulton figures for 'crazing', a network of fine cracks in the glaze – once this starts, it will eventually cover the entire piece.
- Check the legs of Beswick animals: as they are often 'free-standing', models can be vulnerable to damage.

■ Wild Animals ■ Horses ■

**A corgi,** thought to be model 1299. The black, tan, and white version, which is known as 'Black Prince', can fetch £60–80. *1953–94, 14cm (5½in) high.*

**£35–45**

**A lioness,** model 1507. Lioness figures with a golden-brown finish, such as this one, are more valuable than those with a black-glaze coat. *1957–67, 12cm (4¾in) high.*

**£45–65**

**A 'Girl on a Pony',** gloss, 1499. Versions with grey, dappled grey, brown, or tan coats are more valuable; this example has some damage. *1957–65, 14cm (5½in) high.*

**£200–300**

famous racers. Generic horses can cost as little as £20–30, but rare examples with riders, which were produced for short periods, can fetch around £300–500 or more.

## Accent on realism

Royal Worcester have excelled in producing animal figures, concentrating on quality rather than quantity, with some first-class limited editions. Doris Lindner modelled highly realistic animals for the company from the 1930s onwards. She began with dog studies but after the war explored larger subjects. Her early dogs and other animals can fetch £200–500, while her larger, limited-edition pieces from the 1950s, 60s, and 70s, depicting famous racehorses, championship cattle, and equestrian figures, can fetch £700–1,500.

**A Royal Doulton 'Mrs Bunnykins Clean Sweep',** DB6. *1972–97, 10cm (4in) high.* **£20–30**

## Children's favourites

From Squirrel Nutkin to Flopsy and Mopsy, Beatrix Potter's characters are as popular today as when she published her first stories in 1902. Beswick began making Beatrix Potter figures in 1947. The initial series, introduced in 1948, comprised 10 characters including Peter Rabbit and the first Jemima Puddleduck, all of which were modelled by Arthur Gredington. These figures, marked with the gold-coloured Beswick backstamp, are the most desirable. Prices in general have fallen over the past few years, and can vary from as little as £10–15 for a 1970s or '80s 'Tom Kitten', to around £700–1,000 or more for rarer figures such as the black dog known as 'Duchess with Flowers'.

Both the featured character and the production period hold the key to value, with earlier models and those made for only a short time being most sought after. Since most characters were produced over a long period, it is easy to build up a collection of figures costing less than £50–100 each. Car-boot sales, collectors' fairs, and junk shops are good hunting grounds, while specialist auctions are the ideal places to find a particular piece to complete a collection.

## Marks tell all

Beswick Beatrix Potter figures can be dated to a period by the colour, shape, and wording of the backstamp printed on the base. There were many different marks, so it is always best to consult a detailed reference guide, as the subject can be confusing. Collectors have even developed a shorthand, referring to the backstamps as 'BP1', which appeared from 1948 to 1954, through to 'BP11', the most recent variation, used from 2001–2002. (This notation has been used for the figures shown below.)

## Clothing clues

A further clue to dating Beswick Beatrix Potter figures lies in the colour of the clothing. Earlier figures are darker in colour, owing to the lead content of the paint. A pre-1980s Peter Rabbit will have a deeper blue coat and can be worth up to £60, while a similar figure made after lead paint was banned in the 1980s will have a lighter-coloured coat and can cost around £20. In late 2002, Royal Doulton (who had bought Beswick in 1969) ceased production of these figures and the ceramics licence went

## Essential Beswick Beatrix Potter

**PETER RABBIT** This model has a gold BP2a backstamp. Versions made from 1980 onwards have paler-blue coats and are less valuable. 1955–72, 11.5cm (4½in) high. **£100–120**

**MR BENJAMIN BUNNY** This version has a maroon coat and a gold BP2-type backstamp. The one wearing a lilac coat is rare. 1955–72, 10.8cm (4¼in) high. **£80–120**

**PIGLING BLAND** The later version of this figure (1975–98), with a lilac coat, is worth half as much as this rare, early piece (with a BP3a mark in brown). 1973–74, 10.8cm (4¼in) high. **£150–200**

**FLOPSY, MOPSY, AND COTTONTAIL** This group has the BP2-type stamp. Early versions bear a round gold 'Beswick England' stamp. 1955–72, 6.4cm (2¾in) high. **£40–60**

**SIMPKIN** Crafted by Royal Doulton modeller Alan Maslankowski, Simpkin the cat is a rare and valuable character. This piece carries a BP3b-type brown mark. 1975–83, 10cm (4in) high. **£150–200**

**MRS TIGGYWINKLE** This figure bears a brown BP3b-type backstamp. Later examples with Royal Albert markings are only half as valuable. 1974–85, 8cm (3¼in) high. **£15–20**

### *Did You Know?*

*Barbara Vernon's original drawings that inspired the Royal Doulton Bunnykins series were caricatures of her family. The 'Father' figure with round spectacles and a pipe is based on Vernon's depiction of her own father, Cuthbert Bailey.*

to Border Fine Arts. The effect that this will have on prices for the original Beswick creations remains to be seen.

## Funny bunnies

The Bunnykins range by Royal Doulton was the brainchild of the factory manager, Cuthbert Bailey, who used his daughter Barbara's doodles to create a range of nursery ware in 1934. The line was mainly tableware, although a few figures were modelled by Charles Noke in 1939. Now rare, these can fetch between £300 and £700. World War II temporarily limited production to six characters including 'Billie Bunnykins', 'Mother Bunnykins', and 'Farmer Bunnykins'.

In 1972–73, Albert Hallam extended the range by a further 12 characters, including 'Family Photograph' and 'Billie Bunnykins Cooling Off'. Former Beswick modeller Graham Tongue then took over the range, but only 28 characters were produced by the early 1980s. Since then, at least one new figure has been released every year, many of them limited editions. Prices have fluctuated over the last 10 years, peaking around 1997 before falling once more.

Seek out appealing characters, and limited editions, especially those commissioned by the Suffolk-based retailer UK International Ceramics, as these have risen most in value. A 'Sergeant Mountie' Bunnykins figure originally sold for less than £50 but can now fetch £150–200 or more. Look for the scarce and valuable pre-war examples, which do not have the

**A Royal Doulton 'Tally Ho' Bunnykins figure.** *1988–93, 10cm (4in) high.*

**£30–40**

'DB' number used since 1972. Colour variations often fetch more, too.

## SylvaC fancies

SylvaC animal figures, although modestly priced, are no less prized by their owners than those from more prestigious factories. The firm was founded in 1894 and its whimsical ceramic animals were produced from the 1920s and marketed as 'fancies'. They were decorated in bright colours using cellulose paint. The SylvaC name was not used until around 1932. Shortly afterwards, the all-over, single-colour matt glaze that typifies the SylvaC range was created. From the mid-1930s until the 1960s the firm's popularity grew. Towards the end of this period a new, glossy finish known as 'bright glaze' was developed, and pieces started to resemble the figures Beswick. Despite the popularity of SylvaC, the factory went into liquidation in 1982. Production limped on under Longton Ceramics and Crown Winsor but finally ceased in 1989.

## Furry friends

A huge range of animals was produced by SylvaC, but rounded rabbits, pointy-eared hares, and terrier dogs are the most popular. Each piece is stamped with a mould number, but even so it is difficult to date a piece reliably: any date related to a mould number is the date the mould was made, not when the

### *Fact or Fiction?*

*It is believed that a 60cm (24in)-high SylvaC rabbit was once produced for promotional use by Boots the Chemist. Although an example is yet to come to light, its value would certainly be high and competition to own it would be intense.*

piece was produced, and some moulds were used for many years. Nor did mould numbers run consecutively. In general, earlier pieces have a more matt finish and a deeper colour than later ones.

## Prices and pitfalls

Values for SylvaC animals range from £10 to around £300, depending on size, colour, and rarity. Many shapes were made in a variety of sizes within the range 5–30cm (2–12in). Each size

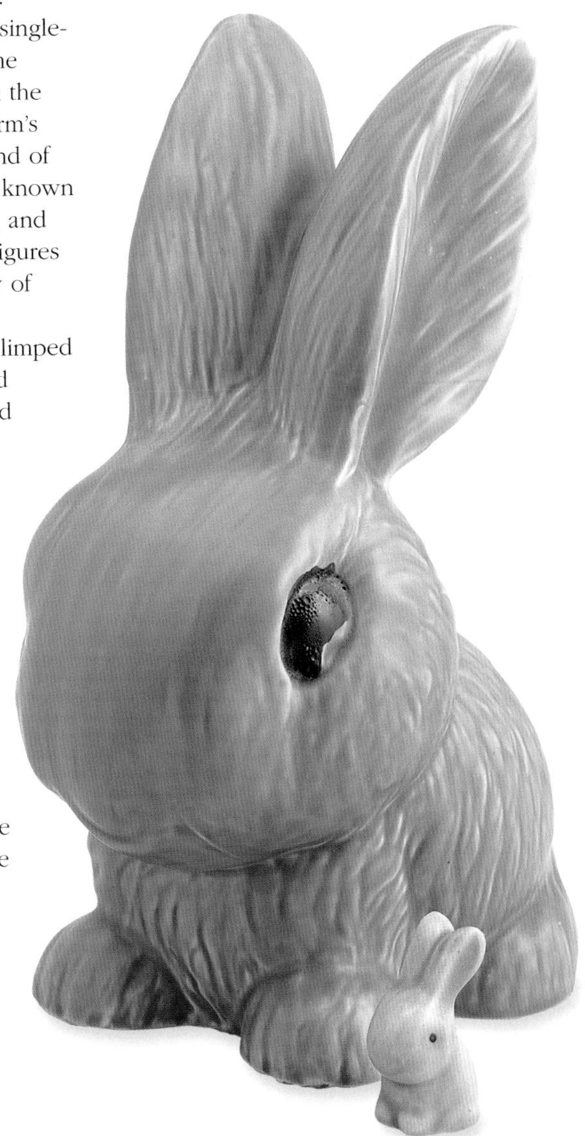

**A large SylvaC green rabbit, with a small SylvaC fawn rabbit,** mould 1028. *c.1960s, larger figure 25cm (10in) high.*

**large figure £50–70**
**small figure £15–25**

## A closer look at... two 'lop-eared' rabbits: one genuine SylvaC, one reproduction

**A genuine SylvaC fawn rabbit,** stamped '1509'. *c.1960s, 10.5cm (4¼in) high.*

**£15–25**

Although original SylvaC animals are still commonly found, modern reproductions are being made from genuine SylvaC moulds. At the same time, fakes are being made from moulds reproduced from the original pieces, resulting in a slightly smaller size than the original. Reproductions and fakes have comparatively little collectable value.

**A modern reproduction SylvaC fawn rabbit.** *c.2000, 10.5cm (4¼in) high.*

**£4–6**

has a different mould number, the larger examples being the most valuable. Colour is important. Most common are green and fawn (or beige). Pink is extremely rare and sought after. Brown and blue are also uncommon and desirable. A 21cm (8½in)-high rabbit cottonwool dispenser in pink, in which cottonwool is pulled from a hole in the tail, can fetch over £100. Some shapes are rare, such as the hippopotamus (mould 1425) and the 'Joey Dog' (mould 1191). These can often fetch up to £100.

Fakes and reproductions are common. Avoid confusing them with period pieces imitating SylvaC, made by firms such as Denby. Although not as sought after as SylvaC, these have some value, usually fetching £30–50 or less.

### Rabbits galore

Pendelfin figures were first produced as gifts for family and friends by Jeanie Todd and Jean Walmsley Heap of Burnley, Lancashire, in 1953. They soon went into commercial production with figures including pixies and witches. In 1955, they produced their first rabbit figure, 'Father Dungaree Rabbit', which was a success. This led to a family of rabbits, and afterwards rabbits became the mainstay of Pendelfin production. Many of the original shapes are still made. Those that have been withdrawn or were produced for only a short time are usually the most valuable.

Prices vary from about £5–15 to around £800 for very rare examples. Early models, such as the original rabbit family from the late 1950s, are the most desirable. Pendelfin also produced a range of animals, which are rare today as they were less popular and soon withdrawn. 'Cyril Squirrel', produced from 1963–1965, can fetch around £300–400, while 'Mother Mouse', produced from 1961–1966, can be worth more than £100 (she is worth considerably more in the rarer grey colour).

Not all figures are so expensive, such as 'Lucy Pocket', produced from 1960 to 1967, and 'Maud', produced from 1967 to 1978, can fetch around £20–30.

Look out for variations, such as figurines with thin necks, or those with

**A Pendelfin 'Puffer' figure,** produced for the Pendelfin Family Circle Collectors' Club and 'model of the year' for 1994. *1994, 11.5cm (4½in) high.*

**£10–15**

clothes of a different colour from the standard versions. 'Uncle Soames Rabbit', whose original clothes were drab, was redesigned with a more colourful outfit to increase sales. 'Midge Rabbit' eating a biscuit was produced between 1956 and 1965 with varying numbers of crumbs on her dress – the more crumbs there are, the more she is worth. Values range from £20 to more than £100.

## The value of exclusives

Special limited editions, such as figurines produced to commemorate Pendelfin events or sold exclusively through the official collectors' club, are less valuable, often fetching £50 or less. They may make a good investment for the future, but they must be in mint condition with their box and any original paperwork.

**A Pendelfin 'Midge Rabbit',** holding a biscuit with two crumbs on her blue dress. *1956–65, 12.5cm (3¼in) high.*

**£20–30**

### Top Tips

- Keep the box and any paperwork issued with the more modern Beswick Beatrix Potter characters produced from the mid-1980s onwards, as this will help to increase value.
- Take great care when handling and moving SylvaC as it chips easily.
- Avoid early SylvaC examples decorated in cellulose paint that is beginning to flake.
- Look out for Pendelfin figurines in the form of animals other than rabbits, as these are usually more valuable.
- Check Pendelfin carefully for damage: the decoration is prone to flaking and chipping, and some models are top-heavy and so may have fallen at some point and been repaired.



## BUY

*Interest in Beswick animals has increased since the factory's closure in 2002. They should make an excellent investment for the future – especially pieces withdrawn from circulation some time previously.*

**A Beswick 'Zebra',** gloss, 845b, modelled by Arthur Gredington. This figure was withdrawn from production in 1969. *c.1960s, 18.4cm (7¼in) high.*

**£100–150**

## BUY

*Some of the currently less valuable but still well-loved Beatrix Potter characters display the desirable early gold-coloured backstamps. They are worth considering as an investment, as they may rise in value significantly as the market grows.*

**A Beswick Beatrix Potter 'Jeremy Fisher',** with a gold BP2a backstamp. This beige version with spots over his body is worth more than the one with striped legs. *1955–72, 7.6cm (3in) high.*

**£50–70**

## BUY

*Later SylvaC figures, produced from the late 1960s onwards in a glossy 'bright glaze', are currently not as popular as earlier pieces decorated in the classic matt glaze. The modelling and colouring are good but prices are still relatively low – though rising. As demand grows further, they may prove a good investment.*

**A SylvaC 'bright glaze' 'Collie' dog.** Dogs are widely liked. This figure bears the mould number '2502'. *c.1970s, 17.5cm (7in) high.*

**£10–15**

## SELL

*The Pendelfin market has been declining for some time, but there are some dedicated collectors who are keen to build collections often started in childhood. Sell now, as the market is unlikely to grow again in the near future.*

**A Pendelfin 'Mother' figure,** dressed in lilac. This thin-necked version of 'Mother' was produced for one year only in 1956. There is minor wear on this example. *1956, 12.5cm (7½in) high.*

**£30–40**

## KEEP

*Limited editions or those produced for short periods are likely to rise in value as the number of Bunnykins collectors grows. This is particularly likely if the piece is part of a series.*

**A Royal Doulton Bunnykins 'King John',** DB91. Part of the desirable second issue of the 'Royal Family' series, this figure is from a limited edition of 250. The range has no certificate. *1990, 10cm (4in) high.*

**£250–350**

## SELL

*Staffordshire animals are out of vogue with many people because they don't fit in with modern interiors, so prices are unlikely to rise in the near future, except for rarities.*

**A pair of Staffordshire King Charles spaniels.** Spaniels such as these are commonly found. One of this pair is also damaged, reducing value. *c.1870s, 19cm (7½in) high.*

**£50–60**

THE AFRICA STAR
THE ITALY STAR
THE FRANCE AND GERMANY STAR
GEORGIVS VI D:G:BR:OMN:REX F:D:IND:IMP:

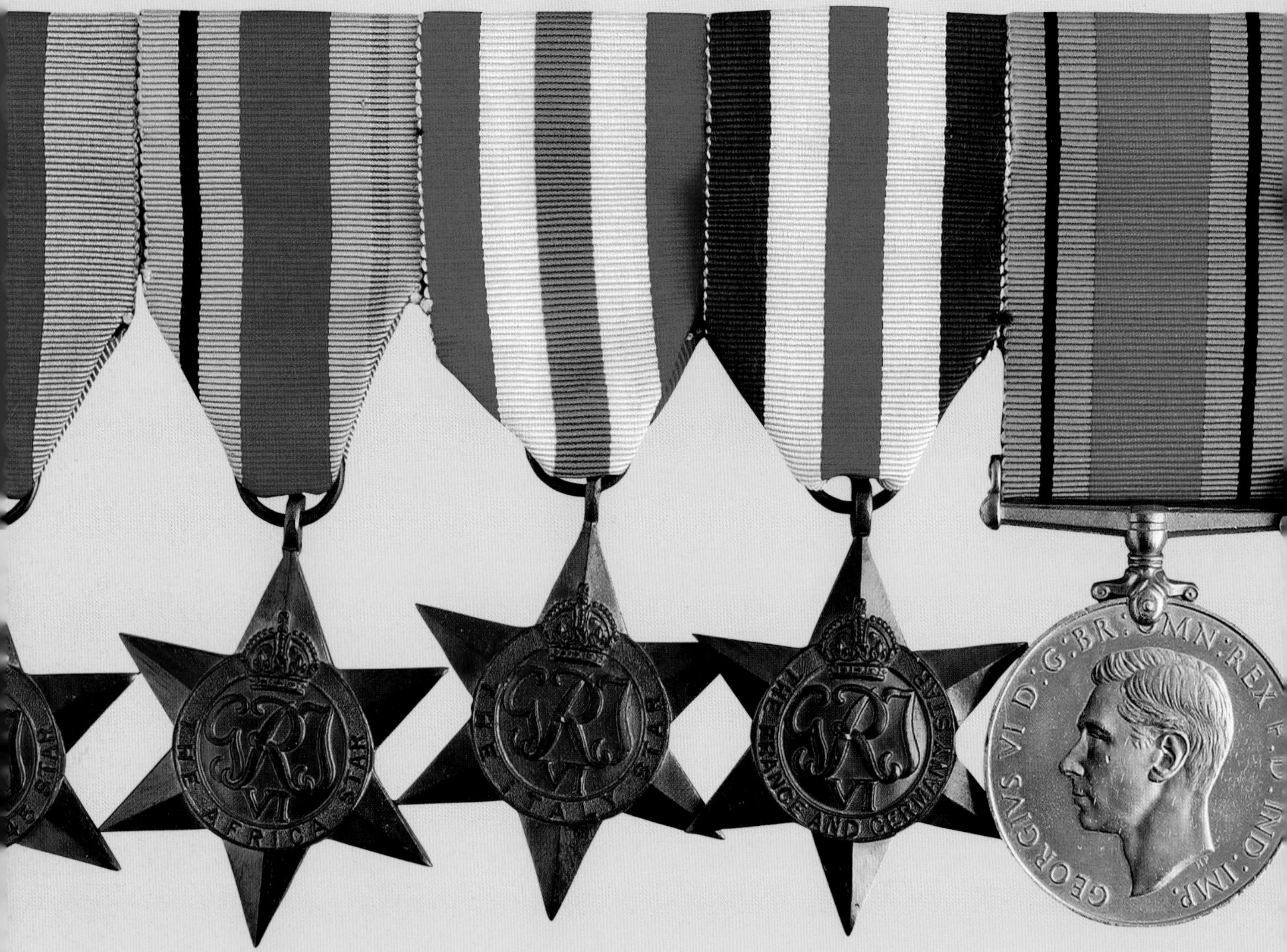

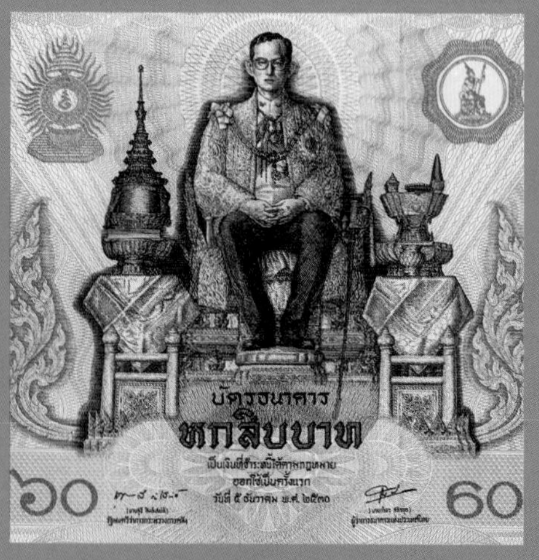

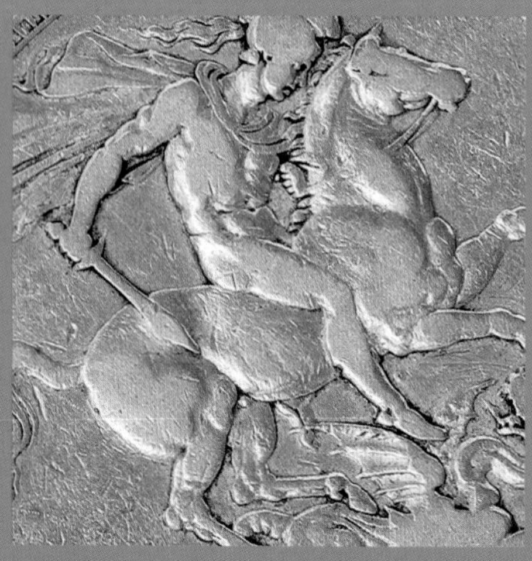

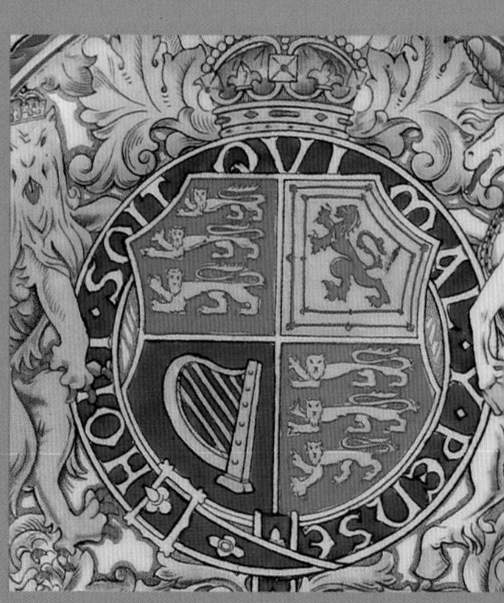

# Historical Memorabilia

Historical memorabilia offers a tangible reminder of key events of the past. It encompasses mugs made to commemorate special events such as royal births and political victories, as well as military medals, holiday souvenirs, and the stamps and coins that were once part of daily life.

1 Wedgwood coronation mug, p.73

2 Coronation teapot, p.75

# Moments of history......

Historical memorabilia shows how important events have been commemorated through the decades. From coronation mugs to Victorian holiday souvenirs, coins, and special issue bank notes, these pieces were treasured when they were created and are still collectable today.

Many of us have a mug we were given to celebrate a royal wedding, or remember a grandparent showing us the medals a relative won during the war. These mementoes are now highly collectable. Many of them have an interesting story attached, which can add to their value.

## Landmarks

Commemorative ceramics have been mass-produced since just before Queen Victoria's reign. Every royal marriage, birth, coronation, and jubilee has been marked with mugs (1), teapots (2), plates, and ornaments.

Politicians such as Sir Winston Churchill (3) are also associated with a huge number of items, ranging from mugs and plates to wartime posters, signed letters, and the front pages of newspapers of the time.

## Holiday souvenirs

The spread of the railways in the 19th century meant that more and more people went on day trips and holidays, leading

5 Mauchline ware money box, p.84

6 Silver lantern Stanhope, p.86

7 Goss crested pot, p.82

Many personal mementoes have an interesting story attached to them which can enhance their intrinsic value.

3 Churchill character jug, p.81

4 Tunbridgeware caddy, p.85

# .brought to life

8 Crimean medal, p.88

to a booming industry in souvenirs. Early examples include Tunbridgeware (4), inlaid wooden souvenirs mainly featuring geometric designs in different colour woods, and Mauchline ware (5), wooden souvenirs printed with picturesque views, originally produced in and around Mauchline, Ayrshire.

Stanhopes (6) were popular souvenirs from Victorian times to the 1930s. These novelty items have a secret feature – a tiny window through which you can see images such as a town, monument, or person.

From the late 19th century onwards, small ceramic items featuring the coats of arms of different towns were mass-produced by firms such as W.H. Goss (7). Attractive to enthusiasts, they were made in many shapes from traditional cups and jugs to coal scuttles, lighthouses, and even army tanks.

## Minted treasures

Old medals (8) – particularly those relating to famous victories or outstanding achievements – have long fascinated collectors. It's worth checking any examples to see if they have extra features which may add to their value.

Many schoolchildren enjoy collecting postage stamps (9) and first day covers. If you still have a parent's or grandparent's collection, it's worth taking a closer look to see if any of the stamps they collected in the past have increased significantly in value over the years.

Old coins (10) and bank notes (11) are sought after for their historical and aesthetic appeal more than for their face value, but rare coins can be valuable and the scarcer banknotes increase in value as time goes by.

9 Penny Black stamp, p.91

10 Victorian crown, p.92

11 Bank of England 10 shilling note, p.93

# Early royal commemorative ware

spans the reigns of Victoria, Edward VII, George V, Edward VIII, and George VI, capturing events such as the 1851 Great Exhibition and the Boer War, along with royal births, deaths, and coronations.

**A Doulton bone-china plate,** produced to celebrate Queen Victoria's Diamond Jubilee. *1897, 22.5cm (8¾in) wide.*

**£40–60**

Many of us are familiar with early commemorative memorabilia, and may even be lucky enough to own a piece or to have inherited a family heirloom. The range of souvenirs produced to mark the many royal and historic events of this period gives plenty of scope for any enthusiast wishing to build a collection. Pieces vary in rarity and quality, but start at around £20–50. The market for these souvenirs, however, has softened with less interest from the USA.

## The dawn of a new era

Queen Victoria's coronation in 1838 was the first royal occasion for which souvenirs were mass-produced in advance. Coronation mugs, still widely available, bear a single-colour transfer portrait of the young queen. Despite their low production cost, they often fetch over £500, but value is halved if a mug has been damaged.

## From grief to jubilation

Queen Victoria's Golden Jubilee in 1887 was subdued, as she was still in mourning for her husband Albert, who had died more than 25 years earlier. Relatively few pieces were produced – usually in brown, black, and other dull colours – and they tend to be much less popular than the more attractive items created for her Diamond Jubilee 10 years later. Doulton's 'Jubilee' beakers were issued in several colours, and enthusiasts often seek to collect one of each. The most valuable (those with fine-quality multicoloured transfers) can fetch more than £150. Single-coloured examples can be worth £50–120.

Copeland wares are well regarded. Their ceramics with a portrait of Victoria against a Wedgwood-like sage-green background included beakers, mugs, jugs, and teapots. Some pieces were made in five sizes. Prices vary according

**A Copeland earthenware jug,** with a raised cameo showing a well-modelled profile of Queen Victoria, made to commemorate her Diamond Jubilee. *1897, 16cm (6¼in) high.*

**£60–80**

**A Crown Ducal earthenware mug,** depicting Princess Margaret on the occasion of her father George VI's coronation. *1937, 7cm (2¾in) high.*

**£50–60**

to size: the smallest teapot fetches about £270, the largest £500. Royal Worcester also made 'Diamond Jubilee' cups and saucers in single colours. These are worth about £300 for a cup and saucer.

## Double dating

Edward VII's coronation, planned for 26 June 1902, was in fact postponed until 9 August. Potteries produced pieces for both the original and the actual coronation date. Issues displaying the August date alone, or both dates, are rarer and can be worth twice as much as those with the June date. An earthenware mug by an unknown maker commemorating peace in the Boer War on one side and Edward VII's coronation on the other can fetch around £50–100.

Some beakers and cups feature a royal portrait in a translucent 'lithophane' base, visible only when held to the light. Four designs were made, for Edward VII, Queen Alexandra, George V, and Queen Mary. The most common, for Edward VII, is worth up to £50; the rarest, for Queen Mary, can fetch over £300.

## The uncrowned king

Wares produced for Edward VIII's coronation (which never took place), are not valuable because so many were produced. Items marking his abdication are worth far more.

**An Aynsley bone-china mug,** made for the coronation of George V. *1911, 7.5cm (3in) high.*

**£20–30**

## A closer look at... a Victorian commemorative plate

Commemorative plates can provide a fascinating window on the past, but they are common and prices have remained static for many years. It is important to look for good-quality, undamaged examples. The 'deluxe' version of this British Empire plate has an all-over multicoloured transfer print and gilding. It can be worth twice as much as the version shown here.

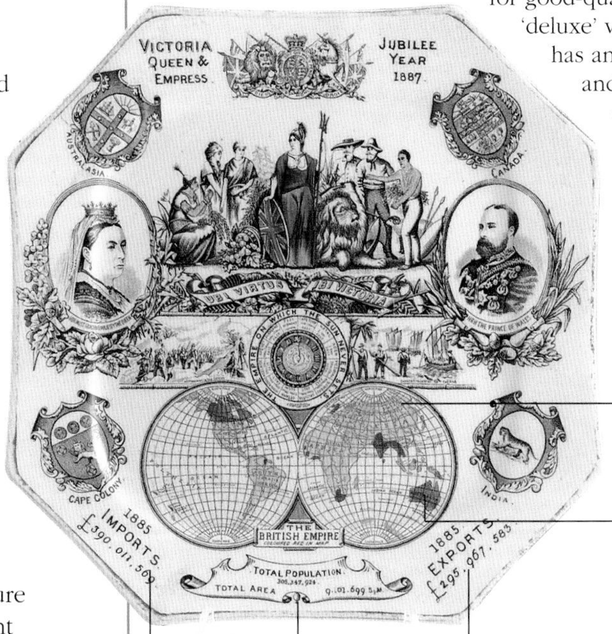

**A 'Balance of Payments' plate,** made by Wallis Gimson to commemorate Queen Victoria's Golden Jubilee in 1887. *c.1885, 24.5cm (9¾in) wide.*

**£60–80**

Added colour increases the plate's value – plates in a single colour are worth less

Red is used to show the extent of the British Empire in 1885 under Queen Victoria

The population of the Empire and its total imports and exports in 1885 are stated

### *Did You Know?*

*The design for Doulton's beakers celebrating Queen Victoria's Golden Jubilee in 1887 was jointly created by John Slater, Doulton's first art director, and the future Edward VII. Some of these beakers were given away as souvenirs to children in London's Hyde Park. Today they can be worth £80–120.*

### *Top Tips*

- Focus your collection on a particular monarch, event, theme (such as a jubilee), or manufacturer, to make it more coherent.
- Judge quality by the fineness of the body and any lithographed decoration – especially when it has several colours and includes portraiture.
- Unless the item is rare, avoid buying pieces that are in poor condition. Also carefully check the quality of transfer-printed portraits.

### BUY

*The death of Prince Albert in 1861 threw queen and country into mourning. Relatively few pieces commemorating his death were made, and these are scarce. Consequently, memorial pieces are in demand and are likely to rise in value.*

**A Prince Albert memorial earthenware plate,** printed in brown. It would be worth more if it had not been restored. *c.1862, 28cm (11in) wide.*

**£80–120**

### KEEP

*Wedgwood produced mugs for the coronations of Edward VIII and George VI, with decoration by the renowned artist Eric Ravilious. These high-quality mugs are typical of the styles of the period. They will at least hold their price, and may rise in value.*

**A Wedgwood earthenware mug,** from a design by Eric Ravilious, made to commemorate the coronation of George VI. *1937, 10cm (4in) high.*

**£200–300**

# Elizabeth II has had every stage of her life commemorated on a rich variety of ceramics. By collecting pieces relating to your own lifetime, you can trace the splendid public history threading through an era of tremendous change.

Have a close look at any early commemorative wares found in the attic or given to you by an elderly relative. Those produced to mark Elizabeth II's birth in 1926 are scarce, apart from a tea service produced by Paragon. Collectors are put off by its unusual decoration of magpies and the lack of any personal imagery. Today, a cup and saucer can fetch £60–80, a teapot more. Two years later Paragon made a set that is more popular with enthusiasts because it features a transfer portrait and the message 'The Empire's Little Princess'. Commemoratives of the princess's 1947 wedding to Lieutenant Philip Mountbatten are also rare, as rationing was still in place and few were made.

**A Wedgwood mug,** designed by Richard Guyatt, issued to celebrate the Coronation. *c.1953, 10cm (4in) high.*

**£150–200**

## Crowning glories

In contrast, a vast number of pieces, especially mugs, were produced for the Coronation in June 1953. Although mugs can form a varied and affordable collection, they are unlikely to rise in value as they are common and often of basic quality. A Denby coronation mug, for example, is worth about £2.

**A Chiswick Ceramics earthenware mug,** made to commemorate the Silver Jubilee. *c.1977, 9cm (3½in) high.*

**£10–20**

Look for reputable makers, well-made bodies, fine detailing, and strictly limited editions. To commemorate the Coronation, Minton produced white orbs with gilt details in a limited edition of 600 that can fetch around £350–450. Coloured examples in burgundy, cobalt blue, and green, which were limited to just 60 pieces in each colour, can fetch a much higher price of over £1,000 each.

Popular wares for the Coronation were also produced by Aynsley, whose

**A Crown Staffordshire bone-china mug,** produced to celebrate the Silver Jubilee. *c.1977, 12cm (4¾in) high.*

**£3–5**

## A closer look at... a Kaiser porcelain vase

Commemorative pieces that were made in editions of 500 or fewer, such as this vase, tend to rise in value as soon as the number of potential collectors becomes larger than the total number of items produced.

The body is made from fine porcelain by a known manufacturer

The unusual shape of this piece hides a secret: the profiles of the Queen and Prince Philip are outlined in the sides of the vase, shown by the lines drawn here (Prince Philip is on the left and the Queen on the right)

Gilt decoration has been skilfully applied, and the coat of arms is finely detailed

**A Kaiser porcelain bone-china silhouette vase,** issued to mark the Queen's Silver Jubilee. It cost around £75 when it was first made. *1977, 21cm (8¼in) high.*

**£80–120**

'Deluxe' plates in different colours, all with gilt details and a photographic portrait, can fetch £200–300. A popular novelty piece is a teapot in the shape of the coronation coach, made in 1953 by both Thomas Hughes and Garden House Pottery. The gold example *(see right)* can be found for around £200–300, but the rarer white-bodied version with gold details and a musical movement can fetch more.

## Investing in silver

The Silver Jubilee in 1977 was widely celebrated by manufacturers of commemorative ware. The high number of surviving pieces – the event took place less than 30 years ago – has kept prices down, so this could be a good time to start an inexpensive collection. Look for higher-quality pieces by Aynsley, Coalport, Royal Doulton, Worcester, and Wedgwood.

## Going for gold

As part of her Golden Jubilee celebrations in 2002, the Queen visited 70 towns and cities throughout the United Kingdom, and many of these places issued commemorative pieces. Look out for those made by established names such as the Rye Pottery of Sussex, whose hand-painted, blue-rimmed, half-pint tankard can fetch £40. These Golden Jubilee commemorative pieces may become the treasures of the future.

### Did You Know?

*The Queen's 1992 'Annus Horribilis' speech was commemorated by a Chown mug showing the lion and unicorn being bombarded by arrows. It also has five slightly bizarre verses, which include:*

*'God save our Queen this Christmastime*
*From the fanatic's knife and bomb*
*And from the more self-serving crime*
*Of perjured Tess and Peeping Tom'.*

**A Caverswall bone-china plate,** issued to mark the Golden Jubilee, from a limited edition of 1,000. *2002, 27.5cm (10¾in) diam.*

**£30–40**

### Top Tips

- Avoid pieces with blemishes such as poor-quality transfers, rubbed gilding, chips, or cracks – unless they are particularly rare.
- Look out for reputable designers, unfussy designs, and unusual or attractive shapes. Generally, loving cups and beakers are more valuable than mugs.
- To give your collection a focus, select a single manufacturer, a theme, or an event, such as a royal visit or jubilee.
- Choose pieces with photographic images – they are often slightly more popular than those with just coats of arms or ciphers.

**An all-over gold-lustre earthenware coach-shaped teapot,** made by Garden House Pottery to commemorate the Coronation. *1953, 13cm (5in) high.*

**£80–120**

### KEEP

*Pieces that display fine quality, a restrained style, and skilled use of gilt decoration will at least hold their value – and may appreciate as collectors seek out the limited number available. If there are other items in the same range, you can start to build a good collection.*

**A Minton bone-china loving cup,** produced to celebrate the Coronation. The design is by John Wadsworth. *c.1953, 10cm (4in) high.*

**£100–150**

### SELL

*A plethora of low-quality mugs has been produced for the Queen's two jubilees. If the mug has a shoddy transfer, thick body, and gaudy colours, its value is unlikely to rise even over the long term.*

**An English mug,** issued to commemorate the Silver Jubilee. *1977, 8.5cm (3¼in) high.*

**£2–3**

# Later royal commemorative ware

has often been created in response to increasing public interest in sensational aspects of the royal family's lives. Manufacturers have drawn on satire as well as affection to produce an inventive selection of collectables.

**A Chown mug,** made to commemorate the divorce of the Prince and Princess of Wales, from a limited edition of 150. *1996, 10.5cm (4in) high.*

**£50–60**

Most households have a piece of royal memorabilia tucked away in a cupboard somewhere. It may be a cheeky *Spitting Image* mug, or a plate celebrating the wedding of Prince Charles and Lady Diana Spencer. Some of these items have undoubtedly now appreciated in value.

Nothing was produced for Diana before her wedding, but hold on to any scarce items showcasing her birthdays. For example, a Caverswall mug with her portrait to celebrate her 21st birthday can be worth £75–95.

The most significant royal occasion involving Prince Charles before his marriage was his investiture as Prince of Wales in 1969. A Royal Crown Derby china bell, sold in a limited edition of 500 to mark this event, can fetch up to £300 in today's market.

Many inexpensive commemoratives were made for Charles and Diana's 'fairytale' wedding in 1981. Prices vary, as does quality – a plain Denby mug would be worth about £20. Towards the other end of the price spectrum, manufacturers include Paragon, Spode, Royal Crown Derby, Coalport, and Royal Doulton. A Spode bone china mug with a double portrait of the pair surrounded by floral and foliate wreaths can fetch up to £50.

## Chronicling less happy times

After the couple separated in 1992, anything featuring an image of the princess alone doubled in price. These prices should at least remain constant and may increase. When the marriage ended in 1996, about six designs were produced to mark the divorce.

Although the quality of some of these pieces is only fair, the fact that so few were made has kept demand – and value – consistent. A mug made by Chown, showing Charles and Diana facing away from each other, is a typical example (see above, right). Any wares made after Diana's death in 1997 should be examined with care, as the quality of portraiture and ceramics generally can be poor.

## Colourful caricatures

A number of irreverent items were produced, and perhaps the best examples are those by Luck & Flaw, who were responsible for the 1980s TV series *Spitting Image*. Egg cups based on the puppets, including Charles with huge, drooping ears, and William as a crying baby, can be worth £60 today. Another well-known item

**A Royal Doulton loving cup,** made for the Queen Mother's 80th birthday. Despite the reputable manufacturer, unknown production numbers have kept values low. *1980, 9.5cm (3¾in) high.*

**£15–20**

## Queen Mother commemoratives to look for:

- 80th birthday
- 90th
- 99th

**A Royal Crown Derby loving cup,** made for the Queen Mother's 90th birthday. The high value is owing to the intricate decoration and the limited-edition run of 500 by a well-known maker. *1990, 7.5cm (3in) high.*

**£80–120**

**A Bradmere House mug,** produced for the Queen Mother's 99th birthday. Only 99 mugs were made, but the maker is not well-known and the decoration is of poor quality. *1999, 9cm (3½in) high.*

**£15–20**

**A J & J May mug,** made to commemorate the birth of Prince William. *c.1982, 9cm (3½in) high.*

**£50–70**

caricaturing Prince Charles is the 1981 Carlton Ware 'Prince Charles ear mug'. Mint, this is worth around £45–60.

## The young generation

Pieces associated with Princes William and Harry are in great demand. The company J & J May made a mug *(right)*, and a limited edition of 50 loving cups, for William's birth in 1982. Both designs show a pram but the loving cup is worth £500–800 because of its limited run and superior quality. More affordable items commemorating the young royals do exist – a Cardigan Pottery mug can be bought for £20–30.

## The best of the rest

Interest in the Queen Mother remained strong as she passed the milestones of old age and many celebratory mugs and plates were produced.

Fewer pieces were made for other royal family members, so rarity value means that prices can be surprisingly high. A mug by Coalport, marking the bestowing of the title 'Princess Royal' upon Princess Anne, can be worth about £50.

### Top Tips

- Avoid smudgy images and poor printing – production and finish are crucial.
- Watch out for hairline cracks, crazing, scratches, and missing bits of transfer.
- When buying royal commemorative wares for investment, note that many American collectors prefer pieces with photographic portraits.
- Look for makers with an established name. Always check for the mark of the factory on the base of the piece.
- With modern wares, look for limited editions made in low numbers, preferably fewer than 100 – these are more likely to rise in value.
- Focus on items that capture the style of their era, such as the *Spitting Image* pieces, that epitomise the 1980s.

### BUY

*Diana's children are eclipsing her in popularity. Fewer pieces were made to commemorate Prince Harry's birth than that of his older brother William, making them scarcer – a low production run often raises the value. Buy now while still affordable.*

**An Aynsley small loving cup,** made to commemorate the birth of Prince Harry. It shows a scene of Balmoral Castle. *1984, 6cm (2¼in) high.*

**£50–70**

### KEEP

*Any humorous commemorative wares, particularly those by Spitting Image such as this double-sided mug, that echoes Charles's large ears in Diana's 'Queen of Hearts' frame, will probably rise in value. They are popular with all collectors.*

**A Kevin Francis 'Charles and Diana' *Spitting Image* mug,** made in a limited edition of 350 to commemorate the couple's divorce. *1990s, 15cm (6in) high.*

**£100–150**

## ▪ 100th ▪ 101st ▪ In memoriam ▪

**A Caverswall lionhead beaker,** made for the Queen Mother's much-celebrated 100th birthday, in a limited edition of 500. *2000, 11cm (4¼in) high.*

**£30–40**

**A Chown mug,** made for the Queen Mother's 101st birthday. The limited edition of 70 makes this collectable. *2001, 9.5cm (3¾in) high.*

**£20–30**

**A Caverswall lionhead beaker,** made in memory of the Queen Mother, in a limited edition of 2,002 (matching the year in which she died). Values may rise as it becomes scarce. *2002, 11cm (4¼in) high.*

**£25–35**

# Political and military ceramics,

made to commemorate outstanding personalities and events, provide a revealing record of the landmarks of British history and popular attitudes of the time, as well as being potentially valuable.

Britain has a long tradition of producing ceramics to commemorate political and military figures and events. Many examples, particularly from the late 20th century, can be found in auctions, antique shops, and collectors' fairs. For older and rarer pieces, specialist dealers and auctions are likely to prove more fruitful. Prices range from about £15 up to around £1,000, with most items costing less than £200.

## Early days

Mass production of commemorative ceramics was made possible by the development of transfer decoration techniques in the late 18th century. Early pieces are scarce and valuable, generally selling for upwards of £500. Even blemished items can be costly: a mug with minor damage marking the 1832 Reform Bill might go for around £300. As the 19th century progressed, commemorative ware became more widely available, owing to ever-improving production and distribution methods. In the late 1800s a number of notable personalities were featured, including prime ministers such as Disraeli and Gladstone. Items relating to Gladstone in particular are fairly common, and some can be picked up for around £25. Rarer pieces in prime condition can be worth more: a Burgess & Leigh plaque dating from around 1898 can fetch £200–400.

Wallis Gimson octagonal plates showing Victorian politicians and personalities are popular. They often sell for more than £100, but pieces can be found for less at fairs and auctions in mixed lots. The production technique will usually affect price: monochrome pieces can be worth around £30–50, whereas many coloured versions in top condition reach £100–150.

**A Wallis Gimson octagonal earthenware plate**, printed in black with a portrait of William Gladstone and details of his achievements; slightly chipped. *1884, 24.5cm (9¾in) diam.*

**£40–60**

## Cult of personality

Many enthusiasts focus on a particular politician. Others choose a style of representation, such as comical and satirical items. Especially sought after are 1930s ashtrays by the political cartoonist David Low, which can raise £50–300, depending on the image. Toby and character jugs are also of interest. A 1940s Neville Chamberlain jug by Lancaster will generally cost around £40–60.

## Some military commemoratives to look for:

■ Napoleonic Wars ■ Boer War ■ World War I ■ World War II ■

◄ **An unmarked pearlware moulded jug** commemorating Lord Wellington and (shown here) General Hill. The Napoleonic Wars remain compelling, and Wellington is still a national hero, so pieces featuring him are perennially popular. *c.1810–15, 13.5cm (5¼in) high.*

**£100–150**

► **A Carlton Ware bone-china dish.** Interest in the Boer War has grown thanks to recent coverage in books and on TV. This plate is colourful, with a harmonious design showing the most important generals – all desirable features. *c.1900, 11cm (4¼in) diam.*

**£50–80**

Sir Winston Churchill is perhaps the most collected British political figure. As so many items were made and kept in good condition, examples can be bought for less than £100. Rarer examples command more – a SylvaC bust to mark Churchill's death in 1965 might sell for around £200–300.

A more recent figure, whose commemorative ware has the potential to rise in value, is Margaret Thatcher. A-Caverswall limited-edition plate made for her election as Prime Minister in 1979 can be worth between £50 and £70, and a goblet from the 500-piece edition by Coalport for her second election victory in 1983 can cost around £100.

## Spoils of war

Since the early 19th century, objects have been produced to mark major wars or campaigns. Early pieces, often satirical in nature, can raise £300–1,500 or more, but later 19th-century (most notably Boer War) and 20th-century items are generally more accessible. A great many World War I pieces were issued in honour of important generals. These are often of lesser interest as many of the men are no longer well known. During World War II, fewer ceramics were commissioned as the production of decorative ware was largely curtailed. Items commemorating major battles or campaigns, such as the Battle of Britain, or key figures, such as Field Marshall Montgomery, tend to be the most popular.

### Collectors' Tales

*'I was wandering around an antiques fair when I spotted a cardboard box full of assorted Victorian crockery. I had a quick look and noticed an attractive octagonal plate. I instantly recognised the decoration as Gladstone. I offered a tenner for it. I later found out the plate was worth nearly £150.'*

**Adrian Jenkins, Frimley, Surrey**

**A Norfolk China anti-Euro mug.** This brightly coloured and humorous piece shows a cartoon with Britain on one side of the English Channel saying 'One says stuff the Euro' while Europe, headed here by Germany, proclaims 'Der pound must die'. *c.1999, 9cm (3½in) high.*

**£15–20**

## Top Tips

- Focus on good-quality, attractive pieces with limited runs by renowned makers, as these are likely to hold their value.
- Invest in current figures or events that you think may be collectable in the future.
- Examine the corners of all square or octagonal plates carefully, as they are vulnerable to damage.
- Learn to recognise significant past politicians.

## BUY

*Major political movements and politicians that change countries forever are likely to be remembered. It can be worth acquiring items that represent these changes, and the forces behind them.*

**A Chown bone-china mug,** made to commemorate New Labour's election victory. *1997, 8.5cm (3¼in) high.*

**£7–10**

## KEEP

*Poking fun at politicians has long been a national pastime, and caricatures are always popular. The cleverest depictions of major public figures have shown consistent prices and should rise in value in the future.*

**A Royal Doulton 'British Bulldog' figurine.** Summing up the spirit of the British nation in the bulldog, this piece was produced after the first year of World War I. Prices have fallen, as these have been reproduced recently. *1915, 15.5cm (6in) high.*

**£150–200**

**A Fielding's novelty miniature chamberpot-shaped ashtray**, marking the Nazi invasion of Poland in 1939. Prices have fallen, as these have been reproduced recently. *c.1939, 3.5cm (1½in) high.*

**£50–70**

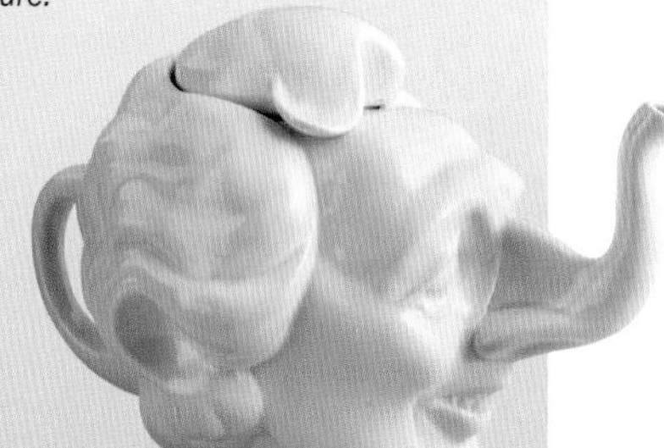

**A Carlton Ware Margaret Thatcher teapot**, designed by Fluck & Law, creators of *Spitting Image*. Features such as the elongated nose/spout make this a popular comical novelty piece. Fluck & Law also designed a Ronald Reagan coffee pot in the same style, which can fetch about £250–300. *1980, 22cm (8½in) high.*

**£80–100**

COLLECTOR'S CORNER

# Sir Winston Churchill has inspired more commemorative wares than any other political figure. His long life and many accomplishments ensure that there is a huge variety of items, mostly emphasising his stocky build or heavy-jowelled features.

▲ **A Kirkland & Co. toby jug.** The top hat has nearly always been damaged and restored on these jugs, reducing their value to about half the amount quoted. *c.1941, 26.5cm (10½in) high.*

**£200–300**

Churchill, born in 1874, is greatly admired for inspiring the nation to victory during World War II. Many people began collecting Churchilliana during or just after the war. Churchill died on 24 January 1965, and more than 350 million people in Britain and around the world watched his state funeral on television.

Pieces produced to commemorate Churchill's wartime leadership, as well as his political life and his death, are sought after. These will often fetch higher prices than tributes to his earlier activities, or items produced 'in memoriam' years after his death. Look for imagery that shows Churchill as he is remembered by the public: with 'bulldog' features, thinly smiling or showing gritty determination, or perhaps resplendent in top hat and tails. Toby jugs, which are as quintessentially English as the man himself, are among the most popular Churchill collectables.

High prices are paid for anything that was owned or used by Churchill (his cigars included), or items otherwise directly associated with him – but only if they come with a reliable provenance.

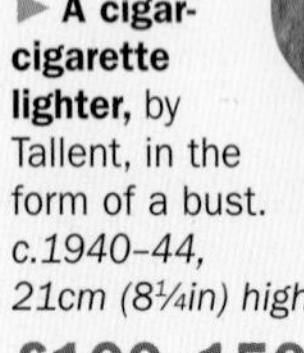

► **A cigar-cigarette lighter,** by Tallent, in the form of a bust. *c.1940–44, 21cm (8¼in) high.*

**£100–150**

► **A Copeland jug** showing three pictures associated with Churchill's wartime activities: the Battle of Britain, the Normandy landings, and his work as First Lord of the Admiralty. *1940–41, 17.5cm (6¾in) high.*

**£220–280**

◄ **A rare English earthenware 'Tuscan' Decoro Pottery Co. bowl**, with a handle. The central image shows Churchill in his characteristic hat and bow tie. *c.1940–41, 15cm (6in) diam.*

**£70–100**

◄ **A carved wooden plaque.** It is unusual to find wooden memorabilia commemorating Churchill. This handcarved piece may well have been homemade. *c.1941, 19cm (7½in) high.*

**£70–90**

◀ **A Wedgwood earthenware 'Chartwell' mug, 'in memoriam'.** This eye-catching mug, unlike other Churchill commemoratives, is bright and colourful, and its design is much less conventional than more commonly found traditional pieces. *1965, 12cm (4¾in) high.*

**£40–50**

◀ **A Caverswall plate,** produced to commemorate the 50th anniversary of Churchill's appointment as Prime Minister. *1990, 22cm (8½in) diam.*

**£30–40**

▶ **A James Kent earthenware plate, 'For Democracy',** produced to commemorate the close links between President Roosevelt and Churchill during World War II. *c.1942, 22cm (8½in) diam.*

**£70–90**

## Collectors' Tips

- Focus your collection on a specific event or milestone, such as Churchill's death
- Look for pieces made around 1941 and 1942. Although unpainted because of wartime rationing, those for the home market are still collectable. Pieces made for export to America are coloured and often more expensive
- Snap up inexpensive pieces showing Churchill characteristics – such as his famous 'V for Victory' sign – as these should gain in value

◀ **A small Cooper Clayton earthenware character jug.** The 1950s date and the trilby hat make this less desirable than earlier jugs or those showing Churchill wearing a top hat. *c.1951–52, 8cm (3¼in) high.*

**£55–65**

▲ **A gilt-metal lapel pin.** After Churchill became a national hero, some people showed their allegiance and gratitude by wearing lapel pins. *1940s, 2.5cm (1in) long.*

**£10–15**

# Goss and crested ware

were once the nation's favourite seaside souvenirs. Their strong nostalgic appeal, frequently low prices, and wide availability ensure their continued popularity with today's buyers.

**A W.H. Goss crested model of an ancient Irish bronze pot,** featuring the crest of Middlesex. *c.1900, 4.5cm (1¾in) high.*

**£5–7**

By the early 20th century, it was said that 90 per cent of British homes had a piece of crested china on display. These wares represent an intriguing aspect of social history, and this adds to their collectability. So many pieces were made that the most common example can still be bought for a couple of pounds upwards. Goss usually commands the highest selling prices of all crested ware makers.

## The crest of a wave

William Henry Goss's Falcon Pottery in Stoke-on-Trent was originally known for its portrait busts of dignitaries, table centrepieces, and elegant vases made from high-quality Parianware, a marblelike porcelain. But in 1881 William's son Adolphus spotted a gap in the booming tourist market for inexpensive ceramic souvenirs. The company switched production to supply one shop in each British seaside town with Goss porcelain miniatures. Their shapes were often derived from an urn or vase in the town's museum. Holidaymakers prized souvenirs based on local themes, so regional dress, activities, monuments, products, and people were modelled. Examples include a Welsh 'chimney' hat, a figurine of Robert Burns, and an Irish colleen with her spinning wheel. All pieces displayed a transfer of the town's coat-of-arms. This type of memorabilia is still popular today.

## Great days out

Goss's porcelain was an instant hit with the public, who were taking advantage of the rapidly expanding rail network to make day trips to the coast on the new Bank Holidays, introduced

## A closer look at... two Goss 'First & Last House' cottages

Goss cottages, introduced in 1893, are sought after and often fetch high prices. Nightlight variations, some with open chimneys to let the smoke from the candle out of the building, tend to be the most valuable. Other key factors to look for include size and the quality of colour and transfers. The two Goss cottages below are from the 'First & Last House' series at Land's End, but one of them is worth four times as much as the other.

**A model of the 'First & Last House' with annexe,** unglazed and sparsely coloured. It has a black-printed goshawk mark on the end wall, together with the text 'Rd.No.521645', which relates to 1908, the year of its introduction. This size was only produced in an unglazed, coloured format. *c.1908, 14cm (5½in) long.*

**£280–320**

The 'First & Last House' came in three sizes: this is the largest and rarest size, and it comes with an annexe

On the versions that carry them you will find a coat-of-arms for Land's End, Cornwall, on the roof

**A model of the 'First & Last House',** glazed with a cream-coloured roof and a green door. It has similar markings to the larger example. *c.1908, 6.5cm (2½in) long.*

**£40–60**

This is the smallest-sized cottage, and also the most common (a rarer middle size was also made)

All cottages of this size are glazed, and sometimes bear the badge of Cornwall

**A Carlton racehorse.** The rectangular base bears the crest of Newmarket. *c.1900, 10cm (4in) high.*

**£50–70**

by Queen Victoria in 1871. The Queen approved of the seaside as a proper and healthy place for the working classes to enjoy their days out. The Goss agent in each town was restricted to selling items depicting the town's coat-of-arms. After 1883 agents could order any model they wanted, rather than being restricted to local shapes, but the crest rule remained in place. So if you wanted a crest of Land's End, the only way to obtain one was to go there and buy it. By 1906, more than 1,000 outlets selling some 7,000 different crests had been established. This marked the beginning of a big collecting craze in Britain.

## The market expands

Keen to cash in on Goss's success, some 330 potteries, including Arcadian, Crescent, Carlton, and Grafton, produced souvenirs of similar appearance. They introduced many novelty shapes, such as lighthouses, shells, miniature tea sets, and animals, and Goss was forced to follow suit. Like Goss's, many items are marked, although more than a third of crested pottery is not.

Goss made the highest-quality pieces, with bright white china and crisp transfers, so their wares form the backbone of most collections. Pieces with good-quality moulding and transfer detail, or with rare and unusual shapes and crests, will often be the most valuable.

## The end of an era

Ceramics manufacturers reacted to World War I by producing a wide range of commemorative ware. War-related items included ammunition shells, despatch riders, and other military subjects. Pieces marking events such as battles and advances sold strongly. Prices for these items now range from around £10 to £200.

**A Savoy model of a postbox,** with a crest for Arras and an inscription commemorating the battle there. *c.1915, 6cm (2¼in) high.*

**£15–20**

### Top Tips

- Limit your collection to one crest – say, your home town, or a particular theme (such as World War I), or the work of a particular factory (such as Goss).
- Look for the Goss mark, which is either a black goshawk above a printed 'W.H. Goss' mark or, on earlier pieces, an impressed 'W.H. Goss'.
- Run your finger across a crest – a Goss crest will be slightly raised from the surface; other makers' transfers are flush with the surface.
- Look out for hairline cracks, chips, and damaged transfers, which can halve value.
- Do not store your pieces in newspaper as the ink can cause crests to fade. Instead wrap them in acid-free tissue.

### KEEP

*Pieces made to commemorate World War I provide fascinating insights into social history of the time and remain highly popular, meaning that they are likely to rise in value. More unusual shapes fetch the highest prices, provided that they are in excellent condition with any protruding parts undamaged. Tanks, for example, are a relatively common shape.*

**An Arcadian model with the ancient arms of the Burgh of Stirling.** This is relatively scarce, which makes it desirable. *c.1914, 7cm (2¾in) long.*

**£40–60**

### SELL

*Crested ware of inferior quality, with unrealistically modelled forms that lack finely moulded detailing, are not likely to be sought after, as so many better examples exist. Pieces dating from around 1920 or later that are unmarked by the factory will also make poor investment prospects.*

**An unmarked model of a kettle,** with the crest of London. *c.1920, 5cm (2in) wide.*

**£1–2**

# Wooden souvenir ware

popular in Britain includes Mauchline ware, made in Scotland, and Tunbridge ware from Kent. Today it is treasured for nostalgic reasons, for the quality of the wood, and for its skilful, often intricate decoration.

Both Mauchline and Tunbridge ware were produced in a range of keepsake items – primarily boxes, but also useful objects such as rulers and inkstands. Although some examples with intricate decoration can be worth hundreds of pounds, common, simply decorated pieces can still be found for around £50 or less.

## Boxing clever

Mauchline ware is made of light, yellowy-beige sycamore, decorated with a dark-toned scene of a building or view, then given a gloss varnish finish. The town of Mauchline (pronounced 'maw-khlin'), near Glasgow, was the heart of the industry – hence the name, which is applied to all Scottish wares of this type. One of the most successful firms was W. & A. Smith, at the Smith Boxworks, in Mauchline. Production began in the early 1800s and centred on quality snuffboxes and tea caddies.

Early works were hand painted. From the 1820s until 1933 (when a fire destroyed Smith's factory), pieces were mostly decorated by transfer printing of designs or, from the 1860s, of photographs. The transfer was applied to an item, then given several coats of slow-drying varnish. The range is wide, so prices vary. A napkin ring can be found for around £10–20. An early hand-decorated box or snuff mull can command £300–900 or more.

**A Mauchline ware turned money box,** with unusual turret design and showing Ravenscraig Castle, Dysart. *c.1890, 8cm (3¼in) high.*

**£30–50**

## Finishing touches

Other finishes were produced by various makers. 'Tartanware' – small wooden objects covered in tartan – was bright and cheerful and satisfied the Victorian interest in all things Scottish. Early examples were hand decorated, but most pieces date from after the early 1850s, when colour-printed paper was glued to the piece, then lightly varnished. Prices vary from less than £100 for a simple 1870s pillbox to £500–800 or more for pieces that are large, early, or hand painted.

'Fernware' – small items decorated with a fern-leaf pattern – was introduced by several factories in the 1870s. Various techniques were applied, such as using an actual fern leaf as a stencil and then stippling dark dye over it in overlapping shapes. Paper printed with a fern design and glued to the box was also common, but pieces decorated this way are less valuable. A small cylindrical box from about 1890 is usually worth up to around £50.

**A Mauchline ware sycamore napkin ring,** with a photographic transfer of Wells Cathedral. *c.1880s, 5cm (2in) diam.*

**£15–20**

## Spa town magic

Kent's historic spa town of Tunbridge Wells produced high-quality wooden mementoes for the Georgian and Victorian tourists who flocked to the town for its curative spring waters.

This ware has its origins in the 17th century, when small, useful pieces of treen (such as drinking vessels) were made by local craftsmen. Production grew as tourism increased. Early pieces (pre-1820s), using the traditional marquetry techniques found in furniture, are much sought after. Most later Tunbridge ware was created using the 'stickwork' method, by which slim rods of different-coloured

### Did You Know?

*In the late 1700s a Scottish inventor, John Sandy, created the 'hidden hinge' snuffbox, using a cutting device that hid the brass pin connecting the lid to the box; this gave the appearance of an all-wood, hingeless box. The resulting box, the first to prevent expensive snuff from leaking into the user's pocket, was exploited by James Stiven of Laurencekirk, Scotland. It was the impetus for the snuffbox industry in Scotland, in and around Mauchline.*

## A closer look at... two Tunbridge ware boxes

Boxes are among the most common objects produced as wooden souvenirs. Of these two Tunbridge ware boxes, one is relatively commonplace, the other rare and carrying a much higher value.

The box is of birch, and is conventional in shape, colour, and design

The geometric lozenges on the lid are created by the standard stickwork technique

**A satin birch tea caddy,** with geometric *tesserae* banding. The piece has not been signed by its maker. *c.1880s, 13.5cm (5¼in) high.*

**£80–120**

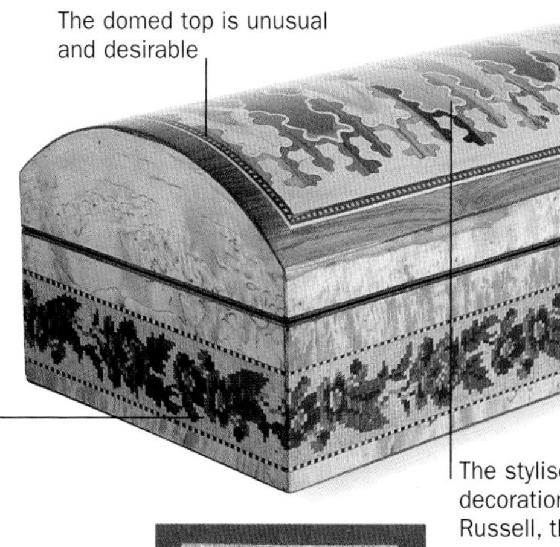

The domed top is unusual and desirable

The box has a superb quality of intricate marquetry

The stylised oak-leaf decoration is typical of Russell, the named maker

R. RUSSELL,
TUNBRIDGE WARE
Manufacturer,
And Inventor of Tunbridge
Ware Marquetry,
*Tunbridge Wells,*

The rare label specifies R. Russell of Tunbridge Wells as the maker

**A burr sycamore box by Robert Russell,** inlaid with a stylised oak-leaf design and bearing the maker's label. The light-coloured burr sycamore is attractive and more unusual than other woods. *c.1863, 25.5cm (10in) long.*

**£1,000–1,500**

woods are cut into paper-thin *tesserae* (tiles) and applied to the surfaces as in a mosaic. At its most popular, between 1840 and 1890, Tunbridge ware used floral designs, stylised natural motifs, local scenes, and profiles – notably of Queen Victoria. The variety is huge, and includes items such as magnifying glasses and paper knives as well as boxes for pills, stamps, matches, tea, and other household essentials. Larger pieces or ones with intricate designs are more valuable, if in good condition. A small trinket box with a simple geometric design can fetch £30–60, a dip pen £40–60, a larger or more complex box £250–650 or more. Notable makers include Henry Hollamby, Thomas Barton, and the Wise and Burrows families.

### Top Tips

- Choose items that cross collecting interests, such as pillboxes or pens, as they hold their values well.
- Look for makers' labels and stamped marks – these add value.
- Closely inspect transfers on Mauchline ware for damage from over-zealous cleaning, as this lowers values.
- Look for Tunbridge ware pieces that have plenty of contrast in the colour of the wood, and fine patterns.

**A late Victorian 'Fernware' box.** *c.1890, 9cm (3½in) diam.*

**£40–60**

### BUY

*Always evaluate the scene on a Mauchline ware item, as some are more popular than others. Scenes of well-known places have wider appeal, and if the piece has strong period associations, so much the better.*

**A Mauchline ware glove box,** with three transfers showing Osborne House in the centre. Osborne House, on the Isle of Wight, has close connections with Queen Victoria. She died there in 1901. *c.1890s, 25cm (10in) long.*

**£50–70**

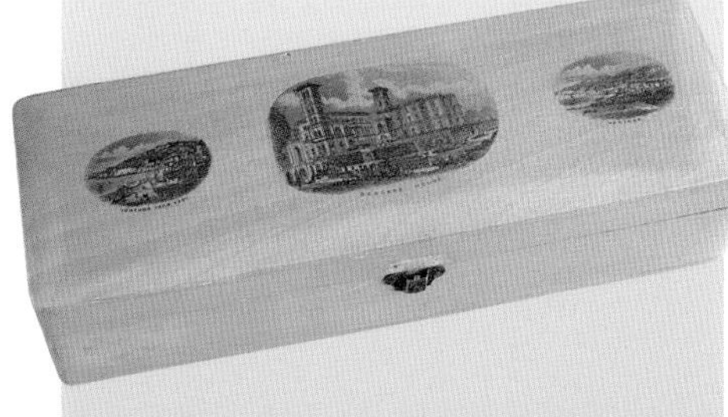

### SELL

*Tartanware prices reached a peak in the 1990s, but they are unlikely to rise again in the short term. Pieces that have interest across markets, such as sewing tools or snuff boxes, will be desirable and their wider appeal may yield higher prices. Sell now and reap the rewards.*

**A Tartanware needle case,** with a label reading 'Prince Charlie'. This relatively simple piece might appeal to a collector of sewing tools. *c.1870s, 8cm (3¼in) long.*

**£60–80**

# Stanhopes, first produced in the second half of the 19th century, are small, novelty mementoes that contain a miniature peephole revealing a 'mystery' photograph. They are an excellent theme for the budget collector.

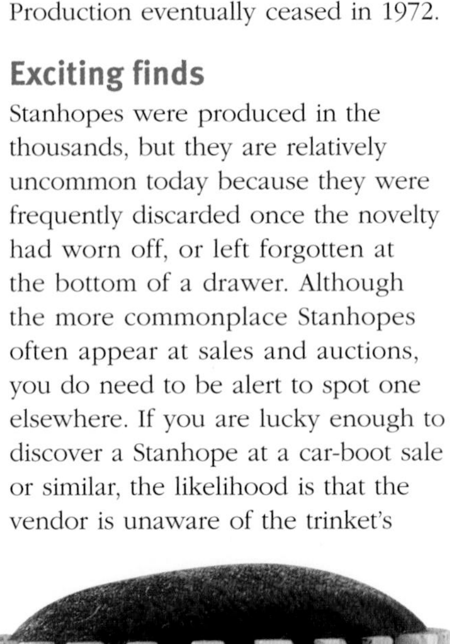

**A British silver lantern charm,** with a Stanhope showing four views of Exeter. *c.1900, 2cm (¾in) high.*

**£40–60**

If you look carefully at the end of a bone needlecase or the top of a dip pen from the 1860s onwards, you may find inset a tiny glass bead. This is the Stanhope proper – a lens just millimetres wide to which one or more minute photographs, which look like black pinheads, are attached. When held up to the light and close to the eye, the lens magnifies the micro-photograph to reveal the picture as if projected on a tiny screen.

## The pioneers

The name 'Stanhope' comes from Charles Stanhope, the 3rd Earl Stanhope (1753–1816), who invented a uniquely powerful hand magnifying lens, achieving enlargements previously possible only with microscopes.

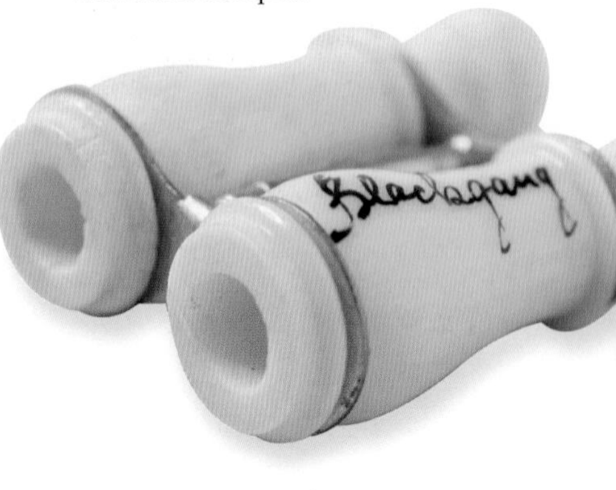


**A pair of French bone binoculars,** with Stanhopes showing views of Blackgang Chine on the Isle of Wight. *c.1920, 2.5cm (1in) long.*

**£10–20**

*Did You Know?*

*Stanhopes such as rings, tiepins, watch keys, and small pencils often contain saucy nudes and other erotic images. Intended for gentlemen, they are a specialist and valuable category with a crossover appeal to collectors of erotica.*

About 50 years after Stanhope's death, his invention was adapted for use in souvenirs. An Englishman, John Benjamin Dancer, invented micro-photography in 1839, but it was a Frenchman, René Dagron, who combined the Stanhope lens with the Dancer micro-photograph in 1860 to make a tiny viewer with an image attached to the lens. He then began setting his device into everyday objects and souvenirs of locations or historic events.

## Booming business

The public's response was so positive that Dagron opened a factory at Gex, on the Swiss border, just two years later. Soon he was employing more than 100 people, producing photographic miniatures known as *bijoux photomicroscopiques*, or 'microphotographic trinkets', fitted into a huge range of inexpensive souvenirs containing views of personalities, resorts, and exhibitions.

The canny Frenchman realised that others might copy his idea once the patent expired, so he marketed 'Stanhope kits' to encourage anyone else who wanted to produce Stanhopes to buy the equipment and supplies from Dagron. As a result, a great variety of Stanhopes was made by various companies during the late 19th century. Business declined from the 1920s to the 60s, although Stanhopes were still manufactured – for example, to commemorate special events such as the Coronation of Elizabeth II in 1953. Production eventually ceased in 1972.

## Exciting finds

Stanhopes were produced in the thousands, but they are relatively uncommon today because they were frequently discarded once the novelty had worn off, or left forgotten at the bottom of a drawer. Although the more commonplace Stanhopes often appear at sales and auctions, you do need to be alert to spot one elsewhere. If you are lucky enough to discover a Stanhope at a car-boot sale or similar, the likelihood is that the vendor is unaware of the trinket's

**A French carved-bone measuring tape and pin cushion,** with a Stanhope of a religious scene. *c.1870, 6cm (2¼in) high.*

**£80–120**

## A closer look at...

### a two-lens erotic Stanhope

The view is always important to a Stanhope's collectability but you should never neglect the object it is set into. This example has a decorative casing as well as several other desirable elements: it features erotic subject matter (a rare and valuable characteristic); and it has an unusual mechanism that gives the appearance of movement – a lady jumping into bed.

**A French base-metal *cinématographe bijou*** ('cinematic jewel'), in the form of a book with two views. *c.1890, 2.5cm (1in) high.*

**£200–250**

Two Stanhope lenses are mounted in the moving metal bar, making it rare – pressing on the bar incorporated into the case alternates the views on offer: in this instance, a lady undressing and the same lady in bed

The 'moving' image is viewed through this peephole

The case is well made, with intricate detailing contributing to the value

**A British 'cranberry glass' perfume bottle** with a Stanhope fitted into the hinge revealing six views of South Shields. *c.1900, 5.5cm (2¼in) high.*

**£140–160**

**A British silver articulated fish charm,** with a Stanhope showing extracts from the Torah (Hebrew scriptures). *c.1900, 3.5cm (1¼in) long.*

**£50–60**

special secret. Most Stanhopes are valued at much less than £100, with only a few rarities exceeding this.

### Lucky dip

Stanhope novelties are predominantly made from bone, base metals, and silver, although plastic was usual after the 1920s. The most commonly found examples are sewing accessories, dip pens, jewellery, smoking accessories, and charms (including tiny binoculars for watch fobs). A pair of miniature bone binoculars with a view of a well-known personality might fetch £60 or more, but those with standard views of scenery may be worth as little as £10. Cigarette holders fall into the £30–90 bracket, depending on the material used (metal and wooden ones are worth slightly more than plastic). Larger items such as walking sticks are rarer and more valuable.

Perfume bottles with Stanhopes can fetch up to £250, thimbles up to £400 – these higher prices can be attributed in part to additional interest from collectors of perfume bottles and sewing tools.

The most frequently found images are of tourist attractions, historic cities, and spa towns. Portraits are rarer and are thus more sought after. Events such as the 1862 London International Exhibition are also unusual and have a wide appeal.

### *Top Tips*

- Before buying, check that the viewer is still set into the novelty. If it has fallen out, the Stanhope will be worth a fraction of a complete example.
- Examine the image carefully – it should be clearly visible, sharp, and unscratched. If it is blurred, bubbled, or crazed, the value of the Stanhope will be much less.
- Ensure that the novelty is in good condition before you buy. Don't wash a Stanhope after buying, as this can remove the gum attaching the image to the lens.

### BUY

*Views of personalities, such as royalty, are rarer and more valuable than scenic views. When the subject is a person, the Stanhope is likely to have been made to commemorate a historic event in their life, which helps to date the item, adding to its collectability.*

**A British brass monocular charm, with a Stanhope showing a portrait of Princess Alexandra** (right). The charm commemorates her marriage to the Prince of Wales. *c.1863, 1.5cm (½in) long.*

**£70–90**

### SELL

*Dip pens, along with binoculars, are among the most widely found Stanhopes. They are a good starting point for a collection, but as dip pens are common, they are unlikely to rise in value, even if they are intricately carved.*

**A French bone penholder, with a view of Crystal Palace.** The Stanhope is set into the shaft. *c.1890, 16.5cm (6½in) long.*

**£10–15**

# British medals, reflecting loyal service and bravery in wars overseas, can create an evocative display that combines historic interest with fascinating personal stories about how the medals were won.

**A one-clasp Indian Mutiny Medal,** awarded for the suppression of the Indian Mutiny. *c.1857–58, 13cm (5in) high.*

**£200–300**

If anyone gives or bequeaths you their medals, count yourself honoured; if you can learn something of the experiences behind the medals, you are doubly privileged.

The first campaign medal issued to every soldier, regardless of rank, was the Waterloo Medal of 1815, which bore the recipient's name and regiment on the rim. The Victoria Cross, from 1856, was the first award for gallantry given to all ranks. Medals of any sort awarded to ordinary soldiers can be worth up to a few hundred pounds; premiums are paid for officers' medals.

## The age of empire

During the 19th century many medals were issued to commemorate Britain's colonial expansion. Single medals start at less than £100, but medal groups awarded to one individual are worth more, especially if they include a decoration for bravery.

Campaign medals come with clasps, or bars, which are stamped with the relevant battles and dates. Some soldiers who served in a long campaign were given several clasps, and these make the medals more valuable. Fake clasps are in circulation, and authentic ones are sometimes added, so multiple examples should be checked against official army records.

Historically significant medals command a premium. If your great-grandfather received a medal for serving with the Light Brigade at Balaclava, expect it to fetch £6,000. Medals with Balaclava clasps for other units will yield only a few hundred pounds.

Medals from the Boer War (1899–1902) fetch £100 for the pair – Queen Victoria died during the war, so another medal was struck for Edward VII.

## On the western front

Millions of British and Commonwealth troops fought in World War I. The 'Old Contemptibles' – the first British soldiers to serve in France and Belgium – were all awarded the 1914 Star. This was followed by the 1914–15 Star, of which 2.3 million were struck. The British War Medal and Victory Medal were also awarded in huge numbers – up to 6.5 million.

**A World War II medal group:** a 1939–45 Star, Africa Star, Italy Star, France and Germany Star, 1939–45 Defence Medal, and 1939–45 War Medal with oak leaf (for a mention in despatches). None of them carry the recipient's name. *c.1939–45, 13cm (5in) high.*

**£100–150**

### Did You Know?

*The Victoria Cross is made from the bronze of Russian cannons captured during the Crimean War.*

## A closer look at... a British medal

A collectable decoration consists of the medal itself and the original ribbon. There may be original clasps, also known as bars, awarded to the same soldier. A clasp was given only to a soldier who had participated in the battle named on the clasp itself.

The more clasps found on a medal, the more valuable it is likely to be. The three battles marked here are the most important battles in the Crimean War (1854–57) and thus make the medal more valuable

**A three-bar Crimean Medal,** awarded to J. Finn of the 77th Regiment, with clasps for the battles of Sebastopol, Inkermann, and Alma. This medal was given to any soldier who participated in the war, regardless of whether they fought in a battle. *c.1856, 13cm (5in) high.*

**£350–400**

The reigning sovereign is pictured on the medal – in this instance, the young Queen Victoria

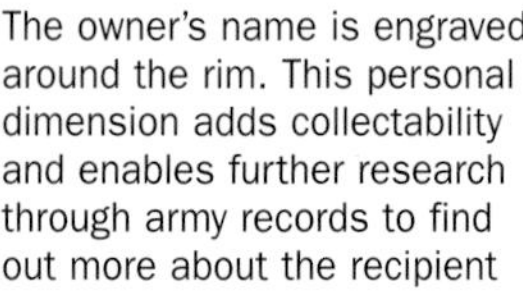

The owner's name is engraved around the rim. This personal dimension adds collectability and enables further research through army records to find out more about the recipient

BUCKINGHAM PALACE

I greatly regret that I am unable to give you personally the award which you have so well earned. I now send it to you with my congratulations and my best wishes for your future happiness.

George R.I

**A World War II medal group with related ephemera.** The medal group comprises a DFC (George VI first-type), a 1939–44 Star with a Battle of Britain clasp, an Air Crew Europe Star with a France and Germany clasp, a Defence Medal, and a War Medal. *c.1939–45, medals 13cm (5in) high.*

**£2,000–3,000**

The three-medal group of Star, War, and Victory is easy to find, and prices start from £25. 'Casualty' medals awarded posthumously, especially on the first day of the Somme in 1916, command a premium, as do those conferred upon men serving with the Royal Flying Corps and the Royal Naval Aviation Service.

## Valiant defence

During World War II, 11 types of medal were awarded. They do not carry the recipient's name, because of the huge number produced, but if the medal is in its original packaging, you can find the name on the allocation sheet. They are an inexpensive starting point for a collection: a Defence Medal for a member of the Home Guard can be bought for about £25–30. A trio made up of a Defence Medal, a 1939–45 War Medal, and a North African Desert Medal can sell for £50–75. Medals awarded to the Air Crew Europe (all Allied air crews who served in Europe) fetch the most. Those related to the Battle of Britain can be worth several hundred pounds.

## In our lifetimes

Campaign medals have also been awarded for Korea, Rhodesia, the Falklands, and the Gulf War. The General Service Medal has clasps for conflicts in Malaya, Northern Ireland, Lebanon, Vietnam, and for Air Operations in Iraq.

**A Hanoverian medal for Waterloo.** This side shows the Prince Regent; the reverse, a stand of arms above Waterloo. *1815, 13cm (5in) high.*

**£350–450**

## Top Tips

- Try turning scruffy medal ribbons inside out to reveal a fresher surface. Also, keep ribbons out of direct sun.
- If you suspect personal details have been faked, inspect the rim of the medal for signs of filing where metal may have been removed. Examine the style of lettering, which may differ from originals.
- Store your medals carefully in purpose-made conservation materials, such as acid-free tissue paper. Many materials, including certain plastics, cloth, and paper, give off corrosive gases.
- Miniature medals – those worn with evening dress – can fetch £10–250.
- If buying a medal, or medals, from a dealer, insist on a detailed receipt with a guarantee of authenticity.
- If you mount a group of medals, check whether the recipient's regiment wore medals 'standard' (hanging freely) or 'court'/'royal' style (stitched onto a backing), and display accordingly.

## BUY

*Collectors will pay a premium for World War I medals with a decoration for bravery, as these were comparatively uncommon. Prices for all World War I medals have been rising steadily over recent years.*

**A World War I medal group,** comprising a George V first-type Military Medal, awarded for bravery, a British War Medal, and a Victory Medal. *c.1918, 13cm (5in) high.*

**£450–500**

## KEEP

*Popular interest in the Zulu War (1877–79), partly owing to the 1964 film Zulu, caused prices for militaria from this conflict to rise. They should continue to do so, as the conflict is often covered in books, articles, and TV programmes.*

**A South Africa Medal**, with a clasp. *1879, 13cm (5in) high.*

**£320–380**

# Philately, the collection and study of postage stamps, is a long-established pastime which is as appealing to the beginner on a limited budget as it is to the serious specialist with thousands to spend.

**An unused George VI 2-cent Malayan stamp,** marked 'BMA MALAYA' (British Military Administration). *c.1945, 2.5cm (1in) high.*

**30–50p**

The first-ever stamp, the Penny Black, was issued on 1 May 1840. Despite its legendary status, it is not rare: around 1.5 million survive. A used stamp can be bought for £20–60, but scarce, unused examples can cost £1,000 or more. The Two-Penny Blue, issued a week later, attracts similar prices.

## A global phenomenon

As such a huge variety is available – more than 350 authorities issue stamps worldwide – collectors often focus on one area, for example stamps of the British Commonwealth. Stamps bearing the head of a British monarch provide a fascinating document of the history of the Empire. Many can be found at low prices: a 1938–44 one-penny George VI stamp from the Gold Coast costs no more than 10p. Generally, the more valuable postage stamps are those with a high face value, as they tend to be rarer.

## Important details

The history of cancellation marks – or postmarks, which are placed over stamps to indicate that they have been used – is studied by many enthusiasts. Numerous cancellation marks were made for propaganda purposes, such as the 'St Lucia – Liquidation of the Empire' mark, which can add around £10 to the value of a stamp.

A rare printing or cutting error can increase a stamp's value. The value of a 1955 one-penny stamp is usually negligible, as it is common, but a small number had perforations cut 6mm (¼in) too high, so the bottom of the design appears at the top of the stamp. These can be valued at about £30–45.

Check stamps on wartime correspondence for any unusual, seemingly trivial details, such as the type of perforation, as these can make a big difference to their value. The wrapping of parcels is also a good source of unusual specimens because their weight necessitates the use of rarer, higher-value stamps.

## All about image

Traditionally, stamps issued by the Royal Mail must not feature images of living people unless they are members of the royal family. There

## Some British stamps to look for:

- Two-Penny Blue
- Half-crown
- Lilac and Greens

**A used Victoria Two-Penny Blue stamp.** All Two-Penny Blues and Penny Blacks have check letters in the bottom corners (an anti-fraud device). Collectors aim to find as many variations as possible. *1840, 2.5cm (1in) high.*

**£70–100**

**A used Victoria half-crown stamp.** Examples that are printed on blue paper are scarce; in good condition they can be worth up to £180–220. This version is lilac on white paper. *1883, 3.5cm (1½in) high.*

**£20–30**

**A used Victoria nine-penny stamp from the Unified series.** This stamp is from the first set issued for both postage and revenue purposes – known as the 'lilac and greens'. The 9d stamp is the most valuable. *1883, 2.5cm (1in) wide.*

**£60–90**

was an uproar in 1999 when Roger Taylor, the still-living drummer for the rock band Queen, was visible next to the late Freddie Mercury on a stamp from the Entertainer's Tale series. Since then the rules have been relaxed and the footballer David Beckham appeared on a British stamp issued in 2002.

Nowadays, you can even stick yourself onto an envelope. The Smilers range of stamps include a feature whereby your favourite family photographs can appear alongside the main stamp image. These have proved popular and some have rocketed in price in recent years. A sheet of 10 Christmas 2000 Smilers stamps can sell for up to £80–120.

## Variations on a theme

Occasionally, the Royal Mail issues a variation, such as a range of stamps with slightly different perforations from previous issues. Collectors often remain unaware of these variations until they appear in the Stanley Gibbons catalogue, the indispensable reference for all philatelists, by which time they are no longer on sale. The subsequent high demand pushes prices up. One example is the 2001 Submarines booklet of six first-class stamps. Two commemorative stamps were self-adhesive, whereas the ordinary stamps were printed on gummed paper. These booklets now sell for £50 or more.

**A set of four unused George VI Jamaican 2½d stamps.** *c.1940, 8.5cm (3¼in) high.*

**£4–6**

## Jubilee Series ▪ George V Half-crown

**A used Victoria two-penny Jubilee series stamp.** The Jubilee series commemorated 50 years of Queen Victoria's rule. This 2d stamp is among the most valuable from the series. *c.1890, 2.5cm (1in) high.*

**£25–50**

**A used George V half-crown stamp.** The design on this series, often called Seahorses, is among the finest. It was reissued in slightly changed form in 1934, with cross-hatching behind the King's head. *c.1913, 4.5cm (1¾in) wide.*

**£60–90**

### Top Tips

- Expect to realise only about 20 to 30 per cent of Stanley Gibbons' catalogue values when selling a stamp – prices quoted are for pristine stamps.
- Prefer unused stamps over used stamps; they are generally worth substantially more.
- Look for unbroken groups of stamps (used or unused); they are more valuable than the same number of single stamps.
- Look for cancellation marks that are well centred and lightly stamped, yet legible. Unusual marks are desirable.
- Soak an envelope briefly in water then gently peel the stamp away before it dries, to remove it – but beware, you may lose the cancellation mark.

### BUY

*There will always be a demand for classic, antique stamps, and as the supply dwindles, prices increase steadily. The value of an early stamp in good condition is almost guaranteed to rise higher than inflation each year.*

**A used Penny Black stamp.** This example has check letters 'C' and 'E' in the bottom corners. The two clear margins at the top and bottom and the good condition of the stamp make it desirable. *1840, 2.5cm (1in) high.*

**£30–60**

### SELL

*The value of some modern stamps has risen rapidly, as collectors seek catalogued items that they missed when first issued. Take advantage of the current market and sell, as value is unlikely to rise any higher.*

**A sheet of unused Christmas Smilers stamps.** This sheet would appeal to a dedicated collector. *2000, 29.5cm (11½in) wide.*

**£80–120**

# Coins and paper money,

as well as stocks and bonds, are more sought after for their historical and aesthetic interest than for any intrinsic value – but there is always the chance that some rare coin might turn up at a fair or a sale.

The study of coins and medals is known as numismatics. This collecting area has broadened in recent years, and now includes paper money (notaphily) and stock and bond certificates (scripophily).

## A penny saved, a penny earned

Some coin enthusiasts specialise in 'type collecting', whereby one coin of each series and design issued for a particular time and place – such as English Victorian coinage – is collected. Others concentrate on coins of the ancient world, commemoratives, minting errors, or other categories. The novice can begin by using coins in circulation, where there is always the faint hope of finding an exceptional specimen – some 1983 2p coins can raise up to £200–250 owing to an error in which a small number were minted with 'NEW PENCE' on the reverse, instead of 'TWO PENCE'. These are not likely to be in circulation as they were only ever issued in commemorative sets.

Condition is vital: 'uncirculated' or 'mint state' coins are usually worth more, although collectors are fond of 'toning'. This is the natural blue-green discoloration that builds up, particularly on silver coins. A good, even tone will increase the value of coins, so never clean or polish them.

## Paper chase

Banknotes are usually intricate, incorporating swirls and flourishes around finely detailed and coloured vignettes, as well as additional security devices. Of these, the watermark is the oldest and most common, but closer investigation will reveal all sorts of subtleties, such as the current US $100 bill, on which Franklin's lapels are micro-printed with the words 'United States of America'. Some possible themes for collecting are battles, monarchs, the Commonwealth, special serial numbers such as palindromic or low numbers, notes with printing errors, or those created for special purposes, such as military currency.

Notes in circulation will only cost face value, and many rarer specimens can be found for £20 or less, rising to around £200. Real bargains can be had by sifting through the boxes of cheap notes kept by many dealers. Opt for the crispest, cleanest notes available.

**A Victorian crown,** with a portrait of Queen Victoria on the obverse and St George slaying the dragon on the reverse. *1898, 3.5cm (1½in) diam.*

**£12–18**

**A certificate for a 7 per cent Confederate States of America Loan for $500.** *1863, 35cm (13¾in) wide.*

**£50–70**

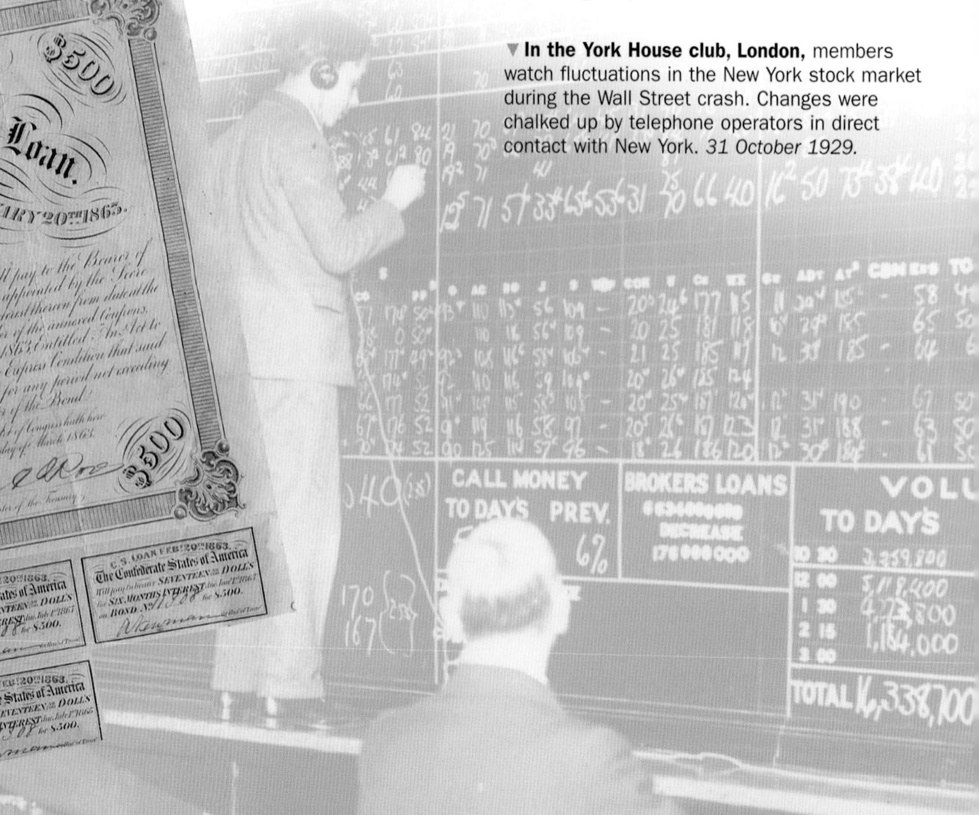

▼ **In the York House club, London,** members watch fluctuations in the New York stock market during the Wall Street crash. Changes were chalked up by telephone operators in direct contact with New York. *31 October 1929.*

## A closer look at... a Romanian commemorative note

Commemorative issues are often produced in large quantities, so to retain their value they must be kept in mint condition. If the note or coin is issued with a presentation case or folder it should be kept safely stored inside. This colourful design by Nicolae Saftoiu depicts the path of the 1999 solar eclipse through Romania, which this note was printed to commemorate.

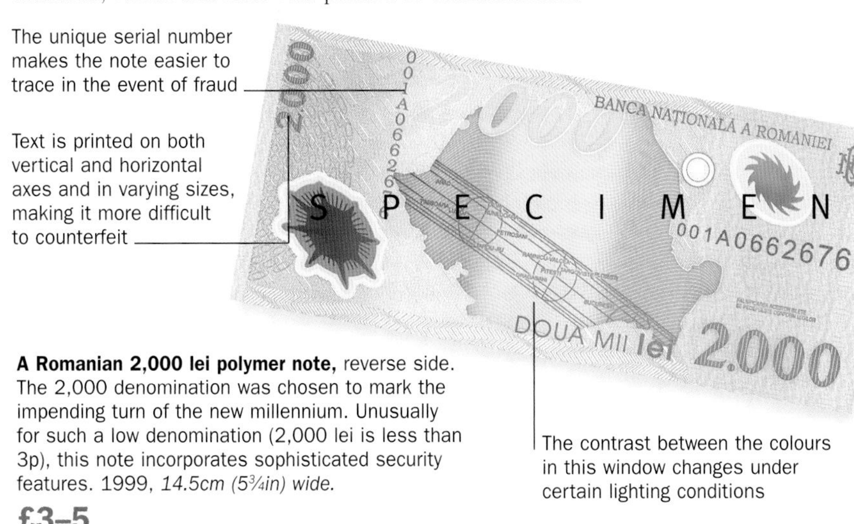


**A Romanian 2,000 lei polymer note,** reverse side. The 2,000 denomination was chosen to mark the impending turn of the new millennium. Unusually for such a low denomination (2,000 lei is less than 3p), this note incorporates sophisticated security features. 1999, *14.5cm (5¾in) wide.*

**£3–5**

### Stock up on stocks

Stock and bond certificates can be attractive, sometimes featuring vignettes depicting the function of the issuing body – such as a ship for a shipping line – and often carrying a security feature in the form of a company seal, watermark, or signature. Most enthusiasts prefer certificates from the early 18th century to the mid-20th century – the period when the great industrial, commercial, and colonial powers flourished and influenced the world.

Headline-making scandals can result in a rise in interest. Nominally worthless certificates for single shares of Enron stock have sold for more than £50 following the disclosure of irregularities involving the company in 2003. Shares in firms with a turbulent history can be more lucrative for collectors than for investors. While shares in Eurotunnel plc fell to less than 60p each in 2003, a 1988 certificate for a single share can fetch up to £50.

Old certificates may be found in excellent condition, as they will probably have been kept in a bank vault for years. Details to look for include the denomination – higher value certificates are usually more desirable – and applied items such as tax stamps and signatures, which can add value. Crossover appeal is another vital factor that can raise value: for example, stock issued by the Great Western Railway Company is attractive to railway enthusiasts as well as to stock-certificate collectors.

**A Thai 60 baht note issued to commemorate the King's 60th birthday,** depicting the King of Thailand in state dress, enthroned, on the obverse. *1987, 16cm (6¼in) wide.*

**£8–12**

### Top Tips

- Choose pieces that you find attractive or interesting.
- Invest in good-quality albums or mounts – coins, notes, and certificates must be kept in the best possible condition.
- Handle coins as little as possible, or use protective fabric gloves. Keep them in the box the dealer provided or in clear plastic wallets.
- Store paper documents flat and ensure that the edges remain crisp and that corners do not become bent – such wear can reduce value.

### BUY

*English banknotes are in demand on the global market and, as time passes, pre-decimalisation paper money is becoming scarcer. Look out for notes that were issued in smaller quantities: 10 shilling notes were less common than pound notes.*

**A Bank of England 10 shilling note,** of the last series printed without the Queen's head, and featuring Britannia. The note has a watermark, and is not dated. This note only appeared with this Chief Cashier's signature in 1955, which, along with its mint condition, makes it an excellent buy. *c.1955, 14cm (5½in) wide.*

**£20–25**

### SELL

*Facsimile coins can be found in abundance and may lower the value of rare coins. The motives behind their creation are often entirely innocent – simply to make a reproduction of an attractive but expensive coin – but it can still be difficult to tell the genuine from the counterfeit. A facsimile is unlikely to rise in value.*

**A silver facsimile Chinese coin with a military bust of Yuan Shih-Kai.** Original coins with this design can cost about £200 but there are many facsimiles on the market. *1914, 4cm (1½in) diam.*

**£2–3**

SALT

MILD LITTLE CIGARS
CANADA

Für
lautes Spiel.

# Household and Kitchenalia

Vintage household and kitchen objects have immense appeal and charm. From softly burnished copper Victorian jelly moulds to 1930s cocktail shakers, they are not only often decorative, but offer a nostalgic reminder of daily life in days gone by.

Cornishware jug, p.104

Brass candlesticks, p.98

Butter-working table, p.101

# The lasting appeal of....

Many people appreciate the beauty and faded charm of vintage household and kitchen objects. There can be great pleasure in decorating the home with unique pieces from the past, such as kitchen scales or an old sewing machine, and many can still be used.

One of the advantages of collecting old kitchen equipment and household paraphernalia is that you don't have to be an expert to appreciate it. Many pieces are both decorative and highly nostalgic, such as the characteristic broad blue and white stripes of Cornishware (1).

## Familiar sights

Hearthside pieces such as coal tongs and horse brasses are seen in pubs the length and breadth of the country, and many people also have them at home. Candlesticks (2) have risen in popularity, but while they were once an essential light source, now they are purely decorative. Kitchen utensils such as bread boards and butter working tables (3), early coffee pots (4), and toasters are all highly collectable.

Old sewing machines (5) and sewing cases (6) remind us of a time when needlecraft was an essential skill for women. If you have inherited an old sewing box, it may

7

Stainless steel goblet, p.124

Sweet box packaging, p.110

Miniature toffee tin, p.115

Copper coffee pot, p.99

Singer sewing machine, p.121

Sewing compendium, p.121



# ...things for the home

well be worth something. Stainless steel pieces (7) from the 1930s to 70s are also sought after: when stainless steel first came out, it was an exciting and resilient new material which, unlike silver, was easy to look after. It also lent itself particularly well to clean, modern designs.

## It's a wrap

Vintage packaging (8) and tins (9) have become a popular collecting area over the last 30 years or so. Late 19th- and early 20th-century pieces tend to be valuable, but it is still possible to find bargains from the 1950s and 60s. Packaging reflects the styles and changing tastes of each period, from sinuous Art Nouveau styles to the functional austerity of the 1940s and the colourful artwork of the 1950s and 60s. It also shows us the kind of things that people bought, the brands they liked, and how advertising has changed over the decades.

Drinking paraphernalia makes a varied as well as useful collection, ranging from vintage corkscrews (10) with their often ingenious designs, to sleek, silvery 1930s cocktail shakers (11) that encapsulate the languid glamour of Art Deco.

Many vintage household objects may be unearthed in your own home. Even everyday objects might be worth something and there are still plenty of fascinating bargains to be found in junk shops, at car-boot sales, and at country auctions.

You don't have to be an expert to appreciate kitchen equipment and paraphernalia. Many pieces are both decorative and nostalgic.

Button corkscrew, p.126

Cocktail shaker, p.129

# Old brass and copper

add charm, warmth, and style to a home, and look good together. Stately brass candlesticks offer a hint of baronial splendour, while homely copper pots and pans conjure up old-style rustic kitchens.

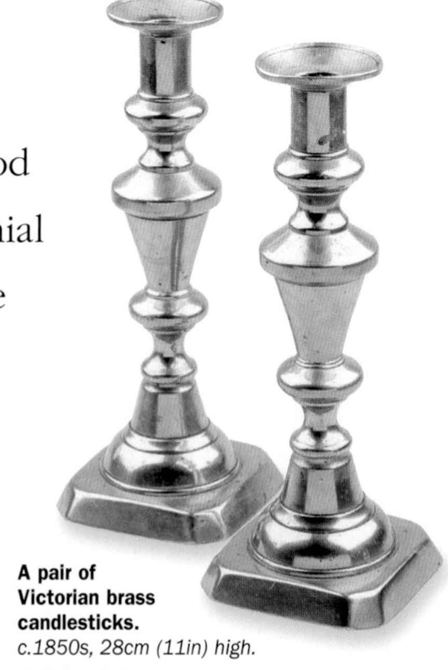

**A pair of Victorian brass candlesticks.**
*c.1850s, 28cm (11in) high.*
**£20–30**

The advent of electricity caused many everyday household items that our grandparents used to become obsolete – which is partly why they are collectable today. It was essential to have a copper or brass warming pan, filled with hot water or embers, to warm the bedsheets. Today these sell for around £70–200, with larger, finely decorated pieces worth the most.

Candles used to be the only light source in a house after dark. Candlesticks were not cast as one piece until the 18th century: before then they were cast in two parts and soldered together. Check hollow ones for evidence of seams, indicating an early date. An 18th-century brass candlestick could fetch up to £300, whereas a similar Victorian one might be worth only £50 or less.

## Kitchen heavyweights

Although saucepans were commonly made of cast iron, wealthy households owned sets made of copper. Vintage copper saucepans might cost from £50 for a small one, up to £300 for a large lidded pan by a noted manufacturer, such as Benham & Froud (1855–1906). A set of six copper pans, with a *bain marie* for making sauces, could be worth more than £1,000. Brass saucepans are generally worth less than copper pans.

**Two brass saucepans with iron handles.**
*1860s–90s, top pan 15cm (6in) diam.; bottom pan 14cm (5½in) diam.*
**£35–45; £60–70**

The kettle developed when tea drinking became popular. Copper and brass kettles rarely appeared in household inventories before the 18th century. Prices now vary but can be high: a mint-condition 1880s kettle by W.A.S Benson could reach £800. Copper samovars or tea urns can be highly ornate. The more intricate an object, the more it tends to be worth, although its value drops if parts are missing or have been replaced.

Iron stands, for holding flat irons as they heated on stoves, were plain at first, but by the 1850s were decorated with complex patterns in brass or copper. The most sought after examples were made by individual craftsmen, sometimes incorporating a horseshoe in the platform.

Mint-condition scales and weights, generally made of iron or brass, are desirable. A set of 10 brass butcher's weights might fetch around £500, whereas a set of plain household weights would probably be worth £100–150 or less. Other kitchen accessories to look for include measuring jugs and copper crumb trays.

## Around the hearth

Brass and copper fireplace accessories included bellows, irons, coal buckets, screens, and fenders. Mullers, used to mull and warm wine or beer, can still often be seen hanging next to a pub fire. They are cone-shaped with a long handle and usually cost £60–100, less if dented or small. Bellows were made of brass and wood, and standard examples often fetch £40–60, whereas larger, more ornate, or mechanical versions can sell for more than £100.

Brass toasting forks could be very ornate. Although they vary in value according to their level of decoration, most tend to fetch £50–100 or under. Pot stands or trivets range from less than £30 up to around £100, depending on decoration and scarcity.

## Lightweight reproductions

Pieces from the 18th and 19th centuries are the most collectable. Many items made in the early 20th century are also popular, although they are generally not as valuable. Because people like to keep their brass and copper polished, it is not always possible to use the patina to date pieces. But modern brass

### Collectors' Tales

*'I once found a big box of brass items at a house clearance. A candlestick poking out of the corner caught my eye. Although most of the pieces were uninteresting, a closer inspection of the candlestick revealed that it was a 16th-century piece. I sold it for the best part of £1,000 – many times more than I paid for the whole lot.'*

**Noel Pullman, London**

## A closer look at... a 19th-century copper coffee pot

Copper coffee pots were made in a variety of shapes and sizes. Ornate examples and unusual styles, such as oriental designs reflecting the Middle Eastern origins of coffee-drinking, often realise the highest prices, particularly if they are by noted designers or makers.

The pot retains its original lid with an acorn-shaped finial echoing the handle

The handle is of boxwood and is attractively turned

The pot has a desirable 'swan's-neck' spout

The condition is excellent, with no dents or splits

**A 19th-century copper coffee pot** by an unknown maker. To differentiate them from the more common teapots, coffee pots were often taller and less bulbous. *c.1860s–80s, 31.5cm (12½in) high.*

**£100–150**

and copper is often lighter because it is rolled more thinly. Run your finger over the surface: is it smooth where you would expect, given its usage? Look for damage or wear: is it believable, or might it have been contrived to fake age? Unlike silver, few copper and brass items were marked by their makers until the Companies Act of 1862. The name on brassware may not be the maker's – many items were engraved to show ownership. Inscriptions and names are often unscrupulously added to genuinely old objects to make them appear more valuable. Modern lettering can appear thin and scratchy compared with authentic lettering.

**A copper crumb tray and matching brush,** for sweeping up crumbs from a tablecloth. *c.1900, brush 34cm (13½in) long.*

**£30–40**

### Top Tips

- Use a magnet when examining old copper and brass to make sure it is not merely plated. A magnet will not be attracted to solid copper or brass.
- Beware of 'over-distressed' copper purporting to be old. New copper is often thinner than old, and so dents more easily.
- Ensure that any set of scales and weights is complete before buying.
- Keep copper pots and moulds for decoration only: there is a risk of poisoning if the protective linings are no longer in perfect condition.
- Avoid common copper or brass items that are split. Repairs can be hard to hide and will reduce the item's value.

### BUY

*One of the joys of collecting vintage metal kitchenalia is that items such as brushes, candlesticks, and trivets can still be used. The range of designs available allows you to build a satisfying collection, adding a period feel to your kitchen. When buying a trivet, look for examples with attractive detail in the legs and the platform.*

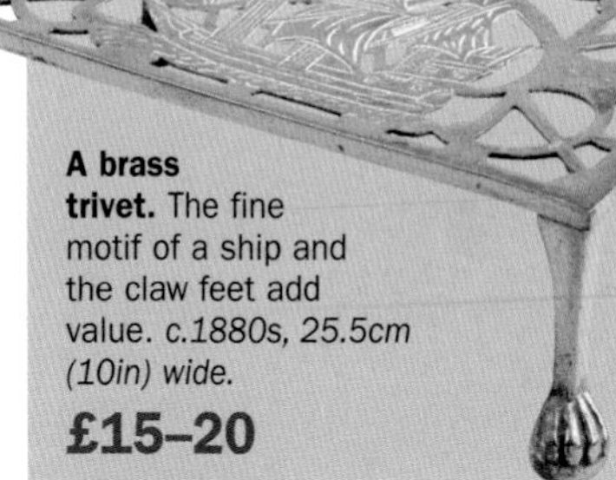

**A brass trivet.** The fine motif of a ship and the claw feet add value. *c.1880s, 25.5cm (10in) wide.*

**£15–20**

### SELL

*Kettles are desirable brass and copper items. As they were heavily used in their day, many were worn and damaged. Examples in good condition are often used as interior decoration in kitchens. Prices are unlikely to rise in the near future, unless the country cottage style of kitchen returns.*

**A copper kettle** with shaped spout and acorn finial on the lid. The floral engraving with the words 'Good Luck' makes this example even more desirable. *c.1870s, 28cm (11in) high.*

**£40–60**

# Vintage wooden objects,

particularly those made for the dairy, hark back to our rural past. The homespun beauty of these satisfyingly tactile pieces and the social history they represent make this an immensely appealing field.

**An oak milking pail** with a pint measure. *c.1880s–1920s, 35.5cm (14in) high.*

**£50–60**

Most of us are attracted by the warmth and natural qualities of wood, and the way it changes so subtly with age. Wooden household objects conjure up images of busy farmhouse kitchens, and a simpler, less stressful way of life.

## Of the tree

Miscellaneous small household items made from turned or carved wood are often referred to as treen, which means 'of the tree'. Although produced since medieval times, few pieces from that period have survived. Most items available today date back to the 19th century and cost from around £20–30 up to £500–700 or more, depending on age, condition, and decorative features.

The type of wood used can help to date a piece. Yew, beech, elm, chestnut, and fruitwoods were used extensively in the 17th century, and boxwood, maple, and pine were popular in the 18th century. Ebony and mahogany came into use in the 19th century, their rich, dark colours suiting Victorian styles.

### *Did You Know?*

*In the 15th and 16th centuries, bread was baked into thin, flat discs. It was served fresh to the head of the house and his guests, and everyone else had to eat day-old bread.*

## Bread and butter

In the 19th century, many rural families kept one or two cows and made their own butter and cheese. Butter was often decorated using a carved stamp or roller that was impressed into the butter pat.

These stamps can be worth from £30–50 to more than £100 for an intricately carved piece in good condition. Butter moulds, in which the pat was shaped and decorated, can sell for even more, especially if the pattern is detailed. Wooden butter dishes are usually worth about £40–60.

## Some dairy collectables to look for:

- Bowls
- Moulds
- Stamps

**A sycamore dairy bowl.** Most wooden bowls acquire an attractive patina and work well as decorative pieces. *c.1910s, 35cm (13¾in) diam.*

**£150–200**

**A sycamore butter mould.** The flower pattern and ribbed edging were imprinted on the butter pat. The level of carved detail makes this piece desirable and valuable. *1850s–80s, 22cm (8¾in) long.*

**£40–50**

Vintage bread boards are either plain or decorated with natural motifs such as leaves and acorns. Simpler examples fetch around £20–60, but boards with mottoes (such as 'God speed the plough') can be worth up to £250–300 if they are rare and have deep, interesting carvings. Vintage bread knives with wooden handles can fetch £30–60.

**A pair of sycamore butter pats for children,** used for 'patting' the butter into blocks. *c.1910s, 14.5cm (5¾in) long.*

**£15–25**

## Spoons for spooning

Wooden spoons and rolling pins were made at home until the 19th century, when they were first mass-produced. The handles of early spoons often had a ball-shaped end which was used to shape a cottage loaf or to settle fruit and vegetables in preserving jars. Basic cooking and eating spoons have changed little over the years. They generally sell for between £2–5 and £20–30. Welsh 'love spoons', which can date back to the 1660s and were made by young men for the girls they loved, were intended for display. They have ornately carved handles: those with more than one bowl at the end are rarer, often fetching £100 or more.

## Grinding down

Mortars and pestles are collectable and come in a number of different styles. Lignum vitae, a close-grained hardwood taken from a tree large enough to yield a bowl at least 30cm (1ft) in diameter, was often used for larger mortars. A late 18th-century mortar in good condition could fetch up to £200–250 or more. On the other hand, a small turned walnut pestle, used for grinding herbs and spices, might cost as little as £40–60.

## Finding fakes

Fake and reproduction wooden items do exist, but are fairly easy to spot. Traditionally, sycamore was favoured for many items because it was unlikely to warp, but modern copies are often made in beech or oak. Another tell-tale sign is wear: it is impossible to fake genuine age and long-term use.

### Top Tips

- Look for decorative carvings and details. If original, they can increase the value, as can names and dates.
- Resist drilling holes in wooden items to hang them up, as this will reduce their value.
- Learn how to recognise different sorts of wood: this can help you to date objects as well as understand what they were used for.

### BUY

*Objects made from fruitwoods and walnut can wear extremely well, showing a rich and varied patina when gently polished. They make superb decorative items, with simple but pleasingly turned designs, and many are still usable.*

**A turned walnut pestle.** The gently curved bulbous end is designed to grind spices. The rich coloration and attractive shape make this a collectable piece. *c.1860s, 22.5cm (9in) long.*

**£40–50**

### SELL

*Items that are roughly carved and show little attention to form, or those with limited decorative value or with an obscure function, are less collectable and unlikely to increase in value. Sell to a person who appreciates their naïve charm.*

**A fruitwood olive spoon** in the shape of a pipe, with a perforated central bowl scoop and a drilled shaft in the handle for draining the liquid from olives. This piece has little decoration or style. *c.1880s–1930s, 40cm (16in) long.*

**£20–30**

## ■ Butter Tables ■

**A West Country sycamore butter stamp.** These usually have geometric or floral patterns to decorate a butter pat. *c.1880s, 13cm (5in) long.*

**£30–40**

**A sycamore butter-working table,** used for consolidating newly churned butter. Unusually, this one is complete. *c.1910, 69cm (27½in) long.*

**£70–80**

COLLECTOR'S CORNER

# Jelly moulds in all their wide variety of materials and shapes bring back memories of birthday parties and feasts, and their appeal is both nostalgic and aesthetic. Not all moulds were just for sweet jellies – some were used for savoury jellies too.

▲ **A salt-glazed 'rabbit' earthenware mould.** The use of moulded animal or vegetable forms dates from an earlier time when the design of the mould would have reflected the savoury ingredients of the jelly. *c.1870s, 16.5cm (6½in) wide.*

**£25–35**

The earliest jelly moulds were made in the 18th century of thin white stoneware. Most jelly moulds found today, though, date from the early 19th century to the 1950s.

In the late 18th century the Staffordshire potteries made deep and increasingly inventive moulds. Shapes and motifs included fruit, animals, wheat sheaves, and classical motifs.

Minton, Copeland, and Davenport were all major manufacturers. They produced cream and white wares from the mid-19th to the early 20th century. Minton pieces are often recognisable by their glaze, which has a bluish tinge. Marked moulds are more desirable.

In the 1840s, decorated earthenware and heavy, brown salt-glaze stoneware were increasingly used. Prices are around £30–60, but highly decorative moulds by major makers can exceed £100.

Copper was another material used as it was light, durable, and easy to mould. From the 1920s onwards, cheaper materials were used and quality declined. Designs also became less intricate, but pieces can still be attractive and are usually priced at around £20 or under. A notable 20th-century maker is Shelley, whose moulds are sought after today, especially if they are well-shaped.

► **A Wedgwood ceramic mould,** with a pineapple motif. Pineapples traditionally represent hospitality and friendship. *c.1880s, 15.5cm (6¼in) wide.*

**£40–50**

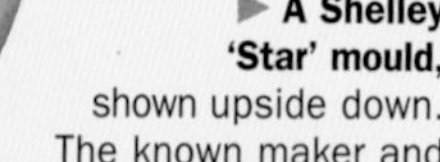

► **A Shelley 'Star' mould,** shown upside down. The known maker and comparatively complex shape increase the value. *1912–25, 14.5cm (5¾in) diam.*

**£30–40**

◄ **A Shelley 'Acanthus' mould.** The acanthus leaf is a classical motif that dates back to antiquity. The attractive design by a well-known manufacturer makes this pottery mould highly desirable. *1912–25, 14.5cm (5¾in) wide.*

**£30–40**

◄ **An aluminium mould.** Many moulds of the 1920s and 30s reflect the simple forms and clean lines of the Art Deco style. *1920s–30s, 17.5cm (6¾in) wide.*

**£5–7**

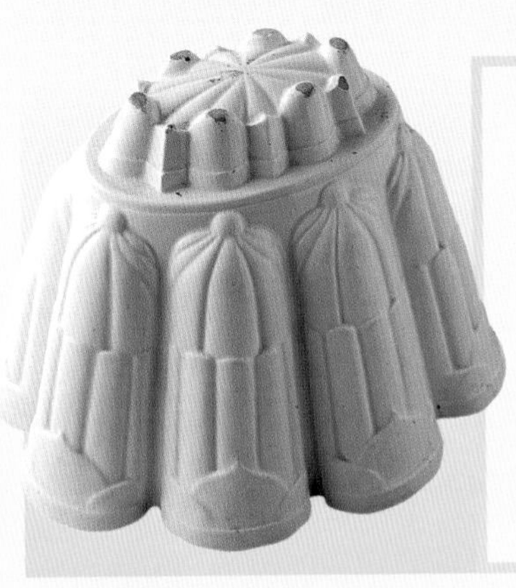

◀ **A Shelley 'Ritz' mould.** The Ritz Hotel in London was opened in 1906 to widespread acclaim. This is an early piece from a notable maker. *c.1912, 18cm (7¼in) wide.*

**£50–60**

◀ **A copper cylindrical 'Charlotte' mould** retailed by T. Aldridge of Brompton Road, London. Charlotte was a 19th-century jelly-like dessert using bread or cake filled with chopped fruits such as apple. *1860s, 8cm (3¼in) high.*

**£50–60**

## Collectors' Tips

- Look out for makers' marks, as notable makers add value
- Feel the weight of copper moulds before buying. Thin, light moulds are probably reproduction. Avoid split and re-soldered pieces
- Look for registered design marks to help date earthenware moulds but bear in mind that marks relate to the date of design, not manufacture

▶ **A Malin mould,** with swan motif. The well-known factory and pentagonal shape, combined with the swan motif, make this a desirable object. *1920s, 17cm (6¾in) wide.*

**£50–60**

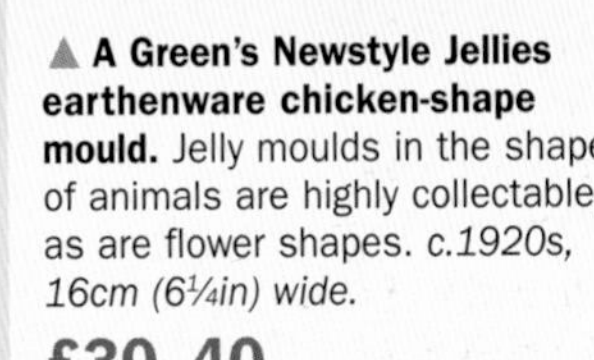

▲ **A Green's Newstyle Jellies earthenware chicken-shape mould.** Jelly moulds in the shape of animals are highly collectable, as are flower shapes. *c.1920s, 16cm (6¼in) wide.*

**£30–40**

▼ **A copper mould.** Copper moulds with complex designs such as this are more valuable than plainer examples. *1870s, 16cm (6¼in) wide.*

**£100–150**

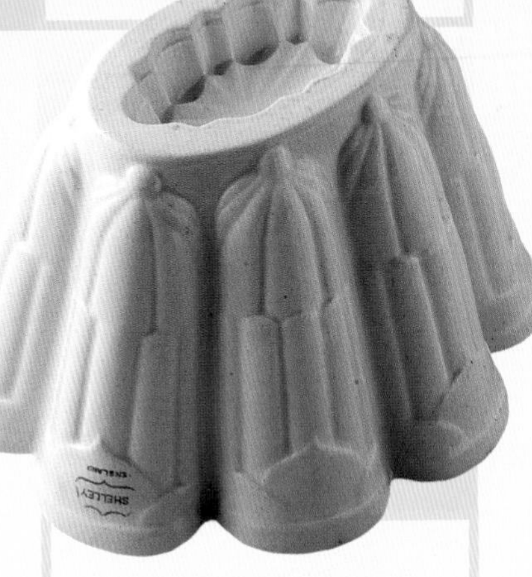

▲ **A Shelley 'Carlton' mould.** The deep indentation at the top created a well into which cream was poured. *1912–25, 15cm (6in) wide.*

**£30–40**

# Cornishware is easily recognised by its simple blue-and-white bands, and is redolent of good old-fashioned country kitchens. The huge range of shapes – and there are even colour variations – gives a great deal of scope to form a collection.

**A milk jug** with the T.G. Green stamp on its base. *1930s–70s, 11.5cm (4½in) high.*

**£20–30**

Most people have one or two pieces of Cornishware tucked away in a kitchen cupboard, or perhaps proudly displayed on a dresser.

True Cornishware was produced by T.G. Green of Church Gresley, in Derbyshire, from the 1920s onwards, its popularity reaching a peak in the 1940s and 50s. The name is said to have come from one of the firm's employees who, on returning from holiday in Cornwall, saw the new range and said that the blue was like the Cornish skies and the white like the crests of Cornish waves.

By the 1980s Cornishware had declined in popularity, and the rights to make it were sold to Cloverleaf of Swindon. In 2001 the rights passed to Mason Cash & Co., who are still manufacturing it. The market for vintage pieces from the 1930s to the 50s soared in the mid-90s. Prices have fallen over the past five years, although they have recently become more stable, and rare pieces will always be popular.

## Cornish miscellany

A vast number of household objects were made, including storage jars, rolling pins, plates, and jugs. The age of an item of Cornishware is often indicated by its shape, since ceramics tend to mirror the fashions of the period. Most pieces before the 1960s were rounded, but Judith Onions, who designed for T.G. Green from 1968, introduced streamlined shapes with clean, modern lines.

## Church and shield

Maker's marks on the bottom of a piece will help with identification and dating. Early marks from the 1920s to the 40s are printed in green and show the church at Church Gresley, the pottery's home. But most original Cornishware bears a printed mark (in black or green) in a shield that incorporates the factory name and is crossed by the words 'Cornish Kitchen Ware'. Be wary of storage jars with named contents ('Sugar', 'Tea', and so on) and the green shield mark: the contents label may have been added later to make a common jar appear to be rare. A 'target'-shaped mark was used between 1968 and 1980 for the range designed by Onions, but from 1980 until 1987 the mark included the church motif once again. Stamped markings that say 'Made in England' or marks including the word 'Chefware' are not authentic T.G. Green Cornishware.

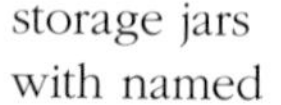

## The price of prunes

Prices range from as little as £5–15 for a blue-and-white mug or plate, up to £300 or more for a storage jar marked with the name of

## A closer look at... a Cornishware jar

Storage jars were produced in large numbers and a huge variety of named pieces exist. But some jars are not authentic Cornishware, while some genuine pieces have had names added later in a bid to increase their rarity. Always examine a jar carefully before buying it, and keep a guide handy for identifying unusual marks.

**A 'MEAL' storage jar** with its lid, in good condition. Most named storage jars have a black shield-shaped mark on the bottom, and some have a green church mark. A green shield mark on a named jar may well be a sign that the piece is not genuine. *c.1940s, 17.5cm (7in) high.*

**£100–150**

an ingredient that is uncommon nowadays, such as lard or meal. Jars for standard ingredients such as flour, tea, coffee, and sugar are easier to find, and usually cost £50 or less. Jars for expensive or uncommon ingredients, such as prunes, cocoa, and borax, are rare: prices often start at about £100.

T.G. Green often undertook special commissions, by request, for unique ingredient names and certain brand names. As these were produced in small runs, they are usually valuable.

## Pot red

Although blue and white is the most characteristic colour combination, Cornishware has been made in other colours. Red bands are the rarest. This range was produced as an experiment during the 1960s and never went into full production. Prices can rise to £200 or more, depending on the shape and type of item. Other colours to look out for include gold, yellow, orange, green, and black, all produced from the 1970s onwards. A yellow-banded egg cup can be worth around £5–10, a green-banded cafetière about £70–100. As well as banded pieces, T.G. Green also launched a blue-and-white range in a polka-dot pattern, known as 'Domino'. Although less popular, it is still collectable, and a small milk jug will usually fetch around £40.

**A 'Domino' sugar bowl** with a T.G. Green stamp on its base. *1930s–50s, 9.5cm (3¾in) high.*

**£20–30**

**A salt box** with a T.G. Green stamp on its base. *1930s–70s, 11.5cm (4½in) high.*

**£60–80**

### Top Tips

- Replace a damaged or missing lid on a named storage jar with an intact lid from an unnamed jar – but check the size carefully as diameters vary enormously.
- Check that there are no chips or signs of repair around the edges of a lid or a stopper and also on the lip of a jug.
- Examine the glaze carefully – a fine network of lines known as 'crazing' reduces value, as do chips or cracks in the glaze.

### BUY

*The simple lines of pieces by Judith Onions from the late 1960s until the 80s often appeal to modern tastes. Many are still relatively inexpensive, and the variety of shapes and colours available adds interest to a collection. These pieces are probably yet to reach their full potential value.*

**A yellow-and-white butter dish, designed by Judith Onions,** with her distinctive target-shaped mark on the base. *c.1970s, 14cm (5½in) high.*

**£30–50**

### KEEP

*The storage jar is one of the most popular and widely collected shapes. Examples with rare contents names will always be worth more. As long as they are in excellent condition, they are worth keeping, particularly as Cornishware may be about to grow in popularity once more.*

**An 'ICING SUGAR' storage jar** with a lid. This has a T.G. Green black shield-shaped stamp on the base, denoting authenticity. *c.1940s, 14cm (5½in) high.*

**£50–70**

# Blue-and-white ware had its heyday in the 19th century, but its familiar, intricate designs still feature in many home ceramic collections. Whether for use or simply for display, it is available in a huge range of shapes, patterns, sizes, and prices.

Few homes are without at least one piece of blue-and-white china, and almost everyone can remember these pieces from their childhood. As prices have fallen over the past few years, a collection of this china can be built up more affordably than ever before. Plates can be found for £10–15, with many other blue-and-white pieces costing less than £500.

The patterns were first used in China to decorate ceramics in the 13th century, when the Chinese hand painted intricate designs onto porcelain, incorporating landscapes, flowers, foliage, and other decorative motifs. Chinese blue-and-white became fashionable in Europe in the 17th and 18th centuries, although the labour-intensive production technique made the ware costly.

## The spreading of a secret

In the mid-18th century, the Worcester factory discovered a revolutionary way of transfer-printing a design onto a piece before glazing, making it possible to produce inexpensive ceramics. It was not long before the secrets of this process leaked out, and soon many factories, including Spode in Staffordshire, and others in Swansea,

**A Davenport 'Muleteer' pattern pepper pot.** *1830s, 12cm (4¾in) high.*

**£40–50**

## Some patterns to look for:

### ■ Asiatic Pheasants

### ■ Death of the Bear

◄ **A Copeland & Garratt 'Death of the Bear' pattern plate.** This pattern is the most commonly found from Spode's Indian Sporting series. *1833–47, 25cm (9¾in) diam.*

**£100–150**

▼ **An 'Asiatic Pheasants' pattern sauce boat,** by an unknown maker. This delicate pattern was produced on a large variety of objects during the 19th century, making it an ideal theme on which to base a collection. *c.1860, 11cm (4¼in) high.*

**£20–30**

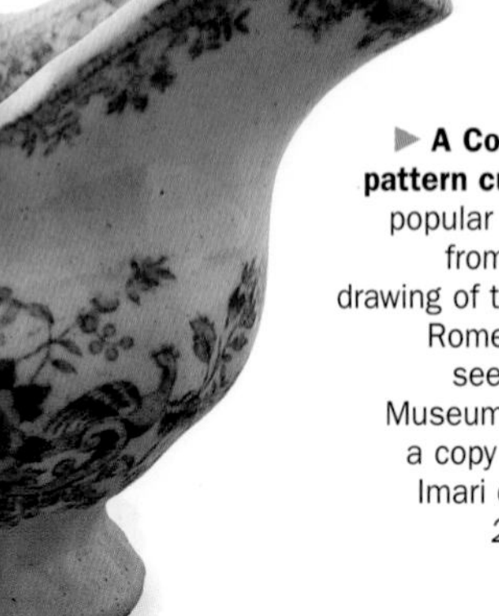

► **A Copeland 'Italian' pattern cusped dish.** This popular pattern was taken from a pen-and-wash drawing of the Coliseum in Rome, which can be seen in the Spode Museum; the border is a copy of a Japanese Imari design. *c.1900, 20cm (8in) diam.*

**£30–40**

Leeds, and north-east England, began printing blue-and-white designs onto mass-produced earthenware pieces.

A huge variety of shapes was produced during the first half of the 19th century, and these are the most sought after. The latter half of the century to the early 1900s also yielded some superb pieces, although changing tastes forced the industry into decline: all-over patterning fell out of fashion and tableware became less ornate, with decoration being limited to the borders.

## Mind the gap

Most early blue-and-white patterns have a decorative border of Chinese-inspired designs, foliage, or flowers that

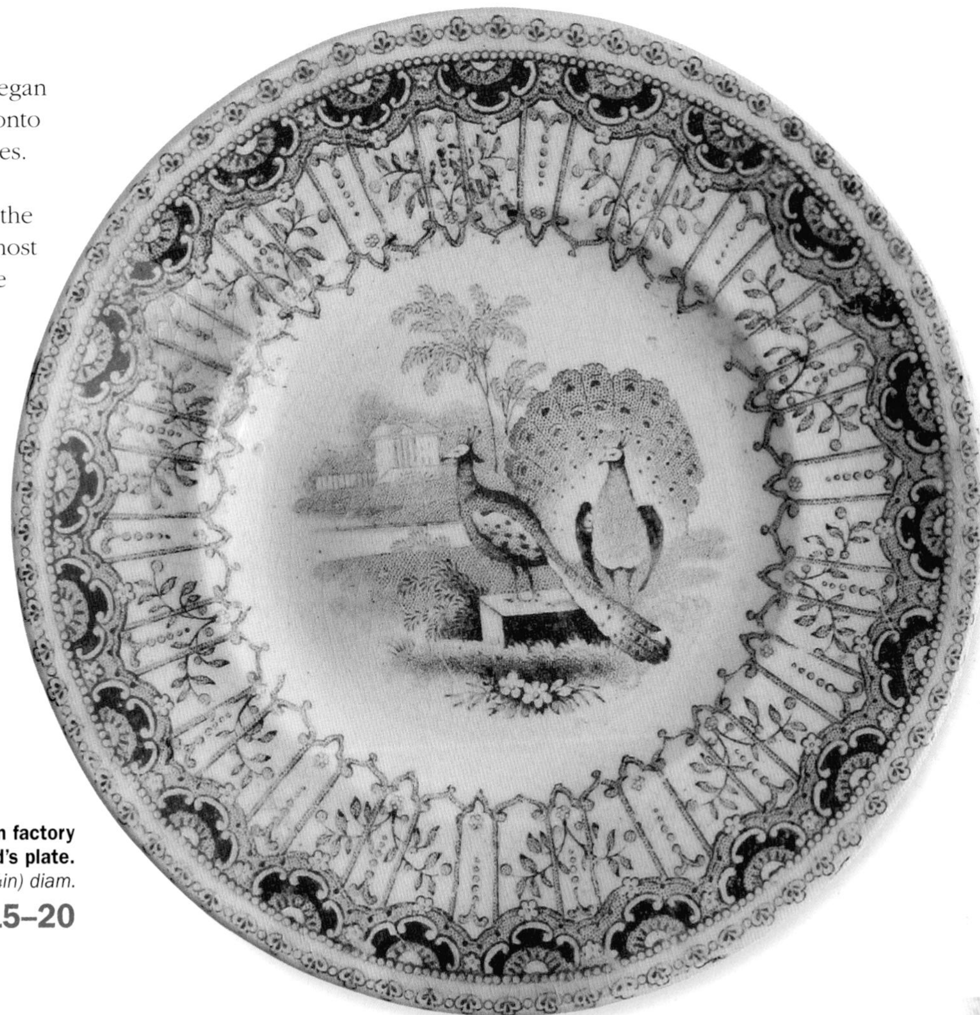

**A Benjamin Godwin factory 'Peacock' pattern child's plate.** *c.1840, 14.5cm (5¾in) diam.*

**£15–20**

## ▪ Italian ▪ Grazing Rabbits ▪ Ponte Rotto ▪ Willow ▪

▶ **A 'Willow' pattern ladle** by an unknown maker. The famed and prolific Chinese-inspired 'Willow' pattern, introduced by Thomas Minton for the Caughley factory in the late 18th century, is perhaps the most common blue-and-white pattern. It will only fetch this price if not broken and restored. *c.1830, 18cm (7in) long.*

**£80–100**

▲ **A 'Grazing Rabbits' pattern plate,** by an unknown maker. This charming pattern of three oversized rabbits eating grass under a tree is not common, making it highly sought after. *c.1820, 24cm (9½in) diam.*

**£80–100**

◀ **A 'Ponte Rotto' pattern tureen stand,** attributed to Rogers. Scenes of landscapes with buildings, often in ruins, were popular subjects. This shows the first bridge across the River Tiber in Rome, which collapsed in 1598. *1815–42, 21cm (8¼in) wide.*

**£40–50**

surround a central scene. From the 1840s, a plain white gap was often left between the border and the central scene, and this can help in dating. Other patterns have an all-over, uniformly repeated design or 'sheet pattern', usually made up of flowers and foliage.

The prolific 'Willow' pattern, introduced by Thomas Minton for the Caughley factory in the late 18th century, is perhaps the most familiar. This is followed by the 'Asiatic Pheasants' pattern, produced by several factories and showing a scene of the birds among flowers, and the 'Italian' pattern, which shows ruined buildings in a landscape – it was introduced by Spode in 1816 but was widely copied.

Some patterns, such as 'Asiatic Pheasants', are in paler colours. This was intentional, as the colour is under the glaze and cannot fade. Before buying a piece, look at the quality of the transfer, which should be crisp and detailed. Pieces decorated with a transfer that is uneven or has obtrusive joins are worth less, as are pieces with blurred transfers.



**Throughout the centuries, blue-and-white ware has withstood the test of time, with old designs resurfacing as timeless classics or being reworked into new ones.**

## Picture perfect

Rarer patterns featuring scenes from well-known stories such as Aesop's fables, mythological scenes, or pastoral scenes such as 'The Beemaster' and 'Grazing Rabbits' can fetch £150 or more for an item such as a plate. Animal and sporting subjects are perennially popular. Designers had rarely seen some of the more exotic species such as elephants and tigers, so the creatures depicted can look strange to modern eyes. Perhaps the most famous sporting designs were in the Indian Sporting series introduced by Spode in the 1820s. Occasionally, an unsavoury subject, such as 'The Death of the Bear', can limit a piece's desirability for some collectors. Nevertheless, a plate featuring this scene may still fetch around £150.

Consult a ceramics pattern book if you need to identify a rare or unusual design. Some patterns – such as 'Willow' and 'Italian' – have remained in almost continuous production. Others were withdrawn but made a return in the 20th century. Some were discontinued and never reintroduced. Recently, Spode has revived a number of 19th-century patterns in a popular range of prestige tableware. These are easy to identify by their marks and also because the pieces show no signs of use and have a strong and even transfer.

## The shape of things

It is important to consider shape, pattern, maker, and size when starting a collection. Blue-and-white ware is often collected by object type, such as jugs. Plates are also popular as they show the pattern clearly and are easy to display. Chargers (large plates), dishes, and platters are desirable for the same reasons, but they are more expensive as they are larger and less common than plates. Some shapes are rare, such as dog troughs, bedpans, and cheese dishes, and these can be worth from £150–400, to upwards of £800.

**A Copeland (late Spode) 'Botanical' pattern plate.** *c.1850, 24cm (9½in) diam.*

**£10–20**

Makers are important, but they are usually secondary to pattern and shape. Look out for major makers such as Wedgwood, Spode, and Minton, as well as lesser-known ones such as Rogers. The name 'Spode' existed until 1833, when Copeland & Garrett bought the factory, but it was reintroduced in the 1970s.

If you want to date the 'Italian' pattern by Copeland & Garrett, it is worth noting that they used marks between 1870 and 1970 that can help you to do so easily. The letter indicates a month, and the numbers the year of production: for example, 'S/03' on an item would date it to September 1903.

**An early 19th-century Spode Dutch-shape jug,** printed in blue with the 'Chinese of Rank' pattern. This is a rare pattern and an excellent quality transfer. *17cm (6¾in) high.*

**£900–1,100**

**An invalid's feeding cup**, by an unknown maker. Must be in perfect condition. *c.1830s, 7cm (2¾in) high.*

**£60–70**

## *Top Tips*

- Display plates and platters on a dresser or use adjustable acrylic plate hangers or stands: metal grips can damage the rim.
- Avoid ceramics with brown, mottled frost stains on them; these cannot be removed.

## KEEP

*Plates and dishes produced during the heyday of blue-and-white ceramics are easy to display, and are collected by a wide number of people. Although the market has declined, prices shouldn't fall any lower and may even rise in the future.*

**A Spode 'Temple' pattern cheese plate.** The chinoiserie scene recalls the Chinese inspiration behind blue-and-white ceramics. *c.1820, 20cm (8in) diam.*

**£10–20**

## BUY

*Large tableware pieces are popular because they are visually impressive and display the pattern well. Blue-and-white ware was made to be used and so damage is common. Complete sets that still have the ladle and are in top condition are especially prized.*

**A Copeland 'Camilla' pattern sauce tureen, stand, and ladle.** This tureen retains its lid, ladle, and stand, which are often missing. *c.1900, 17cm (6¾in) high.*

**£100–150**

# Vintage household packaging

often has a direct, simple charm. The nostalgia of well-known brand names, combined with attractive designs and colours, make this a rich and unusual field.

**An unopened war-time Bird's custard powder sachet.** *1939–45, 10.5cm (4¼in) high.*

**£4–6**

From the idealised 1950s housewife featured on a box of washing powder to a stylish 1960s Biba powder compact, packaging offers a fascinating insight into social history. Following the development of colour printing in the 1840s, companies increasingly used design to devise eye-catching and colourful packaging. Comparatively few 19th-century examples survive, but there are plenty of 20th-century pieces available. Prices can be as low as £3–5 and rarely rise above £100–150. Dummy packaging, used for displays and promotions, is similarly priced and, like retail packaging, valued according to brand, date, and styling.

Vintage packaging gives us a taste of changing styles and prices. A sachet of Bird's custard powder, decorated in the colours still used by the company, cost 1½d during World War II (roughly comparable to current values). Hair cream or gloss, a popular product in the first half of the 20th century, disappeared from the shelves with the advent of the 'freer' 1960s.

## Style wise

If you choose to focus on the 19th century, look for fine lithography on labels and boxes, in many different colours and featuring intricate designs. Items from this period can fetch from £10–20 upwards, depending on brand, style, complexity of artwork and colour printing, and rarity.

The huge variety of 20th-century packaging makes it easy to focus on a specific type, such as sweets, or foods sold during World War II. The style of the artwork is the first factor to consider: it reflects the graphic styles of different periods, from the angularity of 1930s Art Deco to the bright colours of the 1950s and 60s. A soap box from the 1930s can fetch as little as £10–15, while a 1950s glass bottle for Castrol oil tends to be valued at around £10–20.

## Brands and themes

Brand names, particularly ones known internationally, such as Coca-Cola, are popular, and products by one maker can show how styles have changed over time – the Kellogg's Cornflakes rooster is a good example.

**A Bassett's dummy 'Jelly Babies' box.** Bright colours and friendly designs make sweet packaging popular. *1960s, 10cm (4in) wide.*

**£7–10**

## Some packaging to look for:

▪ Sweets ▪ Chocolate ▪

**A Nestlé 'Honey Queen' chocolate bar wrapper.** Chocolate was particularly highly prized when it was rationed during and after World War II. Rationing on chocolate and sweets was not lifted until 1954. *c.1940s–50s, 10cm (4in) wide.*

**£6–8**

You might prefer to concentrate on a specific product. For example, although it may seem an unlikely collecting theme, individual sugar packets can feature company logos, hotels, or famous restaurants. A sugar sachet from a well-known airline such as British Airways can fetch 10p–£2, depending on the period.

## Letter lore

Lettering can help to date packaging. A swirling serif style may suggest the 19th century, while curling, vinelike, Art Nouveau designs may indicate the early 20th century. Bear in mind, though, that some packaging, such as that for Lyle's Golden Syrup, has hardly changed over the years, and that with some products, especially foods, old-fashioned packaging may be part of the commercial strategy.

## Added value

Packaging can carry a higher price tag if it also appeals to collectors in other areas. A celebrity endorsement may attract people interested in celebrity memorabilia, while collectors of Corgi or Dinky toys will want boxes that match pieces in their collection, to increase their value.

### Top Tips

- Avoid damaged items – their value will be considerably reduced.
- A smaller collection of pieces in good condition is better than a large collection of inferior items.
- Look for representative period pieces with a social dimension, such as wartime packaging – this increases desirability.
- Bright, attractive designs and well-known brand names count for more than just the age of an item.

### BUY

*Always look for brightly coloured items with artwork that epitomises the period – in addition to being attractive and nostalgic, they reflect a recognisable phase in the history of design.*

**A box of Lever 'Sunlight' soap.** *c.1935, 15cm (6in) wide.*

**£12–16**

**A card box of 'Oxydol' washing powder.** The brightly coloured vortex and housewife's endorsement are typical of the period. *1950s, 13cm (5in) high.*

**£8–12**

### KEEP

*Well-known brand names are always collectable, and their continued popularity in the marketplace keeps values consistent. Try to track the fashionable trends in brand names – items linked with the key names of the 1960s are currently popular and rising in value.*

## ▪ Processed Food ▪ Cigarettes ▪

**A dummy Birds Eye box for turkey pie.** TV ready-made dinners were first sold in the 1950s. This aspect of social history may make convenience food packaging a popular collecting area. *1950s, 15cm (6in) wide.*

**£3–5**

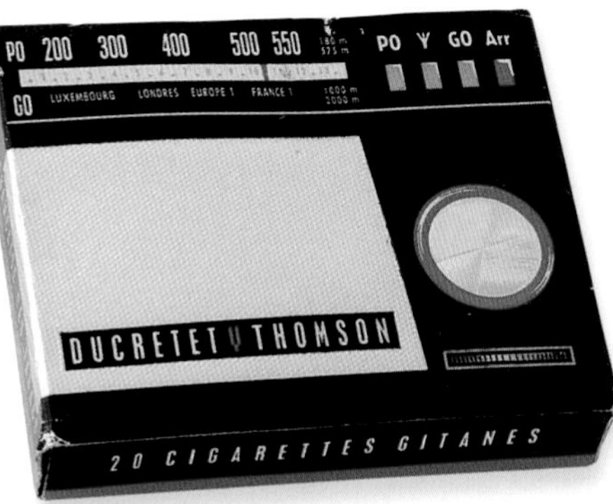


**A French Gitanes cigarette pack,** in imitation of a Thomson transistor radio, with cigarettes. Cigarette packets have become more conservatively styled as health concerns have come to the fore. *1960s, 9cm (3½in) wide.*

**£20–30**

**Three Biba cosmetics containers.** Biba was a household name during the 1960s and 70s, when the London store defined not only a style, but an era. *c.1970, bottle 11cm (4¼in) high.*

**£10–15 each**

# Scottie dogs, always cherished by dog lovers, endeared themselves to a wider public throughout the 1920s to 50s. Consequently, the Scottie motif charmed its way on to a vast array of household objects and some delightful advertising memorabilia.



The Scottie dog motif is still found today on sweaters, jewellery, novelties, and Christmas items, but the heyday of these collectables was from the 1920s to 50s, thanks in part to successful advertising campaigns for Texaco and Black & White Scotch whisky that featured the fashionable Scottish terriers. The appeal of this feisty little animal was enhanced by the fact that many well-known personalities of the time, including Shirley Temple, Humphrey Bogart, and Zsa Zsa Gabor owned Scotties. The most famous of all was President Roosevelt's black Scottie, 'Fala', who went everywhere with him.

A huge number of items embellished with Scotties was produced, from desk accessories to hatpins, ceramic teapots, cufflinks, posters, compacts, and tape measures. Prices can range from around £5–10 for a small item such as a dog-shaped button to around £100–200 or more for a glass lamp offering great scope for a collection.

Lamps are often the most prized and valuable articles, particularly complete examples from the 1930s and 40s. Other popular items include bookends, doorstops, and money banks. Look, too, for Scottie dog artwork by British artist Marguerite Kirmse (1885–1954). A keen collector of Scottie memorabilia, she created pieces that are now highly valued. Prices of Scottie memorabilia have remained steady due to continued interest from the USA.

▲ **A novelty light bulb in an Art Deco-styled base.** Light bulbs using special gases to create a 'neon' effect are not common today, but were popular in the 1930s, often as advertising pieces. In this rare example, the Scottie glows bright orange. *1930s, 18cm (7in) high.*

**£100–150**

► **A German novelty tape measure** with a fabric Scottie dog on the spool. Sewing accessories are extremely collectable. *c.1950, 5cm (2in) long.*

**£15–25**

► **A carved wooden ashtray** with a glass liner. Smoking accessories in the 1930s ranged from stylish and elegant to playful and amusing. *1930s, 16cm (6¼in) long.*

**£50–80**

◄ **A painted cast-iron magnifier** with an adjustable magnifying glass. Desk accessories have a wide appeal, and this piece is well modelled in cast iron. *1930s, 13cm (5in) high.*

**£80–120**

◄ **A set of three framed Marguerite Kirmse Scottie dog etchings.** Kirmse was a noted British dog artist who bred and drew Scotties. Her work is popular and worth acquiring. *1920s, 37cm (14½in) wide.*

**£150–200**

**A glass wall-hanging plaque.** A transfer on the back of the glass shows a fashionable lady in a 1950s A-line skirt and stylish bolero, taking her Scottie for a walk. It captures the spirit of fun that brightened the post-war years. *1950s, 12cm (5in) high.*

**£30–40**

**A ceramic teapot in the shape of a Scottie.** Teapots have a following in their own right, and this one will appeal to collectors of Scotties, too. *1950s, 17cm (6¾in) high.*

**£20–30**

## Collectors' Tips

- As there is such a wide range of Scottie memorabilia, it's best to stick to one theme
- Choose colourful items that represent the style of the period and show the dog clearly

**A Canadian Barry Cigar Factory 'Scotty Mild Little Cigars' tin.** Advertising products such as this have a perennial appeal. *1930s, 8cm (3¼in) high.*

**£25–35**

**Four yellow Catalin buttons.** Early plastics such as Catalin are much sought after today, especially if, as here, they also appeal to specialist collectors. *1930s, 4.5cm (1¾in) long.*

**£15–20 for four**

**A painted and carved wood-effect wall-mounted belt rack.** The American company Swank made a number of gentlemen's accessories that featured Scottie dogs. It is rare to find them on products designed for men. *1950s, 28cm (11in) wide.*

**£40–50**

# Tins of all shapes and sizes were used to store biscuits, sweets, tea, and tobacco in an age before plastic and cardboard containers. Decorative as well as functional, their novel designs have immense nostalgic appeal.

In the 19th century, tins were used to store an increasing range of products, including precious commodities such as tea or snuff, because the near-airtight seal of the lid preserved the freshness of the contents. Early tins were usually plain and had paper labels, but these were easily damaged. In 1868 the first transfer-printed tin was made for the Reading-based biscuit maker Huntley & Palmer, and in 1879 the company was able to print directly onto the tin using offset lithography. Other food manufacturers followed and the decorative tin soon became a familiar form of packaging. Many of these early tins have highly complex and well-detailed printed designs, which makes them particularly desirable today. Because so few of them have survived the ravages of time, they are often valuable.

## Taking the biscuit

Possibly because it was the first, Huntley & Palmer is the best-known brand in tin collecting, but tins were also made by other biscuit makers such as Crawford's, Jacob's, and Peek Frean. Along with tobacco, toffee, and other confectionery tins, biscuit tins tend to be among the most creative, both in their shapes and their artwork. Prices can vary from under £50 to more than £1,000 for a 1920s bus-shaped tin by Carr's.

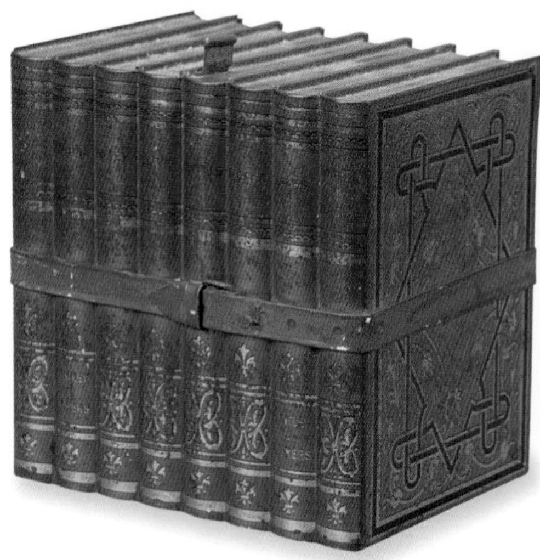

**A Huntley & Palmer 'Library' biscuit tin** with a 'trompe l'oeil' leather strap and buckle. A bookmark acts as a pull-tab to open the lid. *c.1900, 16cm (6¼in) high.*

**£50–80**

## Ship-shape

In the late 19th and early 20th centuries, biscuit tins were made in increasingly exotic shapes and these are the most collectable tins today, often worth about £200–1,000 or more. Among the bestsellers were Huntley & Palmer's book sets, shaped to look like a row of handsome leather-bound volumes. The first set, 'Library', came out at Christmas in 1900, and comprised eight 'books' bound together by a strap *(see above)*. By 1924 the firm had made 10 variations on this theme, including 'Literature' in 1901 and, in 1911, 'Dickens'. One of these 'trompe l'oeil' tins can now fetch up to £200, depending on condition.

Look out for tins in the shapes of cars, boats, or people, especially if they have moving parts such as wheels. Many have richly coloured and detailed decoration. Examining the style of the artwork and typography can help to date different pieces. Huntley & Palmer's 1907 Christmas catalogue featured a tin shaped like an angler's wicker fishing basket, complete with belt loops, handle, and a hinged lid, which may command upwards of £100 today, depending on condition. A Huntley & Palmer

**An unbranded toffee tin** featuring a child in space, a theme typical of the period. *1960s 11cm (4½in) diam.*

**£20–30**

**A Sharp's 'Super-Kreem Toffee' miniature toffee tin.** *1920s, 8cm (3¼in) high.*

**£20–30**

**A Rowntree's 'Cachous' sweet tin** in the shape of a cricket bat. *c.1910. 11.5cm (4½in) long.*

**£55–65**

shell-shaped biscuit tin from about 1912 may be worth more than £400.

## Sweet talk

In 1868 both Fry's and Cadbury's confectionery firms offered decorative printed chocolate tins for the Christmas market. To compete, toffee and boiled-sweet companies also produced decorative tins. In the 1920s Sharp's sold 'Super-Kreem' toffee in a variety of tins featuring a character called Sir Kreemy Knut and his parrot Kreemy. Circular 'Kreemy Knut' tins are usually worth up to around £40, but a cottage-shaped tin can fetch up to around £80.

Prices for other confectionery tins, such as for Dunn's chocolate or Rowntree's, can range from about £50 to £200 for older tins with attractive, detailed artwork. A 1905 golf-club-shaped tin for Clarnico can usually be found for less than £100. Sweet tins tend to be relatively small (often less than 15cm (6in) long), so desirably shaped examples are generally more affordable than shaped biscuit tins – and provide a good starting point for anyone on a limited budget interested in building a collection of novelty-shaped tins.

## Some liked it hot

Tins were also used for tea, cocoa, mustard, and other household products. Many of these had intricate, charming designs, sometimes with images of Europeans in far-off lands. A good example is a Mazawattee tea tin of about 1910 showing a bespectacled granny and her granddaughter sipping tea against an exotic background, which can be worth £15–20 today. Many biscuit and toffee tins were designed to be used as tea caddies once the original contents had been eaten.

## Up in smoke

By the 1880s smoking was a popular habit and there were hundreds of tobacco manufacturers. No effort was spared in the race to make an airtight tobacco tin to keep the 'rough shag', or loose tobacco, fresh. Countless designs were made, and with prices starting from as little as £10–20 for a

## A closer look at... Huntley & Palmer biscuit tins

Tins in novelty shapes are sought after, especially if they look attractive on display and resemble objects around the house. Some makers' or brand names attract a premium, but generally shape and condition are the key indicators of value.

A matching pair like this is worth more than a single tin

The decorative styling is typical of tins intended to be reused or displayed once the contents had been consumed

The colours are still bright, the design is intricate, and the condition is good

**A pair of Huntley & Palmer 'Worcester Vase' biscuit tins, in a tapered octagonal shape.** Each is stamped 'H.B. and S. Ltd Reading' (for Huntley, Boorne, and Stevens, tin manufacturers for the biscuit makers) on the base. *c.1934, 25cm (10in) high.*

**£150–200**

◀ **Huntley & Palmer soldier-shaped biscuit tin,** particularly valuable due to its excellent condition. *1950s, 20.5cm (8in) high.*

**£120–180**

▲ **A Huntley & Palmer 'Kate Greenaway' biscuit tin,** with 'lewd' artwork in the bushes, to the right of centre. *1980, 20.5cm (8in) wide.*

**£20–30**

## Did You Know?

*In 1980 Huntley & Palmer sold a round tin with attractive artwork by Kate Greenaway on the lid, showing a tea party in a summer garden. A mischievous employee surreptitiously added a lewd act being committed in the bushes. Once discovered, the tin was hastily withdrawn and reissued without the offending addition. Today, a tin with the original 'lewd' design is worth around £30.*

▼ **A Chad Valley bus-shaped 'Carr's Biscuits' tin.** This is a rare example. *1950s, 25cm (10in) wide.*

**£350–450**

1930s Player's 'Navy Cut' tin with a printed paper label, tobacco tins are a good choice for a specialised collection. The most famous names to look out for are John Player and W.D. & H.O. Wills, both of whose tins can fetch £50–250 or more, depending on the intricacy and attractiveness of the artwork. Companies vied with each other to give their brands powerful images, such as 'Search Light' and 'Thunder Clouds'.

'Pocket tins' are particularly collectable in the USA. These are pocket-sized rectangular tins with rounded edges in which tobacco could be carried around easily. Some are curved to fit against the body. Prices start at around £50, but rare designs and tins with multicoloured, complex patterns or patriotic artwork may cost £200–800 or more.

## Needlepoint

The tiny needles used in early wind-up gramophones were sold in little tins, and today these containers are inexpensive, with values remaining well under £100. They form an ideal collection theme for people with limited space, as each tin is only about 4cm (1½in) wide. The artwork is often more important than the manufacturer, and its style can help to date a tin. A tin from the 1920s featuring Nipper, the dog representing HMV, may fetch less than £10, while a tin from the same decade decorated with, for example, a striking Art Deco image, can be worth up to £60.

## Modern times

The heyday of decorative tins began to draw to a close in the 1960s, once cheaper packaging, such as plastic and plasticised sachets, was introduced, but tins made before the 1960s are still collectable. A Rowntree's 'Quality Street' or Cadbury's 'Roses' chocolates tin can be bought for around £1–5.

**A 'Salon-Tanz' gramophone needles tin.** *1925, 5cm (2in) high.*

**£40–60**

Look for tins with attractive artwork, particularly those in period styles, such as 1930s Art Deco or the Modern style of the 1950s, as these are sought after not only by tin collectors but also by enthusiasts of graphic design and those with a special interest in collecting pieces from these eras – which tends to inflate the value.

Look out, too, for commemorative tins, such as those celebrating the Coronation in 1953. A Carr's commemorative biscuit tin can fetch around £20. Novelty shapes continued to be produced, such as a 1950s Carr's biscuit tin, made by the well-known toymakers, Chad Valley, in the shape of a bus *(illustrated opposite)*, now worth about £400. Because so many more examples of recent tins exist, it is best to choose ones that are in really good condition.

Tins from the 1960s onwards are not particularly popular at the moment, but there may be an increase in demand for them in the future. Choose pieces that are in mint condition and those that carry popular brand names. Tins that are unusual in shape, decorated in attractive colours, or are for special occasions, are also worth collecting.

### Top Tips

- Avoid tins that are scratched, dented, rusty, or split, or that are missing parts such as wheels or catches.
- Never wash tins in water – this may damage the surface and the metal.
- Keep tins away from direct sunlight, which will make the colours fade, and humid rooms (such as bathrooms and kitchens), which will cause rust.
- Look out for rare images, such as Zeppelins, as these can add value.
- Experiment on already damaged tins to find the best cleaning method.
- Never varnish a cleaned tin – this reduces its value.

### BUY

*Pocket tobacco tins are highly collectable in the USA and are becoming increasingly popular elsewhere through Internet trading. The trend has not picked up to the same extent in Britain yet, but examples do exist, so do some research to find out what prices are being paid for the many different types available.*

**A pocket tin for 'Briggs Pipe Mixture' tobacco,** manufactured by the P. Lorillard Co. in the USA. *c.1940s, 11cm (4¼in) high.*

**£30–40**

### KEEP

*Tins intended for children are often in poor condition as they were played with or carried around in bags. Those in good condition are rarer and worth more. Look out for tins bearing period artwork and well-known brand names, as these will have wider appeal and are likely to increase in value.*

**An Ovaltine school-size tin.** This small tin was probably issued to members of the League of Ovalteenies and would hold enough powder to have with the daily free milk at school. *c.1940, 4.5cm (1¾in) high.*

**£20–30**

# Vintage kitchen equipment

can add a quirky touch to an otherwise modern kitchen. Many items have become objects of curiosity, because their original function has been superseded by new methods.

The kitchens of the 19th and early 20th centuries were packed with gadgets for every need, and there is a multitude of these vintage tools still to be found, many of them in working order. Look out for vintage equipment at collectors' fairs and shops, junk shops, car-boot sales, house clearances, and auctions.

## Pressing concerns

Irons are among the most sought after of vintage kitchen tools. In the 19th century, flat irons were heated on the stove or in the hearth and were often heavy, weighing up to 9kg (20lb). These irons were often simply made, so they are generally less valuable than other types – fetching between £10 and £60. Early box irons held a heated metal 'slug', while later models were filled with hot coals or embers. They were better than flat irons because they stayed hotter for longer. They also eliminated the problem of the base picking up soot from the fire. Box irons can cost £10–100 or more.

## A grinding issue

By the mid-18th century, coffee had become a favourite drink with the upper and middle classes. Some people ground their own beans at home using small wooden grinders, and these are now collectable. In 1815, A. Kenrick & Sons of West Bromwich patented a new box-type cast-iron grinder, which was copied by many other makers, including T.C. Clark, Baldwin, and Siddons. Cast-iron wall-mounted grinders are desirable, as are those by Siddons, since they are much rarer than Kenrick models. Grinders cost from around £35 for a tin model to £300–400 for a more luxurious grinder by a noted maker, especially if it has fine decoration, is made from brass and painted mahogany, and is in good condition and working order.

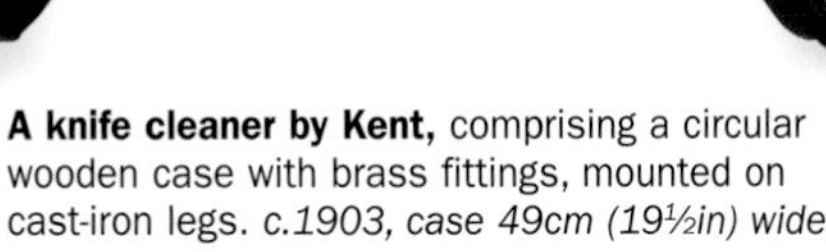


**A knife cleaner by Kent,** comprising a circular wooden case with brass fittings, mounted on cast-iron legs. *c.1903, case 49cm (19½in) wide.*

**£50–60**

## The search for perfect toast

Vintage toasters are growing in popularity with collectors. The electric toaster was developed in the USA in the early 20th century. It became popular in wealthy households because toast made by servants in the kitchen was usually cold by the time it reached the table. The disadvantage was that early toasters only browned one side of the bread at a time, and needed constant watching in case the

**A Continental charcoal box iron,** with a replacement handle and a lion's head catch. *Late 1800s, 20cm (8in) long.*

**£20–25**

**A brass and cast-iron crimping machine,** with heating bars, for crimping fabric. *1870s, 31.5cm (12½in) high.*

**£350–450**

## A closer look at... a goffering iron

The complexity of Victorian clothing and cookery led to the development of many implements that have long since fallen out of use. It is worth familiarising yourself with some of them because they can make good investments.

Hot cylinders warmed in a fire or on a stove were inserted here

It is rare to have two cones. Single examples are more common and less valuable

The cast-iron base is decorative, which is extremely unusual

**A rare double goffering iron,** with a high-relief floral pattern on the base. A goffering iron was used to press ridges or pleats into a garment. In this example, fabric collars and cuffs were wrapped around the cones to set them into shape. The large size of this iron makes it unusual. *1850s–80s, 35cm (14in) high.*

**£300–400**

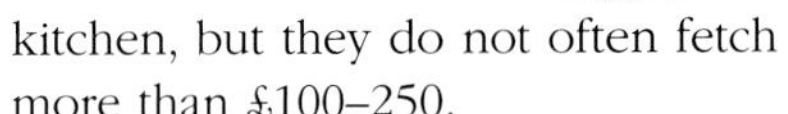

bread burned. Manufacturers raced to introduce new features – turnover toasters, automatic toasters, and toasters that kept the toast warm inside the machine. Values depend on the decorative nature and date of the toaster, and vary from as little as £20 up to £150 or more. A rare US blue-and-white transfer-printed porcelain toaster from the 1920s can fetch up to £800.

### Crimpers, cutters, and scalers

There is a plethora of smaller tools for specific purposes, such as crimping the edges of pies, mincing meat, opening tins and bottles, cutting vegetables, and scaling fish. The more common tools, such as tin openers, can cost from as little as £10 up to around £50, depending on age, material, and decorative value. More unusual items, especially if well made, such as raisin seeders and fish scalers, can generally raise higher prices, reflecting their comparative rarity in today's kitchen, but they do not often fetch more than £100–250.

Knife cleaners, although collectable, are relatively expensive at £100–400. Their size and weight also means they have only limited appeal. Look out for those by notable manufacturers such as Kent and Crowden & Garrod. The value of these implements depends on whether all the parts are still present (as well as the instruction label), condition, and the name of the maker.

### Beware modern reproductions

There are many reproductions on the market and it can be difficult to tell them apart from genuine items. They were not always produced to fool the buyer, but rather to provide decorative, nostalgic pieces that are less expensive and much easier to find than the original. Ironically, though, when there are plenty of reproductions of a particular item available, the original article often becomes less desirable and goes down in value.

**A French 'Le Pratique' steel mincer,** with screw vice to attach it to a tabletop (handle missing). *1920s, 25.5cm (10in) high.*

**£12–15**

### Top Tips

- Check that the bowl of a coffee grinder is in good condition, as it is the weakest part and prone to cracking and splitting.
- Research why and how an item was used originally to make sure you buy the right piece of equipment.
- Choose early examples, as well as transitional prototypes of a particular item, as these are the most desirable.
- Look for pieces bearing a maker's name, as they are often worth more than unmarked or homemade items.

### BUY

*Early toasters are comparatively inexpensive, because the market is small and there is little specialist literature available. Toasters can often be restored to working order, even those with unusual features. Their simple design is attractive, and as interest in the area expands, they may prove to be a good investment.*

**A Rowenta E 5210 folding toaster,** with chrome-plated body and Bakelite handles and feet. The flap on the side opens downwards, causing the toast inside to flip over, so both sides can be toasted by the central heating element. *1940s, 25cm (10in) high.*

**£20–30**

### SELL

*With the recent increase in popularity of coffee made from freshly ground beans, original utensils such as coffee machines and grinders have risen sharply in price. Values have probably peaked, and now may be the time to sell, particularly if tea-drinking makes a comeback.*

**A T.C. Clark & Co. cast-iron, brass, and wood coffee grinder,** with a maker's brass name plate. This example has unusual factory decoration and paintwork. *1880s, 14cm (5½in) high.*

**£80–120**

# Vintage sewing tools

can be highly decorative and ornate. From thimbles to needle cases, they also serve as a reminder of the value once placed on household skills we are now in danger of losing.

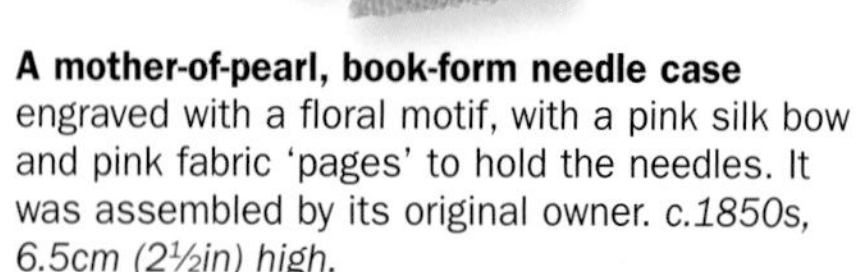

**A mother-of-pearl, book-form needle case** engraved with a floral motif, with a pink silk bow and pink fabric 'pages' to hold the needles. It was assembled by its original owner. *c.1850s, 6.5cm (2½in) high.*

**£80–120**

Sewing tools have been produced for hundreds of years, and until around 30 years ago almost every woman would have owned a sewing box or basket.

Tools were made from wood, ivory, bone, metal, and mother-of-pearl. 'Vegetable ivory', a dense yellow or beige material made from the tropical tagua nut, was typically used for carved needle cases and tape measure covers. Pieces dating from the late 18th and 19th centuries are sought after.

Values vary, depending on age, type of object, material, and decoration, but tend to lie between £20 and £500.

## Thimble talk

Most of today's vintage thimbles date from the 19th century onwards and were machine-made in metal or ceramic. A plain, mass-produced brass thimble may cost around £15–20, but a thimble in gold or silver can fetch up to £500. Hallmarks did not appear until after the 1870s. Before this, thimbles were regarded as too small to require hallmarking. A number stamped into a thimble indicates its size.

Makers to look for include Charles Iles and Charles Horner. Iles was prolific and inventive, producing thimbles with liners and decorative features, which can often be found now for £20–100. In the late 19th century, Horner developed the revolutionary 'Dorcas' thimble, which had a strong steel core overlaid with silver, and lasted longer than softer thimbles of pure silver. Dorcas thimbles may sell for £15–50.

Commemorative thimbles are popular. A base-metal example made for Queen Victoria's Diamond Jubilee (1897) may fetch around £40, while a silver thimble celebrating the Coronation of George V and Queen Mary in 1911 may be worth around £150–200. Ceramic thimbles are also common. Some examples by Royal Worcester featuring birds hand-painted by William Powell can fetch £200–400.

Earlier thimbles do exist, but are rare. They can date back to the 16th century and are often made of leather, bronze, or iron, with domed or onion-

## Some thimbles to look for:

■ Iles ■ Fenton ■ Horner ■ Dorcas ■ Scenic ■

▲ **An 'Iles Patent Ventilated' base-metal thimble.** The ivorine liner – a form of early plastic that looked like ivory – served to ventilate the finger. *c.1909, 2cm (¾in) high.*

**£80–120**

▼ **A silver thimble by James Fenton,** showing a bicycle, and a bird in foliage, and hallmarked Birmingham 1896. This is a valuable example as bicycles are a rare decorative motif. *1896, 2cm (¾in) high.*

**£300–500**

▲ **A silver thimble by Charles Horner,** with a punched dot design, an inset carnelian crown (for decoration), and a Chester hallmark. *1923, 2cm (¾in) high.*

**£50–80**

▼ **A Dorcas steel-cored thimble** by an unknown maker, with a grid pattern and a registered mark for 1887. Hard-wearing Dorcas thimbles were produced by makers other than their inventor, Charles Horner. *c.1887, 2cm (¾in) high.*

**£20–30**

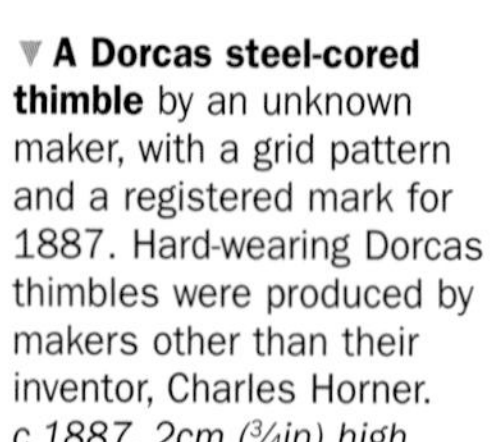

▲ **A sterling silver 'Scenic' thimble by Simons Bros,** featuring a village scene and an unengraved cartouche. This, like almost all scenic thimbles, is from the USA. *c.1880s, 2cm (¾in) high.*

**£30–40**

shaped tops. They can be worth £200–1,000, depending on their shape, condition, and place and period of origin.

## Needle match

When choosing needle cases, look for well-carved or finely modelled examples, made from quality materials such as mother-of-pearl, or those in the shape of figures. Examples can fetch £100–150 or more. Souvenir cases featuring scenic carvings or transfers can sell for £50–100, while beadwork cases can be worth more than £100.

Metal cases, known as 'Averys' (after the maker W. Avery & Son of Redditch), date from the 1870s onwards. They came in three types: 'flats', holding packets of needles; 'quadruples', holding four rows of needles; and 'figurals', which take the form of insects or other novelty shapes and are the most valuable, at around £200–500.

**A 'Spanish walnut' sewing compendium,** including scissors, needle case, stiletto, bodkin, and booklet, all contained in a walnut shell. *c.1850, 4.5cm (1¾in) high.*

**£300–400**

Needle boxes made from card can cost £40–60 or less and feature a variety of printed and embossed decoration. Many cases were homemade, and, depending on the quality, can be worth £30–150. Pin cushions were often made at home, too, but were also produced as commemorative items.

Other sewing essentials include scissors, tape measures, cotton reels, and thread winders. Values depend on materials and decoration, but rarely exceed £100–300. Tape measures are a popular collecting theme: novelty-shaped celluloid ones from the 20th century often fetch around £70–150, while commemorative tape measures tend to be worth £50–70 or less.

## Box of delights

Compendia (compartmentalised boxes) are worth looking out for, as are cased *nécessaires*, which are similar to compendia, but often small, portable, and containing only a few objects. A case with two or three items may sell for £70–100, but a larger collection of finely made tools can be worth £300–500.

## Mechanicals

Sewing machines are a specialised collecting area. Look for examples that were produced for short periods of a few years around the 1850s, as these are among the most valuable. Portable machines such as the 19th-century 'Moldacott' fetch around £100–150 if they have all their accessories.

**A card needle box** with a George Baxter print of Queen Victoria's eldest daughter, Vicky, the Princess Royal and Princess F.W. of Prussia. *c.1880s, 6cm (2¼in) high.*

**£20–30**

### *Top Tips*

- Beware of new thimbles advertised as limited editions or 'collectables'. They are seldom worth collecting.
- Use a magnet to test the authenticity of a Dorcas thimble – its steel core will be attracted to the magnet. A pure silver thimble won't attract, but is often more valuable.
- Examine bone or ivory through a magnifying glass. You should see blood vessels running through bone, while ivory has light striations of colour.
- Make sure the contents of compendia and *nécessaires* are complete and original – replacements are hard to find.

### KEEP

*Needle cases were produced in abundance in various materials, including metal, bone, ivory, and wood. Finely decorated items, or those with mechanical functions, are likely to hold their value, or even appreciate, as demand is growing.*

**A W. Avery & Son needle case,** 'The Quadruple Golden Casket', in gilt, with a leaf and butterfly design, for needle sizes 6, 7, 8, and 9. This is a typically intricate example of an 'Avery' case. It has a sliding nodule at the bottom of the box that moves the rows of needles up and down for easy selection. *c.1870, 7cm (2¾in) high.*

**£150–200**

### SELL

*Despite their often decorative finishes and coloured transfers, sewing machines by makers such as Singer and Jones do not fetch high prices because so many were made. Sell now and consider investing in a rarer machine.*

**A Singer sewing machine.** This example is in excellent condition and retains its decorative transfers; both these factors should lift the price if you choose to sell. *c.1900, 35cm (14in) long.*

**£20–30**

# Salt and pepper shakers

come in a wide range of shapes and materials, as well as prices. They can determine the mood of a table setting, from elegant to whimsical. They are also fun to display – a quality that adds to their appeal.

The salt shaker was a Victorian device invented after free-flowing granular salt was developed in the mid-19th century. The first glass salt shakers were made in the 1850s, with pepper pots coming soon afterwards. Rather like salt mills, early salt shakers had an agitator mechanism that broke down the lumps, a feature that reappeared in the 1960s and 70s.

From the 1930s onwards, new methods of producing cheaper tableware led to the creation of colourful and imaginative shakers. Many were made inexpensively in Japan and the Far East; they are easy to find, often marked 'Foreign'. You can buy them for around £15–50.

Most collectors follow a theme, such as figures, cartoon characters, or advertising; others choose a maker – Royal Winton, Carlton Ware, Midwinter, Beswick – or a look, such as the 1950s. Shakers that overlap with other areas of interests, such as Disney characters, carry high prices, as their appeal is wider.

▲ **A pair of plastic Homepride Flour 'Fred' salt and pepper shakers,** by Spillers. Homepride's bowler-hatted flour-grader, Fred, was a much-loved household name. *1970s, 11cm (4¼in) high.*

**£15–20**

◄ **A Beswick 'Laurel and Hardy' novelty cruet,** on a shaped stand impressed '375' and marked 'Beswick England'. Character-shaped salt and pepper pots are a popular collecting theme. *1930s, 9cm (3¾in) wide.*

**£70–100**

▲ **A pair of 1970s Conrah anodised aluminium salt and pepper shakers,** with incised decoration showing the underlying metal. The 1960s fascination with space-age travel is reflected in the material and design of this pair. *1970s, 9cm (3½in) high.*

**£10–15**

► **A Carlton Ware 'fruity' salt and pepper set.** Carltonware's inventive shapes and designs include novelty pieces such as these pear-and-lemon salt and pepper shakers in a banana dish. *1950s, 17cm (6¾in) wide.*

**£30–40**

◀ **A pair of silver-mounted ivory pepper mills,** made in Birmingham by Hukin & Heath. Ivory objects are out of fashion due to a US ban and general antipathy. However, the silver-mounting adds to its value. The waisted shape of these pieces is traditional. *1935, 8.5cm (3¼in) high.*

**£60–80**

◀ **An orange Catalin early plastic salt and pepper shaker set.** The new plastics of the 1930s brought previously unseen blasts of colour and style to the dining table. *1930s, 6cm (2½in) high.*

**£30–40**

## Collectors' Tips

- Look for animal or bird shapes; their wide appeal should increase value
- Choose complete sets – finding a match to replace a missing piece could take years

▶ **Guinness pottery salt and pepper shakers,** each in the form of a pint of Guinness. Advertising sets – particularly the perennially popular Guinness set – are highly desirable. *1930s–50s, 5cm (2in) high.*

**£50–70**

◀ **A Sydney Harbour 'Water Globe' salt and pepper dispenser.** This souvenir of Sydney, with its sliding lid, is still in its original box. *Late 1950s, 7cm (2¾in) high.*

**£15–25**

◀ **A 'Bonzo' salt and pepper set,** marked 'Foreign', probably Japanese. Cartoon character shakers are extremely popular. *1930s, 7.5cm (3in) high.*

**£45–55**

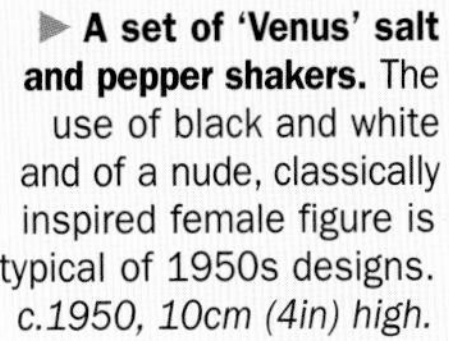

▶ **A set of 'Venus' salt and pepper shakers.** The use of black and white and of a nude, classically inspired female figure is typical of 1950s designs. *c.1950, 10cm (4in) high.*

**£50–70**

▼ **Japanese chrome-plated salt and pepper set, with plastic finials.** The use of chrome and simple shapes such as spheres are typical of the era, as is the use of the Scottie dog. *c.1930s, 11.5cm (4½in) high.*

**£80–120**

# Stainless steel tableware,

the height of fashion in the 1950s, 60s, and 70s, is becoming collectable, largely because the leading designers of the time produced innovative work that complements today's taste for minimalism.

From cutlery and candlesticks to toast racks and teapots, the clean lines, minimal surface decoration, durability, and easy-to-clean nature of stainless steel tableware made it an instant hit with a forward-looking public. As styles changed, many people either stored these pieces or gave them away, thinking them of little value. Prices currently remain fairly low, but this could soon change.

## A stainless reputation

Stainless steel – a basic mild steel to which chromium is added to give rust resistance – was developed in the early 20th century by metallurgist Harry Brearley. Before his invention, table cutlery was plated in silver or nickel, while cutting knives were made of carbon steel that had to be dried thoroughly after being washed.

J. & J. Wiggin Ltd, manufacturer of 'Old Hall', a major name in stainless steel tableware, made the first stainless steel teapot in 1930 and went on to promote this new material for domestic use at the 1934 Ideal Home Exhibition.

In the late 1930s, the industrial designer Harold Stabler created an elegant new range of high-quality tea and coffee services for Old Hall. But expensive manufacturing processes and the advent of World War II soon stopped production, and the factory was turned over to making munitions.

## Master of the art

In 1955 Old Hall appointed Robert Welch as design consultant, and his award-winning designs prompted a resurgence in British metalware. Welch had trained as a silversmith before specialising in stainless steel design at the Royal College of Art. During his time at Old Hall, he won three Design Council awards for his pioneering 'British Contemporary' style.

Welch's stainless steel tablewares were influenced by Scandinavian design: they included the 'Campden' range (1957), notably a sleek toast rack and a striking triple candlestick, a tableware range for the cruise liner *Oriana* (1960) and the award-winning 'Alveston' cutlery range (1964). A pair of late-1950s candlesticks by Welch can fetch well over £100 and the 'Alveston'

**A pair of Old Hall conical salt and pepper shakers.** *1970s, 7.5cm (3in) high.*

**£5–8**

## Some designers to look for:

▪ Stuart Devlin ▪ Robert Welch ▪

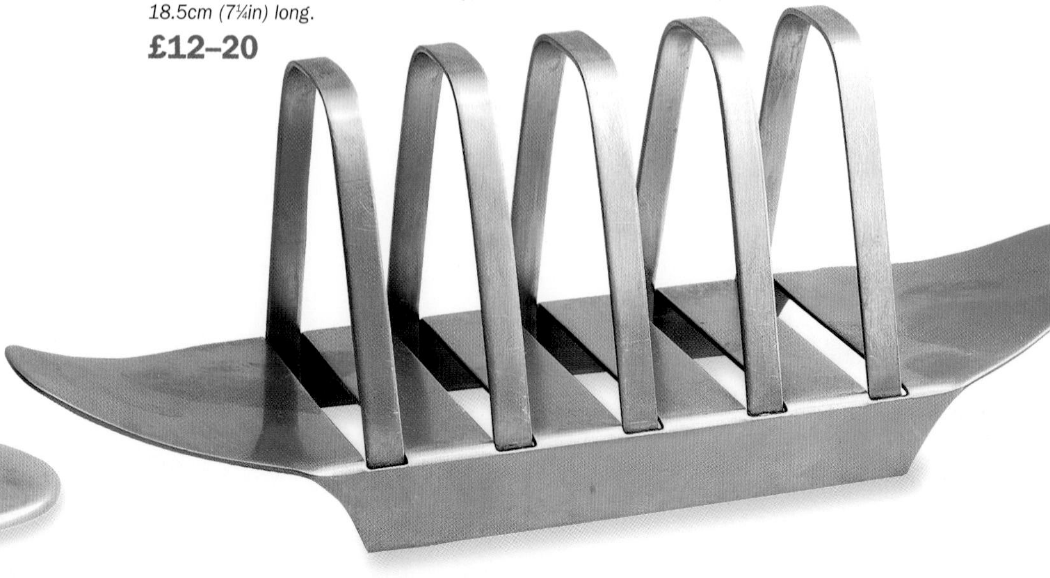

**An Old Hall 'Campden' toast rack designed by Robert Welch.** This award-winning toast rack design was also made in two- and six-section versions. Clean, modern lines were typical of Welch's work. *1960s, 18.5cm (7¼in) long.*

**£12–20**

**A Viners goblet in stainless steel and gold plate designed by Stuart Devlin.** The textured gold plating combined with the shiny steel of this goblet hints at Devlin's other skills as a gold- and silversmith and jewellery designer. *1970s, 17.5cm (7in) high.*

**£35–55**

cutlery is sought after: one seven-piece setting can fetch around £60–70.

## Lots of pots

Old Hall produced a huge range of in-house designed tableware. These pieces tend to cost less than avant-garde items by known designers, and are less likely to rise in value. A 1960s Old Hall in-house designed teapot might sell for about £10–15; many pieces can be found for less than £10.

## Men of steel

Old Hall led the way, but other names to look out for include Viners of Sheffield, who featured the fresh-looking industrial designs of David Mellor, Stuart Devlin, and the leading silversmith and royal-warrant holder, Gerald Benney. The 'Cylinda-Line' tableware by Arne Jacobsen for Stelton of Denmark, launched in 1967, is also worth noting for its modern lines.

The advent of cheap imports from the Far East and its knock-on effect for Old Hall's new owners, US-based Oneida, led to the factory's closure in 1984. But Robert Welch stainless steel tableware continues to be sold by the company bearing his name, which he founded in the mid-1950s.

**An Old Hall 'Connaught' three-quarter-pint teapot.** *1960s, 8.5cm (3¼in) high.*

**£10–15**

## Gerald Benney ■ Arne Jacobsen ■

**A Viners 'Sable' dessert set designed by Gerald Benney,** in its original box. Benney pioneered a textured 'bark' finish in his silver work and achieved a similar effect on the handles of these stainless steel forks. *c.1970, box 13cm (5in) high.*

**£35–45**

**A Stelton 'Cylinda-Line' cocktail shaker designed by Arne Jacobsen.** This design's sleek tubes and perfect brushed surfaces offered a manufacturing challenge that called for special machinery. *c.1970s, 23cm (9in) high.*

**£80–100**

### Top Tips

- Search for wares by notable designers, as they will make better investments.
- If you build up a complete set of cutlery gradually, ensure that all the pieces are in a similar condition.
- Look for pieces in their original boxes – these are scarce as the box was usually thrown away.
- Avoid dented objects: so much stainless steel was heavily used that values can rise by 50 per cent or more for mint examples.
- Keep stainless steel sparkling clean by washing it in warm soapy water and drying it immediately with a soft cloth.

### BUY

*Look for 1950s and 60s designs that would have been considered avant-garde at the time. These items are the most likely to rise in value as a growing appreciation of stainless steel leads to increased demand.*

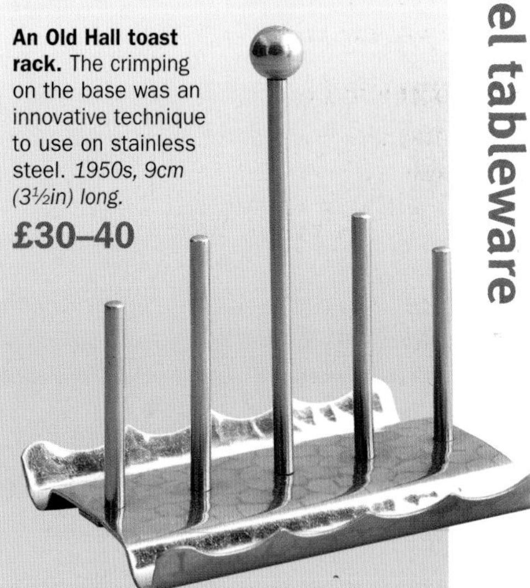

**An Old Hall toast rack.** The crimping on the base was an innovative technique to use on stainless steel. *1950s, 9cm (3½in) long.*

**£30–40**

### KEEP

*Unusual designs with complex shapes were prone to damage, so if you have one in mint condition, it is likely to appreciate in value.*

**A pair of Old Hall triple candlesticks.** If any of the wooden feet are missing, the value will be reduced. The unusual shape and good condition of this pair mean that they should increase in value. *1960s, 23cm (9in) high.*

**£150–200**

# Corkscrews, bottle openers, and pourers can be plain, inventive, or quirky, and their intriguing mechanisms and decorative appearance appeal to many collectors. Corkscrews, in particular, are available in a huge range of materials and styles.

**A Henshall-type button corkscrew,** with a walnut handle and a brush. *c.1840, 13.5cm (5¼in) long.*

**£50–70**

Worldwide, there are 1,000 patents for different types of bottle openers. But the most common form of bottle opener remains the corkscrew. There are two basic types – the straight pull, which relies on the strength of the user, and the often more sought after and valuable versions in which a mechanism of some kind takes the strain. The allure of corkscrews rests in part on the many different devices they use to extract a cork mechanically – including levers, cranked handles, and complex concertina-style contraptions. In addition, handles can be made from a variety of materials, such as silver, brass, steel, carved bone, and wood.

Corkscrews come in many decorative forms, and some carry advertising. There are also artful novelty types, disguised as anything from keys to animals, to conceal their true identity.

New recruits are constantly joining the ranks of corkscrew collectors, so rarities are becoming increasingly difficult to find, but beginners should find many examples priced at £10–40. Numerous novelty or advertising examples sell for less than £10.

**A Lund two-part lever corkscrew.** *c.1880, 20cm (7¾in) wide.*

**£80–120**

## Keeping it simple

The first English corkscrew patent, taken out by Samuel Henshall in 1795, lasted for 14 years and was for a T-shaped straight pull. Henshall's innovation was to add a cap, or button, to the screw. This limited the screw's penetration, but also gripped the cork on contact and turned it, breaking its adhesion to the neck of the bottle. Early versions are rare and can be worth thousands of pounds. When the patent ran out, other manufacturers produced variations on the type until around 1910. Simple all-metal examples can be found for less than £20, while those with ivory or bone handles often fetch £50–120, and those with a maker's name or fine detailing cost about £150. Present-day straight pulls are also collectable if they are decorative and made in fine materials.

## A helping hand

A great many patents were taken out in the 19th century for all manner of corkscrews with levers, arms, and twisting mechanisms. Some enjoyed limited success and are rare today. For example, Robert Jones' design of 1840, which has a brass 'worm', or screw, and three prongs to pierce and grip the cork, can fetch as much as £4,000 if intact and in excellent condition. Another

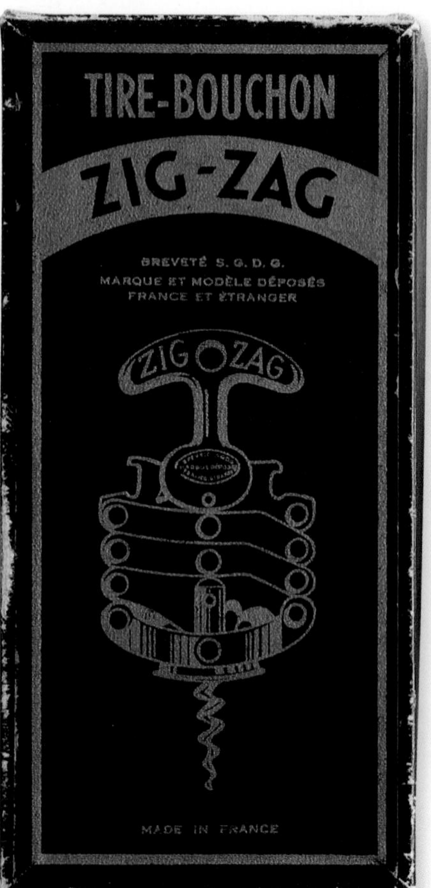

**A French chrome-plated 'Zig-Zag' concertina corkscrew,** with original box and instructions. *c.1920, 15cm (6in) long.*

**£55–65**

## A closer look at... a Thomason-type corkscrew

The inventiveness of corkscrew designs, such as Sir Edward Thomason's 'double-helix' mechanism of 1802, has made 19th-century corkscrews very popular. The Thomason-type is one of the most desirable models.

The bone handle is original: a replacement handle of later date would lower the value

The plain decoration of the brass bottle barrel is relatively common – a more ornate style can add considerably to the value

The brush removes cork, lead, and dust from the bottle neck – the corkscrew's value is not seriously affected if the brush is missing

Thomason's 'double helix' mechanism enables the user to insert the screw and withdraw the cork by turning the handle continuously

**A bone and brass Thomason-type continuous corkscrew by Wilmot & Roberts.** *c.1810, 17.5 cm (6¾in) long.*

**£250–350**

type, often marked 'Lund', combines a simple T-shaped screw and scissor-type handles with a ring to fit around the bottle neck and the screw. After twisting the screw into the cork, you grip the handle and squeeze, which forces the screw and cork up and out. When complete, these corkscrews may fetch around £100. The 'King's Screw' has a top handle that is turned to insert the worm into the cork and a side handle that is turned to extract it. These often sell for £200–500.

Many new kinds of corkscrew, often of simpler design, were designed early in the 20th century. These can usually be bought for £20–80 and could form a wide-ranging collection. Those marked with a maker's name, operated by an unusual mechanism, or finely crafted are all worth looking for.

Corkscrews in the shape of people or animals usually date from the 20th century. Since so many were made for the tourist trade, they tend to be inexpensive.

### One for the butler

Not all openers for bottles with corks use a screw. There are many other types and they are usually less expensive than corkscrews.

A good example is Converse's patent design, with two prongs that slide between cork and bottle. This 'butler's cheat', valued from £30 to £80, enables the unscrupulous user to uncork a bottle and take a drink, then top it up with water and put the cork back.

### After opening

Most bottle pourers date from the early 20th century on. Widely available and inexpensive, they often incorporate human figures or advertise products. Champagne taps were designed to retain the fizz in half-drunk bottles. They have a gimlet which can be screwed through the cork of an unopened bottle, allowing a glass or two to be poured before the tap is closed off. The heyday for these taps was from 1890 to 1920. Silver champagne taps are the most prized.

**A 'Johnnie Walker' whisky spirit pourer.** *1950s, 14.5cm (5¾in) long.*

**£8–10**

### Top Tips

- Before buying a corkscrew, carefully examine the sharp point: damage can reduce the value.
- Look for corkscrews with makers' marks and inscriptions – these always add value.
- Search for the big brass corkscrews used in bars: many collectors place a premium on these.

### BUY

*Colourful and amusing corkscrews that recall 'can-can' dancers at the Moulin Rouge in Paris will appeal to collectors and to anyone who wants to pull a cork with panache. They can be found in a range of colours and should rise in value owing to their wide appeal.*

**A German celluloid lady's-legs corkscrew,** with striped, full-length stockings. *1880–90, 6.5cm (2½in) long.*

**£120–180**

### KEEP

*Bow corkscrews have swing-down accessories contained within a bow-shaped frame. The more accessories they have, the more valuable they are. These corkscrews offer excellent collecting potential as they are available across a wide price range.*

**An English eight-tool folding bow corkscrew,** with a hoof pick, leather hole-punch, gimlet, grooved helical worm corkscrew, spike, auger, screwdriver, and button hook. *c.1820, closed 7cm (2¾in) long.*

**£80–100**

### SELL

*Amusing novelty corkscrews were made inexpensively and sold in great numbers over the 20th century. They are unlikely to appreciate in value, but if you have any, you might be able to sell them to collectors of animal memorabilia.*

**A pair of English novelty corkscrews,** carved in pine as an alert cat and kneeling Scottie dog. *1930s, dog 12.5cm (5in) wide.*

**£10–20 each**

# Decanters and cocktail shakers

conjure up two moods: the classic luxury of Victorian and Edwardian times, contrasting with the dazzle of the Jazz Age. Either offers a way to live the past, not just look at it.

Serving wine in a decanter adds style to any formal meal; and cocktail shakers can create a party mood in, literally, a shake. Whether you want to add elegance or fun to your home, you are bound to find something special, whatever your budget.

## The stamp of quality

Take time to familiarise yourself with the look and feel of a fine decanter. True Regency decanters are heavy for their size, and the quality and design of the cut-glass pattern are obvious when compared to later examples. Decanters from the 1800s to 40s are most desirable, and can be found in a variety of shapes and decoration, including classical-cut designs such as diamonds and 'V'-shapes. Late-Victorian pieces (1880s–90s) are often engraved with exuberant flowers, swirls, leaves, and birds. Prices start at £80–100, but the better the decoration and the quality of the glass, the higher the price. Beware of early 20th-century reproductions inspired by this style – moulding, rather than cutting, is common; clear glass is 'brighter'; and coloured glass may have an ugly tinge.

## Jugs and sets

Decanters with handles are known as 'claret jugs'. Some tall, elegant Victorian pieces are made entirely from glass, often with decorative engraving or faceting, and can fetch £80–200 or more. Bulbous early 20th-century pieces, made by firms such as Mappin & Webb, with silver mounts, can be worth around £150–500.

In the late 19th and early 20th centuries, decanters were sometimes sold as a lockable boxed set (or 'tantalus'), for storing expensive spirits. Prices start at around £150 to £200.

Novelty decanter sets, particularly those from the 1930s and 50s, can be found for around £100.

**A claret jug and cover,** with a rope-twist handle. The body is engraved with a design of grasses. *c.1880s, 33cm (13in) high.*

**£200–250**

**An Edwardian carved oak tantalus and games box.** *c.1910, 37cm (14½in) wide.*

**£450–500**

## Shaken, not stirred

During Prohibition in 1920s and early 30s USA, the only way to render 'bathtub' gin and 'bootleg' whiskey drinkable was to sweeten them. So

## A closer look at... two Regency decanters

Considering their age, Regency decanters are still not excessively expensive, and they add a dash of sophistication and historical interest to the drinks cabinet. It is important to look closely at the design, as well as the overall form.

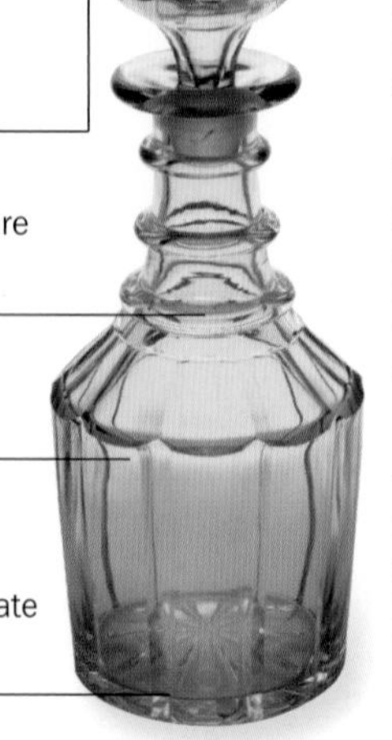


**A flute-cut decanter** with three neck rings, slice-cut shoulders, and flute-cut panels. *c.1835, 26cm (10¼in) high.*

**£80–120**

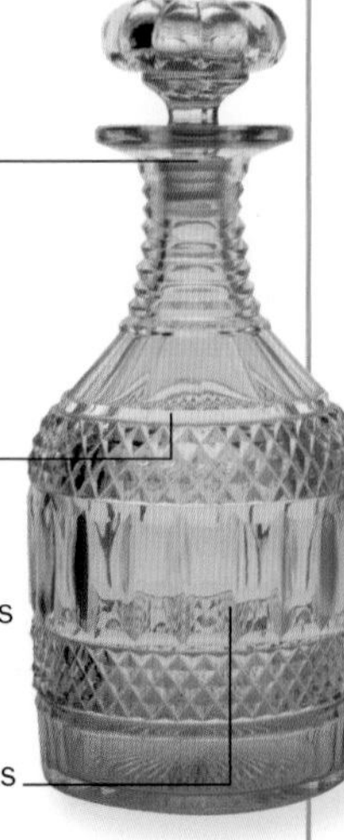


**A pillar-cut decanter** with a step-cut neck. Its body is decorated with cut diamonds, pillars, and slices. The stopper is also pillar cut. *c.1825, 25cm (9¾in) high.*

**£150–200**

cocktails were born. Bar accessories were later invented to accommodate the trend. The most essential accessory was the cocktail shaker. Here, novelty is important, and shape matters more than design. The best examples were produced during the 1920s and 30s and include imaginative forms such as skyscrapers. Such items can fetch £1,000–5,000 or more. If your budget allows (expect to pay £500–1,000 or more), look for rare 'hidden' shakers allegedly used during Prohibition, such as the 'trophy' shaker, where the trophy base turns into the shaker lid.

## A mark of luxury

Shakers that are marked with names of luxury makers such as Asprey are valuable. Designs in chromed metal and copper from the 1930s by the American manufacturer Chase are also popular. Major British makers include Mappin & Webb, Manning Bowman, Kensington, and Chrome Craft. A 1937 promotional Southern Comfort liqueur-bottle-shaped shaker by Chrome Craft can fetch up to £200. American shakers tend to be plated in chrome, and British shakers in silver.

## Plain and simple

Less expensive shakers from the 1940s and 50s were made in anodised aluminium and glass and they now cost about £30, while plain glass and silver-plated 1930s shakers start at around £30–50. Those with recipes printed on are desirable, provided that all the wording can be read.

◄ **A silver-plated cocktail shaker,** with gilt details. The swivelling cover with windows allows individual cocktails to be chosen and the ingredients to be read in the windows. The photograph below shows a shaker in use. *c.1935, 28cm (11in) high.*

**£200–300**

## Top Tips

- Avoid decanters with a mismatched or loose stopper – the stopper should always fit snugly.
- Make sure that pairs of decanters are consistent in design and shape – pairs are more desirable and have a higher value, but only if they match.
- Buy in spring or summer for the best prices: decanters are more in demand around Christmas.
- Check that bases have light criss-crossing scratches consistent with wear through usage – a feature of genuine old decanters.
- Check the pourers on cocktail shakers. They should have closures that fit well, with either a button or screw top. Sadly, many have been lost over time.

## KEEP

*Novelty decanter-and-glass sets are growing in popularity. It is important for sets to remain intact. If they are still functional as well as being fun – few have survived in top condition – prices should rise.*

**An enamelled-metal 'Rolls-Royce' decanter-and-glass set.** The moulded glass decanters and shot glasses are in perfect condition. *1950s, 42cm (16½in) long.*

**£100–200**

## SELL

*Cocktail shakers made from fine materials in novelty shapes from the 1920s and 30s have been fetching large sums recently, thanks to a small band of devoted collectors. Although prices may possibly rise a little further, they are unlikely to go much higher, making this a good time to cash in on your investment or family heirloom.*

**A silver-plated stylised 'polar bear' cocktail shaker,** with a head that can be removed to reveal an internal strainer and to allow pouring. The amusing look and Art Deco feel of the design make this piece highly desirable. *c.1930s, 25.5cm (10in) high.*

**£3,000–4,000**

# Glass

**Once the preserve of the wealthy, glass has been prized for centuries. From Victorian times onwards, mass-production made it affordable to all, and increased competition resulted in a multitude of different styles. More recently, talented artists developed new types of specialised glass which are now highly valued.**

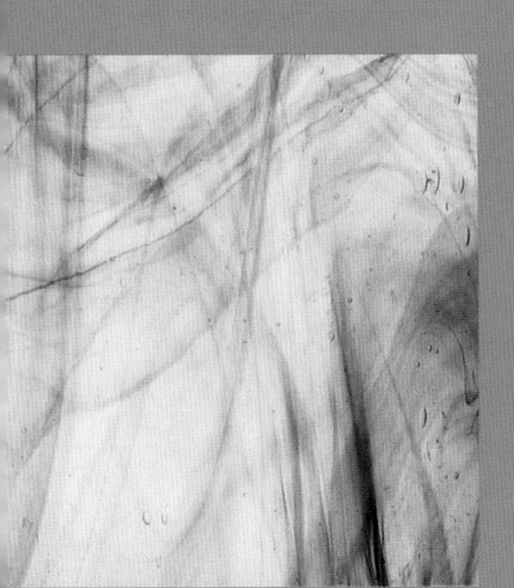

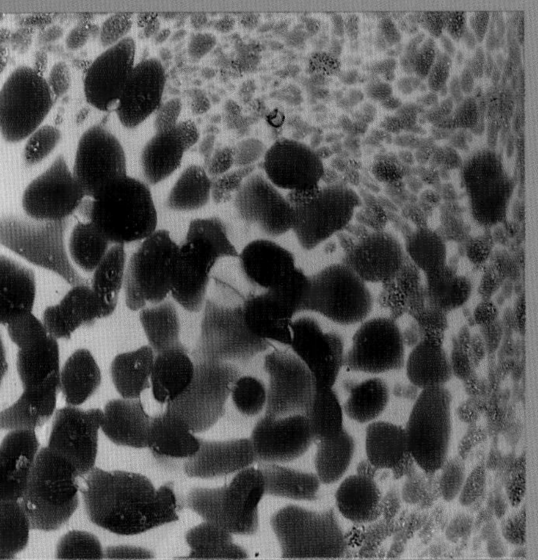

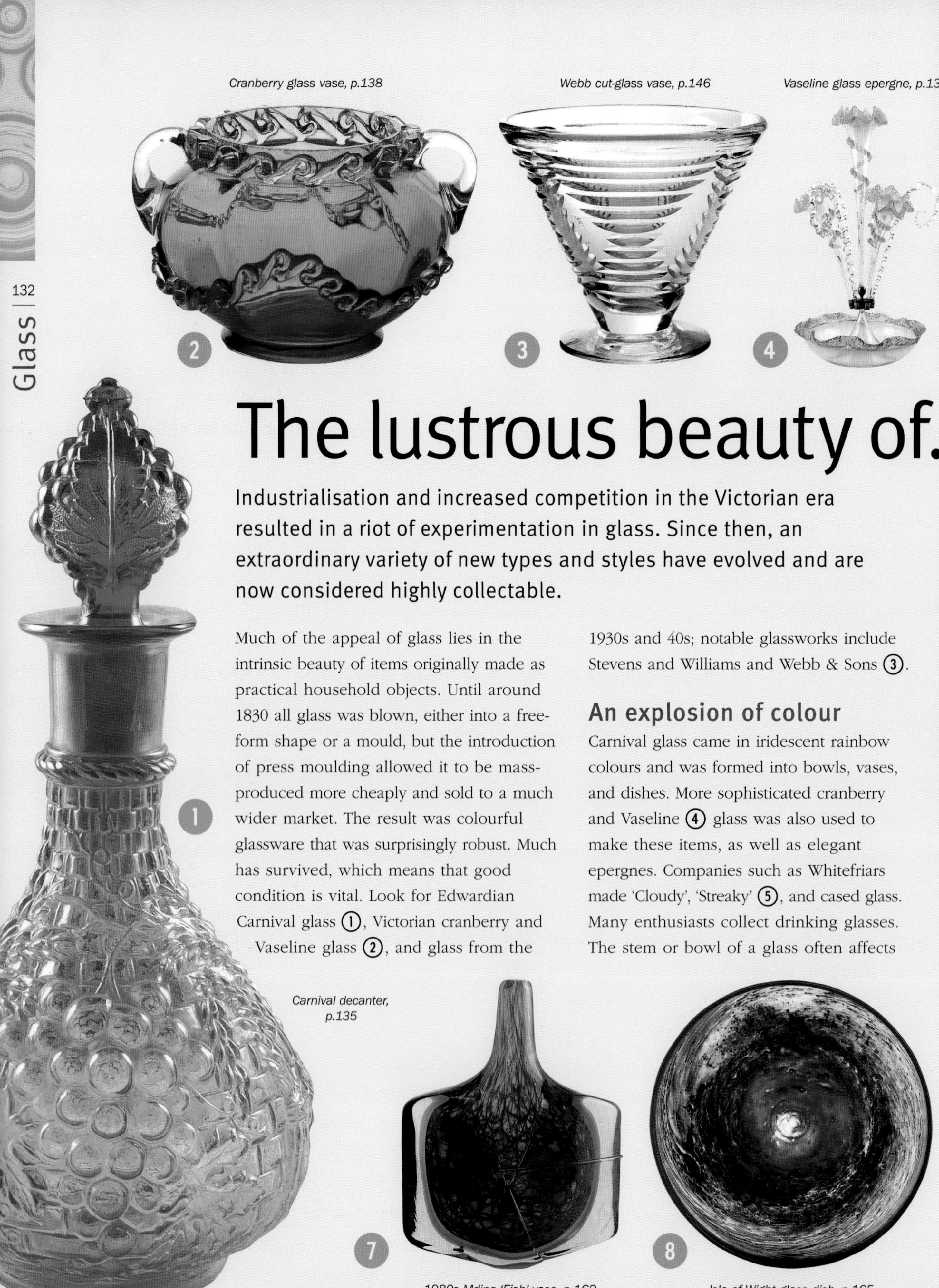

Cranberry glass vase, p.138

Webb cut-glass vase, p.146

Vaseline glass epergne, p.139

# The lustrous beauty of.

Industrialisation and increased competition in the Victorian era resulted in a riot of experimentation in glass. Since then, an extraordinary variety of new types and styles have evolved and are now considered highly collectable.

Much of the appeal of glass lies in the intrinsic beauty of items originally made as practical household objects. Until around 1830 all glass was blown, either into a free-form shape or a mould, but the introduction of press moulding allowed it to be mass-produced more cheaply and sold to a much wider market. The result was colourful glassware that was surprisingly robust. Much has survived, which means that good condition is vital. Look for Edwardian Carnival glass (1), Victorian cranberry and Vaseline glass (2), and glass from the 1930s and 40s; notable glassworks include Stevens and Williams and Webb & Sons (3).

## An explosion of colour

Carnival glass came in iridescent rainbow colours and was formed into bowls, vases, and dishes. More sophisticated cranberry and Vaseline (4) glass was also used to make these items, as well as elegant epergnes. Companies such as Whitefriars made 'Cloudy', 'Streaky' (5), and cased glass. Many enthusiasts collect drinking glasses. The stem or bowl of a glass often affects

Carnival decanter, p.135

1980s Mdina 'Fish' vase, p.162

Isle of Wight glass dish, p.165

The introduction of press moulding allowed glass to be mass-produced more cheaply and sold to a much wider market.

Whitefriars 'Streaky' vase, p.145

Monart vase, p.145

# ..glassware

value: faceted or air-twist stems and engraved bowls command a premium.

Factories such as Monart ⑥, Vasart, and Strathearn in Scotland, and Nazeing in Hertfordshire, used mottled, opaque coloured glass to make decorative items from the 1930s to the 60s. This tradition was continued by Michael Harris at Mdina ⑦ from 1968 and Isle of Wight Studio Glass ⑧ from 1972. At the same time, King's Lynn and Wedgwood ⑨ were creating plain glassware in jewel-like colours. These pieces are becoming increasingly popular.

In the 1950s and 60s, Scandinavian glass-makers such as Orrefors, Kosta ⑩, and Riihimäki experimented with colourful styles of glass, both plain and textured. It is now coming back into fashion.

## New inspiration

The island of Murano ⑪ in Venice has been a traditional centre for glassmaking for more than a thousand years. The industry there received a creative boost in the 1950s and 60s as designers at factories such as Venini and Barovier & Toso created innovative new styles. Pieces from these decades and later, many of them brought home by people who had been on holiday to the city, are now becoming highly sought after. As well as bowls and vases there is also a market for their novelty animal and clown pieces which became popular in the period following World War II.

Wedgwood 'Sheringham' candlesticks, p.159

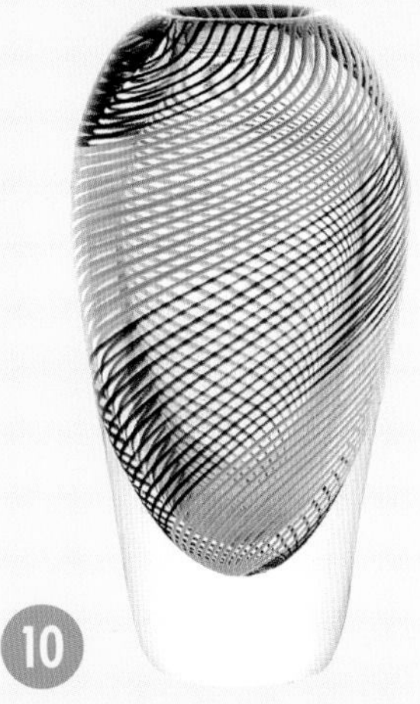

Kosta vase designed by Vicke Lindstrand, p.151

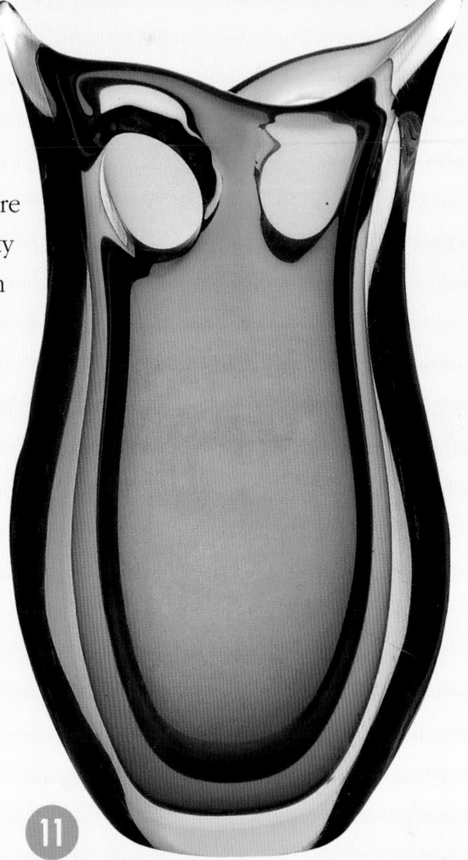

Murano vase, p.169

# Carnival glass has humble origins and was once seen as 'Poor man's Tiffany'. Its attractive patterns, cheerful colours, and generally low prices now make it eagerly collected worldwide.

**A Dugan/Diamond 'Leaf Rays' marigold 'nappy',** a form of shallow bowl. *1920s, 17cm (6¾in) long.*

**£10–15**

With the light behind it, carnival glass can 'warm' and beautify the home with its striking colours and flamboyant patterns. There is always scope for a lucky discovery or shrewd investment, even though these pieces were mass-produced during the 20th century.

## Grand inspirations

At the beginning of the century, Tiffany art glass, with its bright, shimmering hues, was fashionable but expensive. To bring this look to the masses, from about 1905 American glass factories started to spray mass-produced, press-moulded, coloured glass with metallic salts. These iridescent pieces were a huge success, both in the USA and in Britain and continental Europe.

The most popular colours at the time, and the most readily found today, are marigold (orange), amethyst (purple), green, and a rich cobalt blue. Rarer, and so more eagerly collected, are pieces in amber, grey-blue, or with a marbled tortoiseshell effect. The rarest colour is red, launched in the 1920s by Fenton Art Glass.

### *Did You Know?*

*The name 'carnival glass' was not used until the 1950s. It supposedly originated from glassware made in the USA, Australia, Europe, and Argentina in the 1920s and 30s. These inexpensive items were often sold or given away at funfairs as prizes – hence the name 'carnival', which in the USA refers to a funfair.*

## Patterns galore

Different patterns were associated with different makers; and although some apparently identical patterns were made by more than one maker, there are usually slight variations. Particularly collectable are patterns with unusual elements such as classical borders or Japanese-inspired decoration. Shapes are also important, as there are many variations. In general, small bowls and jugs are common and less expensive. Large bowls or flat plates, which are harder to make, are more valuable, fetching up to £1,000 or more, depending on the colour.

## Prime colours

Collectors divide the glass found today into two categories. The 'golden era' of 1911–25 provided the first and most collectable category, known as 'Prime' carnival glass. Leading manufacturers were the Fenton and Northwood companies, both in West Virginia. Early Fenton carnival glass is unmarked but often has unusual patterns, such as

## Some makers to look for:

- Northwood
- Dugan/Diamond
- Fenton

**A small Northwood 'Grape and Cable' milk jug.** A highly popular pattern by a prolific maker, this was made in more than 40 different shapes from 1910 until the 1920s. *c.1920s, 7.5cm (3in) high.*

**£10–15**

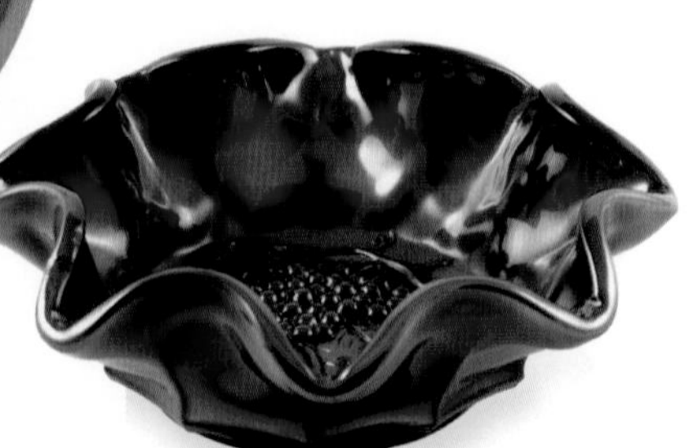

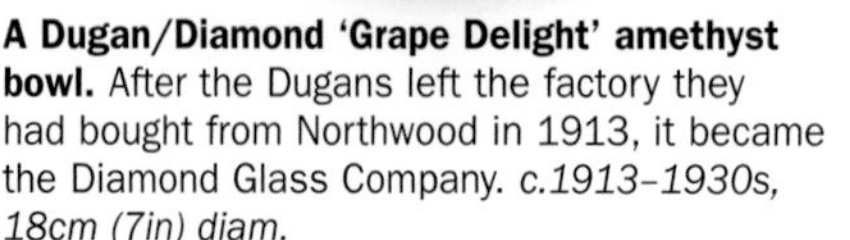

**A Dugan/Diamond 'Grape Delight' amethyst bowl.** After the Dugans left the factory they had bought from Northwood in 1913, it became the Diamond Glass Company. *c.1913–1930s, 18cm (7in) diam.*

**£35–45**

**A Fenton 'Dragon and Lotus' blue bowl.** Along with Northwood, Fenton were one of the biggest producers of carnival glass, and this was one of its favourite and best-known patterns. *c.1920s, 21.5cm (8½in) diam.*

**£50–100**

**A 'Golden Harvest' marigold decanter,** possibly by the Diamond Glass Company. *1920s, 30.5cm (12in) high.*

**£50–60**

'Cherries', and colours, such as red and Celeste Blue; it also frequently had extra hand-finished details.

## 'Grape and Cable'

Northwood marked many (but not all) of its pieces on the base with an underlined 'N', sometimes within a circle or, more rarely, a double circle. One of its best-known patterns was 'Grape and Cable' *(see opposite, far left)*, found on a variety of forms from punch bowls to hatpin holders. As with most carnival glass, Northwood values depend on colour and shape – a large green bowl in this pattern can be worth around £200–400 or more, while a marigold creamer will generally fetch under £30.

Other makers of Prime carnival glass include the Imperial Glass factory of Bellaire, Ohio, which made its name with its ranges of 'Nucut' and 'Nu-Art' pressed glass, and the Millersburg Glass Company, which was also based in Ohio.

From the early 1920s until about 1939, factories in France, Czechoslovakia, and even Argentina made 'Secondary' carnival glass. In England, the Sowerby's Ellison Glassworks at Gateshead also introduced a range. These European pieces tended not to be as crisp as the early American glass, as they were produced with inferior moulds. The work of the Crown Crystal Company in Sydney, Australia, which produced patterns based on native flora and fauna in the 1920s, is often more appealing.

## Lookalikes

By the 1960s, carnival glass had 'arrived' as a popular collecting area. Some makers in the USA, such as Fenton, created new ranges using original moulds. Unlike its earlier products, its new carnival glass is marked, with a script 'Fenton' inside an oval cartouche. Imperial's more recent wares are also marked. Other new items have been made from fresh moulds, or from old moulds not originally used for carnival glass.

## ▪ Imperial ▪ Brockwitz ▪

**An Imperial 'Lustre Rose' bowl.** Imperial made carnival glass between c.1909 and c.1929 and exported many pieces from 1911 onwards – to Britain in particular. *c.1920s, 20cm (7¾in) diam.*

**£45–55**

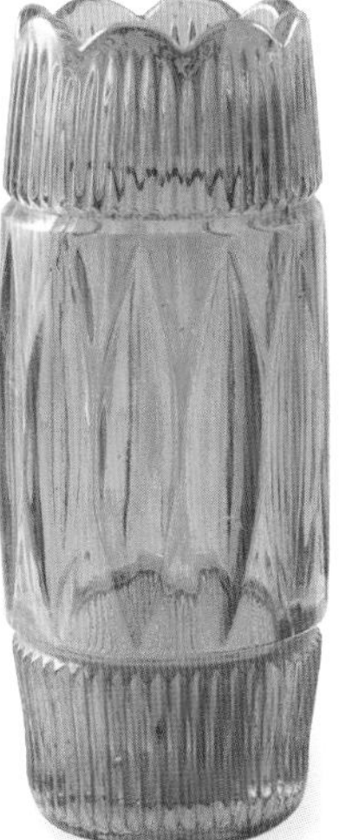

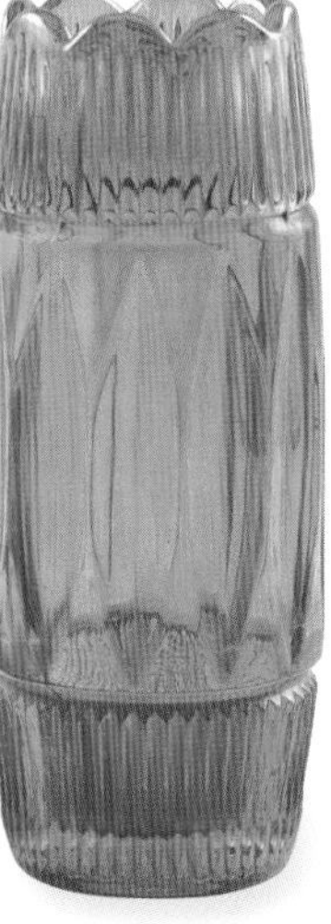

**A pair of Brockwitz 'Triands' marigold vases.** Brockwitz of Germany, opened in 1903, was the largest carnival glass producer in Europe by the late 1920s. *c.1930, 20cm (7¾in) high.*

**£35–45**

### Top Tips

- Look for strong colours in the base glass and shimmering iridescence in the surface finish. The best way to see the true base colour of carnival glass is to hold it up to a light.
- To check for flaws, hold a piece against a strong light and look at it through a magnifying glass.
- Check that holes have not been plugged, or chips repaired using acrylics – a careful inspection will show up any flaws no matter how carefully they have been concealed.
- Look for pattern variants by the same company. They can generate extra interest, which can mean a higher value if the piece is also attractive and in excellent condition.

### BUY

*Pieces with a strong colour, high-quality iridescence, and an identifiable pattern by a well-known maker, such as Northwood, are a good prospect for investment as they are sure to at least hold their value and will probably appreciate.*

**A Northwood 'Good Luck' amethyst bowl.** The deep amethyst colour and good-quality iridescence make this bowl a winner. *c.1920s, 21.5cm (8½in) diam.*

**£80–100**

### SELL

*With so much carnival glass produced, it is important to invest in the best-quality examples. Pieces that lack a strong colour (especially if also a common colour), with a poor level of iridescence, and a faint or common pattern are not likely to gain value. Sell and invest in a more desirable piece.*

**A marigold dish with ruffled edge.** The pattern on the dish lacks definition and the iridescence is poor. Marigold is also the most common colour. *c.1920s, 20.5cm (8in) diam.*

**£8–12**

# Perfume bottles have a powerful allure. From the sparkling flasks of the 1900s to the doves of peace on the stopper of post-war 'L'Air du Temps', they capture the mood of the moment, with plenty of quirky flourishes to adorn the dressing table.



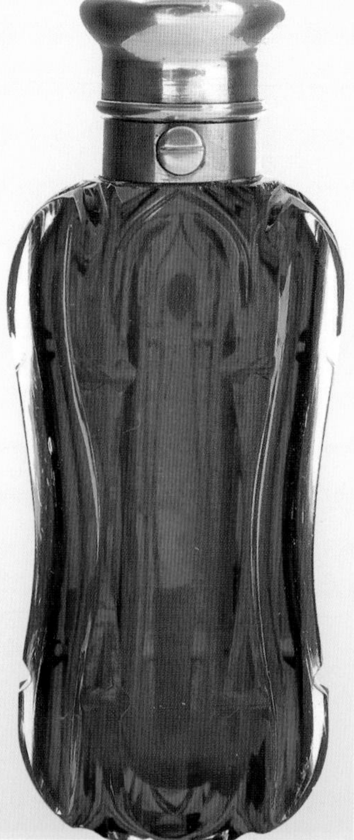

▲ **A Victorian cased ruby glass scent bottle,** with silver mounts. The deep red colour and cut decoration are typical of Victorian styles. *c.1880s, 7.5cm (3in) high.*

**£70–100**

In the 19th and early 20th centuries, fragrances were generally light and refreshing. They were sold in plain packaging, then transferred to more attractive cut or tinted glass bottles for use at the dressing table. In the 1920s several leading Parisian perfumers, such as Coty, began to offer new perfumes in Art Deco bottles. The bottles were made by top glassmakers, such as Lalique, and were designed to complement the new, more sensual fragrances.

By the late 1920s many women aspired to own a bottle of French perfume. Paris couturiers, such as Poiret, launched the first 'designer' perfumes to reach a mass market. Orientalism, then a fashionable style, inspired many perfumes and their bottles, including Guerlain's 'Shalimar', which was named after the gardens of Shalimar in India. The classic Chanel No. 5 bottle has hardly changed since 1921, so even early examples are inexpensive.

During the 1930s, streamlined Modernist designs captured the public's imagination and perfumes came in minimalist bottles, such as Patou's 'Joy'. Surrealism also proved influential. Elsa Schiaparelli's perfume 'Shocking', introduced in 1937, was inspired by the movement and sold in a bottle shaped like a dressmaker's dummy.

After World War II there was a taste for ladylike clothes and sweet fragrances, such as 'Miss Dior', which was launched in 1947. These perfumes came in bottles reminiscent of Victorian fashions.

► **An owl-shaped Bakelite outer case for 'Evening in Paris' perfume, by Bourjois.** By the 1920s manufacturers of inexpensive fragrances realised that stylish packaging and an upmarket name – preferably one with French associations – sold more perfume. *c.1928, 10cm (4in) high.*

**£80–120**

▼ **A Venetian *latticinio* glass scent bottle.** '*Latticinio*' refers to the milky threads in the glass. *c.1880s, 6cm (2½in) high.*

**£70–100**

▲ **A bottle for Caron's 'Les Pois de Senteur de Chez Moi'.** The geometric shape is typical of Art Deco design. The original label enhances the value of this bottle. *c.1927, 11.5cm (4½in) high.*

**£80–120**

▼ **A double-ended cut-glass bottle.** One end was for cologne, the other for smelling salts. *1900s, 12cm (4¾in) high.*

**£70–100**

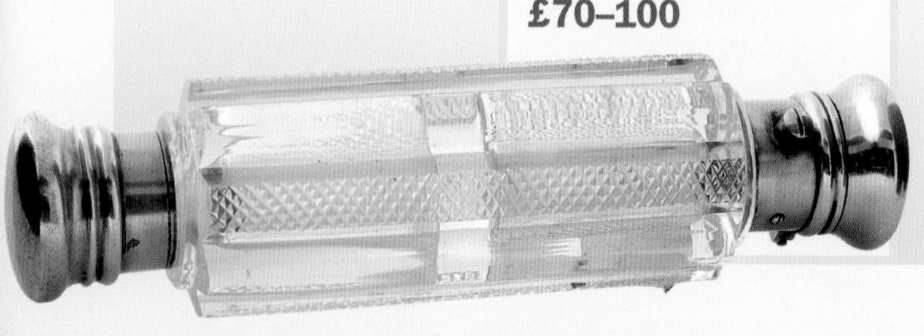

▲ **A Baccarat design for 'Miss Dior'.** The urn shape harks back to mid-Victorian design and echoes Dior's clothes. *c.1947, 14cm (5½in) high.*

**£100–150**

▼ **A gentleman's Baccarat crystal scent flask,** one of a pair, with marks. Baccarat is one of the finest and most desirable French glassmakers. *1900s, 9.5cm (3¾in) high.*

**£80–120 for pair**

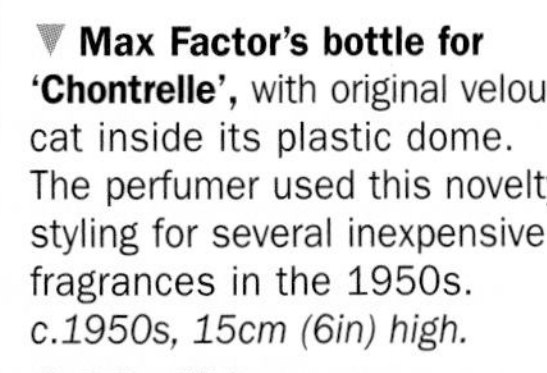


▲ **A Lalique 'L'Air du Temps' bottle for Nina Ricci,** with box. This bottle by Marc Lalique – the son of René Lalique – is highly prized by collectors. *1960s–70s, 10cm (4in) high.*

**£80–120**

▼ **Max Factor's bottle for 'Chontrelle',** with original velour cat inside its plastic dome. The perfumer used this novelty styling for several inexpensive fragrances in the 1950s. *c.1950s, 15cm (6in) high.*

**£40–50**

## Collectors' Tips

- In pre-World War II bottles, look for novelty designs, or an established designer, or a bottle that reflects its period
- Keep current bottles that are celebrity-endorsed or innovatively designed – these may become collectables
- Favour bottles that are full of the original perfume, and still in their box

◀ **A Baccarat bottle for Guerlain's 'Shalimar',** which was launched at the International Exhibition of Decorative Arts in 1925. *1950s, 15cm (6in) high.*

**£50–80**

◀ **Guerlain's 'Parure' bottle.** Limited production runs by leading perfumers always appeal to collectors, and this romantic bottle has been discontinued. *1975, 17cm (6¾in) high.*

**£80–100**

# Coloured glass designed for contemporary tastes was a 'must-have' for the homes of the Victorian and Edwardian middle classes. Today there is still a tempting array of vibrantly hued vases, glasses, bowls, and other items to collect.

A cranberry glass wine glass. 1910s, 12.5cm (5in) high.

£10–15

Opalescent, Vaseline, and cranberry glass dominate this field. As so much was made, you might be surprised to learn that your grandmother's old Vaseline glass vase could be worth £500. Some cranberry glass is more modestly priced and makes a good starting-point for building a collection.

## A milky blue

Opalescent glass has a milky opal-like appearance with subtly graduated colours: thicker areas are opaque milky-white and thinner areas more translucent. An alternative choice of chemical additives produced a yellowish-green variety. A red version is found more rarely.

Opalescent glass was used for a wide range of designs. The term is often associated with inexpensive, mass-produced pieces made in Britain from the 1880s until the 1940s, as well as art glass produced in the late 19th century. Jobling & Co. produced an 'Opalique' range, made of pressed opalescent glass, in the 1930s. It used well-cut moulds, and many of its pieces were of high quality with crisp details. Today, Jobling wares are slightly undervalued and may be a good long-term investment.

## Touches of whimsy

Other factories in the north-east of England made small, humorous, unmarked novelty pieces. These are now popular – particularly the animal shapes – but are difficult to find.

Manchester-based factories such as Burtles & Tate and Molineaux, Webb & Co. produced a whole range of opalescent trinkets such as posy troughs, swans, bowls, and novelty table decorations. An early 20th-century posy trough in the form of a fish can fetch around £150. The firm also introduced rose pink- and yellow-tinted opalescent glass, probably using copper in the mixture. These pieces are growing in popularity. A Burtles & Tate swan-shaped trinket from the 1880s can be worth around £250.

**A cranberry glass two-handled vase,** with slight damage. *c.1880s, 15cm (6in) diam.*

**£40–50**

## A modern alchemy

By using tiny quantities of uranium and metal oxides, makers of Vaseline glass were able to produce a yellow-green glass with a slightly 'greasy' appearance – hence the name, even more appropriate when Vaseline jelly was a greenish yellow. James Powell at Whitefriars Glass (established in 1834) was one of the first British

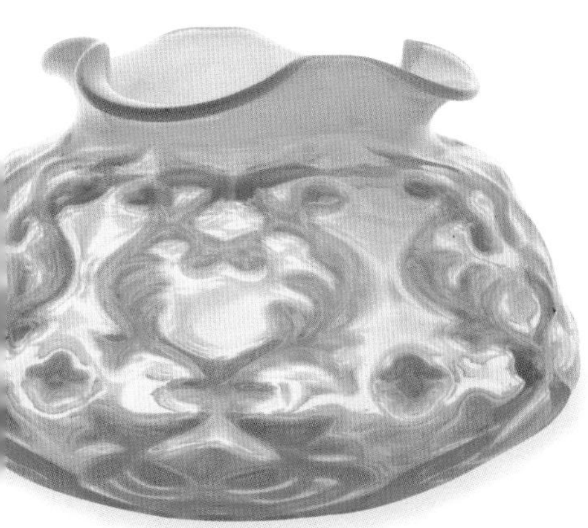

**A John Walsh Walsh Vaseline vase.** *1904, 10cm (4in) high.*

**£100–150**

makers to produce Vaseline glass, in 1877; and Powell and other firms such as John Walsh Walsh and Thomas Webb persisted with it until the 1930s.

Look for examples with fine detailing by major manufacturers. Leaf and flower patterns are particularly effective in Vaseline glass. Vases and bowls can fetch anything from £150 to £500, depending on the quality, level of detail, and size.

Utilitarian tableware, which is usually less finely made and less decorative in its patterning, is among the easiest Vaseline glass to find and can range from £5–20 upwards. Vaseline glass was also used for trinkets such as swans, dogs, and novelties such as fish-shaped flower troughs, many of which can be found for much less than £100.

## Cranberry treats

In Britain a popular glass with a strong raspberry-pink tint was made in Stourbridge in the 19th century. It is most popular in the USA, where it is known as cranberry glass. British manufacturers used it in the late 19th century for drinking glasses with coloured, often engraved, bowls atop clear glass stems. Jugs were also made with coloured bodies and clear glass handles, often decorated with engraved vines. This late 19th-century cranberry glass is the best investment: it has a warmer, deeper hue than later pieces. Carved wares, or those with white enamelled decoration showing children, known as 'Mary Gregory' pieces, fetch up to £200 or more. Enamel decoration of letters, flowers, or foliage can also be found.

## A closer look at...

### a Vaseline glass epergne

An epergne is a table centrepiece used for displaying fruit and flowers. Victorian dinners were often elaborate, with large quantities of decorative glassware complementing the silverware and ceramics.

The frilled edges and large, ornate form are typical of Victorian pieces

The varying colours of Vaseline glass combine well with the frills, twists, and crimpings in the design of this piece

The base was used to hold fruit and the trumpets above to display flowers

A metal collar supports the trumpets

**A Vaseline glass epergne,** with three spiralling, clear, decorative glass canes and four trumpets. *c.1880s, 55cm (21½in) high.*

**£100–150**

### *Fact or Fiction?*

*It has long been thought that Victorian glass-blowers who made Vaseline glass often died of lung cancer at a relatively young age because of exposure to uranium dioxide in the molten glass. But modern experts feel that there must have been other reasons, as radiation tends to affect the thyroid gland rather than the lungs.*

### *Top Tips*

- As prices for quality Manchester-made opalescent pieces are rising, consider buying now before they rise further.
- When choosing a novelty opalescent item, look for good detailing.
- As an opalescent finish cannot be restored, do not buy damaged items.
- Look out for trinkets in Vaseline glass by the Manchester firm of John Derbyshire – any Derbyshire Vaseline piece is worth double any other type of glass they made.

### BUY

*Opalescent glass reached new heights in the 1920s and 30s when French makers such as Lalique produced expensive art glass. Look out for pieces made by Sabino, Etling & Cie, and Barolac, who all produced good imitations of this style. Their pieces often enable you to acquire the Lalique 'look' without paying a Lalique price.*

**A French Edmond Etling & Cie opalescent bowl.** Figures of draped female nudes in this style are highly collectable. *c.1920–30, 23cm (9in) diam.*

**£300–400**

### KEEP

*Webb's Burmese glass contained chemicals that changed colour from yellow to pink when reheated in the furnace. The style has fallen out of fashion, but keep examples if quality is high as they are typical of Victorian styles.*

**A Webb Burmese vase,** with enamelled red flowers and green leaves. The complex shape and scarce enamelled pattern make this a desirable piece. The vase is marked on underside "Thomas Webb & Sons Queen's Burmeseware Patented Rd 67648". *c.1890, 12cm (4¾in) high.*

**£150–200**

# Bottles are endlessly intriguing, partly because of the wide variety of attractive colours and shapes available, but also because they are disposable, everyday household items, so the survival of individual examples is all the more remarkable.

**A Hyde cobalt-blue cylinder ink bottle,** with pouring lip. The bottle is embossed vertically with 'Hyde/London' and is in very good condition. *c.1890s, 15cm (6in) high.*

**£30–50**

Many bottles that are found in antique shops, car-boot sales, or even buried in the garden, date from the 19th and early 20th centuries. Those mass produced from the 1860s onwards are especially common.

Before glass bottles became widespread, pottery vessels were used. These were generally tan or cream in colour, with lettering or decoration. After the mid-19th century, stoneware bottles were underglazed and transfer printed; older, etched versions are rarer. Bottles bearing pictures are sought after, as are those in blue or green, but the majority can be found for less than £50.

**A Watson's whisky jug,** with a Port Dundas pottery mark. *c.1850s, 21.5cm (8½in) high.*

**£20–30**

## Full of minerals

Glass was used increasingly in the 19th century to hold liquids. In 1872 Hiram Codd invented a bottle for mineral water, with a marble used as a stopper – the fizz forced the marble up to seal the lip. Standard aquamarine examples are common and usually fetch under £5. Coloured versions, particularly blue, are more desirable and rare – some are worth up to £2,000 or more. Aquamarine 'codd' bottles with coloured lips are also rare, while amber-coloured examples are more common and sell for about £20–30.

## What's your poison?

Bottles that held poisons are sought after, largely because of their striking colours and unusual shapes. Coloured versions can be found for around £10, but stranger shapes sell for much more. A coffin-shaped, cobalt-blue poison bottle with embossed coffin-nail decoration, recently sold for £10,000. Bottles marked 'Poison' tend to be older and more valuable than those marked 'Not to be taken', a wording that became compulsory in 1908.

## Potions and cures

In the early 19th century, patented medicines were often packaged in attractive bottles to make them more appealing. Before this, barbers dispensed medicine in square or globe-shaped bottles with elongated necks, known as 'carboys'. Some are ornately faceted, and large examples with their original stoppers can be worth £500–1,000. Smaller medicinal bottles often have gilt, painted, or transfer-applied labels with the name of the contents. Values vary from around £15–50 for a clear example, or £60–100 for a blue glass version with a gilt label, up to around £100–200 or more for ceramic examples.

Some Victorian medical substances were known as 'quack cures'. Warner's Safe Cure is perhaps the best known, and standard bottles can be picked up for less than £20. Bottles for William Radam's Microbe Killer, which claimed to 'cure all known diseases' (until the makers were taken to court in 1911), can cost from £20 to more than £500, depending on condition and rarity.

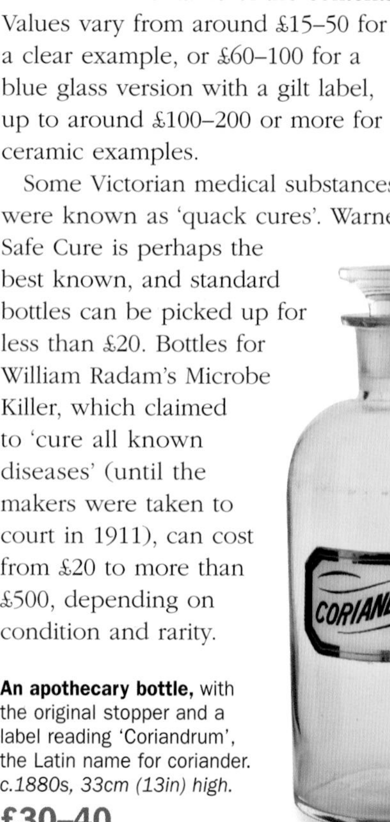


**An apothecary bottle,** with the original stopper and a label reading 'Coriandrum', the Latin name for coriander. *c.1880s, 33cm (13in) high.*

**£30–40**

## A closer look at... a Schweppes Hamilton bottle

When buying drinks bottles, consider shape, colour, and form to ensure the best investment. The Hamilton is an early torpedo-shaped bottle design for holding carbonated drinks.

**A Schweppes dark olive-green glass Hamilton bottle,** with an applied rolled lip. This is a rare, early example of a Hamilton bottle made for Schweppes, still a well-known drinks maker. *1830s, 19cm (7½in) long.*

**£800–1,200**

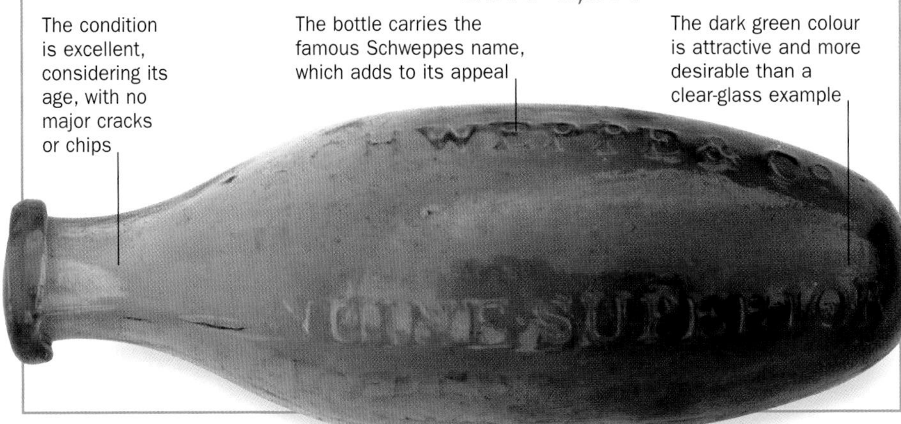

The condition is excellent, considering its age, with no major cracks or chips

The bottle carries the famous Schweppes name, which adds to its appeal

The dark green colour is attractive and more desirable than a clear-glass example

### Wine glass

Wine bottles from the mid-17th century were made from a dark green glass known as 'black glass', and those in good condition may cost £5,000–10,000 or more. Wine bottles from the late 18th century can still be found for about £20–30, though. The original black glass bottles tended to be globe- or onion-shaped, but by the early 18th century the design was a more stable mallet shape (shown below), and by the mid-18th century the familiar cylinder shape was established.

Gin and beer were also packaged in dark glass, which is now thought to have been a ruse to disguise impurities in the contents. A number of bottles were found on shipwrecks during the last few decades; these can be worth £100–800 when they come on sale.

**An English black glass 'mallet' wine bottle.** *c.1730, 20.5cm (8in) high.*

**£400–600**

### Pen and ink

Ink bottles, both earthenware and glass, are desirable and can fetch £5–50 or more. Post-1840 glass examples are especially common, as improving literacy and the introduction of the penny post increased demand for ink. Prices are generally under £30. Novelty-shaped ink bottles are usually worth more – a birdcage bottle can fetch £40–60. Look out for bottles produced by fountain-pen makers such as Waterman and Parker; these are equally popular with pen and bottle collectors and can sell for £5–50 if they are in good condition.

*Did You Know?*

*A Shropshire farmer stumbled across a black glass bottle in the roots of a fallen oak tree. The 17th-century, 19cm (7½in) shaft-and-globe bottle was sold at BBR Auctions for a staggering £19,800 in 1997.*

### Top Tips

- Watch out for cracks or chips, which will reduce the value of a bottle considerably.
- Keep an eye open for bottles of value in attics, gardens, and old cellars.
- Do not use hot water to rinse old glass, and never force anything inside a bottle to clean it.
- Make a small scratch on the base of a coloured glass bottle to check that it is not made of lacquered clear glass.
- Watch out for faked labels by running your fingers over blemishes, tears, and dirt. If you can feel them, they will probably be real; if not, the label may have been photocopied or electronically reproduced.
- Hunt for old bottles at specialist bottle fairs, held throughout Britain, or buy a copy of a collectors' magazine.

### KEEP

*Bottles produced for everyday use were usually thrown away once empty. Paper labels often degraded, stoppers were lost, and bottles were scratched. Items in good condition, such as these, will have the best chance of rising in value.*

**A Savory & Moore boxed bottle,** with a paper label reading 'The Cordial Stomachic Mixture'. As well as retaining its label, it has its shaped wooden box, which is unusual. *c.1860s, 11.5cm (4½in) high.*

**£150–200**

### SELL

*Attractive or striking bottles, or those that fit two or more collecting categories, appeal to a wider group of people. When interest from other groups is strong, it is often a good idea to sell, as values may not rise much more.*

**A rare French Dagron & Cie ink bottle,** with moulded pen rest (not shown). Designed by French inventor René Dagron, this bottle has cross-market appeal. *c.1880, 6.5cm (2½in) high.*

**£50–80**

COLLECTOR'S CORNER

# Vintage drinking glasses

## from the 19th century onwards can make an attractive collection. They often cost the same as good modern examples, but make a better investment because of the huge depreciation of newer pieces.

Drinking glasses have been made in Britain since the 16th century. Early examples are rare and expensive, but 19th- and 20th-century pieces offer plenty of choice. Glasses with faceted stems, popular from around 1825, fetch up to £500 or more. But the Victorian period (1837–1901) offers budget collectors more scope; simple, faceted designs can be found for around £20 or less.

Late-Victorian and Edwardian glasses cost from around £5 up to £30–60. Many are engraved with complex, geometric, looping patterns or natural motifs such as foliage or flowers. Colours tend to be rich blues, greens, reds, and amber.

Numerous new styles and forms emerged during the 20th century: look for clean-lined Art Deco examples, or 1950s and 60s Scandinavian examples.

Nineteenth- and 20th-century drinking glasses can be found at general auctions and collectors' fairs. Due to the huge variety available, it is possible to build up a group of glasses that appear the same until closer inspection – these are known as 'harlequin' sets. Alternatively, pairs or even single glasses can be used to create a varied, attractive, and interesting collection.

▲ **A green wine glass,** machine acid etched and gilded, with a plain stem. Victorian coloured wine glasses tend to have green, red, blue, amber, or amethyst bowls with rounded bottoms on a clear glass stem. This example is made more attractive by the etched band. *c.1890, 13cm (5¼in) high.*

**£15–20**

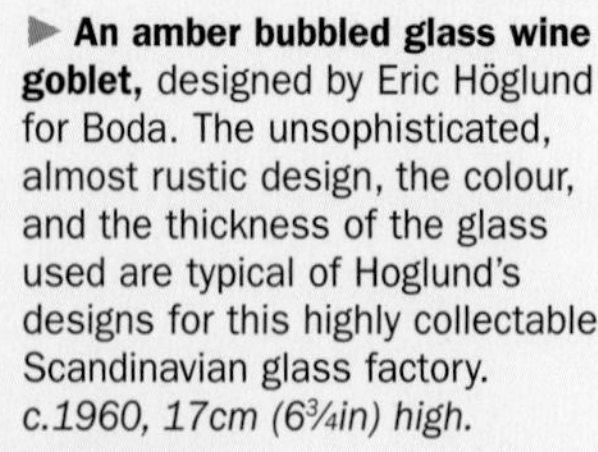

► **A James Powell of Whitefriars ruby wine glass.** The rich colour of this glass and the fact that it was made by one of Britain's most notable glass factories make this piece highly collectable. *c.1870, 11.5cm (4½in) high.*

**£30–40**

► **An amber bubbled glass wine goblet,** designed by Eric Höglund for Boda. The unsophisticated, almost rustic design, the colour, and the thickness of the glass used are typical of Hoglund's designs for this highly collectable Scandinavian glass factory. *c.1960, 17cm (6¾in) high.*

**£40–50**

◄ **A small Victorian bucket-bowl rummer,** on a large foot. Rummers typically have large bowls on short, stout stems – their name probably derives from the German 'römer' or 'wine glass'. Plain rummers like this, intended for use in taverns, can usually be found for around £30 or less. *c.1880, 10cm (4in) high.*

**£15–20**

◄ **A late-Victorian moulded 'penny lick' glass.** Although this glass looks like a small shot glass for spirits, it was actually used for serving dispensed ice cream before the ice cream cone was popularised commercially in 1904 at the St Louis Exhibition. *1880s–90s, 9.5cm (3¾in) high.*

**£15–25**

◀ **A 'deceptive bowl' gin glass with ball knop stem.** Much of the bowl is infilled with glass so that it gives the illusion of containing more alcohol than it actually does. *c.1840, 10cm (4in) high.*

**£25–35**

◀ **A pair of Edwardian engraved sherry glasses.** The thin glass and complex design are typical of Edwardian glasses, many of which are still inexpensive. *c.1905, 9.5cm (3½in) high.*

**£10–15**

▶ **A Georgian champagne flute** with high panel cutting, a collar, and a blade knop stem. The simple but elegant cut panels and the 'blade' shaped knop are typical of glassware of this period. *c.1820, 18cm (7in) high.*

**£50–70**

## Collectors' Tips

- Look for incomplete sets of glasses; these often cost less than a complete set of six or 12
- Look for job lots which contain different types of glasses to start or add to a collection
- Handle authentic pieces to learn how to recognise the look and feel of a period glass

▶ **A Georgian drinking glass** with facet-cut stem and base of bowl, with pontil mark. Facet-stemmed glasses typically have rounded bowls: if the faceting is complex and there is engraved decoration on the bowl, the value will rise. *c.1800, 13cm (5¼in) high.*

**£80–110**

◀ **A petal-moulded dwarf ale glass** with stem. Ale glasses are typically slimmer than today's as they were made to hold a smaller amount – 125ml – of ale, which was drunk as a barley wine. *c.1800, 13.5cm (5¼in) high.*

**£45–55**

▶ **A ruby cased wine glass with petal-cut bowl and hollow sliced cut stem.** The deep red colour which is overlaid onto the clear glass and cut through with the facets would have appealed to mid-Victorian taste; the hollow stem is an attractive feature. *c.1840, 13cm (5in) high.*

**£40–60**

# Glass of the 1930s and 40s

is surprisingly diverse, considering the economic problems of the period. It includes sleek, colourful cased glass, cameo glass with its raised motifs, and crisply sparkling cut glass – much of it available at modest prices.

Many pieces of glass from this period have survived and they are readily available at fairs and auctions.

One of the most collectable forms of cased art glass is Monart. With this type of glass, coloured enamels are sandwiched between two layers of clear glass to produce swirls of colour. Monart was made by the Moncrieff Glassworks of Perth from 1924 to 1961, with a break in output during and just after the war. Products range from large bowls and vases to tiny perfume bottles. Larger pieces, and those in typical greens, blues, and pinks with gold flake inclusions and a good level of 'cloudlike' mottling, are most desirable. With some rarer patterns, such as 'Cloisonné' and 'Stoneware', an extra layer of colour was added to the outside of the piece: items can fetch £200–800. Look out for bands of the coloured swirling 'S' shapes which form a pattern known as 'Paisley shawl'; they are more valuable. Pieces that still carry their paper label are desirable but these are often missing. Fake labels do exist, usually thicker and shinier than the originals.

Similar in style, but less expensive at around £50–250, is Vasart art glass, produced by Ysart Bros of Perth, from 1947. Salvador Ysart had previously worked on Monart glass. The Ysart company name is often engraved into the base of their pieces. Colours tended to be paler than Monart's, with pastels in vogue by this time. In 1965 Vasart became Strathearn Glass, and continued production until 1980. These later pieces are easily identifiable by a 'leaping

**A Vasart vase,** with a two-toned pink body and a decoration of pink and blue swirls. *c.1947–64, 25cm (10in) high.*

**£60–80**

**A Nazeing bowl, in mottled green, with a clear foot.** *1930s, 12cm (4¾in) high.*

**£30–40**

### Did You Know?

*The 'Modern Art for the Table' exhibition hosted by Harrods in 1934 was one of the most important events to affect British cut glass of the pre-war era. Leading artists of the time were invited to submit designs to be produced both in ceramic and glass, and Stuart & Sons were commissioned to make the glass ware. Major painters, such as Dame Laura Knight, Paul Nash, Vanessa Bell, Graham Sutherland, Dod and Ernest Proctor, and Eric Ravilious, took part. All of these exhibition pieces are keenly collected.*

## Essential 1930s Whitefriars

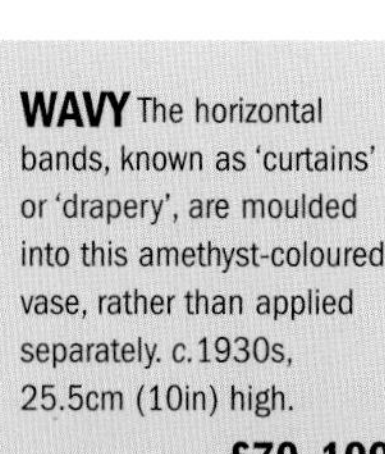

**STREAKY** The colours of this range, typified by the blue vase shown, were derived from Whitefriars' experience in making stained glass. *c.*1930s, 17.5cm (6¾in) high.

**£50–70**

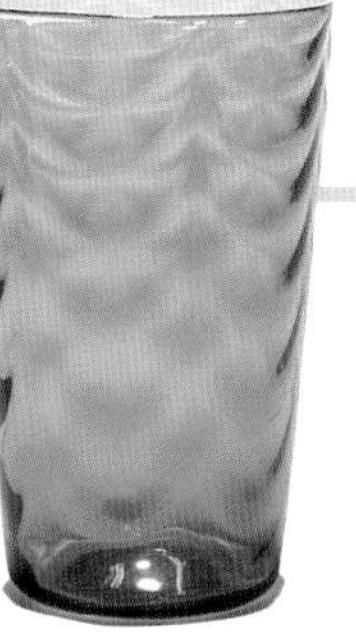

**WAVY** The horizontal bands, known as 'curtains' or 'drapery', are moulded into this amethyst-coloured vase, rather than applied separately. *c.*1930s, 25.5cm (10in) high.

**£70–100**

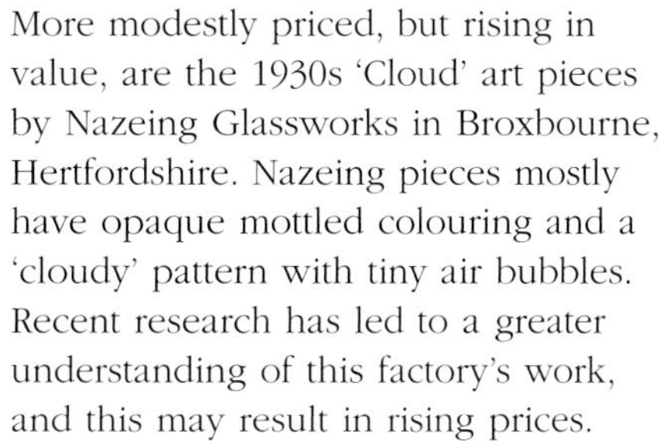

**RIBBON-TRAILED** The decoration used on this range was achieved by trailing molten glass around the body of the item. 1930s, 26.5cm (10½in) high.

**£80–90**

**CLOUDY** The clear glass body of this style of glassware was rolled in powdered enamels, which, on re-firing melted to form a random pattern of bubbles. 1930s, 30cm (12in) high.

**£200–300**

**OPTIC** A large number of thin blue threads applied to the inside surface of the piece creates a wavy effect which is much sought after. 1930s, 33cm (13in) high.

**£200–300**

**CUT** The geometric, clean, modern design on this amber glass vase, by William Wilson, is typical of its period. *c.*1935–37, 31cm (12¼in) high.

**£350–450**

salmon' mark impressed into the base, and pieces can often be found for less than £100.

The Gray-Stan art glass range (1926–36) was developed by Elizabeth Graydon-Stannus, in Battersea, south London. Gray-Stan shapes and patterns are similar to Monart's, but with a different colour range, from pastels to dramatic fiery hues, and a more powdery finish. Signed pieces fetch a premium, although unsigned ones can often be found for £200–300 or less.

**A Monart vase,** of tapering cylindrical form, in turquoise with decorative bubbles and a band of green swirls. *1920s–30s, 26.5cm (10¼in) high.*

**£100–150**

More modestly priced, but rising in value, are the 1930s 'Cloud' art pieces by Nazeing Glassworks in Broxbourne, Hertfordshire. Nazeing pieces mostly have opaque mottled colouring and a 'cloudy' pattern with tiny air bubbles. Recent research has led to a greater understanding of this factory's work, and this may result in rising prices.

### Powell power

Whitefriars Glassworks, known at the time as James Powell & Sons, produced a wide range of popular designs and styles during the 1930s and 40s. Of their 'Cloudy' range of cased-glass bowls and vases from 1928 until 1939, red is the rarest colour, and two-colour examples using powdered enamels also fetch a premium. Their similar 'Streaky' range (designed by Arthur Marriott Powell) is admired for its bold colours and simple shapes. Pieces tend to be unmarked, but company catalogues can be used to identify them.

### Waves and ribbons

Although proud of their cased-glass range, Whitefriars did not abandon the more modest end of the market. They released less expensive mould-blown vases, decanters, bowls, and lamp bases with mouldings that created wavelike optical effects. The appeal of these pieces was enhanced by their cool, watery colours, such as soft greens, blues, and ambers – the rare amethyst is now the most prized.

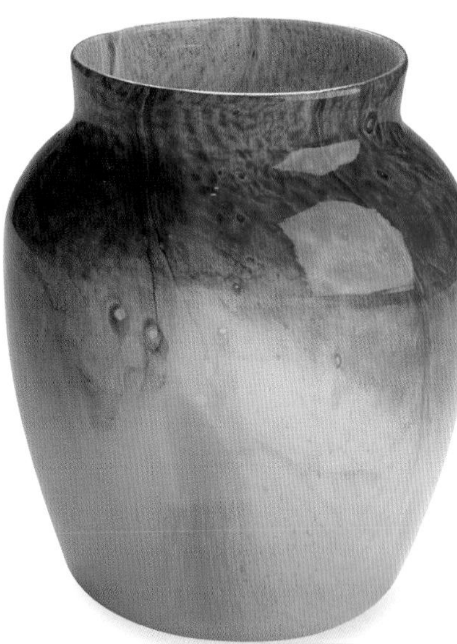

**A Gray-Stan vase,** with etched marks to the base. The clear glass body has turquoise and yellow inclusions. *1930s, 22cm (8¾in) high.*

**£100–200**

Many of these items were made and they are still readily available – so good condition is vital. Large examples with regular and more detailed applied designs in typical colours often fetch £200–400; those in which the wavy pattern is formed within the glass will generally fetch less.

Several other companies made glass in similar 'wavy' designs, and it is possible to distinguish these by slight differences in colour and pattern: Webb Corbett, for example, tended to use more acidic colours.

Whitefriars' chief designer at this time was Barnaby Powell, and he was responsible for designing the 'Ribbon-Trailed' range, in which the exterior is

**A Whitefriars sapphire bowl,** pattern 9034, designed by William Wilson. *c.1935–37, 17cm (7in) high.*

**£350–400**

**A Stuart & Sons cut-glass vase,** with circular and wheat-sheaf patterns. *1930s, 24.5cm (9¾in) high.*

**£100–150**

## A closer look at... a Webb cut-glass vase

During the 1930s and 40s a distinctly modern note appeared in the design of cut glass. Today, such pieces are as popular as they were when first produced. Even excellent examples can be acquired without huge expense.

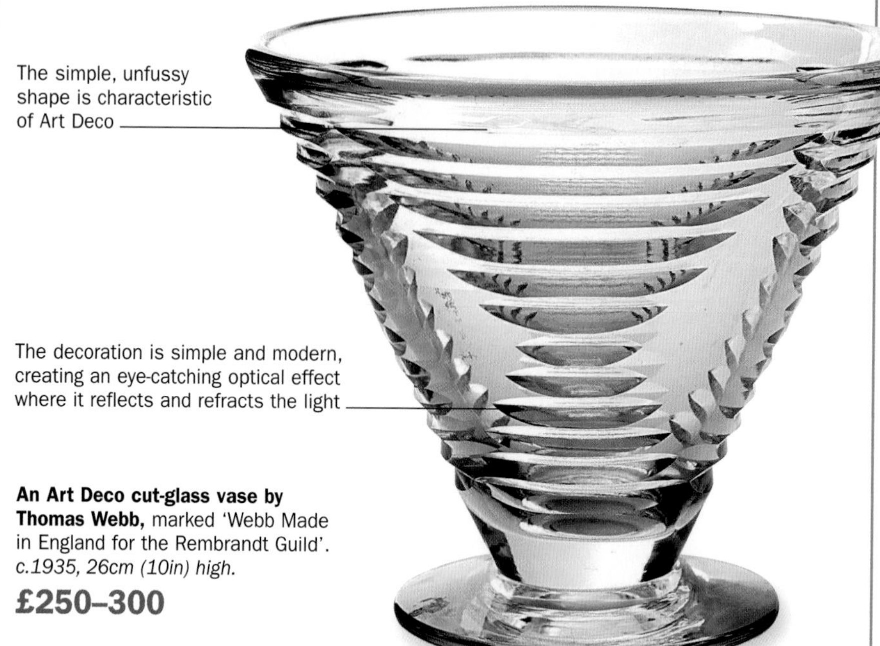


**An Art Deco cut-glass vase by Thomas Webb,** marked 'Webb Made in England for the Rembrandt Guild'. *c.1935, 26cm (10in) high.*

**£250–300**

decorated with applied trails of glass. Examples can be found in sapphire, amber, and emerald-green for less than £100, and pieces in good condition should rise in value. Look for two-colour examples, worth two to three times as much as single-colour pieces.

### Sparkling style

Between the wars, the lower end of the British glass market was flooded with cheap cut glass from Czechoslovakia. Companies such as Webb, Whitefriars, Walsh Walsh, and Stuart & Sons responded by producing luxury glass that combined cutting and engraving, aimed at the higher end of the market. There were two styles: one looked back to Art Nouveau; the other was inspired by Swedish glass and Art Deco. Both are widely available – avoid the many pieces that are an unhappy combination of the two.

Along with much cut glass by leading factories, Whitefriars pieces by William Wilson or Barnaby Powell are admired and fetch high prices (around £300–500). Look for coloured pieces, in which the strong colour works well with the engraved or cut design.

The high lead content of Stuart glass makes it particularly suitable for deep and dramatic Art Deco cut designs. By 1920 the firm had introduced a final acid polish that gave a brilliant, shiny finish. One of the most talented staff designers was Ludwig Kny, the son of a Bohemian glass engraver, who worked for Stuart from 1918 to 1937. His designs ranged from stylised plants to more innovative Art Deco motifs such as zigzags and dashes. His pieces are not always signed but can often be identified by his distinctive cutting method, which used polished intaglio techniques to outline and accentuate olive-shaped mitre cuts. Intaglio is the opposite of cameo, in that the pattern is cut into the glass, rather than the background being cut away.

### Luxury ranges

In Britain between the wars, cut glass was the staple product of Thomas Webb & Corbett, established in 1897 (later called Webb Corbett). Look out for their luxury 'Gay Glass' range in four designs, launched in 1933. The 'Cut Water Lily' pattern, influenced by Art Nouveau and found on vases and bowls, was a favourite at the time and is prized today. Like the other patterns, it was made in crystal, *eau de nil*, dark green, and, most popular at the time, 'sunshine' – a golden amber. In contrast, Anna Fogelberg, wife of the Swedish general manager of Thomas Webb & Corbett, produced striking Art Deco cut and engraved designs, often in the clear and black glass favoured by Swedish designers. Some of these were ahead of British taste and were issued only as prototypes, or made (and marked) for the Rembrandt Guild, a gallery in Birmingham. These pieces are usually rare and expensive. Other makers also produced less adventurous but collectable clear and black glass.

The New Zealand architect Keith Murray, mainly known for his ceramics, worked freelance for Royal Brierley Crystal (previously known as Stevens & Williams) from 1932 to 1940. As well as highly collectable coloured glass in simple bowl, vase, or flower shapes, he produced abstract designs for cut glass, and stylised plant and animal designs for engraved glass. His 'Cactus' vases are rare and cost around £300–600 or more, but his mass-produced tableware designs are less expensive. Any piece by Murray is likely to rise in value.

Look for Art Deco glass by Walsh Walsh of Birmingham. In 1936 the company released pieces designed by William Clyne Farquharson. His distinctive style combines cutting and engraving techniques. He favoured popular motifs, such as wavy lines, olive shapes, and rounded arches.

## Worldwide Webb

Although cameo glass in the 1920s and 30s was almost all French, in 1931 Webb Corbett launched a cheaper, production-line, single-colour 'cameo' range. These 'Cameo Fleur' vases, with raised, coloured lilies or tulips, had a cameo signature, either on the body of the vase or on the foot. Webb's 'Rich Cameo' vases and bowls have flat decoration. Initially made by H.G. Richardson, their mark still appears on items made after the Webb takeover in 1930. Look out for red pieces, as these are rare.

**A Keith Murray for Stevens & Williams bubbled rose vase,** made in Stourbridge. *c.1930s, 22cm (8½in) high.*

**£200–250**

### Top Tips

- Collect documented pieces that are traceable to company catalogues, as these are more likely to hold their value. Collectors' clubs often know how to get hold of these publications.
- Look – and feel – carefully for blemishes on what should be a totally smooth outer surface, as these are detrimental to value.
- Check inside vases for limescale which interrupts the smoothness and clarity of the glass. These rough-textured deposits are hard, sometimes almost impossible, to remove.
- Enlist an expert to polish away light scratches on cut glass (except for those on the base or around the rim).

### BUY

*Hartley Wood pieces are bright and colourful, and the almost free-form shapes and swirls make each piece unique. The factory has only recently become popular, so prices may rise as collectors learn more.*

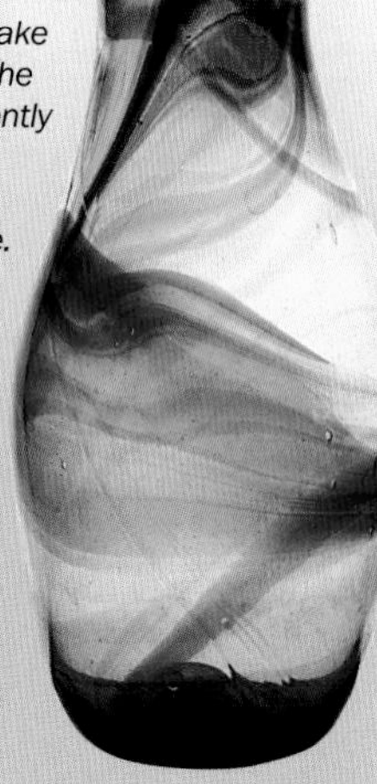

**A Hartley Wood vase.** This Sunderland factory was experienced in making stained-glass windows. *1936, 10cm (4in) high.*

**£150–200**

### KEEP

*Interest in Art Deco-influenced pieces has rather eclipsed those inspired by Art Nouveau. But well-made Art Nouveau-style 'cameo' pieces from the 1930s and 40s are sought after. Identified ranges by renowned makers in excellent condition should rise in value.*

**A Webb Corbett 'Cameo Fleur' vase.** This piece typifies the Art Nouveau style in its curving, stylised floral motifs. *1930s, 23cm (9in) high.*

**£150–200**

### KEEP

*Modern-looking pieces that broke new ground were often overlooked and undervalued. Collectors are only just beginning to realise the importance of these cutting-edge designs and so they are likely to appreciate in value.*

**A Webb Corbett vase, designed by Irene Stevens.** A series of deep, horizontal mitre cuts undulate gently around the vase, intersected by concave discs. *c.1940s, 31cm (12¼in) high.*

**£150–250**

# Paperweights are unique examples of virtuoso glassmaking, available in countless colours and designs. The finest are from 19th-century France, but the work of a younger generation from Britain and elsewhere is more attractively priced.



Paperweights have a thick, clear, domed glass casing, which magnifies the colourful design within. The most popular type contains multicoloured glass canes cut in short sections to create an effect known as *millefiori* (Italian for 'a thousand flowers').

A different style of manufacture is the sulphide weight, which is also popular with collectors. Sulphide weights encapsulate a small portrait made from a white porcelain-like material.

The French factories of St Louis, Clichy, and Baccarat produced superb paperweights in the mid-19th century. Today they can fetch anything from a couple of hundred pounds for the simpler designs to thousands for the larger, finest pieces with dense, complex patterns. Many European glassmakers settled in the USA in the 1850s, and the best American examples can also be expensive.

The collector on a budget has plenty of scope within the 20th century. One outstanding designer was the Spanish-born Paul Ysart, who worked for the renowned Montcrieff glassworks in Scotland. Their weights bearing the label 'Monart' can be found for little more than £100 – a good investment, as prices are rising. Ysart moved to Caithness Glass in 1963, staying with the company until 1970 and then set up on his own in 1971. Other Scottish makers worth looking out for include Vasart, Strathearn, and Selkirk. English makers to look for are John Deacons, Wedgwood, Langham Glass, and Isle of Wight Studio Glass.

19th- and early 20th-century Chinese paperweights are still relatively modestly priced. High-quality, clear pieces may be a good long-term investment.

▲ **A Ronald Stennett-Willson paperweight for King's Lynn Glass.** The organic, budlike shape shows the influence of mid-20th century Scandinavian style on this British glassmaker. *1967, 10cm (4in) high.*

**£80–120**

► **A miniature Clichy *millefiori* paperweight.** Clichy often used soft colours, concentric rings of *millefiori*, and sometimes a cane with a 'C' on the end, or a cane cut like an open rose (the 'Clichy Rose'). *c.1860s, 4.5cm (1¾in) diam.*

**£150–200**

► **A Chinese black clipper ship paperweight.** Among early paperweights, Chinese examples are probably the best executed outside France, Britain, and the USA. *c.1880s, 6.5cm (2½in) diam.*

**£200–300**

◄ **A Lalique 'Reynard' clear glass paperweight,** moulded as a fox. The circular base bears the signature 'R. Lalique'. After Lalique's death in 1945, the 'R' was no longer used. *c.1930s, 4cm (1½in) high.*

**£200–250**

◄ **A Bohemian sulphide portrait paperweight,** with a cameo of the German religious reformer Martin Luther. *c.1880s, 9.5cm (3¾in) diam.*

**£80–120**

◀ **A Selkirk *millefiori* paperweight.** This glassworks was established in Scotland in 1977. Pieces by Selkirk can be identified by a cane bearing a small 'S' or the signature of Peter Holmes. *c.1980s, 5.5cm (2¼in) diam.*

**£60–100**

◀ **A Baccarat 'Dupont' garlands paperweight.** Dupont weights are often more affordable, and use smaller canes, than other Baccarat weights. *c.1850s, 7cm (2¾in) diam.*

**£200–300**

## Collectors' Tips

- Choose weights with closely packed canes
- Check canes for makers' marks or dates
- Look for canes bearing animal silhouettes
- Avoid cracked weights – they cannot be repaired (although tiny chips can be fixed)

▶ **A Whitefriars concentric *millefiori* paperweight.** High-quality *millefiori* weights from this English maker are less common and more valuable than their abstract designs. *c.1970s, 8.25cm (3¼in) diam.*

**£220–280**

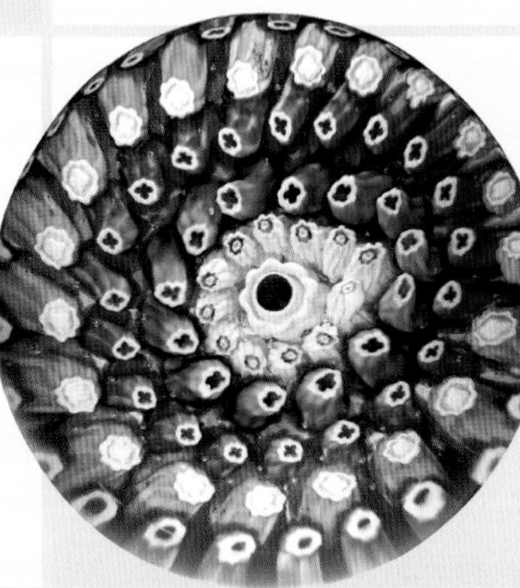

◀ **A Clichy 'posy' weight,** with two pink roses and a pink-and-white cane set among five green leaves. *c.1860s, 6.5cm (2½in) diam.*

**£200–300**

◀ **A Perthshire scattered *millefiori* paperweight.** The canes are on a ground known as 'tossed muslin'. Note the tiny elephant and kangaroo profiles – a desirable feature. *c.1970s, 5cm (2in) diam.*

**£100–150**

▶ **A Monart *millefiori* paperweight.** Monart paperweights are sought after – especially those designed by Paul Ysart. This one has a paper label on the base. *c.1950s, 7cm (2¾in) diam.*

**£400–450**

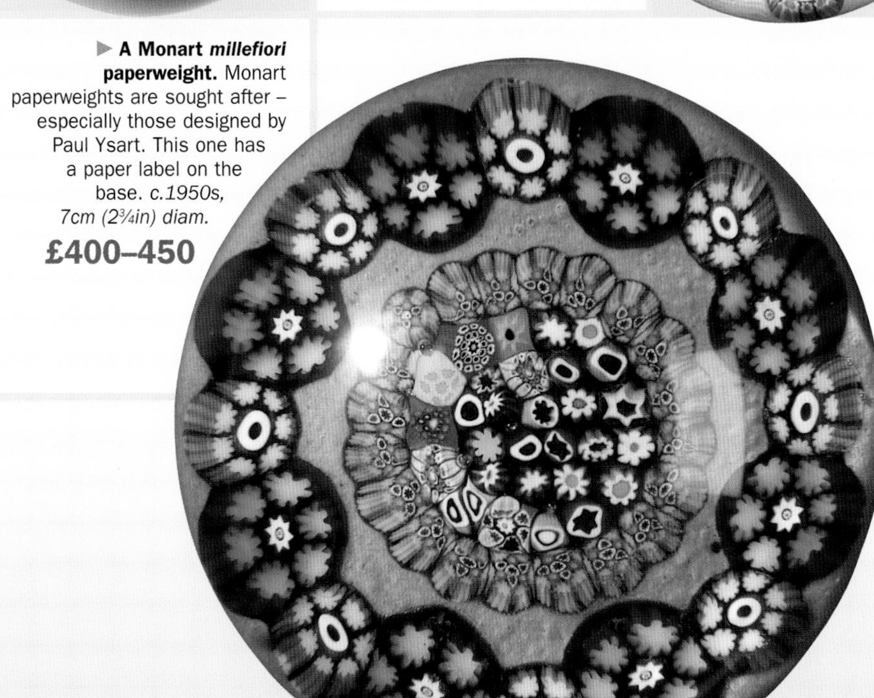

▲ **A Paul Ysart butterfly paperweight.** This designer produced some of Britain's finest paperweights in the 1960s and 70s, most featuring *millefiori*. Animal subjects, such as this butterfly, are rare. *1970s, 7cm (2¾in) diam.*

**£300–400**

# Scandinavian glass includes some of the 20th century's most exciting work in this medium. With classic yet innovative designs, jewel-like colours, and tactile textures, it has become a magnet for lovers of clean, modern design.

**A bark-pattern Finlandia vase designed by Timo Sarpaneva for Iittala.** *c.1964, 17cm (6¾in) high.*

**£100–150**

The twin forces of industrialisation and urbanisation had a huge impact on the West in the early 20th century, but in the Scandinavian countries tradition never lost its force. So, in the 1930s, Scandinavian glassmakers began a drive to bring hand-crafted quality to factory-produced designs affordable by ordinary people. The result was the quiet, restrained elegance that has become synonymous with Scandinavian glass. The success of this initiative quickly led to a boom in design, production, and exports.

Thanks to its particular chemical formulae, Scandinavian glass has an extraordinary clarity of tone, and can be engraved, carved, and blown into moulds. There are four categories: organic forms, geometric forms, textured glass, and engraved glass.

## Budding designs

Curving, naturalistic shapes were considered 'cutting edge' in the 1940s and 50s, and this style was adopted by Scandinavian glass designers. Sven Palmqvist's Selina range and Nils Landberg's Tulpenglas (Tulip glass) range for Orrefors, Sweden, are now classics, as are Timo Sarpaneva's asymmetrical vases for Finland's Iittala.

Per Lütken created fluid vases, bowls, and ashtrays, often with 'pulled' rims – sections of the rim are pulled out, creating softly angular protrusions – for the Danish Holmegaard glassworks. His glass was typically cool, subtle, and transparent, in grey, smoked, or brown-tinged colours. These pieces can often be found for less than £100, as can his tableware. Other notable designers working in this organic style were the Swedish husband-and-wife team of Edvard and Gerda Strömberg at their factory Strömbergshyttan. Their pieces have a subtle blue, grey, or brown tint.

## Some designers to look for:

- Tamara Aladin
- Nanny Still

◀ **Tamara Aladin's undulating, or flanged, vases for Riihimäen Lasi Oy, Finland.** Aladin is perhaps best known for the geometric style popular during the 1960s. *1960s, 28cm (11in) high.*

**£60–70 each**

**Vases designed by Nanny Still for Riihimäen Lasi Oy, Finland.** From the 1950s, Still's style became increasingly geometric, with strong, bright colours. *1970s, 28cm (11in) high.*

**£70–100 each**

## Optical effects

Scandinavian designers were interested in optical effects, especially those created by internal bubbles. Cased within layers of clear glass, the linear or swirling patterns they formed appear like rows of little pearls. Gunnel Nyman at Nuutajärvi-Notsjö in Finland was one of the leading exponents, and her work is often copied. It is sought after today, and large vases can fetch more than £200. Other optical features include broad internal ribs or waves and thin swirling threads, a style most commonly associated with Vicke Lindstrand.

## Solid geometry

Geometrical designs, with angular lines and projections and clean, unadorned surfaces, were commonly produced – in vibrant reds, blues, greens, and yellows. This style became hugely popular in the 1960s. Now easy to find, such pieces make a good subject for a new collection.

One of the key factories producing geometrical glass was Riihimäen Lasi Oy of Finland, whose pieces were nicknamed 'Lasi' from the Finnish word for 'glass'. Most of its glass is unsigned, but there may be a mark etched into the base incorporating a stylised lynx above the factory name. Prices are still low, usually ranging from about £15 to £100, depending on size, colour, and form.

At Holmegaard, as well as his naturalistic forms, Per Lütken created clean, sharp pieces in the Palette and Carnaby ranges in bright colours such as pillar-box red. These can be bought for around £100, often less. Another successful and accessible Holmegaard range is the Gul vases designed by Otto Brauer. Price depends on size and colour; cased-glass pieces often fetch twice as much as clear glass. A large green bottle may go for £100–120, a smaller one £30–40.

## A closer look at... an Erik Höglund 'Sun Catcher'

Although designers were inspired by, and even copied, each other's designs, there are a few with unique styles, such as Sweden's Erik Höglund. Thickly rendered glass, deep colours, and primitive motifs are all trademarks of his work. Höglund designed for several Swedish firms including Kosta and Strömbergshyttan.

The glass is usually thick on pieces designed or made by Höglund

**A Boda 'Sun Catcher' designed by Erik Höglund,** signed 'H866/F', which was made to hang in a window with sunlight passing through it. *c.1960s, 30cm (11¾in) high.*

**£100–150**

Höglund decorated pieces with impressed or moulded primitive animal or human figures

His palette is strong, typically using orange, blue, or red

## ▪ Vicke Lindstrand ▪ Per Lütken ▪ Helena Tynell ▪

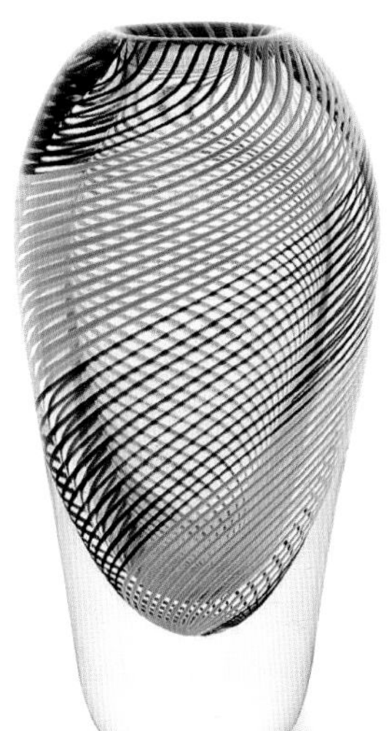

**A Vicke Lindstrand vase for Kosta, Sweden.** Lindstrand produced many styles, including glass with internal threads, as in this example. *c.1960, 16cm (6¼in) high.*

**£200–250**

◄ **A Per Lütken vase for Holmegaard, Denmark.** Lütken is renowned for organic forms. His work is often signed, with a date. *1960, 13.5cm (5¼in) high.*

**£60–100**

► **A Helena Tynell vase for Riihimäen Lasi Oy, Finland.** Tynell is known for her vases with undulating rims or strong optical effects. *c.1970s, 21.5cm (8¼in) high.*

**£80–120**

## Finlandia

The rugged landscape and harsh climate of Finland inspired the talented designers Tapio Wirkkala and Timo Sarpaneva. They translated natural shapes and textures – particularly from ice and bark – into one-off sculptural studio pieces, as well as making inexpensive mould-blown production-line domestic glass. They worked for the three major Finnish glassworks – Iittala, Riihimäen Lasi Oy (sometimes referred to as 'Riihimaki' or 'Lasi'), and Nuutajärvi – from the 1940s until the 60s. Look out for Sarpaneva's landmark Finlandia range with its barklike texture and clear, cool colours, and Wirkkala's evocatively named 'Stump' vase. Colours are clear or in earthy green or smoked tones.

Wirkkala designed a wide range of textured tableware for Iittala from the late 1960s through to the mid-1980s. Look out for his 'Ultima Thule' carafe, with its textured surface and knobbly feet, introduced in 1970, and glasses produced from 1968; also, Sarpaneva's Iittala ranges, which include 'Festivo' candlesticks.

Textured pieces became popular in the 1960s and 70s, and the fashion spread overseas. Other designers such as Nanny Still, known by then for her geometric styles, began to follow the trend. Her textured pieces can still often be found for less than £100.

**Even during World War II, Scandinavia had both the continuing resources and the political and imaginative freedom to create stunning designs.**

**A vase designed by Vicke Lindstrand for Orrefors,** with an engraved decoration of a naked male swimmer. *1930s, 22cm (8¾in) high.*

**£200–250**

## Cutting edge

Resilient new glass formulae stimulated Scandinavian manufacturers to produce engraved glass from the 1920s onwards. The Swedish factory Orrefors excelled at producing clear-glass pieces with engraved designs using a spinning cutting wheel. Important designers include Simon Gate and Edward Hald, whose stylish engravings – often featuring figures or decorated bands known as friezes – were influenced by designs from ancient Rome and Greece. Today, these can fetch thousands of pounds. You should also look out for engraved pieces with sparsely decorated, more modern designs by these two designers.

Vicke Lindstrand joined Orrefors in the 1930s. His range, including Art Deco-style figures and engraved nude divers, is as popular today as it was in the 1930s. Items usually sell for upwards of £200, depending on the design and condition.

**An aqua-blue vase from the Fossil range designed by Helena Tynell for Riihimäen Lasi Oy.** *1960s, 16cm (6¼in) high.*

**£100–150**

## A closer look at... an Ariel pattern cased-glass vase

From the 1930s, Scandinavian glass factories were centres of innovation. One of their major triumphs was at Orrefors, where a new technique known as Ariel was developed. Ariel patterns lent themselves to more dramatic effects than traditional engraving techniques.

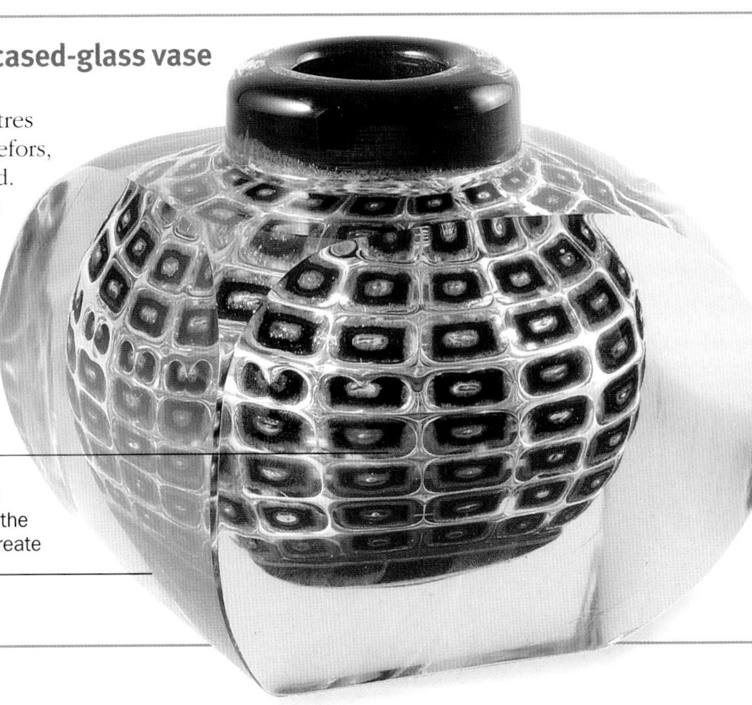

**An Ariel vase designed by Edvin Öhrström for Orrefors,** with green glass decorated with bubbles. The base is engraved with the designer's initials, maker's marks, and pattern numbers. *c.1960, 11cm (4¼in) high.*

**£1,200–1,800**

The pattern, composed of trails, or rows, of squares within the glass, was sandblasted onto a coloured body known as a 'blank'

The heavy, clear casing on the outside interacts with the coloured glass inside to create interesting optical effects

### Delicate lines

Engraved glass was not unique to Orrefors. Tapio Wirkkala, whose designs are most often inspired by nature, began his career at Iittala with a range including the mushroom-shaped 'Kantarelle' vase of the mid-1940s and the similar 'Foal's Foot' vase in 1946. The surfaces of both are engraved with delicate lines. His original limited editions are museum pieces, but later and smaller items from the 1950s onwards, including curling leaf-shaped bowls, can still be found for a few hundred pounds and are expected to rise in value.

After leaving Orrefors in 1950, Vicke Lindstrand joined the Swedish factory Kosta. His vases with finely engraved figures reinvigorated the business; many smaller items from the 1950s or later can be found for less than £100.

### Innovative etchings

Abstract designs in glass were also produced using new techniques. Most important are the Graal and Ariel methods, which were used to create engraved, sandblasted, or etched designs in coloured cased (layered) glass. If you are on a budget, look for good-quality examples that are either unmarked or by lesser-known factories – prices for these pieces will be much lower.

### Top Tips

- If the lettering on a signed piece is hard to read, try examining it using a magnifying glass and a piece of black paper or fabric placed inside the piece.
- Learn to spot the style of leading designers by visiting museums and reputable dealers to look at their work.
- Engraving cannot be restored, so check the design all the way around the piece. Unusual flattened areas on a curved piece indicate restoration through polishing.
- Look for original engraved designs that capture the spirit of the time – such as skyscrapers, circuses, or skiers.
- Tableware is a good starting point for a collection. Sets can be built up over time and are useful and decorative.

### BUY

*Vases with 'pulled' rims epitomise the Scandinavian interest in budlike forms and appeal to today's minimalist tastes. Even large pieces are still fairly inexpensive. Avoid scratched, scuffed examples, or those with limescale stains inside. These vases should increase in value as the demand outstrips supply.*

**A vase with a pulled rim designed by Edvard Strömberg for Strömbergshyttan.** *1930s–50s, 22cm (8¾in) high.*

**£20–30**

### KEEP

*Natural forms were favoured by many Scandinavian designers, as demonstrated in this vase shaped like a curling leaf. When considering pieces such as this, look for hand-made and signed examples by notable designers, as these are more likely to increase in value.*

**A leaf vase designed by Tapio Wirkkala for Iittala,** engraved with fine lines. It is engraved 'Tapio Wirkkala-Iittala' on the underside. *1953–59, 18cm (7in) long.*

**£300–400**

### SELL

*Mould-blown vases in basic geometric shapes are typical of Scandinavian styling and love of colour, and interest in them has grown. But owing to the large number produced, the recent rise in value is unlikely to continue. Sell if prices do not rise soon.*

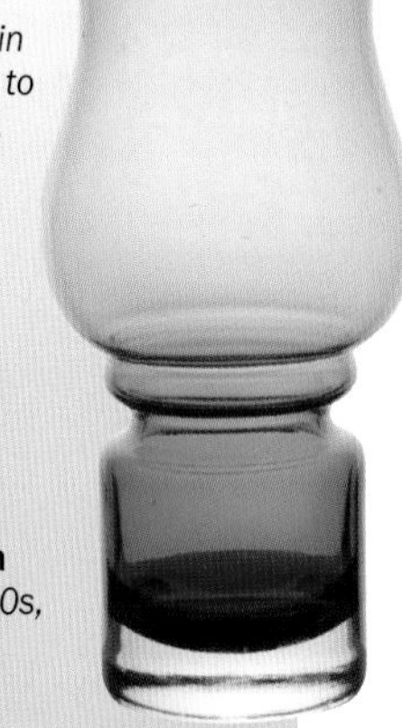

**A green mould-blown vase designed by Tamara Aladin for Riihimäen Lasi Oy.** *1960s, 20cm (7¾in) high.*

**£30–50**

# Post-war Whitefriars

glassware embodied a fresh approach to glass design. Drawing on the influential Scandinavian and Italian styles of the time, it gave post-war Britain a 'new look', but at affordable prices.

**A vase** with bubbled decoration and pull-up rim designed by Geoffrey Baxter. *c.1954, 20cm (8in) high.*

**£40–50**

The contribution made by Britain to modern glassware in the 1950s is best summed up by the work of Geoffrey Baxter of Whitefriars. A graduate of the Royal College of Art, Baxter was keenly aware of new design trends and introduced them to Whitefriars when he joined in 1954.

By 1957 the company was producing designs by both Geoffrey Baxter and by the factory's managing director William Wilson. Influenced by contemporary Scandinavian glassware, they created organic, asymmetrical vases, with 'pulled' rims and heavy casing (one layer of glass encased inside another). Many had internal 'bubble' decoration (usually an easy way to spot a Whitefriars piece), and were regular in pattern; pieces with irregularities were usually graded as 'seconds'. The vases were produced in cool, classic colours with evocative names such as 'Arctic Blue', or they were made in an entirely new palette of rich ruby, dark blue, and dark green, quite unlike anything Whitefriars had produced before. Smaller pieces can be found for around £30, while larger pieces cost about £50–150, depending on their shape and size. When buying clear glass items, particularly in lighter colours, make sure that they are unscratched; damage of this sort detracts from the purity of the glass and the delicacy of the colours.

**A vase** with internal air bubbles. *1950s, 13cm (5in) high.*

**£25–35**

## Clear-cut style

Around the same time, Whitefriars launched Baxter's designs for clear cut-glass in the 'Contemporary' style which was prevalent in the late 1950s. His motifs and patterns included stylised English wild plants such as grasses and cow parsley, engraved fish designs, and star-shaped cuts, which were popular at the time. Baxter's designs followed the Scandinavian practice of leaving much of the object's surface uncut. These pieces are often mistaken for genuine Scandinavian glass. Despite the fine-quality engraving and crystal-clear glass of Baxter's cut-glass ware, it is currently neglected in favour of his coloured glasswork. Examples can be found for as little as £100. Bubbles and scratches reduce the value.

## Angular appeal

Baxter's great skill in interpreting current trends in a way that found favour with the British public was summed up in an article in *House & Garden* magazine in 1964. It said: 'Whitefriars ... designs are good, gentle, British, without a sign of Nordic starkness.' From 1961–63 Baxter designed thinly blown 'Angular' soda-glass vases in the now-established strong, dark colours. These were based on old lighting moulds, and their 'bulb cover' shapes often hint at this origin. Still comparatively inexpensive (usually found for less than £100), they can form an affordable collection that represents an important – and popular – period in the company's output.

## A closer look at... two Baxter vases for Whitefriars

These two similar 1950s Whitefriars vases were designed by Geoffrey Baxter. The gently curving, bud-like shape, along with the purity and clarity of colour, recalls the work of Per Lütken for the Danish factory, Holmegaard. Look closely at colour to learn to spot valuable examples.

This combination of colours is rare, as the different-coloured glass layers often broke down in the furnace when joined

The 'organic', bud-like form was popular

The body of the vase is made from green glass and the heavy foot from blue glass

**An Aquamarine vase designed by Geoffrey Baxter** combining two colours – only five examples have been found. Another rare colour combination using pink and grey glass is known as Evening Sky. *c.1957, 9.5cm (3¾in) high.*

**£900–1,200**

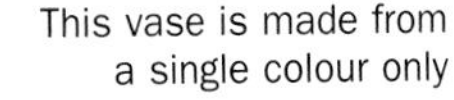

This vase is made from a single colour only

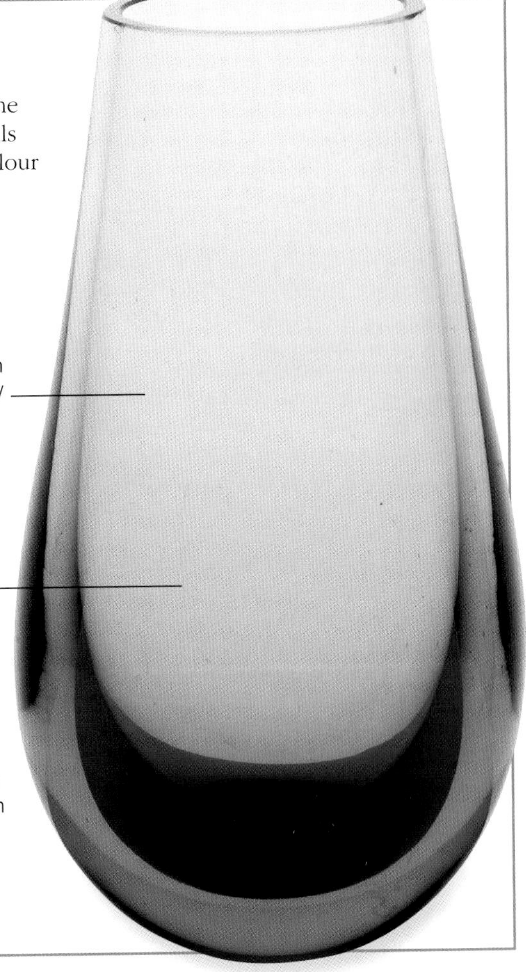

The colour is common

**An Ocean Blue vase designed by Geoffrey Baxter.** It appeared in the 1957 Whitefriars catalogue. *c.1957, 15.5cm (6in) high.*

**£30–50**

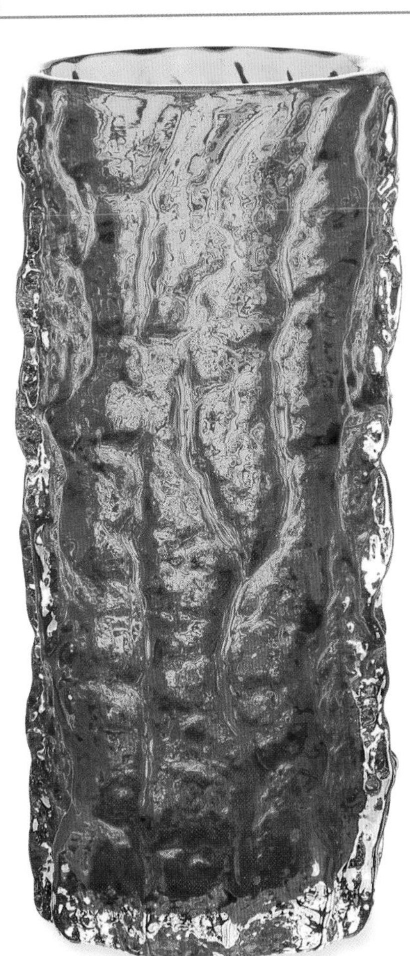

### From tree bark to glass vase

Whitefriars' biggest breakthrough was the textured mould-blown glass range designed by Baxter in 1966 and launched in 1967. Textured glass was immensely fashionable in the 1960s and 70s and was also produced in Scandinavia at roughly the same time (although it's difficult to pinpoint where textured glass was first launched). Today this type of work often commands high prices to match the demand. Cylindrical-cased 'Bark' vases were made from 1967 to 1980 and, although highly characteristic of Whitefriars, they are still modestly priced at less than £50 for a small example. There are three sizes: the largest, rarest, and most sought after was only made until 1974.

The Birmingham-based company of Jones & Co. commissioned Swedish-made textured vases to compete with Whitefriars' best-selling 'Bark' vases. The Jones version, which is less sought after, is not cased, and is square rather than cylindrical.

**A 'Bark' vase,** in Tangerine, designed by Geoffrey Baxter. *1967–80, 19cm (7½in) high.*

**£40–50**

*Fact or Fiction?*

*Inspired by the textures of tree bark in woods near his home, Geoffrey Baxter made the original 'Bark' vase moulds, lined with bark, in his garage at home in 1967. He had the trial pieces made up at the factory and left them on director William Wilson's desk to await his return from holiday. Fortunately, Wilson liked them.*

### First impressions

Other Whitefriars textured glass designs of the 1960s were made in moulds that had been lined with wire and nails. These left impressions and texture in the glass once it was blown into the mould. When buying a vase of this type, seek out unusual shapes, as they are likely to be worth more.

The 10-sided 'Banjo' vases *(shown opposite)* are particular favourites and can command up to £1,000 or more, depending on size and colour. These were launched in 1967 in Cinnamon, Willow, and Indigo, with other colours added later, such as Kingfisher Blue and Tangerine in 1969, and Aubergine in 1972.

The 'Drunken Bricklayer' vase – another superb 1960s asymmetrical design – was produced in two sizes and several different colours from 1967 until about 1977. Although slightly less expensive than the 'Banjo' vase, it is still one of Baxter's most popular and characteristic designs.

'As chief designer at Whitefriars I have more scope than probably any other glass designer in Britain ... I have a completely free hand to create.' Geoffrey Baxter

## Proud as a peacock

Whitefriars also produced a limited-edition 'Studio' range, created by the young designer Peter Wheeler, which was launched in 1969. Look out for the two-colour 'Peacock Studio' range with trailed decoration that was produced until about 1970. All Studio pieces are marked with an engraved pattern number and the year of production.

Whitefriars continued production through the 1970s, but by the end of the decade orders fell away and the company closed in 1980.

▼ **Whitefriars glassworks,** established in 1834, was particularly noted for its simpler, sparser designs dating from the 1920s onwards. The photograph shows designer J.H. Hogan at work in the upper studio at Whitefriars in the 1920s – he would probably have been astounded by the extraordinary new-look glassware that was produced by his successors at Whitefriars during the 1950s, 60s, and 70s. *c.1920.*

► **A Sage Green vase from the 1964 'Knobbly' range.** *c.1964, 19cm (7½in) high.*

**£30–40**

▲ **A Geoffrey Baxter Cinnamon vase.** *c.1962, 24.5cm (9½in) high.*

**£250–300**

## *Top Tips*

- Look for textured glass pieces with crisp definition. Moulds often deteriorated with use, resulting in less desirable, 'flatter' textures over time.
- Choose colours that are typical of the period: tangerine is quintessentially 1960s and 70s.
- Examine textured surfaces for smooth areas that could indicate restoration using polishing – this lowers value.
- Identify Studio-range items by their engraved marks. Many other pieces have paper labels incorporating the name and the 'White Friar' figure.
- Check prices carefully: some Whitefriars pieces are almost indistinguishable from Scandinavian glass, but they are generally more moderately priced.
- Keep your eyes peeled in local auctions, as you can sometimes find mixed 'job' lots of Whitefriars glass.

◄ **A 'Banjo' vase,** designed by Geoffrey Baxter. *c.1957, 32cm (12½in) high.*

**£1,500–2,000**

## KEEP

*Some uncoloured or partly coloured Whitefriars vases are mistaken for Scandinavian glass, because of the high-quality wheel-engraving and modern designs. Although largely ignored until now in favour of other coloured and textured pieces, and often undervalued (because they are not always recognised as Whitefriars), prices for these are rising.*

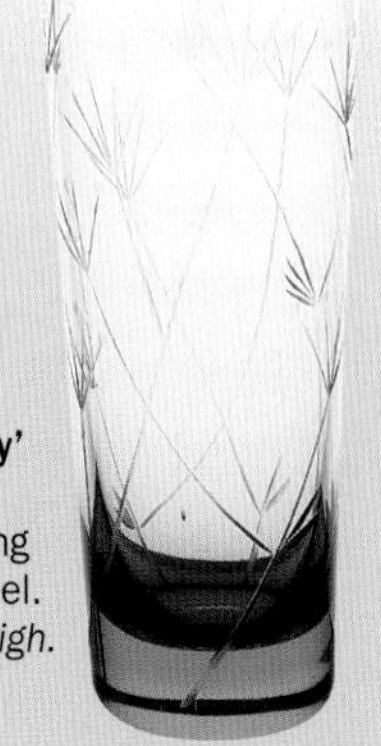

**A Geoffrey Baxter engraved 'Cow Parsley' vase.** The pattern is engraved by hand, using a spinning cutting wheel. *c.1955, 22cm (8¾in) high.*

**£200–300**

## KEEP

*Textures and colours that are reminiscent of the 1960s and 70s represent a major part of Baxter's work. Pieces that are typical of Baxter's designs, the factory, and the period should rise in price and are worth keeping.*

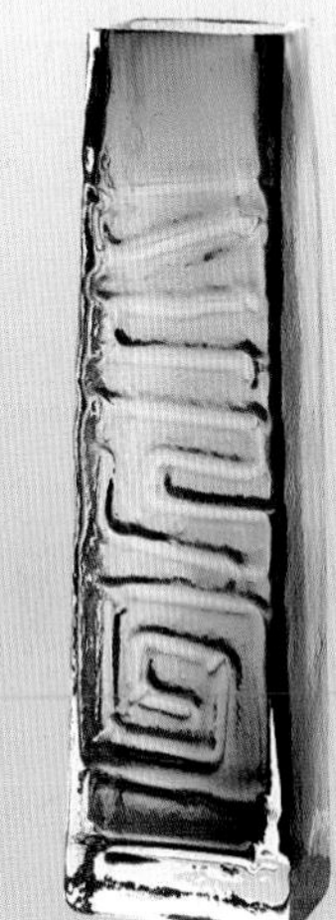

**A Geoffrey Baxter 'Totem Pole' Cinnamon glass vase.** The pattern on this vase was an innovation of Baxter's and is unique to Whitefriars. The texture was made by nailing a thick curling wire to the inside of the glass mould. *c.1967, 26cm (10in) high.*

**£180–220**

## SELL

*Although the internal bubbles are typical of Whitefriars during this period, small desktop items are relatively common. Pieces that have become less useful are unlikely to rise in value. Sell to a collector of writing accessories, and invest in one of the many more decorative and typical pieces instead.*

**Glass 'Parker 51' pen holder.** These glass deskbases were made by Whitefriars for the Parker Pen company. *1950s, ball 7cm (2¾in) high.*

**£20–30**

# Studio and factory glass

in Britain after World War II showcases great British design. It is colourful, modern, and often excitingly experimental. Much of it remains relatively affordable, although this could change as it becomes better known.

**A Wedgwood blue glass fruit bowl,** with knopped stem. *1970s, 23cm (9in) high.*

**£50–80**

During the 1950s and 60s, many British glassmakers were heavily influenced by the newly fashionable Scandinavian styles. Their bright colours, pure clarity, and clean lines struck a chord in optimistic post-war Britain. One of the leading British glass designers to fall under their spell was Ronald Stennett-Willson. Elegantly restrained, his designs offered a distinctly English slant on Scandinavian modernism and were very popular in their day. He designed for two different factories: King's Lynn and Wedgwood. Examples of his work can be found at collectors' fairs and car-boot sales from as little as £10–20 for a small 'Brancaster' candlestick, to around £100 or more for a larger vase. His most characteristic designs, such as 'Sandringham', are likely to fetch more.

## Modern production

Stennett-Willson set up King's Lynn Glass in Norfolk in 1967, specifically to produce glass in the modern style. As well as being typical of his work, the 'Sandringham' service is also one of his most successful, along with the now eagerly collected, technically demanding 'Sheringham' candlesticks. Made in various sizes and colours, 'Sheringham's' outstanding feature was the series of glass discs that make up the stem. These range in number from one to nine: the more discs there are, the higher the value of a piece. Examples in clear glass with one or two discs are generally worth around £10–20 but larger examples with nine discs can fetch over £1,000. The simpler, hollow-stemmed 'Brancaster' candlesticks, also in various heights and clear colours, are notable, too. They range in value from £10–20 for a small coloured example, to around £100 for larger pieces. Sets are highly prized and cost more. The designs are fragile, but the clarity of the glass ensure that any damage is usually easy to spot.

The 'Studio' range of large, mould-blown floor vases is also popular. These came in a variety of colours and finishes from a highly coloured, striated, tortoiseshell effect, to single colours used in the Scandinavian manner to show off the pure and varying intensity of the glass. Many pieces are cased and are similar to the Scandinavian examples that influenced them, although they are often more symmetrical in form. In 1969, King's Lynn Glass was taken over by Wedgwood Glass, which continued to produce Stennett-Willson's designs, but with an acid-etched Wedgwood mark.

**Two Dartington Glass candle holders,** design attributed to Hans-Eric Anderson in 1968. *c.1970s, tallest 18.5cm (7¼in) high.*

**£30–40 each**

### *Did You Know?*

*As part of his commitment to Scandinavian design, the English maker Ronald Stennett-Willson employed Swedish glassworkers to train his workforce at his King's Lynn glassworks in Norfolk.*

## Surface value

Influenced by the Scandinavian trend for textured surfaces in the 1960s and 70s, Stennett-Willson produced pieces with a variety of textures ranging from bark to the lunar surface. These usually have a shallower relief than examples by Whitefriars, a useful identifying feature. Prices are still low compared to many Scandinavian pieces. His textured glass wares can range from £50–70 to around £100–150 depending on size, colour, and form. Any clear glass pieces must be in

## A closer look at... two textured 1960s vases

Textured surfaces, often inspired by Scandinavian glass of the period, were popular in the 1960s and 70s. But why is one of these textured vases twice the price of the other? Important considerations include the pattern, the factory, and the designer.

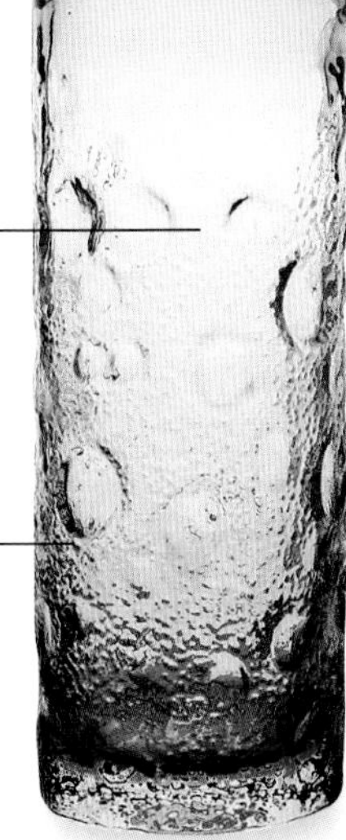

This vase is brightly coloured with excellent clarity and attractive variations

The abstract moulded design is well executed, showing good variation in the relief

**A King's Lynn Glass yellow textured glass vase**, designed by Ronald Stennett-Willson. This range was designed to commemorate man landing on the moon, hence the lunar texture. *c.1969, 26cm (10in) high.*

**£80–120**

The colour is dull, uniform, and less attractive

The glass is thinner and of inferior quality

**A grey/green textured glass vase, with abstract flower and geometric patterns.** The two patterns do not work well together. It is unmarked and is not by a notable maker or designer. *1960s, 30cm (11¾in) high.*

**£20–30**

perfect condition because chips and scratches will be all too obvious. An unusual pattern, shape, or a large size will add to a piece's value.

### The Devon connection

A former colleague of Stennett-Willson's, and another devotee of the Scandinavian style, Frank Thrower went on to set up the Dartington glass factory at Torrington in Devon in 1966. Together with Peter Sutcliffe, who ran the Dartington Hall charitable trust, they hoped to bring commercial prosperity to the area. Thrower was appointed director and chief designer.

During his 20-year career until the late 1980s, Thrower was responsible for over 90 per cent of the designs produced by Dartington, creating more than 500 designs. These were mainly for tableware, such as wine glasses, and their simple lines combined the modernism of the period with the principles of Scandinavian design. Thrower's work met with popular acclaim and many designs remain in production today.

During the 1960s and early 70s, his vase designs for Dartington were often cylindrical or square, with concave and convex moulded patterns or textured surfaces, many of them in the form of stylised flowers such as daisies. They were produced in a range of rich colours, from 'Kingfisher' turquoise to 'Midnight' smoked glass.

These are commonly found today, and often feature trumpet-shaped lips. Values are still low compared to other makers, with vases regularly fetching around £30–50 to £300 for rare, early examples.

**A Wedgwood pink glass 'Sandringham' candle-holder, designed by Ronald Stennett-Willson.** *1970s, 18.5cm (7¼in) high.*

**£40–60**

### Top Tips

- Identify Stennett-Willson's work in company catalogues and specialist literature by the initials RSW and a model number.
- Look at marks to find out when your piece was made. From 1969, King's Lynn Glass used a short-lived etched mark and paper label incorporating a crown above the word 'LYNN'; 'Wedgwood Glass' was etched on the bottom from 1969–87.
- Check glass candlesticks and holders carefully for heat cracks from burning candle stubs; never allow candles to burn right down.

### BUY

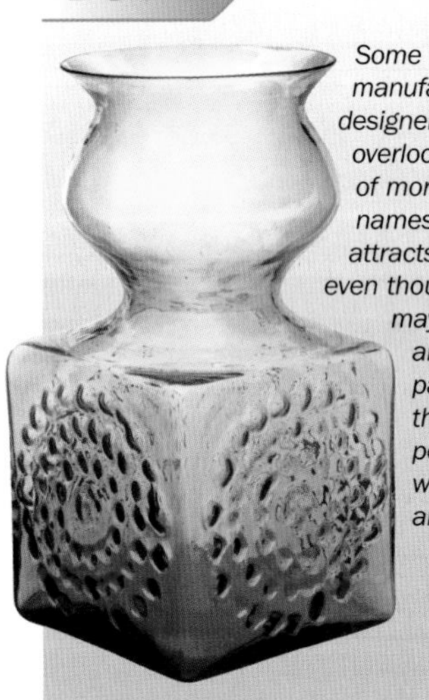

*Some influential manufacturers or designers are often overlooked in favour of more famous names, so their work attracts lower values, even though they may have played an important part in creating the look of the period. Buy while prices are low.*

**A Dartington Kingfisher blue vase,** with moulded dots pattern and shaped top with flared rim, designed by Frank Thrower. *15cm (6in) high.*

**£50–80**

### KEEP

*Key designs by notable designers will always retain their value. Look for designs that sum up the age, and are also representative of, or possibly unique to, that designer and factory. Many fine-quality designs from the 1960s still have some way to rise in value and certainly won't fall.*

**A Wedgwood 'Sheringham' candlestick designed by Ronald Stennett-Willson.** This was one of his most notable designs for a major manufacturer. *c.1967, 23cm (9in) high.*

**£200–250**

## A Scottish slant

During the 1960s, the newly-established Caithness Glass factory began producing its own range of Scandinavian-influenced glass in John O'Groats, Scotland. It was designed by Domhnall O'Broin who worked for Caithness in the early to mid-1960s. Its distributor, Edward Bowman, was also the British distributor for the Scandinavian factories Holmegaard and Kastrup, so he was able to advise Caithness on best-selling styles.

As with Scandinavian examples, Caithness vases and glasses were mould blown and had thin lips and heavy, cased bases in a range of strong, pure colours. But the shapes and colours were much more Scottish in inspiration: there were ranges called 'Stroma' and 'Lochsheil' (both historic Scottish sites) made in colours called 'Heather', 'Peat', and 'Loch Blue'. The subtle tints and clean lines of these early ranges, produced from the mid-1960s until the 1980s, have a timeless appeal but also capture the understated good taste that was a key feature of modern post-war design. Today, Caithness is better known for their paperweights, and appreciation for its earlier pieces is only just materialising. Recognition has also been hindered because most of these pieces are unmarked, although some still retain their original factory labels: these bear the letters 'CG' and the words 'Made in Scotland'.

### Did You Know?

*Do you remember those 1960s drinking glasses with the bright yellow, round 'smiley face' motif? A psychedelic symbol during the 1960s, the smiley face has been recognised and reproduced ever since. It was originally devised in 1963 by the American artist Harvey Ball for a company who wanted to give staff a morale boost by handing them badges printed with the face. Drinking glasses bearing the 'smiley face' motif are worth around £3–6 today.*

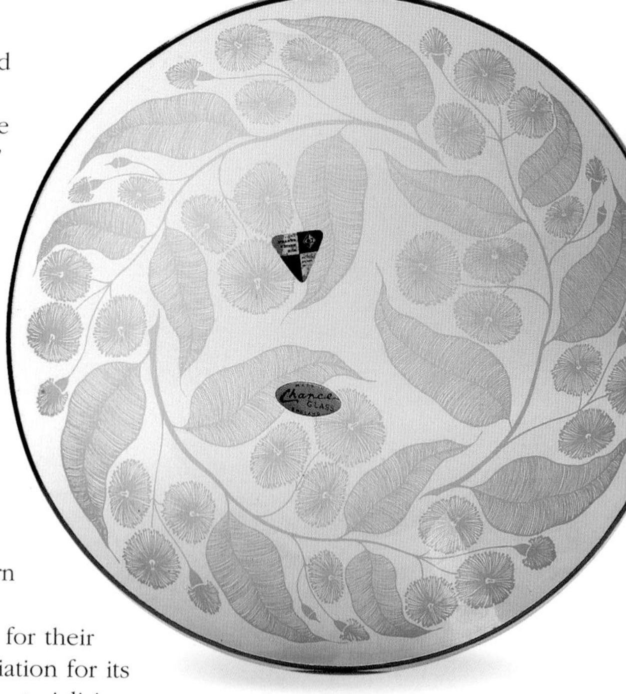

**A Chance 'Calypto' pattern plate,** designed by Michael Harris in 1959, with 'Design Centre' sticker. *c.1960s–80s, 23cm (9in) wide.*

**£8–12**

## Taking a Chance

Chance Brothers of Birmingham produced a vast amount of popular, inexpensive domestic glassware from the 1950s to the 1970s, which has now become collectable. In 1951 the Festival of Britain was awash with graphic patterns and scientific motifs, and Chance caught the mood of the time with its winning range of 'Fiesta Ware'. This had gilded rims and linear designs in thin, clear glass that was 'sag moulded': flat plates of glass were heated until they literally sagged into the shape of the mould. Modern patterns were then applied to the under- or inside by screen printing. Flattish dishes dominate, although items such as carafes and glasses are also found. All of them share simple lines with a minimum of moulded decoration and fitted perfectly with the Modern aesthetic prevalent in the 1950s. Different patterns were regularly added to keep the range up to date. Most of the designs were printed in white, with floral designs dating from the mid-1950s onwards; different colours, such as turquoise, are mainly from the 1960s onwards. Look for examples that capture the style of

**A Chance Glass ruby flashed intaglio cut dish.** *1950s, 22cm (8¾in) diam.*

**£15–20**

the decade, such as 'Swirl', introduced in 1955 and 'Night Sky', introduced in 1957 and designed by Margaret Casson. As well as Casson, Chance also employed designers such as Michael Harris, who went on to found the Mdina Glass and Isle of Wight Studio Glass factories. Harris was responsible for a number of designs, such as 'Calypto' with its curving leaf motif, introduced in 1959, and 'Anemone', one of the colourful floral patterns that he brought out during the 1960s.

**A Chance black-and-white psychedelically striped 'Handkerchief' vase.** The form was copied from the Murano vases designed at Venini & C. *1960s, 10cm (4in) high.*

**£30–50**

## A major production

Chance glass was produced for more than 30 years in a huge variety of patterns, and many people could afford it. Since there is so much of it still around, in people's homes or at popular venues such as car-boot sales, good condition is essential. This proliferation also keeps values comparatively low: expect to pay from £10–15 for a plate, with mint-condition pieces often fetching around £30–50. More unusual shapes such as carafes and letter racks will usually fetch more but they rarely rise above £70–100.

Its well-known and instantly recognisable moulded 'Handkerchief' vases can fetch more, perhaps due to their eye-catching colours and patterns. Introduced in the 1950s, they often had striped or chequered patterns screen-printed on the outside. One of the last patterns, 'Gingham', was introduced in 1977. Values range from around £5–30 for small pieces, up to around £30–50 for larger examples. The rarest patterns will receive £50. Its post-war glass is marked with labels printed 'Chance' or 'Chance Glass', except for the 'Fiesta' range which has its own 'Fiesta' label.

## Bohemian rhapsody

Another form of factory-produced glass that was very popular, and is still commonly found today, came from Czechoslovakia. The most affordable pieces were made from pressed glass. In 1965, the small number of factories that produced it were amalgamated under the name 'Sklo Union', and it is by this name that the glass is known to collectors.

Recent research has uncovered the names of designers, and interest is growing rapidly. Forms tend to be modern and clean-lined, with geometric or abstract moulded patterns that focus on the optical properties of glass. Colours were often bright, including green, orange, and sky blue. The most collectable pieces are vases, but ashtrays and tablewares were also produced. Values range from £10 upwards, with a very few by notable designers such as Frantisek Vizner, fetching over £100. Cut glass also

### Top Tips

- Caithness Glass made in the 1960s had labels bearing a 'CG' logo and 'Made in Scotland'. Glass from the 1970s–90s was labelled 'Caithness'.
- Look for original Chance boxes: these increase desirability and value.
- Consider buying Czech glass from the 1950s–70s as pieces from this period are often modestly priced.
- Give preference to brightly coloured Czech glass, or their clear engraved or textured clear glass; it is more sought after.
- Only buy Czech factory glass that is in excellent condition, unless very rare.

### BUY

*Some mid-20th-century factories are still being researched, so few people are familiar with their work. Pieces by notable factories that were not produced in vast numbers could make excellent buys and should rise in value as interest and demand grow.*

**A 'Heather' Caithness Glass lamp base, designed by Domhnall O'Broin, with its original factory label by the lip.** The clean lines and colour, which was inspired by Scottish heather, are typical of this factory's designs. *c.1967, 25.5cm (10in) high.*

**£50–60**

### BUY

*Interest in, and values for, Sklo Union designs have risen over the past few years. Keep an eye out at car boot sales and charity shops, as many people do not recognise them yet. Prices should continue to rise as demand grows.*

**A Sklo Union Rodolfova glassworks green pressed glass vase**, designed by Rudolf Jurnikl and produced from 1964. This is typical of the avant garde designs being produced at the time. *1970s, 23cm (9in) high.*

**£60–80**

underwent a transformation, becoming similarly geometric and abstract, and moving away from traditional natural or heraldic motifs.

The work of designers such as Vladimir Zahour and Josef Pavec is sought after, and may fetch £200–1,200 depending on size and quality. Also look out for vibrantly coloured 'freeblown' glass that resembles Murano glass of the period. Curving, bud-like forms are typical, and many pieces are cased in colourless glass, and heavy in weight. Designed by Jan Berànek for the Skrdlovice glassworks, Miloslav Klinger for the Zelezny Brod glassworks, or Josef Hospodka for the Chribská glassworks from the 1950s–70s, prices currently range from £30–150 depending on size, shape, and colour, although these may rise.

**A Sklo Union Rosice glassworks light blue pressed glass vase,** designed by Vladislav Urban in 1967. *1970s-80s, 20cm (8in) high.*

**£50–80**

**A Chlum u Trebone mould brown 'garnet' glass vase,** designed by Jan Gabrhel in 1962. *c.1970s, 16cm (6¼in) high.*

**£30–40**

## Mdina magic

The designer Michael Harris was the force behind two increasingly popular post-war names: Mdina Glass in Malta, and Isle of Wight Studio Glass. Still very affordable, their designs are colourful and handmade, making each one unique. Many people may have pieces at home which they bought on holiday; they are now commonly found at carboot sales, and collectors' fairs.

Mdina glassmakers produced glass in bright colour combinations such as the blues, greens, golds, and ochres inspired by the Maltese coast.

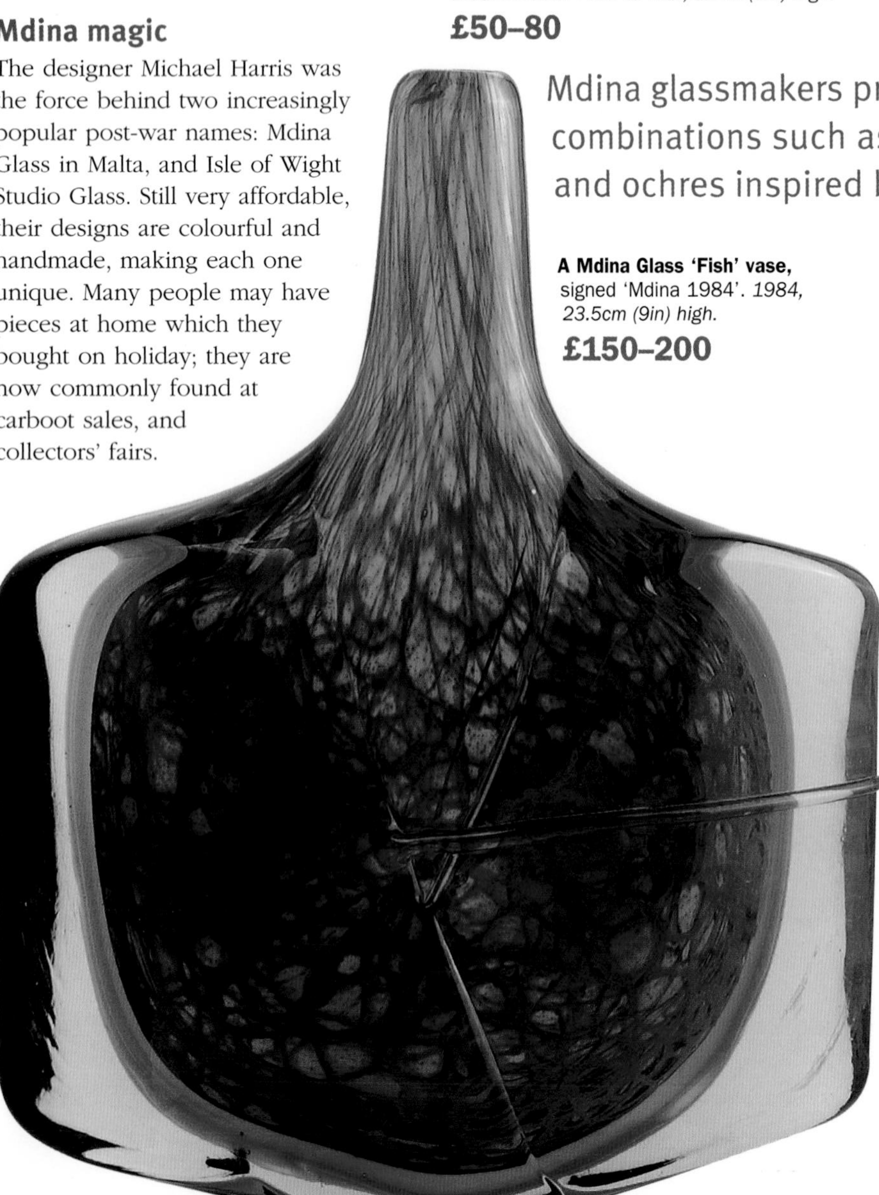

**A Mdina Glass 'Fish' vase,** signed 'Mdina 1984'. *1984, 23.5cm (9in) high.*

**£150–200**

## A fresh approach

In the 1960s, Harris was a glass tutor at the Royal College of Art, and went on to set up Mdina Glass in 1968 with the intention of exploring glassblowing in a new community.

With a financial backer, Eric Dobson, and two Italian glassblowers from Whitefriars, Ettore and Vicente Boffo, Harris trained local glassmakers from scratch. Because these glassmakers had no preconceptions, Harris was able to encourage them to approach the subject in an unconventional way, and free from bad habits. The Mdina glassmakers produced pieces in bright colour combinations such as the blues, greens, golds, and ochres inspired by the Maltese coast and the sunbaked landscape of the island.

These early Mdina pieces, including dishes, cylindrical, and curving 'Fish' vases, and goblets with unusual craggy stems are the most avidly collected. Many of the pieces are boldly inscribed 'Mdina' on the bottom, or bear Mdina paper labels; others are unmarked but their colours instantly identify them.

## On the rise

In the 1960s and 70s, Mdina produced textured vases, often in the sand or brown colours in vogue at the time. Values vary, but although still low, they have been creeping upwards over the past five years; this trend shows signs of continuing. A small vase may fetch around £10–30, while very attractive pieces may rise to around £40–100. Larger examples tend to be rarer, mainly because more small, easy-to-pack pieces were made for Malta's burgeoning tourist industry.

A large piece in typical colours and one of Harris's characteristic shapes can fetch up to £150 or more. Pieces signed by Harris himself command a premium and are extremely rare because he was there for only four years. A curving Mdina 'Fish' vase made from 1969–72, and signed in the usual way may fetch around £400–600, but Harris's signature can make the price leap to around £1,500, depending on size and complexity.

**A Mdina Glass goblet**. *1970s, 19cm (7½in) high.*

**£60–90**

## Modern times

Harris left Malta in 1972 but production continues to this day, initially under the management of Eric Dobson and after 1981 under one of his apprentices, Joseph Said. Many of Harris's original designs are still being produced but, as they tend to be undated, it can be difficult to tell which pieces are old and which are new. The new ones are much less desirable so look out for the classic colours and styles associated with Mdina. Older pieces often show signs of wear such as a light criss-crossing network of scratches on the bottom, caused by moving pieces around during cleaning or use.

**A sand and tortoiseshell-coloured Mdina Glass vase.** *1970s, 20cm (7¾in) high.*

**£40–60**

### *Did You Know?*

*In addition to the signature, two logos may be found on labels stuck to Mdina glass: the Maltese Cross for Malta and a tower. The tower showed the real-life one that Harris had originally chosen as the home for Mdina glass when he moved to the island with his family in the 1960s. But the Maltese government intervened and the factory ended up being set up in a disused airfield.*

## A closer look at... an Isle of Wight Studio Glass vase

Studios such as Isle of Wight Studio Glass are highly creative, and many unusual variations of various ranges were produced. A number of these are highly sought after, particularly if in large sizes or rare colours. To determine whether a piece falls into this category, look closely at its colour, size, style, and any markings.

The large size of this vase makes it very rare

This colour was unpopular, which means comparatively few examples were sold

It shares the iridescent finish of other designs in this range

**A large Isle of Wight Studio Glass 'New Kyoto' vase,** designed by Michael Harris. This range was produced for only two years from 1986, and was unpopular when released. Unusually, the base carries a 'broken' pontil mark, and also has an Isle of Wight Studio Glass black triangular sticker, which helps to date it. *c.1986–88, 35cm (13½in) high.*

**£200–300**

## Island studio

Harris's next move was to set up the Isle of Wight Studio Glass factory near Ventnor in 1972. His first ranges, such as the blue 'Seaward', 'Tortoiseshell', and 'Blue Aurene', are similar in colour to some of his Mdina pieces. Despite this, Isle of Wight glass is generally thinner than Mdina glass, weighs less and is often more finely blown. From around 1974, the base was stamped with an impressed pontil mark of a stylised gather of glass in a flame – the gather is the lump of glass from which the glassmaker produces his art. Paper labels were also used from the mid-1970s and their style can help to identify the manufacturing date; in the 1980s, for instance, triangular stickers were used. From 1981, the impressed pontil mark was discontinued and bases were machined and polished flat. Values vary from around £30 upwards; plenty is still available at well under £100, such as small vases. Larger pieces, or those signed by Harris, will fetch around £100–400 or more.

As well as the early ranges, look out for key designs such as 'Undercliff' and 'Azurene', a 1979 Design Council award winner. Produced in many different colours including pink, blue, and black, its surfaces are decorated with overlaid squares of fused silver and gold leaf. It was also produced in various shapes including 'onion' and curving 'Fish' vases – shapes originally designed at Mdina – as well as cylindrical vases, paperweights, and miniature perfume bottles. Values for Isle of Wight glass are rising fast but smaller pieces can be found for around £15–30.

## Going solo

Due to the profound influence of the American studio glass movement of the 1960s, many British artists at that time began working on their own. The development of a type of low-temperature, hot-blown glass allowed a generation of young glassmakers to abandon factories and work independently in studios, hence the name studio glass. Here they were free to follow their own ideas and explore the random nature of glassblowing. Although expensive, studio pieces may

**A striated studio glass bottle with a spherical stopper,** by American Scottish glassmaker, Ed Iglehart. *1990s, 20.5cm (8in) high.*

**£70–100**

become the 'antiques' of tomorrow, particularly the one-offs. Over the past decade, they have started to appear more often at auctions and collectors' fairs. Limited editions will often be more modestly priced than one-offs as there are more of them.

This is still a developing area, although the top end of the market is already well established, with prices ranging from £300–800 into the thousands of pounds. For example, some works by celebrated artists such as the American, Dale Chihuly, can cost tens or even hundred of thousands of pounds. Look instead for pieces by some of the less well-known but established British names; their pieces often cost less, fetching anything from £200–300 upwards.

**A 'Blue Aurene' Isle of Wight Glass dish,** with a 'gather of glass' impressed pontil mark visible in the centre. *1974–c.1982, 16cm (6½in) wide.*

**£70–100**

## Cream of the crop

'The Glasshouse', which was set up in London's Covent Garden in 1969, was a studio, gallery, and glassmaking co-operative that attracted the cream of young British glassmakers. Early members included Annette Meech, Steven Newell, Pauline Solven, Peter Layton, and Sam Herman. Herman, who introduced a glassblowing course at the Royal College of Art, revelled in the freedom of blowing hot glass. He made brightly coloured vases with decorative swirls in an almost painterly style, as well as more subdued coloured pieces. His glass is usually signed and highly sought after, fetching anything from £200 upwards, depending on the size, date, shape, and pattern. Other collectable names include Tessa Clegg and Anna Dickinson. More affordable designers include Anthony Stern, Siddy Langley, and Ed Iglehart, whose works can often be found for around £50–150. John Ditchfield of 'Glasform' also has a large and dedicated following. With a career stretching back over 35 years, he is still producing today and is known for his vases, bowls, and paperweights in iridescent glass; he often uses natural motifs and animals as inspiration.

**A Peter Layton flattened oviform cased glass vase** decorated with a freeform blue and yellow patination. *1980s, 17cm (6¾in) high.*

**£150–200**

### Top Tips

- Look for blue, turquoise, and green Mdina glass; these are the most popular, followed by 'tortoiseshell'.
- Consider investing in unique signed studio pieces; although more expensive they should appreciate in value.
- Studio glass should be marked; examine the base carefully because signatures can sometimes be hard to read or recognise.
- Limited editions should have marks to show the number of the piece and how many were made.

### BUY

*Isle of Wight glass is generally finer blown than Mdina glass and comes in a larger range of colours. Designs by Michael Harris are becoming more desirable, particularly those from discontinued ranges. Prices are likely to rise.*

**A 'Seaward' range Isle of Wight Studio Glass vase with a rough, unimpressed pontil mark.** 'Seaward' was one of the first ranges designed by Harris at Isle of Wight and was produced for a short period of time, so makes a good buy. *1973, 11cm (4½in) high.*

**£80–120**

### KEEP

*Signed pieces by notable protagonists of the studio glass movement are growing in popularity. Each piece is usually hand blown, so its colours and patterning will be unique. Look for items that are typical of an artist, and check that the piece is signed; prices for representative works hold their value well and are likely to rise.*

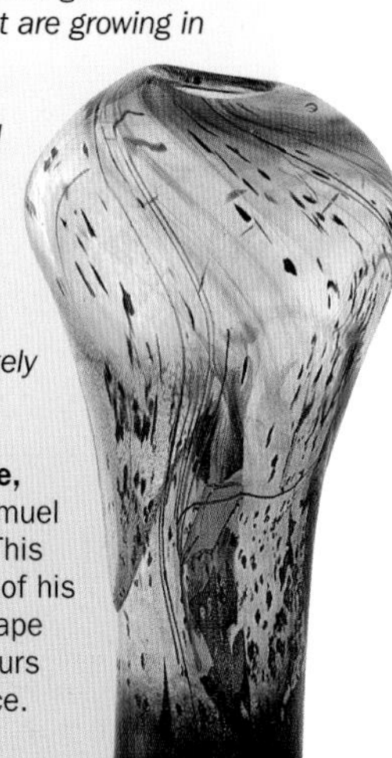

**A Sam Herman glass vase,** signed on the bottom 'Samuel Herman' and numbered. This vase is a typical example of his work, with its freeform shape and swirling different colours with patches of iridescence. *1970s–90s, 27cm (10½in) high.*

**£500–700**

# Murano glass brought Italian art glass back to the forefront of international design. Some of the best-crafted, most vibrant, and desirable examples were made during the post-war boom from the late 1940s to the 60s.

**A Fratelli Toso *murrine* vase,** with yellow and white *murrines* over an amber base, and two yellow handles. *c.1910, 10cm (4in) high.*

**£400–500**

If you are lucky enough to own some Murano glass from this golden period, it could be worth a small fortune – especially if it is by a top studio, such as Venini & C.

The small island of Murano in the Venetian lagoon has been home to glassmakers since the 14th century, and its glassworks have always borrowed freely from each other. Studying the best wares will help you to spot good-quality pieces by lesser-known designers and factories, which are available at more modest prices *(see overleaf)*.

Dramatic colour combinations were used in stripes, patchworks, swirls, and free abstract designs. Talented designers used glass in original ways, sometimes applying traditional Venetian decorative techniques to new fluid forms.

## Leading the revival

Paolo Venini, co-owner of the Venini & C glassworks, was also a designer, and his glassworks employed other fine designers such as Carlo Scarpa and Fulvio Bianconi. Scarpa developed the techniques that Venini was known for, such as *tessuto*, which uses criss-crossing, finely striped canes to create an effect resembling woven fabric. In 1934, he started using the *sommerso* (submerged) technique, casing (that is, covering) the main colour with a thin layer of another colour and then a layer of clear glass.

Bianconi used coloured *tesserae* (tiles) to create the dramatic 'Pezzato' (patchwork) vase and the bold stripes on the 'Spicchi' (segments) vase. The *fazzoletto* (handkerchief) vase series – shaped to resemble a scrunched-up handkerchief – was designed by Bianconi and Venini and produced in various sizes and styles from the 1950s. Originals fetch around £200 or more but good copies are available for less.

## A change of scale

The leading studios also produced less expensive, often witty, items. In the 1950s and 60s, Venini made fish-shaped paperweights, giant eggs, and two-colour egg-timers in different sizes. Prices start at £150 for smaller sizes.

## Some designers to look for:

- Paolo Venini
- Carlo Scarpa
- Dino Martens

**A Venini decanter, or stoppered bottle, designed by Fulvio Bianconi** in 1952 and produced into the 1960s and beyond. *1952, 21.5cm (8½in) high.*

**£700–1,000**

**A *tessuto* vase designed by Carlo Scarpa for Venini & C.,** with etched mark 'Venini Italia 81' and labels. Scarpa's design dates from 1940. The 1980s reissues, like this one, fetch less than the originals. *1981, 32.5cm (12¾in) high.*

**£600–900**

**A vase designed by Dino Martens for Arte Vetraria Muranese,** with white spirals (*latticinio*) and coloured canes. Martens' designs in the 1950s are typified by his abstract use of bright, contrasting colours and by his asymmetrical shapes. He also created designs for the company Aureliano Toso. *c.1952, 35.5cm (14in) high.*

**£1,500–2,500**

## A closer look at... a *murrine* vase by Vittorio Ferro

The designer-led tradition at Murano continues today, with contemporary names becoming as sought after as their predecessors. One of the most prestigious designers of today is Vittorio Ferro. As well as looking for notable designers, it is worthwhile learning about the decorative techniques they use. In a *murrine* piece, slices of glass canes are used to form a mosaic. A hot clear glass body is then rolled in the tiles, so that they stick to the glass surface.

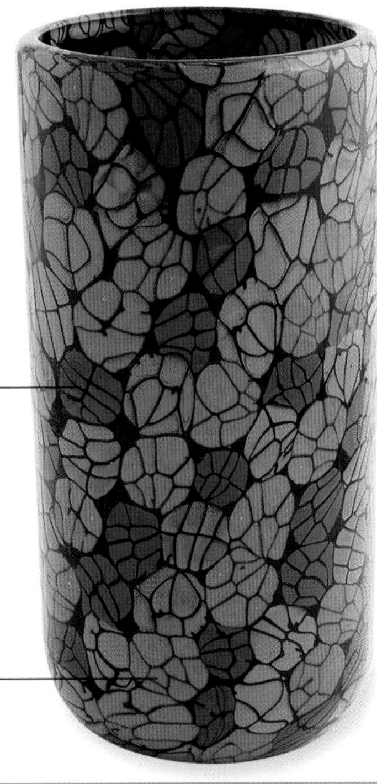

These tiles started off as long, multicoloured glass canes, which the glassmaker cuts into mosaic-like pieces and 'melts' onto the body of the vase in a furnace

The contrasting, bright colours, which are typical of the 20th-century Muranese tradition, and the black lines in each section, are hallmarks of Ferro's designs

**A contemporary *murrine* vase,** in blown glass, designed and made by Vittorio Ferro. Ferro comes from an established glassmaking family and his work is increasingly sought after around the world. The vase is signed and dated on the base by the artist. *2000, 26cm (10¼in) high.*

**£800–1,200**

### Top Tips: the finest art glass

- Check Venini pieces for an acid-etched identification stamp on the base – look closely because this mark can be difficult to find and read.
- If you find a Murano piece with a label (some Murano originally had a paper label with an outer layer of foil, often now missing), you can use the style of the label to help identify the period.
- Examine fine-quality Murano pieces to familiarise yourself with the size, weight, thickness, and close-up appearance of originals. This will help you to identify unmarked pieces.
- Because many top designs have been skilfully copied, only buy expensive investment pieces from reputable dealers or auction houses.
- If you cannot afford substantial pieces from the quality makers, consider smaller-scale items from anonymous factories. Small unmarked eggs can be picked up for less than £100. Egg-timers can be found for £150–200.

## ▪ Flavio Poli ▪ Gio Ponti ▪ Fulvio Bianconi ▪

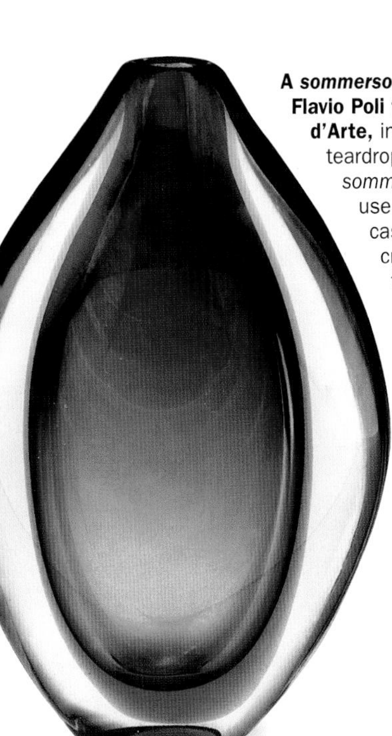

**A *sommerso* vase designed by Flavio Poli for Seguso Vetri d'Arte,** in the shape of a teardrop. Poli, known for his *sommerso* designs that use contrasting coloured cased glass, often created curving, flowing forms. *c.1955, 26cm (10¼in) high.*

**£700–1,000**

**A Venini & C. bottle vase designed by Gio Ponti,** marked 'Venini Murano ITALIA'. Work by Ponti is often characterised by broad bands or stripes in bright colours. *1946–50, 29cm (11½in) high.*

**£300–500**

**A Venini & C. 'Pezzato' vase designed by Fulvio Bianconi,** made from joined panels of coloured glass. His 'patchwork' vases are among his most sought-after designs. *1950s, 22cm (8¾in) high.*

**£3,000–4,000**

## Starting small

The colour, vibrancy, and wit of post-war Murano glass was not the sole preserve of major factories and designers. A host of traditional, smaller workshops produced quantities of more affordable Murano pieces, and although these shared some of the same features as more luxurious pieces, they were often aimed at the tourist trade. They also borrowed and adapted new designs by the great names. These pieces epitomise the style and colour of Murano glass, if not always the quality of the originals.

Modestly priced Murano glass can be found at collectors' fairs, charity shops, and car-boot sales. Striking colours and innovative designs are sometimes combined with traditional Venetian decorative techniques, such as stripes and *latticinio* (a white, milk-coloured glass made in thin threads and arranged into a spiral or net pattern), and cut facets and contrasting colours.

## The *sommerso* menagerie

The *sommerso* technique used by the leading glass designers was also used by other Murano glassworks to make a wide variety of decorative glass items, including animals. While a signed piece by a well-known factory will be expensive, there are plenty of good unsigned or unattributed items that cost much less than £100. Larger pieces are more likely to appreciate in value than smaller ones, as they are less common and their visual impact also makes them popular.

*Sommerso* ashtrays were produced in vast quantities in the 1950s and 60s at a time when smoking was still stylish. These are readily found in rounded shapes and with facet cutting, and often cost less than £60.

*Sommerso* vases come in a variety of shapes from geometric to abstract free-form, often incorporating generous curves. Free-form pieces with extending rims or peaks tend to cost more; they are also vulnerable to damage. The geometric vases have cut facets that reflect the light in eye-catching scintillations. They can be picked up for £25–100.

### *Did You Know?*

*Venetian glassworks were set up on the nearby islands, rather than in the city itself, to protect Venice from the fire hazard posed by the glassmaking furnaces.*

## Colourful characters

Animals and character figurines have been a staple of novelty and souvenir items since the 1950s. They were produced in large numbers by skilled workers. Their appeal and price depend on the quality of workmanship and their condition. Look for fine detail, originality, and complexity of design. Clowns and musicians were favourite subjects. The figures were made in pairs, usually male and female, often depicted in elaborate historical costumes. A pair is more desirable and valuable than a single figure, and they can range from £15 to around £100 each.

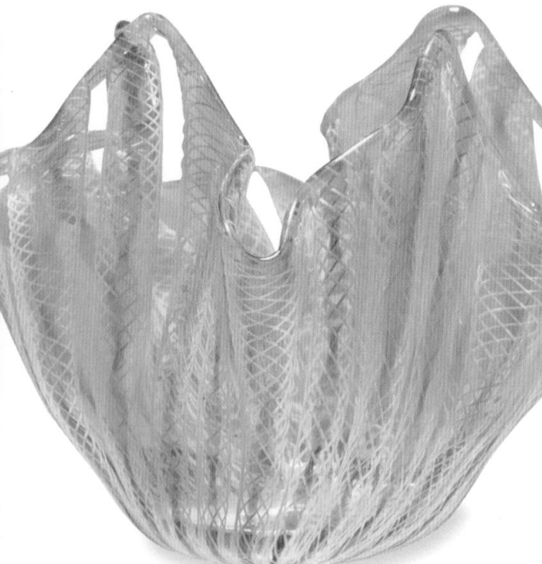

**A Murano *fazzoletto* vase,** decorated with bands of *latticinio*. *1950s–70s, 10cm (4in) high.*

**£50–120**

**A Murano yellow geometric *sommerso* vase.** *1960s, 16cm (6¼in) high.*

**£50–60**

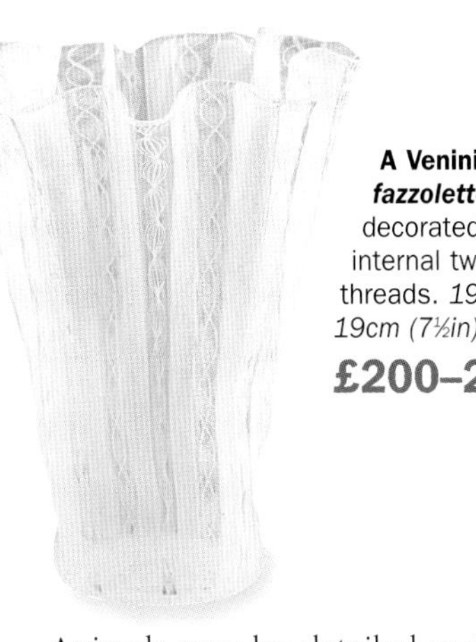

**A Venini & C. *fazzoletto* vase,** decorated with internal twisted white threads. *1950s, 19cm (7½in) high.*

**£200–250**

Animals may be detailed and realistic, or more stylised. Dogs, cats, and birds are popular, as are fish. A 25cm (9¾in) high 'Scottie' dog from the 1950s may fetch around £80–100.

These wares were often assembled from small pieces of glass, so are vulnerable to breakage. Any damage or repair will reduce the value, so check carefully before buying a piece by feeling along any potential fracture sites – sharp edges are a warning sign.

## Novelty value

There are no hard and fast rules when it comes to collecting novelties. The more ingenious, charming, or humorous they are, the greater their appeal and the higher the price they are likely to fetch. Size and quality also affect price. Most pieces command less than £100. Typical Murano novelties include glass eggs (copied from the successful Venini range of the 1950s and 60s), egg-timers, and animals.

Many of these novelties are still made today. To be sure that you buy a genuine vintage piece, check it carefully for signs of age, such as light and criss-crossing scratches on the base, accumulated from years of being slid across the surfaces on which they have stood.

Souvenirs and small novelties made in the last 20 years are unlikely to rise in value. It is best to buy or keep them because you like them, rather than as an investment.

## A closer look at... two 1950s *sommerso* novelties

Many novelty-shaped *sommerso* pieces were produced in the 1950s, and can make a colourful display. Smaller pieces are more common, as they were mass-produced as souvenirs – impulse buys that could easily fit into a tourist's well-packed suitcase. The larger pieces, more refined in design, were produced in smaller numbers and were also more vulnerable to damage, making them scarcer today.

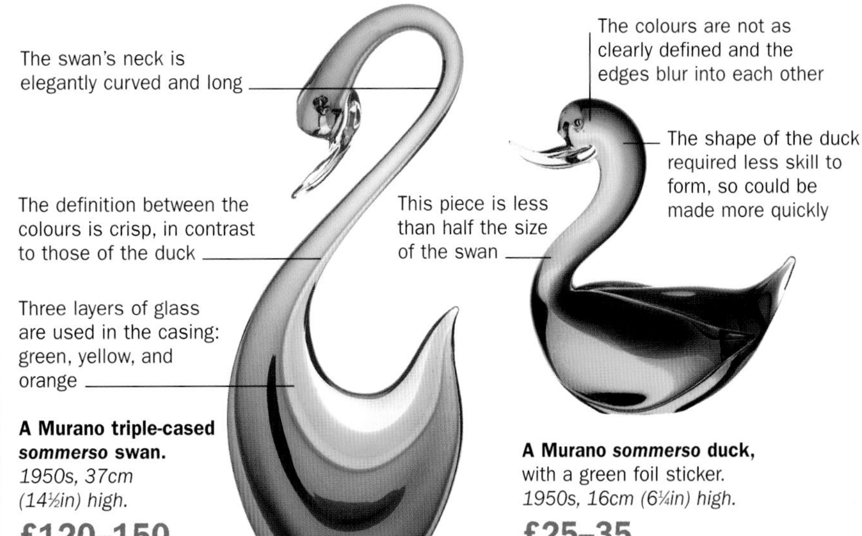


**A Murano triple-cased *sommerso* swan.** *1950s, 37cm (14½in) high.*

**£120–150**

**A Murano *sommerso* duck,** with a green foil sticker. *1950s, 16cm (6¼in) high.*

**£25–35**

### *Top Tips: lesser factories*

- Look for pieces with bright, contrasting colour combinations, fluid shapes, and exuberant designs.
- Avoid *sommerso* glass with rough patches or scratches – the glass should be smooth.
- Run your finger along the top, bottom, and any sharper edges to check for tiny chips.

## BUY

*Although many unsigned* sommerso *pieces have been produced, large, impressive examples are worth buying, especially those with strong colours that show off the technique to its best advantage. Pulled, extending rims and fluid, curving forms are also popular. Pieces in excellent condition should rise in value.*

**A Murano triple-cased green, amber, and red *sommerso* vase.** The shape of this vase resembles a stylised owl, with its typically large eyes. *1950s, 27cm (10½in) high.*

**£150–200**

## KEEP

*The* fazzoletto *vase is Venini's most popular design. Signed pieces are becoming harder to find and, with so many copies available, signatures are vital. It is worth keeping the larger pieces and those with differently sized frills. As demand outstrips the limited number of good signed pieces available, prices should rise.*

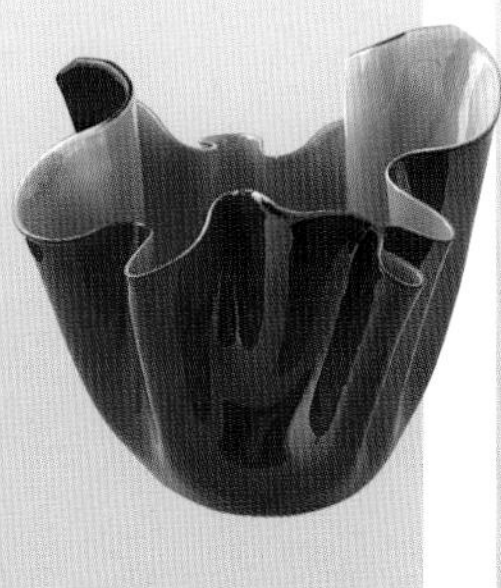

**A Venini cased *fazzoletto* vase,** with red exterior and white interior, and acid etched mark. This piece is unusually coloured, with a contemporary look. *1950s, 19.5cm (7¾in) high.*

**£300–400**

## SELL

*Murano glass is less likely to increase in value if it does not have the characteristic colours and forms. If a piece is made by a minor factory or is unsigned, its appeal lessens still further. But pieces that have retained their foil labels will be fairly easy to sell.*

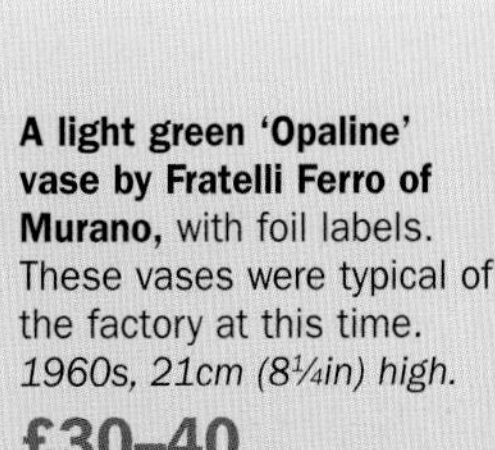

**A light green 'Opaline' vase by Fratelli Ferro of Murano,** with foil labels. These vases were typical of the factory at this time. *1960s, 21cm (8¼in) high.*

**£30–40**

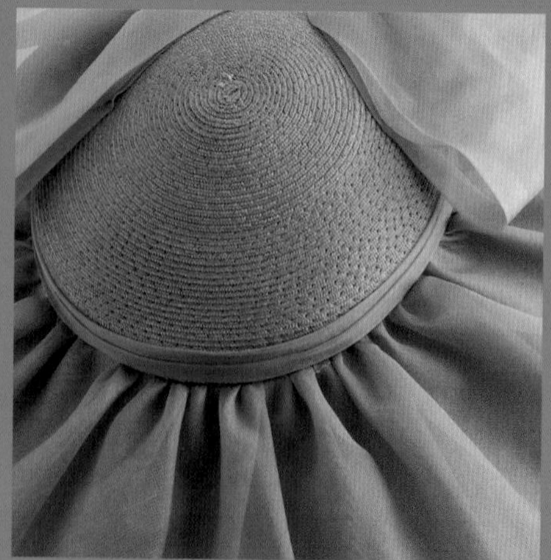

MOVADO

# Beauty and Fashion

The whole spirit of a decade is captured in its fashions. From the frivolity of the 1920s to the austerity of the war years, the optimism of the 1960s to the brashness of the 80s, clothes, jewellery, and fashion accessories are the perfect barometer of their time.

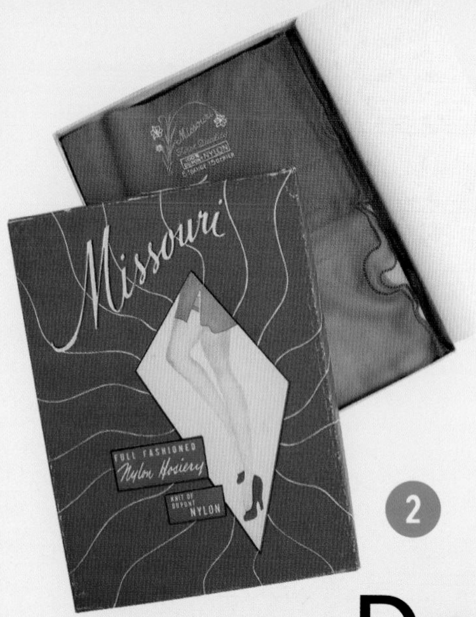


1950s nylon stockings, p.176

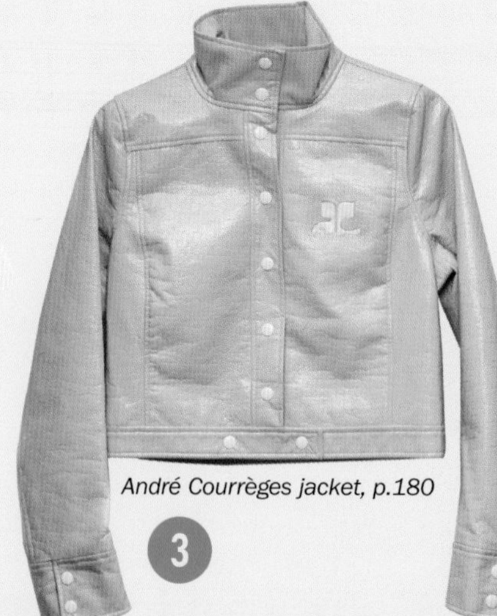


André Courrèges jacket, p.180

Art Nouveau brooch, p.202

# Dedicated followers....

**Fashions may change, but the trend for vintage clothes shows no signs of diminishing. Much of the attraction lies in wearing unique clothes that help you stand out from the crowd; another advantage is that they are often beautifully made.**

Beaded flapper dress, p.175

Twenties flapper dresses ①, nylon stockings from the 1940s and 50s ②, 1960s miniskirts, and even punk bondage trousers from the 1970s are becoming increasingly sought after as more and more people want to own a piece of fashion history.

Look for pieces that are in good, and, where possible, original condition. Part of the appeal of Victorian shawls and flapper dresses lies in the beauty and cut of the fabric and the quality of decoration. Even vintage underwear has a market, so do not overlook a pair of bloomers which has been passed down through the family.

## All in a name

If you enjoy poking around in charity shops and at jumble sales, bear in mind the names people often look out for. For couture outfits, the crème de la crème – Chanel and Christian Dior from the 1930s onwards, and Schiaparelli from the 1930s to the 60s – are the ones to spot. Iconic 1960s designs by Pucci, Pierre Cardin, Courrèges ③, Biba,

1940s wedge-heeled mules, p.188

1960s Gucci bag, p.187

Look for pieces that typify an era and are in good and, where possible, original condition.

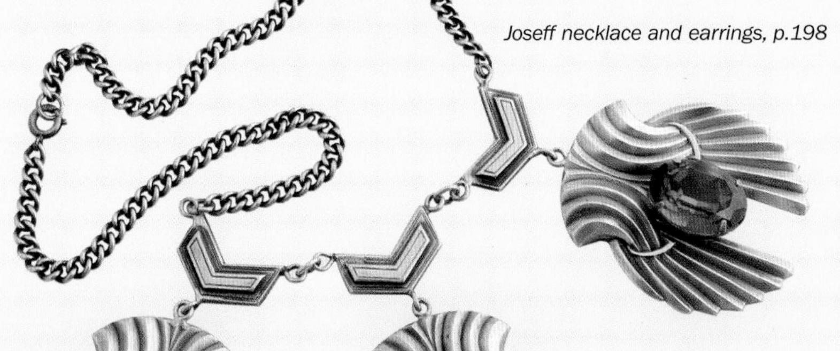
Joseff necklace and earrings, p.198

# .of fashion

and Mary Quant are highly desirable, while pieces by the queen of punk, Vivienne Westwood, from the 1970s onwards have become increasingly collectable. But labels are not everything. Flared jeans and platform shoes from the early 1970s are hotly contested when they come up for sale.

## All that glitters ...

Vintage jewellery ④, whether real or costume, is another growing area. Gold and silver rings, earrings, necklaces, and brooches set with precious or semi-precious stones have an intrinsic value which is enhanced by good design or a famous name. Although costume jewellery ⑤ is not made from precious stones, stylish pieces and those by named designers which typify a particular period are popular. Look out for pieces by Trifari, Miriam Haskell, and Christian Dior.

Accessories such as shoes ⑥, handbags ⑦, hats ⑧, and powder compacts ⑨ are also prized. Distinctive, stylish, well-made pieces are always a good buy and are worth holding on to if you are lucky enough to inherit them. Labels are less important here; many early 20th-century bags are not labelled at all and others are by makers who have long been forgotten.

Watches – ranging from gentlemen's hunter pocket watches ⑩ to early wristwatches – have always been collectable. Today, even 1970s steel digital watches are sought after by enthusiasts.

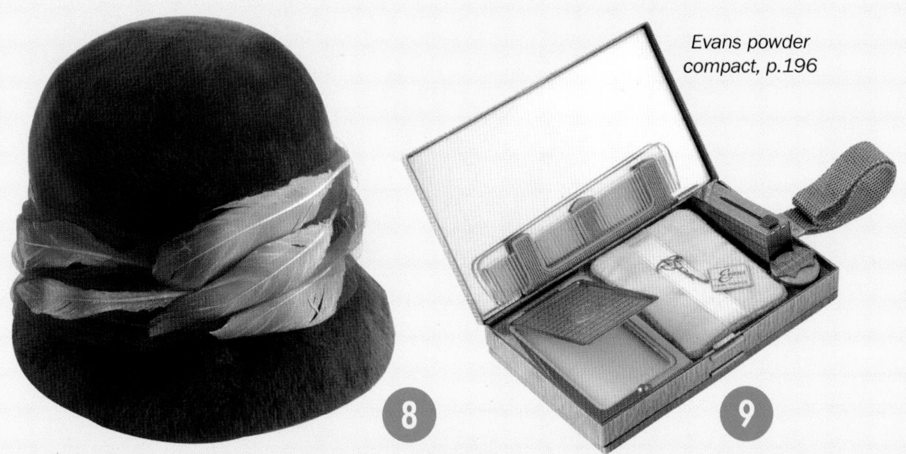
1950s Christian Dior hat, p.178

Evans powder compact, p.196

Waltham hunter watch, p.204

# Vintage fashions from the early part of the 20th century reflect radical social changes, as well as being often beautiful. Many pieces were worn only once or twice and it is still possible to find gorgeous garments at relatively low prices.

**Black silk evening jacket, embroidered with ivory oriental motifs.** *1930s, 61cm (24in) long.*

**£100–150**

Between 1910 and 1930 women went from wearing figure-hugging, full-length clothes made from reams of fabric to the slim shimmer of the beaded shifts beloved of the 'flappers'. Fashions changed so fast that dresses were often discarded after a season, so many are still in top condition. Prized pieces can be picked up in house clearance sales and specialist street markets. At the top end of the scale, auction houses and vintage clothes shops have reaped high prices for exquisite, well-preserved items.

Late Edwardian women were tightly corseted into long dresses, or jackets and blouses with a long skirt. Pastel colours were fashionable, but in an era when mortality rates were high, black predominated. Early 20th-century clothing is trimmed with buttons, bows, pleats, puffs, lace, and frills, all of which are easily damaged or lost. Expect to pay £200–300 for a black silk-velvet cape from the early 1900s, and £200–500 for an Edwardian embroidered white cotton dress.

One drawback with much early clothing is that it is usually small by today's standards, and unlikely to fit anyone taller than 1.60m (5ft 3in) with a waist larger than 65cm (26in). This is irrelevant to some collectors who feel

**An American *eau de nil* green chiffon dress, with train.** *1910s, 127cm (50in) long.*

**£100–200**

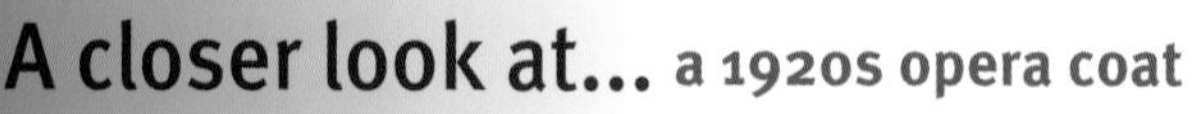

## A closer look at... a 1920s opera coat

Many sumptuous creations were designed for ladies to wear in the evenings, and some are still wearable today. As well as shape, consider the material used and any decoration, as this can increase desirability and value.

The striking pink silk-velvet material is a hallmark of quality

The decoration is hand worked, with fine and intricate curling foliage and a geometrical pattern in metal beadwork, highlighted with pearls and diamanté

The shape is both extravagant and typical of its period, with scalloped 'bugle'-shaped sleeves and tails

**A pink silk-velvet opera coat.** The value would be higher if it were by a notable designer and bore a label. *1920s, 101.5cm (40in) long.*

**£500–800**

**A silk-velvet rose-print dress,** with decorative gathered panels. *1920s, 101.5cm (40in) long.*

**£200–300**

that these clothes should be preserved, not worn.

## Couture culture

Many women made their own clothes, or patronised a trusted dressmaker. Couture, which was worn only by the wealthy, was the finest bespoke fashion, and Paris was its capital.

Garments made from the mid-19th century onwards by the top couturiers, such as Charles Frederick Worth, Paul Poiret, John Redfern, and Jeanne Paquin, originally had labels, so check any likely garments carefully.

Paul Poiret stripped away decoration and banished the corseted shape. He created straight, high-waisted oriental-inspired dresses and loose kimono coats, using jewel colours, bold prints, and rich fabrics. When the European dance company Ballets Russes took Paris by storm in 1909, their Arabian costumes gave the public a taste for exoticism. In response Poiret took his designs a step further, creating kaftans, turbans, lampshade tunics, and harem pants. His garments are much loved but rare, with a powder blue chiffon and ivory silk tunic dress from about 1911 fetching upwards of £1,500.

Gabrielle 'Coco' Chanel gave fashion a sporty flavour, and her simple, chic creations suited the austerity of the World War I period. She designed sailor's-style boaters, berets, plain shirts, chemise dresses, overcoats, blazers, and two-tone shoes (based on men's spats). She also offered the earliest version of her famous cardigan suit, which came with an ankle-length skirt. Her early work (1910–20) is rarely seen outside museums: a major auction house or dealer might sell a piece for £1,000–1,500 or more.

## The Roaring 20s

Post-war exuberance fuelled the partying mania of the 1920s, when energetic new dances, such as the Charleston, raised hemlines to the knee. Flappers' dresses can be found for £200–800 or more, depending on the complexity of the design and decoration, and the quality of the fabric. In this decade, stylised floral and bold geometric prints were in demand for daytime dresses, which can often be found for less than £100.

Poiret's brand of exoticism and Chanel's casual elegance dominated clothing design in the 1920s. Shapes were simple and tubular. Well-endowed women bound their chests to flatten them.

Waistlines – if they existed at all – dropped to hip level. Sleeveless, beaded, shift-like dresses were popular for eveningwear. Bold young women started wearing wide-legged pyjama-style trousers on casual occasions. Examples can be found for £100–600, depending on the quality, but items by the top designers will cost more.

## Sleek silhouettes

In the early 1930s women's clothes became more streamlined and elegant. Couturiers such as Madeleine Vionnet and Gilbert Adrian started using fabric 'on the bias', particularly for evening gowns, as it enabled garments to be form-fitting yet comfortable. Hollywood stars promoted the look.

By the late 1930s couturiers such as Elsa Schiaparelli and Edward Molyneux began to look to Victorian styles for inspiration, and produced fitted suits and evening dresses with tight bodices and long, full skirts.

Good representative 1930s dresses can cost less than £100, but expect to pay around £1,000 or more for pieces by top designers.

### Top Tips

- Store beaded dresses flat – hanging them will encourage tears. Wrap them carefully in acid-free tissue paper.
- Expect tiny holes or some staining on pre-war garments, but avoid any garment that has extensive damage.
- Avoid any silk items with splits in the fabric or missing sections of thread: once damage starts, it is irreversible.
- Treat clothing well: light, dust, dirt, and the stress of handling can lead to deterioration.
- Do not wash or dry-clean clothes without consulting a textiles expert.

### KEEP

*Dresses or other items of clothing that are typical of the period in both style and fabric are desirable. Pre-war pieces were often altered during World War II when clothing was rationed. This reduces value considerably.*

**A silk dress and matching bolero.** The fabric of this unaltered day dress has an abstract pattern that was typical of the period, making it a desirable item which is likely to increase in value. *1930s, 119cm (47in) long.*

**£400–500**

### SELL

*Heavily beaded silk dresses were popular in the 1920s but they are difficult to keep in perfect condition – this is essential to retaining value. Prices have risen over the past decade for those garments still in top condition, so sell now while they are still looking good.*

**A beaded silk dress,** decorated in an Art Deco pattern. This dress is attractively beaded in an intricate pattern, so it would be appreciated by a serious collector for as long as the beadwork survives. *1920s, 81cm (32in) long.*

**£1,000–1,500**

# 1940s and 50s fashions

for women encapsulate the contrasting styles of these two decades. From severe wartime suits to feminine, full-skirted dresses, there is a wealth of fabulous, wearable clothes for discerning buyers.

**A pair of Missouri nylon seamed stockings,** with the original packaging. *1950s, box 18cm (7in) high.*

**£35–45**

A purist might prefer to keep her fine 50-year-old dress unworn, to avoid wear or damage. Some owners wear a prize garment only on special occasions; others, whenever the chance arises. It all depends on personal preference, or on the value of the item. Many collectors focus on a particular decade or style of clothing, and garments from the 1940s and 50s are both stylish and easy to obtain. Austere wartime designs can be very different from the ladylike elegance of 50s fashions, but pieces from both decades are highly sought after.

## Rationed fashions

In 1941 the British government announced the wartime Utility scheme, under which everyone was given 66 coupons a year to buy clothes. A wool dress 'cost' 11 coupons, a non-woollen one, seven. The scheme rationed the amount of fabric and number of buttons used to make a garment, and decorative trims were not allowed. All Utility fashions carry a 'CC41' mark.

Leading London couturiers, such as Norman Hartnell and Hardy Amies, created simple, elegant designs for the scheme. A typical suit had a long jacket with square, padded shoulders and a slightly flared knee-length skirt. The tailoring was particularly fine and these suits and coats still offer value for money, often costing less than £100. Some surviving 1940s fashions came from America, where there was little rationing and fewer shortages. Wartime evening wear was low-key and restrained and ranges in price from £50 to £100 or more, depending on quality, material, and style.

**An American embroidered, black velvet full-length dress.** *1940s, 124.5cm (49in) long.*

**£60–120**

## Head to toe

In this era of utility and thrift, hats were rarely worn. Turbans and headscarves were practical and inexpensive alternatives. A 1940s rayon scarf by Jacqmar of London may fetch £60–100, while a less well known name such as Thirkell can cost £20–40 or less. Headscarves were commonly tied under the chin, a fashion popularised by the royal family in the 1950s.

Silk and nylon stockings were scarce during the war years (1939–45), although American GIs seemed to have a ready supply of nylons. A boxed pair of unused nylon stockings from the 1950s will usually fetch £20–40.

## The 'New Look'

After the austerity of wartime, Christian Dior's first collection in 1947 was an explosion of nostalgic opulence. Inspired by Worth, the 19th-century couturier, Dior produced crinolined evening dresses, fitted jackets, and long, full skirts, all in understated, elegant colours. He accessorised his outfits with wide-brimmed hats, gloves, and stiletto heels. With its structured lines, stiff fabrics, round, padded shoulders, and cinched waists, this style was so different from wartime wear that it was christened the 'New Look'. An original Dior suit can be worth £800–1,200 at auction and an evening dress up to £5,000. But clothes made by less well known makers in imitation of Dior can often be found for under £100.

## Fifties femininity

Early 1950s fashion took its inspiration from the 'New Look' and was characterised by a feminine, hourglass

### Collectors' Tales

*'I was on the way home when I spotted a fantastic red tweed coat in a charity shop window. I've been collecting vintage clothes for ages so I could tell it was late 1950s. It came from Aquascutum, a brand popular with the "ladies who lunch". I bought it for £30, but it would probably have cost £300 from a specialist.'*

**Naomi Cartwright, Maida Vale**

silhouette, with full skirts over layered net petticoats, tiny, belted waists, and fitted tops. In reaction to Dior's retro corseted style, Coco Chanel came out of retirement in 1954 and relaunched her classic, straight-skirted suit to great acclaim. 1950s Chanel suits can now fetch £600–800 at auction.

Italian Emilio Pucci produced some of the first designer leisurewear and his 'ski slacks' and cropped Capri trousers are now synonymous with the 1950s. His simple sundresses and shirts were also widely copied. Pucci introduced the 1950s look of separate co-ordinates in bold colour combinations, such as orange and pink, or lemon and red.

## Early street style

By the mid-1950s, teenage girls began to rebel against ladylike fashions. They wore circle skirts, ankle socks, and penny loafers. Artistic types dressed in a uniform of dark glasses, polo necks, skinny black trousers, and ballet pumps. All this heralded the street styles that dominated fashion in the late 20th century.

## Bargain buys

As with all vintage fashion, general condition and the quality of the fabric affect prices, as do a piece's provenance and scarcity. It is also worth looking out for items made when a talented designer was working at a particular couture house, such as clothes designed by Yves Saint Laurent for Christian Dior in the late 1950s. Clothing by designers can be expensive, but if you avoid the big names, you can find some wonderful clothes at reasonable prices, often cheaper than their modern equivalents. The best places to look are large markets, vintage clothes shops, charity shops, and car-boot sales.

**A red and green rose-print dress.** *1950s, 100cm (39½in) long.*

**£100–150**

## Top Tips

- Buy what you like and what suits you. Always try things on, as dress sizes have changed over the years.
- Check for damage and avoid clothing with major alterations, worn fabric, stains, or broken zips or fastenings.
- Use a steamer to remove creases from clothing: do not iron as this can leave a shine on some fabrics.



## BUY

*Worn by everyone from the Queen to Hollywood stars such as Grace Kelly, scarves are emblematic of the 1950s look. Hermès scarves were among the most popular, and today they are increasingly hard to find, especially in good condition, and their prices are steadily rising.*

**A Hermès 'Chiens et Valets' pattern silk scarf,** designed by C.H. Hello. The design of this scarf is typical of Hermès, reflecting its equestrian heritage: the company began as a saddlery. *1950s, 89cm (35in) wide.*

**£100–200**

## KEEP

*Fashions that are representative of their period are worth keeping. During the 1950s, teenage styling was a new force in fashion. Look for baby blue and shell pink clothes, which were among the decade's most popular colours.*

**A felt full skirt,** with an appliqué poodle motif. Poodles are a classic feature of 1950s design. *1950s, 48.5cm (19in) long.*

**£50–80**

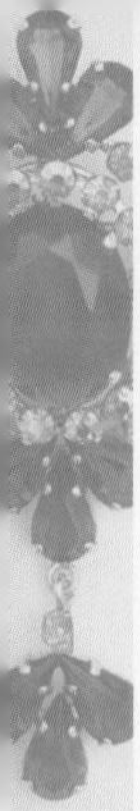

# Hats appeal to our sense of drama – and there's nothing like a vintage hat for turning heads. No longer an essential accessory, hats are still desirable and are becoming an increasingly popular collectable.

At the beginning of the 20th century, the hat was integral to women's fashions. Going out bareheaded was unthinkable and Edwardian ladies donned large hats decorated with finery ranging from ribbons to stuffed birds. Even in the 1920s, the emancipated flapper would not consider leaving home without her cloche hat.

In the early 1930s, wide-brimmed hats were in vogue, but by the end of the decade they had become much smaller and were accented with feathers and veils. During World War II, female factory workers wore scarves tied up in a turban style for safety reasons, which soon became a fashion statement. Although they were not rationed, hats were difficult to obtain during this period; some women contented themselves with eye-catching trims, while others felt justified in going bareheaded like their favourite screen actresses, such as Veronica Lake and Lana Turner.

Except for formal occasions such as weddings or the races, most 1960s women abandoned the hat in favour of exotic hairstyles and even wigs. But the hat was back a decade later. Designers of the 1970s emulated retro glamour – especially the famed New York milliner, Adolfo.

▲ **A Christian Dior blue plush hat with netting over the feathers.** In the late 1950s, hats based on the cloche became chic. This hat was probably originally purchased to match a navy coat. *1950s–1960s, 19cm (7½in) high.*

**£50–100**

► **A pale pink wool felt hat decorated with a feather and a black dotted veil.** The hat's dramatic decoration is inspired by Victorian millinery. *1930s, 40cm (15¾in) wide.*

**£120–180**

► **A brown straw cloche hat decorated with a satin band and lined with silk.** Cloche hats were so popular during the 1920s that they came to symbolise the decade. *1920s, 13.5cm (5¼in) high.*

**£100–150**

◄ **A black woven horsehair hat decorated with a velvet band and supported by a wire frame.** Older hats are often shaped using wiring or inner stuffing. Damaged or missing supports and linings lowers the value. *1930s, 49cm (19¼in) wide.*

**£40–60**

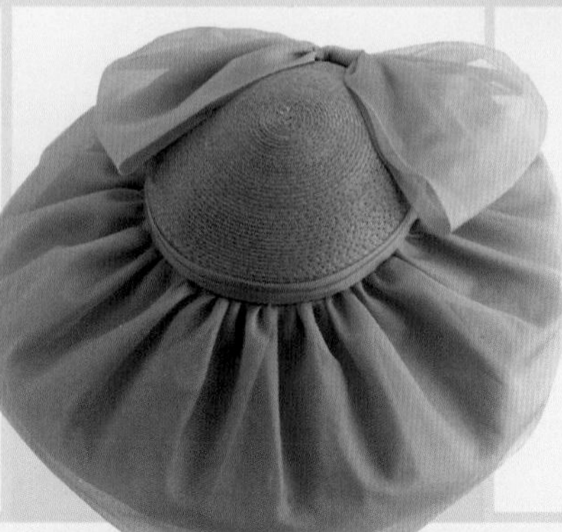

◄ **A grey/blue wide-brimmed straw hat covered with organza.** Wide-brimmed hats such as this one accented the elegant 1950s silhouette perfectly. The organza decoration is a reworking of a popular Victorian design. *1950s, 35cm (13¾in) wide.*

**£40–50**

◀ **A wide-brimmed straw hat decorated with a velvet band and roses.** This would have been worn to complement a formal outfit. Beware of holes in straw hats; they cannot be repaired. *1950s, 38cm (15in) wide.*

**£50–100**

## Collectors' Tips

- Look for 1920s cloche hats; these are now highly collectable
- Store hats in hatboxes, stuffing the crowns with acid-free tissue paper to retain their shape
- Use a hand-held steamer to reshape straw and felt hats; if badly crushed, ask a professional

▶ **An Adolfo blue straw hat decorated with simulated pearls, geometric shapes, and a simulated pearl hat pin.** As one of New York's best-known milliners, Adolfo's hats appealed to conservative, wealthy socialites. *1970s, 31cm (12¼in) wide.*

**£35–45**

◀ **A Kaystyle rayon scarf decorated with a wartime pattern.** Colourful wartime propaganda print scarves are now highly sought after. *1940s, 84cm (33in) wide.*

**£200–250**

▲ **An Elsa Schiaparelli multicoloured turban decorated with beads and faceted blue 'jewels'.** Shocking colours and outrageous design were a Schiaparelli hallmark. Her best-known hats from the 1930s looked like lamb chops, ice cream cones, and shoes. *1950s, 21cm (8¼in) wide.*

**£300–400**

# 1960s fashions marked a dramatic change in clothing styles for women. Today's designers are raiding the Sixties for inspiration, and authentic items by well-known names are in great demand.

Clothes from the 1960s represented either the dawn of the age of Aquarius or a hippie trip to Marrakech. The first look was minimal and futuristic. The second was flamboyant with ethnic overtones. Clothing in these styles and other key looks of the decade, including the A-line dress (like the 'Buy' dress: opposite) and the denim jacket (below), are collectable.

**A Levi's women's blue denim jacket.**
*1960s, 54cm (21¼in) long.*
**£50–100**

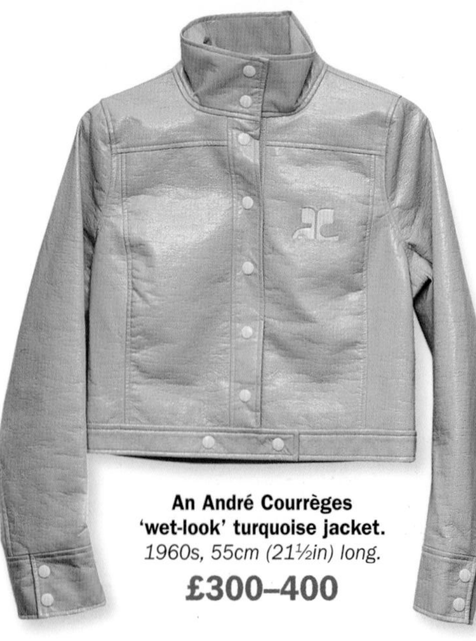

**An André Courrèges 'wet-look' turquoise jacket.**
*1960s, 55cm (21½in) long.*
**£300–400**

Have a rummage through the wardrobe of a willing 'Sixties child' for items of value. A wet-look jacket by Courrèges can fetch around £300, while an Ossie Clark blouse might be worth up to £750. It might be more economical to choose clothing inspired by the top designers or to look for stylish items from the original 1960s boutiques.

## Futuristic designs

America's mission to send a man to the Moon propelled fashion into the Space Age. In the mid-1960s the Parisian couturier André Courrèges created a look for sci-fi heroines – trouser suits, tunic dresses, miniskirts, and white go-go boots. His designs were stark and angular, often in white accented with Day-Glo colours. He embraced new synthetic materials, such as wet-look vinyl.

Pierre Cardin, another Parisian designer, made helmet hats, jumpsuits, and tunic dresses. He experimented with stiff, synthetic knits and used bold, contrasting colours, substituting black for Courrèges's white. Cardin also introduced geometric cut-outs and circular zip fasteners.

## Wearable fashion

British fashion designer Mary Quant opened her first boutique, 'Bazaar', on the King's Road, London, in 1955. She is credited with popularising the miniskirt, and her inexpensive, cutting-edge fashions were bright, simple, and well co-ordinated. In the early 1960s she designed the first range of British co-ordinates, with sleeveless and pinafore dresses in unique colour combinations.

**A black and white minidress,** in a bold geometric print inspired by Mary Quant's designs.
*1960s, 89cm (35in).*
**£50–100**

## Emilio and Ossie

Emilio Pucci's widely copied clothing combines futuristic and hippie styles. This Italian designer was known for his psychedelic prints, inspired by stained glass and Aztec art. Pucci's tunics, caftans, and harem pants regularly featured in classic 1960s *Vogue* photo shoots. He made his originals with silk in natural colours, but also used new fabrics and dyes.

Ossie Clark, in his heyday (1965–74), created floral gypsy dresses and peasant blouses with a sophisticated twist. He rejuvenated the elegant bias-cut of the 1930s and was a master of draping difficult fabrics such as crêpe and chiffon. His signature touch was a secret pocket for a key. Look for printed fabric designs created by his wife Celia Birtwell, a textile designer.

## Boutique glad rags

In London in the 'swinging Sixties', boutiques showcasing marvellously individualistic clothes were fashionable. Barbara Hulanicki's Biba store was influential, selling her floaty fashions, feather boas, and handbags. Today, anything linked to Biba is collectable. Quorum was another popular boutique, and Ossie Clark designed for them. Today's vintage boutiques are ideal places to search for 1960s clothing.

## A closer look at... two 1960s Biba dresses

Here are two dresses designed by Barbara Hulanicki for her London boutique Biba, which opened in 1964 and sold inexpensive fashionable clothes. Items with Barbara Hulanicki's unique 'retro' glamour are more sought after.

The elegant flowing lines and Deco-influenced pattern are typical of Biba

**A floral dress for Biba.** The romantic look and nostalgic print are characteristic of the late 1960s. *134cm (52¾in) long.*

**£200–300**

Short puffed sleeves and checked fabric date this mid-1960s dress

The brown checked pattern and shape of this rather plain dress are not in tune with today's fashions

**A brown checked dress for Biba.** *Mid-1960s, 138cm (54¼in) long.*

**£80–100**

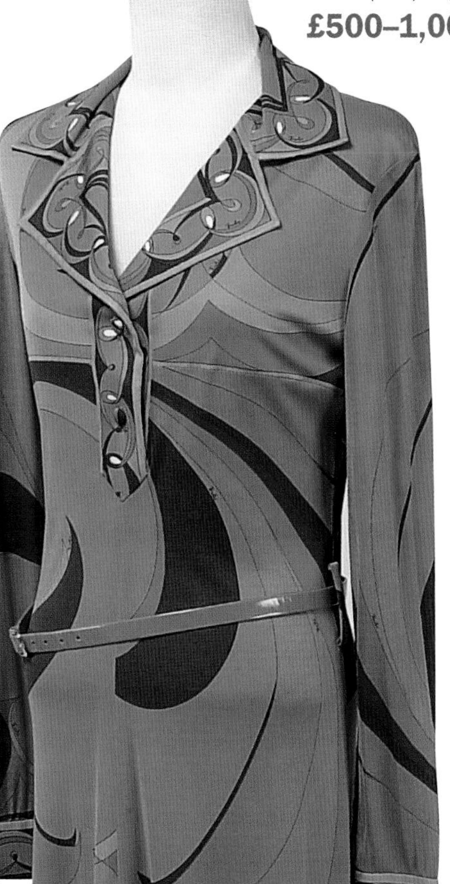

**An Emilio Pucci silk jersey dress,** made for Saks Fifth Avenue. *1960s, 112cm (44in) long.*

**£500–1,000**

### Top Tips

- Beware of rips and stains, particularly under the armpits: these lower the value.
- Avoid repaired, altered, or customised items – these change the original nature and design of the piece, making it worth less.
- Get to know the key looks and labels of the period – those from less-expensive, lower-quality ranges may not be so valuable now, but are likely to increase in price in the future.
- Be careful when handling clothing made of plasticised materials from the 1960s – it is fragile and may be brittle. Damage affects the value.

### BUY

*Vintage clothing that sums up the age is highly desirable. Consider the quality of the garment – the fabric, cut, and stitching – and buy the best you can if investment is the aim. If a piece is by a designer who led style, rather than followed it, the garment is sure to rise in value.*

**An André Courrèges navy and white dress.** The severe A-line cut is typical of the period. *1960s, 108cm (42½in) long.*

**£400–500**

### KEEP

*In the 1980s and 90s, Cardin hired out his name for use on just about anything, including frying pans, and this promiscuity devalued his original designs. Nevertheless, he was an innovative fashion designer and couture pieces from his 1960s collections are a good investment.*

**A Pierre Cardin Space-Age green and black block dress.** *1960s, 105cm (41¼in) long.*

**£600–1,000**

# Post-1960s fashion is a new collecting phenomenon among women. Clothing from the 1970s and 80s, once declared 'the decades that taste forgot', are fashionable once again, and owners are eager to wear their amazing vintage dresses.

**A Valentino print jacket** from a two-piece suit. *1980s, 48cm (19in) long.*

**£80–120 for two-piece suit**

Although designer clothing from the 1970s and 80s can fetch top prices, some items are more affordable: a Sonia Rykiel knit dress can fetch about £120–180. Learn about the top designers to recognise elements of fashion styles that represent the era. The best designers were imitated by major manufacturers such as Max Mara and Jaeger: these copies are available at reasonable prices – look in vintage or secondhand clothing shops. Top-quality pieces are often found at specialist dealers and auctions.

## Romance and elegance

During the 1970s, the British fashion designer Ossie Clark introduced a romantic look – wraparound dresses tailored to drape around the body. Bill Gibb, another British designer, created colourful layered dresses based on ethnic costumes and the traditional styles of the Scottish Highlands. These designs spawned many imitators and were key looks of the decade.

The Parisian Yves Saint Laurent was renowned for his chic trouser suits and *le smoking* – a tuxedo similar to those worn by glamorous 1930s stars such as Marlene Dietrich. Look for his flattering close cut and fit, using fine fabrics. The 'sophisticated peasant' look of the 1970s 'Russian' collection is popular, fetching from the low hundreds to many thousands of pounds for couture pieces or garments worn on the catwalk at major fashion shows.

## American style

Wraparound dresses were as ubiquitous as flares in the 1970s, and those by the American Diane Von Fürstenberg were bestsellers. Many can still be found in the USA and are often offered for sale on the Internet for around £150. Often associated with the decadent New York nightclub Studio 54, Roy Halston is another leading American designer

## Some designers to look for:

Gianni Versace ▪ Bill Gibb ▪ Diane Von Fürstenberg ▪ Vivienne Westwood ▪

**A Gianni Versace matching top and trousers.** Versace's extrovert style is apparent in the bright pattern. He was also known for first-rate craftsmanship and using quality materials. *1980s, 126cm (49½in) long.*

**£300–500**

**A Bill Gibb floral print dress.** Gibb was acclaimed throughout the 1970s for his skilful blending of colour, pattern, texture, and ornament. *1970s, 150cm (60in) long.*

**£100–150**

**A Diane Von Fürstenberg dress and matching jacket.** Von Fürstenburg wore a green version of this print on the cover of Newsweek in 1976. Her trademark design was the wraparound dress, of which more than 5 million were sold in the 1970s. *1970s, jacket 71cm (28in) long.*

**£100–200**

**A Hanae Mori blue diaphanous kaftan.** *1970s, 135cm (53in) long.*
**£400–450**

from this era. Look for his minimalist halter-neck dresses, kaftans, and flared jumpsuits, worth around £300–1,000.

## Punk rebellion

In the late 1970s, young people frustrated with establishment values dressed to shock. Torn T-shirts and jeans were worn and accessorised with safety pins. British designer Vivienne Westwood, along with Malcolm McLaren, promoted the punk and bondage craze on the catwalk. Today, tartan clothes, bondage trousers, and 'cheesecloth' T-shirts are snapped up at auctions. A bondage suit can be worth about £500–600 or more, while a cheesecloth 'Destroy' or 'Anarchy' shirt can fetch about £300–500.

## Dressed to impress

In the 1980s, designer labels were attached to everything from jeans to ballgowns and reflected the affluent mood of the decade. The Parisian designer Karl Lagerfeld joined Chanel in 1983, and his version of the classic Chanel suit, with a collarless jacket and short skirt, became a key look. These suits can be found for upwards of £300. The Italian designer Giorgio Armani is the other leading classicist. His suits were equated with success in business, and his early 1980s shoulder padding summed up the 'power suit' look.

The Italian Gianni Versace had a reputation for exquisite craftsmanship and design, often using loud colours and unusual materials and styles to create extravagant, showy clothing.

**A Vivienne Westwood bow dress,** with a printed tulip design, from her 'Pagan 1' collection. Westwood is known for giving traditional designs a new twist – as seen here in the innovative treatment of the bow. *c.1978, 92cm (36¼in) long.*
**£500–800**

### Top Tips

- Choose garments that define the look of a designer or an era.
- Look for items that are well tailored.
- Check that designer labels are original – although rarely cut out of garments, as they add value, they are sometimes sewn into non-original clothing to increase the price.
- Avoid garments that are torn or stained – don't forget to check under the arms for perspiration marks.

### BUY

*The French designer Christian Lacroix is credited with introducing the lavishness that was a hallmark of 1980s fashion. He is well known for using fabrics printed with bright multicoloured patterns. His distinctive pieces from the 1980s are increasing in popularity (and therefore value) as they sum up the era so well.*

**A Christian Lacroix *prêt-à-porter* jacket and shirt.** The bright colours and bold pattern are typical of this designer. *1980s, 45cm (17¾in) long.*
**£200–250**

### KEEP

*Missoni is an Italian family firm renowned for knitwear that uses intricate patterns. Their designs haven't changed much since its launch in 1969 and pieces tend to hold their value.*

**A Missoni knitted dress in blue, orange, and white.** The colours and the use of stripes are typical of this company. *1970s, 150cm (60in) long.*
**£600–700**

# Sunglasses of vintage quality have never been more collectable. From early Ray-Bans to 'Aviators' and 1950s novelty sunglasses, there is a huge variety of retro shades available and they may prove to be an invaluable investment.



Sunglasses first appeared in the 1880s, but only became popular in the late 1920s. Hollywood stars such as Joan Crawford and Cary Grant wore round sunglasses in the 1930s and the leading American brand Ray-Ban was founded in 1937. 'Aviator' sunglasses, worn by military pilots, first became popular during World War II.

Wraparound sunglasses were popularised by jazz musicians in the 1950s. In the late 1950s, novelty shades with decorated plastic frames were all the rage and are now highly collectable. Classic styles by Foster Grant and Ray-Ban generally fetch from £20 to £200–300. In the early 1960s, the trend was for space-age sun goggles. Later in the decade, John Lennon sparked a trend for wire-framed 'granny glasses'.

Designer shades were the 'must have' of the 1970s, especially those by Emmanuelle Khanh. *Playboy* was a big phenomenon in the 1970s, and memorabilia connected to the name is collectable today, fetching from around £30 to £150–200. The 1980s saw a return to retro shapes such as the 'Aviator' and Ray-Ban 'Wayfarers'. Cazal produced large frames that are now popular with hip-hop lovers, and a vintage pair can command up to £500 today.

▲ **French plastic wraparound sunglasses.** These glasses are made from a yellow snakeskin-effect plastic, and the 'wings' wrap around the wearer's face – both are unusual features that add to the sunglasses' desirability. *1950s, 12cm (4¾in) wide.*

**£150–200**

► **Women's novelty sunglasses.** 1950s and early 1960s novelty shades, such as this pair with fabric petals around the frames, are now very collectable. *1950s, 12.5cm (5in) wide.*

**£100–150**

► **Women's sunglasses with bronze spotted plastic frames,** made in America. The film star Lana Turner popularised this style and the 'bow tie' shape was much seen in the 1940s and early 1950s. *1950s, 13.5cm (5¼in) wide.*

**£20–30**

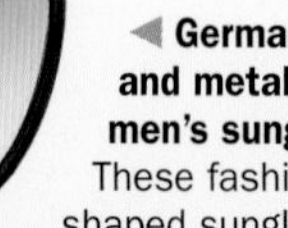

◄ **German black plastic and metal 'Playboy' men's sunglasses.** These fashionably shaped sunglasses, with a discreet bunny logo by the arms would have been a big hit. *1970, 14cm (5½in) wide.*

**£50–70**

◄ **Ray-Ban women's sunglasses** with blue flecked frames. Vintage shades from Ray-Ban command a premium. *1950s, 14cm (5½in) wide.*

**£70–100**

◀ **Yves Saint Laurent laminated plastic 'Aviator' sunglasses made in Italy,** with their original graduated coloured lenses. This large squared-off look was fashionable in the 1970s, and the fact that these sunglasses were made by a designer of international renown makes them even more collectable. *1970s, 14cm (5½in) wide.*

**£200–300**

▲ **Men's glasses,** in tortoiseshell plastic, made in Italy. *Late 1950s, 14.5cm (5¾in) wide.*

**£40–50**

## Collectors' Tips

- Watch out for scratched lenses, or damaged frames as these reduce value
- Look out for styles that are typical of a particular period
- Fakes of top names are common, so check a new pair against a pair you know is genuine

▶ **French diamond-shaped, laminated plastic sunglasses.** These sunglasses follow the avant-garde 'Op Art' movement of the 1960s, and are eye-catching and desirable. *1960s, 15.5cm (6in) wide.*

**£150–200**

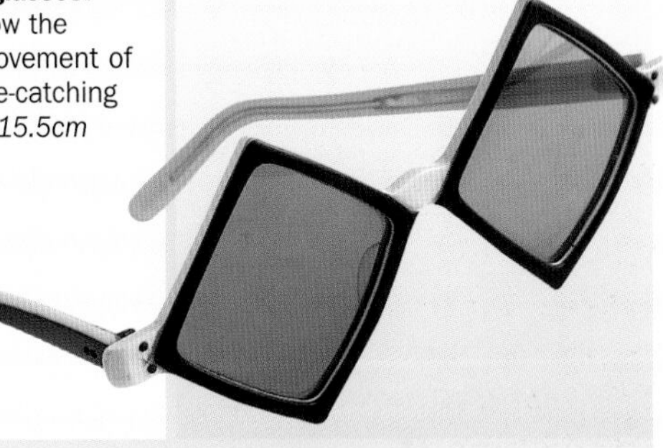

◀ **French 1960s tartan plastic sunglasses.** Made from tartan fabric laminated between layers of clear plastic, glasses like these were all the rage in the 1960s. *1960s, 13cm (5in) wide.*

**£100–150**

◀ **A rare pair of André Courrèges sunglasses,** with white plastic frames and slit lenses, marked 'France'. These are typical of the 1960s Space Age look. *c.1964, 15cm (6in) wide.*

**£200–300**

▼ **French pearlised, bow-tie shaped, laminated plastic spectacles.** Large sunglasses that covered the eyes, and often the eyebrows, were fashionable in the 1960s, as were bright colours. *1960s, 13cm (5in) wide.*

**£150–200**

# Handbags capture the glamorous fashions of the past century. A Hermès 1950s Kelly bag can be worth more than £1,000, but many desirable bags cost much less than £100.

**A beadwork bag** with a tortoiseshell-patterned plastic clasp and Art Nouveau shape and motif. *1900s, 15cm (6in) wide.*

**£100–150**

Handbags have grown in size and complexity in proportion to women's independence. In the early 20th century, most women were largely financially dependent on men. Handbags were correspondingly small and dainty, as they needed to hold very little. Some were so tiny that they could be clipped to belts or dangled from finger-rings.

The most popular styles from this period were the drawstring bag and the square, flat bag with a chain handle. Both types were often made of satin or leather, but most of the examples that survive are of fashionable beadwork, or metal mesh, which is like a delicate chain-mail.

Floral-patterned beadwork bags generally cost £100–200, but rarer designs, such as those with an unusual beadwork picture, tend to be slightly more valuable.

Mesh was sometimes chemically tinted or decorated with enamel discs. Most mesh bags, made from a base metal, fetch between £100 and £200; rarer gold and silver examples are usually worth substantially more.

By the 1920s a growing number of women were earning their own money, which gave them more independence. Meanwhile smoking had become a fashionable pastime and the use of cosmetics was all the rage. This resulted in a trend for larger bags, to accommodate the necessities of women's busier lifestyles. Daytime bags were made of cloth and leather, while glamorous, brightly coloured beadwork bags with Art Deco patterns were favoured for the evening.

**A 'beehive' bag** with a clear top inset with golden bees. *1950s, 14cm (5½in) high excluding handle.*

**£300–400**

## Look, no handles

Clutches – bags without handles – were predominant throughout the 1930s. These were some of the first women's bags to be given interior divisions to organise their contents. Clutches came in many sizes and in simple, geometric shapes. Some examples can be bought for less than £100 but expect to pay more for fine-quality materials. Simple, modern designs were sometimes given an exotic twist with materials such as snakeskin. Finely made bags of this type may sell for more than £100, while standard pieces often start at around £50. Seek out models with brightly coloured details such as clips in plastic (a new material at the time), as these can add value.

## Wartime wonders

World War II limited bag production in Europe, so most surviving 1940s bags come from the USA, which was less affected by rationing. British bags of the time were often made at home from items such as old clothes. Colourful felt appliqué bags, made

## A closer look at... a Gucci handbag

The Florentine maker Gucci has produced quality leather goods since the early 20th century, but the price of success has been a flourishing trade in fakes. Genuine Gucci bags have a leather or suede lining, which bears a gold stamp reading 'Made by Gucci in Italy'. Below are some further tips for distinguishing the real thing from counterfeits.

**A Gucci dark-navy-blue leather clutch bag.** The double 'G' logo signifying the luxury Gucci brand is recognised – and copied – globally. *1960s–70s, 28cm (11in) wide.*

**£100–200**

Examine the stitchwork, which on genuine examples will be perfectly regular and tightly sewn. If the stitching is coming apart or is cracking, the bag is probably a fake

Real Gucci is hand-finished and made from high-quality materials. The best leather is used – if the leather feels cheap, the bag may be a copy

Check the quality of the gold-plated trim – a fake Gucci bag will often have thin, worn gold plating even when the bag itself shows no signs of wear

from recycled fibre, were another wartime choice. These inventive bags tend to be less costly than those of the 1930s, as they are often inferior and less attractive.

### From frivolity to women's lib

In the 1950s, austerity gave way to frivolity and unabashed elegance. Novelty bags were the latest craze, especially in the USA – from wicker bags with felt fruit to rigid plastic box-shaped bags in bright colours. The latter were mostly made from an early transparent plastic called Lucite, and are much sought after, with prices starting at around £150–200.

The Hermès Kelly bag (named after Grace Kelly) was hugely popular for dressy occasions, and is possibly the best-known and most luxurious bag in the world. Genuine examples can command prices of more than £1,000.

The 1960s 'youthquake' favoured futuristic designs and ethnic decoration. Enid Collins' wooden boxes and Emilio Pucci's psychedelic patterned bags are among the most desirable examples from this era and often fetch around £50–400, depending on the condition, design, and rarity.

In the 1970s, with the advent of the Women's Liberation Movement, tote and shoulder bags became popular as practical alternatives to the briefcase. As with bags from the 1960s, many items are usually available for less than £50, although those by well-known names will usually be worth more.

### Status symbols

In the 1980s and 90s, women rose to top positions in business for the first time, and indulged in expensive outfits and luxury handbags. These status bags from élite makers are highly collectable in the current brand-conscious age. Names such as Gucci were popular in the 1980s, and the Prada rucksack was a highlight of the 1990s. Both often sell for more than £50–100. Look, too, for glitzy, witty handmade evening bags from the 1990s. One top-of-the-range example is Judith Lieber's crystal-covered animal handbags, known as 'minaudières', which often fetch around £400–1,000.

### *Top Tips*

- Don't buy mesh and beadwork bags with holes or missing sections – they are hard to repair.
- Avoid leather bags with dry, cracking, or rubbed surfaces – restoration is difficult and costly.
- Store handbags flat to avoid damage, especially to the handles.
- Keep handbags away from damp, heat, and direct sunlight, as exposure to these conditions can cause damage.

### BUY

*Many 1930s cloth bags, especially those made in costly metallic lamé, are still undervalued in comparison to beadwork examples. They make a shrewd buy for collectors on a limited budget.*

**A gold lamé evening bag.** The clip is made from paste, rather than precious stones. *1920s–30s, 16cm (6½in) wide.*

**£50–100**

### KEEP

*Collectors value 1940s felt bags, but it is difficult to find examples in good condition. If you have one that is, and you can keep it that way, the chances are that you will be rewarded with a good price when you eventually decide to sell.*

**A felt bag, with appliqué fruit.** The fresh colours of the appliqué motif make this bag both eye-catching and collectable. *1940s, 34cm (13¼in) wide.*

**£100–200**

# Vintage shoes appeal to women who want a unique accessory, as well as to collectors searching for display pieces. From delicate Edwardian items to 1970s trainers, there is plenty to choose from.

**A pair of novelty wedge-heeled mules,** made as souvenirs in the Philippines after World War II. *1940s, 31cm (12¼in) long.*

**£100–200**

Shoe styles have changed frequently since the 1900s, responding to the fashions of the day with startling rapidity. Whether for display or to wear, there are plenty available.

## Fashionably French

In the early 1900s women's footwear was robust. Lace-up boots were the first choice for everyday wear and had sturdy, waisted 'Louis' heels, a style that originated at Louis XIV's court in 17th-century France.

Shoes of the 1900s, which were reserved for formal occasions and evening wear, were also inspired by Louis XIV styles and modelled on 17th-century heeled slippers. They were often made from silk and decorated with embroidery, bows, and elaborate buckles. They came in pale colours, such as lilac and *eau-de-nil* green, and were worn with saucily patterned stockings. Prices start at around £100 and rarely exceed £300, unless the shoes are exquisitely decorated or made of fine materials, and can be found at auctions, costume dealers, and antiques and collectors' fairs.

## Straps and pumps

When hemlines rose in the 1920s, strappy shoes became fashionable. These came in dazzling colours, such as scarlet, emerald, and gold, and are highly collectable. Louis heels were still in vogue, and some shoes featured cut-away sides or peep-toes.

In the 1930s strappy designs were still popular, but streamlined pumps were the dominant style. Also known as court shoes, pumps were plain slip-on shoes with flat or raised heels, based on 18th-century footmen's slippers. They had rounded toes with slightly tapering heels and enclosed most of the foot.

## Platforms and wedges

Wartime rationing in the 1940s required leather to be reserved for the forces. So designers came up with statuesque platform shoes, made from cork, wood, fabric-covered plastic, felt, and straw. Forces' pin-ups, such as Betty Grable, made platforms seem glamorous and hugely desirable. Examples can often be found in charity shops, car-boot sales, and jumble sales for around £50 or less. Finer items, or those in better condition, can also be found at vintage and second-hand clothes shops and dealers.

The wedge heel, introduced by legendary Italian shoemaker Salvatore Ferragamo in 1936, was also popular. Examples by Ferragamo and his imitators can be found, generally at vintage clothes dealers, for around £50 and rarely exceeding £100–150.

The 1950s are associated with low-cut pumps with pointed toes and dainty stiletto heels. The heels on some stilettos were so sharp that women were banned from wearing them in certain buildings because of the damage they did to flooring. Roger Vivier, a Parisian shoemaker, made

## Essential shoes through the decades

**1900s** American glacé kid-leather day shoes, from Lord & Taylor of New York, with eyelets and ribbons. The Louis heel is typical of this period. c.1905, 22cm (8¾in) long.

**£200–300**

**1940s** A pair of grey peep-toe slingback platforms. Platforms of the 1940s were more streamlined than 70s versions. 1940s, 24cm (9½in) long.

**£20–40**

**1960s** A rare pair of Biba boots. A big fashion statement of the 1960s, boots were equated with youthful rebellion. 1960s, 58cm (23in) high.

**£400–500**

**1920s** Multicoloured lamé shoes with Louis heel, ribbon laces, and rosettes. The bright colours and fancy lacings of these evening shoes sum up the times. 1920s, 22cm (8¾in) long.

**£200–250**

**1950s** A pair of Pandora Footwear purple dévoré velvet evening shoes with stiletto heels. 1950s style is captured in these spiky-heeled shoes. 1950s, 25cm (9¾in) long.

**£100–150**

**1970s** A pair of wooden platform sandals decorated with plastic cherries. 1970s platforms scaled bizarre new heights. 1970s, 24cm (9½in) long.

**£50–100**

some of the finest examples. His gem-encrusted pumps are highly sought after and often exceed £2,000. You can also find simpler styles from around £20–30 upwards.

## A decade for boots

The youthful styles of the 1960s were reflected in the 'Mary-Jane' look (based on a child's button-up flats), often worn with mini skirts. Pumps with squared toes and heels were also typical of the time. Boots played a major role in 1960s style – from futuristic white plastic go-go boots to 'New Age' hippie boots – and, with the current fashion for retro styling, they can be expensive. Boots by popular names such as Biba and Mary Quant may cost £100–300 or more, and those by their imitators can cost almost as much, as they capture the sought-after look of the decade. Despite this, good examples can be found for about £50–100.

## Timeless soles

By the 1970s fashion had stepped back into platforms and wedge heels, and the new versions of these 1940s styles were much more extreme than the originals. A pair of Terry de Havilland pale green, pink, purple, and orange snakeskin-effect wedge sandals from the early 1970s may cost around £200–300 or more. These, and wooden platform Candie's shoes, are a good investment, as the profile of 1970s fashions is rising.

Disco-mania swept Europe and the USA in the latter part of the 1970s, and dressy dance shoes became fashionable once more. The French designer Maud Frizon was acclaimed for the striking cone heels and colourful, decorative designs of her disco shoes, which can now be found in many second-hand clothes shops for around £50–80.

During the 1980s, styles such as the pump and strappy shoes with towering or Louis heels were dusted off and given a flashy makeover by Ferragamo and Chanel, among others. Examples of these can be found at around £50–100, or less. Manolo Blahnik, known for his dainty, open, strappy shoes with high heels, is still prominent, and his shoes from the 1980s can fetch £100–200 or more.

**A pair of Anne Klein paisley pumps.** *1980s, 27cm (10½in) long.*

**£80–120**

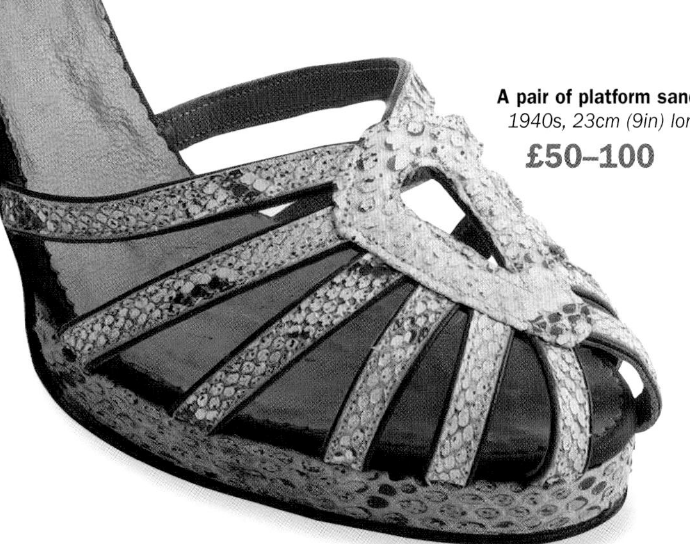

**A pair of platform sandals** *1940s, 23cm (9in) long.*

**£50–100**

### Top Tips

- Go for slightly worn, less expensive examples of vintage shoes if you are intending to wear them. Those in mint condition should be for display only.
- Store your shoes using wooden shoe trees or stuff the toes with acid-free tissue to help retain their shape.
- Look out for vintage shoes by Ferragamo, as they are highly desirable. Other pre- and post-war names include Bally, Charles Jourdan, Rayne, and Gucci.
- Check shoes for leather soles – a mark of quality footwear. But note that until World War II, most shoes were made with leather soles.
- New brand-name limited-edition trainers may make a good investment.

### BUY

*Trainers are among the most desirable collectables at the moment, and prices are rising rapidly. Look for retro trainers like Puma 'Clyde', Adidas 'Superstar', and Nike 'Cortez'.*

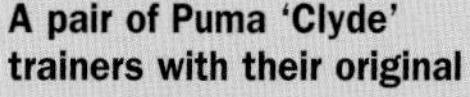

**A pair of Puma 'Clyde' trainers with their original box,** named after the American basketball hero Walt 'Clyde' Frazier. Many vintage styles from the 1970s are being revived or adapted for today's trainer-wearers. *1970s, 27cm (10¾in) long.*

**£30–60**

### KEEP

*Transparent-heeled shoes first made an appearance during the 1950s; most were made in the USA to match plastic handbags. Those in good condition usually increase in value over time.*

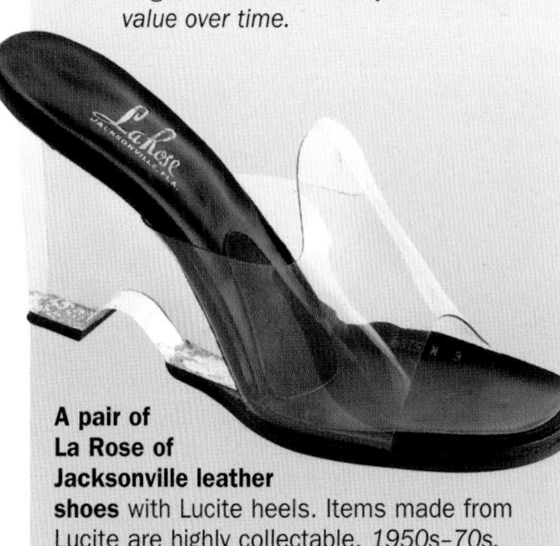

**A pair of La Rose of Jacksonville leather shoes** with Lucite heels. Items made from Lucite are highly collectable. *1950s-70s, 22cm (8¾in) long.*

**£80–120**

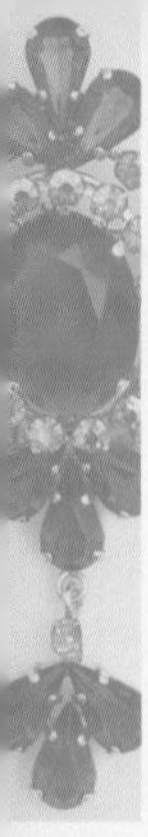

# Fans are worth getting into a flutter over – they have always been as much about the fashion and etiquette of the day as about keeping cool. These delicate and intriguing accessories still excite interest, and often display remarkable artistry and craftsmanship.



Gentlemen courted ladies with gifts of fans. Opera-goers hid behind them while watching each other. Lovers used them to flirt with. The language of the fan became so developed in the 18th century that you could converse without saying a word.

The fan's decorated fabric or paper is known as the 'leaf', while the framework upon which the leaf is mounted is made from 'sticks'. 'Guards' are the two outer sticks, and these may be decorated. Brisé fans are made entirely from sticks.

The painting and calligraphy on fans were prized by the Chinese centuries ago, but it was only in the second half of the 19th century that Western enthusiasts began to collect them. Today, sought-after items include leaves painted by famous artists, such as Degas and Toulouse Lautrec, along with fans advertising specialist areas such as early ballooning and travel.

Unusual examples for any collection include celluloid fans from the 1920s that unfold to reveal lipstick, powder, and a mirror, and fans from the 1920s and 30s made from exotic materials such as feathers. Early 20th-century fans promoting products and places are also collectable.

▲ **An 18th-century paper fan,** with a scene of 'Rebecca at the well'. The hand-painted scene from the Bible and the ivory sticks make this fan desirable, as does its age. *c.1790, 28cm (11in) wide.*

**£200–300**

► **A late 18th-century fan,** with decorated ivory sticks and guards carved as figures. This fan would be worth more if the hand-painted leaf were not damaged and the colours were not faded. *c.1790, 30cm (11½in) wide.*

**£100–200**

► **A fan with a lace leaf and mother-of-pearl sticks.** Lace fans were popular from the 18th century onwards. Handmade lace fans are rare. This machine-made lace fan (with Irish lace from Carrickmacross) is the most common type found today. *c.1850, 31.5cm (12in) wide.*

**£100–150**

◄ **A mid-19th century fan,** with a paper leaf printed with a picture of a fisherman flanked by two ladies next to a river. The fan has gilt detailing and pierced bone sticks applied with silvered decoration. One guard is damaged. *26.5cm (10½in) high.*

**£50–100**

◄ **A Victorian black fan,** with a leaf decorated with flowers, and ebony sticks. Sombre fans were popular when Britain mourned the death of Prince Albert in 1861. *1860s, 32.5cm (12½in) wide.*

**£40–50**

◀ **A late-Regency hand-coloured fan,** showing a typically French-style pastoral scene. The bright colours of the decorated leaf and the ivory sticks inlaid with silver make this fan a desirable item. *c.1820–30, 27cm (10¾in) wide.*

**£180–220**

◀ **A Victorian printed fan,** with a scene showing a gathering of ladies. This fan is not as valuable as some: it has bone sticks, and the design is printed, rather than hand-painted. *1870s, 26cm (10in) wide.*

**£50–60**

▲ **A red feather fan** with ivory sticks. Fans from the 'Roaring 20s' can make superb display pieces. *1920s, 32cm (12½in) wide.*

**£50–100**

## Collectors' Tips

- Store fans in acid-free tissue to prevent deterioration and protect them from insect damage
- Leave cleaning and repairs to professionals
- Check that sticks and leaves match, and that the fan is free of any breakage, tear, or mark

◀ **A Cantonese lace leaf fan.** The colours and scene, showing Oriental people in typical dress, are characteristic of some Far Eastern fans, as are the ornately carved ivory sticks (detail shown in inset). *c.1890, 28cm (11in) wide.*

**£200–300**

◀ **An Art Nouveau fabric fan,** with a painted pastoral scene of dancing figures. Mother-of-pearl sticks and gilt-highlighted period decoration add to its desirability. *c.1910, 23cm (9in) wide.*

**£250–300**

# Gentlemen's accessories

range from ties and cufflinks to hip flasks and walking canes – the means by which men have displayed personality and flair for more than 100 years. Many of these are now highly collectable.

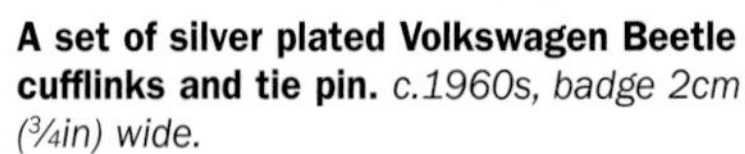

**A set of silver plated Volkswagen Beetle cufflinks and tie pin.** *c.1960s, badge 2cm (¾in) wide.*

**£100–200**

Cufflinks and ties are still popular, but men looking for something special can also choose from studs (for shirts), tie clips, and even hip flasks. An expensive pair of cufflinks or set of studs could cost you £1,000 or more, but most items are much less costly.

## Up your sleeve

Cufflinks are made in all designs and materials, including glass, mosaic, ivory, gold, enamel, and jewels. Collectors often focus on certain styles, such as Art Deco, or jewellers such as Fabergé, Tiffany, Cartier, or Van Cleef & Arpels. Prices for such names can be high, often £300–800 or more, but there are many less expensive items at around £200–300 or less. Silver sets with simple enamelling can cost less than £100. More modern items are generally less expensive than their original retail prices.

Look for 'four vices' enamelled cufflinks, with symbols representing the 'gentlemanly' vices: playing cards, horse-racing motifs, cocktail glasses or champagne bottles, and elegant or scantily clad ladies. A gold Victorian or Edwardian set can fetch up to £1,000–1,500 or more.

**A pair of base-metal oval cufflinks** decorated with ocean liners; they are probably a souvenir from the *Queen Mary. 1930s, 2cm (¾in) wide.*

**£40–60**

Early 20th-century cufflinks were sometimes gold-plated, with printed scenes under a clear glass covering on one or both faces. These can fetch between £10 and £50. Similarly valued are plastic sets from the 1930s onwards, often in novelty shapes.

## All dressed up

Before the 1960s, men wore dress-shirts with studs in place of buttons. There were two types: those for wear with tailcoats and white ties, and those for dinner jackets and black ties. White-tie sets are pale, usually made of mother-of-pearl or snowy enamel set in a platinum or white-gold mount. Black-tie sets are frequently set with

## A closer look at... two early 20th-century gentleman's canes

A cane was an essential outdoor accessory for a typical middle- or upper-class Victorian or Edwardian gentleman. The materials used in canes and the quality of their decoration displayed the owner's wealth and social status. These factors also contribute to their value today.

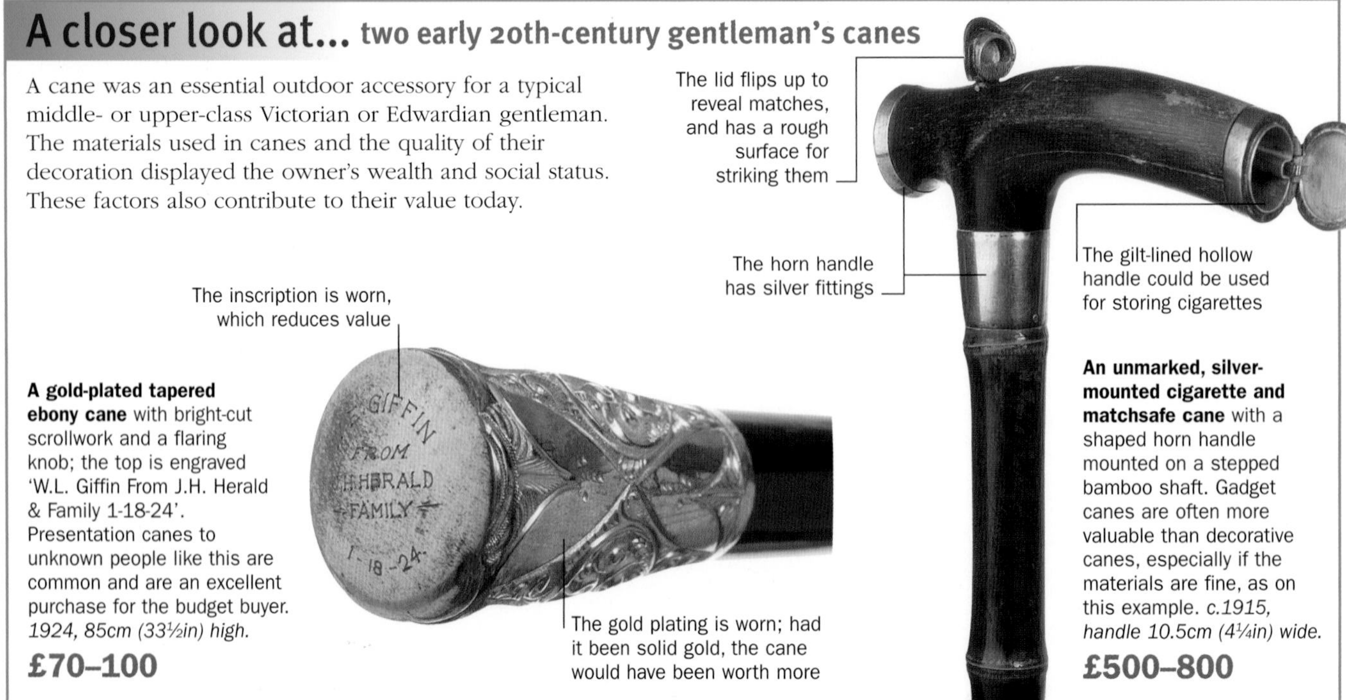


**A gold-plated tapered ebony cane** with bright-cut scrollwork and a flaring knob; the top is engraved 'W.L. Giffin From J.H. Herald & Family 1-18-24'. Presentation canes to unknown people like this are common and are an excellent purchase for the budget buyer. *1924, 85cm (33½in) high.*

**£70–100**

**An unmarked, silver-mounted cigarette and matchsafe cane** with a shaped horn handle mounted on a stepped bamboo shaft. Gadget canes are often more valuable than decorative canes, especially if the materials are fine, as on this example. *c.1915, handle 10.5cm (4¼in) wide.*

**£500–800**

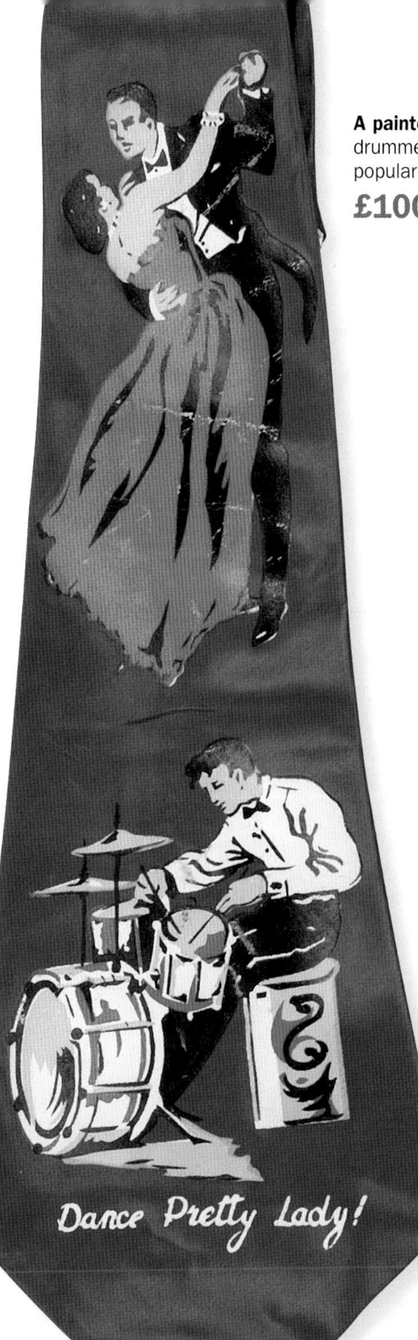


**A painted silk tie** decorated with a dancing couple and a drummer, with the caption 'Dance Pretty Lady', from a popular song. *1940s, 140cm (55in) long.*

**£100–150**

onyx or ebony enamel in a white- or yellow-gold mount. Cheaper variations, often pastes set in a silver or gold-plated mount, can also be found. Values can vary from around £100–200 for a paste set, up to £1,000 or more for finer sets in precious materials.

## Tied in knots

Bow-ties have a limited following and prices are low, with fine silk or rayon examples costing less than £30–50. Look out for patterns from the 1930s with Scottie dogs, aeroplanes, or cars.

The long neck-tie was introduced between 1890 and 1900, but came into its own in the USA in the late 1940s with a craze for ties with hand-painted tropical scenes and risqué images. These are now sought after. Collectors also look for 1960s psychedelic designs from Pucci and Mr Fish, and Surrealist designs by Fornasetti, as well as élite names such as Hermès. Values vary from £5–10 for 1970s and 80s ties, up to £150 or more for original hand-painted 1940s ties. Look for 'peek-a-boo' ties, with a semi-clad or naked lady on the underside of the tie.

## Pinned down

Tie clips and pins were popular from the 1930s to the 60s, especially in the USA. Most are plain with perhaps a single stone or paste to enliven them. They are usually gold- or silver-plated, but occasionally solid gold, silver, and platinum ones can be found. Solid examples can fetch several hundred pounds, or even £1,000 or more, while plated pieces will usually cost around £30–100, depending on the style and decoration.

## All in a day's sport

The majority of vintage hip flasks found were produced between 1890 and 1930 and were designed to hold brandy or whisky. Most are silver, silver-plate, or pewter. They come in a variety of shapes and sizes, including glass examples, encased in silver or leather. Values depend on the maker, the material used, the decoration, and the condition, but hip flasks can usually be found for around £50–300.

### Top Tips

- Avoid enamel cufflinks that are chipped: they cannot be easily repaired, so the value falls.
- Look on the back of cufflinks for makers' marks and hallmarks.
- Make sure the stones in tie pins and clips are secure in their settings – missing stones are hard to replace.
- Fill hip flasks with water before purchasing to make sure there are no leaks.

## BUY

*Wearable or usable accessories are popular, especially if they are well made and in classic designs. Prices rarely fall and pieces in the best condition or by notable makers ought to rise in value over the years.*

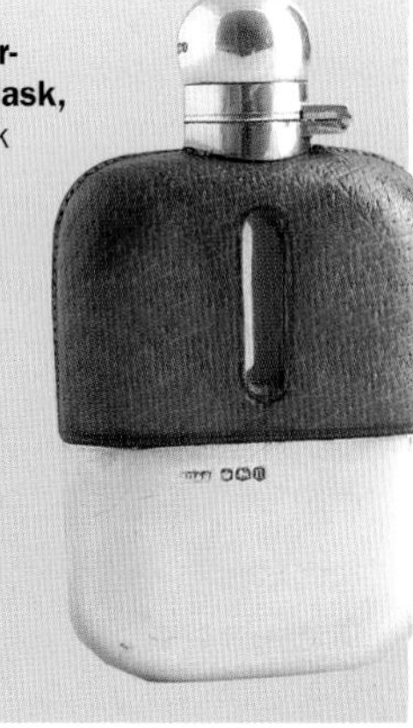

**A silver- and leather-covered glass hip flask,** with a maker's mark for 'J.D. & Sons' and London hallmarks. This is a classic functional and decorative design for a hip flask; there is a small window to check the level of liquid. *1930s, 15cm (6in) high.*

**£60–100**

## KEEP

*Authentic hand-painted silk ties from the 1940s are now being reproduced and surviving originals are highly sought after by collectors. Prices for originals are climbing steadily.*

**A hand-painted silk tie** decorated with a dancing girl among palm trees. The bright colours and well-posed naked lady make this an excellent example. *1940s, 140cm (55in) long.*

**£150–250**

## SELL

*Cufflinks by the best-known makers generally fetch the highest prices, but the style and design should be typical of the maker. Wearability aside, if you are looking for investment potential, sell these and buy more representative pieces.*

**A pair of Georg Jensen silver cufflinks** decorated with horseshoes. The horseshoe, a symbol of luck, is not typical of this globally known company of Danish silversmiths. *1960s, 2cm (3/4in) diam.*

**£150–200**

# Smoking accessories

have become highly collectable, perhaps because of the decline in popularity of smoking itself. It is not difficult to find beautifully designed, imaginative, and unusual pieces at prices to suit all budgets.

**A silver vesta case** with an engraved foliate pattern and engraved initials; it has a hallmark for Birmingham. *1903, 5cm (2in) high.*

**£50–100**

Many desirable smoking accessories such as cigar, cigarette, and match cases, as well as lighters and cigarette dispensers, can be found at collectors' fairs, antiques shops, general auctions, and even car-boot sales. Finer or rarer pieces are available from specialist dealers or auctions.

**An Italian clockwork cigarette dispenser** with feet shaped like small devils' heads and an angel-shaped finial. *c.1950s, 34cm (13½in) high.*

**£80–120**

## From tin to tortoiseshell

Made for storing matches, vesta cases (named after a type of match and also known as 'matchsafes') have a rough or ribbed strip at the base for striking the match. They were made from a variety of materials including tin, brass, ivory, wood, and tortoiseshell. Silver and gold vesta cases – ranging from simple pieces with a scrolled engraving to a novelty shape such as a crown – are the most sought after. These can be found for as little as £20–40 for a plain silver or plated example, but generally cost around £30–150. High-quality cases were often decorated with coloured enamels: these can sell for around £100 or more, depending on the complexity and quality of the enamelling.

## Cedar fresh

Rather than leaving cigars in the wooden boxes in which they were shipped, smokers stored them in elaborate boxes made of wood, silver, and hardstone. These were lined with cedar to prevent the cigars from drying out, and some – known as humidors – featured a water container to keep the cigars fresh. Values usually depend on type of material used, maker, decoration, and size. Ornate boxes in fine materials, by noted makers such as Dunhill and Mappin & Webb, or by a good Victorian or Edwardian central London retailer such as Finnigans or Leuchars, can sell for around £200–800 or more.

## A night on the town

Cigar cases were often moulded in cigar shapes. Cases designed to hold three or four cigars were produced from the mid-19th century onwards in materials such as leather, wood, papier mâché, silver, and gold. From time to time, single cigar cases are found, sometimes with an extinguisher, so a half-smoked butt could be saved. As these cases are still usable today, prices can be high, even for leather examples. A mock-crocodile-skin holder can cost £80–200 or more, while silver and gold cases can cost upwards of £50–250, depending on condition, maker, and decoration.

## Cutting edge

In the late 19th century, novelty cigar cutters were made in such shapes as animals, people, and liquor bottles. Popular because they are still usable, silver table-mounted novelty cigar cutters can sell for £100–800 or more. There are also many pocket versions made from brass in shapes such as shoes and champagne bottles, which are available for around £30–200.

## Slim cases

Cigarette cases were mainly of gold, silver, or were silver- or chrome-plated. The flat surface was perfect for decoration, including enamelled or engraved designs. A simple silver-plated early 20th-century case can

## A closer look at... a Dunhill lighter

Dunhill is one of the most collectable lighter manufacturers, and has a heritage going back to the 1920s. Look out for unusual combinations of function and fine materials. The company marked many of the parts on complex examples with a matching serial number, so check that these are consistent.

The casing is made from solid silver

The integral watch is a rare feature, introduced around 1927

The chimney protects the flame from wind, indicating that this is the Sports model

The matching serial number is stamped on different parts

**A Swiss-made Dunhill 'Unique' Sports manual petrol pocket-watch lighter.** If the filler cap that screws into the bottom had been a replacement, the value would have been reduced. *1927, 5.5cm (2¼in) high.*

**£3,000–4,000**

cost less than £20, whereas a finely lacquered piece from the same period made under a partnership between Dunhill and Namiki of Japan may be worth in excess of £500–800.

### Lighting up

Portable lighters appeared in the early 20th century. Dunhill is the most collectable name: it first issued its 'Unique' lighter (still produced today) in 1923. Look for lighters with extra functions, such as watches or powder compacts, especially if they are concealed. These can fetch high prices, often in excess of £500–1,000. Models with lacquer or coverings such as shagreen and leather cost around £100–500 or more and are more sought after than plainer versions, which can be worth £50–150. Solid-silver or gold lighters can cost around £150–500. Later gas-filled versions, such as the brick-shaped 'Rollagas', are usually of less interest than 1920s–40s models, but precious-metal examples can fetch around £50–200. Other names to look out for include Thorens, Ronson, and the American Zippo.

Table lighters by leading potteries such as Wedgwood and Carlton Ware can be found for £50–100, or less. Those with attractive decoration or designs characteristic of the firm or the period, such as the 1930s or 50s, are likely to rise in value the most.

### Did You Know?

*In 1919 Frederick Charles Wise and Willey Greenwood developed a lighter that could be struck with one hand, using a horizontally placed flint and striking wheel. This prototype for the Dunhill 'Unique' lighter was made from a discarded mustard tin and can still be seen in London's Dunhill Museum. It marked a turning point for the Alfred Dunhill company.*

### Top Tips

- Check the interior of metal vestas and cigar and cigarette cases for signs of wear to the gilding; this reduces value.
- Examine all enamelled items carefully for chips and dents.
- Learn to spot the difference between English, European, and American vesta cases: English examples usually have a ring for hanging from a watch chain.
- Look for fine detailing and a deep striker on novelty animal-shaped vesta cases; plainer pieces with shallow strikers are probably reproductions.
- Use vintage boxes for display or serving only – do not store cigars in them, as they are not usually airtight.
- Check lighters for major wear, dents and splits as well as missing or replaced parts, which lower the value.

### SELL

*Cigar smoking is growing in popularity, despite the general decline in smoking. Now is a good time to sell classic vintage accessories to collectors or cigar smokers.*

**A Russian silver gilt enamel cigarette case** by Khlebnikov, St. Petersburg, vesta case and strike. This is an excellent time to sell anything Russian. This is particularly desirable, with a portrait of Czar Alexander II. *1876, 10cm (4in) wide.*

**£10,000–12,000**

### KEEP

*Prices for lighters by notable makers, in good condition, have risen over the past decade, and they should continue to do so as this area becomes more popular and attracts new collectors.*

**A Swiss-made silver-plated Dunhill 'Unique' Standard pocket lighter.** The plating on this example is in good condition and the casing has no scratches or dents, adding to its value. *1940s, 6cm (2½in) high.*

**£100–200**

# Powder compacts first

appeared in the 1900s, but it was the growing popularity of the car in the 1920s and 30s that helped to take them out of the boudoir and into the realm of fashion accessories.



Increasing mobility after World War I created a demand for portable grooming kits. More women began to use cosmetics and it became socially acceptable to reapply make-up in public. The first powder compacts were imported from France and the USA, but in the 1930s there was an upsurge in British production. Most compacts were made of sterling silver, silver plate, chrome plate, or gold plate, but other metals were also used, as well as tortoiseshell, mesh, and Bakelite.

From plain to detailed, stylish, and bejewelled, compacts came in all shapes, sizes, and prices. Some even had mechanisms that allowed them to play music. Elegance gradually gave way to souvenir-led designs and novelty items: both vintage soft toy and compact enthusiasts, for example, would relish finding a Schuco soft toy with a concealed powder container.

If these are a little extreme, however, you should aim to seek out stylish compacts with intriguing mechanisms and novelty value. Coty, Kigu, and Stratton are among the leading names. Slender compacts from the 1930s decorated in a typical Art Deco style are particularly popular.

By the 1960s, the advent of compressed powder and disposable containers meant that powder compacts had, for practical purposes at least, had their day. But their beauty and the nostalgia they evoke continue to appeal both to collectors and the fashion conscious.

▲ **An Evans 'silvertone'-plated** starburst design 'Standard Carry All' compact, with chain-link handle and original card tag. This compact was designed to hold other accessories and has space for cigarettes. *c.1950, 14cm (5½in) long.*

**£200–300**

▼ **An Evans Tapset lady's compact,** with plated Scottie dog motifs on the lid. Scottie dog items are hugely collectable in their own right. *c.1930s, 5.5cm (2¼in) wide.*

**£50–60**

▼ **An American mother-of-pearl compact by Ansico.** Mother-of-pearl cases often have missing sections or splits in the covering – original and complete examples command a premium. *1950s, 5cm (2in) wide.*

**£30–50**

▲ **A musical compact and lipstick with musical mechanisms by Thorens.** The compact plays 'The Night They Invented Champagne' and retains its original box (not shown). *1950s, 10cm (4in) wide.*

**£150–250**

▲ **A Schick Mfg Co. mother-of-pearl covered compact,** with gold link chain. It is unusual to find compacts in mint condition and complete with all their accessories, such as the fabric purse and lipstick holder. This one also has space for cigarettes in a compartment on the underside. *c.1949, 15cm (6in) long.*

**£200–300**

◀ **A Georg Jensen silver compact.** Jensen was a notable Danish silversmith, and anything by him is highly sought after. He often used animals and natural motifs. *c.1925, 5cm (2in) wide.*

**£300–400**

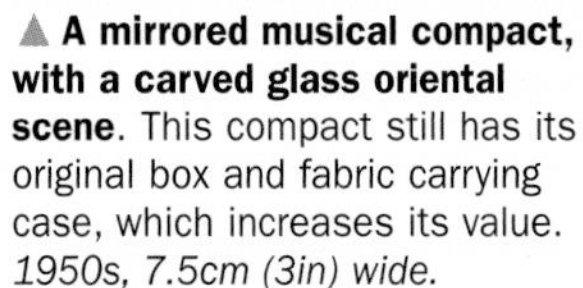

▲ **A mirrored musical compact, with a carved glass oriental scene**. This compact still has its original box and fabric carrying case, which increases its value. *1950s, 7.5cm (3in) wide.*

**£100–150**

## Collectors' Tips

- Use an old toothbrush and cottonwool bud to clean powder traces from compacts
- Make sure the compact's hinge is sound and that it opens and shuts easily
- Do not wash any part of a compact, including powder sifter and puff

◀ **A Coty brushed gold compact and lipstick.** Manufacturers often ingeniously combined other features into compacts, such as the lipstick holder in the hinge. This can add value and interest. *1950s, 8.5cm (3¼in) wide.*

**£50–100**

▲ **A Pilcher circular gold-plated compact**. Condition will usually determine the value – this compact, with its polished horse design on the lid, is in mint condition, which is unusual for such a practical item. *c.1950s, 9.5cm (3¾in) diam.*

**£100–150**

▼ **An enamelled compact and cigarette case** by Chelsea Cigarettes. In the 1920s, smoking was fashionable and combined cases were common. *1920s, largest 8.5cm (3¼in) wide.*

**£100–150 the pair**

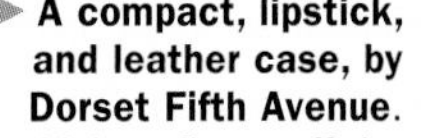

▶ **A compact, lipstick, and leather case, by Dorset Fifth Avenue**. Light reflects off the finely engraved pattern on the surface of this compact, creating an interesting visual effect. *1950s, 17cm (6¾in) wide.*

**£50–100**

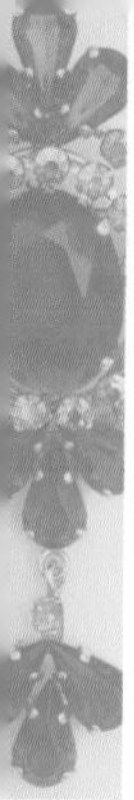

# Costume jewellery was glamorised by Hollywood in the 1930s and is still highly prized. Many women wear their glorious costume pieces as proudly as if they were crafted from genuine gold, diamonds, and precious jewels.

**A pair of Chanel gilt button earrings,** with Chanel's classic double-C motif. *1980s, 2.5cm (1in) diam.*

**£100–200**



The fashion for 'frankly fake' jewellery was popularised by Coco Chanel, who turned replicas of precious jewellery into accessories in their own right.

## Paris leads the way

Chanel thought of jewellery as decorative rather than a display of wealth. She mixed the faux with the priceless and wore lots of bold jewellery. Wealthy trendsetters loved the look and by the early 1920s she was selling costume jewellery in her Paris couture house. Many of her signature designs – button earrings, outsized pearls, gilt chains, and *pâte de verre* (moulded glass) crosses – date from this era. Pieces made during her lifetime are generally of fine quality, and sell for about £300–1,000 or more.

Fellow Parisian fashion designer Elsa Schiaparelli also produced costume jewellery in the 1930s. Although her pieces had a big impact on fashions of the time, they were produced in limited numbers and can now fetch between £500 and £1,000. After the 1950s, her designs were produced under licence by other makers who often featured abstract leaves, shells, and snails made from flamboyant stones and iridescent crystal. Pieces sell for about £100–500.

Chanel's and Schiaparelli's early work was exciting and innovative, but it looked like an exaggerated version of precious pieces. The impetus for change came from the USA.

## New York style

During the 1920s, New Yorker Miriam Haskell designed jewellery aimed at America's most stylish women. She used inexpensive materials, such as artificial seed pearls, in lavish quantities and daring new ways: necklaces, earrings, bracelets, and brooches were layered with stones resembling glitzy bunches of grapes.

Jewellery by Haskell is extremely well made, being assembled by hand with hidden wires and attached to a gold-plated filigree base. Pieces from the 1920s to the 1940s are rarer than later items, but the complexity and detail in Haskell's jewellery are more important than the date. A small 1940s brooch and earrings with large faux pearls surrounded by smaller pearls in the form of a fruit with leaves can be worth around £100, whereas a 1960s necklace from the 'Shooting Star' range, with a built-up central motif and strings of faux pearls hand-wired to look like ears of wheat, can be worth £800–1,000.

## Some designers to look for:

- Joseff
- Miriam Haskell
- Hobé
- Schiaparelli

**A Joseff of Hollywood necklace and matching earrings.** Bold, fan-like motifs are characteristic of 'Cocktail' jewellery. The moulded pattern and boldly set single-colour stone typify Joseff's work. *1940s, earrings 9cm (3½in) long.*

**£600–1,000**

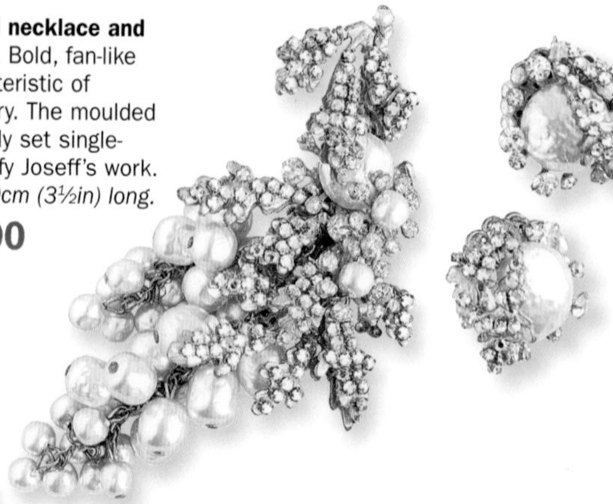

**A Miriam Haskell diamanté and simulated seed pearl brooch, with matching earrings.** A layered, three-dimensional effect is a classic element of Haskell's work. *1940s, earrings 3cm (1¼in) long.*

**£300–400**

*Did You Know?*

*Lucite, Plexiglass, and Perspex are brand names of the same type of transparent acrylic plastic. This relatively expensive material was first made commercially in the 1930s. Acrylic is transparent, lightweight, and shiny, and can be moulded, tinted, and carved. Jewellers were quick to take advantage of these properties. Beware, acrylic can yellow or crack with age.*

Haskell started marking her pieces with 'haskell' in an oval stamp in the late 1940s. Unmarked designs are attributed to her by the quality of workmanship and distinctive look. Values vary from around £80–120 for a simple pair of clip earrings to more than £2,000 for a complex necklace, earrings, and bracelet set.

## The age of plastics

During the 1920s and 30s, Bakelite was used for costume jewellery. A wide variety of brooches, bracelets, and chain-necklaces with small fruit charms were produced in jazzy colours of jade, orange, yellow, red, and chocolate brown. Look for deeply cut pieces with geometric or whimsical designs, or bright colours. Items can be found for £50–80 or less, and the majority sell for less than £500.

Bakelite jewellery is highly prized and modern copies abound. Vintage pieces rarely carried a maker's mark, but can often be identified by signs of wear, such as light scratches on the surface. Most genuine articles are heavier than modern period-style pieces, and the clasps are usually attached with screws or pins rather than glue.

## Hollywood greats

Movie moguls liked their stars to be seen wearing pieces that conveyed a larger-than-life glamour, both on and off the screen.

Eugene Joseff, the leading supplier of costume jewellery to the movie industry, made pieces that photographed well. Using simple designs, he kept the stones to a minimum to show off the metal's shape and texture. Most Joseff pieces have a gold-matt finish, developed to minimise the glare from studio lights.

The majority of his designs are stamped 'Joseff of Hollywood' or 'Joseff'. Pieces that once belonged to, or styles that were worn by, film stars are the most valuable. A Russian gold sun-shaped pin made from clear rhinestones and worn by Pier Angeli can fetch around £250–350.

Joseff's fellow Hollywood designer, William Hobé, took 18th-century jewellery designs such as sprays, ribbon garlands, and floral baskets and reworked them in quality materials like silver and silver-gilt. Hobé is noted for his hand-setting and finely executed metalwork. His 1930s pieces can fetch £200–500, but those from the 1960s onwards can cost as little as £30–50.

**A 'laminated' cast phenolic bangle,** in coloured stripes. *1930s, 7.5cm (3in) wide.*

**£200–300**

## ▪ Trifari ▪

**A Hobé silver bow pin,** set with multicoloured crystals. Romantic bows covered with flowers are one of Hobé's hallmarks. *1940s, 10cm (4in) long.*

**£100–200**

**A Schiaparelli red and iridescent crystal bracelet, with matching earrings.** Unusual colours and leaf shapes are typical of 1950s Schiaparelli costume jewellery. *1950s, bracelet 19cm (7½in) long.*

**£300–500**

**A Trifari brooch in vermeil** (gold-plated sterling silver), with rhinestones and blue enamel. Trifari often made fruit-shaped brooches after World War II. *1940s, 3.75cm (1½in) long.*

**£100–200**

## Cocktails for two

When the USA entered World War II in late 1941, European supplies had already dried up and restrictions were placed on the use of materials such as base metals, which were needed for the war effort. Even so, costume jewellery thrived, with designers turning to new materials such as Lucite for stones, and using sterling silver instead of base metal.

The major makers of American costume jewellery in the 1940s were Coro and Trifari. Both started out making copies of Art Deco jewellery, then came into their own when they created 'Cocktail' jewellery, worn by glamorous socialites to evening parties. This bold sculptural style featured raised draped motifs and curving lines, along with bizarre combinations of vivid coloured stones and the extravagant use of gold.

Coro's double clips ('Duettes'), which could be worn individually as two separate brooches or combined as a single piece, were a huge hit. Values range from around £100 to £700. Other definitive Coro designs include a donkey cart brooch, a blow-fish brooch, and a brooch in the shape of a hand. Pieces from the 1950s onwards can often be found for less than £50, while pieces from the 1930s and 40s often reach £200–300 or more.

Trifari is closely associated with 'tutti-frutti' jewellery, set with carved pastes and *pâte de verre* pieces made from moulded glass. Crowns, inspired by historical movies of the time, were specialities, made from the 1930s to the 50s. The 'Coronation Gems' range was introduced in 1953 to mark the coronation of Elizabeth II. However, Trifari's 'jelly-belly' animals designed by Alfred Philippe are by far the most sought after – these have Lucite centres modelled to form the animal's abdomen. Silver-gilt 'jelly-bellies' from the 1940s and 50s command the top prices of more than £200–300.

## A closer look at... a Stanley Hagler necklace and earrings

Hagler's fantasy jewels have an international cult following. The New York-based costume jeweller worked briefly for Miriam Haskell before setting up on his own in the late 1950s. Picking up on Haskell's layering and intricate design, Hagler took it one step further to create bigger, more opulent, highly colourful pieces.

Seed beads were combined with larger ornaments like glass leaves or crystals – a Hagler characteristic

The beaded areas are built up in the centres, so that they appear three-dimensional

The colour is typically bright and eye-catching

**A Stanley Hagler floral motif necklace and earrings,** with faux coral glass petals, beads, cabochons, and drops. Each individual piece is hand-wired to a filigree backing, a characteristic of Hagler's style. *1980s, necklace 57cm (22½in) long.*

**£600–1,000**

## To Europe and back

Christian Dior produced some of the most innovative costume jewellery of the 1950s, recreating 18th- and 19th-century designs with obviously non-precious stones, such as iridescent crystals in place of diamonds. He made costume jewellery for two markets: exclusive couture pieces and the more easily found licensed pieces made for upmarket shops. Mitchell Maer in Britain and Kramer in the USA held the first licences, and from 1955 onwards the German firm Henkle & Grosse acquired all rights.

Dior designs are stamped with a date. Pre-1970s pieces are the most desirable, although post-1974 pieces are less expensive at about £50–100 and offer an affordable way to start a collection. A pair of earrings simply set

### *Did You Know?*

*Metal-frame Christmas jewellery in seasonal greens and reds first appeared in the late 1940s. In 1950 the wives and mothers of American servicemen stationed in Korea sent their husbands and sons corsage-shaped pieces for Christmas or wore them as a reminder of their loved ones overseas. Even now, many designers introduce Christmas tree jewellery in their collections.*

**A Coro 'Duette' bouquets of flowers pin,** in enamelled silver with red glass beads, green glass, and clear rhinestones (shown front and back). *1930s, 7cm (2¾in) long.*

**£200–300**

**A Dior pendant brooch,** rhodium-plated with royal blue glass stones and iridescent rhinestones. *1958, 7.5cm (3in) long.*

**£150–250**

with coloured stones may fetch around £40–80. Pieces that are intricate or date from the 1960s or before often sell for about £500–1,000.

When selecting a piece, check the quality of the stones, which are usually rhinestones. It is their clarity, cut, and sparkle that attract collectors.

## Into the Space Age

The futuristic designs of early 1960s costume jewellery featured geometric forms in chic combinations such as black, white, and red. Enamel, plastics, and white metal were used and designs included solid plastic bracelets and rings, rectangular and circular pendants on long chains, and necklaces and belts made from discs and squares. Geometric earrings were especially popular. The Parisian couturiers Pierre Cardin, André Courrèges, and Paco Rabanne are some of the most important names in Space Age costume jewellery. They produced limited-edition pieces as well as more readily available licensed designs. The more common mass-produced items can be found for around £50–100.

## Larger than life

Kenneth Jay Lane's outrageous, outsized interpretations of valuable pieces were a big hit with the 1960s jet set, and they were often featured in the fashion magazine *Vogue*. Lane used flashy gilt and flamboyant enamels with abandon. He liked massive plastic cabochons in gaudy turquoise, pink, and coral. His larger-than-life panther brooches and animal-head pieces now fetch £100 or more.

Look for pieces with bright colours and sparkling stones, as well as oriental-inspired designs. A pair of earrings can usually be found for around £50–70, but many of Lane's pieces, such as his necklaces, can exceed £100–200, with a few reaching £500.

## Retro revival

The English company Butler & Wilson was at the forefront of the retro costume jewellery revival of the late 1970s and 80s, taking old favourites and updating them with a slightly brash 1980s twist. Its signature piece was a salamander pin. Many tip Butler & Wilson as a good name to collect, so it is worth keeping an eye open for its work, which can sometimes be picked up in car-boot sales. Expect pieces to command around £30–50 and upwards.

### Top Tips

- Look for makers' marks on clasps, earring backs, or brooch backs, and inside catches or on closures.
- Avoid altered or damaged pieces.
- Ask a jeweller or specialist restorer to re-set loose stones.
- Expect a bit of wear and tear on enamels, but avoid pieces with significant chipping or touch-ups.
- Keep hairspray, perfume, soap, and body lotion away from costume pieces.
- Avoid soaking costume jewellery in liquids, which can loosen crystals from their settings and discolour the finish.
- Clean paste jewellery with a lightly dampened cloth or cotton bud.
- Remove tarnish from silver-gilt pieces with a jeweller's polishing cloth; don't buff hard – gold plating can rub off.
- Store pieces individually in padded bags and boxes to avoid damage.

### BUY

*Christmas tree jewellery is growing in popularity with plenty of variety and scope for collectors. Pieces are available at a range of prices, and growing interest is likely to push up value.*

**An unsigned Austrian brooch,** with multi-coloured and clear rhinestones. This is an early piece in an unusual design, with clear, baguette-cut stones for the candles. *1950s, 7.5cm (3in) high.*

**£50–60**

### BUY

*Lobsters were a favourite with the Surrealists during the 1930s and the motif also features in much costume jewellery. Animal subjects are consistently popular, so they are likely to hold their value, or appreciate.*

**A pink enamel lobster brooch,** with claws on springs. Look out for lobster brooches with spring 'snapping' claws, like this one, as they command higher prices. *1930s, 8cm (3¼in) long.*

**£60–70**

### KEEP

*Classic pieces by Miriam Haskell are rising in value as the look is in vogue and her work is usually of fine quality.*

**A Miriam Haskell three-strand necklace,** with faux and baroque pearls and poured-glass beads. Haskell is known for her faux pearls, and combinations of faux pearls with coloured beads are sought after. *1940s, 51cm (20in) circ.*

**£300–400**

### KEEP

*Butler & Wilson's pieces are still comparatively inexpensive, but values may rise as 1980s styles are being revived by fashion houses.*

**A Butler & Wilson dancing couple pin,** with clear paste heads and black and clear rhinestones. The movement in the skirt and the classic glitzy black-and-white design make this piece typical of Butler & Wilson. *1980s, 12cm (4¾in) long.*

**£50–80**

# Jewellery ranges in style from the traditional to the avant-garde. Not only can pieces represent an excellent investment, but they can also be worn on special occasions without compromising their value.

**An Art Nouveau enamelled silver brooch** in the shape of a pansy. *c.1890, 6cm (2½in) high.*
**£50–70**

Victorian and 20th-century jewellery embraces everything from sentimental remembrances of the late-Victorian era, through the ground-breaking fashion changes of the 1920s and 30s, to sleek modern-day designs.

## Victorian keepsakes

Nothing epitomises Victorian jewellery more than the cameo: a carved miniature relief sculpture, usually made from a hard stone, a gem, or a shell, with the subject in a colour that contrasts with the background. Good-quality Victorian examples can be worth £300–500 and upwards. Early 20th-century pieces, often made as souvenirs, can be found for £50–100, although the carving can be crude.

Tokens of remembrance reached new levels of popularity after the death of Prince Albert in 1861. Jewellers favoured enamel, amethysts, and seed pearls (a symbol of tears), and all decoration had to be black, purple, or white. Carved jet chains, crosses, and brooches were especially popular. Mourning pieces were often inscribed with the name of the deceased and contained a lock of their hair. Prices start at about £40–60 for a small, rolled-gold mourning brooch, but can rise to £200–800 or more for earlier Georgian items.

The Victorians also admired Scottish agate jewellery, which was made of silver or gold, set with inlays of colourful stones, and based on Celtic designs such as Luckenbooth or Witch's Heart. Pieces may still be found for about £150, but the average value is now around £300–800.

**A mourning brooch,** with human hair in the form of a wheatsheaf, in a gold-plated mount. *1880s, 5.5cm (2¼in) high.*
**£10–15**

## Finely crafted jewels

Originating in the 1890s and recognisable by their flowing lines, Art Nouveau pieces often depict sinuous plants, dragonflies, and mysterious maidens. Designers such as René Lalique created naturalistic pieces in which craftsmanship was paramount. Art Nouveau jewellers were highly skilled with enamel, especially *plique à jour* (a technique similar to *cloisonné*, which created a stained-glass effect). Pieces of this type can be found from £500 upwards. Objects by leading names can fetch between £2,000 and £100,000 or more.

Much Arts and Crafts jewellery from the 1890s to about 1910 was handmade and fine hammer marks were often left on the finished piece deliberately, to endorse the authenticity of the craftsmanship. Silver was often used, set with cabochons of agates or moonstones, or mother-of-pearl. Small brooches and pendants can be found for less than £200. Named pieces, such as those by Arthur & Georgina Gaskin, usually command from around £200–400 to £3,000–5,000 or more.

## Dazzling days

The bold Art Deco style of the 1920s and 30s gave rise to dazzling jewellery. Platinum was a popular material, along with diamonds, clear rock crystal, and pearls. The look was sometimes accented with black onyx, red coral, and stones such as sapphires, rubies, and emeralds. Art Deco pieces can sell for thousands of pounds, although pieces in less expensive materials, such as paste and silver, can fetch from around £100–200 upwards.

## Daring designers

Values for jewellery made during the 1950s and 60s depend on the maker, material, and design, and can range from around £150–300 up to many

**A Victorian-style gold, ruby, and seed-pearl charm** in the shape of a lady's hand, with a later 18ct-gold chain. *c.1910, pendant 4cm (1½in) long.*
**£150–200**

## A closer look at... a Georg Jensen silver brooch

Brooches (called pins in the USA) have long been popular. Art Deco brooches are particularly sought after for their striking, modern design. In order to buy wisely, look at a number of features, including the material, form, details, and maker.

**A Georg Jensen silver brooch of a grazing deer,** with the design number 298 and bearing the maker's mark. The popularity of the maker and the fact that this is typical of his work make this a sought-after piece. *1930s, 5.5cm (2¼in) wide.*

**£400–500**

The simple form, clean lines, and lack of intricate surface decoration are typical of Art Deco design and Jensen's style

The legs crossing the roots of the tree add perspective – a sign of good quality

thousands of pounds for names such as Boucheron, Van Cleef & Arpels, and Asprey. Designers to look for include the Americans Tony Duquiette, a Hollywood interior decorator (a small piece may be found for £2,000–3,000), and Courts & Hackett, who began designing one-off pieces for rock stars, and whose items can often be found for £200–300 or less.

Jewellery by the Danish company Georg Jensen continues to be popular, with its modernist styles, usually in silver, incorporating naturalistic motifs and themes. Examples can be found for around £100 for a small, simply designed post-war silver brooch, to £2,000–4,000 for a more decorative brooch from the 1930s. In general, pre-war pieces are worth more.

### Contemporary names

One of Britain's leading contemporary jewellery designers is Dinny Hall. Characterised by a simple elegance, her pieces are handmade, usually from silver, resin, gold, and gold plating. Pieces from the late 1990s can be found for £50–200 and look likely to become classics. Other names to look for include Wright & Teague, launched in 1984; Dower & Hall, launched in 1990; and Monty Don, who designed jewellery in the 1980s and has since found fame as a gardener. Pieces can often be found for about £50–150.

### *Did You Know?*

*Diamonds were rare until the discovery of abundant South African mines in the late 19th century. Some antique diamonds have as few as three facets and can be mistaken for glass or marcasite. Older diamonds tend to be less sparkly and have fewer facets than modern equivalents, and you may just pick up a bargain if you spot one that has been mistaken for an imitation stone.*

**A pair of Dinny Hall gold-plated silver earrings** in the shape of elongated, stylised leaves. *c.2001, 3.5cm (1½in) long.*

**£80–100**

### *Top Tips*

- Look for original cases for antique pieces. These may be stamped with the jeweller's or retailer's name.
- Ask a specialist to test gold content.
- Check the back of a piece for repairs and alterations, which reduce value.
- Watch out for 'improvements', such as replacement modern stones, which can look out of place in older settings.



### BUY

*Silver brooches from the 1880s and 90s are representative of the period, yet comparatively inexpensive. No two hand-engraved pieces are identical. These pieces may increase in value as demand grows.*

**A silver double-horseshoe brooch.** The good-luck theme of the horseshoe is as popular today as it was in the Victorian era. *1880s, 4cm (1½in) wide.*

**£30–40**

### KEEP

*Many Art Deco diamond and platinum designs were reproduced in paste and silver. Paste pieces with fine workmanship and good detail are highly collectable. They offer excellent value for money if you want the sparkly Art Deco look but can't afford diamonds, and they will remain in demand as period pieces.*

**A paste-and-silver bow brooch.** The simplified shapes, strong lines, and bold contrasts of colour are characteristic of the period. *1920s, 5cm (2in) wide.*

**£60–80**

### SELL

*Many Victorian pieces can be worn in more than one way – a brooch might convert into a hairpin or pendant, for example. If the design is unbalanced or has been altered, sell it and buy a better piece.*

**A gold almandine garnet-and-pearl brooch.** The design is uneven and the pendant fitting is missing. *1860s, 5cm (2in) wide.*

**£400–600**

# **Watches** evolved from 19th-century pocket timepieces, through 1930s Art Deco wristwatches, to designer sports models. Although they all share the same basic function, they include remarkably varied examples of human ingenuity and craftsmanship.

**An American gold-plated Waltham gentleman's full-hunter pocket watch.** *c.1910, 4cm (1½in) high.*

**£80–120**

Large numbers of pocket watches were produced in the 19th and early 20th centuries. Most were open faced, but there was also the hunter (with a flip-open cover protecting the entire face), and the half-hunter (a flip-open cover with a central aperture so that some of the watch face is visible).

## Pocket pieces

A pocket watch's value is affected by its maker, and its functions, materials, and decoration. A plain silver- or gold-plated example from the 1890s to the 1920s, either unmarked or by a prolific maker such as Waltham or Elgin, can be found at collectors' fairs, auctions, or antiques shops for about £40–100. Those made of precious metals such as silver, gold, or platinum are worth more – gold watches can cost £100–500 or more. Decorative features such as enamel or jewels can add value, depending on the quality of workmanship. Look for hallmarks inside the casing, but take care when opening the back, or ask an expert.

## Something for the ladies

Ladies' pocket watches, introduced in the late 19th century, are smaller and more decorative and are often enamelled or set with stones. Novelty case shapes, such as beetles or violins, or pendant watches hanging from a pin, can sell for £150–500 or more.

Rectangular 'purse' watches, which were carried in a handbag, are popular. A plain leather-covered example can cost £80–120, while finer models are worth about £200–300.

Apart from timepieces by notable names such as Abraham-Louis Breguet or Patek Philippe – whose watches can reach a staggering £10,000 or more – the most valuable pocket watches are often those with added features. An extra dial showing the current phase of the moon, a chronograph, a calendar, and features such as a 'repeating mechanism', add to the value. An unmarked gold watch with all these functions from around 1900 can sell for up to £1,000 or more.

## Changing shapes

Wristwatches became popular in the 1920s, especially those with square, rectangular, or octagonal shaped faces, often with Art Deco styling. In the 1940s, watches often matched a

## Some 1970s watches to look for:

- Spaceman
- Pierre Cardin
- Sicura

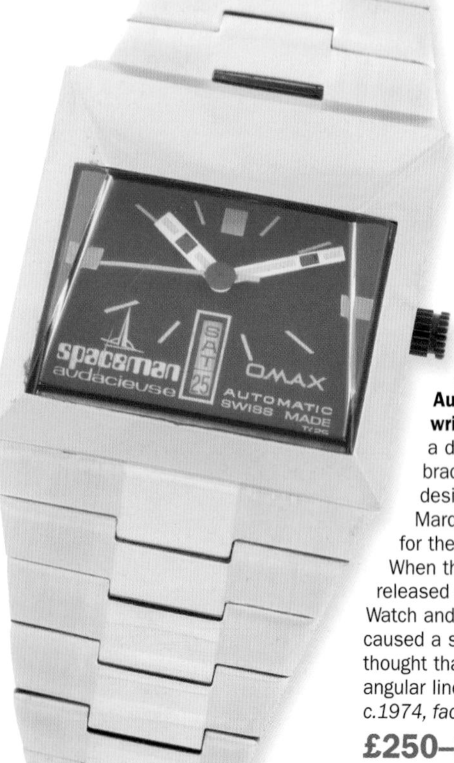


**A Spaceman Audacieuse automatic wristwatch by OMAX,** with a date function, on a metal bracelet. This model was designed by André Le Marquand in 1972, originally for the Catena watch company. When these watches were released at the 1973 Basel Watch and Jewellery Show they caused a sensation – nobody thought that such avant-garde angular lines would sell. *c.1974, face 5cm (2in) wide.*

**£250–350**

**A Pierre Cardin wristwatch,** with a movement by Jaeger-LeCoultre. This watch combines a stylish look with a fine-quality mechanism. The strap has been replaced. *1970s, face 5cm (2in) wide.*

**£200–300**

**A Sicura wind-up wristwatch,** with a gold-filled bezel and bronze dial, on a black patent plastic strap. Sicura are known for their stylish period designs and quality mechanisms. *1970s, face 4cm (1½in) wide.*

**£100–150**

woman's jewellery, or were designed for military use. Futuristic styling arrived in the 1950s.

Watches made from the 1930s to the 60s by known makers range from £50 to £500 or more. A stainless steel Rolex from the 50s may sell for around £250–500. Gold watches by the Swiss company Longines can be worth £150–400.

**An Art Deco Movado lady's silver gilt and black enamel purse watch.** There is damage to one corner. *1928, case 5cm (2in) wide.*

**£150–250**

## Top watches

Many people collect by the maker: Rolex, Patek Philippe, Audemars Piguet, Vacheron & Constantin, and Jaeger-LeCoultre are the most notable and expensive. A gold Patek Philippe chronograph from 1939 can command up to £20,000. Look for watches by American companies, too, such as Elgin and Hamilton, whose prices are commonly up to around £100–300.

Watches from the 1960s and 70s often have visually exciting cases. The top names and finest-quality examples can command high prices (£500–1,000 or more), but sports models often cost less and are a good way of owning a top brand-name watch – a 1970s Heuer 'Carrera' can be found for around £200–400.

### Top Tips

- Keep all sales material and any details of restoration work; these add value.
- Check the condition of the case as this is vital, and remember that a clean dial may indicate either a well looked-after watch or a replaced dial.
- Buy from reputable dealers – there are many fakes on the market.
- Look out for the government-issue 'arrow' mark inscribed on the back or printed on the face of a watch; this denotes that it is a military watch.
- Look for popular makes that combine cutting-edge design, representative of the era, with a good-quality mechanism.

### Collectors' Tales

*'I knew a dentist who went to Petticoat Lane and bought a Rolex as a present for his wife. It was an 18ct-gold perpetual watch. He got a jeweller to check the strap and it was genuine, so he assumed the rest of the watch was too. He thought he'd got a good deal for £6,000, so he bought it. But when he showed it to a watchmaker he discovered that the strap was the only part of the watch that was genuine and it was only worth about £500–600.'*

**Mo Hedariah, London**



### BUY

*Watches produced from the 1930s to the 50s by big names, with simple styles and little ornamentation, are growing in popularity. Examples in good condition with original cases and mechanisms will hold their value, if not rise.*

**A Rolex gentleman's watch.** This example has a 9ct-gold case, which makes it highly desirable. Both the dial and the movement were made and signed by Rolex, which adds to the value. *1950s, 4cm (1¾in) high.*

**£300–400**

### SELL

*Accessories for pocket watches such as 'Albert' chains and watch stands are of little practical use today. Sell to a collector with an interest in period accessories and invest in a watch from an area that is growing in value.*

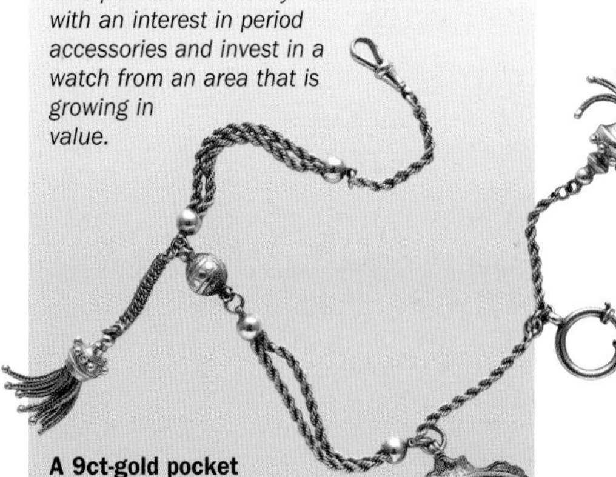

**A 9ct-gold pocket watch fob chain,** with an older unengraved revolving citrine seal fob. The addition of the Victorian seal makes this piece attractive to specialists. *c.1900, 20cm (8in) long.*

**£100–150**

## ▪ Sorna ▪ Buler ▪ Vulcain ▪

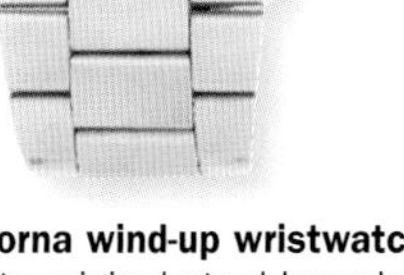

**A Sorna wind-up wristwatch,** on its original steel bracelet. Watches by good makers with extra features, such as an alarm, are desirable. *1970s, face 4cm (1½in) wide.*

**£150–250**

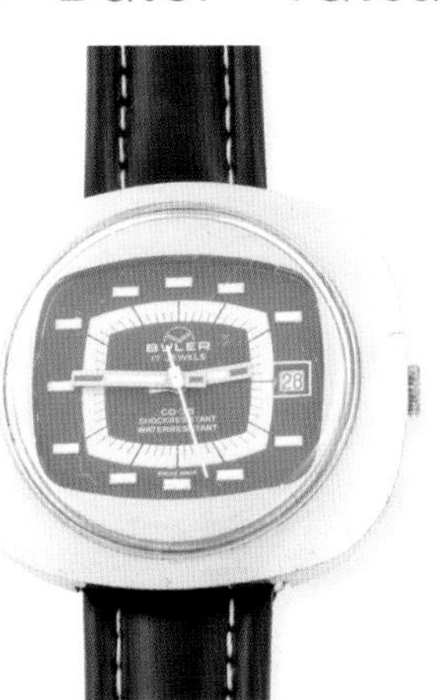

**A Buler wind-up wristwatch,** on a black leather strap. The face is shaped like a TV, a design feature characteristic of the era. *c.1970, face 4.5cm (1¾in) wide.*

**£70–100**

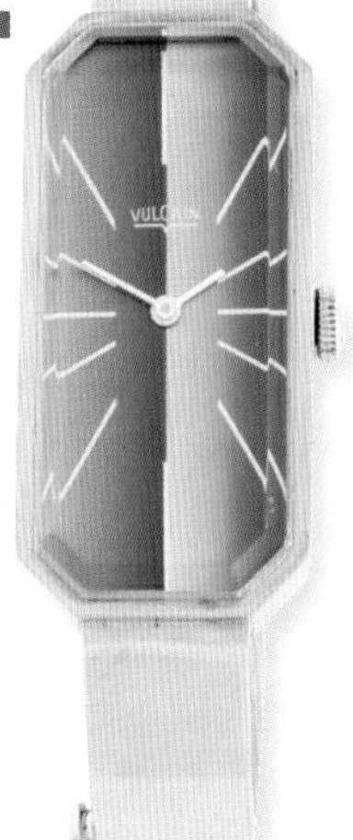

**A Vulcain lady's wristwatch,** on a gold-plated bracelet and with its original tag. The known maker, the 1970s shape, and the bracelet make it desirable. *1970s, face 2cm (¾in) wide.*

**£100–150**

COLLECTOR'S CORNER

# Digital watches are stylish, often chunky, and typical of the 1970s. They were the first watches to adopt the advances in electronic micro-circuitry – state of the art 70s technology that introduced light emitting diode (LED) displays.

When quartz-driven LED digital watches arrived at the beginning of the 1970s, American and Swiss manufacturers were the first to harness the new technology. In 1971 the Hamilton Watch Company in the USA starting producing the Pulsar, the world's first wristwatch with no moving parts. Limited-edition 18-carat gold Pulsars can now fetch anything up to £800–1000. A year later, Longines released its first LED model and by the mid-1970s most Swiss makers had begun introducing digital ranges.

Other notable early digitals include Omega's 1601, 1602, and 1603 models and Citizen's Quartz Crystron LED; a mint-condition Omega 1601 can fetch upwards of £500. But the ever lower cost of the technology meant that liquid crystal display (LCD) digitals from the Far East soon flooded the market. By the end of the decade, most quality watch-makers in Switzerland had reverted to making traditional watches.

Compared to mainstream watch collecting, the digital market is not yet widely known or understood. Pieces can still be found for sale in a range of venues from car boot sales and collectors' fairs to vintage clothing and accessory shops.

But increasing interest from both those subscribing to retro fashion trends and hardcore collectors is already pushing up prices.

▲ **A rare Casio 52 LCD wristwatch on a steel bracelet.** Casios with original metal bracelets are always worth keeping – this watch includes time, day/date, stopwatch, and chronograph functions. Casio produced many versions, and collectors are eager to collect all the variations. *c.1981, face 4cm (1½in) wide.*

**£80–150**

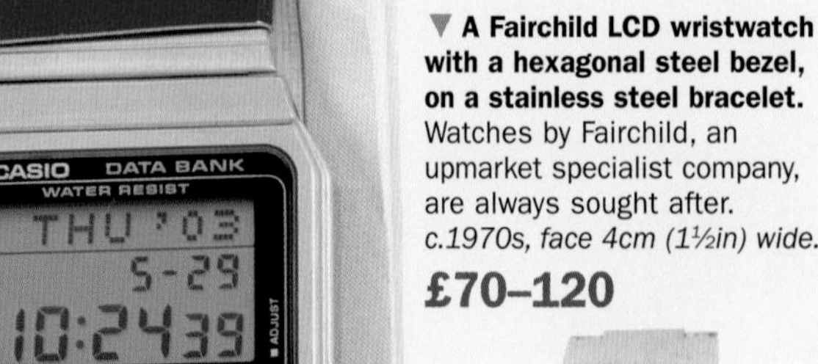


► **A Casio 505 Data Bank LCD wristwatch on a steel bracelet.** Casio is a leading name in the digital watch collecting market – always look for the original papers and labels. *c.1980, face 4.5cm (1¾in) wide.*

**£70–120**

▼ **A Fairchild LCD wristwatch with a hexagonal steel bezel, on a stainless steel bracelet.** Watches by Fairchild, an upmarket specialist company, are always sought after. *c.1970s, face 4cm (1½in) wide.*

**£70–120**

► **A Fairchild Timeband LCD wristwatch with gold-plated bezel on a gold-plated bracelet.** One of the earliest, and top range, LCD watches. Its value is likely to rise in time. *1978, face 4cm (1½in) wide.*

**£50–80**

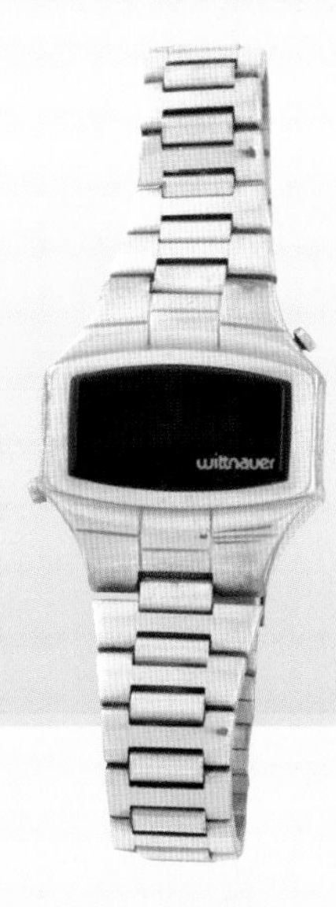


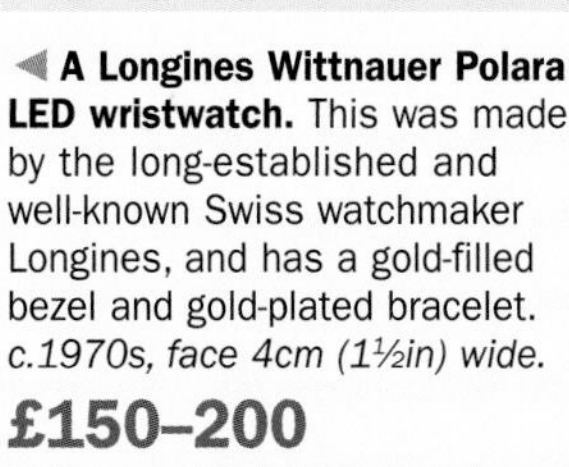

◀ **A Longines Wittnauer Polara LED wristwatch.** This was made by the long-established and well-known Swiss watchmaker Longines, and has a gold-filled bezel and gold-plated bracelet. *c.1970s, face 4cm (1½in) wide.*

**£150–200**

◀ **A Junghans Mega 1 LCD wristwatch with a hexagonal steel bezel on an original black leather strap.** This is the British version of the first radio-controlled watch and was fashioned by Frog Designs. It synchronises itself daily between 3am and 6am to the atomic clock in Frankfurt, Germany. *1991, face 4.5cm (1¾in) wide.*

**£200–300**

▶ **A Fairchild LCD wristwatch with a steel bezel and black face on a steel bracelet.** This is one of the earliest LCD watches, and from a prestigious manufacturer. *c.1970s, face 4cm (1½in) wide.*

**£80–150**

## Collectors' Tips

- Before buying a vintage digital watch, check that all the functions work and that there is no battery leakage
- Replace or remove watch batteries as soon as they run out

◀ **A Pulsar Sport Timer LCD wristwatch on an original black plastic strap.** This rare watch was designed for sports use and was novel at the time: it can time four people at once, thanks to the combined stopwatch settings. *c.1970s, face 4cm (1½in) wide.*

**£80–150**

▶ **A Synchronar 2100 solar-powered driver's watch with a LED readout on a stainless steel bracelet.** This unusual watch designed by Roger Riehl has two solar panels on top *(see right)* which power it for up to a year. The digital display *(see far right)* is on the side so it is easily read while driving a car. The watch is fully calendar-programmed until 2100, hence its name. *1973, face 4cm (1½in) wide.*

**£1,000–1,500**

HORNBY
SOUTHER
516
2
1
3
MATTEL, INC.

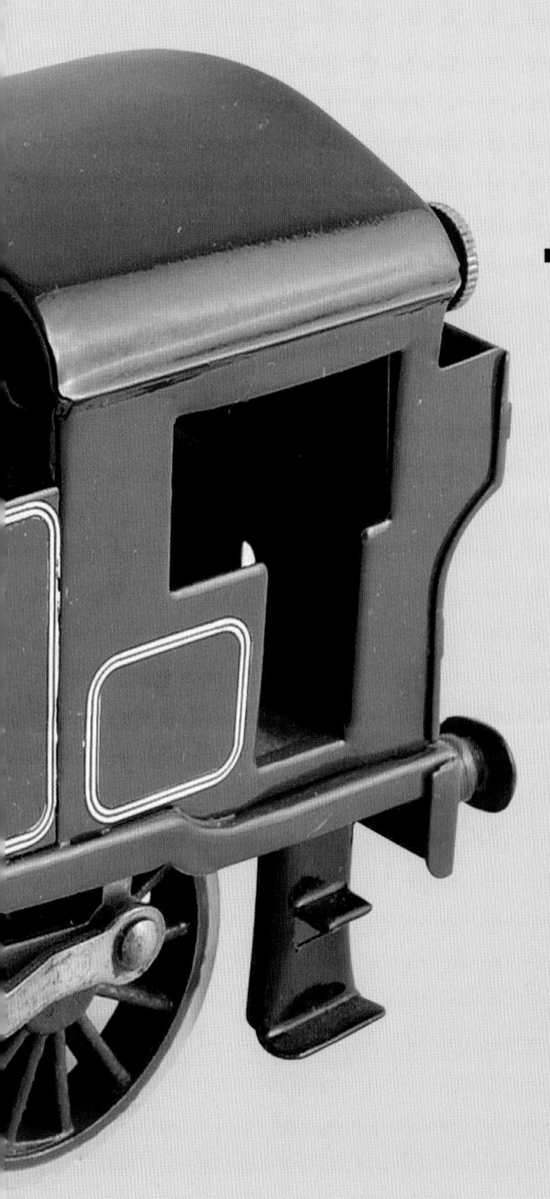

# Toys, Dolls, and Teddies

**Nothing evokes childhood more immediately and vividly than an old toy. Each generation harks back to the playthings it enjoyed – the old-fashioned cars, dolls, and teddy bears of the early 20th century, or perhaps the Barbies and Tiny Tears of the 1960s and 70s.**

1
Penny toy, p.213

2
Dinky van, p.215

# The nostalgic charm of...

Toys bring back fond memories of rainy afternoons in the past spent playing with a dolls' house, a favourite teddy bear, or a fleet of model cars. Each generation harks back to the playthings it especially enjoyed, and many of them are now sought-after collectables.

Toy cars and trucks are not only fun to play with; they also show how real cars have changed over the years. From early tinplate toys ① to die-cast versions – the Dinkys of the 1930s onwards ②, Corgis ③ of the 1960s onwards, and Matchbox toys of the 1960s and 70s – they offer a parade of vintage cars for the living-room floor. Although early tinplate toys can be scarce and valuable, later toys and those that are smaller are still affordable. But to reach the highest values, toys should be in good condition and retain their original box.

Model trains show how locomotives and carriages changed with the introduction of diesel although, for many, steam trains remain the most appealing. Trains by reputable makers such as Märklin, Hornby ④, and Bassett-Lowke are as popular today as they were when first produced.

## On parade

Boys used to enjoy playing with toy figures ⑤, especially armies. Even battle-weary examples can be worth keeping. Farm and zoo animals were popular as well as soldiers.

5
Lead circus figures, p.225

6
Bisque doll, p.237

7
Käthe Kruse doll, p.241

Just as toy cars show how technology has developed over time, dolls from the past century show how fashion has evolved.

Corgi gift set, p.217

3

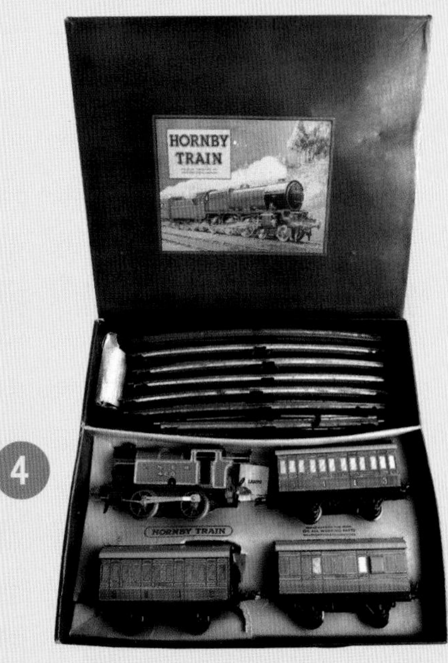


4

Hornby train set, p.220

# .toys and teddies

Just as toy cars and trains show how technology has developed, dolls from the past century show how fashion has evolved.

## From bisque to Barbie

In the early 20th century, bisque dolls ⑥ were the preserve of the wealthy and were cherished. As a result, dolls by makers such as SFBJ, Jumeau, Heubach, and Kestner can still be found today.

By the 1950s, these dolls had been replaced by affordable, mass-produced fabric ⑦ and plastic dolls, dressed in more casual clothes. Makes such as Lenci, Barbie ⑧, Sasha, and Tiny Tears were on every girl's wish list.

Many of these dolls were advertised on the new commercial TV stations which started broadcasting in the 1950s. The spread of TV also brought a new range of characters to life. Companies such as Pelham Puppets had already been making toys under licence from Disney ⑨. Now, popular TV characters such as Muffin the Mule and Sooty were made into toys.

## Childhood friends

Teddy bears ⑩ are the sort of childhood friends who often accompany us into adulthood. From the Steiff bears of the 1900s to the Chad Valley and Dean Rag Book Co. teddies of the 1930s onwards, there is always a market for old bears, even those that have been so well loved that they look a little ragged.

J.K. Farnell teddy bear, p.228

8

Barbie doll, p.244

9

Pelham puppet, p.226

10

# Tinplate toys

are among the earliest mass-produced toys available. They evoke nostalgia for a childhood of imaginative games. The best combine fine detailing, period styling, and renowned makers.

Tinplate toys began to eclipse wooden toys in the early 19th century. Formed of sheets of tinplated steel which were cut out, shaped, and then decorated, they were easier and cheaper to make. Although tinplate toys from the early 19th century onwards are scarce today and mostly expensive, later, smaller toys are accessible to many. Expect to pay £50–100 for a small wind-up animal-shaped toy of the 1930s–50s.

## The toy pioneers

The late 19th and early 20th centuries are the 'golden age' of the tinplate toy. Many of the most important producers were German – notable names include Märklin (founded 1856), Gebrüder Bing (1863–1933), Carette (1886–1917), and Ernst Planck (1866–c.1935). Toys by Märklin and Bing are particularly sought after. The American makers Marx and Strauss, and C.I.J. in France, also made fine examples.

Before the 1890s, tinplate toys were hand painted, which allowed for a high level of detail. Boats were among the most popular toys at this time. Often expensive in their day (with portholes that opened and convincing rigging), examples can now fetch £3,000–20,000 or more. Similiarly detailed early toy cars, produced as the motor car gained popularity in the early 20th century, featured lamps, doors that opened, running boards, and wheels with rubber tyres. Today these can fetch around £2,000–4,000 and often more.

From the 1900s, makers increasingly used the printing technique of colour lithography to decorate their toys with a transfer. It was faster and more economical but tinplate toys became lighter and less complex. Prices for such toys remain comparatively high today, fetching from a few hundred pounds to thousands of pounds, depending on the type and size of toy, and its complexity and condition.

## Penny for them

If you are looking for an inexpensive way to start collecting tinplate toys from the golden age, try 'penny toys'. Often based on their larger counter-parts, these small, simply made toys were sold by street vendors. They included lorries, cars, and horse-drawn carts, as well as novelties such as gramophones and babies in prams. They measure around 10cm (4in) long, are often brightly coloured, and are usually decorated with a lithographic transfer. Production peaked around the beginning of the 20th century. Today, examples with detailed designs and embossed areas are the most valuable. A tiny German Meier sewing machine on a stand might fetch £40–50, while a detailed car or lorry by a noted maker can be worth up to £500 or more.

**A Distler 'Goose on Platform'** penny toy with embossed lithographed decoration and an amusing bobbing-head action. *c.1900, 9cm (3½in) long.*
**£200–250**

## The later years

Although quality had declined by the 1920s and 30s, there are still many excellent examples from this period and the 1950s and 60s. Again, German manufacturers, such as Schuco, Karl Bub, and Distler, led the field. Britain's Hornby, Mettoy, and Tri-ang, along

**A battery-powered Bristol Bulldog aeroplane,** by Straco of Japan. The powered action includes a stop-and-go switch and a turning propeller. There is some minor rubbing to the finish. *1950s, 30.5cm (12in) long.*

**£100–200**

with numerous Japanese makers, also produced colourful, inexpensive models. Cars and motorcycles are often seen: examples by Masudaya in Japan or Schuco in Germany could fetch £100–200 or more. Many were driven by wind-up or (from the 1950s) battery-powered mechanisms. Small, basic, wind-up vehicles or animals have a whimsical charm. These can be less costly – though if in their original boxes the value can range from £30 to £150, depending on maker, size, date, and condition.

## A closer look at... a clockwork tinplate motor coach

Tin cars are among the most collectable type of tinplate toy. Before the classic 'limousine' styles of 1900 to the 1920s, cars were made that mimicked the earliest 'horseless carriages' on the roads. These can be highly desirable and valuable.

**A painted French motor coach,** with a clockwork mechanism, original glass, tufted upholstery, and opening doors. The paint wear on the roof and dashboard exterior does not affect the value much since the age, size, and shape of the coach make it highly desirable. *c.1890, 39.5cm (15½ in) long.*

**£6,000–10,000**

The model has a clockwork motor drive (detail above), making it one of the earliest automotive toys seen.

The decoration is hand painted, indicating an early toy

The motor coach is finely detailed with lamps and opening doors

### Top Tips

- Look for brushstrokes, an uneven application of paint, and slight bumps on the surface – these are all signs of handpainting.
- Watch out for repainting (giving a bright and fresh appearance), as this reduces value.
- Always buy pieces in the best condition, as rusted or worn toys are difficult to restore. With penny toys, mint condition often adds more value than rarity.
- Look for cars, lorries, and limousines – all tend to be popular and valuable.

### BUY

*Penny toys in the form of cars, lorries, and buses are worth seeking out. Look for undamaged pieces with intricate decorative details applied by transfer lithography and finely cut details such as a driver, passengers, and opening doors.*

**A German Meier limousine penny toy,** with embossed lithography, a fully modelled driver, and cut-out passengers. The toy is in excellent condition, but needs cleaning by an expert to reach its full potential. *c.1900, 11cm (4¼in) long.*

**£200–300**

### KEEP

*Pieces like this clockwork motorcycle and rider are sure to retain their popularity. Their bright colours, realistic lithographed detailing, mechanical movement, and automotive subject matter make them immensely popular. If in excellent condition, they're likely to grow in value.*

**An Arnold Mac 700 clockwork motorcycle,** with a movable rider in period clothing. In good working order, and only slightly worn, it has its key and original instruction sheet. *c.1948, 23cm (9in) long.*

**£200–300**

# Dinky toys have enthralled children since the 1930s. Many of us love to acquire and handle the models that once so tantalisingly tempted us in toyshop windows.

**A Ford Capri 1:25 Rally Special,** 2214, in red with a black bonnet and roof. Its original bubble pack is slightly damaged, but the car is in excellent condition. *1974–76, 17cm (6¾in) long.*

**£100–200**

Dinky toys are still produced, but the pre-1980s models are the ones to look for. Those dating from before World War II are especially desirable. Dinkies can be worth £10 to £10,000 or more, so any old play toys or car-boot buys are worth close examination.

## Transport your imagination

The forerunners to Dinky, known as Modelled Miniatures, were launched by Hornby in 1931 as accessories to its train sets. The first cars appeared in 1933 and were such a hit that by the following year they were given their own brand name – Dinky.

With the growth in the motor industry, toy cars caught the imagination of children everywhere. The range, made in 1:42 scale, expanded rapidly: by the late 1930s there were more than 200 varieties of cars, as well as planes and boats. By 1939 wayside buildings, road signs, and animals were available. The 1930s is often deemed Dinky's 'golden age', but production was halted during World War II.

After the war some pre-war models were reissued, tending to have fatter wheels, black-finished base plates, and dull colours.

## On the right lines

In 1947 the slightly smaller Dinky Supertoys were launched – with a 1:48 scale. Clear plastic windows and spring suspension were introduced in the late 1950s, while the 60s brought opening doors, bonnets, and boots, and working steering wheels. By 1963 competition

**A Supertoys Euclid Rear Dump Truck,** 965, with its box. *1955–61, box 15cm (6in) long.*

**£100–200**

## A closer look at... a Dinky Big Bedford 'Heinz' van

Minor design variations (in particular, in colours and transfers) affect the value of Dinky toys, sometimes leading to great disparity in value between two similar pieces.

The roof has been retouched (restoration reduces value)

This model with the baked-bean can transfer was produced for longer and is more common than other versions

The box adds value – which would be higher if the corners were not scuffed

**A Big Bedford 'Heinz' van in standard livery,** 923, with baked-bean can transfers. *1955–58, 14cm (5½in) long.*

**£200–300**

Look for models bearing the ketchup transfer: they are rarer and more valuable.

from Corgi had resulted in financial trouble, and the company was bought by Tri-ang, who continued making Dinky toys until 1980. In 1988 Matchbox acquired the rights to the name and relaunched some of the Dinky range.

### Survivors

Pre-war toys in good condition are rare and can be worth up to £500 or more. Series 25 lorries and series 28 delivery vans are particularly desirable.

Individual Dinky toys were not sold boxed until the mid-1940s (before then they were sold unboxed, out of 'trade boxes' containing six models). Gift sets comprising models and accessories were always sold in boxes. Original packaging, in good condition, can add 40 per cent or more to the value.

Most of the standard toys from the 1950s to 70s tend to fetch £30–100, with values unlikely to rise. Boxed toys in excellent condition from the 1950s and early 60s make better investments, as do toys with rare variations. Uncommon transfers can add value – a Supertoy 514 Guy Van with a 'Slumberland mattress' transfer (1950–52) can fetch around £150 in mint condition with a box, but the value could be trebled if the van had a 'Weetabix' transfer (1952–54).

### A perfect match

Matchbox-made Dinky toys are of high quality, although perhaps lacking the charm of earlier models. In 1991 Matchbox decided to restrict output and limit colour reissues in order to enhance collectability. Its limited editions often fetch £10–30 or less and are unlikely to gain much as so many have been kept pristine.

**A P47 Thunderbolt,** 734, with red plastic propeller, in excellent condition, complete with bombs. The 'blister pack' is slightly discoloured. *1975–78, box 15cm (6in) wide.*

**£200–300**

### Top Tips

- Beware of less valuable models that have been repainted to look rarer. Tell-tale signs are fresh and bright colours, and (often) thicker paint. Original paint tends to flake off.
- Consult a reference book for rare colour and design variations. Also look for export-only models which can be worth far more.
- Examine wheels to date models: the first toys had all-metal wheels, moving to white rubber up to 1939. Many post-war cars had black rubber tyres.

### KEEP

*Gift sets are sought after if a genuine set (all the models are correct), complete with its box. As models were often lost by children playing with them, only a limited number of complete sets survive.*

**A Post Office Services Gift Set,** 299, complete, with its box, all in excellent condition. Unusually for a post-office set, a pillar box model was not included. *c.1957–59, box 30cm (11¾in) wide.*

**£500–800**

### SELL

*Trends in toy collecting change as generations age. Although many toys become classics collected by different age groups, scarcer pieces are often best sold to the generation that originally loved them as children.*

**A rare 1930s Dinky Shell Aviation Service refueller,** in good condition. It has white solid rubber wheels and a black base. Although rare and valuable, this is not a classic pre-war Dinky toy and interest in it may diminish in the future. *1938–40, 12.5cm (5in) long.*

**£200–300**

# Corgi toys, launched by Mettoy in 1956 to rival Dinky's domination of the toy car market, have an extra touch of refinement that has won them a loyal fan-base. Tiny working parts, combined with generally low prices, make for a winning formula.

**A BMC Mini Cooper S 1966 Monte Carlo winner,** 339, in red with white roof and with a roof rack and spare wheels; mint, in its box with paperwork. *1967–71, 7cm (2¾in) long.*

**£60–100**

To differentiate its models from Dinky, Corgi produced vehicles with clear plastic in the windows – a dramatic departure! Later innovations included 'Glidamatic' spring suspension, bonnets and boots that actually opened, and 'jewelled' headlights.

Details like these were thrilling to boys all over the world and, by the end of the 1960s, Corgi were exporting their toys to more than 120 countries.

In collecting terms the 1960s currently has an edge over later decades. The key factor is a vehicle's rarity – some were only produced in six-month runs.

A standard Corgi in mint condition, still in its box, can fetch between £30 and £85. Boxes add as much as 40 per cent to the value, but, as with other die-cast toys, even the condition of the box has to be taken into account. In general, prices have levelled off in recent years: no one should expect to make a quick profit in this field. But the good news is that many Corgis can be bought for just a few pounds.

## Rise and fall

In the 1960s Corgi prospered. A new range, called 'Corgi Classics', issued to celebrate Mettoy's 30th anniversary in 1964, won the 'Queen's Award to Industry'. But after a warehouse fire in 1969, which destroyed stock and upset the distribution system, many retailers turned to Dinky. In 1983 the receivers were called in, but the company was re-formed as Corgi Toys Ltd in early 1984.

In collecting circles, Corgi has traditionally been overshadowed by Dinky. During the 1980s and 90s even Matchbox eclipsed Corgi in popularity. But the balance is now shifting, partly because people who loved these toys

## Some TV and film Corgi toys to look for:

■ Batman ■ Popeye ■ James Bond ■ The Avengers ■

**A Batmobile with Batman and Robin,** 267, the first issue, with its pictorial box. The Batmobile was made from 1966 until 1979 in many variations. Later Batmobiles produced for longer periods would fetch half this value or possibly less. *1966–67, box 15cm (6in) wide.*

**£300–500**

**A James Bond Aston Martin DB5,** 270, silver with tyre slashers, ejector seat, front-mounted machine gun, and other accessories, all in good condition, with box. This variant of the box was fragile, so few have survived. *1968–76, box 15cm (6in) wide.*

**£500–700**

**A Popeye Paddle-wagon,** 802, with all its original parts and in working order, in a reproduction box. The Popeye, Olive Oyl, Swee' Pea, Bluto, and Wimpy figures move as the toy is pushed across the floor. The price reflects moderate wear and chipping. *1969–72, box 15cm (6in) wide.*

**£100–150**

as children of the 1960s have now become adults, with cash to spend.

## TV times

Where Corgi had the edge over Dinky was with its TV- and film-related toys. This is another reason why Corgi's star is rising: many people are mesmerised by these novelties. Reaching much higher prices than ordinary cars, such toys in their boxes and in mint condition are worth looking out for. One of the most successful models, reaching sales of 5 million, was the 1966 Batmobile *(see opposite, far left)*. Other top earners included the 1969 Noddy car (now worth around £700), the Chitty Chitty Bang Bang car (around £150–250), The Man from U.N.C.L.E.'S 'Thrushbuster' Oldsmobile (around £250–300), and Dick Dastardly's Mean Machine racing car from the Wacky Races cartoon series (around £80–120).

## Special gifts

Keep your eyes open for Corgi's gift sets. A complete transporter set, which consisted of a lorry and four cars to load and unload, can be worth up to £300, whereas the same models sold separately might only raise about £250.

**A Ford Consul Cortina Super Estate Car,** 440, in dark metallic blue with 'wood' side-panels, complete with golfer, caddie, clubs, and trolley; mint, in its box. *1966–69, box 15cm (6in) long.*

**£150–200**

Also of great interest are the variants that were released; most tend to be more valuable, often because they are rarer. The 1964 range of 'Corgi Classics' was discontinued after 1969 but re-released in 1985 with 'Special edition' on the base-plate. Originals are usually worth £15–25, while re-releases fetch much less than £10. In the 'Chipperfield's Circus' range, released in 1960, animals add an extra dimension to the hardware. Many collectors relish the challenge of building up the complete set.

### Top Tips

- To fetch the highest price within its range, a model should come with its box and both should be in mint condition.
- Look out for rare variations, such as in the body colour, wheel hubs, and seats, as these increase value.
- Avoid unattractive cars, such as the Marlin Fastback. They are unlikely to rise in price.
- Keep abreast of new Corgi releases. Most of them are limited editions and they often sell out within a matter of weeks.

### BUY

*Corgi's 'Whizz Wheels' range offered wheels that turned faster so vehicles travelled faster for longer. Examples can be bought for £10–100 but prices look set to rise.*

**A Rover 2000TC 'Whizz Wheels',** 281, mint; with its window box (the back is shown). This model is uncommon, since it was only produced for about a year. *1971–72, 9.5cm (3¾in) long.*

**£80–120**

### KEEP

*Corgi's 'Chipperfield's Circus' range is popular. Some models were heavy and damaged their packaging, so few boxes have survived. Demand for the range looks likely to outstrip supply, so prices may rise.*

**The Avengers, a gift set,** 40, with Bentley, Lotus Elan, two figures (John Steed and Emma Peel), and three umbrellas; the box is damaged, which reduces the value. The set with a green painted Bentley is worth around 20 per cent more than this. *1966–69, box 15cm (6in) wide.*

**£200–300**

**A 'Chipperfield's Circus' Scammell with Menagerie Trailer,** 1139, with three animal cages, with its window box. This model is harder to find than other examples, so its relative scarcity makes it more valuable. *1968–72, 23cm (9in) long.*

**£300–400**

# Matchbox and other die-cast makers

challenged the dominance of established brands Dinky and Corgi in the battle for schoolboys' pocket money. Some of these smaller makers are worth looking for.

**A pair of Matchbox 'Superfast' Ford Mustangs 8,** red and orange-red, with white and red interiors; both boxed. *1970–71, boxes 11cm (4½in) long.*

**£200–300**

The Matchbox range was established in 1953 by Lesney Products, which had started making die-cast toys in 1948. Although millions of the original series of 1:75 scale models were made, values have been rising steadily. Most early models fetch at least £20, if boxed and in mint condition. A boxed, 1960s London Routemaster bus with a rare 'Players Please' advertising transfer may fetch up to £100 if mint. Still rarer Routemasters (if also mint and boxed) can fetch three or four times more.

## Casting the past

In 1956 Lesney released a new line called 'Models of Yesteryear', initially limited to 15 pre-1930 vehicles. The high standard of casting and detailed hand-paintwork make these first series 'Yesteryear' models extremely attractive: mint-condition boxed examples are worth at least £50. The next series was started in 1960 and marked a shift to plastics for some of the components. Models from the early 1960s are highly desirable.

## The need for speed

In response to US manufacturer Mattel's successful 'Hot Wheels' line, Lesney launched its 'Superfast' range in 1969. The models in this series had 'frictionless' axles and therefore ran faster. The first issue of 'Superfast' models, made from 1969 to 1974, was produced in high numbers, so prices are low at just a few pounds each – making the range a good starting point for collecting Matchbox toys. Limited-edition models can fetch £500 or more.

**A Tri-ang 'Spot-On' LWB Land Rover 161,** in pale blue with a white roof; in good condition and with a fair box (there is some damage to one end). *1961, 11cm (4½in) long.*

**£80–120**

**A Lesney 'Models of Yesteryear' Horse Bus,** 12, boxed and in very good condition. *c.1959, 10cm (4in) long.*

**£60–100**

## In search of days gone

Lesney's demise in 1982 prompted the original director Jack Odell to create a company named Lledo (his surname reversed). Although it made only 30 models in its first six years, hundreds of colour and style variations were released. As with other die-cast models, unusual colour variations and transfers add value. Lledo's ranges include 'Vanguards' and 'Days Gone'. Most are valued at about £5, but limited-edition promotional models based on the 'Days Gone' series can

## A closer look at... a Matchbox 'Superfast' vehicle

The Matchbox catalogue of 1970 listed 75 items in the 'Superfast' range. In addition to cars by well-known makers such as Ford, Volkswagen, Pontiac, Mercedes, and Rolls-Royce, the range included trucks and trailers, an ambulance, a horsebox, and a crane.

**A Matchbox 'Superfast' Leyland petrol tanker 32C,** in metallic purple with silver tank, NAMC transfers; boxed. *1970–73, 10cm (4in) long.*

**£150–200**

fetch considerably more. Lledo is still manufacturing today. As with Matchbox, newly released limited editions could be worth investing in.

Tri-ang Toys, active from 1924 to 1971, released a new range of 1:42 scale die-casts in 1959 under the name 'Spot-On'. These detail-perfect models were only made until 1967. Tri-ang's innovation was to introduce correct scaling on each vehicle and their models are highly sought after. Mint toys in boxes range from about £20 for an Austin A40 up to around £450 for a 1963 'Ovaltine – The World's Best Nightcap' Routemaster bus.

Hornby, which also launched the 'Dinky' name, took over Tri-ang in the early 1970s. After this, the Hornby brand was used again on die-cast toys such as the Hornby 'Minic Ships' range *(see below).*

### Few and far between

Although harder to find, die-casts made by lesser-known British makers are also collectable. Lone Star models (1960–88) fetch around £5–50. Morris and Stone produced the 'Morestone' (1954–59) and 'Budgie' (1959–65) ranges, now selling for about £5–30. Chad Valley made high-quality die-casts with clockwork motors in the early 1950s; now scarce, these items can fetch up to £200 each.

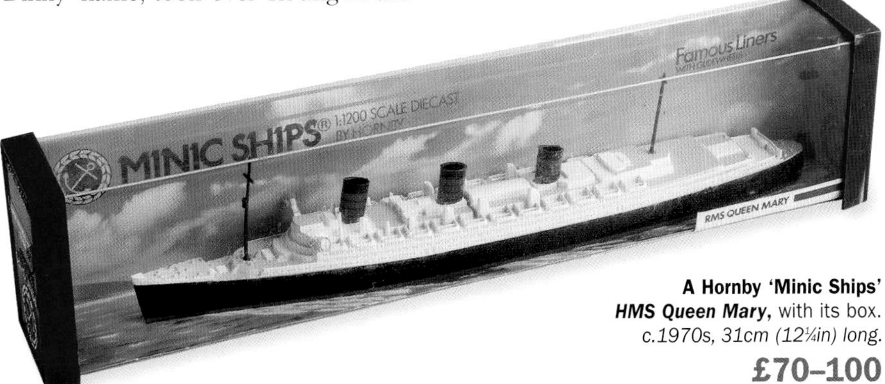


**A Hornby 'Minic Ships' *HMS Queen Mary*,** with its box. *c.1970s, 31cm (12¼in) long.*

**£70–100**

### Top Tips

- Consider investing in past and present limited-edition production runs by major makers; values are likely to rise.
- When buying a boxed example, check that the box and the model match.
- Check the condition of mint models still in their blisterpacks: paintwork may have rubbed off against the inside of the pack.
- Sell models one by one, rather than in batches, to make the most on each. But if they are in a presentation set, they should always be sold together.

### BUY

*Look out for models with unusual variations such as rare colours, flashes (panels of contrast colour), wheels, and transfers.*

**A Matchbox Bedford removals van,** series MB17, with silver trim and metal wheels. The van is in good condition, with minor rusting to the axles. Its rare colour and silver (instead of gold) flashes increase its collectability. *c.1956, 6.5cm (2½in) long.*

**£60–100**

### KEEP

*'Spot-On' presentation sets were relatively expensive in their day. Complete sets in original condition sell for a premium as few have survived. Prices should rise as demand is strong.*

**A Tri-ang 'Spot-On' presentation set,** comprising a Bentley, Jaguar 3.4, Austin Healey, Austin A40, and BMW Isetta, all in good condition, complete with box. *1960, 26cm (10¼in) wide.*

**£500–600**

# Model trains from makers such as Hornby and Märklin are very popular with enthusiasts. If you have assembled a collection of trains over the years, whether on a working track layout or kept in the attic, it may prove to be an excellent investment.

**A Hornby 0-gauge No 101 tank passenger set,** in the scarce LNER teak livery, with a clockwork locomotive, two coaches, a guard's van, and the original box. *1930s, box 46cm (18in) wide.*

**£150–250**

Model trains were first produced in the 1850s. Since then, they have been driven by steam, clockwork, or electricity, and made in a variety of gauges. Early versions were made in Germany by companies such as Märklin. Today, model trains can be picked up at toy fairs, car-boot sales, charity shops, and specialist auctions.

## Clockwork 0-range

Frank Hornby launched the first fine-quality 0-gauge Hornby train sets in 1920 and they are immensely popular. Hornby's early clockwork trains were toylike, but he soon produced more realistic designs. Prices vary: a 1930s Hornby LMS tank locomotive is worth about £45–55, while a rare 1938 Eton Southern Railways locomotive and tender might cost £600–800.

Hornby's scaled-down mass-produced trains soon cornered the market: compact and competitively priced, they were ideal for the more confined home. During the 1930s the company introduced the even smaller, realistic Dublo range with superior detailing. This had to compete with the 00-gauge trains of the German companies Märklin and Trix. Post-World War II 0-gauge Hornby trains were of poor quality and were phased out by 1969.

Hornby models to look out for include clockwork Dublo trains produced before 1940: a 1935 Hornby 0-gauge can fetch more than £1,000. 'Three rail' sets (the centre track being the electricity pickup) are very desirable. They were produced from the 1930s until the late 50s, when Hornby resorted to cheaper plastic-based track with two rails. The introduction of plastic trains in the mid-1950s was a disaster for the company and it was taken over by Tri-ang, which eventually went out of business in 1971. The Hornby name lives on today under 'Hornby Railways'.

### *Collectors' Tales*

*'I once saw a chap pay £500 for an empty box at Christie's. I thought he was mad. But it turned out he had the Märklin pre-war engine to go in it. The engine on its own would be worth about £1,500 but the box would push the price up by much more than what he paid for the box!'*

**Jeff Williams, London**

## Mail trains

In the early 1900s, W.J. Bassett-Lowke realised the potential of marketing model trains for adults and sold toy trains made in Germany by mail order. This move prompted Märklin to

**A Hornby 0-gauge 0-4-0 tank loco,** a well restored clockwork No 1 Special, finished in Southern Railways 516 green and black livery. *c.1930, 30.5cm (12in) long.*

**£150–200**

## A closer look at... a Bing train

**A Bing gauge II live steam 4-4-0 L.S.W.R. 7096 locomotive and 6-wheel LSWR tender,** handpainted in green and brown with yellow lining. The paint is crazed and there is some denting. Bing is one of the most notable German train makers and its trains are second in quality only to those by Märklin. *c.1910, 58.5cm (23in) long.*

**£4,000–6,000**

produce models specifically for export to Britain. Bassett-Lowke trains remain popular – even an 00-gauge locomotive in the standard range can raise around £150–400 at auction.

### Wrenn designs

G. & R. Wrenn Ltd formed in 1950 and ceased trading in 1992, but it has since been bought by a group of enthusiasts and some collectable limited editions have been produced. Average prices for Wrenn trains are currently about £100–400. They are often harder to find than Hornby models because they were produced in small runs, sometimes of only 200. One of the highest prices raised for a Wrenn train was over £1,500 for a 264 tank engine – only eight or nine were ever made. Values tend to range from £200–400.

From 1993–94, Wrenn advertised the 'last chance to buy original Wrenn wagons in Wrenn boxes', at around £10 per item. Although the wagons were in original boxes, most of them had Dapol printed labels. There are 58 different wagons, catalogued as 'The Winsford Wagons' and they are now highly collectable.

### All change!

One of the best respected names is the German company Märklin. In 1891, Märklin standardised track gauges and sold ready-made track sections, engines, coaches, and accessories. Early models were made in three gauges, called I, II, and III. They were fairly successful but around 1910, Märklin added a smaller gauge of 0. The 00-gauge was introduced in 1935 and the H0-gauge in 1948. Of the early models, scarce, large, and fine-quality trains fetch the highest prices, at around £300–800; larger steam-trains fetch about £3,000–10,000.

### Bing brings competition

The German company Bing rivalled Märklin in the early 20th century. Many Bing trains have English or American markings. Mass-produced Bing engines from the bottom end of the ranges, together with rolling-stock, can be worth £50 to £400, depending on the model and condition.

### Grateful dad

By the 1950s thousands of trains were being produced, but as planes and cars became more commonplace, toy trains gradually lost their mass appeal and the market shrank. Companies that survived the 1960s either aimed their products at adults, or, like Hornby, moved their production to countries such as China, where labour is cheaper. Generally, trains from the 1980s onwards by makers such as Rivarossi and Joueff are not collectable; so many of them exist that they look unlikely to rise in value in the forseeable future.

### Top Tips

- If you are planning an investment, check you are not buying a repainted train: turn it over to see if the parts have been taken apart.
- Consider repainted trains if you wish to build a collection on a budget.
- Check that early trains have their original mechanisms and that the springs are intact.
- Preferably, buy trains from major manufacturers and buy examples made before 1970.
- Watch out for metal fatigue in some pre-war trains, where the metal cracks.

### BUY

*Post-war sets could rise in value. They are often still found for less than £100, so buy sets in good condition because they are more likely to rise in value. Always buy post-war sets boxed as this increases their value.*

**A Tri-ang 00-gauge train set RS1,** containing a Princess Victoria locomotive, two coaches, and track, in its original box. *c.1960, box 51cm (20in) wide.*

**£100–150**

### KEEP

*The Hornby Dublo range is highly collectable and has a huge following, with prices continuing to rise for pieces in mint condition. If your loft contains a good-quality example, keep it and watch the price go up.*

**A Hornby Dublo EDLT20 'Bristol Castle' locomotive and tender,** in BR lined green livery, number 7013. *1950s, 33cm (13in) long.*

**£100–150**

COLLECTOR'S CORNER

# Marbles strike a chord, not only for their vivid, swirling colours, but also because they are so evocative of childhood. The multicoloured glass balls produced from the mid-19th century onwards are avidly sought after.

The most desirable marbles are handmade, mostly in Germany from around 1850 until World War I. Made from brightly coloured glass rods that created swirling patterns of colour, they can be identified by a slightly rough area called a pontil mark where the marble was removed from the rod. There are many different types of marble, all with descriptive names, such as swirls, onion-skins, or corkscrews.

Collectors look for marbles with complex patterns. Symmetrical patterns increase a marble's value and large marbles command a premium. 'Suphides' are also highly sought after. These clear marbles contain a small white figure, human or animal, and can fetch from £80 to more than £2,000.

As German imports tailed off, the USA began to export machine-made marbles, the first of which reached Britain after World War II. Machine-made marbles can usually be distinguished from handmade ones because they do not have a pontil mark. They have become popular because of the increasing scarcity and expense of handmade marbles. Nostalgia also plays a role, as many of today's collectors played with machine-made marbles when they were young.

Look for marbles by the Akro Agate Company, M.F. Christensen & Son, and the Peltier Glass Company. Values vary enormously, ranging from £1–5 for an Akro Agate Co. 'Slag' marble to more than £200 for a Christensen 'Guinea'. It is also worth looking at the innovative work of today's marble makers, which has become increasingly popular since the 1990s, with brisk trading via the Internet.

▲ **An Akro Agate Company machine-made 'Swirl Oxblood' marble.** During the company's lifetime (1910–1951) Akro Agate was the USA's largest marble producer. 'Oxblood' refers to the deep rust colour with black striations; the 'Swirl Oxblood' is thought to have been produced later in the company's history. *c.1940s–1951, 1.5cm (½in) diam.*

**£5–10**

► **A German handmade 'Orange Latticinio Core Swirl' marble.** The pontil mark, which shows where this marble was removed from the rod, can be clearly seen. Made from twisted strands of coloured glass, a marble's most common core colour is white; orange is comparatively scarce, and blue extremely rare. *1860s–1920s 1.5cm (½in) diam.*

**£20–30**

► **A handmade 'Indian' marble**, with a black base and swirls of navy and white, and green and yellow. 'Indian' marbles usually have a dark glass base with coloured strands applied on top of it. The more colours there are, the more valuable the marble usually is. *1860s–1920s, 2cm (¾in) diam.*

**£80–120**

◄ **A German handmade 'Solid Core Swirl' marble.** This fairly complex example has a pink, white, and blue inner swirl overlaid with an outer swirl made up of thin white strands in white glass known as 'latticinio', after the Italian word for milk. *1860s–1920s, 2cm (¾in) diam.*

**£20–40**

◄ **A German handmade 'End of Day' Onionskin marble.** 'End of Day' marbles use stretched flecks of coloured glass rather than rods, which are used in 'Swirls'. The flecks tend to be red, blue, or green; other colours are rarer. *1860s–1920s, 1.5cm (½in) diam.*

**£80–120**

◄ **A German handmade 'Banded Lutz' marble,** with yellow and white bordered Lutz swirls. Lutz marbles have copper flakes suspended in glass, creating the impression of gold. *1860s–1920s, 2cm (¾in) diam.*

**£100–150**

◄ **A German English-style 'Joseph's Coat' marble** with blue, orange, and white strands and two pontil marks. Named after the biblical coat of many colours, handmade 'Joseph's Coat' marbles have a layer of tightly packed coloured strands beneath the surface. *1860–1920, 1.5cm (½in) diam.*

**£50–70**

## Collectors' Tips

- Seek out solitaire boards, but ensure that the marbles are old, as sets are often replaced
- Avoid marbles such as 'cat's eyes' that were mass-produced after the 1960s
- Look for original packaging. It adds value but is usually only found for machine-made marbles

► **A German china marble with blue painted circles** and a band of brown elongated teardrops. China marbles from around the 1860s tend to be glazed and have more complex designs, but as time passed and competition grew, the designs became simpler and glazing stopped. *1870s–80s, 2cm (¾in) diam.*

**£20–30**

► **A contemporary glass marble by Edward Seese,** with a ribbon swirl and a green aventurine band, signed 'FES 2003'. *3cm (1¼in) diam.*

**£20–30**

▲ **A machine-made 'Corkscrew' marble,** made by the American Akro Agate Company. Akro Agate made the most marbles during the 1930s and 'Corkscrew' marbles were the most common, with over 1,000 colour variations. *1930s, 1.5cm (½in) diam.*

**£10–20**

◄ **A German handmade sulphide marble** with a white standing lion. Making sulphides took great skill. Named personalities and painted figures are the most valuable. *1870s–1920s, 3.5cm (1½in) diam.*

**£100–150**

# Toy figures, initially in lead, were first produced as mementoes in the 18th century. Many became boys' most treasured toys. Enthusiasts rekindle childhood memories by adding a regiment to their armies or an animal to their zoo or farm.

**Two John Hill farm figures:** a drover with a red handkerchief and a tramp with a stick and bundle, both in good condition. *c.1950s, 5.5cm (2in) high.*

**£50–100**



Lead-figure making began in Germany: Johann Hilpert's commemorative figure of Frederick the Great on horseback, in 1777, heralded the start of an industry that continued until the mid-1950s. These early figures were two-dimensional *Zinnfiguren* – or 'flats'.

## German supremacy

Despite their promising start, German firms lagged behind their French counterparts until about 1870, when the German firms Heyde and Haffner began to cast three-dimensional figures. Georg Heyde's firm produced military figures based on armies from all over the world and throughout history. Its catalogue also included civilian figures, animals, and scenery. These late 19th-century items are among its most sought-after pieces.

Heinrichsen, market leader from around 1870 to 1910, also produced a huge catalogue of armies and books of war games. A single pre-World War I German figure in good condition can fetch £15–25.

## Little Napoleons

The Napoleonic Wars of the 18th and 19th centuries inspired Lucotte, a Paris-based company, to create the French armies in lead alloy. These figures became market leaders, at home and abroad, and were among the first to be made in the '*ronde-bosse*' or 'solid' style. In 1825 Lucotte merged with CBG, a rival firm, and in 1875 both became part of Mignot – the oldest toy soldier firm still in operation today.

Early solid figures by Lucotte are sought after: a single figure can cost £40–80, and a small regiment of Napoleonic soldiers might sell for £200–500 or more. The later Mignot figures were made in greater numbers and over a longer period, so they are not as desirable; but a single boxed Mignot figure can sell for £30–50.

## Battle of Britain

In 1893 William Britain, Jr introduced his 'hollow-casting' method, which released the molten lead from the centre of a figure and halved the cost of a box of figures. William Britain became the largest maker of lead soldiers in the world, making more

## Some makers to look for:

▪ Britains ▪ Otto & Max Hausser ▪ Charbens ▪ Timpo ▪

◄ **A Britains Royal Horse Artillery group,** Set 39, comprising a six-horse team. Britains became synonymous with the English toy-soldier business. The company was noted for its accurate depictions of British uniforms. *c.1930s, 30cm (12in) long.*

**£150–200**

► **An Otto & Max Hausser group of five mounted Native Americans, including a squaw and papoose.** Otto & Max Hausser's so-called Elastolin figures, of which these are an example, have a reputation for being finely detailed as well as being made of high-quality composition. *c.1920s, 5.5cm (2in) high.*

**£100–150**

**Knights of Agincourt by Britains,** including 1659, a mounted knight with a mace, and 1663, a mounted knight with a lance broken in battle; all are in good condition. *c.1930s–50s 6.5cm (2½in) high.*

**£100–150**

than 100 British Army regiments and setting the standard size (54mm/2in) for toy soldiers. Boxed sets in good condition can be found for less than £500, with smaller sets often selling for about £100–250. A set of Irish Guards (Set 124) in good condition, but with signs of wear, can be found for £80–120 or less.

## Animal magic

By 1910 imports of lead figures had fallen in the UK and William Britain – which became Britains Ltd after 1912 – was soon exporting its products.

Following World War I, interest in military subjects waned, and makers created new lines of farm and zoo animals. Britains introduced its 'Home Farm' figures in 1923; Pixyland issued a range of wild animals; and Taylor & Barrett added zoo keepers, cages, and children's rides to its list.

Animal figures from between the wars can be found at auction for around £20–40, although early circus and zoo sets can fetch £3,000–4,000 or more.

Toy-soldier makers also turned to merchandising. Excella struck a deal with Walt Disney to make replicas of characters from *Three Little Pigs* (1933).

During the 1950s, there was a boom in toy-figure production, influenced by the coronation of Elizabeth II, the growth of children's TV, and a buoyant film industry. These factors provided inspiration for new metal toy makers such as John Hill and, of course, for Britains. In 1966 the use of lead in toys was banned, and firms such as Britains, John Hill, Timpo, and Cherilea switched to safer metals as well as composition and, later, plastic. Some composition and plastic figures were derived from metal-figure designs. Plastic figures are now increasingly collectable.

▲ **Charbens nine-piece circus ensemble.** This London-based manufacturer is noted for its non-military pieces such as circus performers and farm figures. *c.1930s, tallest figure 9cm (3.5in) high.*

**£400–500**

▼ **A Timpo group of nine railway passengers.** The British company, Timpo, marketed its products to both war-game players and model-railway enthusiasts. The scale used for each figure was the same. These figures are all in excellent condition. *c.1930s, tallest figure 5.5cm (2in) high.*

**£200–300**

## Top Tips

- Beware of oxidation on lead figures – 'lead rot' can destroy fine details and painted finishes.
- Check that sets of figures match – paintwork can vary subtly from batch to batch.
- Look for makers' marks on bases and boxes in particular – vintage figures are often stamped.
- Seek out original boxes, as this will add value, especially for smaller firms.
- Check for 'customisation', such as replaced heads or arms – you may feel a lump and the area of the join may have been repainted, lowering value.

## BUY

*Earlier lead figures in good condition, especially those with thin, easily damaged limbs or parts, are hard to find. Buyers prefer boxed items, so always consider a figure with its original packaging. Pieces evocative of historical events should attract attention.*

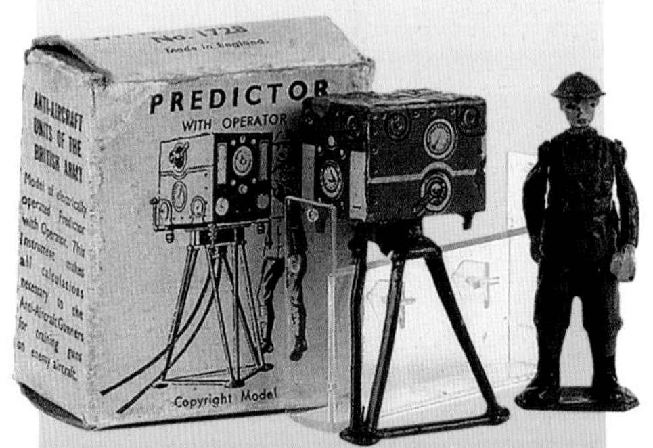


**A Britains model Predictor, used to direct anti-aircraft fire, with operator,** Set 1728. One part of the stand is missing, but the figure, with its box, is in reasonable condition. *c.1940s, 5.5cm (2in) high.*

**£80–120**

## KEEP

*Dig for hidden treasures in a box of old toys. A single lead figure made by one of the dominant manufacturers as late as the 1950s would be a lucky find and, if kept in good condition, will increase in value.*

**A Britains army staff car,** Set 1448. The steering wheel and windscreen are missing, but the firm's name makes it desirable. *c.1930s, 12.5cm (5in) long.*

**£200–250**

# Puppets have always held a certain fascination, perhaps because we can 'bring them to life'. The archetypal maker was Pelham Puppets, which produced a host of children's favourites, from Noddy and Pinocchio to Muffin the Mule.

An old puppet coiled in a toybox or trunk in your attic evokes a lost age of home theatricals. Before you repaint it and replace the original strings, think twice: it may be worth much more exactly as it is. The real treasures are puppets that were never played with, still have their strings and boxes, and are not worn or blemished.

## Pelham power

Pelham started life in 1947 when Bob Pelham set up a small puppet-making firm in Marlborough, Wiltshire. His products found favour with the London toy store Hamley's, and by 1951 more than 50,000 had been sold.

By 1953 the firm had acquired the rights to make Disney characters. The Pinocchio puppet became a big seller and still fetches reasonable prices: a boxed Pelham Pinocchio in good condition can cost at least £30–50. Various versions of Mickey Mouse were produced over the years; Minnie Mouse, Donald Duck, Cinderella, and Snow White and the Seven Dwarves were also popular.

In 1963 the 'Animal' series of 31 new characters was released, in a distinctive yellow box. They were designed by Peter Carter-Page, a Canadian artist who had previously worked for Disney. Prices today range from as little as £50 up to around £200 or more for the rarer examples.

## Wealth of characters

Despite a commercial hiccup in the mid-1960s, the firm carried on making puppets into the early 1990s, after the death of Bob Pelham in 1980.

Puppet types are classified by variations in the appearance of the

**A Pelham puppet type SL 'Pinocchio',** with plastic legs; with original control bar and coloured strings; excellent condition in good but incorrect 2nd-type yellow box with lid (marked 'Tyrolean Boy', not shown). *1960s–70s, 30cm (11¾in) high.*

**£50–80**

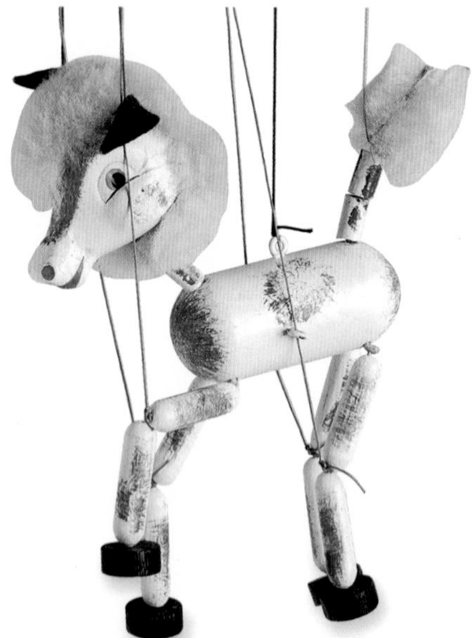

**A Pelham puppet jumpette type 'Foal',** A5, with its original crossbar and coloured strings, and with a fair-to-good yellow box with a lid (not shown). *c.1960s, 20cm (7¾in) high.*

**£30–50**

## A closer look at... a Pelham puppet

As well as those in mint condition, the most valuable Pelham puppets are often those produced for a limited time, or in comparatively small numbers. Look also for original clothes and strings.

**A rare Pelham puppet type SM 'Renaldo the Fox',** with carved head, hinged mouth, and wooden carved hands and shoes. The box (not shown) is plain. *c.1953, 51cm (20in) high.*

**£400–500**

**A Lesney Products 'Muffin the Mule' metal puppet,** complete with original tail, strings, and finger rings; in original box; minor wear. *1950s, 15cm (6in) high.*

**£200–300**

### Did You Know?

*Pelham Puppets started life as Wonky Toys but changed its name in 1948. Bob Pelham recruited fellow ex-servicemen and -women who were unable to return to their pre-war occupations owing to injury or ill health. Initially, the puppets were made out of army surplus materials.*

head. They include the common SS type, around 30cm (12in) high with simple, painted wooden ball heads; the SM type, with an opening mouth to add realism; and the SL type with a moulded head, initially used for TV and film characters.

With 50 years of puppet making to its name, there is no shortage of Pelham puppets, but they vary hugely in value from £10 to £1,000 – key factors being condition, age, and rarity. At its peak the company produced thousands of each of its many characters, and this, combined with the fact that many people have kept their puppets since childhood, means that examples are common. You can still, if you are lucky, pick them up for a few pounds at a car-boot sale. Generally, early puppets are more valuable than later ones – but since some of the more recent types were made in relatively small numbers, these are now quite scarce and valuable too. Several of the characters brought to life by Pelham Puppets over the years were already children's favourites – for example, Muffin the Mule, Noddy, and Pinky and Perky.

## Muffin the magnificent

An unlikely cult figure for the 21st century, Muffin the Mule has become extremely collectable, partly because of his comparative rarity. Although he was an iconic puppet of the 1950s, Muffin's history dates back to 1933. His heyday began in 1946 when Annette Mills, older sister of the actor John Mills, discovered the puppet, christened it Muffin, and made it the star of a new children's TV show. The series lasted until 1955. An early boxed Muffin by Pelham Puppets in good condition might fetch £300 today.

Muffin puppets were also made in die-cast metal by Lesney Products in the 1950s. They are often hard to find, but do occasionally appear in online auctions and toy and juvenalia sales, fetching around £150–200.

### Top Tips

- Look out for rare Pelham puppets such as 'Wolf', 'King', 'Crow', 'Frog', and the original 1960s Thunderbirds puppets.
- Keep and study boxes: they not only add to value but also help to date the puppet, if correctly matched. For example, brown cardboard boxes were used between 1947 and 1956, followed by yellow card boxes between 1956 and 1969; a yellow box with a see-through window was introduced in 1968 and used until 1986.
- Examine puppets' hands. Lead hands with no fingers date from the late 1940s. Large hands with individual, bulbous fingers date from the late 1940s to the early 1950s.

### KEEP

*Despite being produced in large numbers, Disney's cartoon figures are very popular with puppet collectors, who have to compete with Disney fans. Prices for a Disney puppet in mint condition with its box should rise as demand outstrips supply.*

**A Walt Disney's 'Mickey Mouse' type SL Pelham puppet;** mint condition, in box. *1960s, 23cm (9in) high.*

**£200–300**

### SELL

*Puppets that are unknown characters tend to be less popular, especially if produced for a long period. Their potential is limited, so sell now and invest in another, scarcer puppet.*

**A Pelham puppet type SS 'Gypsy',** with coloured strings, in good condition in its original yellow box with a lid (not shown). Signs of wear reduce its value. *1960s, 31cm (12¼in) high.*

**£30–40**

# Teddy bears have comforted the young since the early 20th century, but now they can offer financial solace, too. Vintage bears may fetch thousands of pounds, but post-war, miniature, and promotional bears can be found for much less.

The special appeal of teddy bears is that each one has its own characteristic charm. Enthusiasts may benefit from learning to recognise shapes and forms of different makers, but 'cuddle' appeal should not be underestimated. Original pads, eyes, and stitching and intact fur are all desirable. Also vital are size, maker, and condition.

## Bear essentials

Pre-World War I bears are rare and expensive; even inter-war bears fetch high prices, especially those by German makers such as Steiff, Gebrüder Bing, and Schuco (trademark of Schreyer & Co.). Prices start at around £200–300 for a 1920s or 30s bear, rising to £10,000 or more. British bears made by Chiltern Toys, Dean's Rag Book Co., and J.K. Farnell can fetch £200–600 or more. Chad Valley and Merrythought bears usually cost upwards of £100, depending on age, size, and condition. Small, much-loved bears with balding fur and replaced pads, eyes, and noses usually sell for well under £100, unless by a notable maker.

**A J.K. Farnell bear,** with features typical of Farnell's early bears: jointed arms and legs, humped back, padded paws, and stitched claws – as well as cardboard inserts in the feet to enable it to stand. *c.1912, 28cm (11in) high.*

**£500–600**

**A Steiff mohair bear**, with a stitched mouth and claws, a black felt nose, a button in the left ear, and a swivel head. Typical of this maker are the humped back, long bent arms, and pointed snout. *c.1909, 31cm (12¼in) high.*

**£500–700**

## Lifelong friends

Steiff bears are the most sought after. They are usually solid and well stitched (but stuffing and stitching can degrade over time), with thick mohair, long, slim bodies, elongated arms, large feet,

## Some makers to look for:

- Steiff
- Bing
- Chiltern

**A Bing plush bear.** Before 1920, these bears resembled Steiff's in shape and appearance, but later the smile grew wider. *c.1920, 69cm (27¼in) high.*

**£1,000–1,500**

**A Chiltern mohair bear.** The two stitches at the top of the nose are typical of the bears that Chiltern made in the 1920s and 30s. *c.1930, 51cm (20in) high.*

**£300–400**

## A closer look at... a 1920s and a 1950s teddy bear

Familiarising yourself with the different features of bears will help you to distinguish between early examples and those of the late 1940s, 50s, and beyond. Early bears are especially desirable and often fetch a premium. Convincing signs of wear and tear are a reliable sign of authenticity.

**A golden mohair bear,** probably English, with a fully jointed body, felt paw pads, and wood-wool stuffing. Early bears were made from mohair and stuffed with firm materials such as kapok. *c.1920s, 33cm (13in) high.*

**£700–800**

The snout is longer than on later bears

The arms are long and bend slightly at the wrist

The paws are slightly upturned

**An Austrian light-brown mohair bear,** with jointed limbs and head, a black stitched nose and mouth, and plush pads. Post-war bears were usually made from shinier, softer plush. *c.1950, 61cm (24in) high.*

**£80–120**

The rounder face and shorter snout suggest a post-World War II bear

The arms and legs are shorter

The round, plump body is typical

a humped back, and a pointed nose. They have a Steiff button in the ear – or a hole where it once was. Unusual colours or variations add value, such as the rare 'centre seam' bear (*c*.1905–7), which can fetch up to £5,000: every seventh bear had a seam down the centre of its head, to avoid fabric wastage.

Bing's plush-covered bears (*c*.1920s) usually included a mechanical element (walking or kicking) – and often wore smart outfits. Many Schuco bears of the 1920s to the 50s also moved – for example, the nodding 'Yes/No' bear.

### The best of British

British bears tend to be dumpy, with short arms and legs, and flat faces. The nose and snout, and the paw detailing, can help with identification – for example, Chiltern bears often have shaved muzzles. Look for Chiltern's 'Hugmee' mohair teddies (1920s–60s). These can fetch £100–500 or more.

### *Top Tips*

- Always sniff an old bear – it's impossible to fake the smell of years of love, attention, and accidents.
- Get to know the defining features of well-known makers.
- Avoid suspiciously clean 'old' bears, or any bear with an old label on new paw pads – pre-World War II bears are often faked.
- Beware of fake logo buttons and incongruous modern logo buttons that look shiny and new.

## ▪ Schuco ▪ Merrythought ▪ Chad Valley ▪

**A Schuco 'Yes/No' bear** made out of mohair with a straw filling. The tail controls his head movements. Damage has reduced the value. *1920s, 38cm (15in) high.*

**£150–200**

**A Merrythought jointed bear,** by one of the most popular and prolific makers of the post-war era. A Merrythought label is, typically, on the right foot. *1950s, 38cm (15in) high.*

**£100–200**

**A Chad Valley mohair bear.** This popular British manufacturer made bears that typically have flat ears and chunky limbs. *1930, 51cm (20in) high.*

**£300–400**

## Essential miniature bears

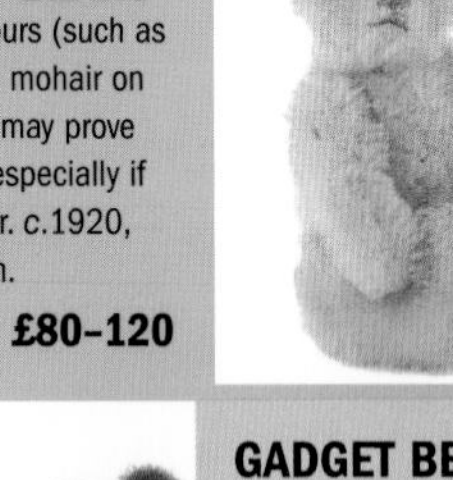

**COLOURED BEARS** Unusual fur colours (such as red, or the white mohair on this Steiff bear) may prove more valuable, especially if by a good maker. *c.1920, 9cm (3½in) high.*
**£80–120**

**BERLIN BEARS** First made in the 1950s, Berlin mascot bears wore a crown and a 'BERLIN' sash. This Schuco bear's lost sash lowers its value. *1950s, 7.5cm (3in) high.*
**£50–100**

**NOVELTY BEARS** Two-faced 'Janus' bears by Schuco feature heads that turn around, revealing a second face, complete with protruding tongue. *1950s, 9cm (3½in) high.*
**£450–650**

**GADGET BEARS** Schuco were masters of the miniature jointed bear, which was often designed to hold items such as lipsticks or perfume bottles. *c.1950, 14cm (5½in) high.*
**£120–180**

**UNKNOWN BEARS** Miniature bears in standard colours by unknown makers can be an effective and economical way to expand a collection. *c.1940s, 9.5cm (3¾in) high.*
**£20–40**

**PANDAS** Panda bears became popular from the 1930s onwards, when live pandas started appearing in zoos. This model was made by Schuco. *1950s, 8.5cm (3¼in) high.*
**£80–100**

Dean's bears, often mousey-looking, had ears sewn lower down on the sides of the head. In the 1920s and 30s unusual colours were common. Farnell's large-footed Alpha range (early 1920s to 60s) are the most desirable English bears. Large early examples can be worth up to around £2,000. Early Chad Valley bears fetch £200–600 or more.

### Tiny treasures

Miniature and novelty bears are popular collectables. Schuco specialised in miniatures – sometimes designed to store make-up. Steiff also made miniature bears, as did several other makers. Prices start at about £20–30 for an unmarked bear.

During World War II, factory production of bears was interrupted, owing to a shortage of materials such as mohair. Instead, many bears were made at home – often out of felt, sheepskin, or wool. These homemade bears currently fetch modest prices, but are gaining in popularity.

### Synthetics

From the 1950s onwards, most bears were given washable fillings and synthetic fabric bodies. Many had rubber and plastic noses and, by the late 1960s, locked-in plastic eyes. Makers such as Wendy Boston, who pioneered the safe eye and the washable bear in 1954, even

▼ **Children listen to the radio** at home with their child-sized teddy bear. *1920s.*

► **A Steiff jointed 'Zotty' bear** (derived from *zottig* – the German for 'hairy' or 'furry'), with the original Steiff tag and button in its ear. *c.1960s, 18cm (7in) high.*
**£80–120**

abandoned jointed arms and legs. Most collectors prefer traditional 'jointed' teddies, made in mohair, so post-war bears, except those by the main makers, usually fetch less than £100–200. Coloured bears exported from the Far East after the 1950s are usually poor in quality and are not collectable at present.

**A Merrythought 'Cheeky' bear,** with a fully jointed, dark-gold mohair body, brown felt pads, a black wool-stitched mouth on a velvet snout, and a printed label reading 'Merrythought/ Ironbridge, Shropshire' on its right foot. *1970s, 39cm (15¼in) high.*

**£150–200**

## Cheeky chappies

Post-World War II teddies by Steiff had a printed fabric label in the left ear (as well as the traditional button), and a card swing tag around the neck. As with other makers, the form of these bears grew rounder during and after the 1940s and 50s. Prices remain high, but examples can be found between £150 and £800. Chad Valley bears from the 1950s are also sought after, especially the rainbow-coloured range, which normally fetches £100–200 or more.

Look out for Merrythought's 1950s Cheeky bears, with wide, stitched smiles, costing from about £100 to £1,000 depending on size and age. Chiltern was taken over by Chad Valley in 1967, and bears were marked 'Chiltern Chad Valley'. All Chad Valley records were destroyed when the company was taken over by Palitoy in 1978, so identification can be difficult. A bear that has charm, and is in good condition with the maker's marks intact, is the best investment.

## Barely collectable

Around the late 1970s bears started to be made as collectors' pieces, as distinct from toys. These 'new' bears fall into two broad groups: 'artist's' bears, created by designers, and limited editions and replicas, made by leading names. Both may be good investments, but the majority are yet to show any significant gain. Top of the range is Steiff, who launched a limited-edition series in 1980, and added replica bears in 1991 (offering the chance to own an example of rare early designs, such as the 'Somersault Bear' of 1909). Merrythought's limited-edition ranges, such as 'Bingie Bear' (1930s), are rising in value, as are Dean's replica bears, launched in 1981. Limited-edition bears in low runs (for example, less than 1,000) may provide good returns. But beware, replicas can be confused with, or occasionally even misrepresented as, original early bears.

Small promotional bears, often made in Japan, Taiwan, or China, form a niche area that may appreciate in the long term. Look for quality, a good maker, and scarcity. The Schuco miniature bear given away by BP in the late 1950s can now fetch upwards of £300, depending on its condition.

### *Top Tips*

- Look out for homemade bears from the World War II period, as they offer charm and are growing in popularity.
- Never immerse a bear in water, whatever its age. This can cause damage, and may affect the stuffing.
- Keep bears you have bought brand new for investment in the original, unopened packaging, together with receipts. Mint condition and authentication are important.
- Look for bears with an interesting or heart-warming provenance. A photograph of the original owner and the bear together adds to the value.

## BUY

*An appealing or unusual face often adds to a bear's value. Many such faces are unique to the individual toy, so if you find a characterful bear in good condition, it is likely to be a sound investment.*

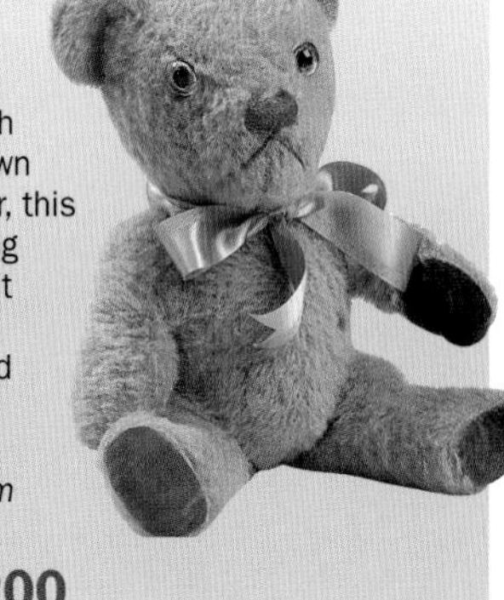

**A British 'glum' bear cub.** Although by an unknown manufacturer, this bear's striking face makes it a desirable purchase and a worthwhile investment. *c.1950, 28cm (11in) high.*

**£100–200**

## KEEP

*It is usually worth keeping large bears if they are in reasonable condition, especially if they have their original pads and are by a well-known maker. Bears dressed by their original owner are also popular.*

**A Steiff bear dressed in military clothing,** with signs of wear. The unusual uniform makes this bear desirable. It would be worth having him restored. *c.1920s, 43cm (17in) high.*

**£700–800**

## KEEP

*Rare bears with an interesting story behind them can be valuable. This pair of bears was produced to celebrate the birth in 1949 of Brumas, the first polar bear cub to be bred at London Zoo.*

**Two Dean's Rag Book Co. mohair plush polar bears, 'Ivy & Brumas'.** It is very unusual to find this mother-and-cub set still intact. *c.1949, cub 16.5cm (6½in) high.*

**£150–200**

# Soft toys, with their simple, nostalgic charm and sometimes bizarre appearance, appeal to young and old alike. It is possible to find many unexpected treasures, by major makers, at affordable prices.

**A soft toy lamb,** by an unknown maker, with its original box. *c.1930, 18cm (7in) high.*

**£20–30**

Traditional soft toys date only from the second half of the 19th century. Their golden age was from the 1920s to the 60s, after which quality declined as inferior goods were imported from the Far East. So, although your child's 90s giraffe may never be collectable, your own childhood 'Peggy' penguin made by Steiff in the 50s could be worth up to £200.

## Unwavering quality

Steiff, a German company established in 1877 and best known for its teddies, started out by making other soft toys. The firm has made some of the best-quality animal toys, including cats and dogs, wild animals, dinosaurs, lobsters, reptiles, and insects. Margarete Steiff's first toys were homemade presents for her family. A felt elephant made as a pin cushion for her sister-in-law in 1880 trumpeted the beginning of the Steiff empire and was featured on the button used on toys made in 1904–5.

Penguins joined the Steiff range in the 1920s, with 'King Peng'. Some toys, such as the insects, produced in the 1950s to 60s, are often undervalued by those who associate Steiff with bears, and can be found for £50 or less; others have fetched £400 or more. Well-known characters are sought after – a felt Steiff 'Mickey Mouse' from the 1930s can fetch £2,000–3,000, depending on size and condition.

## Monkeys and acrobats

Germany was also home to Schreyer & Co., known as Schuco, established in 1912. As well as bears, they made a range of miniature monkeys. Some valuable examples were designed to conceal hidden features such as compacts or lipstick holders, and others had wind-up mechanisms that made them tumble or perform acrobatics. The limbs on toys made in the 1950s are sometimes thinner and the bodies and heads rounder than on earlier models, but this is not always the case. Look out for Schuco monkeys in unusual colours such as blue – they are more valuable than those in traditional colours.

## Some makers to look for:

▪ Steiff ▪ Schuco ▪ Merrythought ▪ Chad Valley ▪

**A Steiff elephant.** Even after the war, when many makers were using cheaper fabrics, Steiff continued to use quality materials, so it is safer to date these toys from the style, tag, or button in the ear (introduced in 1904). *c.1918, 25cm (9¾in) high.*

**£150–200**

**A Schuco 'Yes/No' monkey,** with felt clothes, painted metal eyes, and a tail lever that makes its head nod or shake. Many of Schuco's soft toys had such mechanisms, enabling them to move. *c.1920, 20cm (7¾in) high.*

**£80–120**

**A velveteen Merrythought 'Jerry' mouse,** with a label. This top British maker is noted for its wide and varied range of soft toys. *1930s–c.1970s, 23cm (9in) high.*

**£60–80**

**A 1960s Chad Valley plush 'Sooty',** wearing red dungarees, with original paw pads. *17.8cm (7in) high.*

**£20–30**

## Did You Know?

*When the traditional black-faced golliwog became increasingly unacceptable in the racially sensitive atmosphere of the 1960s, Dean's Rag Book Co. produced an alternative white-faced 'Mr Smith' golly to challenge the traditional Chad Valley version. The white-faced golly never enjoyed the same popularity. Far fewer were made and so they are now rare.*

## The best of British

Merrythought, a British toymaker established in 1930, is renowned for the quality of its soft toys. It made toys based on the characters from Disney's film *Winnie the Pooh* between 1965 and 1976. Look out for 'Kanga and Roo' from this period, which can be worth up to around £100 when found together – 'Roo' is often lost.

Chad Valley, established in 1897, is another notable British toymaker. It began to make soft toys after 1915, and, from the early 1920s to the mid-30s, produced comic velveteen 'Bonzo' dogs with painted-on facial expressions. These can fetch around £100 and upwards, depending on size and how much of the painted face is still intact. Along with a large range of other toys, they also made 'Tim Tale', a mouse character with large ears, a black jacket, and a red waistcoat, seen in *Daily Mail* cartoons in the 1930s. Today he's hard to find and can fetch up to £200.

## Pick your favourites

As well as seeking out favourite makers, some people collect by animal type – cats, dogs, and monkeys being especially popular. Cartoon and comic characters are also sought after.

Look for toys made from early materials: mohair, felt, and kapok or wood-wool stuffings are generally pre-1950s, while silk plush and softer stuffings date from the 1950s onwards. During wartime, when mohair and other 'fur' materials were scarce, toys' bodies were made using cheaper fabrics, formed into 'clothes'.

**A Steiff 'Peggy' penguin.** *1950s, 33cm (13in) high.*

**£100–150**

## Top Tips

- Choose a soft toy that is undamaged, clean, and retains its button or label if it had one. Condition is all-important.
- Invest in unmarked early toys if they are in good condition and come with an original box. If they also have a pleasing appearance, it is likely that they will retain their appeal and make sound investments.
- Don't undertake restoration work yourself, such as sewing up a split seam, as this can reduce value. Also, never immerse a toy in water. Find a teddy bear or doll hospital to restore or clean a soft toy.
- When storing a soft toy collection, use lavender bags rather than moth balls to deter moths, as the smell is more pleasant. Destroy insects by sealing toys in plastic bags and then putting them in the freezer overnight.

## BUY

*When buying modern limited editions, look for low edition numbers, short-lived editions, or those that commemorate events such as anniversaries. Always keep the toy in mint condition with its tags, paperwork, and box, if applicable, as these will ensure the highest prices if you sell in the future.*

**A mechanical Steiff elephant** from an edition of 4,000. Modern limited-edition toys, like this elephant, have yet to reach a peak in interest, with most still fetching less than their original price. *1988–90, 33cm (13in) high.*

**£80–120**

## KEEP

*Toys associated with TV programmes are always a hit with nostalgic fans who watched them as children. But many of these toys have been forgotten and consigned to a box in the loft. Today, shows from the 1950s to the 80s are being re-run, so this revival may extend to popular characters made into soft toys.*

**Wendy Boston's 'Basil Brush'.** Although popular during the 1970s and early 80s, this anarchic fox is now rarely seen, but a revival means that Basil may rise in value. *1970s, 40cm (15¾in) high.*

**£20–30**

# Snow domes and globes capture charming, miniature little worlds. From religious subjects to the frankly kitsch, they make delightful souvenirs and are even more popular now than they were when they originated in France in the 1870s.



The first souvenir snow domes were sold at the 1889 Paris Exposition and featured miniature Eiffel Towers. But, sadly, none appears to have survived.

The central subject is key to a snow dome or globe's appeal, and today these tiny worlds feature everything from Hawaiian snow scenes to Harry Potter.

Early domes were made from hand-blown glass and filled with water. They had a wooden, ceramic, rubber, metal, or marble base and plaster-moulded interior scenes. The 'snow' was made of chipped bone, porcelain, treated wax, rice, or sand. Today, it comprises fragments of white plastic or glitter in distilled water. The water evaporates over time, affecting values to some extent. Later models may be refillable, though.

Production accelerated in Europe during the early 20th century, followed by the USA in the late 1920s, and Japan in the late 30s. Since the late 1950s, domes have been made of plastic with injection-moulded interior scenes. Taiwan, Hong Kong, and China have led production since the 1970s.

▲ **A rare, early 20th-century Continental glass snow globe.** Domes and globes with religious themes were most popular at the turn of the 20th century. This one has wax angels on wire tremblers with gold leaf 'snow flakes'. *c.1910, 12.5cm (5in) high.*

**£40–60**

► **A souvenir sailor and sea captain snow globe.** Examples with appealing characters are always popular. This piece has a seesaw fishing scene. *1970s, 12.5cm (5in) high.*

**£35–45**

► **A Walt Disney Productions 'Mickey and Donald' snow dome.** Mickey Mouse and Donald Duck, two of Walt Disney's most popular characters, sit astride a moving seesaw. *Early 1970s, 7.5cm (3in) high.*

**£10–20**

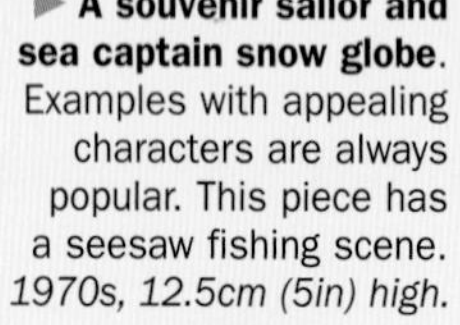

◄ **A Walt Disney Productions 'Pinocchio' snow globe.** This is one of a set of five snow globes that includes Raggedy Ann and Bugs Bunny. *Early 1960s, 12.5cm (5in) high.*

**£50–60**

◄ **A set of three McDonald's snow domes.** These domes were given away with Happy Meals in Germany only. *1980s, 5.5cm (2¼in) high.*

**£10–15 each**

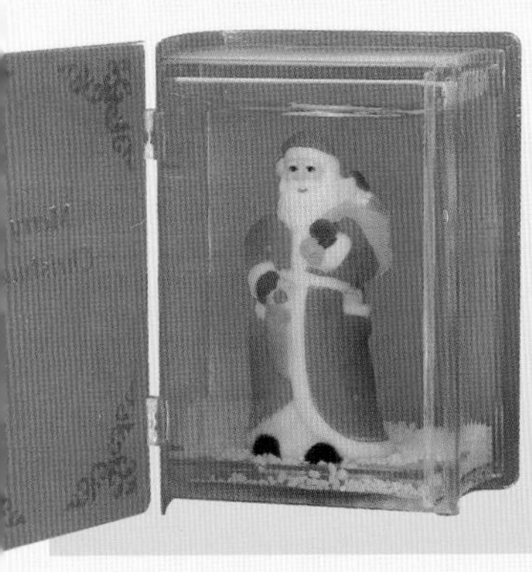

◀ **A book-shaped snow dome with Santa.** Although not domed (or global) in shape, this novel commemorative Christmas item has an unusual shape and a festive theme. *1970s–80s, 9cm (3½in) high.*

**£7–10**

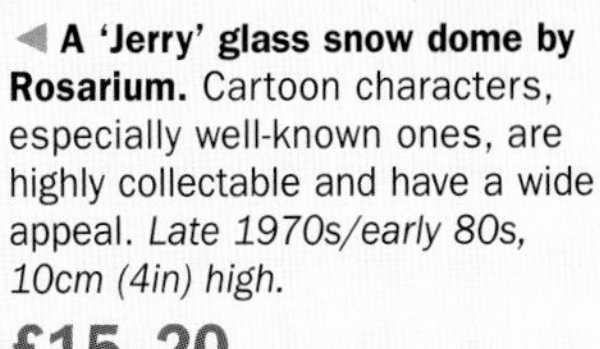

◀ **A 'Jerry' glass snow dome by Rosarium.** Cartoon characters, especially well-known ones, are highly collectable and have a wide appeal. *Late 1970s/early 80s, 10cm (4in) high.*

**£15–20**

## Collectors' Tips

Look out for these desirable features:

- Attractive designs featuring both a foreground and a background
- Domes with unusual shapes, moving parts, or scenes that fill the entire dome

▶ **An illuminated religious snow dome.** Religious subjects and souvenirs from pilgrimage sites, such as Lourdes, are still in demand. This dome shows the Last Supper and the Crucifixion. *c.1970s, 9cm (3½in) high.*

**£8–12**

◀ **A snowman snow globe with seesaw action.** There are plenty of Christmas scenes around. The rocking action of this globe gives it extra charm, as does the cheerful snowman. *Late 1960s, 12.5cm (5in) high.*

**£15–25**

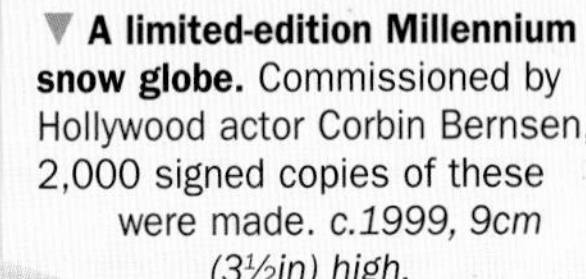

▼ **A limited-edition Millennium snow globe.** Commissioned by Hollywood actor Corbin Bernsen, 2,000 signed copies of these were made. *c.1999, 9cm (3½in) high.*

**£10–15**

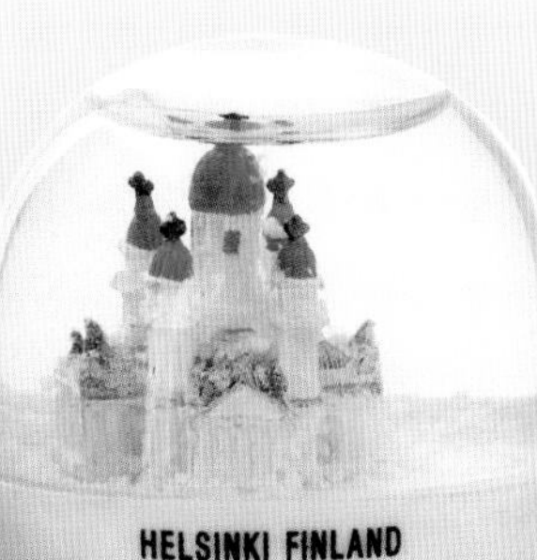


◀ **A Helsinki, Finland, souvenir snow dome.** Don't underestimate the interest in basic tourist-attraction domes – even if inferior in quality, these items are still collectable. *1990s, 5cm (2in) high.*

**£4–8**

# Bisque dolls were first made in France and Germany, but soon captured the hearts of children everywhere. With their period costumes redolent of childhoods long past, they represent an important area of interest for doll enthusiasts and investors.

**A late 19th-century character doll** in contemporary sailor dress. It has a cloth body, an open mouth, and a mark that looks like 'Alma'. *c.1880s, 32cm (12¾in) high.*

**£35–45**

Bisque, the material used to make the heads of these dolls (and sometimes their hands and feet, too), is unglazed tinted porcelain. Bisque dolls were popular from about 1850, and were made by all the leading French and German dollmakers.

## Bisque basics

There are three types of bisque doll: French fashion dolls (miniature adults), *bébé* (baby) dolls, and character dolls, which tend to be more expressive or dressed as a certain type of character. Fashion dolls are extremely expensive today. Early *bébés* are perhaps the most popular type of bisque doll, with prices to suit all pockets. Later *bébés* can be expensive, but those by lesser-known firms are more affordable. Character dolls offer the widest range of prices and styles. An appealing face or expression will always add value.

## Bonny *bébés*

French *bébés* reigned supreme from 1860 to the 1890s. Leading makers include Jumeau, Bru Jeune et Cie, Gaultier, and Steiner; early examples from any of these now cost thousands of pounds. Early *bébés* often have no identifying marks, and authentication is a matter for experts.

In 1899 French dollmakers formed the Société Française de Fabrication de Bébés et Jouets (S.F.B.J.) to produce 'economy' dolls to compete with German imports. S.F.B.J. dolls tend to have cruder faces, with rosier cheeks and parted lips. The bisque heads (often made in Germany, ironically) are usually attached to jointed wood and composition bodies. Most S.F.B.J. dolls made after 1905 bear these initials on the back of the head. Prices often start at about £200.

## Some makers to look for:

▪ Armand Marseille ▪ Simon & Halbig ▪ Steiner ▪ S.F.B.J. ▪ Jumeau ▪

◄ **An Armand Marseille 'Dream Baby' doll.** Marseille often manufactured in high volumes to meet the demand for less expensive dolls. In series such as the charming 'Dream Baby' range (from 1926) they maintained high overall quality. *c.1930s, 17.5cm (6¾in) high.*

**£100–150**

**A Simon & Halbig girl doll,** with original ► Edwardian clothes. Examples made before the early 20th century have open mouths and solid heads. Later dolls have closed mouths and socket-type heads. *c.1920, 32cm (12½in) high.*

**£150–200**

◄ **A Steiner doll,** incised 'SCS', series C. Steiner dolls always have the nose set close to the mouth, and hands with stubby fingers. *c.1870, 62cm (24½in) high.*

**£3,000–3,500**

**An S.F.B.J. toddler doll,** 236. ► S.F.B.J.'s character dolls tend to be popular. *c.1911, 51cm (20in) high.*

**£400–500**

## Living dolls

Character dolls with more expressive faces appeared around 1900. This market was dominated by German makers, such as Kammer & Reinhardt, who issued its first dolls of this type in 1909. Rare examples of these early dolls can fetch tens of thousands of pounds. Look out for dolls with mould numbers 117 or 117/A.

The character dolls made by Simon & Halbig carry the initials 'SH' on the back of the head. Its black and Asian dolls are much sought after.

## Dolly mixtures

Character dolls by the German maker Armand Marseille are less expensive. From 1890, it made bisque heads, usually marked 'AM', both for its own company and others. Its 'Dream Baby' (produced until the late 1940s) came in many sizes, as well as in four ethnic types. The 341 model, up to 60cm (24in) high and with a composition body, is the most popular and can fetch around £100–500. Black versions are desirable, especially those with coloured and fired (rather than painted) bisque heads. They can fetch around £200–600.

Other makers include J.D. Kestner and Gebrüder Heubach. Kestner dolls are largely known by their mould numbers, with very few having names. One exception is the highly prized 'Hilda', which can fetch £800–1,000 or more. Prices for genuine Gebrüder Heubach dolls have suffered from the existence of good fakes, made from moulds taken from the originals.

**A Jumeau *bébé*,** in size 9. Jumeau dolls are prized for their delicately painted faces and charming expressions. *c.1885, 61cm (24in) high.*

**£2,500–2,800**

### Top Tips

- Check the back of the bisque head for a mould number and perhaps a maker's mark.
- Examine dolls for pale-coloured bisque and detailed painting – bold colours and crude features are less valuable.
- Try to buy dolls with original bodies and original or appropriate clothing.
- Look for black and Asian dolls still in their original costumes, as they are much sought after.
- Avoid dolls with repainted facial features or details – the repainting will reduce value.
- Choose dolls with jointed limbs – they are easier to stand or sit for display.

### KEEP

*Character dolls are popular, especially those with expressive and cheerful faces. Relatively large sizes by known makers are the most sought after and should rise in value.*

**A 1920s S.F.B.J. French character doll,** known as a 'Laughing Jumeau' (Jumeau was one of the firms in the S.F.B.J.). Its mint condition and original body both add to the value. *1920s, 41cm (16¼in) high.*

**£400–500**

### SELL

*Armand Marseille dolls from the 390 mould series (from around 1900) are among the most common antique dolls, and are unlikely to rise in value over the foreseeable future. Finely painted dolls in larger sizes, with more realistic faces, will have more potential.*

**An Armand Marseille doll,** 390, with original clothing. It is larger than the smallest size, which is 23cm (9in), but the quality is below that of many dolls of the period. *c.1910s, 60cm (23½in) high.*

**£80–120**

COLLECTOR'S CORNER

# Half Dolls, dainty porcelain figurines, were fashionable early in the 20th century and were produced in their thousands at the height of their popularity. By the end of the 40s, however, production had virtually ceased.

▲ **A porcelain half doll of a lady wearing a pink dress.** Although it is neither particularly well painted nor modelled, this doll's fan and tall wig enhance its appeal. *c.1925, 9.5cm (3¾in) high.*

**£10–15**

Intended for ornamental use around the home, half dolls were usually made from porcelain or bisque: they had upper bodies, heads, and arms, but no legs. They were sometimes known as pin-cushion, dresser, or tea-cosy dolls, as the voluminous skirts sewn onto them were used as decorative covers for everyday household objects, such as teapots, pin-cushions, and powder boxes. The most popular half dolls were modelled on pretty ladies, but male dolls were produced too, as well as children and a variety of animals.

The most prolific manufacturers of half dolls were German factories, such as Dressel & Kister, Heubach, Goebel, and Kestner.

Values start from around £10–20 for basic dolls (made from a single mould so the arms lay against the body). Mid-price dolls have arms set further away from the body, while the finest dolls have delicately sculpted outstretched arms and can be worth up to around £300. Detailed painting and smooth bisque are also good indicators of quality. Large dolls are particularly sought after, as are those with their original skirts, which are often elaborate and made from a wide variety of fabrics.

▼ **A porcelain half doll** of a lady wearing a hat and dress. Unusually, this doll has legs and her original clothing. She is sitting in an attractive position with her arms bent, and her dress and hat have an attractive, lustred finish. *c.1910, 9cm (3½in) high.*

**£40–50**

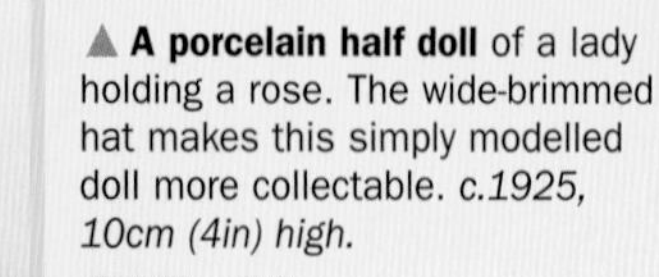

▲ **A porcelain half doll** of a lady holding a rose. The wide-brimmed hat makes this simply modelled doll more collectable. *c.1925, 10cm (4in) high.*

**£15–20**

▼ **A ceramic half doll** of an elegant young woman mounted on an upholstered fabric skirt. Dolls dressed in their original clothes, usually homemade, are much sought after. *c.1935, 14cm (5½in) high.*

**£15–20**

▲ **A porcelain half doll** of a naked lady with painted feathers in her hair. This finely painted doll has expressive arms, which makes it very desirable. *c.1910, 10cm (4in) high.*

**£60–70**

◀ **A porcelain half doll of a blonde lady mounted on an upholstered fabric skirt base.** The porcelain legs added to this doll are an unusual feature, making it more desirable. *c.1935, 13cm (5¼in) high.*

**£15–20**

◀ **A pair of porcelain Dutch boy and girl half dolls.** National dress is a feature much sought after by collectors, as are pairs of dolls. *c.1925, 4.5cm (1¾in) high.*

**£15–20 each**



▶ **A porcelain half doll of a young lady.** This doll's finely modelled face, thoughtful expression, and the rose she is holding in her outstretched hand, make it valuable. *c.1910, 7.5cm (3in) high.*

**£80–120**

## Collectors' Tips

- Look for dolls with period details and clothing, such as 1920s hairstyles or 1930s outfits
- Dolls' features were prone to damage, so check them carefully for signs of chips or re-gluing
- Examine dolls' back waists for manufacturers' identification marks

◀ **A porcelain half doll of a 'flapper' in a yellow painted 1920s cocktail dress.** This doll's hairstyle dates it to the 1920s, a period when half dolls were extremely popular. *c.1925, 7cm (2¾in) high.*

**£20–25**

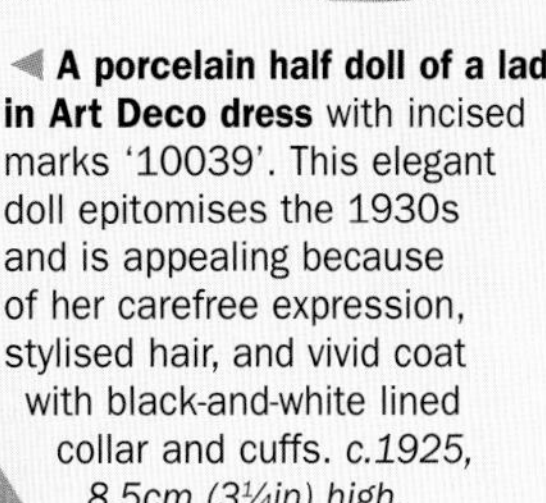

◀ **A porcelain half doll of a lady in Art Deco dress** with incised marks '10039'. This elegant doll epitomises the 1930s and is appealing because of her carefree expression, stylised hair, and vivid coat with black-and-white lined collar and cuffs. *c.1925, 8.5cm (3¼in) high.*

**£100–150**

▲ **A porcelain half doll of a young lady** with incised marks '15460'. The wealth of detail, from bows on the doll's chest and sleeves to her floppy, wide-brimmed hat, make it desirable. *c.1925, 12cm (4¾in) high.*

**£15–20**

# Fabric dolls are direct descendants of the homemade rag doll – that huggable confidante of children down the centuries. While some fabric dolls can have a high price tag, English fabric character dolls – to take just one of the many types – can be found for less than £50.

Dolls made of plush, pressed cotton, or printed felt are classed as fabric dolls. These materials are fragile, so older examples are rare. Most of the fabric dolls available today were made between 1900 and 1950. Prices for marked dolls with maker's labels or marks by well-known companies, such as the Italian firm Lenci, rose in the 1990s, but inexpensive dolls still exist.

## Wardrobe of felt

Felt dolls made by Lenci, established in 1908, were designed for display. Typically, they have elaborate costumes and expressive painted faces, often with sideways glancing eyes. Dolls with glass eyes are more valuable than those with painted ones.

The most desirable Lenci dolls, made in the period from 1920 to 1941, tend to fetch £200–500, but rare examples can be worth up to £5,000. Those made after 1941 are usually valued at less than £200. Reproductions of early designs, issued in the 1970s, may prove to be a good investment.

Lenci dolls have a black or purple stamp on the foot and often a label attached to the costume. Early dolls may have a Lenci pewter button sewn on to the costume, too.

## Who stole my sheep?

Starting in 1926, in Shropshire, Norah Wellings made high-quality fabric dolls. Those modelled on nursery rhyme characters, such as Little Bo Peep, can fetch £300. Character dolls, such as cowboys and Indians, are generally less expensive. Smaller sizes can be found for less than £100; larger sizes can cost up to £300.

Look for dolls with accurate detail, colourful costumes, and all their accessories. Little Bo Peep should have her sheep. Copies exist – especially of the sailor doll, often marked 'Imperial' – so check the labels. All Norah Wellings dolls have a cloth label on the foot or wrist, although sometimes this is missing.

From 1920, Chad Valley made a range of fabric dolls, often with mohair wigs and glass eyes. Those based on the young princesses, Elizabeth and Margaret Rose, or on Mabel Lucie Attwell characters, can cost up to £500.

**A Nora Wellings 'Mountie' doll,** with his original hat and clothing. *c.1930s, 25cm (10in) high.*

**£15–20**

**A Norah Wellings brown velvet doll,** with fixed brown glass eyes and painted mouth, wearing integral green velvet dungarees, and a label attached to the foot. This one is slightly worn, which reduces the value *c.1920s, 29cm (11½in) high.*

**£20–30**

## Alpha types

Two teddy bear manufacturers, Alpha Toys and Dean's Rag Book Co., also made fabric dolls. Alpha Toys is renowned for its costumes. Its dolls date back to the 1930s and include ones that play music. Look for its George VI doll from around 1937, which can fetch about £200.

From 1905 to 1995, Dean's Rag Book Co. also produced printed fabric dolls designed to be cut out and sewn up at home. Its post-war dolls often had features such as shoes and socks printed on the fabric. Dean's also specialised in ready-assembled promotional dolls. It introduced

## A closer look at... a Käthe Kruse cloth doll

Käthe Kruse dolls are worth more if they are in fine condition. Dirty, worn dolls can be worth as little as half the value. Examples complete with box and clothing carry a premium. All Käthe Kruse dolls are marked with a signature and number on the left foot.

The doll is in excellent condition, with strong, brightly painted facial features

The original box is present, as are many of her original clothes

**A Käthe Kruse cloth child doll,** 7534. She is wearing a flannel tartan skirt and red shirt. Some clothes have been added to her original wardrobe. Her excellent condition accounts for much of the value. *c.1930, 51cm (20in) high.*

**£500–600**

a large range of felt dolls around 1920, readily found today for £50–300.

### Fireman, soldier, dreamer

The German company Steiff made felt dolls such as firemen and military figures. They have distinctive painted felt faces with a centre seam, sewn-on ears, and felt hands. Recent limited editions of its earlier dolls from the 1920s to the 50s have the script 'Steiff' button, used since 1986. Larger dolls can fetch £500–700.

Another famous German maker is Käthe Kruse, who introduced her fabric dolls in 1912. Look for early examples produced before 1929 with three hand-stitched seams on the head. Her *Du Mein* ('You are Mine') and *Traumerchen* ('Little Dreamer') dolls are desirable. Early dolls in good condition are very expensive. Dolls from 1948 onwards have plastic heads and tend to fetch £100–300.

**A Dean's Rag Book Lupino Lane fabric doll,** with dog-tooth checked suit and printed face. *c.1939, 29cm (11½in) high.*

**£80–120**

### Top Tips

- When examining a Lenci doll, check that the pewter button from an early doll has not been attached to a later one. A tell-tale sign is new stitching.
- Be wary of unmarked 'Lenci' dolls – they may be Chad Valley copies.
- Do not wash a fabric doll.
- Wrap dolls in acid-free tissue and store them in a box.
- To eradicate insects, seal the doll in a bag and place it in a freezer overnight.
- Look for characters from fairy tales, nursery rhymes, and stars of stage and screen: these are especially collectable.

### BUY

*Look for a Lenci doll that has a face full of character – a scowling child can be worth up to £600. A rare costume and the original label also add value.*

**A Lenci 'Mascotte' doll** holding a red rose, in good condition. *c.1930s, 51cm (20in) high.*

**£80–120**

### SELL

*Many companies produced sailor dolls, including firms that made advertising props. They are too common to rise in value, so it is worth selling to a collector of advertising memorabilia.*

**An 'Invicta' marine doll.** This late example was produced as an advertising doll and is not by a noted maker. It has no maker's label or stamp. *1950s, 23cm (9in) high.*

**£10–15**

# Plastic dolls have delighted generations of little girls since they first appeared in the 1940s. The huge numbers produced over recent decades – first in America and then Britain – allow plenty of scope for anyone interested in adopting these pretty creatures.

Plastic was the toymakers' ideal material, allowing them to produce dolls that were light, hygienic, hard-wearing, and inexpensive. Post-World War II dolls in this novel medium were snapped up by an enthusiastic public. By the late 1950s, the hard plastic of the early years had been replaced by a softer vinyl. With so many of these dolls still in existence, condition is vital. Desirability is also increased by a rare or appealing design, or by a well-known maker.

## American beauties

The American doll designer Mary Hoyer began making hard plastic dolls in 1946. They were distinguished by curled hair and elaborate outfits, often homemade by their owners, using special knitting or sewing patterns.

In 1945 Beatrice Behrman – trading as Madame Alexander of the New York-based Alexander Doll Co. (established 1923) – introduced one of the earliest ranges of currently collectable plastic dolls. She featured characters from films, books, and cartoons, as well as celebrities. Her dolls are marked either on the back or elsewhere on the body, and some have name tags attached to their clothes. Among her most sought-after dolls are the 'Little Women' series based on Louisa M. Alcott's books. Examples in mint condition with their original clothing and hairstyles can fetch anything between £30 and £500.

Dolls made by the Vogue Doll Co. in the 1950s will now generally cost £200–500, again if in good condition with their clothes and hair unchanged.

Sasha dolls were a triumph of the 1960s. These realistic-looking dolls – a boy ('Gregor') or a girl ('Sasha') – had dark or fair hair, brown or blue eyes, different skin colours, and everyday play clothes. They were designed to break down cultural stereotypes, and were made by different manufacturers in different countries. In Britain they were produced by Trendon Toys from 1965. Authentic clothing and a swing tag on the wrist will add value, as will the doll's general condition, especially if the long hair on the female model is uncut.

### *Did You Know?*

*Kewpies began life as doodles in the love stories that Rose O'Neill illustrated for the American magazine, 'The Ladies' Home Journal'. Asked to develop them into a children's series, Rose redesigned them as dolls. They were so successful that they were even commemorated on a US postage stamp.*

► **A vintage Mary Hoyer hard plastic doll,** with her original dress and tag, and marked on the back with the maker's mark. *1950s, 35cm (14in) high.*

**£150–200**

◄ **Two plastic Rosebud Kewpie dolls,** with moulded hair. *1950s, 15cm (6in) high.*

**£20–25**

## A closer look at... a Madame Alexander doll

Dolls produced by this renowned New York maker are known for their detailed costumes and accessories – the example here even has a hairnet and hair curlers.

The doll still has its presentation box, which is in excellent condition

The hair is set in its original style and retains its floral band and hairnet

The clothes and accessories are still intact, including the hatbox

The tag is still attached, which adds value.

**A Madame Alexander 'Margot Ballerina' doll,** with her original clothing, accessories, and box. She is in mint condition, which is rare for a doll of this age. *c.1953, 35.5cm (14in) high.*

**£500–600**

### Pedigree chums

During the 1950s the Pedigree brand was a favourite in Britain, and its Rosebud dolls were well loved by many young children. As a result, the condition of these dolls is often poor – check them for damage to fingers and toes, as many owners painted their baby's nails. Some types had washable hair, so make sure that it hasn't been spoiled by any washing and that it is still in its original style. Sleeping eyes should open and close and eyelashes should be intact. Missing or replaced clothes will lower the value.

### Newborn babes

British National Dolls Ltd specialised in newborn baby dolls with hair that was shaped and moulded as part of the doll's head, then sometimes given a painted finish. Many dolls even had 'mama' voice boxes. Most are missing their original clothes, which reduces their already modest value (£30–50 or less). Other 'newborns' include Palitoy's 'Tiny Tears', launched in 1965 with accessories such as a bottle, travelling kit, and bath.

### Kewpie cuties

Cartoons and illustrations gave rise to many character dolls. One of the most popular was Kewpie, with her starfish-shaped hands, small 'wings' over the ears, tiny eyebrows, and appealing face. As a result of the variety of different types, sizes, and materials available, as well as the range of prices, Kewpie dolls make an excellent collection on their own. Licences were issued to various companies who produced inexpensive plastic Kewpies from the late 1940s and 50s; some pirate versions were also made.

### The eyes have it

Googly dolls, with their large, 'goo-goo' eyes, were first produced in bisque by various German makers. Later plastic versions were made by a number of lesser-known manufacturers. These plastic dolls can often be found for under £100. Googly dolls with mischievous expressions are more collectable.

### Top Tips

- Avoid any doll with hair that has been altered by its owner – cut, restyled, or damaged by washing or brushing.
- Choose dolls that are clean, with unstained plastic. But also make sure that over-enthusiastic cleaning hasn't damaged the surface of the plastic.
- Look for original accessories and packaging – especially the box – as these will enhance the value.
- Search for dolls with makers' tags still attached, as this also adds value.
- Look for one of the following marks to indicate Madame Alexander dolls: 'Mme Alexander', 'Alexander', or 'Alex'.
- Beware of unauthorised Japanese-made Kewpies without a proper label.

### KEEP

*Madame Alexander is now one of the most desirable names in the plastic-doll market, and those models with eye-catching, brightly coloured clothing are especially popular. Prices are rising fast, as interest in plastic dolls grows, so an example such as this is sure to at least retain its value.*

**A Madame Alexander 'Morocco' bent-knee doll.** The original clothing is in excellent condition and the doll still has its tag, making this piece well worth keeping. *1950s, 20cm (8in) high.*

**£200–250**

### BUY

*Many dolls made since the 1960s do not currently fetch high prices, but good-quality examples of models that were particularly popular in their day have the potential to rise in value as yesterday's children become tomorrow's collectors.*

**A 'Tiny Tears' doll.** Valuable earlier examples of this doll by Palitoy have hard, solid heads. Look out for mint-condition 'Tiny Tears' from the 1960s, marked 'Made in England 16D'. *1980s, 30cm (12in) high.*

**£70–100**

# Barbie is the most successful doll ever made. A generation of little girls abandoned their baby dolls for Barbie's fashion-conscious look and wardrobe of 'must-have' clothes. She has now turned 50, and has her own website and publications, and admirers of all ages.

Launched in 1959, Barbie was the first teenage doll. She evolved from a nubile German cartoon character, Lilli, who was unsuccessfully launched as a doll in 1955. Her American maker Mattel has issued many Barbies each year since then – plus accessories, as well as family and friends, including her boyfriend Ken, first launched in 1961.

The most prized Barbies are those from 1959–72, especially examples from the 'ponytail' era (1959–66). Special limited-edition dolls (fewer than 35,000) are also desirable, as are early 1960s gift sets, Barbies and Kens with bendable legs (made in 1965–67), and 'fashion model' Barbies, dressed in couture clothing (these must have their original labels). Also sought after are accessories such as Barbie's Dream Kitchen and Dinette and her tiny necklaces, shoes, and tiaras. Red-haired Barbies, introduced in 1961, are rare and desirable.

Condition is crucial: a mint-condition doll, costume, or set of accessories in an unopened box will be worth two to four times more than one without its box. Standard 'pink box' Barbies are rarely a good investment: go for limited editions instead.

▲ **A boxed 'SuperSize' Barbie.** The extra-large Barbie was launched by Mattel in 1977 but never caught on. *c.1977, 47cm (18½in) high.*

**£80–120**

► **A 'Growing Up' Skipper.** This version of Barbie's sister, Skipper (1964), grew taller if her arm was twisted. The missing shoes lower the value. *c.1970s, 23.5cm (9¼in) high.*

**£20–30**

► **A rare, dressed Mattel Barbie No. 1.** The first Barbie was usually sold in a swimsuit. Dressed versions were for shop display. This doll is complete with box, clothes, and shoes. *1959, 30cm (12in) high.*

**£4,000–6,000**

◄ **A *Barbie Sings* 45rpm record set,** with the 'pages' made as record sleeves and printed with lyrics. Among the many Barbie collectables featured at fairs, sales, and on the Internet are posters, books, jigsaws, wrist-watches, and records. *c.1961, 20.5cm (8in) wide.*

**£30–40**

◄ **A 'Hawaiian' TNT Barbie,** in its original box. TNT is short for 'Twist 'n' Turn', a moving-waist feature that was introduced in the mid-1960s. *c.1975, box 31.5cm (12½in) high.*

**£40–60**

▲ **An *Exclusive Fashions* brochure.** Mattel issued a short series of fashion brochures in 1963 and 1964. *1963, 10.5cm (4¼in) high.*

**£7–10**

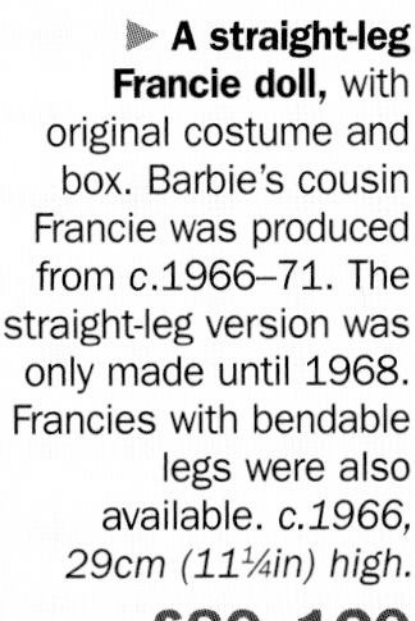

▶ **A straight-leg Francie doll,** with original costume and box. Barbie's cousin Francie was produced from *c.*1966–71. The straight-leg version was only made until 1968. Francies with bendable legs were also available. *c.1966, 29cm (11¼in) high.*

**£80–120**

## Collectors' Tips

- Check the Barbie mark, usually on the buttock but occasionally on the shoulder
- Barbie's friends and family – including Ken, Midge, and Scooter – are less valuable but rarer, and their values could rise

▲ **A flock-haired Ken,** with clothes. Ken was introduced in 1961. The hair of this example is slightly rubbed away, which reduces the value. *c.1961, 31cm (12¼in) high.*

**£15–20**

◀ **A brunette 'bubble-cut' Barbie,** with original box and brochure. The hairstyle indicates a date of 1961–67. The complete packaging, in good condition, increases the value. *1963, box 31cm (12¼in) high.*

**£80–120**

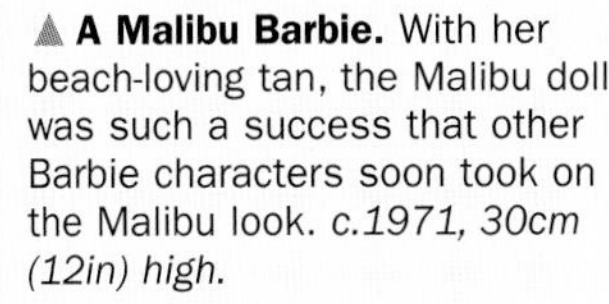

▲ **A Malibu Barbie.** With her beach-loving tan, the Malibu doll was such a success that other Barbie characters soon took on the Malibu look. *c.1971, 30cm (12in) high.*

**£15–20**

# Dolls' houses reached the peak of their popularity from the Victorian era to the 1950s. Many mass-produced examples – and their furnishings – from the late 19th century onwards survive in good condition, and they are much sought after.

The first dolls' houses, constructed by cabinet-makers in the 16th and 17th centuries, were models of the homes of the wealthy, created purely for display. It was not until the 19th century that the dolls' house became a toy. Many examples made from the 1930s to the 1950s can be found today for about £100–400.

## Home, sweet home

The age and rarity of early dolls' houses make them valuable: a simple 17th-century William and Mary dolls' cabinet – essentially a sort of cabinet of curiosities – was sold at auction in 1999 for more than £17,000. Size, quality, and original furniture and decoration contribute to the overall value, whatever the era. A simple late-Victorian house may be found for between £500 and £1,000, but most will cost around £1,000–5,000 or more.

Many Victorian, Edwardian, and some later houses were repainted or repapered, and these will be worth less. Style, colour tone, and patterns provide clues to decoration that is not original.

## Household names

British toymaker G. & J. Lines included dolls' houses in its list of toys from about 1895. These were made from wood covered with paper and printed to look like bricks. Many were expensive in their day and remain so, often commanding £500–1,000 or more. Those produced by Lines Brothers (founded in 1919 by George Lines' sons) under the Tri-ang brand are sought after. Produced in different styles for 30 to 40 years, they were made from wood and tinplate, which was painted or covered with printed paper. From the late 1950s and early

**A wooden dolls' house bureau by Walterhausen,** with a drop-down writing slope, in good condition. *1890s, 14cm (5½in) high.*

**£180–220**

**A Mettoy lithographed tinplate dolls' house,** with an open back. *1950s, 47cm (18½in) wide.*

**£100–200**

## A closer look at... two Tri-ang dolls' houses

Tri-ang was one of the most prolific makers of dolls' houses in the 20th century. When buying a house by this manufacturer, consider its style and individual elements, as well as the materials, paint, and finish – all factors that will affect its value.

**A large Tri-ang mock Tudor gabled house** (63), with four rooms, a staircase, a card 'thatched' roof, and electric lighting. This example is typical of the company's desirable and well-proportioned 'Stockbroker Tudor' style and is sought after today. *1930s, 68.5cm (27in) long.*

**£250–350**

All pieces are original: the windows even have metal frames that open

The original paintwork decorates the front – an attractive feature

The house is double-fronted, with gabled windows and a built-in garage

Plastic is used for the roof, door, and window fittings

The proportions are unrealistic, particularly around the door and annexe

**A Tri-ang two-storey dolls' house** with four rooms, a detachable roof, and a tinplate twin sliding front, on a green base. This house has been repainted and transfers of flowers have been added to the walls, which reduces the value. *1960s, 66cm (26in) long.*

**£70–100**

60s onwards, many had plastic features. 'Stockbroker Tudor', copied from the new suburban houses of the 1920s and 30s, was a style associated with the company. Values range from as little as £80 to over £400. Larger, more complex houses in original condition are the most desirable.

Companies such as Mettoy produced printed tinplate houses covered in coloured transfers for the brickwork and roof slates, window frames, and flowers. A colourful 1950s-style Mettoy house in good condition may be worth around £80–120. Other manufacturers to look for include Cooper, Frederick & Sons, Joseph Evans & Sons, Everrest, J. Tattershall, and C.E. Turnbull & Co. Prices for houses from the first half of the 20th century range from about £200–500 up to around £2,000.

### Room service

Items of dolls' house furniture from the late 19th and early 20th centuries by Tri-ang, Barton, and Everrest are available for about £5–50. Plastic pieces from the 1960s onwards can cost less than £10–15. Complete sets of furniture attract the highest prices.

The 19th-century manufacturer Walterhausen used lithographed paper applied to wooden furniture to create the look of marquetry – desks and bureaux can be worth around £80–200.

### Top Tips

- Start with modern replica period furniture if you are on a tight budget.
- Always have any electrical components checked by a qualified electrician.
- Examine the style, decorative features, materials, size, and condition to date a house. Look at real houses of the era to identify period features.

### BUY

*Original period dolls' house furniture is always worth buying, as it is usually well proportioned and often detailed. Objects connected with the running of a house, such as domestic appliances included to help educate little girls, are particularly popular.*

**A lithographed tinplate sewing machine on a stand.** The transfers are in comparatively good condition, particularly on the machine itself, and add to its value. *c.1900, 7cm (2¾in) high.*

**£20–30**

### KEEP

*Small dolls made as accessories for dolls' houses add realism and life to a house. Period examples were handled a lot, so those in good condition with their original accessories and clothing – usually indicating their role in the house – should at least hold their value.*

**A cloth dolls' house 'cook' doll,** with original clothing and holding a knife and fork. This example is clean; a dirty, worn, or damaged doll will be worth less. *1920s, 16.5cm (6½in) high.*

**£30–40**

# Nursery playthings,

especially traditional toys such as rocking horses, wooden building blocks, and Noah's arks, have seen an upsurge of interest in recent years but many inexpensive objects can still be found today.

**A Victorian doll's pram.** *c.1880s, 84cm (33in) long.*

**£120–180**

Nursery toys first became popular in the late 18th century. In the 19th century vast numbers were produced for the growing middle classes. Pieces from the 19th century are valued, both for their charm and craftsmanship – especially if they are undamaged. Toys from the 20th century can be a desirable, and less costly, option.

## Horsey, horsey

Rocking horses are great favourites. The first finely crafted 'bow rockers' were produced in the mid-18th century. These are now rare and can cost thousands of pounds. By the 1870s the bow-shaped stand had been largely replaced by a metal cradle on a wooden stand. F.H. Ayres, Collinson, and Lines Brothers (under the names Sportiboy and Tri-ang) mass-produced horses into the 20th century. Prices for these range from £100 to about £800, but Edwardian and earlier examples with attractive features, such as turned heads and fine painting, can command more than £1,000–2,000.

Rocking horses from the 20th century offer value for money. Patterson Edwards, for example, created the 'Leeway' range, which was made until the mid-1970s. A good example can cost about £200–300. Rocking/ride-on horses made by mid-20th-century toymakers in materials other than wood, such as metal or rubber, are less expensive. Those by makers like Tri-ang can be found for about £50–80, although these are usually less than full size.

### Did You Know?

*For many children in the 19th century play was forbidden on the Sabbath. Instead, a child read Bible stories with the family, or enjoyed a special Sunday toy with a religious theme, such as a Noah's ark.*

## The animals went in two by two

A few Noah's arks were made in the 18th century, but many more appeared during the Victorian era. Few craftsmen had seen the creatures they were carving, so figures can be oddly shaped. Prices depend on quality of decoration, condition, age, and size: a large, complete 19th-century ark will cost at least £600–1,000, and a rare, top-quality model up to £10,000.

## Piecing it together

Jigsaw puzzles originally showed a world map, but in the 19th century

## A closer look at... a rocking horse

Rocking horses make delightful and enchanting toys for children, and buying one can prove to be an excellent investment. Consider the condition, shape, and the maker to ensure that you make the best choice.

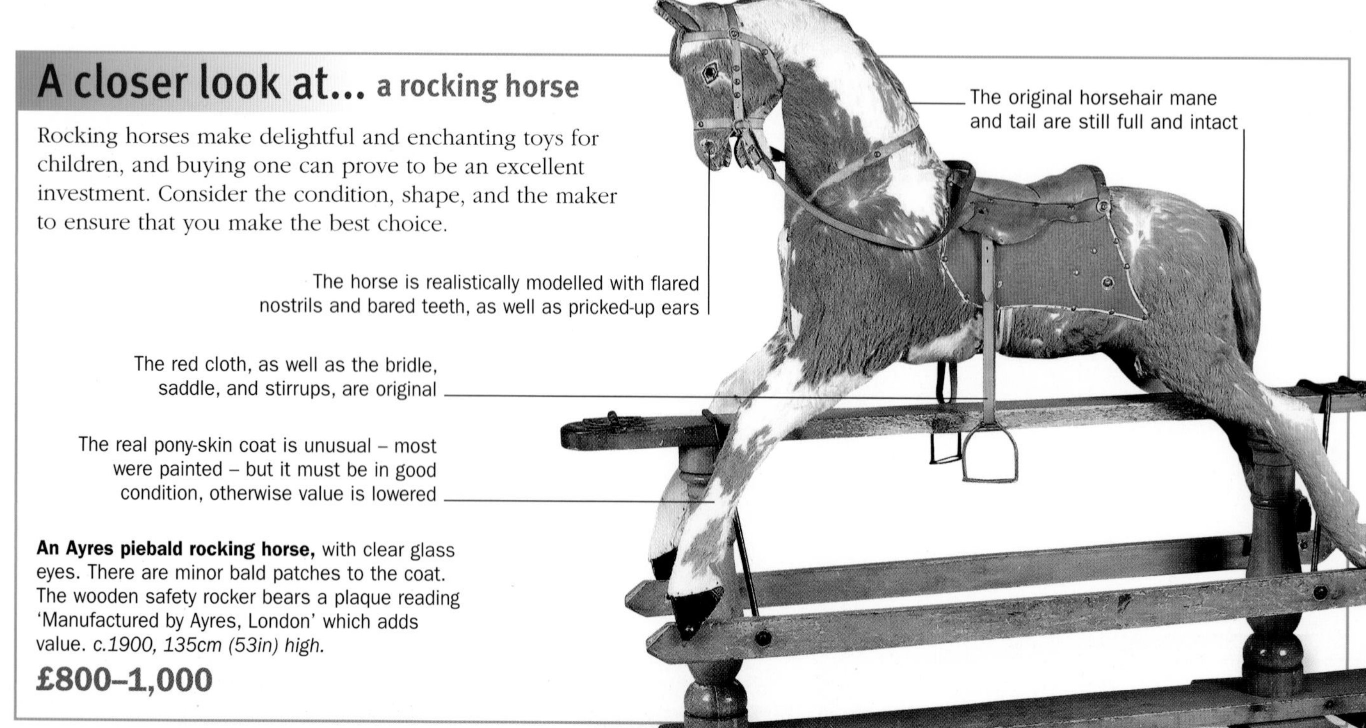


**An Ayres piebald rocking horse,** with clear glass eyes. There are minor bald patches to the coat. The wooden safety rocker bears a plaque reading 'Manufactured by Ayres, London' which adds value. *c.1900, 135cm (53in) high.*

**£800–1,000**

**A German painted wooden Noah's ark,** with eight wooden people and 90 pairs of animals. *c.1870s, ark 19cm (7½in) high.*

**£600–900**

other themes such as animals and nursery rhymes were introduced. With chromolithography, which was widely used by the 1870s, puzzles became more colourful and varied. British puzzles from this era include Tuck's 'Zig-Zag' and these are now worth up to £150–300. Hand-cut, hand-painted wooden puzzles sell for the most – from around £200–400 to £1,000 or more for special examples.

The introduction of cardboard in the late 19th century, and new die-cutting techniques, led to an increase in puzzle production. British makers such as Chad Valley began selling puzzles in the 1920s, which can now cost about £30–50. If a puzzle has crossover appeal, such as a nautical, military, or railway theme, it can sell for £50–300 or more. Exceptional value can currently be found in puzzles from the 1960s and 70s made by companies such as Waddingtons: they may fetch £10–20.

## Learning to build

Children's building blocks from the 19th century in original boxes can be worth up to £400 a set, but early 20th-century examples often cost as little as £10–50. More recent sets of non-wooden blocks also have some value: the 1950s Minibrix range from the Premo Rubber Company, with box and manual, can be worth around £20–40.

## Tea-time favourites

Children's tea sets have great appeal, especially those by noted 19th-century ceramics manufacturers such as Derby, Worcester, or Copeland, and can cost £100–500 or more. China tea sets from the 20th century are often worth up to £50, but sets featuring Disney or other popular characters can cost £200–400 or more, depending on the date, with the 1930s being the most desirable. Plastic and aluminium sets from the 1940s to the 60s can be found for £30–50 or less.

Doll's prams and other wooden or metal toys, from 'cup and ball' games to musical instruments, are popular – look for good quality and condition and original boxes.

**A child's miniature white glazed ceramic tea set,** with floral transfer decoration, in original box. *c.1950s, box 21.5cm (8½in) wide.*

**£10–20**

## *Top Tips*

- Expect to find real horsehair tails and manes on rocking horses: carving usually indicates fakes, most often made in Southeast Asia.
- Ask the dealer if the jigsaw puzzle is complete – if two or three pieces are missing, the price drops.
- Look for jigsaw puzzles in their original boxes – these increase the value.
- Examine the material carefully – toys made of ivory or finely carved lustrous hardwoods are desirable.

## SELL

*The Victorians and Edwardians made toys for amusement, such as spinning tops and 'teetotums' – a six-sided 'top' with numbers. Items such as these are often ignored and sold in boxes of assorted pieces for a few pounds. Check carefully as pieces can sometimes be worth more than the price of the box, especially if they are in good condition, or in materials such as fruitwood or ivory.*

**A carved ivory spinning top.** This would be more valuable if it was made of bone. Most were made from wood or tin. *c.1910, 2.5cm (1in) high.*

**£20–25**

## KEEP

*As toys and games from Victorian and earlier times are consistently popular, cherish any that you find or inherit. Prices are unlikely to fall and may well rise, especially if the game is complete and in good condition.*

**An early Victorian English jigsaw or 'dissected puzzle',** of the British Isles, in a painted wooden box. As well as being complete, this puzzle has its original box, making it desirable. *c.1820s, box 17.5cm (6¾in) wide.*

**£100–150**

# Games played by the whole family celebrate childhood and the best aspects of family life. Victorian and Edwardian card games, board games, and chess sets are in demand, especially those in good condition.

**A 'Tiddly Winks' game by John Jacques & Sons,** with its original box. *c.1890, box 10cm (4in) wide.*

**£25–35**

The mix of chance, skill, and rivalry that characterises indoor games has fascinated people for centuries. Games that are visually interesting, such as decorative Victorian and Edwardian examples, are generally the most desirable. The good news for collectors is that many vintage games can cost £100–200 or less and rarely reach more than £1,000.

## Keep in check

Many chess sets were produced in the 19th century; earlier examples are hard to come by. Prices for collectable sets start at £30–50 for a plastic example from the 1950s. By contrast, an 1840s ivory set can raise £800–1,200 or more.

Sets made of ivory and exotic woods, such as rosewood, are prized, while more basic examples made of common woods, such as boxwood, and bone are generally less desirable but form the staple of many collections. An intricately carved set may be worth three times as much as a comparable set with basic carving.

Sets by the English maker John Jaques & Sons (known as 'Staunton' sets because they were endorsed by the chess celebrity Howard Staunton) are almost a collectable area in themselves. They were made from the Victorian period until the early 20th century and vary in value from around £150 to £600. Look for original boxes with green labels and stamped pieces to indicate an authentic Jaques chess set. Similar sets were produced by other makers; these are known as

## Some card games to look for:

- Famous Five
- Happy Families
- Snap

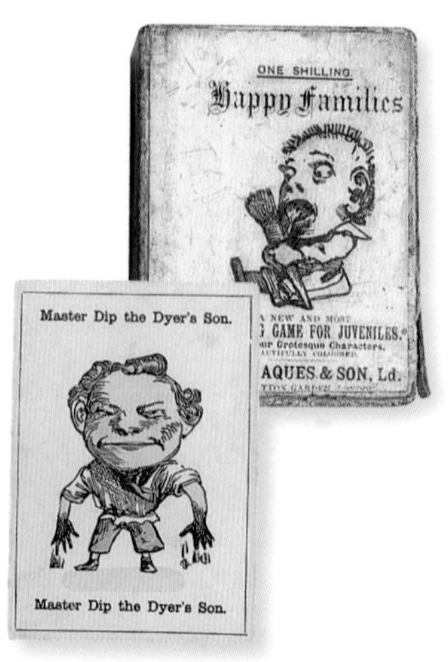

**A 'Famous Five' card game,** with its original box. The popularity of Enid Blyton's storybook characters and the superb artwork on each card make this set highly sought after. *1950s, box 9cm (3½in) high.*

**£35–45**

**A 'Happy Families' card game,** by John Jaques & Sons, with its original box. The amusing and grotesque illustrations and the notable maker increase the value of this set. *c.1890, cards 8cm (3½in) high.*

**£30–40**

**A 'Snap' card game,** with its original box. Each of the 24 colour-lithographed cards depicts a strongly characterised figure. Early sets with well-drawn figures in period clothing are collectable. *c.1900, cards 8cm (3¼in) high.*

**£25–35**

**A John Jaques & Sons carved boxwood and ebony 'Staunton' chess set.** The white king is stamped 'Jaques London'. *1880s, king 8cm (3¼in) high.*

**£150–250**

'Staunton pattern' and can be found for about £80–300.

### Take a chance on Monopoly

Commercial board games appeared in Britain in the early 18th century, but the enduring leader in this category, 'Monopoly', dates from the 1930s. With the exception of rarities such as the Alfred Dunhill version with gold houses and silver hotels (these sets can sell for well over £5,000), 'Monopoly' is unlikely to make a great profit. Used, but complete, vintage sets are worth about £30–50. Its sister game, 'Totopoly', based on the world of horse racing, never sold as many copies. Today a pre-war set in good condition can fetch around £100–200.

### Holding the right cards

Limited-run, high-quality, and unusual card games from the 19th century are desirable. For example, a pack of 'Happy Families' playing cards by John Jaques & Sons from the 1890s can fetch £30–40. Packs produced by De La Rue and the 'Multum in Parto' Company in the early 1900s are also worth looking out for.

### Top Tips

- Look for vintage editions of games at your local antique centre, flea market, or car-boot sale.
- Avoid exposing board games and playing cards to sunlight, heat, damp, and dust – they are easily damaged.
- Don't try to repair boxes or boards yourself – seek help from a professional paper conservator.
- Look for vintage board games in their original boxes with all their original pieces, dice, and instructions.
- Examine chess pieces closely to see whether any has been repaired or is a replacement – it may have glue marks or be a different colour or shape.

## ▪ Playing Cards ▪

**A set of De La Rue playing cards.** These cards do not have numbers, suggesting that they are pre-1900. The two-headed figures were first used in the late 19th century – earlier cards had single figures. *1870s, cards 9.5cm (3¾in) high.*

**£15–25**

### BUY

*Small hand-held games from the 1920s and 30s rarely survive in good condition, as parts were often broken and pieces lost. Commonly found for £10–50 or less, those in original condition make an excellent and amusing collection and may be a good investment for the future.*

**A 'Ringtail Cat Puzzle' dexterity game.** This paper-covered wood, card, and glass game was made by R. Journet & Co., a highly collectable name, which adds to its value. *1920s, 11cm (4¼in) high.*

**£30–50**

### KEEP

*Magic sets are as popular with children today as they were more than 50 years ago. The subject has become a collecting area in its own right and the market looks set to grow. Look for vintage sets with attractive artwork and ensure that all the pieces are present.*

**A 'Hokus-Pokus' magic set** complete with its box and lid depicting a young magician entertaining his friends. The attractive artwork on the box, as well as the age of the set, adds to the value. *1930s, box 39.5cm (15½in) wide.*

**£80–120**

Dreamcast

# Entertainment and Sports

Entertainment and sporting memorabilia is a diverse area that covers many modern passions. From rock groups and football teams to films, TV programmes, and even computer games, the interests which have filled our spare time are intriguing to look back on and experience all over again.

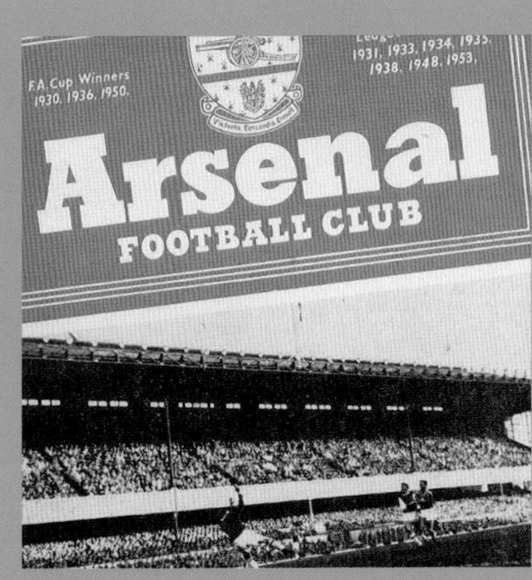

1

Toy car, p.259

Tardis toy, p.263

2

Items connected to the plethora of modern boy bands will probably hold no more than curiosity value in future.

# Spotlight on the world.

Entertainment and sporting memorabilia such as film posters, signed record albums, football programmes, and old golf balls are the sort of mementoes we all keep as reminders of special events in our lives. But these items may have a value which is more than just sentimental.

Cult TV series ① and films have a loyal fan base keen to own props and original merchandise. *Doctor Who* ②, *Star Trek*, *The Prisoner*, and *Thunderbirds* have all had a dedicated following for many years. As old films and TV programmes such as *Charlie's Angels* are remade or re-released, spin-off items such as lunch boxes, annuals, and toys emerge from attics and garages to be appreciated again. Some TV series may even benefit from being off the air; the fact that no new programmes have been made for decades adds to their cachet. But this is not the case with long-running series of films such as *James Bond* and *Star Wars* ③ which have been popular since the beginning.

## All in a name

Film props offer an exciting way for fans to own a piece of their favourite movie – whether it's crockery from the dining room on *Titanic*, a sword from *Gladiator*, or a letter addressed to Harry Potter.

Film posters ④ also attract a dedicated band of enthusiasts who look for examples

Donald Duck money box, p.269

5

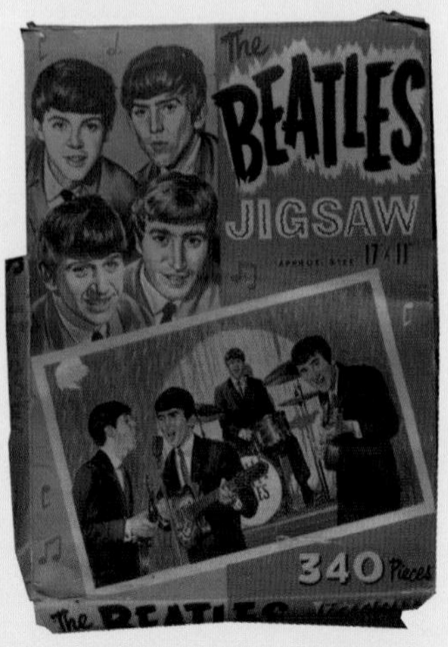


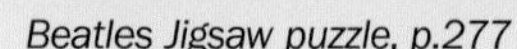

6

Beatles Jigsaw puzzle, p.277

7

Graceland security badge, p.274

3 Star Wars toy and box, p.256

Film posters, p.266

4

# ..of entertainment

from blockbuster, cult, or classic films, or those that are typical of their era or have a striking design.

## Rock around the clock

Walt Disney films have been delighting children for 80 years. Since the 1930s the company has licensed toy and other manufacturers to create products to complement its films. These include soft toys, puppets, and money boxes (5). If you were a fan of The Beatles (6) or Elvis (7), and still have your old LPs and fanzines, you are fortunate: most items associated with these pop icons are worth at least a little money today to fans old and new. Memorabilia connected to bands that are truly representative of their era, such as Abba in the 1970s and Wham! in the 1980s, is also worth keeping, but items connected to the plethora of modern boy bands will probably hold no more than curiosity value in future.

## Sporting souvenirs

Souvenirs such as World Cup tickets, cup final programmes, signed bats, balls, or kit (8) connected to players such as David Beckham are often valuable. There is also a thriving market for vintage sports equipment (9) such as fishing tackle.

Don't throw out old computer games (10) either: classic pioneers are continually rising in value as advances in technology make early examples rarer.

8 Signed football shirt, p.287

9 Wilson tennis balls, p.292

10 Computer game, p.272

# Star Wars is one of the most merchandised film franchises of all. An immense variety of products can be found with a *Star Wars* theme – from soaps and lunchboxes to toy figures, vehicles, and spacecraft. Any collector is spoilt for choice.

**A *Star Wars* R2D2 figure and C-3PO action figure.** *c.1978, largest 9.5cm (3¾in) high.*

**£10–15 each**

For collectors of *Star Wars* items, there are two names to look for: Kenner in the USA and Palitoy in the UK (both now part of Hasbro). Their products are the most popularly collected and include action figures, board games, and puzzles. Many other foreign companies secured *Star Wars* licences too, and because of the strict control that the films' creator George Lucas exercises over the rights to his trademarks, quality is high.

## The figures add up

There are many tales of mothers disposing of supposedly priceless *Star Wars* toys. In reality, Kenner/Palitoy's original 1977 line-up of 12 figures are still available for £10–20 each, although the less common characters and variations can raise £50–200, or more for truly exceptional items, such as a vinyl-caped Jawa or 'Power of the Force' Yak Face. As so many were opened up and played with, the highest prices are reserved for figures still sealed in their packaging. Today, these figures can realise from £100 to £800. Again, rare variations can be worth more, depending on the figure. Look for packaging that shows the original 12 figures on the back of the pack, as this usually indicates an early example from the first series. Han Solo is among the rarest figures from the original line-up and a sealed and unopened example in mint condition can be worth £300–500.

## Completing the scene

*Star Wars* figures were complemented by a range of vehicles and play sets based on scenes from the films. Many contained small parts that were easily lost, and so intact surviving examples are valuable. There is even a thriving trade in the accessories, and the tiny guns that came with the figures can now sometimes fetch up to £10–20.

The 'Power of the Force' range – the figures made by Kenner/Palitoy after the first trilogy of films had come and gone – are also sought after. These did not sell in such high numbers as

## *Star Wars* toys to look for:

▪ AT-AT ▪ Luke Skywalker ▪ Jawa ▪ Han Solo ▪

▼ **A *Star Wars: The Empire Strikes Back* AT-AT (All Terrain Armoured Transport) by Palitoy, with its box.** An AT-AT must be in near-mint condition and complete with its box and all parts to reach this price. *c.1980, 45.5cm (18in) high.*

**£100–200**

**A *Star Wars* C-3PO bath-size bar of soap**, unused and in its box. *c.1978, 14cm (5½in) high.*

**£2–5**

previous lines and so are harder to find. A collector's coin was included in the packaging and these coins are the most keenly pursued *Star Wars* secondary collectables.

## May the flask be with you

For children in the early 1980s, a *Star Wars* lunch box was the height of fashion. Today, an *Empire Strikes Back* vacuum flask and lunch box can sell for £80–120 if in excellent condition. Other household items that bore the *Star Wars* name include soap, toothbrushes, and bed clothes. Items made by better-known companies tend to be more valuable, and perishable items must be unused to retain any value. In general, the price for a *Star Wars* product that falls outside the more clearly defined categories of toy figures and comic books depends largely on what a particular enthusiast is willing to pay to own it.

## A galaxy of pictures

So many *Star Wars* posters were printed, and yet so few saved, that there is always a chance of coming across something new. Categories include posters for film releases from various countries, advertising, and commemorative posters produced after each film's release. Values vary widely, depending on age, condition, and, crucially, rarity. The original poster from the US release of *Return of the Jedi* bore the film title 'Revenge of the Jedi', until George Lucas decided that revenge was something a Jedi knight would not seek. Comparatively few survive, so prices are high: around £300–500, depending on condition. A different, more common, US one-sheet poster for the same film can cost up to £100.

Original props from all the films are hard to come by, as their availability and sale is strictly regulated by George Lucas's production company.

**► A *Star Wars* Jawa action figure, with a vinyl cape by Kenner.** If the cape were missing, or made of fabric, the figure would be worth less than £15. *c.1978, 6.5cm (2½in) high.*

**£200–300**

**◄ A *Star Wars* Luke Skywalker 'Early Bird' action figure by Palitoy.** This example, from the first batch of toys, is a rare variant with a long extending light sabre. *c.1978, 9.5cm (3¾in) high.*

**£120–180**

**▲ A *Star Wars: The Empire Strikes Back* Han Solo (Bespin Outfit) action figure by Palitoy, with packaging.** Out of its packaging, the figure would be worth less than a tenth of this value. *c.1981, packaging 22.5cm (9in) high.*

**£70–100**

### *Top Tips*

- Look for props used in the more recent films – they are more readily available and less expensive than earlier ones. Ensure studio documentation accompanies any prop.
- Seek out issues of Marvel and Darkhorse comics featuring Star Wars – these can be found for reasonable prices.
- Invest in mint-condition and boxed action figures released for the new films after the initial rush, when prices have been lowered. These may be tomorrow's must-have collectables.
- When trying to identify a variant of a figure, use the serial number printed on the packaging as a guide.

## KEEP

*Older* Star Wars *merchandise, particularly anything from the early 1980s or before, has powerful nostalgia value for today's generation of thirty-somethings.*

**An *Empire Strikes Back* flask and lunch box made by Thermos.** Condition is all important – dents, scratches, and other damage reduce value considerably. *1981, 22cm (8¾in) wide.*

**£50–70**

## BUY

*The Kenner brand has come to be a badge of quality among* Star Wars *merchandise, and portable computer games are becoming more collectable and valuable. Early spin-off games that straddle these two collecting fields may well increase in value over the coming years.*

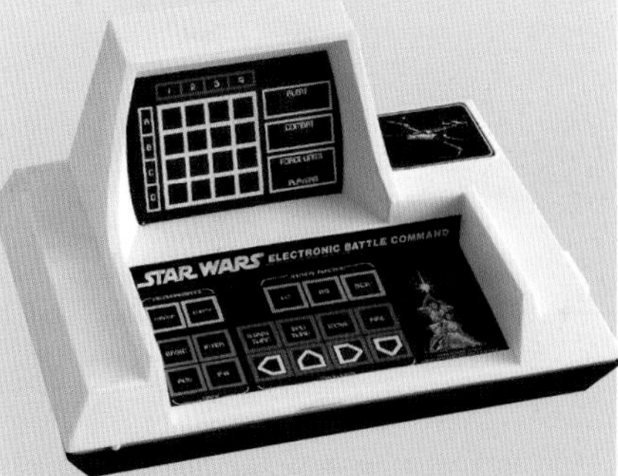


**A Kenner *Star Wars* electronic Battle Command game.** Check that the battery cover is present. *c.1979, 21cm (8¼in) wide.*

**£60–80**

# Cult TV

From *The Avengers* to *Z-Cars*, certain TV programmes inspire a long and loyal following. Because of their nostalgia value and the cult status of their protagonists, the merchandising associated with them is a major source of interest.

It is probably our age that determines the period of TV history which really interests us. Anyone who grew up in the 1960s is likely to remember *The Prisoner*, *The Saint*, or *The Avengers* with affection, while children of the 1980s may have a soft spot for *Knight Rider* and *The A-Team*. The current trend for re-runs, new films based on TV classics, and even pastiches of TV programmes, often creates a boom in prices for original memorabilia.

## Cult collections

Enthusiasts tend to be fanatical about their collections, which may include storybooks, annuals, magazines, original toys, or posters based on characters or series. Owning a prop used in the filming of the original series is the dream for many, but prices are in a higher league than those for general memorabilia and fetch from £200 to £900, or even thousands of pounds. Annuals, books, and other memorabilia, however, can often be found for under £50–100.

Many cult TV series appealed mainly to boys, so cars and action figures are often a good place to start a collection. Values can range from £10 to £500, depending on condition and the popularity of the series. Corgi was known for its popular range of TV- and film-related vehicles produced during the 1960s. Many are still available, so look for examples in mint condition complete with their original boxes in similar condition.

Both *The Avengers* of the 1960s and *The New Avengers* of the 1970s were popular, so memorabilia attracts a lot of interest. Always look for pieces representative of the characters: Steed, for example, was known for his umbrella which doubled as a sword stick: the toy version produced by Lone Star can be worth £350–400. Even the packaging card attached, with artwork of Steed brandishing the umbrella, can fetch around £70.

Action figures are always popular. Hasbro's 1970s range of *Charlie's Angels* figures sold particularly well because they were the first major TV action heroines. Dolls of the main cast members are likely to appreciate in value; they are currently available for around £20–60 each.

**A badge showing 'The Fonz',** made in the USA. *1970s, 2.5cm (1in) diam.*

**£8–10**

## Some cult TV toy cars to look for:

- Knight Rider
- The Man from U.N.C.L.E

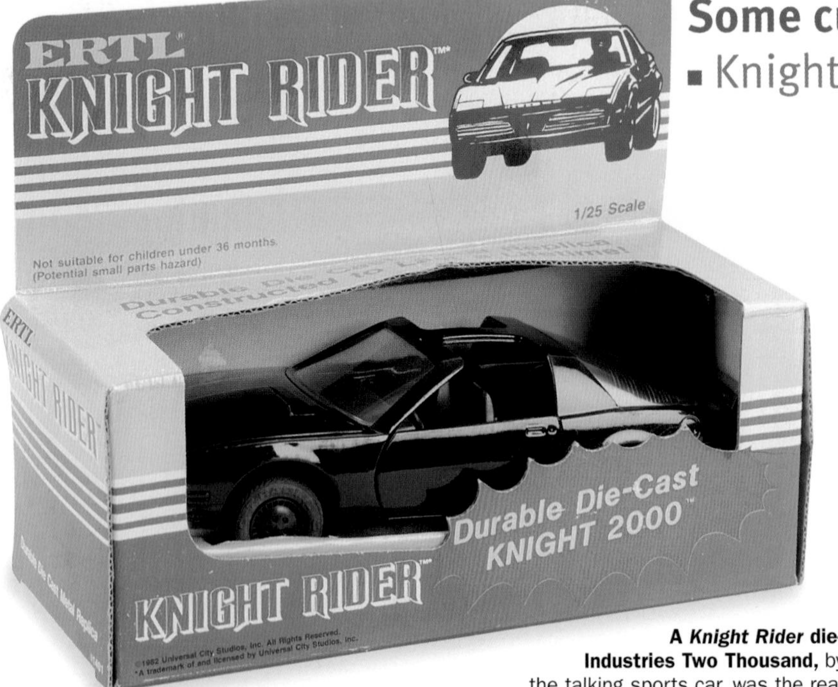


**A *Knight Rider* die-cast Knight Industries Two Thousand,** by ERTL. KITT, the talking sports car, was the real star of this 1980s TV show. *c.1982, 12cm (5in) long.*

**£50–70**

**A Corgi No. 497 *The Man From U.N.C.L.E.* blue Thrushbuster,** in excellent condition and boxed. Look out for the rarer white version of this car. *c.1966, 12cm (5in) long.*

**£200–250**

**A *Charlie's Angels* lunchbox and vacuum flask,** by Aladdin Industries. *c.1978, 20cm (8in) wide.*

**£40–60**

## Look ahead

Cult TV programmes of today include *Buffy The Vampire Slayer*, *The X-Files*, and the new series of *Star Trek*. When buying merchandise, consider which programmes are the most popular, because the children who watch them today will often become the nostalgia-driven collectors of tomorrow.

## Bringing back memories

Other TV collectables include tie-in books and comics, especially those with stories based on existing series, such as *TV Comic*. Books and comics from the 1970s and 80s in good condition range in value from £1–3 to £20–30. Cigarette cards and old copies of *Radio Times* featuring the main characters from TV series are also popular, but it can be hard to find a magazine in good condition.

A growing trend since the early 1990s has been to collect lunch boxes decorated with images from popular children's programmes. A 1979 *Buck Rogers* box could be worth more than £100, while complete boxes in mint condition from the 1950s, such as *The Lone Ranger*, may fetch up to £300–400.

### Did You Know?

*You can re-enact favourite scenes from 'The Prisoner' on the perfect stage: the bizarre and colourful village it was filmed in is not a set, but a real place – Portmeirion – built between 1925 and 1975 on the Welsh coast south of Snowdonia.*

### Top Tips

- Look for memorabilia from the most popular or cult shows.
- Always look for products in original packaging, particularly toy cars.
- Beware of fake boxes and packaging. If a box looks new, it probably is.
- If you buy a jigsaw or game, make sure that all the pieces are still there.
- Look for pieces that are representative of the characters or the series.

### BUY

Buffy the Vampire Slayer *has a cult following. If in mint condition with its box, a limited-edition piece that has gone out of production such as this figurine should rise in value.*

**A *Buffy the Vampire Slayer* limited edition figurine,** by Steve Varner, from an edition of 4,500. *2000, 23cm (9in) high.*

**£60–70**

## ▪ The Dukes of Hazzard ▪ The Prisoner ▪

**A *Dukes of Hazzard* Hazzard County Sheriff car,** by Ideal in its original packaging. *1981, 12cm (5in) long.*

**£15–20**

**A Dinky Toys 106 *The Prisoner* Mini-Moke,** boxed and in very good condition. *1967–70, 8.5cm (3in) long.*

**£180–220**

### KEEP

*When older TV series are revived through remakes, interest in original toys and memorabilia often increases - and prices with it. Hold on to original pieces until the time is right to sell.*

**A 1980s Galoob '*A-team*' Mr T action figure.** There is currently talk of the A-team being remade. Mr T was one of the most popular characters, and this example is made more desirable, as it is in mint condition and unopened. *Box 38cm (15in) high.*

**£30–40**

# Sci-fi TV memorabilia

has been in demand since science-fiction shows first burst onto the small screen in the late 1950s. The appeal is just as strong today, as new viewers discover the magic.

**A *Space 1999* Annual,** by World Distributors. *1970s, 23cm (9in) high.*

**£4–5**

When Yuri Gagarin became the first man in space in 1961, 'astronaut' ousted 'train driver' as the most-coveted job for children everywhere. It's not surprising that TV science-fiction shows soon became popular.

## Puppet TV

Gerry Anderson was responsible for several 1960s 'Supermarionation' (from 'super', 'marionette', and 'animation') puppet series in Britain, including *Stingray, Captain Scarlet and the Mysterons, Joe 90*, and *Thunderbirds*. A new generation of fans is created every time they are aired on TV.

During the 1970s live actors replaced puppets in sci-fi series such as *UFO* and *Space 1999*, which were also Anderson productions.

The successful American TV series *Buck Rogers in the 25th Century* and *Battlestar Galactica*, both by Glen A. Larson and featuring live actors, also still have their fans and a band of devoted collectors.

## Making their name

From the earliest days, themed merchandise was popular and included everything from games and comics to action figures and toy versions of the vehicles, which were often major stars of many of these shows. Original toys in good condition are sought after, and merchandise in mint condition can command astonishing prices because of its rarity – few toys are left untouched in their original packaging. Prices vary depending upon the popularity of the show, and examples can fetch anything from around £25 to £500. Original Supermarionation merchandise – especially vehicles – is always of interest. A 1960s Stingray submarine bath toy can cost £50–70, while a Lady Penelope FAB1 car from the same period can fetch around £200–300, provided that it is in mint condition with its packaging.

**A *Star Trek* Champions pewter figure of Captain Kirk,** inspired by the 1979 film *Star Trek: The Motion Picture*; from a limited edition of 9,998. *1998, box 23.5cm (9¼in) high.*

**£40–60**

Stickers, badges, trading cards, and other small items are often available for £1–5 or less, and original 1960s annuals usually cost about £1–10. Model kits are reasonable buys, but only if boxed and in mint condition. Airfix kits from the 1970s *Space 1999* and the 1990s *Battlestar Galactica* kits by Revell can often sell for £10–20 if unused.

## Rocketing prices

The rarest merchandise is that from *Fireball XL5*, Gerry Anderson's first Supermarionation show, launched in 1962. Fairylight made a Fireball XL5 spaceship which, if boxed and in mint condition, can command up to £2,000–2,500. Even without its packaging, it may be worth £300–600. *Fireball XL5* hasn't been broadcast in Britain for nearly 20 years, but its release on DVD in 2003 may push prices higher.

Shrewd investors may prefer to gamble on more recent ranges. A mid-1990s Thunderbirds model by Matchbox, kept in immaculate condition with its box, can now cost £20–30. When choosing current toys, look for lots of detail, gadgets, and moving parts; toys that are popular now are likely to be collectable in

## A closer look at... a Thunderbirds Dinky toy

Dinky made dozens of film and TV tie-in toys that were popular with children of the time and are sought after by today's collectors.

The toy retains its outer packaging (left) and inner card box (below) with a panel showing attractive artwork

**A Dinky Thunderbirds 2 and 4 toy, 101.** Thunderbirds 2 is green with yellow plastic legs that fold into the base and red thrusters. The Thunderbirds 4 craft (yellow) fits inside the belly of the 2 craft. *1967–73, 18cm (7in) wide.*

**£400–500**

This green version is more valuable than the later blue model in the same condition

years to come, but only if kept boxed and in excellent condition.

### Thunderbirds are go

Far more merchandise was produced for *Thunderbirds*, but mint-condition toys can still cost up to £500, with some reaching around £3,000. A 1966 Thunderbirds rifle made by Crescent was sold in perfect condition a few years ago for £2,000. Given its rarity, even a used rifle without its illustrated box can fetch £300–600. With a new *Thunderbirds* film due out, expect prices to rise. In addition, Disney has bought the rights to *Joe 90*; Anderson Productions is working on a computer-animated *Captain Scarlet* film; and a *UFO* movie is in production in the USA. Hold on to any collectables related to these shows, as they may increase in value.

**A Dinky Lady Penelope's FAB 1 car, 100.** The car is in excellent condition but the box is damaged. *1967–75, box 20cm (8in) long.*

**£100–150**

### Beam me up

*Star Trek* launched a galaxy of films, spin-off shows, merchandise, and fanzines. First shown in 1966, the programme became popular on both sides of the Atlantic. The continued interest in all things 'trekkie' means it is still worth searching for bargains. A complete set of the five 1960s promotional cards distributed by TV stations can fetch up to £30–60, while a Mego Klingon action figure issued in 1974 can be worth £50–80 if complete and in mint condition. Later figures, such as those issued alongside The *Next Generation* series, are generally less expensive. Try attending *Star Trek* conventions to learn what's popular.

### Top Tips

- Buy the latest Thunderbirds toys and figures and keep them in their original packaging, as these may increase in value.
- Look out for Gerry Anderson characters from the 1990s range of 'candy toys' by Konami, as these look set to rise in value.
- Try to find unused transfer books – those featuring Joe 90 and Space 1999 now sell for about £30.
- Look for 'Playmates' – the most collected Star Trek figures. Expect to pay about £5–15 for characters in good condition.

### KEEP

*The price of original memorabilia can leap following re-releases and remakes of films or series. Pieces linked to the original series may rise in value as a result.*

**A Battlestar Galactica story book,** by Brown Watson. It dates from the original series, making it desirable, and a revamped mini-series is due. *1978, 26cm (10¼in) high.*

**£2–3**

### SELL

Buck Rogers *is not a favourite, and there are no revivals planned. Pieces may not increase in value, so sell now and invest in promising items, such as those from* Thunderbirds.

**A Buck Rogers Laserscope Fighter**, made by Mega Corp. In mint condition, with its box. *c.1979, box 30cm (12in) high.*

**£30–40**

# Doctor Who and his time-travelling machine, the Tardis, first appeared on BBC TV in November 1963. *Doctor Who* books, videos, and figurines can all be found, but the big merchandising success story was the Daleks.

The first Dalek toy, introduced in 1964, retailed at 17s 11d and sold out within days. There were Dalek tins, make-it-yourself Dalek kits, and even Dalek bubble bath. Online auctions are a good place to hunt for such items, which usually sell for less than £50. Original Palitoy 'talking Daleks' from the 1970s are highly collectable, fetching up to £150. One of the most sought-after Dalek items is the 1.5m (5ft) playsuit, launched for Christmas 1964.

Other collectables include metal lapel badges showing the Doctor and various other characters, given away in boxes of Kellogg's 'Sugar Smacks' cereal in 1971. The Denys Fisher Company produced a set of figures in 1974 showing the Doctor, Leela his assistant, a Dalek, the dog K9, a Cyberman, and the Tardis.

Eight actors have played the Doctor over the years: William Hartnell (1963–66), Patrick Troughton (1966–69), Jon Pertwee (1970–74), Tom Baker (1974–81), Peter Davison (1981–84), Colin Baker (1984–86), Sylvester McCoy (1987–89), and Paul McGann (in the 1996 TV film).

Everyone has a favourite – perhaps the one they watched as a child – and some fans limit themselves to collecting items representing a specific period.

The new series of *Doctor Who* launched in 2005 has been a great success. It has revived interest in models and various character products amongst collectors.

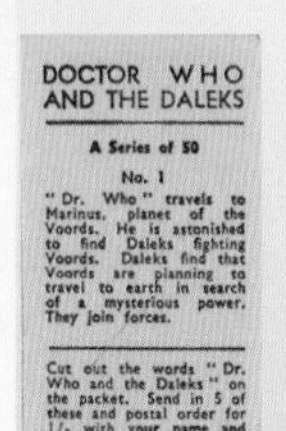
DOCTOR WHO AND THE DALEKS

A Series of 50

No. 1

" Dr. Who " travels to Marinus, planet of the Voords. He is astonished to find Daleks fighting Voords. Daleks find that Voords are planning to travel to earth in search of a mysterious power. They join forces.

Cut out the words " Dr. Who and the Daleks " on the packet. Send in 5 of these and postal order for 1/- with your name and address to CADET SWEETS, Trading Estate, SLOUGH, Bucks., for an album.

▲ **A set of 50 'Doctor Who and the Daleks' trading cards,** for Cadet Sweets. The series was re-issued in 1983 with 'Goodies' replacing 'Cadet Sweets' on each card. Unusually, a complete re-issue set is worth more than the original, fetching around £100–150. *1964, cards 6.5cm (2½in) wide.*

**£100–200**

▶ **A life-size replica black dalek.** This unique model was commissioned privately to be displayed at *Doctor Who* exhibitions. *2001, 150cm (60in) high.*

**£1,000–1,500**

▶ **An LP of the *Doctor Who* theme music** from the TV series. The well-known bass line and swooping melody have been featured on a number of *Doctor Who* albums. This one has a hologram cover. *1986, 30cm (12in) wide.*

**£8–12**

◀ **A rare 'Doctor Who Give-a-Show Projector',** by Chad Valley. Toys and games from the 1960s are hard to find, especially in good condition. *1965, 54cm (21in) wide.*

**£150–200**

◀ **A *Doctor Who: The Five Doctors* video gift pack.** This rare gift set was produced by Dapol for Boots, and came with a plastic Dalek figure. The figure had slightly different colourings from a Dalek produced by Dapol in 1989. *1990, 25.5cm (10in) wide.*

**£55–65**

▲ **A limited-edition *Dalekmania* box set,** by Lumiere, with a video (including an interview with the creator of the Daleks, Terry Nation), a colour booklet, and six postcards. *1995, 42.5cm (16¾in) wide.*

**£60–100**

▼ **A figure of Draconian,** one of the Doctor's adversaries, by Product Enterprises, in its 'Classic Moments' range. Such figures are still being made years after they were last seen on TV – a healthy sign of their collectability. *c.2002, 18cm (7in) high.*

**£20–30**

▼ **A limited-edition *Doctor Who: Daleks* video box set,** signed by Sophie Aldred, who acted in the series. *1993, 21.5cm (8½in) wide.*

**£45–60**

◀ **An audio cassette of *The Evil of the Daleks,*** featuring the voice of Patrick Troughton. This was one of the first of the BBC's 'Missing Stories' range. The box has been signed by Deborah Watling, who played one of the Doctor's assistants. *1992, 14cm (5½in) wide.*

**£15–25**

▼ **A hand-crafted model of the Tardis.** Seven years after the last *Doctor Who* TV series, and around the time of the ill-received TV film, Britannia Miniatures brought out a model Tardis. *c.1996, 14cm (5½in) high.*

**£30–50**

## Collectors' Tips

- Search the Internet for videos and posters, which are easily found; they cost from £2
- Look for memorabilia still with its original box
- Avoid items that look worn or used

◀ **A set of nine *Doctor Who* 'Premier' trading cards** by Cornerstone**.** When turned face down, the cards can be arranged to form a composite image of the first actor to play the Doctor, William Hartnell. Released at a time when interest in *Doctor Who* was low (especially among children), this set is rare. *1994, 9cm (3½in) high.*

**£220–280**

# James Bond, 007, has proved to be a licence to print money – for merchandisers. Ian Fleming's MI6 franchise has been so successful that, 50 years after the first publication of *Casino Royale*, the English gentleman spy is still big business.

Maybe it's the cars, the girls, or the gadgets. It could be the music, the villains, or the exotic locations. Whatever the reason, James Bond films loom large in the public imagination. Most enthusiasts were probably children when they saw their first Bond film, so nostalgia plays a significant part in their desire to accumulate mementoes. What is more, the latest Pierce Brosnan releases have helped to create new fans and inspire older collectors.

## The name's Bond, James Bond

Bond's enduring popularity makes memorabilia connected to the films much sought after. Anything from the 1960s Sean Connery period is desirable, especially posters and toys.

For many Bond fans who grew up in the 1960s, the satisfaction lies in buying toys they perhaps could not afford at the time. The Corgi gold Aston Martin, originally priced at 10 shillings, can now be worth around £100–150 with its box and in excellent condition. Other 1960s merchandise such as puzzles, costumes, and lunch boxes, can attract prices from £30–300. A 1960s puzzle by Arrows with a scene from Thunderball or Goldfinger may fetch around £50–70, if complete and with its box. Although 007 only ventured into space once (in Moonraker), several of the films have featured space sequences and space merchandise is a perennial favourite. Deluxe versions of Mego's 1979 space-suited James Bond figures with the rocket pack and helmet can fetch up to £200–250.

**An American 'C'-style one-sheet poster for *You Only Live Twice*,** with artwork by Robert McGinnis. *1967, 104cm (41in) high.*

**£800–1,200**

## The last international playboy

First editions of Fleming's early novels are expensive, running into thousands of pounds for the rarest, but you can still own a genuine piece of Bond literary history for a more modest sum. A Jonathan Cape first British edition of *Octopussy* and *The Living Daylights* issued together in one volume might only cost £50–70, and even a 1961 *Thunderball* can be had for £300–500. Old numbers of *Playboy* magazine,

## Some film posters to look for:

▪ From Russia With Love ▪ The Living Daylights

**A British one-sheet poster for *From Russia With Love*,** linen-backed. The original UK release poster is hard to come by, so it attracts high values. *1964, 102cm (40in) wide.*

**£700–1,000**

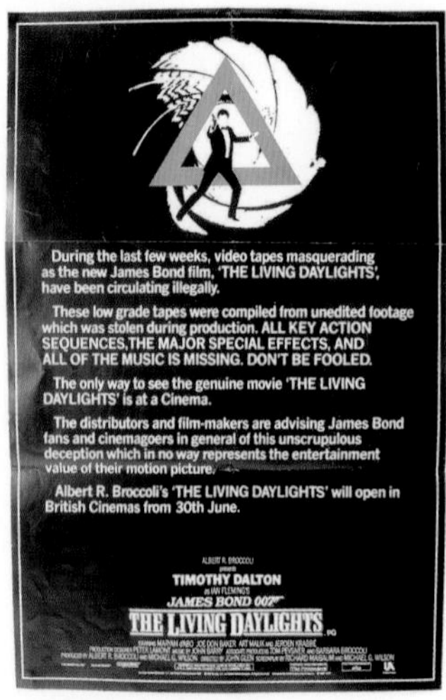


**A teaser and illegal-release warning poster for *The Living Daylights*.** *1987, 51cm (20in) wide.*

**£100–200**

**A British quad poster for *Tomorrow Never Dies*.** This version was withdrawn from circulation as 'Tomorrow' was spelt wrongly in the credits, making it hard to find. *1997, 102cm (40in) wide.*

**£60–80**

which was licensed to serialise Fleming's work, are less expensive still. Between 1960 and 1966 at least six James Bond stories were featured in *Playboy*, illustrated by Daniel Schwartz and Howard Mueller, notable *Playboy* graphic artists, among others. The relationship between *Playboy* and 007 is so close that Bond is seen carrying a *Playboy* card in *Diamonds Are Forever*, and the 1999 Raymond Benson short story featuring James Bond was not only published in *Playboy* but was actually set in Hugh Hefner's mansion. Many of these magazines cost less than £10, although the older and more sought-after issues can command prices of £40–60 and even higher.

**A signed Pierce Brosnan publicity photograph.** *c.1996, 25.5cm (10in) high.*

**£40–60**

## Sound and vision

James Bond posters are a high priority for enthusiasts. Early posters have become classics and can fetch high prices at auction, from around £50–100 up to around £3,500 or more. The first, produced for *Dr. No* in 1962, set the standard for the entire series, featuring Bond with a gun and girls. The artwork on these early examples ranged from superb paintings to photomontage by artists such as Robert McGinnis and Frank McCarthy. Posters from the 1980s and 90s have not yet matched the cult status of the 1960s examples, but may become classics in time. Look for the classic films – *Thunderball* (1965) was remade in 1983 as *Never Say Never Again*, and many aficionados spurn the second version as inferior.

The signature of a Bond actor across posters increases their value. Signed publicity stills of the current Bond, Pierce Brosnan, may fetch £30–80.

As Bond films are re-released on DVD, the enthusiast can start to build a collection of boxed sets. It's likely that many of the limited-edition 'Blue', 'Gold', and 'Silver' MGM sets produced in the last few years are being stored away in the hope that they will one day rise in value, but this will not happen unless demand exceeds supply.

The price of original vinyl soundtracks might climb sooner. A 1979 *Moonraker* LP in good condition will fetch around £8–12, and the rarer Japanese release of the album can be worth three times more. An original French 7in single release of the *Goldfinger* theme can fetch £30–40. More obscure items attract higher prices as they are harder to find.

■ Tomorrow Never Dies ■ Dr. No

**An American one-sheet poster for *Dr. No*,** the first James Bond film poster, with art by Mitchell Hooks, linen-backed. A seminal piece of Bond iconography, this classic poster is the one that started it all. *1962, 104cm (41in) high.*

**£1,500–2,000**

### Top Tips

- Try to buy posters in good condition, without pinholes or tape marks, and don't consider those that have been trimmed or dry-mounted.
- Look for rare variations in poster artwork, which can add to the value.
- Some firms are reproducing original packaging for vintage Bond toys, so pay close attention to copyright notices when considering purchase.

### BUY

*007 and Playboy have shared a passion for glamorous women, hi-tech gadgetry, and the finer things in life. Back issues of the magazine in excellent condition with a strong 007 theme are a promising investment.*

**A November 1965 copy of *Playboy* magazine.** This was the first issue of Playboy to feature Bond girls and has a wonderful cover image. *1965, 28cm (11in) high.*

**£40–60**

### KEEP

*Toy cars are highly collectable, especially the cars used in the Bond films. As so many were produced, look for those in near mint condition, with the box and any other accessories that came with them.*

**A Corgi James Bond Aston Martin DB5, No 261,** with its original picture box. The Aston Martin DB5 is perhaps the most famous Bond car of all. *1964, 102cm (40in) wide.*

**£80–120**

# Film memorabilia, from *The Wizard of Oz* in 1939 to *Terminator 3* in 2003, yields a rich vein of collectables; enthusiasts want a piece of their favourite blockbuster, and the range is huge, with objects and prices to suit everyone.

Once the sets are cleared, props and memorabilia can be sold at auction. The market is extremely volatile, and although simply owning a keepsake from a film can be fun, it is even better if it is likely to rise in value.

## The big screen

Some people focus on a particular star, while others collect by genre, such as horror films. Objects linked to film stars go for the highest prices and make the best investment. Props, autographs, posters, photographs, and costumes are the mainstays, with photographs and autographs often costing £50–100. Almost anything is collected, including film scripts and crew T-shirts – a T-shirt from *A.I. Artificial Intelligence* can cost around £10–20.

Props that play a small role in the film can be inexpensive. A life jacket from *Titanic* can be worth £40, and an ammunition clip from *Saving Private Ryan* can cost £10–20. Iconic items can carry a heavy price tag: Harrison Ford's whip from the Indiana Jones films raised £12,000 at auction.

**A gold-coloured 'gold ingot',** from *The Mummy*, impressed with the design of a scarab beetle. *1999, 28cm (11in) high.*

**£30–50**

## Poster appeal

Film posters have evolved their own collectors' cult, with prices to match. An original *King Kong* poster was sold for a staggering £35,000, because of its rarity and its stunning artwork. Values depend on the featured stars, the popularity of the film, and the impact of the artwork. Look for foreign posters with striking designs: studios sometimes produce different layouts for each country, although this practice is dwindling.

British quad posters (76cm/30in x 101.5cm/40in) and US one-sheet posters (68.5cm/27in x 104cm/41in) are the most popular sizes. Only pristine posters will fetch high prices, although it is difficult to find mint-condition pre-1970s examples. Creases, tears, pinholes, and sticky-tape damage all reduce value.

## Some film posters to look for:

▪ The Godfather ▪ The Shining ▪ Gladiator

◂ ***The Godfather,*** British quad poster. This is a classic image from a seminal film that united some of the best talents working in the industry at the time. A poster for this film is bound to hold its value. *1971, 101.5cm (40in) wide.*

**£500–700**

▾ ***The Shining,*** British quad poster. Posters showing key scenes or central characters are desirable. This image of the deranged Jack Torrance (played by Jack Nicholson) breaking through the bathroom door with his fire-axe is evocative of the terror inspired by this film. *1980, 101.5cm (40in) wide.*

**£200–250**

***Gladiator,*** promotional poster. The addition of important signatures, such as on this poster, signed by Russell Crowe, can add value, particularly if it is a less common pre-release promotional poster. *2000, 106cm (42in) high.*

**£400–600**

## Costume collection

Prices for clothing vary. A suit worn by Al Pacino in *The Recruit* sold for about £500, but interestingly there was more demand for costumes worn by his co-star Colin Farrell, an up-and-coming star. At the other end of the scale, a pair of beige trousers worn by James Dean in the 1955 classic *East of Eden* sold at auction in the USA for $15,000 (almost £10,000).

## Quality goods

The quality of film memorabilia varies greatly. Props that featured prominently in a scene or were in the foreground of a shot are likely to be more detailed and better made than background props, and so are more valuable. Weapons are especially sought after.

When buying props or costumes, look for studio tags or certificates. For example, large numbers of props from *Titanic* were sold, but a studio certificate accompanied each item. Any item that does not come with a guarantee is probably not authentic.

## Popularity shifts

When a blockbuster opens, there can be a clamour for collectables and prices can rise, then fall when the publicity dies down. If the film is released on video or DVD, interest – and prices – may soar again. There are exceptions, such as the James Bond films, but price fluctuations are common.

Look for items linked to cult (or potential cult) films. *Blade Runner* bombed at the box office, so few props were kept. Today it is a cult film and anything associated with it is now sought after – and difficult to find.

**A used prop White Star Line, Moët & Chandon champagne bottle, from *Titanic*.** *1997, 30cm (12in) high.*

**£150–200**

## ▪ A.I. ▪ The Lord of the Rings ▪

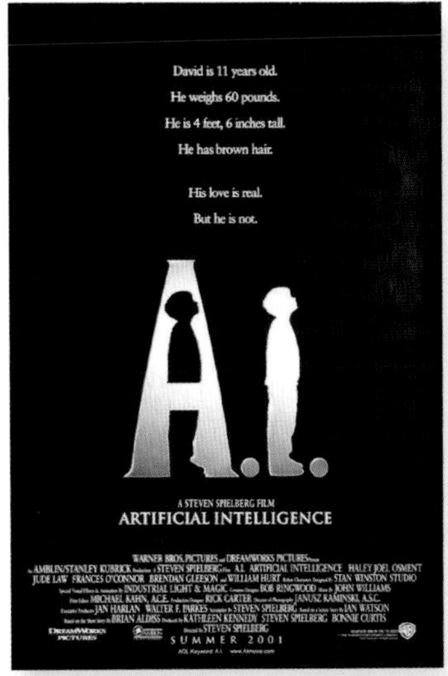


***A.I. Artificial Intelligence,*** advance US one-sheet poster. The film was preceded by interactive hype on the Internet and in other media. The credits on this poster contain hidden symbols that unlock information on a website. *2001, 104cm (41in) high.*

**£60–80**

***The Lord of the Rings: The Fellowship of the Ring,*** style A, teaser one-sheet poster. Teaser posters, issued before the film's release, are more desirable than a standard poster. The style B poster shows Frodo looking down at the ring. *2001, 104cm (41in) high.*

**£70–100**

### *Top Tips*

- Autographed photographs may not be genuine – many are signed by assistants, or stamped, or printed.
- Before buying, carefully track prices for memorabilia linked to Hollywood blockbusters, such as souvenirs given away before the film is released.
- Look for the name of an actor (or the character's name) inside the collar of any unique costume from a film.
- Search the Internet for online prop auctions held by major film studios.

### BUY

*Look for props from or showing key moments in a film, as these are likely to have enduring popularity and consistent values. Certain films and characters never fall out of fashion, but inexpensive items can be found and may rise in price if they fulfil these criteria.*

**A prop copy of the 'Daily Planet' from *Superman III*** recalls the memorable scene from the film in which Superman straightens out the Leaning Tower of Pisa. *1983, 58.5cm (23in) high.*

**£100–150**

### BUY

*Observe what children – tomorrow's collectors – are watching, as nostalgia is an important motive for collecting. Buy pieces that are present in key scenes, or that give a strong flavour of the film as a whole.*

**A wand box from *Harry Potter and the Philosopher's Stone.*** This first Harry Potter film is almost certain to become a classic. *2001, 36cm (14in) long.*

**£400–600**

# Animation – in particular, animation art – is a popular collecting area, with often high prices justified by good investment prospects. The emperor of the craft is Disney, whose artefacts, artwork, and merchandising attract a passionate following.

**A yellow Catalin Disney 'Donald Duck' pencil sharpener.** *c.1930s, 3.5cm (1½in) wide.*

**£30–40**

When Mickey Mouse first appeared in the black-and-white cartoon short *Steamboat Willie* in 1928, who could have foretold that this endearing little rodent would one day become a collectable with extremely good investment potential?

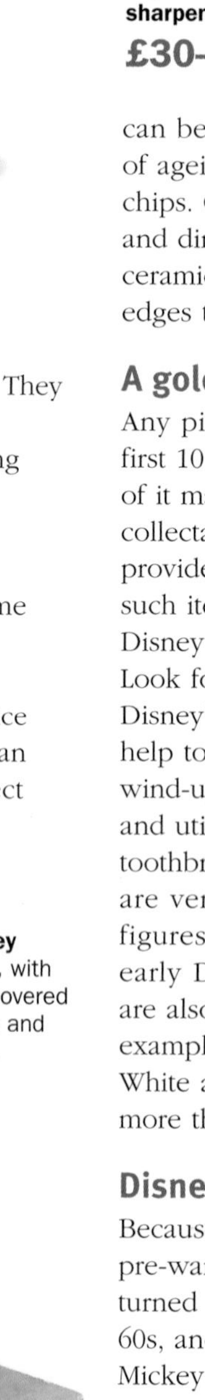

**A rare baby's rattle,** with painted celluloid figures of Snow White and the Seven Dwarfs suspended from the brass ring. *1940s, 8cm (3in) high.*

**£60–80**

## The mouse that roared

Mickey Mouse's creator, Walt Disney, must have had some inkling of his invention's commercial potential, since the great Disney merchandising bandwagon started to roll as early as 1930. This was due to a wealthy New York businessman named George Borgfeldt. Luckily for Disney, who was struggling financially, Borgfeldt had two young children who liked the early Mickey and Minnie shorts. So he decided to license their image from Disney and started producing toys, books, and items of clothing. They sold spectacularly well.

If you want to start collecting Mickey memorabilia, it's worth familiarising yourself with his changing looks over the years. Generally speaking he has become more rounded and cuddly in appearance. Mickeys that have eyes shaped like pies with one slice removed usually indicate an early date. But this effect can be faked, so also check for signs of ageing, such as old scratches or chips. Genuine scratches acquire grime and dirt over time, while chips on old ceramics are less sharp around the edges than new ones.

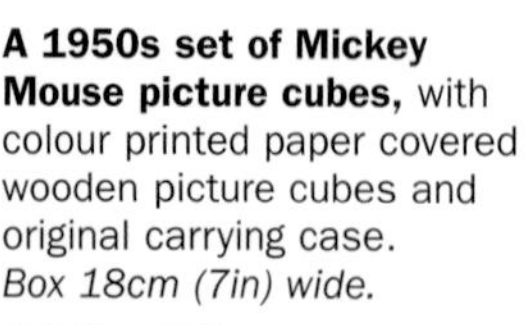

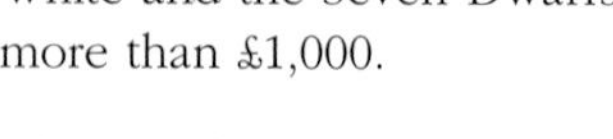

**A 1950s set of Mickey Mouse picture cubes,** with colour printed paper covered wooden picture cubes and original carrying case. *Box 18cm (7in) wide.*

**£20–30**

## A golden decade

Any piece of merchandise from the first 10 years of Disney output – much of it made in Germany and Japan – is collectable and can fetch high sums, provided it is all in one piece. Most such items are in the USA, where Disney dominates popular culture. Look for printed marks indicating Disney's copyright details, as these help to date pieces. Mickey and Minnie wind-up toys, ceramic figures, dolls, and utility items such as egg cups and toothbrush holders from this period are very scarce today. Ceramic figures of characters from early Disney feature films are also highly sought after – for example, a good, vintage set of Snow White and the Seven Dwarfs can fetch more than £1,000.

## Disney for the masses

Because of the increasing scarcity of pre-war Disneyana, collectors have turned to merchandise from the 1950s, 60s, and 70s. During this period Mickey Mouse became even less mouselike, and plastic overtook tin as the favoured material. Other Disney characters, making their screen debuts in films such as *Pinocchio* (1940),

## Essential Mickey Mouse

**EARLY DESIGNS** This early Steiff Mickey Mouse soft toy with an angular face is large and in excellent condition making it highly desirable. c.1930s, 30.5cm (12in) high.

**£1,500–2,000**

**POTTERY FIGURES** The value of ceramic figures like these depends on their age and size. Early and large figures command the highest prices. c.1970, largest 8cm (3in) high.

**£35–40**

**TINS** Mickey Mouse tins can fetch a considerable sum. This example has bright, attractive artwork and is in good condition. 1930s, 15cm (6in) wide.

**£200–250**

**DIE-CAST** Toys in die-cast include novelties such as this Mickey and Minnie barrel organ. The figures are separate from the organ. c.1940s, box 10cm (4in) high.

**£180–220**

**MONEY BANKS** Early money banks were often used as toys, rather than for saving. This rare French cast aluminium model is by the Depeche Company. c.1930s, 15cm (6in) high.

**£150–200**

**BADGES** Many badges were made and they are still common. This one is marked 'Walt Disney 1937' and made by Kay Kamen Ltd of New York and London. c.1937, 3cm (1¼in) diam.

**£15–25**

*Dumbo* (1941), *Bambi* (1942), *The Lady and the Tramp* (1955), *101 Dalmations* (1961), and *The Jungle Book* (1967), also became major subjects for merchandising.

Mass-market merchandising arrived in the 1950s and 60s, so don't expect your treasured 1980s plastic Pluto lunch box to be worth much more than you paid for it originally. But if you're lucky enough to have a scarcer 1950s metal box depicting Mickey Mouse, expect it to fetch up to £200 if it's in excellent condition.

Inexpensive and commonly found items such as badges, pens, rubbers, and greetings cards, may rise in value in the long term, particularly if from the 1930s–50s. But the best investment potential for modern pieces lies with larger or more unusual items and limited editions, provided they are in mint condition with original packaging.

### Computer creatures

Is it worth keeping merchandise and memorabilia from the computer-generated cartoons of today, such as *Toy Story*, *Dinosaur*, and *Monsters Inc.*? It certainly is – provided you keep the presentation box and the item is well preserved, be it a cuddly toy or a comic book. Such classic animations represent the nostalgia of tomorrow.

*Did You Know?*

*Walt Disney originally wanted to call his mouse 'Mortimer' but his wife felt that was rather pompous and preferred 'Mickey'.*

**A pair of Dean's Rag Book Mickey and Minnie Mouse poseable dolls,** in excellent condition. *c.1931, 32cm (12½in) high.*

**£800–1,000**

**KEEP**

*Attractive boxed sets with all their original pieces are likely to rise in value, even if produced comparatively late.*

**A boxed set of Mazda Disneylights, manufactured by the British Thomson-Houston Co.** This consists of 12 bell-shaped Christmas tree lights, each printed with Disney characters, including Mickey Mouse, Dumbo, the Seven Dwarfs, and Bambi. The box adds value. *c.1960s, box 25cm (10in) high.*

**£40–60**

**BUY**

*Although produced in vast numbers, paper and card items are often damaged. When in good condition, they make excellent display pieces, showing artwork characteristic of their period.*

**A Hallmark Cards Disney Mickey Mouse 5th birthday card.** Well preserved and with a charming subject, this is likely to appreciate in value: its current price is low for a vintage piece. *c.1930s, 11cm (4¼in) high.*

**£10–20**

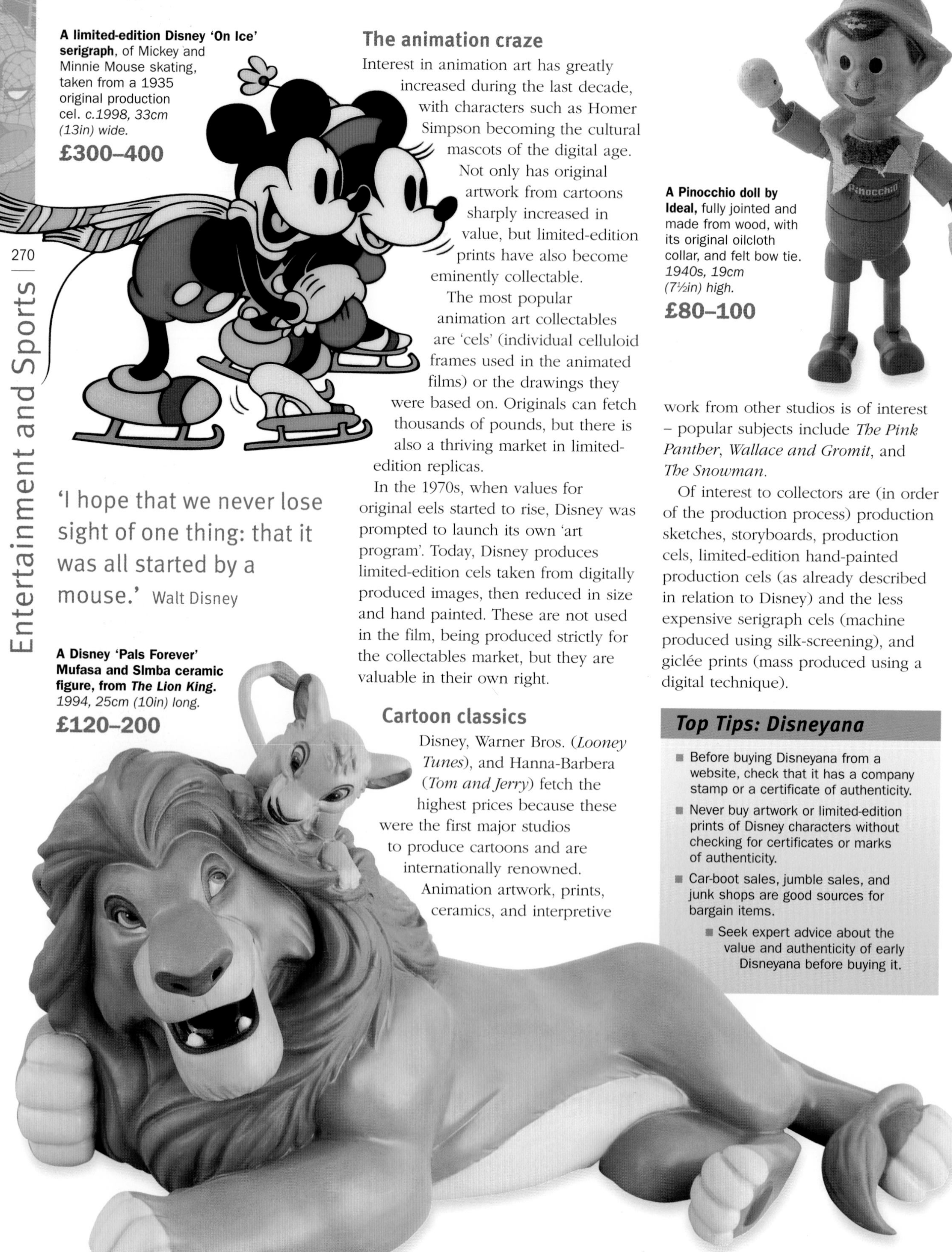

**A limited-edition Disney 'On Ice' serigraph**, of Mickey and Minnie Mouse skating, taken from a 1935 original production cel. *c.1998, 33cm (13in) wide.*

**£300–400**

## The animation craze

Interest in animation art has greatly increased during the last decade, with characters such as Homer Simpson becoming the cultural mascots of the digital age.

Not only has original artwork from cartoons sharply increased in value, but limited-edition prints have also become eminently collectable.

The most popular animation art collectables are 'cels' (individual celluloid frames used in the animated films) or the drawings they were based on. Originals can fetch thousands of pounds, but there is also a thriving market in limited-edition replicas.

In the 1970s, when values for original eels started to rise, Disney was prompted to launch its own 'art program'. Today, Disney produces limited-edition cels taken from digitally produced images, then reduced in size and hand painted. These are not used in the film, being produced strictly for the collectables market, but they are valuable in their own right.

**A Pinocchio doll by Ideal,** fully jointed and made from wood, with its original oilcloth collar, and felt bow tie. *1940s, 19cm (7½in) high.*

**£80–100**

'I hope that we never lose sight of one thing: that it was all started by a mouse.' Walt Disney

**A Disney 'Pals Forever' Mufasa and Simba ceramic figure, from *The Lion King*.** *1994, 25cm (10in) long.*

**£120–200**

## Cartoon classics

Disney, Warner Bros. (*Looney Tunes*), and Hanna-Barbera (*Tom and Jerry*) fetch the highest prices because these were the first major studios to produce cartoons and are internationally renowned.

Animation artwork, prints, ceramics, and interpretive work from other studios is of interest – popular subjects include *The Pink Panther*, *Wallace and Gromit*, and *The Snowman*.

Of interest to collectors are (in order of the production process) production sketches, storyboards, production cels, limited-edition hand-painted production cels (as already described in relation to Disney) and the less expensive serigraph cels (machine produced using silk-screening), and giclée prints (mass produced using a digital technique).

### *Top Tips: Disneyana*

- Before buying Disneyana from a website, check that it has a company stamp or a certificate of authenticity.
- Never buy artwork or limited-edition prints of Disney characters without checking for certificates or marks of authenticity.
- Car-boot sales, jumble sales, and junk shops are good sources for bargain items.
- Seek expert advice about the value and authenticity of early Disneyana before buying it.

## Did You Know?

*All production artwork at Walt Disney was drawn by hand until 'Beauty and the Beast' in 1991. From that date, only characters, special effects, such as rain, clouds, smoke, and shadows, and backgrounds have been hand drawn. The drawings are then scanned into a computer, which adds the colour, and the finished scene is finally transferred onto film. This new process has made production cels redundant, increasing their value as collectables.*

*The Simpsons* probably has the biggest mass-market appeal at the moment, and many pieces are released for sale to dealers, galleries, and websites by 20th Century Fox, including original production cels, drawings, storyboards, and special-edition prints. Prices can start at around £200 for a production cel. Since this series may be around for many years to come, pieces probably won't appreciate in value quickly, but if you have a collection, it may be the start of a generous bequest to your grandchildren.

**A Marvel Studios official Marvel Collector's Edition cel,** given away free in a magazine. *1990s, 27.5cm (10¾in) wide.*

**£200–300**

### Top Tips: animation art

- Look for cels that show the typical poses or expressions of famous characters: a good example is Homer Simpson's 'Doh'.
- Invest in first-rate limited-edition prints, as they can sometimes be worth as much as an original cel.
- Display original cels out of direct sunlight as they can fade, and consult a professional framer on the use of conservation glass and mounts.
- Concept artwork or sections of a storyboard are also collectable. Look for strong images, ideally showing faces.
- If you are storing cels, keep them flat and covered with acid-free tissue paper. Other materials such as polythene and normal paper can damage them over time.

**A 20th Century Fox original production cel from *The Simpsons*,** featuring the family in their Sunday best. *c.2000, 42cm (16½in) wide.*

**£600–800**

### KEEP

*Choose cels of famous characters, such as Tom and Jerry, especially if depicting characteristic activities. If a cel is hand painted, reproduced from a rare production cel, or from a notable limited edition, its value will hold, and may well rise.*

**A limited-edition Hanna-Barbera hand-painted cel, from *Yankee Doodle Mouse*,** signed by animators Bill Hanna, Joe Barbera, and Iwao Takamoto. *c.1996, 30.5cm (12in) wide.*

**£1,000–2,000**

### SELL

*Although well liked in the UK, DangerMouse is unlikely to increase in popularity, partly because this 1980s TV series was short lived but also because it is less popular in the USA and Europe.*

**A Cosgrove Hall original production cel from 'Once Upon a Time Slip'.** This cel has action and implied danger, so would have great appeal to *DangerMouse* fans. *1980s, 32.5cm (12¾in) wide.*

**£150–250**

# Computer games have fascinated adults and children since the 1960s. Even the simplest and earliest games still appeal to today's high-tech enthusiasts, and as their popularity is likely to increase, so is their value.

The first significant computer game, the outsized 'Space Wars', was introduced in the early 1960s, but it was only in the 1980s that manufacturers started producing compact gaming systems for the home. By 1990, Nintendo and Sega had introduced their first consoles and the popular game 'Tetris' was on sale.

The Nintendo 'Game & Watch' range, and other simple games that use liquid crystal displays (LCDs) are popular among enthusiasts. The first of almost 60 'Game & Watch' consoles, 'Ball', was released in 1980. Widescreen versions included 'Snoopy Tennis', 'Fire Attack', and 'Popeye'. These games can be worth £20 to £150, with rarer examples fetching more than £200. From 1991, Nintendo concentrated on developing its Gameboy console.

Of the huge range of games consoles, the Sega Dreamcast is popular, despite being made until recently. Peripheral Dreamcast objects and attachments, generally issued in small numbers, have increased in value.

Neogeo's consoles have become popular with enthusiasts. Its Pocket Colour, a rival to the Gameboy, can fetch from £20 to £80, while the company's home system often fetches around £200–300.

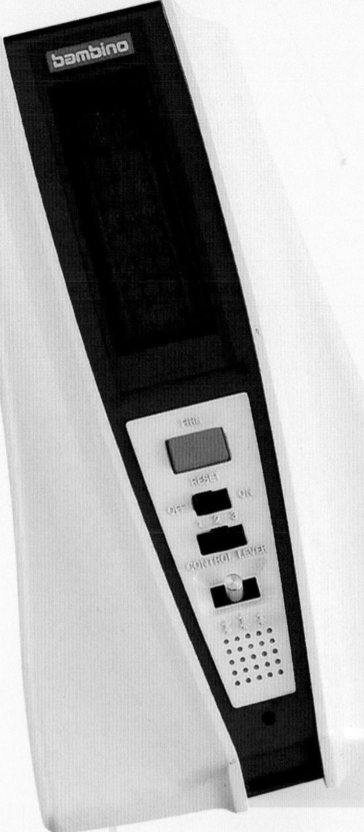


▲ **A Bambino 'UFO Master-Blaster Station' hand-held game,** with a uniquely designed 'space ship' plastic body and a large screen. *c.1980, 13cm (5in) wide.*

**£30–40**

► **A CGL 'Earth Invaders' hand-held game,** based on the successful 'Space Invaders' and similar games. *c.1980, 20cm (7¾in) wide.*

**£30–50**

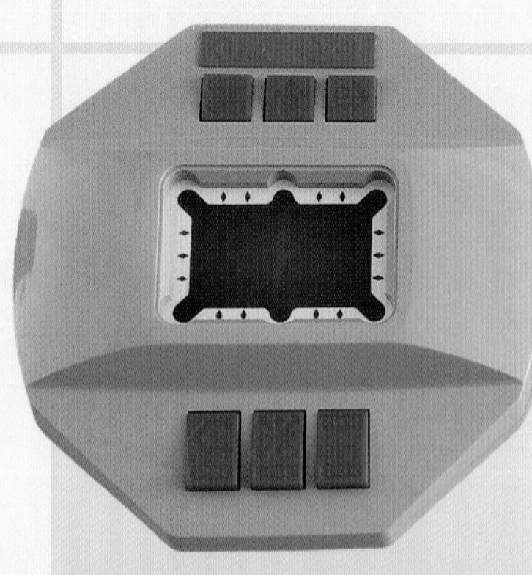

► **A Palitoy 'Alex Higgins Cue Ball' tabletop game,** endorsed by the snooker player. Games that recreated sports were fashionable in the 1980s. *c.1980, 15.5cm (6in) wide.*

**£40–50**

◄ **An Atari 2600 game console.** This is a smaller version of the 'woodgrain'-cased model, which is more common and usually worth around 20 per cent less than this version. *c.1986, 26.5cm (15in) wide.*

**£50–70**

◄ **A Grandstand 'Munchman' tabletop game,** with two skill levels. The success of the arcade game 'Pac-Man' led to companies releasing similar games such as this one, which even has a Pac-Man-shaped case in identical yellow. *c.1981, 20cm (7¾in) wide.*

**£30–40**

◀ **A Bambino 'Boxing' tabletop game,** with a six-button control that enabled the players to attack their opponents from various different positions. *c.1979, 30cm (11¾in) wide.*

**£30–40**

◀ **A Nintendo 'Snoopy SM-91' panorama-screen 'Game and Watch'.** As well as being one of the desirable 'Game and Watch' series, the addition of popular characters such as Snoopy adds interest. Other versions of the game use Disney characters. *c.1983, 11.5cm (4¼in) wide.*

**£100–200**

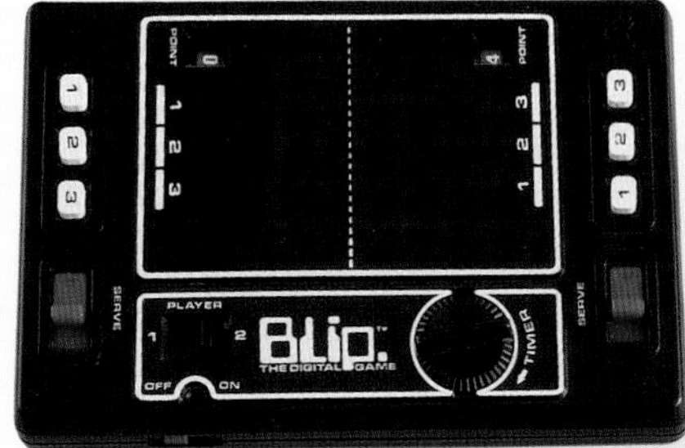


▶ **A Tomy 'Blip' hand-held analogue game.** Early games often used simple graphics of a randomly moving dot that had to be kept away from the sides of the screen. *c.1977, 17.5cm (6¾in) wide.*

**£20–30**

## Collectors' Tips

- Games should be complete, have their battery covers, and be in full working order
- Remove batteries when games are not in use
- Try to protect serial numbers and stickers

◀ **A Nintendo Micro Vs 'Donkey Kong Hockey' HK-303, two-player 'Game and Watch'** with two controls (not shown). *c.1984, 15.5cm (6in) wide.*

**£100–150**

◀ **An SNK Neogeo Pocket-Color 16-bit portable game console.** First released in Japan, this console enjoyed limited success in the US and Europe. Features include an alarm clock and a customized horoscope. *c.1999, 13cm (5in) wide.*

**£30–40**

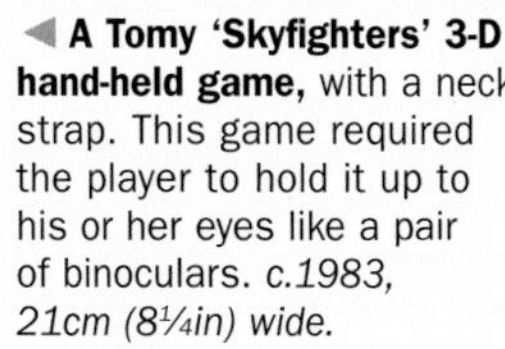

◀ **A Tomy 'Skyfighters' 3-D hand-held game,** with a neck strap. This game required the player to hold it up to his or her eyes like a pair of binoculars. *c.1983, 21cm (8¼in) wide.*

**£20–30**

▲ **A Nintendo 'Parachute PR-21' wide-screen** from the highly collectable 'Game and Watch' series. The player has to save parachutists falling from a helicopter by catching them in a rowing boat. *c.1981, 11cm (4¼in) wide.*

**£40–60**

# Elvis Presley dominated the pop charts in the 1950s and his movie-star status in the following decade created a multi-million dollar industry, generating a wealth of memorabilia – from wrist watches to Christmas cards – for his fans and enthusiasts to explore.



As well as records, items including badges, watches, and postage stamps have been adorned with Elvis Presley's image. There's even a Monopoly game based on him. If you know fans who followed the star during his lifetime, find out if they have any memorabilia: it might be worth something.

**A Summer Festival at the Las Vegas Hilton souvenir concert menu,** signed by Elvis Presley. *1970s, 38cm (15in) high.*

**£500–700**

## The King

Presley was brought up in a poor working-class family in Tupelo, Mississippi, where he was influenced by the pop and country music of the time as well as the gospel music in his local church. In 1953 he paid $3.98 to make his first record, 'My Happiness'. The following year he signed up with the Sun Records label in Memphis, Tennessee, and his singing career began in earnest, managed by the self-styled 'Colonel' Tom Parker.

Presley's bluesy vocal style, sexy image, and electrifying live shows opened up a new era in popular music and culture. In 1956, at the age of 21, Elvis had his first US No.1 hit with 'Heartbreak Hotel'. In the same year he broke the UK charts and made his movie debut in *Love Me Tender*.

In 1958 Presley was called up for military service. While this interrupted his career as a live performer, it heightened his appeal among his legions of fans. Items used by Elvis during his army service are extremely rare, but Tom Parker produced a run of ankle bracelets with replica Elvis Presley army 'dog tags', which can be found for less than £20.

When he left the army, Presley embarked on his 'Hollywood years': he made 27 movies between 1960 and 1969. Original Elvis movie posters and lobby cards are highly sought after and can fetch upwards of £100.

**A Swiss-made 'Forever Elvis' commemorative wristwatch,** by the Precision Watch Company Inc. *c.1980s, 5cm (2in) diam.*

**£20–25**

**A Graceland security badge,** marked 'Caughley 5'. James Caughley was a security guard at the Presley mansion. *c.1961, 10cm (4in) high.*

**£700–1,000**

## The Vegas years

After an 11-year hiatus, Elvis returned to live performance with the 1968 'Comeback Special'. This final period of his career was characterised by

Elvis remains the undeposed 'King of Rock 'n' Roll'. It is estimated that he has sold more than one billion records, and his Memphis mansion Graceland attracts more than 600,000 visitors each year.

An Elvis Presley Panel Delux double-album boxed set (RP-9201-2), produced by RCA for the Japanese market. The albums are in near-mint condition. *c.1970, 40cm (15¾in) high.*

**£1,000–1,500**

## Top Tips

- Be cautious when buying souvenirs relating to Elvis's most famous performances, such as his 1968 'Comeback Special', as these items are commonly targeted by forgers.
- When buying concert memorabilia, note that Elvis performed only five concerts outside the USA in the whole of his career – in Canada in 1957.
- Seek third-party authentication – particularly for high-price items.
- Do not buy any item originally sold in the 1999 Graceland auction unless it comes with a certificate of authenticity.

extensive touring and his downward spiral into obesity and ill health.

Elvis played throughout the USA in the 1970s but was particularly popular in Las Vegas, where the glitzy atmosphere suited his style. Souvenirs from his Vegas shows, such as the menus printed for his two- and four-week residencies at the Hilton Theater, are highly collectable. Presley died at his home, Graceland, Memphis, in 1977 at the age of 42.

## Sweet charity

Items that belonged to or were used by Presley are far more valuable than the merchandising. In 1999, at a charity auction of 2,000 items from the Graceland archives, a set of balls from Elvis's billiard table fetched $7,500 (£5,000), his old football helmet sold for $10,000 (£6,700), and a credit card raised $11,000 (£7,300). Even a receipt for a TV set went for $650 (£450).

## Sun singles

Prices for Elvis memorabilia may level out as lifelong fans get older, so it is essential to invest carefully.

Personal items are valuable if the link can be proven beyond doubt, and any merchandise from the 1950s will command impressive prices. Souvenirs produced since Elvis's death are less likely to fetch large sums of money.

The collectables market is swamped with Elvis Presley's music. Most of his records are worth less than £50,with some fetching as little as £2–5.

Among the most valuable items are mint-condition Sun singles, which can sell for up to £2,500. But, none of Elvis's LPs reaches these dizzy heights: the rarest can sell for around £500.

## BUY

*Key events in the Presley story, including his untimely death, are still being commemorated in various media. Attractive pieces by well-known makers, in limited-edition runs of 200 or fewer, are likely to rise in value, mainly owing to Elvis's enduring popularity even among people born since his death.*

**An enamel box depicting Elvis,** made by Halcyon Days, with Andy Warhol-style artwork. The box was issued in a limited edition of 500 to mark the 25th anniversary of Presley's death in 1977. *2002, 5.5cm (2in) long.*

**£150–250**

## KEEP

*Keep items with strong visual impact, such as any showing a young Presley in the first phase of his career in the 1950s. An authentic Presley signature will make the item even more desirable. The piece is likely to rise in value, especially if it was produced in limited numbers and can be displayed easily.*

**A Christmas card signed by Elvis.** This is addressed to 'Mary' by Elvis. *1966, 16cm (6¼in) high.*

**£600–800**

# The Beatles burst onto the scene in 1962 and changed pop music forever. Their superstar status, especially in the 1960s, led to a huge array of memorabilia, and this – along with their records, of course – can make an impressive collection.

**A painted plaster figure of George Harrison,** with a nodding head. *1960s, 20cm (8in) high.*

**£60–90**

The Beatles – John Lennon, Paul McCartney, George Harrison, and Ringo Starr – dominated the popular music scene from the early 1960s until they disbanded in 1969. Nowadays, their domination of the rock and pop memorabilia market is similarly pronounced. John Lennon and Paul McCartney's pianos headlined the first rock memorabilia auction in 1981, and Beatles items continue to lead the way.

## Marketing the Beatles

Countless products bearing their portraits were manufactured, from souvenir buttons and coins to dolls, serving trays, and even a *Yellow Submarine* pop-out decoration book. You may still have some item of memorabilia in your family. If so, it could well be worth more now than the price originally paid for it.

A cloth badge, made to tie in with the 1967 *Sgt. Pepper* album, could have been bought with pocket money at the time, but today can fetch £150–200.

## Spin city

Collecting Beatles records can be a minefield. For example, the American edition of 'She Loves You' (released on Swan in 1964) was pressed at several factories, resulting in a number of label variations. To increase the confusion, this single was frequently forged. An authentic, signed 'She Loves You' recently fetched £1,500 in mint condition – the signatures adding greatly to the value.

Millions of Beatles records have been released over the years, so most are of relatively low value and rarely fetch more than £50, but some at least are highly sought after by serious collectors. For example, any records produced in small runs, such as promotional copies of singles used by DJs, have a high value, as do those withdrawn from sale, such as the notorious edition of the American compilation *'Yesterday' and Today,* with a cover showing the Beatles in butcher's overalls, surrounded by dismembered dolls. It is said that the band requested this cover as a protest at the way in which their American record company, Capitol, was 'butchering' their albums by recompiling them. Early copies were withdrawn and replaced with an innocuous version showing the band standing around a storage trunk, with Paul sitting inside it, but in some cases the new image was simply pasted over the offending cover.

Other collecting areas include programmes, magazines, and posters. A programme for the group's 1964 Australian tour can be worth £80–120,

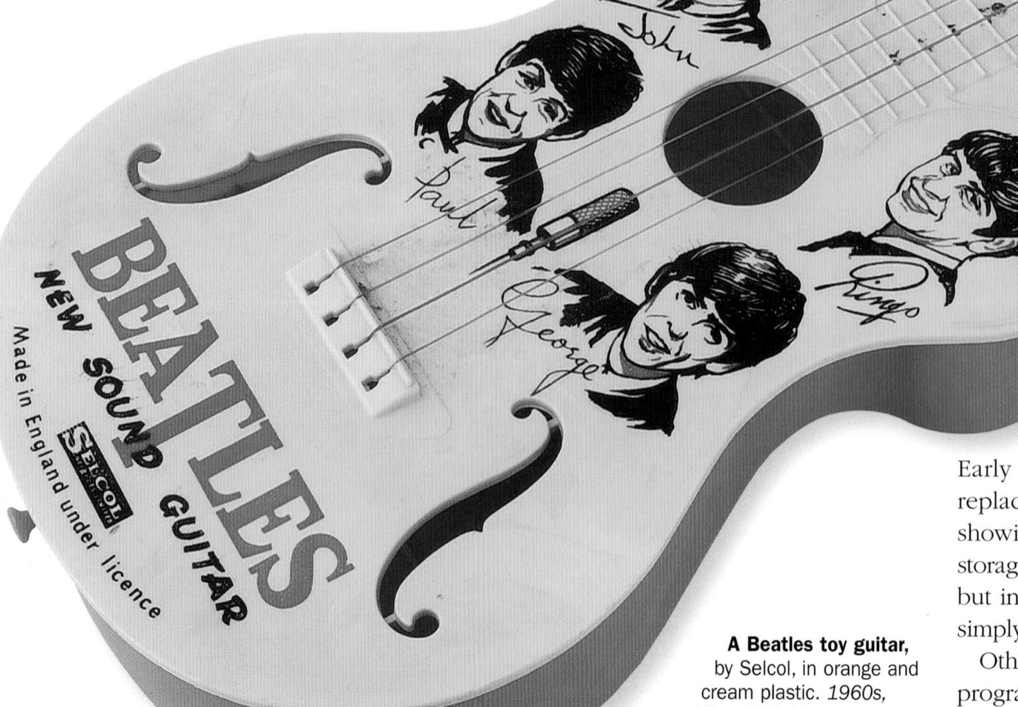


**A Beatles toy guitar,** by Selcol, in orange and cream plastic. *1960s, 60cm (24in) long.*

**£200–300**

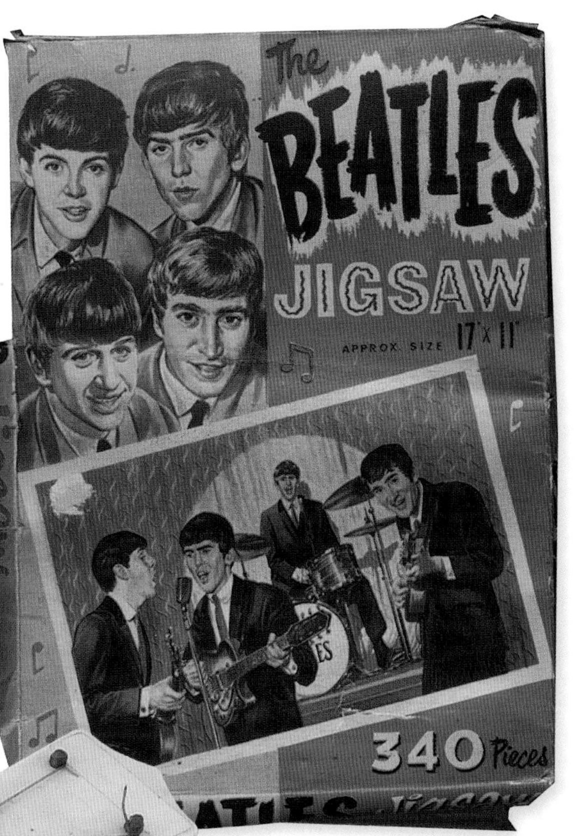


**A Beatles jigsaw puzzle**, with a worn box. *1960s, 35cm (12in).*

**£80–120**

and a complete set of the original 77 issues of *The Beatles Book Monthly* magazine, published from 1963 to 1969, can fetch £400–500. A film poster for *A Hard Day's Night,* signed by Paul, George, and Ringo, has fetched more than £1,500.

## Personal touches

Items of significance to, or owned by, members of the band are usually valuable, particularly if they are representative of their lifestyle at the height of 'Beatlemania'. Examples include clothes, musical instruments, and documents such as contracts and plane tickets. The link and provenance must be cast-iron, though.

## Autograph alert

A band member's signature or handwriting will increase the value of any item it appears on. A note by Paul carrying lyrics from 'Penny Lane' sold for £1,350, and a copy of the album *Please Please Me* signed by the entire band can be worth £1,000–1,500. A cartoon Christmas card of John and his first wife Cynthia drawn by Lennon, with an eight-page letter enclosed, fetched £8,000.

Band members were known to sign for each other in the early days, and a photocard signed for all the Beatles by Paul has sold for £500. A word of warning: Beatles autographs are among the most commonly faked, so be sure that anything with a signature comes from a reliable source.

## Top Tips

- Join a Beatles fan club to keep informed about collectors' events and auction sales.
- Stay up-to-date with current album prices by checking auction sites on the Internet.
- Familiarise yourself with the distinguishing features of the most collectable pressings, such as misspellings of song titles and minor variations in recording credits.
- Don't be fooled by 1970s reprints of *The Beatles Book Monthly.* Each reprint issue contains four extra pages, but these can be removed. Other tell-tale signs are that the photos are less clear than the originals; and some copies vary slightly in size from the original 15.25 x 21cm (6 x 8¼in).

## BUY

*Beatles images appeared on the packaging of a vast variety of products. Relatively few disposable items survive, so they may well rise in value. Look for items that show the faces and signatures of the Beatles and that are representative of the styles of the time.*

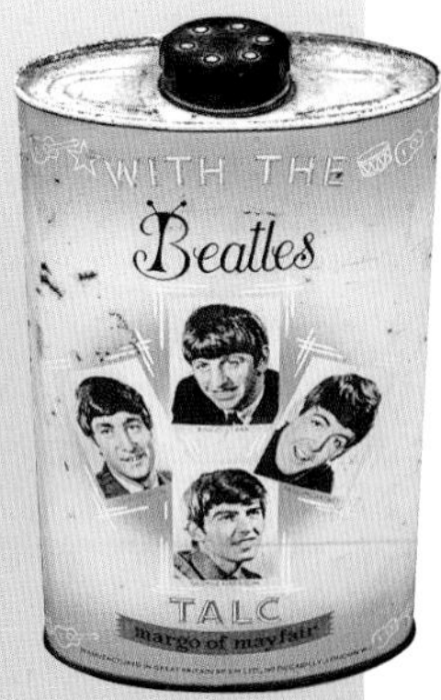


**A British Beatles talcum powder tin.** Tins such as this are prone to damage, which makes one that is in mint condition especially valuable. *1960s, 18cm (7in) high.*

**£60–100**

## KEEP

*If you were lucky enough to have seen the Beatles in concert, hunt out any memorabilia you might have kept. Original programmes, or even ticket stubs, can be of value, and, as they are in limited supply, prices are likely to continue rising.*

**A programme for the 'Another Beatles Christmas Show'** season at the Hammersmith Odeon, London (24 December 1964 to 16 January 1965), together with a ticket stub from the show on 8 January. The printed artwork on the cover is by John Lennon. *1964–65, programme 30cm (12in) high.*

**£200–300**

# Essential Beatles

**MERCHANDISE** The 'Fab Four' were so famous that their faces appeared on even the most mundane objects. This tea towel captures 'Beatlemania'. 1960s, 60cm (23¾in) wide.

**£40–60**

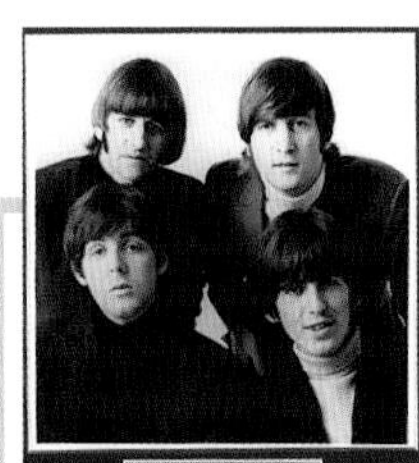

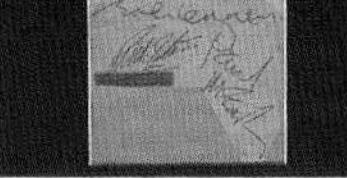

**SIGNATURES** Genuine signatures are desirable, especially if, as with these framed with a photo, they don't overlap each other. 1960s, frame 40cm (16in) wide.

**£1,500–2,000**

**PERSONAL ITEMS** Even pre-fame artefacts, such as John Lennon's employment card from his job at a waterworks, can be highly sought after. 1959, 25cm (10in) wide.

**£8,000–10,000**

**RECORDS** Rare pressings and unusual foreign editions, such as this Italian version of the album *With the Beatles*, fetch high prices, but only if in excellent condition. 1965, 32cm (12½in) wide.

**£220–280**

# Rock and pop music

## have commanded an often fanatical following since the birth of rock 'n' roll in the 1950s. More and more fans are turning to collecting memorabilia relating to the artists they most admire.

**A large Royal Doulton 'Buddy Holly' character jug,** in a limited edition of 2,500. The removable spectacles (not shown) have been broken. *1998, 15cm (6in) wide.*

**£50–80**

Collectors of rock and pop memorabilia usually specialise in particular artists, eras, or genres, and although reports of record-breaking sales suggest otherwise, this remains an accessible area of the collectables market. With thousands of artists, and more than half a century of material to choose from, there is plenty to collect for those of every popular music persuasion. Even fans of artists who have died (which increases the value of memorabilia associated with them) are able to pick up items such as ticket stubs and concert programmes at relatively low prices.

### Rock 'n' roll is here to stay

In the late 1950s, artists such as Elvis Presley, Buddy Holly, and Bill Haley ushered in the rock 'n' roll era. Although memorabilia associated with Buddy Holly and Bill Haley is not as highly priced as Elvis material, collectors still expect to pay up to around £100–300 for tour brochures and concert programmes. A signature adds to an item's value: a signed Buddy Holly programme can cost up to £800. Early memorabilia related to Cliff Richard, who was launched in the 1950s as the 'British Elvis', can still be picked up inexpensively, usually for less than £100.

### Like a rolling stone

In the 1960s the influence of rock 'n' roll, as well as blues, hit Britain as bands like The Beatles and The Rolling Stones emerged. Early Stones memorabilia, such as guitars and items of clothing, is rare and sought after, but there are less expensive alternatives. Souvenir booklets and tour brochures from the mid-1960s are available for around £25–60, and a programme with a ticket stub can often fetch £80–120. Unlike most bands from the era, The Rolling Stones are still recording and touring, so there is almost 40 years' worth of material to choose from. In general, items from the 1960s have the highest value (a 1960s guitar signed by the original members of the band might fetch £3,000–5,000 or more, especially if it was used by the band), but memorabilia from later

◄ ► **A Bill Haley photograph and autograph;** mounted together and framed. *c.1960s, frame 40cm (16in) high.*

**£100–150**

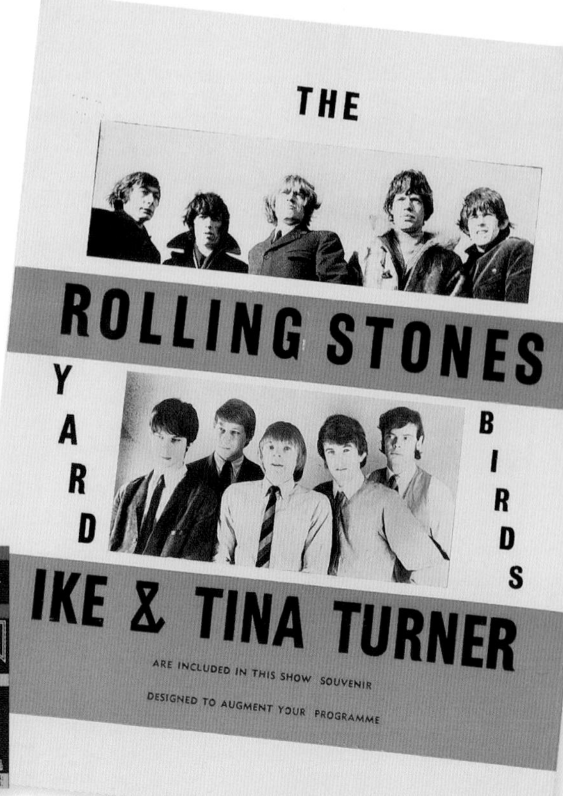


► **An original souvenir programme** for a tour featuring The Rolling Stones, Ike & Tina Turner, The Yardbirds, The Small Faces, and others. *c.1965, 20cm (8in) high.*

**£100–150**

▼ **A Rolling Stones poster,** to promote the release of the CD and video *Rock and Roll Circus. 1996, 94cm (37in) wide.*

**£300–500**

## A closer look at... a psychedelic poster

The desirability of a late-1960s psychedelic poster is based on the profile of the designer, the significance of the concert or event being promoted, and the extent to which the design and colours are typical of the era.

Famous names like The Jimi Hendrix Experience and Pink Floyd make this poster more desirable

Bright, often acidic colours were most often used

Scrolling Art Nouveau-like motifs and shapes are typical

Integrating the font and the type's layout into the design – an Art Nouveau technique – is common

**A silkscreen poster advertising two concerts at the Saville Theatre, London,** for Pink Floyd and The Jimi Hendrix Experience. It was designed by 'Hapshash and The Coloured Coat', the pseudonym of notable designers Nigel Weymouth and Michael English, and published by Osiris Visions. All these factors add to its value. *1967, 140cm (55in) high.*

**£500–800**

decades will also attract premium prices if rare.

### The shock of the new

The American singer and guitarist Jimi Hendrix is one of the most collectable artists from the 1960s. He spent some time living in London, so there are many British items of memorabilia available. A framed flyer and booking form for a 1967 Jimi Hendrix Experience/Cat Stevens/Engelbert Humperdinck concert in Leicester can fetch £600–700, and similar prices are paid for signed photographs. A membership card and pass issued to someone who went to see a Jimi Hendrix gig at London's Revolution Club in 1968 is less expensive at around £80–90.

Other American artists from the 1960s whose memorabilia still attracts great interest include The Doors, Grateful Dead, The Monkees, and Bob Dylan. Along with British names such as The Who, Deep Purple, and Pink Floyd, these are 'A-list' artists for whom concert tickets and posters can fetch £100–400 or more. A less expensive alternative can be to collect lesser names, or tickets for music publications' poll-winners concerts or for TV music shows. Audience tickets for the TV show *Ready, Steady, Go!* are often available for less than £50, with higher prices paid for broadcasts in which a famous artist made his or her debut.

**An American one-sheet poster** for Pink Floyd's *Live at Pompeii* concert film. *1973, 104cm (41in) high.*

**£200–300**

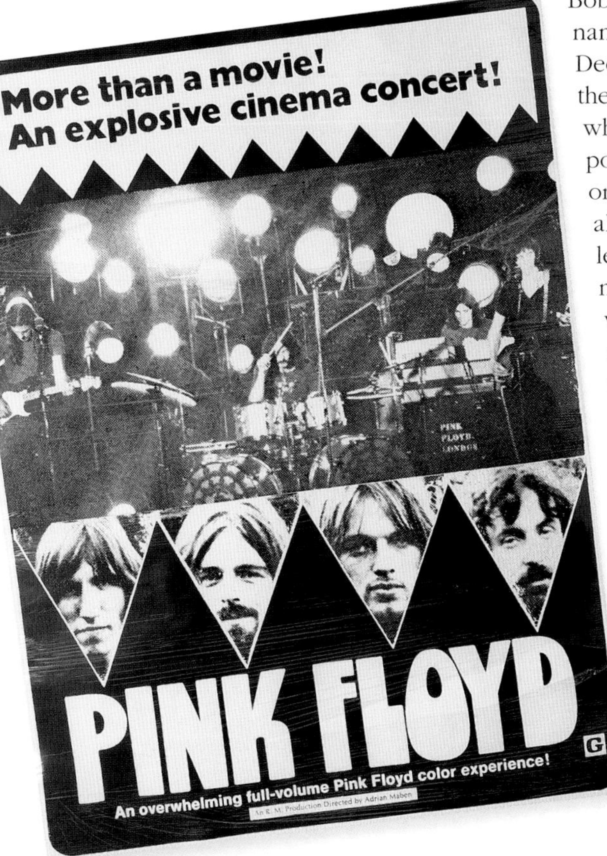


### Writing on the wall

Original late-1960s concert posters that employ psychedelic patterns and colours have become highly collectable, especially those by renowned American designers such as Rick Griffin, or Stanley Mouse and Alton Kelley, who worked together as a pair. Griffin's work is found on posters for seminal events such as the 1967 'Human Be-In' in San Francisco, as well as for many of the early San Francisco shows by bands such as Jefferson Airplane and Grateful Dead. He was also a prolific record-sleeve artist. As with other deceased artists, the value of his work increased after his death in 1991. Any damage such as rubbing or wear to the design (especially on 'mirrored' or reflective areas), tears, or fading reduces value considerably. Rarer examples can fetch £1,000 and more, but others with the same look can be found from about £30–50, with the majority worth around £100–400.

The 1960s was also the decade of the first music festivals, and although memorabilia from the most famous of them all – Woodstock – is costly, items from the Isle of Wight festivals held in 1969 and 1970 are less

#### Did You Know?

*Unexpected treasures can still be found. In 1996 a rock and pop dealer discovered 20 tapes of one of the last Jimi Hendrix concerts stored in a barn in Delaware, USA. They were later sold at auction for £1.5 million.*

expensive – an original poster can be found for around £50–100.

## Rock giants

In the late 1960s, British bands such as The Who, Deep Purple, and Led Zeppelin developed a heavier guitar sound, but it wasn't until the 1970s that they became rock superstars. Any musical instruments or clothes connected with these artists or other notable rock bands, such as T. Rex, Black Sabbath, and Queen, command top prices. A guitar autographed by members of The Who can fetch £1,000–1,500 or more. Similarly, prices for 1970s posters advertising the most notable bands and artists are sought after. A poster for Pink Floyd's 1972 film *Live at Pompeii* will usually be worth around £200–250 and a 1979 Led Zeppelin Knebworth concert poster will often fetch £200–300.

Concert tickets tend to be less expensive, but significant gigs attract a premium. A ticket for Led Zeppelin's 1970 show in Dallas can be found for around £50–60, yet a ticket from Madison Square Garden for the same year – when lead singer Robert Plant dedicated a song to Jimi Hendrix, who had just died – can fetch more than £100.

Tickets for concerts at which a member of a band played for the first or last time will often fetch around twice as much as a standard ticket. For example, two members left Deep Purple and were replaced in 1970, two more in 1973, and one in 1974. Expect to pay up to around £100 or more for a Deep Purple member's debut or farewell concert.

**A Led Zeppelin poster** promoting a concert at Knebworth Park in 1979. *1979, 66cm (26in) high.*

**£300–500**

## Changes

Some musicians and singers transformed their image as they changed their style of music, and this can be reflected in an item's value. David Bowie is a prime example, and prices have been rising since his death. His incarnation as Ziggy Stardust lasted from 1971 to 1973, and prices for memorabilia from this era are usually higher than for any other period in his career. As with

**A David Bowie 'Serious Moonlight' tour concert programme.** *1983, 30cm (12in) high.*

**£50–100**

▼ **A Led Zeppelin promotional photograph** for their *Houses of the Holy* album. *1973.*

*Did You Know?*

*A sale of The Who memorabilia in 2003 included 180 guitars, the largest number ever sold at one auction. The highest price was paid for a 1958 Gibson Explorer, which fetched more than £95,000.*

**A sleeve for the U2 live album *Under a Blood Red Sky*,** signed by all four band members. *1983, 34cm (13½in) wide.*

**£200–300**

**A giant colour Madonna poster** for the Spanish leg of her 1990 'Blond Ambition' world tour. *1990, 137cm (54in) high.*

**£40–60**

other stars who are still performing, there is a great deal of Bowie memorabilia on the market, the most valuable pieces often being those with a story behind them. The original cover for Bowie's 1970 *Man Who Sold The World* album, on which he wore a dress, was hastily withdrawn. A copy of the album sold in 2003 for £320.

Elton John is another artist at the height of his popularity during the 1970s who is still recording. Images of him wearing his colourful glasses and platform shoes will forever be associated with the flamboyance of the era. Top-quality memorabilia fetches high prices: a pair of his platform shoes worn on stage in the 1970s can fetch up to £2,000 or more. But Elton John is a conspicuous consumer, buying hundreds of pairs of shoes, and it is possible to pick up a pair for £200–400.

## Pistols and pogos

One interesting area for collectors of the 1970s is punk rock, especially items associated with the influential bands The Clash and, above all, the notorious Sex Pistols. The Pistols were only on the scene for about three years from 1975, and the death of their bassist Sid Vicious in 1979 added value to the band's memorabilia. They played few concerts, so even tickets are worth considerable sums: a ticket for a 1976 gig featuring the Sex Pistols and The Damned can fetch £100–200. Promotional album posters are collectable – a poster signed by a band member can go for around £150–200 if in excellent condition. Pistols fanzines are also sought after: the first issue of *Anarchy in the UK* may be only 12 pages long, but it can still often fetch around £150.

## Global superstars

From 1981, MTV was a key influence on the development of popular music. Through videos channelled into people's homes, pop artists such as Michael Jackson, Madonna, and Prince became global superstars with greater emphasis on image. But rock bands continued to flourish, too, as U2, Nirvana, and Oasis came to the fore. New music styles such as house and rap also emerged, so the period from the 1980s onwards provides collectors with a rich variety of material.

## Variations on vinyl

Recordings made for individual markets became widespread in the 1980s. Along with the growth of the picture disc and coloured vinyl, these offer plenty of scope for collectors. The Police, for example, released 'De Do Do Do De Da Da Da' in 1980 as a 7-inch single; a French version can be bought for around £5–10, a Japanese version for around £20–40, and a rare 12-inch Spanish-language version produced for the Colombian market can be worth more than £200.

Rare promotional records and first pressings are also sought after, with artists as varied as Madonna, The Clash, and U2 all putting out limited-edition vinyl. The standard version of U2's 1983 *Under a Blood Red Sky* LP can usually be found for about £10, but the first Mexican pressing, with its unique sleeve artwork, can fetch more than £100. Signed standard album sleeves without the vinyl record can fetch around £150–200.

## Recognition and reward

The rise in the profile of musicians over the last 20 years has been accompanied by the growth of awards

## Essential rock memorabilia

**ALBUMS** 1960s and 70s rock albums are notable for their often futuristic cover artwork. This debut LP by the blues-rock trio Cream has been signed by the band. c.1967, 34cm (13½in) wide.

**£200–300**

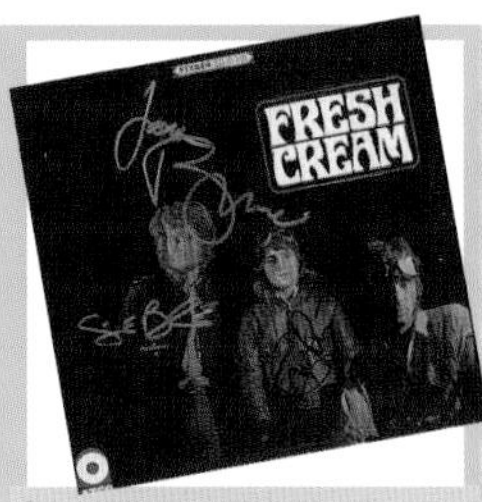


**MAGAZINES** Issues recording major events are popular. The Stones' 1967 Hyde Park concert came two days after the death of band member Brian Jones. 1970s, 30cm (12in) high.

**£80–120**

**INSTRUMENTS** Rock stars are often asked to sign the tools of their trade. These drumsticks have been signed by Mick Fleetwood, drummer for Fleetwood Mac. c.1980s, 36cm (14¼in) long.

**£20–40**

**POSTERS** The most successful posters give a strong impression of the music they promote, as in this example for the annual 'Monsters of Rock' festival. 1984, 150cm (59in) high.

**£150–200**

events. As a result, awards memorabilia has attracted much interest. A silk suit worn by Prince at the 1998 Grammys, for example, can be worth around £5,000, partly because a global television audience saw him wearing it. For the budget buyer, programmes for the same event are available for just a few pounds.

## Cult followings

Some bands gain a mystical aura that generates a passion in their fans for everything and anything to do with them. Grateful Dead, formed in the 1960s, are one example. 'Dead' memorabilia has always been highly prized, but the death of lead singer Jerry Garcia in 1995 pushed prices even higher. While tickets, posters, and fanzines from the 1980s and 90s are within the price range of most collectors, memorabilia from the 1960s can be expensive: a ticket for a 1966 Grateful Dead concert in San Francisco can be worth up to around £300–500 and one of Garcia's Hawaiian print shirts can fetch more than £1,000.

Since their explosion onto the music scene in the early 1990s, the rock band Nirvana have enjoyed a huge cult following, and the suicide of lead singer Kurt Cobain in 1994 has done little to dampen fans' enthusiasm. Pieces signed by Cobain attract the highest prices – a British Airways Concorde life jacket that Cobain gave to his wife, the rock singer and actor Courtney Love, as a Valentine's Day present is a quirky piece of memorabilia worth more than £500. Other items are less expensive: an unused ticket for a 1994 Paris concert, for example, might sell for around £20–30, and original photographs often fetch less than £20.

## An eye to the future

Memorabilia from recording artists who have been successful for a long time will almost always be worth more than

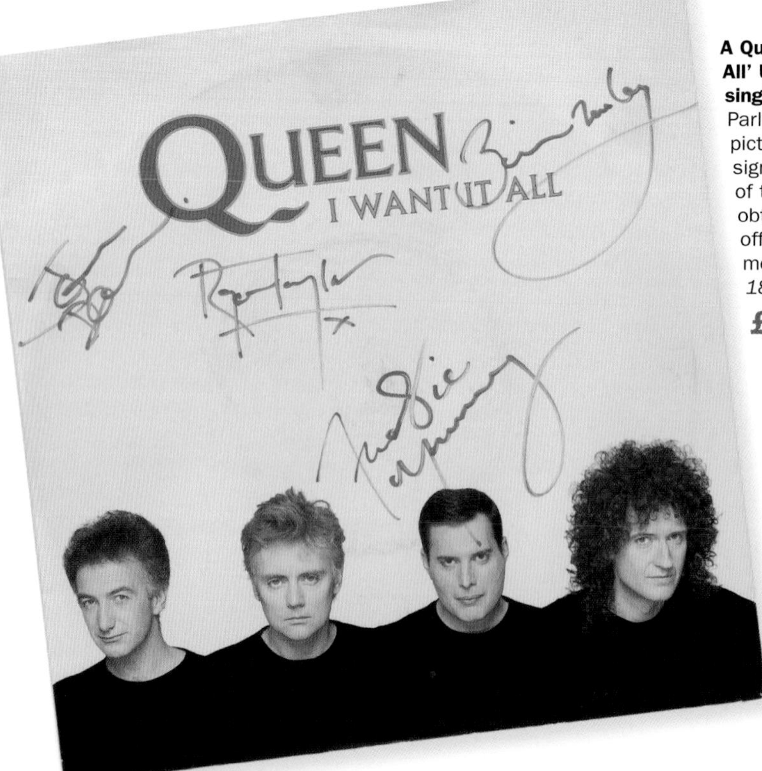


**A Queen 'I Want It All' UK QUEEN 10 single**, released by Parlophone, the picture sleeve is signed by members of the group, obtained from an official fan club member. *1989, 18cm (7in) wide.*

**£400–500**

## Some pop groups to look for:

▪ Wham! ▪ Abba ▪ Genesis ▪

**A Wham! colour photograph,** signed 'George Michael' and 'Love Andrew Ridgeley'. With their series of catchy, 'sing-along' pop tunes written by George Michael, Wham! were one of the first 'boy bands', a genre that is now ubiquitous. *1980s, 25cm (10in) wide.*

**£80–120**

**An Abba publicity photograph,** signed by all four members of the group. One of the most successful pop groups of the 1970s, Abba's memorable lyrics and catchy tunes ensure their perennial popularity, which is likely to continue. *c.1980, 15cm (6in) high.*

**£200–300**

**An album sleeve for *Abacab*,** signed by Phil Collins, Mike Rutherford, and Tony Banks. Originally a 1970s progressive-rock band, Genesis moved to a softer pop sound in the 1980s. *Abacab* is typical of their new style and was a bestseller. *1981, 34cm (13½in) wide.*

**£70–100**

that from bands and solo artists who have been 'manufactured' by record companies. Oasis have an enormous fan-base and their special limited editions can often fetch high prices. While a CD with a bonus track can be worth around £10–15, a 1995 one-track promotional CD of the song 'Acquiesce' – limited to 300 pressings – may fetch more than £200. Radiohead, owing to their loyal following and the consistent quality of their music, are also highly collectable.

Owing to their extraordinary popularity and unprecedented 'girl band' success at the time, items signed by all the Spice Girls are highly prized. A poster for their 1997 film *Spiceworld* often fetches in excess of £200–300. Of the current crop of pop stars, signed photos by artists such as Sophie Ellis-Bextor, Westlife, and Blue can be found for about £50 and less. Whether prices will rise is debatable, as the length of their careers and continued popularity cannot be guaranteed.

### Top Tips

- Be aware that a star's signature on an instrument does not necessarily mean that he or she used it: those that were definitely used will fetch more. Seek authentication for valuable items.
- Look for items that are identifiable from a video, TV appearance, or album cover – these attract higher prices.
- Choose undedicated autographs, not written to a specific person. These are usually preferred by collectors.
- Read the music press to get a feel for acts who might be 'the next big thing'.

## BUY

*Original memorabilia associated with infamous or shocking events in pop history often becomes highly collectable, and usually increases in value if the notoriety of the episode endures.*

**A German Frankie Goes to Hollywood tour poster.** This 1980s pop group shocked the world with the explicit lyrics of their debut single 'Relax', which was banned by the BBC in 1984. The tour poster was banned in Germany. *1985, 117cm (46in) high.*

**£100–200**

## KEEP

*The outrageous punk movement defined the late 1970s and is still memorable. Pieces from key bands, in particular those owned by a band member, should rise in value, especially at times when punk is back in vogue.*

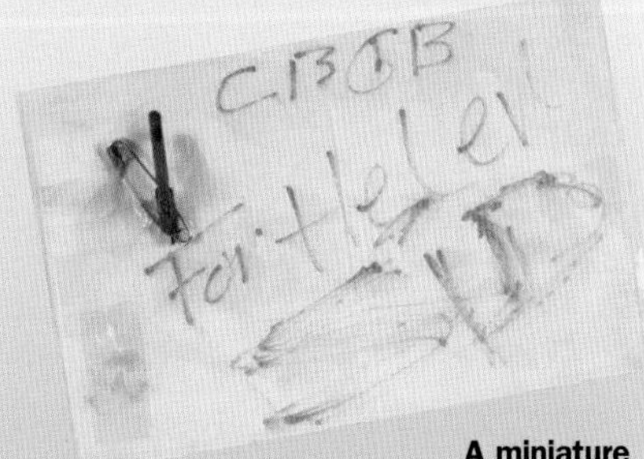


**A miniature pistol-shaped pin charm** with attached safety pin, originally given to Sid Vicious by his friend Helen Wheels. The pin was given back to Wheels at the CBGB club in New York with a note written by Sid Vicious. *1970s, card 18cm (7in) wide.*

**£1,000–1,500**

## KEEP

*Autographs are commonly found in attics and drawers. If they are authentic and belong to major stars who are unlikely to fall out of favour, they will probably increase in value.*

**A Jimi Hendrix autograph,** mounted with a colour photograph. Hendrix's guitar skills and his enduring popularity make items associated with him well worth keeping. *1960s, 40cm (16in) high.*

**£1,000–1,500**

## SELL

*Not all stars are able to attract younger fans once their heyday has passed. Sell to the loyal fans who follow the star through thick and thin, as such memorabilia is unlikely to rise in value.*

**Two 1950s magazines featuring Cliff Richard.** Items that are associated with the star's early life are likely to appeal to loyal Cliff Richard fans. *c.1950s, 25cm (10in) high.*

**£20–30**

## SELL

*Some bands that were huge in their day but are no longer popular attract a cult following, with die-hard fans competing to own memorabilia. As the number of these fans dwindles, pieces will become less valuable. Sell now before prices fall.*

**A Lynyrd Skynyrd *Tribute* LP** signed by Allen Collins, Leon Wilkeson, Artimus Pyle, Gary Rossington, and Billy Powell, together with a sheet of paper signed earlier by lead singer Ronnie van Zant. Lynyrd Skynyrd's career was cut short by a plane crash in 1977, which killed three members of the band. *1987, 31cm (12¼in) high.*

**£200–300**

## KEEP

*Memorabilia associated with bands that have consistently strong recognition and respect is worth keeping as they are likely to gain new listeners, adding to their already large fan-base.*

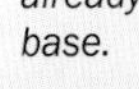

**A copy of The Clash's LP *Combat Rock*,** signed by the band members on the front cover. Values keep on rising for items associated with this influential British punk band, especially since the death of their songwriter Joe Strummer in 2002. *1982, 34cm (13½in) wide.*

**£150–250**

# Football memorabilia

appeals as much to team supporters who are passionate about the 'beautiful game' as to canny investors pursuing the sporting chance of a worthwhile investment.

**An England international cap,** decorated with an embroidered rose, and the date 1902 on the peak. It has a Young & Co. maker's label inside. *c.1902, 18cm (7in) wide.*

**£300–500**

It is not often in the world of collectables that a modern-day item exceeds the values reached by comparable historical finds, but it can happen with football memorabilia. This may be a result of the aura of fame, wealth, and glamour that surrounds today's top players and clubs.

Football fanaticism is nothing new: when the 'wizard of the dribble' Sir Stanley Matthews was due to play, attendances were estimated to go up by 10,000. The 1953 FA Cup Final has gone down in history as the 'Matthews Final', because of the way he inspired his team, Blackpool, to beat Bolton 4–3. The strip he wore that day sold for £10,321 in 2003.

## United approach

Manchester United is the most collectable of British clubs, partly because of its vivid history of triumph, tragedy, and outstanding, charismatic players, such as George Best and Eric Cantona, but mainly because of its recent domination of the English game and its huge global fan-base.

There was a national wave of sympathy for the club following the 1958 Munich air disaster, which killed eight players and seriously injured legendary manager Sir Matt Busby. The Arsenal v Manchester United match programme for 1 February 1958 is highly sought after – it was the last game played in England by the 'Busby Babes' before the tragedy. Much rarer is the following Saturday's programme, officially pulped as a result of the accident. It is likely to fetch at least £4,000 apiece in today's market.

## Some football programmes to look for:

- Manchester United
- FA Cup Finals
- Pre-War

**Manchester United v Fulham, 25 December 1951.** Manchester United programmes are always popular – particularly pre-1960s examples like this one, and those for big games, such as their 1968 European Cup Final victory over Benfica. *1951, 23cm (9in) high.*

**£40–60**

**Leicester City v Manchester United, FA Cup Final, 25 May 1963.** Traditionally, the FA Cup Final is the climax of the English football season: memorabilia prices reflect its special place in fans' hearts. *1963, 23cm (9in) high.*

**£20–30**

**Fulham v Exeter City, 7 May 1932.** Many programmes were lost during World War II, so any that survive, especially if commemorative, are highly collectable. *1932, 22cm (8½in) high.*

**£75–85**

## In contention

Other famous clubs likely to attract interest among collectors include the fierce Glasgow rivals, Celtic and Rangers, as well as leading English Premiership sides, such as Liverpool, Arsenal, Chelsea, and Newcastle United. But, any club will have fans keen to buy mementoes of its greatest achievements. For example, around the 1950s, Wolves were the most successful club of the day. As well as winning the League three times and the FA Cup twice, they laid the foundations for European club competition by playing a series of games known as 'floodlit friendlies' against top overseas sides, such as Honved of Budapest. Memorabilia associated with these matches can be valuable.

At the other end of the scale, programmes and other memorabilia involving clubs that have slipped out of the top four divisions, or even folded, will be worth a little more than if they had remained successful.

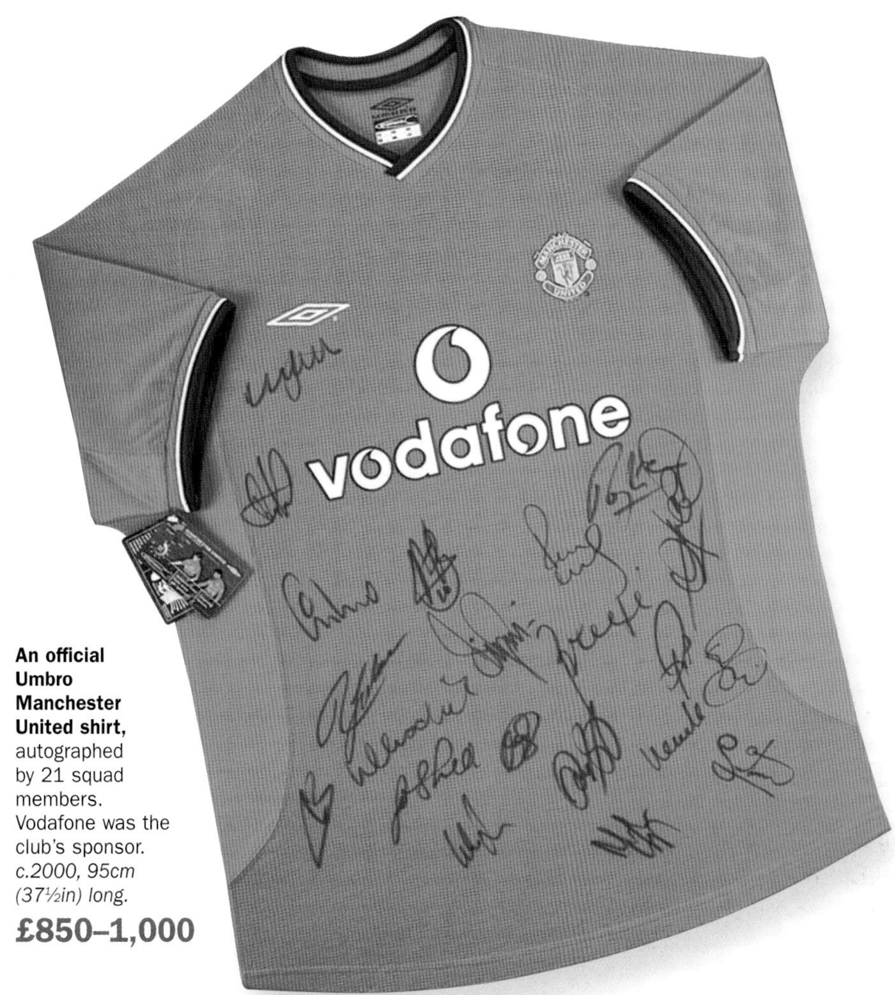


**An official Umbro Manchester United shirt,** autographed by 21 squad members. Vodafone was the club's sponsor. *c.2000, 95cm (37½in) long.*

**£850–1,000**

Matches ■ Internationals ■ Big Clubs ■ Early 'Floodlit Friendlies' ■

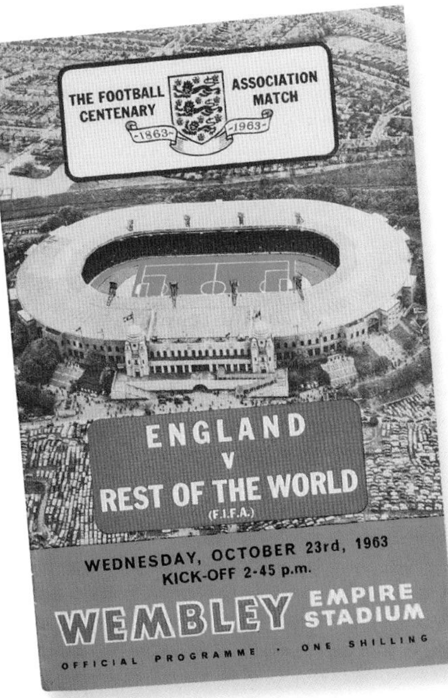


**England v Rest of the World, 23 October 1963.** Some collectors focus on international matches, such as this friendly to mark the centenary of the FA – the world's first football governing body. *1963, 23cm (9in) high.*

**£10–20**

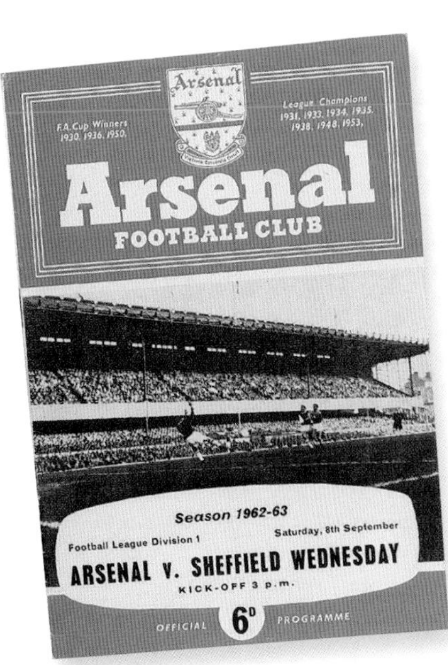


**Arsenal v Sheffield Wednesday, 8 September 1962.** Arsenal is a big club and so is more collectable than most. Even so, programmes from the 1960s onwards tend to be interesting rather than valuable. *1962, 18cm (7in) high.*

**£5–10**

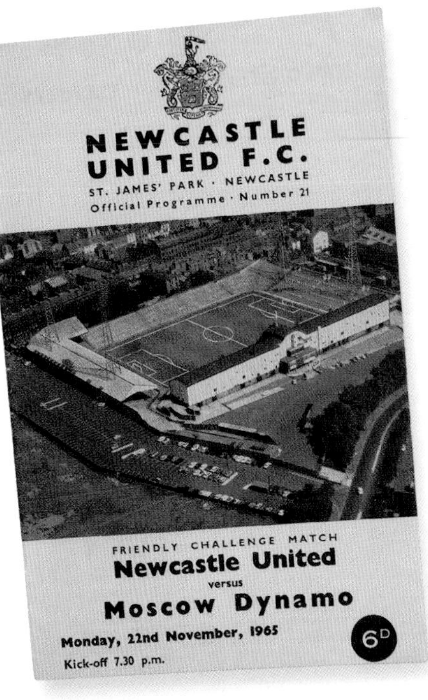


**Newcastle United v Moscow Dynamo, 22 November 1965.** Even after the introduction of the European Cup in 1955, English clubs continued to hold prestigious 'floodlit friendlies' against foreign sides. *1965, 23cm (9in) high.*

**£5–10**

## From rags to riches

The value of an item of football memorabilia is affected by the condition and age of the piece, the prominence of the featured team, and (for match-specific items) the importance of the match. Even with a limited budget, you can still build up a collection from the wide array of items on offer. Choose from tickets and programmes, medals, badges, collecting cards and stickers, mugs, scarves, shirts, autographed pieces, teamsheets (which are still produced for press and VIPs), magazines, club handbooks, and scrapbooks.

Match clothing, particularly if worn by a star player, is especially desirable – a pair of boots worn by David Beckham can reach an astonishing £14,000. Kit issued to players but not actually worn is next in popularity and value (an unworn Beckham England shirt has been known to sell for £2,280), with replica kit at the lowest end of the price scale.

Medals often fetch the highest prices – an FA Cup winner's medal will tempt only the dedicated collector, with prices ranging from £2,000 to the £20,000 paid in 2001 for Sir Stanley Matthews' 1953 medal. Note that medals will probably become increasingly scarce, as few of today's phenomenally well-paid stars will need to sell off their honours.

## Mementoes of the game

Programmes are keenly collected. Pick a theme: either a specific team or a competition, such as the FA Cup. Prices for Cup Final programmes range from a few pounds up to the £11,500 paid for one from the 1915 'Khaki' Cup Final between Chelsea and Sheffield United (so called because many of the crowd were soldiers on leave or about to set off for the World War I trenches).

Early programmes or teamsheets from the 1870s onwards have values matching their rarity. Indeed, any pre-

### *Did You Know?*

*Memorabilia from the 1966 World Cup – when England beat West Germany 4–2 in the final at Wembley – can prove to be hugely profitable. At Christie's, South Kensington, in 2000, a winner's medal presented to England goalkeeper Gordon Banks fetched £124,000 and Sir Geoff Hurst's match shirt raised £91,750. Hurst remains the only man to score a hat-trick in a World Cup Final.*

▲ **A 1921 Yorkshire Football Challenge Cup medal,** in nine-carat gold. *c.1921, box 7.5cm (3in) long.*

**£300–500**

▲ **A 1966 World Cup Final ticket stub,** for Wembley's South Terrace. There is a central fold in the ticket, otherwise it is in good condition. *1966, 10cm (4in) high.*

**£200–300**

**A collection of 19 Manchester United badges,** mostly of enamel, including 1967 League Champions and 1968 European Cup Winners badges. *c.1960s, frame 30cm (12in) wide.*

**£150–200**

**A first-edition book entitled *The Cup*,** documenting 50 years of the FA Cup. The competition began in 1871, but Blackburn Olympic's win in 1883 was the first by a professional club. *c.1932, 25cm (10in) high.*

**£50–80**

World War II examples should be valuable. Manchester United programmes tend to be the most popular – pre-1939 examples can fetch between £200 and £300.

It's worth remembering that mint-condition programmes or teamsheets are more valuable if they do not have the final score and the goal scorers written on them by an ecstatic or despondent spectator.

As well as age, historical significance adds value to pieces. For example, a programme from the 1912 Spurs v Woolwich Arsenal match held in aid of victims of the *Titanic* disaster sold for £4,600. But a programme for England's triumphant 1966 World Cup Final against West Germany can be found for a more modest £50: this is due to the fact that so many have been kept in good condition.

## Modern times

Historic games apart, programmes from the 1960s onwards are not worth much in themselves and are unlikely to appreciate for some time. This is partly because many more fans started to keep programmes from this time onwards and also because clubs now print extra copies to sell in bulk to dealers. Collecting modern programmes offers an inexpensive way to build your own archive and record the fortunes of your club. They cost from £2 a copy. Look out for specials, such as those produced for pre-season 'friendly' matches. Rounding off a complete season's worth is not only satisfying but it is also a way of increasing the overall value of your programmes.

## The write stuff

Autographs are always popular and will increase the worth of any sporting memorabilia, from balls to shirts, especially if they are signed by top players and can be authenticated. A collection of 1950s teamsheets, portraits, and pictures signed by players from Chelsea, Birmingham City, and Coventry City was sold in 2003 for £120.

Another good collecting focus is scrapbooks, especially those that evoke a particular era and contain a good selection of newspaper match reports and other football stories.

## Stadium for sale

In recent years, many clubs – Manchester City, for example – have moved to a new stadium. When they do so, they often auction off parts of their old ground, such as squares of turf and seats from the grandstand. If your team is planning to move and holds such an event, take the opportunity to get hold of a unique piece of memorabilia.

### Top Tips

- Keep any unused tickets for big games – they tend to be more valuable if they are complete rather than just stubs.
- When selling at auction, submit your items for viewing in plenty of time – serious collectors won't buy on impulse and will always do their homework.
- Scan the small ads at the back of football magazines. Many fans advertise their collections for sale in this way.
- Join a supporters' club – members often trade items privately.
- Never wash an autographed shirt. You cannot be certain that the player who signed the shirt used indelible ink. Even if he did, the ink might still fade.

### KEEP

*Clothing worn by a player is always highly desirable, especially if it has a certificate of authenticity to prove it. If the player is immensely popular, or predicted to have a long and influential future in the game, the value should certainly hold, if not rise.*

**A Thierry Henry Arsenal 'home' shirt,** worn in a Premier League game in 2001, with a letter of authenticity. *c.2001, 71cm (28in) long.*

**£1,000–1,500**

### SELL

*Memorabilia such as handbooks, especially recent ones, are unlikely to rise in value. But an example such as this is saleable, because it is a superb reference work.*

**A Champions League 2001/2 official statistics handbook,** held in a lever-arch file. The handbook provides in-depth data on all the teams that qualified for Europe's premier club competition in the 2001–2002 season. *2001, 30cm (12in) high.*

**£50–80**

# Golf has a long history, and its enduring popularity has produced a wide variety of equipment and related items to collect. Although antique pieces are rare and expensive, there is plenty to suit even the most modest budget.

**A German ceramic bottle** in the shape of a golfer. *1920s, 13cm (5in) high.*

**£120–180**

Many of us have inherited a passion for golf from our parents or grandparents. Some may even have been lucky enough to have been passed on something more tangible, such as a well-worn set of clubs or a cherished memento of an early Open.

## A time-honoured pursuit

By the late 19th century, golf had become tremendously popular. Enthusiasts eagerly pursue the wide range of equipment, such as clubs, balls, bags, and club-head covers, sold during the Victorian era.

Absolutely anything with a golfing theme – including books, artworks, ceramics, and silverware – is of interest. Antique equipment catalogues make a fascinating addition to any collection, for example, with some dating from the late 19th century available for £150–250; later examples usually cost less.

Established ceramic factories such as Royal Doulton, Spode, and Clifton started producing wares decorated with golfing images in the 1890s. Early pieces in perfect condition can sell for £100–1,000 or more, whereas golfing ceramics from the 1950s onwards can often be bought for around £10–50.

**A silver golf-themed smoker's companion,** with an attached lighter and covered ashtray in the shape of golfballs. *1923, 12.5cm (5in) high.*

**£700–1,000**

## Competitive edge

Not a week goes by without a professional golf tournament being played somewhere, and each one produces more memorabilia: tickets, trophies, programmes, and posters. Many of these items can be picked up relatively inexpensively – a British Open Championship programme from the early 1980s might set you back around £10–20.

Older pieces, or those linked with significant competitions and golfing landmarks, will attract higher price tags – a programme from the 1962 Open Championship might sell for £400–600, but one from the 1930s or earlier will generally be worth about £800–1,200 or more.

## Clubbing together

Clubs, of which there are 14 distinct varieties, form a central feature of many collections. Market prices are linked to age, rarity, quality, and condition. Iron-headed clubs that pre-date the introduction of the steel shaft in the 1920s are particularly prized, as are the early long-nosed woods that were in use until the mid-19th century. These can be worth from £2,000 up to £50,000. Later examples, such as 1930s steel-shafted clubs, can be found for less than £50, but they may rise in value as they become rarer.

Modern clubs can also be collectable. Rare early Ping putters from the 1960s can sell for more than £1,000, with some more recent examples from the 1980s already reaching around £100–200.

## From feathers to dimples

The first golf balls, called 'featheries', were hand made from stitched animal-skin casing stuffed with boiled feathers. Featheries with no identified maker can be picked up for around £800–1,200, but the mark of a recognised manufacturer such as Andrew Dickson or Henry Mills can often boost this to £10,000 or more.

Featheries were replaced in the mid-19th century by balls made of

### Collectors' Tales

*'One of my better buys was a table croquet set for £45. When I got it home I discovered that instead of four croquet balls, there were two croquet and two golf balls. The golf balls turned out to be two beautiful, hand-hammered "Forgan" pattern gutta-percha balls in mint condition and worth around £1,000 each.'*

**Manfred Schotten, Oxfordshire**

# A closer look at... a Spalding jigger

This jigger (old-fashioned golf terminology for a club that gives high loft) is a good example of an early steel club. The famous name and distinctive features make this a valuable piece.

The hexagonal shaft was bored through the centre and drilled with more than 1,000 holes in order to reduce its weight

Hand-punched dots like these (to impart spin to the ball) help to date a club – most later examples were punched mechanically

**A Spalding Gold Medal no. 4 jigger,** with a hammer stamp and patent marks. *c.1918, 100cm (39½in) long.*

**£1,500–2,500**

**Three Dutch Delft tiles** showing gentlemen golfers. *1880s, 12.5cm (5in) wide.*

**£200–300**

gutta-percha (a whitish, rubbery substance). A genuine 'gutty' can fetch more than £1,500, especially if it carries the stamp of a notable maker, such as Archie Simpson or Allan Robertson. Unbranded examples can be found for around £300–500.

At the end of the 19th century, rubber-core balls made by Haskell arrived on the scene and these were used until the more controllable dimple-patterned balls came into play some years later. Haskell balls are scarce: a standard example in good condition may fetch more than £80–120.

## Celebrity links

Golf has been a favourite celebrity pastime since the mid-20th century when Hollywood stars such as Bing Crosby and Bob Hope helped to popularise the sport. Any golfing items with a celebrity pedigree are attractive both to fans of the star and the sport. Equipment associated with professionals does have some worth, but unless it's linked to a truly international name, such as Jack Nicklaus or Tiger Woods, the effect on value will be minimal.

There is a strong market for golfing publications, particularly classic instruction manuals and books by renowned course architects and famous players. Books written by or about modern greats such as Seve Ballesteros, Tony Jacklin, or Nick Faldo can be picked up for £5–10 or less. But they could be worth around £20–100 if endorsed with a celebrity signature.

### Top Tips

- Keep an eye out for the major sales, which are often scheduled for the week leading up to the Open Championship in July.
- Inspect golf clubs with wooden heads and shafts for undue wear and tear, as well as woodworm; irons should be checked for extensive rusting.
- Never clean antique golf clubs yourself: collectors value the soiling and patina accumulated over a lifetime of use. Ask a specialist to do the job for you instead.
- Look for golfing publications that are in excellent condition – with a strong binding, a clean, unmarked cover, and all the pages present and intact.

### KEEP

*Although now frowned upon, gathering stray balls from the edges of golf courses was a lucrative pursuit at one time and elderly relatives or friends might have indulged in this activity. If these balls are still around, hold on to those in good condition as prices should rise.*

**A North Berwick square-mesh rubber-core ball.** Although produced after the scarcer 'featheries' and 'gutties', values for early 20th-century balls in good condition such as this one can still be relatively high. *1900–20, 4.5cm (1¾in) diam.*

**£100–150**

### KEEP

*Golfing memorabilia depicting women is at a premium. Modern young women took up the game in the 1920s. A golfing theme may add further period interest to an already attractive Art Deco figure.*

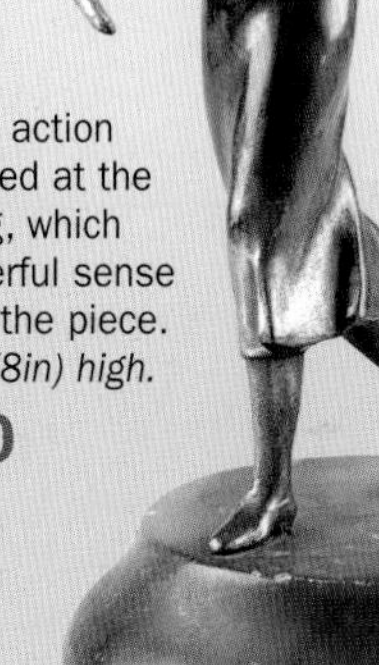

**A zinc Art Deco lady golfer on a plinth base.** The action has been captured at the end of the swing, which imparts a wonderful sense of movement to the piece. *1920s, 20.5cm (8in) high.*

**£200–300**

# Fishing gear is a recent addition to the collectables market, and it is a growing niche. At one end of the price range are reels by renowned makers, costing thousands; at the other extreme, obscure but intriguing items of equipment can be had for pounds.

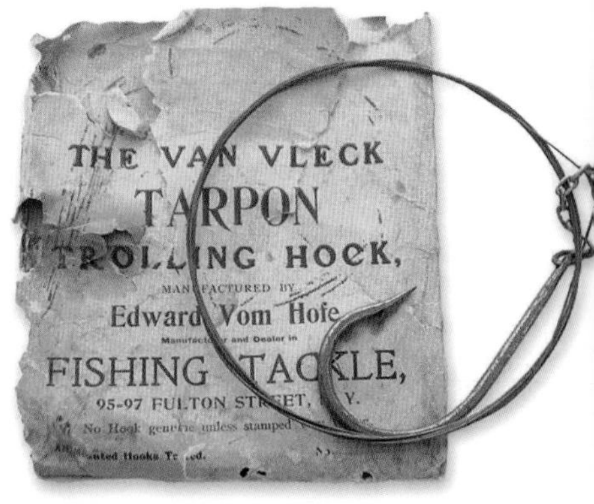


**The 'Van Vleck' Tarpon Trolling Hook from Edward Vom Hofe,** complete with original linked chain and wire trace and in the maker's paper packaging. *c.1920–40, packet 2.5cm (1in) high.*

**£100–150**

Rods and reels are beautiful objects, and they showcase the ingenuity and design skills displayed by previous generations. English rods from the 15th century were about 6m (20ft) long and fashioned from heavy, native British wood. Rods remained the same until the 19th century, when treated bamboo canes were cut and planed to form fly rods of exceptional quality. Split cane rods from this period sell for around £80–120 for an unmarked example, but a particularly fine piece, such as an H.L. Leonard trout rod, can command as much as £400–500.

### Reel differences

The first written record of reels, also called winches, is in Thomas Barker's *The Art of Angling,* published in 1651. Metal reels are more durable than wooden rods, which is why there is such a range available. Many of the finest designs and mechanisms were developed in the late 19th to mid-20th centuries, including 'multiplying', 'half-crank', 'cage', and 'freespool clutch' reels. Prices range from less than £100 to several thousand pounds, depending on rarity, quality, and condition. A rare Allcock 'Aerial Match' centre-pin reel listed for only one season (1939–40) can command £2,500–3,000 in top condition, but a more common Hardy 'Elarex' freshwater multiplying reel, from the same era, is only worth about £90–150. Reels marked with a maker's name are more desirable than those without. Both Allcock and Hardy Bros are names synonymous with quality fishing gear, and their equipment is sought after.

### Something fishy

Most anglers' tackle boxes are full of bits and bobs: line driers, floats, flies, and landing nets, even priests – for killing fish with a blow to the head – and curates – tools with cutters and tweezers used for tying flies for fly fishing. Craftsmen first started producing fishing tackle in the mid-17th century. Charles Kirby, who had a shop in London around 1650, was famous for his reliable hook, and his brand is still the world's favourite.

There are few reliable indications as to what might be the next area of

## Some fishing reels to look for:

▪ 'Spitfire' Finish ▪ Variants ▪ 'Aerial' Design

**A Hardy 'Perfect' alloy trout fly reel,** with ebonite handle, smooth alloy foot, and 'Spitfire' finish, in good condition. Hardy's celebrated 'Spitfire' finish has a metal surface which is hand-papered and then lacquered for an exceptional shine. *c.1960, 10cm (4in) diam.*

**£700–900**

**A variant Hardy 'St George' alloy trout fly reel,** with an ebonite handle and ribbed brass foot, stamped on the interior 'D.W.' (Denys Ward). Fly reel enthusiasts are attracted by any unusual or scarce variations of more common reels. *1920s, 8.5cm (3¼in) diam.*

**£600–800**

**An Allcock 'Aerial' alloy centre-pin reel,** with a spoke tension regulator and brass foot; the back plate is stamped with a circular logo and patent information. Allcock's 'Aerial' design first appeared in 1896, apparently inspired by the spoked bicycle wheel that had been introduced at that time. *c.1930, 10cm (4in) diam.*

**£1,000–1,500**

### Collectors' Tales

*'I love trout fishing so much my nickname is "Fisheroy". Some friends gave me an old-fashioned trout basket called a "creel" for helping out with a house clearance. It's made of wicker with a leather shoulder strap and has a hole in the top to put trout through. I'd never sell it because it was a gift, but I was flicking through an antiques price guide and was thrilled to discover it's worth about £100.'*

**Fitzroy Cooper, London**

**An Allcock Aquatic Spider,** mounted on an original card with instructions on the reverse and complete with the original tin box. *c.1920–40, box 7.5cm (3in) long.*

**£80–120**

interest. Victorian baits and spinners were unregarded just 10 years ago, but now all sorts of examples can be found. A standard bait fetches about £100, but more intricate examples, popular brands, and those in excellent condition can fetch £300–400 or more.

## The written word

Manufacturers' catalogues are an important source of information and can be collectable. Early 20th-century examples are worth around £70–150. Instructional books and memoirs can also be worth finding. A 1971 first edition of *Pike* by Fred Buller, with its original dust jacket, can cost £220–280. Older books usually fetch more, especially if signed by the author. A signed 1906 first edition of *My Fishing Days and Fishing Ways* by J.W. Martin can cost around £400–500.

## The one that didn't get away

Preserved and mounted fish can fetch a lot of money, depending on the quality of the taxidermy and the type and size of the fish. A 9.5kg (21lb) perch mounted by F.W. Anstiss can cost about £2,200–2,800, while a 60cm (24in) jack pike by J. Cooper & Sons might be worth twice that figure.

### Top Tips

- Browse through old tackle catalogues to learn about antique fishing gear.
- Avoid items that show signs of heavy restoration, such as re-varnishing, soldering, or painting.
- Beware of 'marriages' – where a missing piece has been replaced with a piece from another model. These are sometimes passed off as originals.
- Familiarise yourself with the workings of fishing reels and the names of all the component parts. This will help you understand what you are buying.
- Do not use abrasive creams or scouring pads when cleaning fishing gear, as rods can be fragile. You may remove an attractive patina.

### KEEP

*Old catalogues, particularly those of popular and respected manufacturers and retailers, are valuable collector's tools, as well as fascinating historical documents. Look for an example with an interesting cover, as it should hold its value, if not appreciate.*

**An Allcock trade catalogue,** 34. This is the large octavo edition, and it has attractive, stylised imagery on the cover showing a fish about to take some bait. *1937, 23cm (9in) high.*

**£100–200**

## ▪ 'Cone' Design ▪ Original Finishes ▪

**A Kenton's 'Cone' centre-pin reel,** with a mahogany drum on a brass spindle and a cone-shaped milled wheel tensioner; the brass foot is stamped 'Cone Patent No. 24776'. Kenton's 1903 patent refers to the use of cones to eliminate 'drum shake'. This is one of the few known examples. *c.1903, 11.5cm (4½in) diam.*

**£400–600**

**A Hardy 'Longstone' sea centre-pin reel,** with ebonised wooden drum, knurled nickel silver drum screw, ebonite handle attached to elliptical brass receivers, and alloy backplate and foot. This reel retains nearly all of its original finish, making it particularly sought after. *c.1921, 10cm (4in) diam.*

**£300–500**

### SELL

*Paraphernalia without a maker's mark is not usually as attractive to fishing enthusiasts as branded gear. It is unlikely that the value of such items will rise significantly.*

**An angler's tackle box, made of zinc.** The compact nature and range of accessories should appeal to a new enthusiast, making an excellent start to a collection. *c.1900, 15cm (6in) wide.*

**£60–80**

# General sporting memorabilia

is often kept by sports fans for purely nostalgic reasons, but bats, balls, gloves, hats, programmes, and other sporting souvenirs can be valuable too if rare or associated with an important game or player. It is never too late to start collecting tomorrow's treasures.

**A sealed tin of three Wilson tennis balls.** *c.1950, 20.5cm (8in) high.*

**£70–100**

From tickets for a world championship boxing match, which can be worth £10–60, to horse-racing annuals from the 1950s that can fetch about £5, there are collectable ephemera for those of every sporting persuasion.

## The wisdom of Wisdens

Cricket memorabilia has generally risen in value since the mid-1990s, with John Wisden's *Cricketers' Almanack*, published since 1864, attracting some of the highest prices. Rare early editions can be worth up to £1,000. Post-1950 Wisdens can be picked up for £20–30, but original copies covering a noted Test series or club centenary are worth more.

Bats haven't changed much since cricket evolved into its modern form in the mid-1800s, so they need other features, such as autographs, to add value. The most valuable bats are those used by top players in renowned matches. Bats signed by teams are more common – a 1994 bat signed by the England team can be worth £60. Prices for miniature commemorative bats with team signatures are usually just below those for full-sized versions.

Scorecards range from a few pounds for county games about 60 years ago to higher values for 19th-century cards. A rare scorecard for the Surrey and Essex versus England match at the Oval, in 1867, can be worth £250. Completed cards and those signed by the teams command the highest sums. Programmes can cost less than £10, but games featuring legendary teams or incidents are worth more: a brochure from the infamous 1932–33 'Bodyline' Test series in Australia can fetch up to around £1,500.

## The oval ball

Some people specialise in particular rugby union teams or themes such as the Oxford versus Cambridge Varsity matches. A rare 1896 Varsity match programme can be worth up to £100. Signed menus from official pre- and post-match dinners can top £100–150, and early 19th-century rugby-themed ceramics can fetch £200–400.

A modern rugby shirt worn by a key player can be worth up to £200, and

## Some sporting memorabilia to look for:

▪ Almanacks ▪ Signed Ephemera ▪ Ceramics

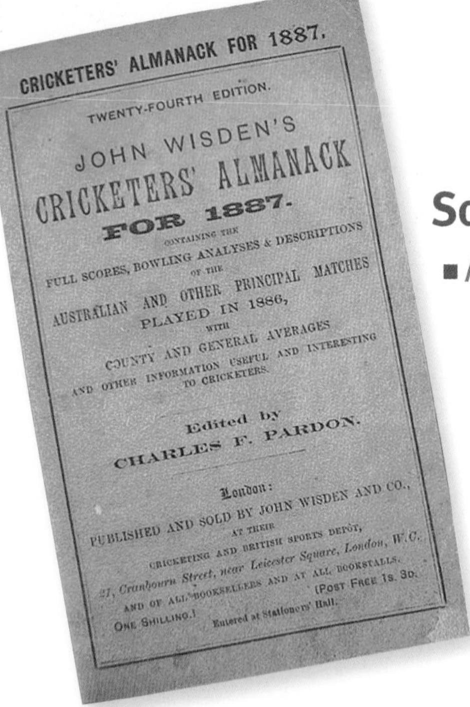

CRICKETERS' ALMANACK FOR 1887.

TWENTY-FOURTH EDITION.

JOHN WISDEN'S
CRICKETERS' ALMANACK
FOR 1887.

CONTAINING THE
FULL SCORES, BOWLING ANALYSES & DESCRIPTIONS
OF THE
AUSTRALIAN AND OTHER PRINCIPAL MATCHES
PLAYED IN 1886,
WITH
COUNTY AND GENERAL AVERAGES
AND OTHER INFORMATION USEFUL AND INTERESTING
TO CRICKETERS.

Edited by
CHARLES F. PARDON.

London:
PUBLISHED AND SOLD BY JOHN WISDEN AND CO.,
AT THEIR
CRICKETING AND BRITISH SPORTS DEPÔT,
21, Cranbourn Street, near Leicester Square, London, W.C.
AND OF ALL BOOKSELLERS AND AT ALL BOOKSTALLS.

ONE SHILLING.] (POST FREE 1s. 3D.
Entered at Stationers' Hall.

***John Wisden's Cricketers' Almanack for 1887.*** Sporting annuals are sought after, and none more so than the cricketing 'bible'. This 24th edition with original wrappers is in fairly good condition. *1887, 23cm (9in) high.*

**£350–450**

**Original W.G. Grace postcard,** signed and dated. There is a huge market for ephemera signed by leading sports figures. The legendary cricketer W.G. Grace's signature adds value to this tatty postcard. *1903, 13.5cm (5½in) high.*

**£40–80**

**A Copeland Spode jug,** with a golfer on one side and a cricketer on the other. Ceramic pieces add variety to a sporting collection. Two sports appear on this jug to make it appealing to a larger market. *1901–10, 17.8cm (7in) high.*

**£80–120**

**Three Cambridge University sporting cloth caps.** *1920s, 25cm (10in) wide.*

**£50–80**

an international shirt many times more. Kit worn by England's winning team in the 2003 World Cup is sure to fetch high prices. Other prized memorabilia includes match-balls, programmes, and limited-edition colour prints.

## Tennis, anyone?

Tennis racquets from the 1870s can fetch up to £1,000 or more. Early aluminium racquets from the 1920s can be worth £100–200, those from the 1930s about one-third less. These are rare as most pre-1980 racquets were wooden. Fibreglass racquets were introduced in the 1970s: early Wilson examples can cost around £30–70.

Unopened tins of tennis balls from the 1930s can cost about £50, and a 1960s tin of Dunlop balls can sell for about £30. Programmes from major tournaments usually cost only a few pounds, but a signature adds value.

## Formula One

A Grand Prix programme from the last 30 years or so often fetches £20–50, but the one for the 1994 Imola race at which Ayrton Senna was killed can be worth £200. Press kits from the 1980s can fetch about £20; helmets worn by star drivers may cost £2,000 or more.

## In the ring

Signed boxing gloves and shorts are sought after. Signed photos of world champions from the 1950s to the present day can cost £50–200 or more.

## Top Tips

- Make sure the Wisden *Almanack* you are buying is not a reprint, which will be worth only about 15 per cent of the value of an original.
- Consider collecting items for future Olympic events, World Cups, and world championships, as values could rise.
- Establish the authenticity of equipment used by players – buy from reputable dealers and ask for proof of provenance.
- Bear in mind that just because a sportsperson signed an item, he or she didn't necessarily own or use it.

## BUY

*Look for photographs signed by sports heroes, especially those capturing a great sporting moment. A signature adds authenticity and value.*

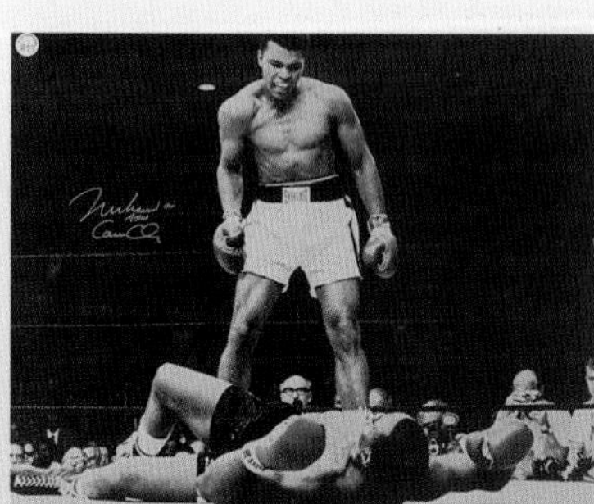

**A Muhammad Ali/Cassius Clay signed press photograph.** This photo shows a triumphant Muhammad Ali, who changed his name from Cassius Clay in 1964, standing over the prone Sonny Liston during their World Championship bout in May 1965. It is a terrific keepsake of one of the great nights in boxing history. *1965, 55cm (21½in) high.*

**£200–300**

## ▪ Replicas ▪

**A full-size replica Michael Schumacher Grand Prix racing helmet.** This helmet, complete with Ferrari, Marlboro, and Asprey logos, is more valuable because, unusually, Schumacher signed the visor, rather than the helmet itself. A real helmet would not have the lipped base found on this replica. *c.2000, 43.5cm (17in) high.*

**£1,800–2,200**

## SELL

*Cycling has always been a niche sport – despite the efforts of Olympic gold medalist Chris Boardman in recent years. Now may be a good time to pass on cycling memorabilia as prices are unlikely to rise.*

**A rare autographed sepia photograph of national cycling champion H.W. Payne.** Although this is a superb image, Payne is no longer widely known. *1899, 25.5cm (10in) high.*

**£60–100**

The beauty of Madeira and . . .
du MAURIER
du MAURIER
THE MOST WIDELY SMOKED FILTER
CIGARETTE IN THE WORLD

CUT TRAVEL
LING TIME
Victoria line
a free leaflet includes an Underground map with details
of Victoria Line times, fares and how to use the automatic
gates. Ask at any of the London Transport Travel Offices
or write to the Public Relations Officer 55 Broadway SW1
Phone Travel Enquiries: 01-222 1234, any time, day or night

Drink
Coca-Cola
Delicious and Refreshing

# The Written Word and Ephemera

From precious first edition books to calling cards, both the written word and ephemera are rich and diverse fields for collectors. Ephemera is an umbrella term for printed or handwritten objects, usually on paper or card, made for a specific, often short-term, purpose before being discarded.

1 First edition Agatha Christie book, p.298

2 J.K. Rowling Harry Potter book, p.301

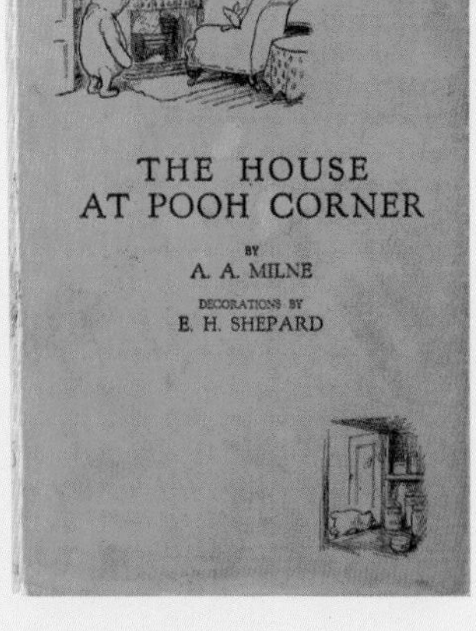


3 First edition A.A. Milne book, p.301

# Words and pictures......

**From first editions of much loved books or favourite childhood comics to saucy seaside postcards and old Valentine cards, there are publications both vintage and modern to suit all tastes. Charming to read and look at, they bring back fond memories of leisure time in the past.**

A first edition – the very first printing of a book – is the most valuable version. Titles by authors such as Agatha Christie (1), Ian Fleming, Beatrix Potter, J.K. Rowling (2), and A.A. Milne (3) are highly sought after.

Cookery books, especially those by Mrs Beeton, and old travel guides such as Baedekers offer a fascinating insight into the days before convenience foods and charter flights. Children's annuals, especially perennial favourites such as the *Rupert* annuals, have become valuable because they are only available for a limited period of time each year and have a loyal following.

## Childhood memories

Old comics such as *The Dandy* (4) and *The Beano* are much appreciated by nostalgic adults keen to revisit the characters and jokes they enjoyed as children. Like comics, old magazines (5) have their fans and the fact they are usually thrown away once read makes some surviving copies valuable.

6 Victorian Valentine card, p.311

7 Postcard of a post office, p.313

8 Seaside postcard, p.312

Children's annuals have become valuable because they are only available for a limited period of time each year.

4

1945 copy of The Dandy, p. 304

5

1963 Life magazine cover, p.307

# .to treasure

The introduction of the unifom Penny Post in 1839 made posting letters affordable. Soon manufacturers started creating commercial greetings cards, the most decorative of which were Christmas and Valentine cards ⑥. The intricate designs inspired many recipients to keep their most beautiful cards, and these often come up for sale today.

## Dropping a line

Sending postcards became a popular way for people to keep in touch when they went away on holiday. Cards featuring local views ⑦ or saucy seaside cartoons ⑧ are sought after.

Advertisers keen to persuade us to drink everything from Guinness ⑨ to Coca-Cola ⑩ have used increasingly sophisticated and striking illustrations and slogans to attract the public's attention through the years. Promotional posters, glasses, badges, and trays are all worth keeping hold of.

Posters ⑪, particularly those for railway lines and the London Underground, offer a nostalgic trip back in time. Look for those by well-known artists or redolent of a particular era.

The condition for all books, cards, magazines, and ephemera is very important to collectors, as items made of paper and card can be easily damaged.

9

Guinness advertising figure, p.318

10

Lithographed tin sign, p.320

11

French railway poster, p.326

# Modern first editions

are probably the most accessible area of book-collecting for the newcomer. English-language books published since the 1890s are particularly sought after if they are in good condition and are by notable authors.

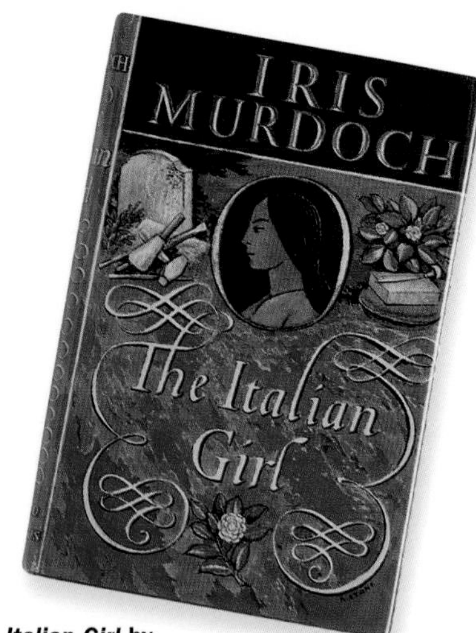

***The Italian Girl* by Iris Murdoch,** published by Chatto & Windus, London. *1964, 20cm (8in) high.*

**£100–150**

When collecting new first editions, the trick is to spot up-and-coming writers who are likely to capture the public's imagination. Buying a first edition on publication and keeping it pristine may prove to be a good investment. And for collectors of older books, there are many bookshops and websites that specialise in first editions.

## Dust proof

Collectors generally define a first edition as the very first print run, or impression, of a book. Condition is vital, and the book must retain its original dust jacket. In the 19th century these were plain, but later they became more colourful and eye-catching to increase sales. The jacket on a second, or later, impression may differ from the first edition, perhaps with quotes added from book reviews. Print runs for post-war books were larger than for pre-war runs, so there is less of the scarcity factor that leads to high prices. Look also for 'extras' such as the author's signature.

## A new generation

Some of the finest post-war writers, including the Britons Lawrence Durrell, Anthony Burgess, Kingsley Amis, and William Golding, and the Americans Jack Kerouac, William Burroughs, and Allen Ginsberg, began their careers in the 1940s and 50s, and are sought after. A first edition of John Osborne's 1957 play

## Some authors to look for:

▪ Agatha Christie ▪ Colin Dexter ▪

***Towards Zero* by Agatha Christie** (Collins Crime Club, London). Christie was hugely prolific. Her detective novels have sold more than 100 million copies worldwide. *1944, 19cm (7½in) high.*

**£300–500**

***Service of All the Dead* by Colin Dexter** (Macmillan, London). Dexter wrote the Inspector Morse books which were adapted for the popular TV series. *1979, 20.5cm (8in) high.*

**£200–300**

***From Russia, with Love* by Ian Fleming** (Jonathan Cape, London). First editions by the creator of James Bond are desirable, even when slightly damaged, like this copy. *1957, 19cm (7½in) high.*

**£2,000–3,000**

### Did You Know?

*Collectors are as fascinated by the personality of Ian Fleming as by his books. His gold-plated typewriter sold at Christie's in London for £55,750 in 1995. The buyer was the current James Bond, Pierce Brosnan.*

*Look Back in Anger* can cost around £40–60. Kingsley Amis's first novel *Lucky Jim* (1954) and two earlier volumes of poetry can each sell for £1,000–3,000, but much of his other work costs around £30–50. A first edition of Anthony Burgess's *A Clockwork Orange* (1962) can command £1,000–1,500.

## Contemporary interest

Look out for early works by today's popular writers such as Martin Amis, Vikram Seth, Sebastian Faulks, Salman Rushdie, Nick Hornby, and Irvine Welsh. Contemporary women authors are also popular – the film of the life of Iris Murdoch has introduced her to a new generation. Other top female writers include Margaret Atwood, A.S. Byatt, Zadie Smith, Donna Tartt, Helen Fielding, Pat Barker, and Fay Weldon.

Books often rise in value when made into films. A US first edition of Patricia Highsmith's *The Talented Mr Ripley* (1955) can reach up to £1,000 following the 1999 film adaptation.

## Shock, horror

Science fiction, horror, spy stories, and detective fiction are popular themes. Ray Bradbury, Terry Pratchett, Brian Aldiss, Stephen King, and Arthur C. Clarke are top names in the science fiction and horror genres. With the exception of *The Colour of Magic* (1983), most of Terry Pratchett's titles from the mid-1980s onwards are easy to find. Spy novels by John Le Carré, Frederick Forsyth, and Len Deighton are favourites, but Ian Fleming heads the field. A pristine copy of *Casino Royale* (1953), the first James Bond novel, can fetch £7,000. Later books usually go for less: *Goldfinger* (1959) can cost £100.

Agatha Christie, Ruth Rendell, and P.D. James are queens of crime writing. Prices for Agatha Christie can vary from £30–50 up to £2,000 or more. Her early novels from the 1920s and 30s are the most valuable.

### Top Tips

- Seek out first editions signed by the author – these are often highly prized.
- Be aware that inscriptions or notes can reduce value, unless the person who wrote them is well known.
- Look for the earliest works of major writers that were printed in small runs before the author became famous.
- Ensure that any post-1950 book has its dust jacket; it is possible to be more lenient before this date.
- Search for earlier works by Booker Prize winners – the prize increases interest in the works and adds value.
- Check out winners of, or titles shortlisted for, other fiction awards, such as the Whitbread Novel Award.

### KEEP

*Celebrated poet Ted Hughes was greatly influenced by the natural world. As well as his writing, his relationship with American poet Sylvia Plath ensures that he continues to fascinate people. His death in 1998 and a film about him have led to renewed interest.*

***Birthday Letters* by Ted Hughes,** first edition (Faber & Faber, London). This is Hughes' last book of poetry and was well received on its release. *1998, 22.5cm (8¾in) high.*

**£1,500–2,000**

### KEEP

*Memoirs are an increasingly popular literary genre, and books that describe successful attempts to overcome real-life setbacks appeal to a wide range of readers and should rise in value.*

***Angela's Ashes* by Frank McCourt** (Scribner, New York). The story recalls the author's impoverished childhood in Ireland. The UK first edition, published by HarperCollins, is currently less valuable than the US, fetching around £30–50, but prices are likely to rise. *1996, 22.5cm (8¾in) high.*

**£200–250**

## Ian Fleming ■ Graham Greene ■ Stephen King ■

***Travels with my Aunt* by Graham Greene** (Bodley Head, London). Greene is highly admired, and wrote several novels inspired by his travels and experiences working for MI6. *1969, 20cm (8in) high.*

**£50–80**

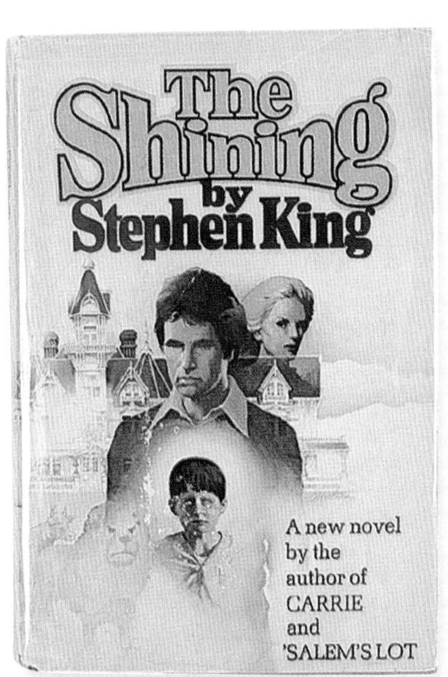


***The Shining* by Stephen King** (Doubleday & Company, Garden City, New York). This American author has written a wide variety of horror stories, many of them adapted for film. *1977, 19cm (7½in) high.*

**£650–750**

# Children's books, treasured for generations, are now highly sought after, both by collectors of first editions and by those for whom the rich heritage of children's literature is filled with nostalgia.

From beloved classics with rabbits or bears as main characters to tales of adventure and fantasy, there's plenty of scope for collecting children's books. Some, both traditional and modern, can reach high prices, but there are books to suit all budgets.

## Enduring classics

Created by Beatrix Potter, the much-loved Peter Rabbit, followed by a host of other animal characters, hopped into children's lives in 1901, when Potter made a private printing of *The Tale of Peter Rabbit*. This edition comprised just 250 copies and one of these can be worth £40,000. The average price of most pre-1920s editions is around £300–500. Other children's classics, especially rare or early books by Lewis Carroll, Kenneth Grahame, J.R.R. Tolkien, A.A. Milne, and Rudyard Kipling, are also sought after. A first edition of Tolkien's *Lord of the Rings* can cost £10,000 or more. Kenneth Grahame's *Wind in the Willows* and the fantasy tales of C.S. Lewis are desirable, too.

## Tales of adventure

Adventure stories for girls and boys are perennially popular and books by Angela Brazil, Elsie Oxenham, and Elinor Brent-Dyer sell for good prices. The most successful British children's author of the 20th century, however, is Enid Blyton – best known for her Famous Five books (1942 onwards), and her Noddy series (1949 onwards). Prices for Famous Five titles range from around £35 to £500, while *Noddy Goes to Toyland* (1949) often tops £70–100, with other early Noddy books raising around £20–40.

The adventures of Biggles by Captain W.E. Johns remain popular. The earlier books (1932–43) are hard to find; print runs were increased for later titles, so they are easier to locate and less expensive, at around £50 or less. The most sought-after Biggles

***The Tale of Squirrel Nutkin* by Beatrix Potter,** first edition (F. Warne & Co, London). *1903, 14.5cm (5¾in).*

**£300–400**

## Some children's series to look out for:

▪ Babar the Elephant ▪ Famous Five ▪ Biggles ▪

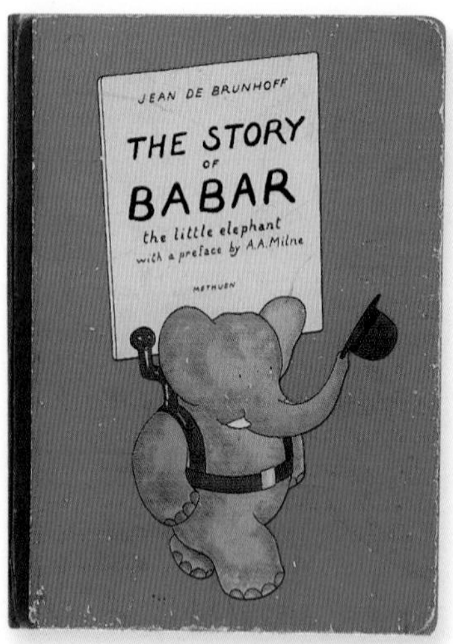


***The Story of Babar, the Little Elephant* by Jean de Brunhoff,** first UK edition (Methuen, London). Babar, created by de Brunhoff and his wife Cécile for their young boys, first appeared in French. *1934, 28cm (11in) high.*

**£100–150**

***Five Go to Demon's Rocks* by Enid Blyton,** first edition (Hodder & Stoughton, London). The Famous Five titles are probably the best known of Blyton's more than 700 books. *1961, 19cm (7½in) high.*

**£90–120**

titles are those published by John Hamilton in the 1930s.

**Harry Potter and the Chamber of Secrets by J.K. Rowling,** first edition (Bloomsbury, London); slightly damaged. This is the second book in the series. *1998, 24cm (9½in).*

**£2,000–3,000**

## Bear necessities

A.A. Milne's Pooh stories appeared in 1926, illustrated by E.H. Shepard, and were an instant hit. A 1973 colour edition of *Winnie the Pooh*, published by Methuen, can command £70–100.

Rupert the Bear began life in 1920 as a comic-strip in the *Daily Express*. The first Rupert the Bear annual, from 1936, can be worth up to £3,000 for an original. Facsimiles of the early annuals are now produced regularly and the earliest (1985), a reprint of the 1936 volume, now costs about £150.

## Modern originals

Books by Roald Dahl are sought after, particularly *James and the Giant Peach* (1961), worth around £150–250, and *Charlie and the Chocolate Factory* (1964), which can cost £200–300. Those illustrated by Quentin Blake, from 1991 onwards, sell for around £30–50 or less.

Raymond Briggs created some innovative picture books, particularly the Snowman titles published from 1978 and *Fungus the Bogeyman*, published in 1977. The 1978 first edition of *The Snowman* can sell for £30–50.

## World of wizards

First editions of J.K. Rowling's early Harry Potter books, particularly the first two volumes, can command high prices. Bloomsbury issued an initial print run of only 500 copies of the first book, *Harry Potter and the Philosopher's Stone* (1997). In 2003 one of these was sold for £19,500.

In some cases, prices have not increased dramatically since 2000, perhaps because collectors are waiting to see if Harry has staying power. Prices for a 1999 special limited edition of 4,000 copies of *Harry Potter and the Chamber of Secrets* range from around £75 to £100.

### Top Tips

- Buy books by the best-known authors as these are likely to be a better investment.
- Choose works featuring popular characters (such as Peter Rabbit), as these will be more desirable than those about lesser characters.
- Seek out limited editions, often with lavishly bound slipcases – these will be worth less than first editions, but more than standard print runs.
- Focus on hardbacks rather than paperbacks, as they tend to be rarer, more durable, and more collectable.
- Look out for pre-war signed copies – a plain inscription raises the value by 25 per cent, and up to 50 per cent for the more sought-after authors.

### BUY

*Published from 1903 to the mid-30s, Dean's fabric books – (or 'rag books') are hard to find in good condition. Those that are should appreciate, especially those from the 1920s.*

**A to Z in the Puff Puff by R. James Williams,** book no. 211 (Dean's Rag Book Co., London). This book will also appeal to railway collectors, which may increase demand. *1921, 18cm (7in) high.*

**£80–100**

## Thomas the Tank Engine ▪ Winnie the Pooh ▪

**Biggles and the Plane That Disappeared by Captain W.E. Johns,** first edition (Hodder & Stoughton, London). The World War I flying ace, Biggles, is a classic hero. *1963, 19cm (7½in) high.*

**£150–250**

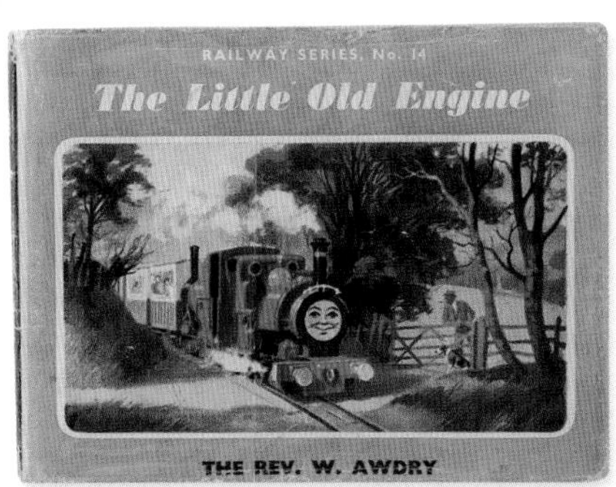


**The Little Old Engine by Rev. W. Awdry,** no. 14 in the 'Railway Series', first edition (Edmund Ward, London). The Thomas the Tank Engine stories have been turned into a popular TV series. *1959, 14.5cm (5¾in).*

**£70–100**

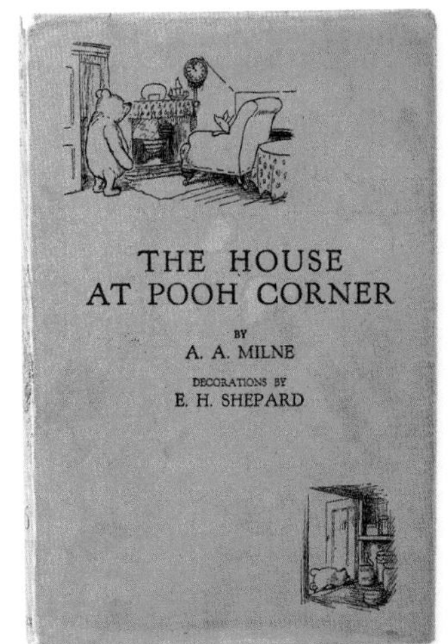


**The House at Pooh Corner by A.A. Milne,** first edition, illustrated by E.H. Shepard (Methuen, London). Winnie the Pooh has appeared in more than 25 languages and has been made into a series of Disney films. *1928, 19cm (7½in) high.*

**£800–1,000**

### SELL

*Roald Dahl, creator of characters such as Willy Wonka, has thrilled generations of adults and children with his imaginative tales. Many experts consider him to be one of the few modern children's authors who will stand the test of time.*

**James and the Giant Peach by Roald Dahl,** a first edition (Allen & Unwin, London). This was Roald Dahl's first book for children, based on bedtime stories invented for his own children. *1967, 24cm (9½in) high.*

**£500–600**

# Cookery and other books,

such as those on travel and sports, from the late 19th century onwards, are perennially popular. They also give rare insights into previous eras. But beware: just because a book is old and a first edition does not mean that it is valuable.



**Practical Cooking and Dinner Giving, by Mrs Mary Henderson,** first reprint (Harper & Bros, New York). *1878, 19cm (7½in) high.*

**£50–60**

Increased TV coverage of cookery and lifestyle topics has stimulated interest in books on these subjects, with prices being affected by factors such as rarity, desirability, and fashion.

## Recipe for success

Despite their popularity, first-edition cookery books from the late 19th and early 20th centuries can often be found for less than £15–25.

Mrs Beeton is the best-known Victorian author of domestic science books, and a top-condition, first edition of her *Book of Household Management* (1861) can cost more than £1,000. The book was rewritten and reissued several times, though, and these later editions can be found for about £20–40. Modern reprints will usually cost less than £10.

Others to look out for include the 19th-century writer Mary Henderson, whose books fetch around £20–150, and 20th-century authors X.M. Boulestin, whose works can sell for £10–50, and Ambrose Heath (about £5–15).

## Modern cooks

From the 1960s, the number of cookery books rocketed. Authors of interest include Elizabeth David, Theodora Fitzgibbon, Primrose Boyde, and Patience Grey. Values usually range between £5 and £30. The books of early TV chef Fanny Craddock tend to fetch around £10–20.

## The armchair traveller

Travel guides can fetch high prices. Baedeker produced a range of travel books between 1860 and the outbreak of World War II, at a time of increased interest in travel. The series is known for historical information, attention to detail, and its early star-rating system. The first and only English edition on Russia (1914) can be worth up to £600 or more. The classic 1929 guide to Egypt, which includes information on the discovery of Tutankhamun's tomb in 1922, is worth around £100–300. Later printings of other Baedekers,

***The Mary Frances Cook Book, or Adventures Among the Kitchen People,* by Jane Eayre Fryer,** (Harrap & Co.), with illustrations by Margaret G. Hayes and Jane Allen Boyer. *c.1912, 23.5cm (9¼in) high.*

**£100–200**

## A closer look at... two travel books

Although travel books are popular with collectors, historians, and the casual browser, examples are not equally collectable. Look at key features of the book to ensure that you make the wisest choice if buying for investment. These two travel books highlight some of the reasons why prices can vary.

The corners are bent and scuffed

The single-colour cover is dull and faded, and its design is unappealing

**Guide to *Lucerne, the Lake and Environs*, by J.C. Heer** (H. Keller's Foreign Printing Office). The book covers a smaller, less visited location, so has limited appeal. *1906, 18cm (7in) high.*

**£10–20**

The Art Nouveau cover is beautifully designed and brightly coloured

***Italy* by Frank Fox, with illustrations by Alberto Pisa** (A. & C. Black, London). The subject of Italy will appeal to a wide range of people. The illustrations make this book more attractive and of historical interest. *1918, 23cm (9in) high.*

**£70–100**

The cover is in good condition, with no signs of wear or damage

such as an 11th edition on northern Italy (1899), can sell for £10–30 or more, although some can cost up to £300 if in good condition.

Thomas Cook also produced travel guides, and a pre-1930s first edition, such as *Cook's Traveller's Handbook: Venice* (1923), can be worth £10–300, depending on condition and rarity. Titles in good condition with illustrations or photographs of well-known sights are the most desirable.

### Leisure pursuits

Sports books – especially on golf, cricket, football, and tennis, or ones commemorating a particular event – are popular. William Tilden's tennis classic *Aces, Places, and Faults* (1938) can fetch £150–180, while Teddie Tinling's *Sixty Years in Tennis* (1983) is worth about £30–60. Sports annuals are also worth keeping.

Fishing books are almost as popular as the sport itself. First editions of Frederic M. Halford's *Dry Fly Fishing in Theory and Practice* and *The Dry Fly Man's Handbook* can fetch £200–400.

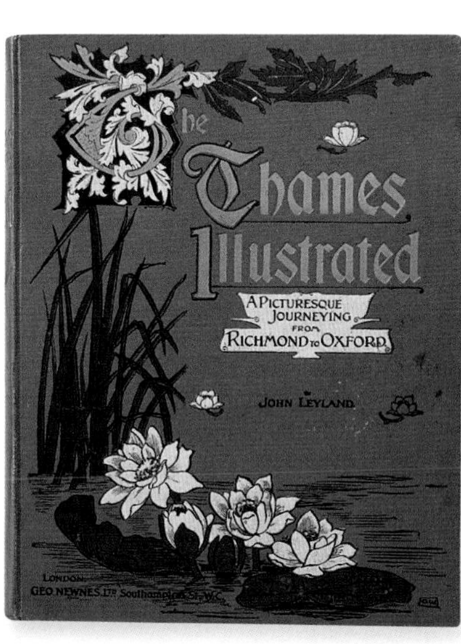


***The Thames Illustrated, A Picturesque Journeying from Richmond to Oxford*, by John Leyland** (Newnes, London). *1901, 20.5cm (8in) high.*

**£50–100**

### *Top Tips*

- Look for first editions in good condition with their dust jacket.
- Keep books away from damp to preserve them in top condition.
- Buy a book for its subject matter or author rather than as an investment: the book market can be unpredictable.
- Be aware that although charity shops can be an excellent source of old and rare books, experienced dealers are more reliable if you want a valuable edition.
- Avoid books with notes or inscriptions in them as these lower value (unless written by or for a well-known person, or by the author).

### BUY

*More people began to travel abroad in the 1920s. Look for books that recall this period. Thomas Cook guides were once overshadowed by Baedekers, but interest is now growing and should continue to do so.*

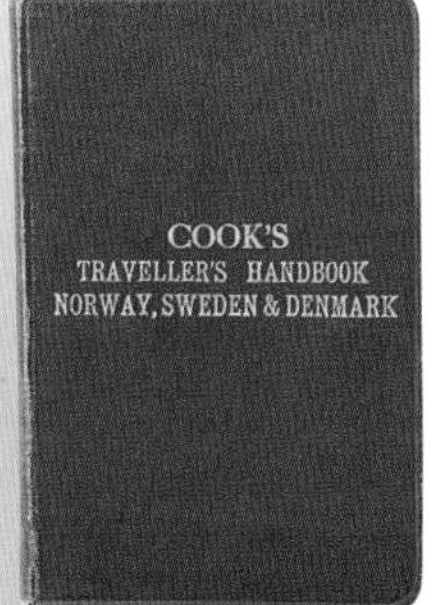


***Cook's Traveller's Handbook: Norway, Sweden and Denmark*** (Thos Cook & Son, Ludgate Circus). This first-edition guide, from the golden age of European travel, is likely to rise in value. *1923, 16.5cm (6½in) high.*

**£150–200**

### KEEP

*Instructional books on running a household successfully became popular during the Victorian era. They give a fascinating insight into everyday life. Values are likely to stay the same or even increase.*

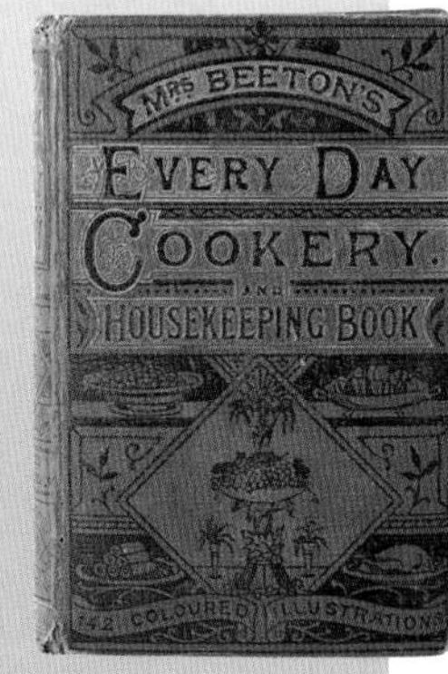


***Mrs Beeton's Every Day Cookery and Housekeeping Book*** (Ward Lock & Co, London). As well as being a first edition, the notable name of the author makes this a book worth keeping. *c.1880, 19cm (7½in) high.*

**£80–120**

# Children's comics were produced in profusion during the 1950s, 60s, and 70s, and appreciation of them is greater than ever. Search the attic for old boxes full of vintage *Beanos* or *Eagles* and you could be in for a pleasant surprise.

**The Dandy.** *1945, 29cm (11¾in) high.*
**£100–150**

Interest in British comics has increased in the last few years, and those from the 1970s are now sought after by people wanting to revisit or own items they enjoyed as children. Comics from the 1950s and 60s are slightly harder to find, but today they are prized for the quality of their artwork and stories.

## Colourful capers

*Mickey Mouse Weekly* (1936–55) was the first full-colour comic. The 1930s are considered to be the golden age of the comic, with titles such as *Tiny Tots* (1927–59) and *Crackers* (1929–41), followed by D.C. Thomson's *The Dandy* and *The Beano*, which introduced a new style of drawing and a colourful cast of characters.

*The Dandy* first appeared in 1937. It introduced 'Korky the Cat', 'Keyhole Kate', and 'Desperate Dan', and used speech balloons instead of captions.

While a first issue of *Mickey Mouse Weekly* may cost £200–250, vintage comics can be found for under £5.

## Eggo mania

*The Beano* arrived in 1938 with 'Big Eggo' on the cover. 'Lord Snooty' featured in the first issue but many recognisable characters came later, including 'Dennis the Menace' (1951), 'Roger the Dodger' and 'Minnie the Minx' (both 1953), and 'Billy Whizz' (1954). A first issue of *The Beano* fetched £7,565 in 2003. Issues from the 1960s and 70s are worth about £5 or less, with examples from the 80s onwards worth only 20–50p or less.

## Dan Dare to the rescue

*Eagle* (1950–69) introduced 'Dan Dare', 'The Mekon', and 'PC 49'. The comic was so popular – because of its quality

**Bunty,** leading British comic for girls, which outlived all the others. *1959, 29cm (11¾in) high.*
**£5–10**

**The Wizard,** one of the original series, which ran from 1922 to 1963. *1961, 29cm (11¾in) high.*
**£10–15**

**A first issue of *Mickey Mouse Weekly*,** published on 8 February 1936. *1936, 38cm (15in) high.*
**£300–400**

## A closer look at... a copy of *Eagle*

*Eagle* was a publishing phenomenon from the start: its first issue, in April 1950, sold 900,000 copies. Eye-catching and vivid design, as well as exciting stories that managed to retain a worthy and informative tone, set new standards for the genre.

Superb artwork by Frank Hampson gave *Eagle* its big, bold, and colourful look

The *Eagle* masthead makes a strong impact: the red corner 'block' and airborne eagle remained unchanged for more than a decade

'Dan Dare' was probably the most popular British fictional character during the 1950s

**A 1950s copy of *Eagle*.** This comic had a large print run, so always look for examples in pristine condition; these have the best chance of appreciating in value. *1953, 34cm (13½in) high.*

**£10–20**

artwork, which is itself collectable – that many readers saved their weekly copies. They are now easy to find; expect to pay £2–8 for a 'standard' copy. Older and rarer issues from the early to mid-1950s can go for more. A first-issue copy sold for £576 in 2002.

### Girl guides

During its heyday in the 1960s, *Bunty* sold a million copies a week. In general, girls are less possessive about comics, so most were discarded. *Bunty* usually came with a cut-out doll or doll's clothing on the back page, so many copies were cut up. A complete *Bunty* from the late 1950s or early 60s might sell for £5–6 and one from the 1980s £1–2. *Misty*, a supernatural comic for girls first issued in 1978, has developed a cult following and copies can be picked up for £3–5.

### Classic tales

The Classics Illustrated series was introduced into the UK in 1951 and featured 168 titles, including *Moby Dick*, *Macbeth*, *Robin Hood*, and *The Time Machine*. They are noted for memorable front cover artwork. Copies are available for about £3–4, but some hard-to-find issues, such as *Gulliver's Travels*, can cost £20 or more, and the rare *The Argonauts* can fetch £250.

### Superstars

There is a huge interest in US comic-book superheroes such as Spider Man and The Incredible Hulk. Original issues of *Action Comic*, in which Superman took his bow in 1938, are now changing hands for £100,000 plus, but examples from the 1960s can often be found for around £3–5 or less.

***Mutiny on the Bounty,*** from the Classics Illustrated series. *c.1950s, 25cm (10in) high.*

**£5–10**

### *Top Tips*

- Store comics out of direct sunlight to prevent fading. Make good-quality colour photocopies of your favourite pages for display purposes.
- Do not store comics in plastic bags; they have a chemical content that could adversely affect the paper.
- Look out for Christmas or Easter editions and summer 'specials', particularly of *The Dandy* and *The Beano*, as these can be worth more.
- Avoid comics that have pieces cut out, or have added cartoons, colourings, or doodles – these all reduce value.

### BUY

*A host of British comics were produced in the 1970s and early 80s but with children having more playthings available, comics such as* Corr!!, Scorcher and Score, Smash!, Roy of the Rovers, *and* TV21 *met with varying success. Such comics are still inexpensive.*

***Wow!*** This short-lived comic ran for 56 issues in 1982–83 and has nostalgic appeal. *1982, 28cm (11in) high.*

**£5–10**

### KEEP

*Comics that have enduring appeal are worth holding onto, especially if they have cross-market interest. Collectors of James Bond memorabilia will find this of interest, as well.*

***Doctor No,*** from the Classics Illustrated series. This is a classic among 'Classics'; the *Doctor No* series booklet is rare and does not appear on the market often. *c.1950s, 25cm (10in) high.*

**£300–400**

# Vintage magazines transport the reader into an almost forgotten world. Their individual styles and contents provide a fascinating glimpse of the outstanding events, celebrities, fashions, and endlessly changing lifestyles of past decades.

**A *Tit-Bits* magazine from January 1954,** featuring Zsa Zsa Gabor on the cover. *1954, 31.5cm (12½in) high.*

**£5–10**

Dedicated collectors save magazines because an issue has an intriguing article or photograph, or because of other specialist interests such as fashion or film stars.

## In vogue

Fashion magazines offer a unique record of period styles and are filled with excellent photography showing the designs of the day. *Vogue*, launched in 1916, has documented decades of evolving fashions. The 'vintage' of the edition is important, as is the style and subject of the cover – striking covers are often associated with *Vogue*. Values vary from about £2–10 for a copy from the 1980s or 90s, to around £20–30 for a copy from the 1960s. An issue from the 1930s featuring the designs of a leading couturier like Elsa Schiaparelli can be worth £30–100. Other notable fashion magazines include *Queen*, *Nova*, and *Harper's Bazaar*, but these are often less valuable than *Vogue*.

## Star attraction

Magazines featuring well-known personalities can attract anyone who collects subjects such as royalty or movie stars. The face on the cover is a good indicator of value. The first issue of *Playboy* (December 1953), featuring

**Vogue from April 1964.** The 'fashionista's bible', *Vogue* is renowned for its coverage of the changing world of fashion. An eye-catching, well-photographed cover – as many were – makes an issue more collectable. *1964, 29cm (11½in) high.*

**£35–45**

## Some magazines to look fo

■ Vogue ■ House & Garden

***House & Garden* from January 1956.** This magazine has a long-established reputation for covering the best in period styling – look for issues that show the work of noted designers. *1956, 29cm (11½in) high.*

**£10–15**

a nude centrefold of Marilyn Monroe and a cover image of her waving, sold more than 54,000 copies, ensuring a second issue. The first issue is rare and can command £500–1,500. Another sought-after example is the October 1961 issue of *Life* with a cover shot of Elizabeth Taylor as Cleopatra, which can be found for about £20–30. *Radio Times* and *TV Times* usually fetch less than £10, but covers showing *Doctor Who*, *Steptoe and Son*, and James Bond can command up to £30.

The value of music magazines is often determined by the cover story. Following a revival of interest in music – and magazines – from the 1960s, magazines from the 1970s are becoming valuable. It may be worth hunting out 1980s issues of magazines such as *Smash Hits* and *Record Mirror*, as interest in this era may grow too.

Newspaper colour supplements are rarely worth keeping – mainly because so many people have been doing so for years. There are a few exceptions, like those featuring enduring icons such as Marilyn Monroe or Audrey Hepburn. They can sell for £5–15.

## Landmarks in history

The history of vintage magazines recording national events goes back more than 100 years – *The Illustrated London News* commemorated Queen Victoria's Diamond Jubilee in 1897. From the 1950s onwards, so many people kept royal souvenir issues that they are worth little, but values may rise. An issue of *Vogue* covering the wedding of Prince Charles and Lady Diana Spencer can be worth £20–25, while a *Life* magazine from 1969 showing the Earth from Apollo 8 can be worth £40–60. Look for events of lasting importance.

## On the domestic front

Lifestyle and interiors magazines are generally not as valued as other niche publications, but *Ideal Home*, *House & Garden*, and *Good Housekeeping* have a small following. The value of 1950s, 60s, and 70s issues may rise, as there is a growing market in retro styles.

Many people collect by cover image or inside illustrations. Values vary depending on the artwork, but range from about £5–10 for a lesser-known publication with simple artwork up to £100 or more for classic examples of Art Nouveau or Art Deco.

Some people buy magazines for their advertisements, focusing on a brand name or a particular product. Values can vary from as little as 50p to around £20–40. Wear and tear is to be expected and will affect value.

### Top Tips

- Choose early issues: the first 10 issues – before a publication's sales became established – are rare and can be more desirable.
- Keep issues that feature modern celebrities with enduring popularity, such as Madonna and Kylie Minogue, on the cover – you could realise a profit in a few years.

### BUY

*Key titles featuring outstanding photography of well-known personalities are sought after. Examples that were not marketed as 'specials' or 'souvenir' issues are the most likely to appreciate as demand will continue and the supply will be limited.*

**Vogue from December 1991,** featuring the Princess of Wales. The continuing interest in Diana and the iconic photography by Patrick Demarchelier make this issue likely to rise in value. *1991, 30cm (11¾in) high.*

**£20–30**

### SELL

*Issues of magazines covering unpopular people or distasteful events often sold poorly. This makes them rare today. Specialist collectors may be prepared to pay a premium for them.*

***Life* from 19 December 1969,** with a Charles Manson cover and story. This is a rare issue: few copies were sold or kept. *1969, 35.5cm (14in) high.*

**£10–15**

## ■ Life ■ Harper's Bazaar ■

***Life* from 6 December 1963,** with a cover commemorating John F. Kennedy's funeral. *Life* covers often depict memorable historic or topical events, or people, in a dramatic, hard-hitting way. *1963, 35.5cm (14in) high.*

**£20–30**

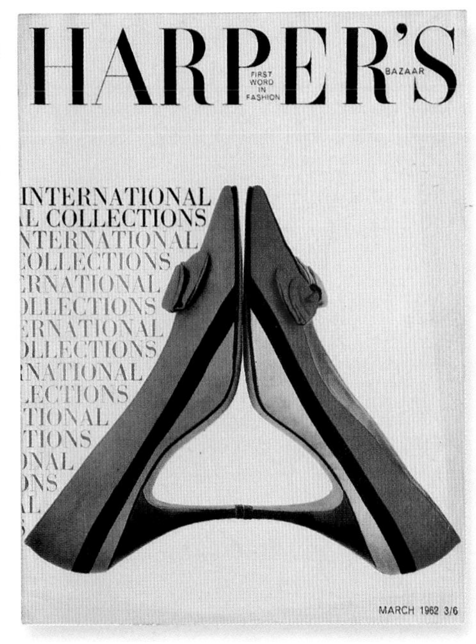


***Harper's Bazaar* from March 1962.** Now known as *Harper's & Queen*, this magazine offers an insight into high society. Early examples with attractive covers, or showing key fashions or events, are popular. *1962, 32cm (12½in) high.*

**£10–15**

# Printed ephemera allows a glimpse into past events, interests, styles, and trends. Small, easy to store and display, and often rare, these items appeal, through their fleeting nature, to design historians and enthusiasts alike.

**A trade card for Harrison,** a saddler and harness maker of Norwich. *c.1800–10, 9cm (3½in) high.*

**£120–150**

Ephemera, such as cards, menus, and invitations, has been produced in large quantities for the last 200–300 years. Values vary from less than £5–10 to upwards of £1,000–2,000. Most examples date from the late 19th and early 20th century, with items fetching £300–500 or more.

## Stock-in-trade

Originating in London during the early 17th century, trade cards, advertising products and services, were among the first forms of publicity. Rare 18th- and early 19th-century woodcut or letterpress cards can fetch more than £200–500. Later, more common, items cost around £30–80 or less.

Chromolithography, an 1840s printing technique, enabled the production of colourful trade cards. Many had a blank space for the trader's details. By the 1900s, other forms of publicity, such as magazine advertisements and posters, took over and the pictorial trade card declined. Examples with well-printed, complex designs can cost £5–50 or more.

## Sentimental scraps

Scraps, also known as 'swaps' or 'die-cuts', are brightly coloured, shaped cards printed with designs such as flowers, animals, and people. Their popularity peaked from the 1870s to the early 1910s. They were either cut from cards or torn from pre-cut strips, and were placed into albums, made into book marks, or used to decorate screens and small pieces of furniture or boxes – a decorative process known as 'découpage'. Prices start at less than £10 and rarely exceed £20–40. Look for large, well-printed, intact examples. Scraps can be found at collectors' fairs, junk shops, or specialist dealers.

## Some Victorian scraps to look for:

▪ Ladies ▪ Animals ▪ Flowers ▪ Exoticism ▪

**A large scrap of an elegant lady.** Ladies that featured on scraps often conform to stereotypes of Victorian beauty, with flawless porcelain-like skin, tiny noses, heavy-lashed gentle eyes, rosebud mouths, and delicate flower-encrusted gowns. *c.1880s, 10cm (4in) high.*

**£10–15**

**Four die-cut, joined cockerels.** Complete pages of scraps are desirable and generally fetch more than the equivalent sum of individual pieces. *c.1880s, 12cm (4¾in) wide.*

**£20–25**

## Mourning glory

The Victorian preoccupation with mourning reached its height after Prince Albert's death in 1861, and funerals of high-profile figures were marked with sombre, formal invitations, tickets, and printed announcements. A ticket for Queen Victoria's funeral can be found for around £50–100, depending on its condition. Printed funeral cards with spaces for filling in details cost around £30–50 or less.

**One of a series of 25 'Polar Exploration' cigarette cards,** issued by John Player & Sons. *1915, 7cm (2¾in) high.*

**£50–100 for the set**

## Smokers' addictions

Cigarette cards originated in the 1880s, when 'stiffeners' were inserted in paper packets of American cigarettes. Soon these cards carried advertisements and, later, collectable picture cards, to encourage brand loyalty.

The pioneering British company was W.D. & H.O. Wills, whose first general-interest cards, 'Ships', were colourful, with informative text on the reverse. Other tobacco firms soon followed, and the trend reached its peak in the 1920s.

Early cigarette card themes included war, sport, actresses, art, and transport. The key to their collectability then (and now) was in making up the set – usually 25 or 50 cards. Production of cards by cigarette firms ceased in early 1940 because of wartime restrictions.

The condition of the cards is vital to their value. Their popularity as 'swaps' meant they were handled a lot. Many colourful cards can be found for less than £100 per set, with some costing as little as £20–40 per set. Look out for a 20-card clown series issued by the London tobacco supplier Taddy around 1914, which can raise up to £15,000 – currently only 15 sets are known to exist.

**An oriental lady with fan.** The Victorians loved exotic places and customs, and scraps featuring people in traditional dress or objects from a foreign country are often found. *c.1880s, 6cm (2¼in) high.*

**£5–10**

**A large scrap of a man's hand bearing a lily-of-the-valley bouquet.** Flowers are a common subject for scraps: the largest examples and those with finer detailing and intricately cut shapes are the most valuable. Flowers offered by a man are a symbol of romance. *c.1890s, 12cm (4¾in) high.*

**£5–10**

### Top Tips

- Avoid damaged ephemera (unless it is rare). Tears, creases, missing pieces, and crinkled edges all reduce value.
- Store pieces in an acid-free paper folder and keep them away from strong light and damp conditions.
- Never write on ephemera, or stick notes on items, as this discolours and marks them.
- Do not use glue or sticky tape to fix ephemera into albums or onto display cards, as the adhesive will cause staining – use stamp-style mounts.
- Handle pieces with clean, dry hands.

### BUY

*Inexpensive Victorian ephemera can be found. Choose good-quality printing and design, and items in still-vibrant colours and unusual shapes. Victorian sentimentalism is still popular, and pieces with all these qualities should rise in value.*

**A die-cut card in the form of a tambourine.** This card is unusual in shape; and the well-printed image makes it a good example of Victorian sentimentalism. *c.1895, 15cm (6in) wide.*

**£20–30**

### KEEP

*Ephemera produced for events of national importance has a wide appeal, in particular items relating to notable personalities who still capture public interest today. Pieces in the best condition should hold their value and may rise.*

In Memoriam.

In Memory of
OUR BELOVED QUEEN,
VICTORIA,

Born at Kensington Palace, May 24th, 1819.
Succeeded to the Throne, June 20th, 1837.
Crowned at Westminster Abbey, June 28th, 1838.
Married to Prince Albert, February 10th, 1840.
Died at Osborne, January 22nd, 1901.
Having Reigned 63 years and 7 months.

"She brought her People lasting good."

Interred at Windsor, February 2nd, 1901.

**A Queen Victoria memorial card.** The design of this card, with its regal portrait and chronology of the key events in Victoria's life, is typical of funerary tastes of the period. *c.1901, 13cm (5in) high.*

**£20–25**

# Valentine cards of the 19th and early 20th centuries often feature unique, intricate, hand-made designs. Their delicate beauty, linked to expressions of undying love, have great appeal for latter-day romantics.



Although romantic verse and love messages have been exchanged for centuries, one of the first references to Valentine's Day tokens came in Samuel Pepys' diaries of the 1660s. Valentine cards probably evolved from religious devotionals of the 16th century, which were made of paper intricately cut to look like lace, with a holy image as the centrepiece.

Early cards were usually illustrated with engravings, which were either left plain or coloured by hand. Subjects varied from flowers and cherubs to more abstract designs. By the early 19th century, embossed paper with a relief pattern was used, as well as intricately cut 'lace paper'. Cards were embellished by the wooer, using silk, ribbons, shells, or trinkets. Often, a few lines of romantic poetry were added.

By the 1870s, after chromolithography was established in Britain, printed Valentines replaced hand-made ones. Boxed cards also appeared, decorated with silver and gold lace paper. Some quilted cards even contained a small pendant or a seed pearl bracelet.

Messages are part of the social history of cards, and can add to their desirability. The original envelope with its postmark will also increase the value of a card. The postmark helps to date it, too.

▲ **A card showing a basket of flowers** with embossed lace paper and original hand colouring. The hand-painted flowers, the heart-shaped frame, and the texture of the lace paper, make this a valuable card. *c.1850–60, 17cm (6¾in) high.*

**£100–150**

► **A hand-coloured wood-cut 'cricketer' card.** Comic Valentines were produced in large numbers by 1840. Wood block printing was a favoured method. *c.1840–50, 18cm (7in) high.*

**£70–80**

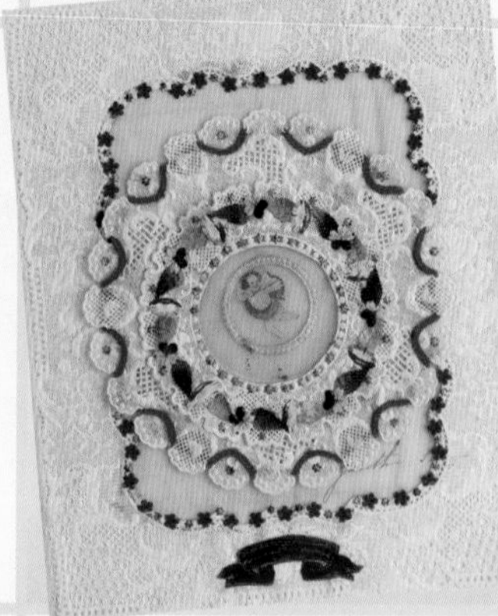

► **A Valentine of hand-painted flowers,** with lace paper and a background of silk mesh. The unusual design of the lace paper and the card itself, and the fact that it is dated, make this card desirable. *c.1851, 25.5cm (10in) high.*

**£150–200**

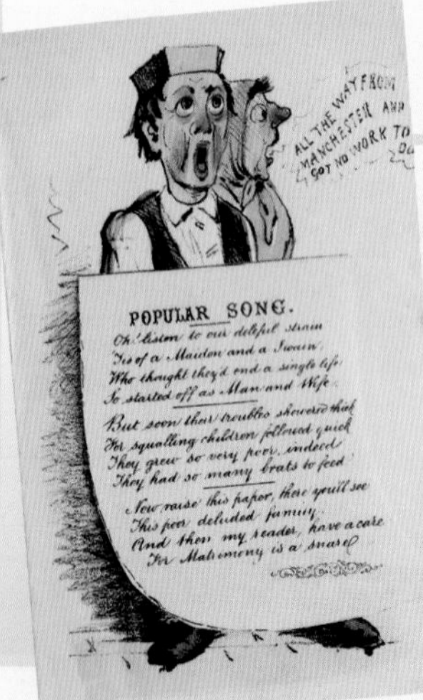


◄ **A card entitled 'All the way from Manchester and got no work to do'.** This comic card hints at the problems that family life brings after the initial romance has worn off. *c.1840–50, 18cm (7in) high.*

**£50–70**

◄ **A pair of Valentine poetry booklets,** in mint condition. Booklets like these offered verses and messages that could be copied into Valentine cards. *1840–50, 17.5cm (7in) high.*

**£150–200 each**

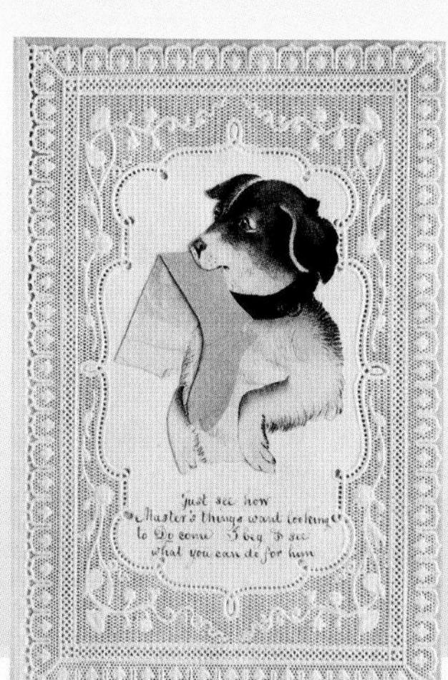

◄ **A Dobbs & Co. card** with embossed lace paper and original hand colouring, showing a dog with a stocking in its mouth. Dobbs & Co. provided fancy paper for Valentines as early as 1803. *c.1850–60, 13.5cm (5¼in) high.*

**£70–100**

◄ **A hand-coloured card featuring a floral vignette,** with embossed swirls of lace paper on a delicate pink background. *c.1850–60, 17cm (6¾in) high.*

**£80–100**

► **An English Valentine made by Wood,** with embossed lace paper and hand-painted die-cut detail. The die-cut lace paper on this card is complex and, surprisingly, still intact. *1850–60, 17cm (6¾in) high.*

**£90–100**

## Collectors' Tips

- Store cards away from strong light, in non-polythene sleeves from a photographic shop
- Inspect cards with mechanical, moving, or pop-up parts carefully for damage

◄ **A card decorated with lace paper leaves and fronds** and embossed lace paper. The colours of the card have not faded, despite its age, and the delicate fronds around the edge of the centre are all still intact. *c.1850–60, 17cm (6¾in) high.*

**£70–100**

◄ **A card showing a hand-cut figure of a lady** with embossed lace paper and original hand colouring. Cards with figures are popular, especially if they have applied features, such as the silk and gauze overskirt on this example. *c.1855–60, 17cm (6¾in) high.*

**£80–100**

► **A card with a glove motif,** embossed lace paper and die-cut, silvered leaves. Gloves have been tokens of love since the 16th century. *c.1850–60, 17cm (6¾in) wide.*

**£120–150**

# Postcards are still a great way to say 'Wish you were here', but early cards carry historical images of society, events, and places. They are treasured for the nostalgia they evoke and for their occasional flashes of artistic brilliance.

**A coloured postcard of a young courting couple.** *c.1910, 14cm (5½in) high.*

**50p–£1**

Up to the early 20th century, postcards were plain, as the Post Office required that the address be on one side and the message on the other. From 1902, postcards with a message and address on one side, known as 'divided backs', were allowed, and the reverse carried photographs and illustrations of considerable artistry. Today, pre-1900 cards are especially sought after.

## Town and country

Cards that offer a snapshot of daily life, such as a townscape, were commonly produced. But it is the detail – such as how people dressed and the forms of transport of the time – that creates interest. These cards can fetch from £3 to £40, depending on the location, with pre-1950s railway stations being a good buy. Postcards of one-off events, such as village fairs, social gatherings, and even disasters, are rarer, as fewer would have been printed; they can be worth £10–40.

Landscapes, castles, and churches are usually less popular, as they tend not to change as much over time. Values are often less than 50p and rarely more than £1–2. Alfred Robert Quinton, known as 'ARQ', painted British landscapes and was published in the early 20th century. His cards are numbered, so are easy to collect. They fetch from around £1.50 up to £50.

## A military message

During World War I, many propaganda and patriotic cards were printed. Values are around £3–10 or less, because of the number produced. Look out for those showing military subjects, especially Zeppelins, as these usually go for between £5 and £30. Cards showing one-off events are desirable too, with an image of a German U-boat aground often worth

## Some postcards to look for:

- Saucy Seaside
- Propaganda

◄ **'The Good Old Summer-time' postcard.** Saucy seaside cards are popular and quintessentially British. The racier the image the better, but most look tame by today's standards. *c.1900s, 13.5cm (5¼in) high.*

**£2–5**

► **A World War II propaganda postcard.** Cartoons were used to raise public morale. *c.1940, 13.5cm (5¼in) high.*

**£10–15**

up to £15. Patriotic cards with the Union flag and a quote from Burns can cost about £1, while embroidered silk cards may be worth about £4–6.

## The tourist trade

Scenes of holiday resorts were sold in large numbers, so their value is usually low. Often more collectable are the typically British 'saucy seaside' cards, in particular those by Donald McGill. Because of the popularity of this genre from the 1910s to the 1930s, there are many to choose from, with values ranging from 50p to more than £5.

## Stylish designs

Advertising and artistic cards are popular, particularly if they show the styles of the period – such as the sinuous lines of Art Nouveau around 1900–10, or the clean forms of Art Deco from the late 1920s and 30s.

Designs by the Art Deco poster artist Adolphe Mouron (known as 'Cassandre') can be worth £30–50.

Original Louis Wain postcards featuring his cat illustrations can range from £30–60. Mabel Lucie Attwell, with her images of chubby children, is another popular name, and her cards may be worth £3–30.

Although postcards are not usually collected because of their manufacturer, there are some notable exceptions, such as Raphael Tuck of London, and Valentine of Dundee, which are known for the quality of their printing. Avoid buying modern reproductions.

**A 'Cassandre' postcard with fish motif.** *1930s, 19cm (7½in) high.*

**£55–65**

**H.M.S. *Centurion* and Zeppelin L.3,** Kiel, June 1914. Military cards are of interest not only to postcard enthusiasts but also to collectors of wartime memorabilia. The addition of a Zeppelin makes this card particularly rare and desirable. *1914, 14cm (5½in) wide.*

**£6–10**

**The Dymock Flower Show and Sports,** 25 August 1910, showing the 'Grand Stand'. Postcards showing local village events are collectable, as few were produced and sold. Always look for good composition, as in this example. *c.1910, 14cm (5½in) wide.*

**£15–20**

### Top Tips

- Try to find cards in mint condition, as these will usually fetch the highest prices. Generally, a message will only add value if the sender or addressee is famous.
- Pay attention to postmarks, as these help to date a card, and some are rare. Make sure the stamp has not been torn off, as this can lower value.
- Look out for postcards with views of areas that have changed dramatically, as these are often collectable.
- Look for good artwork and fine-quality printing when buying artistic or non-photographic cards.

### BUY

*Postcards showing certain types of building are popular and form an excellent focus for a collection. Some are fairly rare and it can be well worth tracking them down.*

**A postcard of West Tytherley post office,** published by A.E. Brundle, dated 6 August 1912. Cards featuring post offices – often the centre of a rural community – are rare and desirable. *c.1912, 14cm (5½in) wide.*

**£20–25**

### KEEP

*Look for postcards that cross collecting interests and fields, such as those with aeronautical, railway, motoring, or sporting images, as these will appeal to more people, leading to consistent and often rising prices.*

**A postcard featuring a 1932–3 Everton FC team photograph,** published by Corbonora Co. This sport-related card is made more desirable as it includes 'Dixie' Dean, famous for scoring the most goals (60) in an English football season. *c.1933, 14cm (5½in) wide.*

**£70–100**

# Christmas memorabilia –

Victorian Christmas cards, glistening glass baubles, and Santa Claus figures – is much sought after for its charm and nostalgia. Mementoes of a bygone age, these often fragile pieces conjure up visions of snowy Christmases past.

Sir Henry Cole, founder of the Victoria & Albert Museum, is credited with sending the first illustrated Christmas card in 1843. About a thousand were printed, a dozen of which survive. In 2001 one fetched £22,350 at auction.

Sending cards only became popular when cheaper postal rates were introduced in 1870, and soon millions were being sold. Charles Goodall & Son was an early manufacturer, as were Marcus Ward and Raphael Tuck & Sons. Late 19th-century cards are fairly easy to find and range from £5 to £50. Look for intact Victorian cards that fold in a complex way or have moving parts.

From the early 20th century onwards, other Christmas items were produced on a large scale. Santa figures from the 1930s and earlier are particularly desirable. Look for German 'Belsnickles' made from plaster or papier-mâché: they are valuable and can fetch from around £300 to £1,000. Large plaster Santas or those with clockwork parts are also prized, as are celluloid Santas produced in Japan from the late 1940s.

The tradition of a Christmas tree also came from Germany. Early German trees made from coloured goose feathers are valued. Other memorabilia, usually priced from £3–10 upwards, includes early glass baubles, cake decorations, tree lights, tins, and even Christmas crackers. By the 1960s, cheaper glass and plastic ornaments were being mass-produced and the 'golden age' of the Christmas decoration was over.

▲ **A German Christmas snowman sweet container** made from pressed card coated with plaster. Novelty-shaped containers that used to contain treats are a relatively common and very collectable form of memorabilia for both Christmas and Hallowe'en. *1940s, 14cm (5½in) high.*

**£80–120**

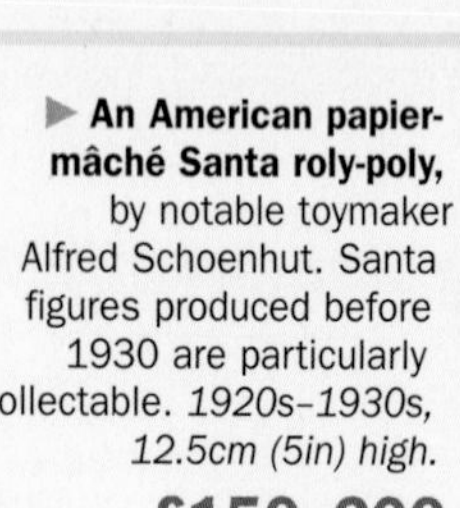

► **An American papier-mâché Santa roly-poly,** by notable toymaker Alfred Schoenhut. Santa figures produced before 1930 are particularly collectable. *1920s–1930s, 12.5cm (5in) high.*

**£150–200**

► **An early English moveable Christmas card,** by Goodall, with four vignettes of little girls. Charles Goodall first made Christmas cards in 1859 and its cards are marked 'CG & S'. *c.1870, 12cm (4¾in) high.*

**£40–50**

◄ **A Japanese Suzuki wind-up cycling Santa**, made from celluloid and tinplate, with a ringing bell. Many festive toys were produced in the late 1940s and 50s. Moving toys with tinplate parts like this are sought after. *c.1946, 10.5cm (4¼in) high.*

**£150–200**

◄ **An early English Christmas card,** by playing card maker Charles Goodall, featuring a moveable bouquet of flowers. Undamaged cards with moveable panels are scarce and highly desirable. *c.1870, 12cm (4¾in) high.*

**£40–50**

◀ **An unusual die-cut English card,** by Earnest Nister. Robins have adorned Christmas cards since the early days of the postal service. The robins on Victorian Christmas cards came to represent the postmen who delivered them. The maker, the complex shape of this card, and its fine printing make it desirable. *c.1895, 12cm (4¾in) high.*

**£10–15**

▲ **A chromolithographic Christmas card,** made by Raphael Tuck & Sons who first produced Christmas cards in 1871. The company was known for its fine lithographic printing and won the royal warrant in 1893. *c.1890s, 13.5cm (5¼in) high.*

**£10–15**

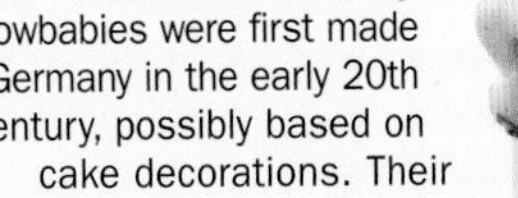

▶ **A ceramic snowbaby.** Snowbabies were first made in Germany in the early 20th century, possibly based on cake decorations. Their condition and size affect their value, and larger sizes fetch higher prices than the standard 3.5cm (1½in) sizes. *1930s, 3.5cm (1½in) high.*

**£30–40**

## Collectors' Tips

- Look out for incomplete sets of Christmas tree decorations as full sets are rarely found
- Seek out fine quality printed cards, preferably with complex cut-out details
- Take care when storing Christmas cards: those that have been stuck in albums lose value

▶ **A German Christmas feather tree,** made from green-dyed goose feathers. Larger versions of such trees are more valuable, as are those in unusual colours such as blue or burgundy. *1920s, 21.5cm (8½in) high.*

**£50–70**

◀ ▲ **Two Victorian chromolithographed paper 'scraps'.** Scraps were popular 'cut-out and collect' objects stuck in albums or used as bookmarks. Santa in a different coloured suit is unusual and desirable. *1880s, largest 7cm (2¾in) high.*

**£10–15 each**

◀ **A card showing a woman with a candle looking at the moon,** made by the London firm De La Rue. This firm was also well known for printing British stamps and bank-notes, so the quality of its lithography and printing was extremely good. *c.1895, 7cm (2¾in) high.*

**£10–15**

# Autographs are the trophies of today's celebrity-obsessed culture – whether scribbled on a napkin or sold as part of the luminary's PR. A star's signature in a rare medium can fetch an aptly astronomical price.

**A black-and-white photograph of Barbara Cartland,** signed in her customary pink ink across the upper left corner. *c.1970s, 14.5cm (5¾in) high.*

**£50–70**

Famous personalities sign their names on a wide variety of collectable artefacts, including handwritten or typed letters, official documents such as contracts, driving licences, photographs, manuscripts, books, and programmes, as well as items such as guitars and menus – and, of course, autograph albums.

## Focus group

Many new collectors concentrate on one subject, such as royalty, film stars, or sportspeople. Enthusiasts often take into account the accessibility of the personalities involved if they are still alive – for many, the 'thrill of the chase' is as important as the satisfaction of ownership. Anyone considering collecting should look into prices before choosing their special interest: it can cost as little as £10–20 to buy a page from an autograph album signed by a minor star, but thousands of pounds for a rare document or object with biographical interest – such as a letter or a contract.

## Reaching for the stars

Before the 20th century, it was fashionable to collect the letters and autographs of writers and political figures. The advent of modern media shifted the focus to entertainers. By the 1930s and 40s many film stars and, later, TV personalities, pop stars, sporting heroes, and models became so besieged by autograph hunters that a minion signed their photos for them.

In the past, film stars working with the major studios were often contractually obliged to sign autographs and be friendly to fans, but today's entertainers are freer to opt out of what many regard as the irksome business of signing their name. A handful of celebrities, among them

**Main image:** Brigitte Bardot signs her autograph for admiring fans. **Inset: A postcard-sized colour photograph of Brigitte Bardot,** signed by her across the lower portion of the image in bold black ink. *1960s, 15cm (5¾in) high.*

**£200–250**

## A closer look at... two Marilyn Monroe signatures

The kind of item, wording, presentation, and display appeal are important to a signature's value. Monroe's enduring fame and the rarity of her autograph influence value, but other characteristics cause price differences too. Cheques, for example, make excellent display pieces, as they are larger and visually more interesting than autograph album pages.

**A cheque signed by Marilyn Monroe,** drawn on her company's account at the Bankers Trust Company in New York, dated 11 August 1961. It is made payable for the sum of $127.90 to May Reis, who is known to have been a close friend of Monroe. *1961, 25cm (9¾in) long.*

**£5,000–8,000**

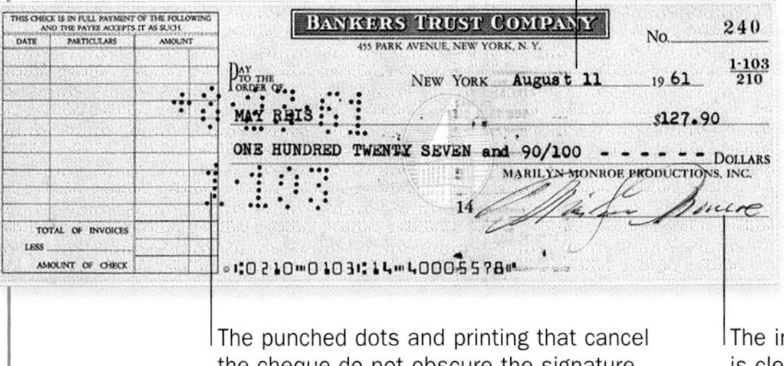
THIS CHECK IS IN FULL PAYMENT OF THE FOLLOWING AND THE PAYEE ACCEPTS IT AS SUCH.

| DATE | PARTICULARS | AMOUNT |
|---|---|---|
| TOTAL OF INVOICES | | |
| LESS | | |
| AMOUNT OF CHECK | | |

BANKERS TRUST COMPANY
455 PARK AVENUE, NEW YORK, N. Y.
No. 240
NEW YORK August 11 19 61
1-103
210
PAY TO THE ORDER OF MAY REIS $127.90
ONE HUNDRED TWENTY SEVEN and 90/100 DOLLARS
MARILYN MONROE PRODUCTIONS, INC.
14

The date of the cheque helps attest to its period authenticity

The punched dots and printing that cancel the cheque do not obscure the signature

The inked signature is clear and complete

The personal dedication to someone whose relationship to the star is unknown reduces the appeal to buyers

The signature, which is cramped to one side and on the diagonal, is less well placed here

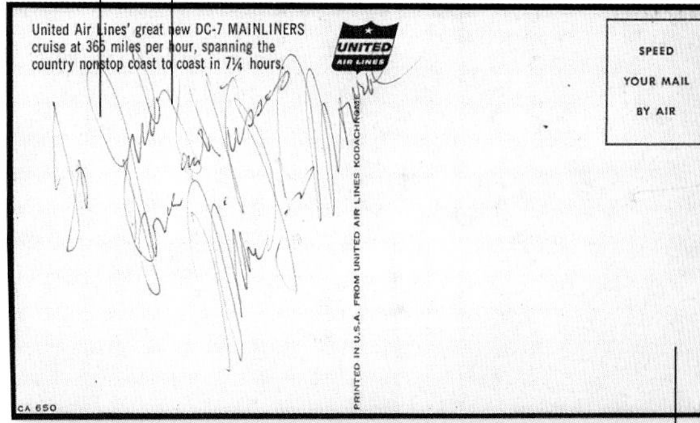


The back of a picture postcard is less attractive to display

**A Marilyn Monroe signature on a United Airlines DC-7 postcard.** The card is signed and dedicated in blue ballpoint pen on the reverse (shown here) 'To Judy Love & Kisses Marilyn Monroe'. *1960s, 15cm (5¾in) wide.*

**£2,000–3,000**

Britney Spears and Tobey Maguire, simply refuse to sign autographs. Others, such as George Clooney and Angelina Jolie, give them as 'payback' to their fans.

The value of an autograph often depends more on rarity than historical status. Trends also play a part: prices rise as people become more popular or are 'rediscovered'. An autograph including all the members of the band Abba can fetch up to £200 today, more than it would have done during the late 1980s. Signatures on artefacts with added visual appeal such as photographs are also desirable.

In America, professional autograph collectors can make six-figure salaries simply by selling signed photographs to fans. Be warned, autograph collecting provides easy pickings for forgers and con men too, especially through Internet sites devoted to sales.

### Golden rule

It can be difficult to distinguish between fakes and the real article – few signatures are consistent – so seek the advice of a reputable dealer first. Experts will spot clues such as styles of lettering or, in the case of historical documents, old inks and papers.

### Top Tips

- Examine the signature to ensure it was written and not printed.
- Look for a complete, clear signature.
- Consider whether the signature's position on the object allows for easy display.
- Handwritten letters tend to be more valuable than typed, hand-signed ones.
- For maximum investment value, pick signatures that are not dedicated to an individual.
- Only choose a dedicated signature if there is a relationship between the signer and recipient, or if the recipient is also famous.

### KEEP

*Autographs enhanced with drawings or images are often highly sought after, particularly if the image is associated with the artist. Here, an Oscar-winning cartoon artist and illustrator has drawn one of his best-known characters.*

**A white cotton handkerchief** embroidered with an image of Gromit the dog, with a signature and original drawing of Wallace in bold black ink by Nick Park (a detail is shown here). *1990s, 45cm (17¾in) wide.*

**£600–1,000**

### SELL

*Beatles material is consistently collectable, but signatures by other people on their behalf reduce the appeal.*

**An autograph album page signed by Paul McCartney and George Harrison.** Harrison also signed 'Ringo Starr' (who signed 'John Lennon' is unknown). Stains and damage reduce appeal. *1967, 11cm (4¼in) wide.*

**£1,000–1,500**

### SELL

*Leonardo DiCaprio is a major movie star, with roles in such films as Titanic, but he is still young, with the prospect of a long and high-profile career. He will almost certainly produce many more autographs to add to the large number already in circulation, so a plain DiCaprio signature is unlikely to appreciate in the long term.*

**A Leonardo DiCaprio autograph on a plain white card.** *1990s, 15cm (5¾in) wide.*

**£100–150**

# Guinness advertising

has adorned posters and promotional products ever since the 1930s. Not only does it have a strong period look; it is colourful, clever, humorous, and above all, memorable.

Long regarded as witty and stylish, Guinness advertising has become an enormously popular collecting area.

Although the company was founded in Dublin as early as 1759, its first advertisements did not appear until the late 1920s. These were in national newspapers and were text-based, with a small picture of a pint of Guinness. The advertising agency S.H. Benson took over in 1929, launching the brand with amusing, colourful advertisements that often played on the drink's claimed health benefits. S.H. Benson designed so many Guinness advertisements and promotional products that plenty remain on the market today, from posters to ceramic figurines, beer mats, and trays. Prices range from £3–5 for a 1930s beer mat to £500–700 or more for a poster from the same decade.

## Poster power

The designer John Gilroy was responsible for most of the images and themes associated with early Guinness advertising. Many were first used on posters, by then a booming form of advertising. Some of the best-known 1930s posters promoted Guinness's supposed ability to build strength. A 1934 poster shows a man walking along effortlessly carrying an iron girder – hinting, perhaps, at the beneficial levels of iron the drink was said to contain. By this time, the poster format had been established – a plain white background with a striking slogan in simple lettering. Slogans included 'Guinness is Good for You' and 'Guinness for Strength'. Examples of these now celebrated posters can often be found for between £100 and £700.

## From A to zoo

In 1935 a visit to London Zoo inspired Gilroy to develop a new range of posters. These legendary designs featured a befuddled zoo keeper with different animals, each of which makes off with his pint of Guinness.

**A metal Guinness advertising tray** with smiling pints of Guinness blooming from flowers. *1950s, 27cm (10½in) diam.*

**£50–100**

The first, released in late 1935, shows him chasing a jolly sea lion, with a pint of Guinness balanced on its nose. Today, these posters can fetch around £100–700 or more, depending on their condition and size. Perhaps the best-known Guinness animal was the toucan, which was reused for a short period in the late 1960s and 70s. Posters featuring the toucan are often the most popular.

During the 1940s, Guinness posters continued to emphasise strength: one poster showed a Guinness man moving huge bombs onto a trolley. In the 1950s and 60s, new artists were employed, such as Abram Games and Tom Eckersley. Abram Games' posters show ingenious designs and typography, and witty images. Gilroy's animal posters and posters from the 1950s and 60s usually fetch between £150 and £700.

### Did You Know?

*Although John Gilroy developed the idea of using animals to advertise Guinness, the most memorable of them – the toucan – was developed by an S.H. Benson copywriter, Dorothy L. Sayers, who went on to become a notable crime writer.*

**A Carlton Ware Guinness turtle** advertising figure. *1930s, 7.5cm (3in) high.*

**£200–250**

## A closer look at... a Guinness advertising figurine

The popularity of Guinness has spawned many reproductions and fakes. Although they have decorative value, and offer an affordable way to acquire examples of landmark advertising, they have no collectable value and will not rise in value. Examine them carefully to ensure that you are buying an authentic example, and remember that reproductions do not usually carry Carlton Ware marks.

The orange and red on the beak is carefully blended and graduated. In reproductions, it is over-delineated or smudged

The white part of the neck is bright white. In reproductions it is often cream

The correctly applied typical Guinness slogan on the base shows that the figure is authentic

**A Carlton Ware Guinness toucan** advertising lamp base. This example is authentic and unusual, making it both collectable and valuable. *1930s–50s, 30.5cm (12in) high.*

**£600–800**

### Ceramics and more

Gilroy's animal campaign was not restricted to posters. From the 1930s to 50s, Carlton Ware made small ceramic figurines of the Guinness animals. Most of these cost from £150–350; but popular animals such as the toucan or penguin can fetch up to £300–400. Lamp bases and pull-along toys were also produced, but perhaps the best known are the set of three wall-mounted flying toucans; an original, mint set can fetch around £300–500.

Other promotional objects are less expensive. These include a 1940s plate based on the Chinese 'Willow' pattern, a 1950s wooden clothes brush in the shape of a Guinness bottle, and ceramic cruet sets, often decorated with animals and slogans. Prices range from £30–80. Look for paper objects, such as menus, calendars, and beer mats, using the artwork styles, slogans, and characters of the period. These often cost under £10–20. A huge number were made, but many were thrown away, so they are probably rarer than they should be. Another of the most common promotional objects is a set of six Guinness buttons, which can fetch around £50–80 for a complete set. It's worth buying an incomplete set, provided it is priced accordingly, then building up a set gradually.

### Drink to the future

Guinness has continued its strong advertising campaigns, using well-known agencies such as Ogilvy & Mather and J. Walter Thompson. Pieces related to campaigns from the 1980s and 90s currently fetch lower values, usually under £30–50, but if interest in memorabilia associated with the brand continues, they may well make a good investment.

**A Guinness advertising clothes brush** in the shape of a bottle of Guinness. *1950s, 20cm (8in) high.*

**£15–20**

### Top Tips

- Look for posters from the 1950s and 60s by the leading poster designer Abram Games. They feature clever use of simple graphics and typefaces.
- Choose objects and posters with familiar slogans; they are usually more valuable, particularly those from the 1930s and 50s.
- Look out for items featuring Gilroy's animal series.

### BUY

Although posters can be expensive, you can own examples of key period artwork by looking for memorabilia such as calendars, notepads, card advertising standees, beer mats, and menus. Always look for artwork by the key designers such as Gilroy and Games, especially if it features well-known slogans.

**A Guinness pocket calendar, 'My Goodness My Guinness'.** With artwork featuring part of the animal series designed by John Gilroy, as well as a popular slogan, this calendar should rise in value. *1959, 9cm (3½in) high.*

**£30–50**

### KEEP

Such is the quality of advertising and memorabilia that even recent Guinness examples are worth collecting. These should rise in value if they are typical of their period, were popular, and especially if they feature key images used in campaigns.

**A 1990s set of Guinness playing cards.** The backs of these cards show the pint of Guinness used in many 1990s advertisements, and the major cards show the most famous poster artwork designs from the 1930s and 50s, making this a collectable deck. *1990s, 9cm (3½in) high.*

**£10–15**

# Coca-Cola is one of the world's most recognised brands. Ranging from Hamilton King's advertising calendars in the early 20th century to the Coca-Cola millennium bottle, this collecting area continues to grow.

▲ **A lithographed tin sign.** This incorporates a thermometer and its imagery and relatively early date make it sought after. *1930s, 42cm (16½in) high.*

**£300–400**

Originally developed as a pick-me-up drink in 1886 by Dr John Pemberton of Atlanta, Georgia, Coca-Cola's popularity grew swiftly from the 1900s onwards, partly due to its long-standing rivalry with competing brands, such as Pepsi. Coca-Cola is now found in more than 200 different countries, with advertising, promotional material, and packaging designed specifically to reflect the culture of each market.

Coke memorabilia can be separated into either promotional advertising or packaging but, due to the vast amount available, collectors often focus on an object type or area, such as trays or items linked to a specific country. Pieces from the 1890s and early 20th century are rare; most objects date from the 1950s onwards. Items displaying Coke's varying slogans are popular, and can also help to date the pieces. Since the 1970s, Coca-Cola has produced reproductions of vintage designs. It has also produced designs specifically to look old, so check for signs of wear to identify truly vintage pieces. Cans and promotional material produced for special occasions are particularly collectable: 200 cans were made to mark the presence of Coca-Cola on the space shuttle Challenger in 1985, and the empty cans often now sell for more than £150.

► **A Coca-Cola 'push plate',** which would have been placed on the doors of shops that sold Coca-Cola, to advertise the product as the customer entered. This example is made of enamelled metal. *1950s, 30cm (12in) high.*

**£200–250**

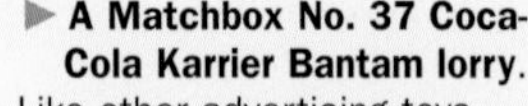

► **A Matchbox No. 37 Coca-Cola Karrier Bantam lorry.** Like other advertising toys, this crosses collecting fields, appealing to both collectors of the toy manufacturer and the product it advertises. *c.1960s, 12cm (5in) long.*

**£70–90**

◄ **An American colour lithographed tin sign.** Card six packs for Coca-Cola bottles, as shown on this sign, were introduced in 1929. Condition is important; if this example had not been faded, the value would have been higher. *1930s, 33cm (13in) wide.*

**£50–60**

◄ **A free sample cup.** An enormous number were made so they remain more common than other pieces. Although this example is more than 50 years old, it is still affordable. *1950s, 7cm (2¾in) high.*

**£5–10**

◀ **A tray** made for the Mexican market. Although trays showing smiling ladies are relatively common, this example features rare artwork. *1950s, 33.5cm (13¼in) high.*

**£250–300**

◀ **A card advertising Coca-Cola.** These command a premium when found in good condition, due to their fragile nature. If Santa had been cut out and assembled, this piece would have been worth a fraction of its value. *1950s, 18.5cm (7¼in) high.*

**£100–150**

▶ **A laminated card sign** made for the German market. This card's artwork is indicative of the varying styles produced for different countries. *1950s, 33cm (13in) high.*

**£250–300**

## Collectors' Tips

- Beware of fakes: tin trays, novelties, and mirrors are the most commonly faked items
- Handle as many different objects as you can to learn the feel and appearance of authentic pieces

▲ **A boxed bottle opener** of the kind that would have been fitted to dispensing machines or to a bar. The box is rare, and without it the value would be lower. *1950s–60s, 20cm (8in) wide.*

**£20–25**

▶ **A rare, restored American card advertising standee**. The model is Lupe Velez, a popular film star from the 1920s–40s, who starred in The Mexican Spitfire in 1939. Unrestored and mint-condition examples are rarer and worth more. *1930s, 52cm (20½in) high.*

**£800–1,200**

# Vintage advertising is worth tracking down for its vibrant artwork, quirky slogans, and the nostalgia that it evokes for bygone days. From tin signs to ashtrays and novelties, there is a vast wealth of small advertising treasures to collect.

Posters and tins weren't the only forms of advertising used by manufacturers during the first half of the 20th century. Packaging, catalogues, and a host of other small items helped them to establish their brands and imprint their company names on the public consciousness. Most of these promotional items were produced for a short time only, yet were familiar to many people at some point in the past. Often still inexpensive, yet rich in design and period detail, they are an ideal choice for a collection. Try focusing on a particular brand, era, or product.

## Art from the past

The artwork is a vital factor to consider when collecting advertising ephemera. Usually bold and colourful, it reflects the style of the period in its imagery and lettering. An interesting collection might show how design developed through the decades. The style can be used to date a piece. A label or sign from 1900 may have traditional motifs, while 1930s artwork may be simpler and more modern, in keeping with the Art Deco taste of the period. The artwork also gives an insight into life in the past, showing what people wore and used in their homes. Such nostalgia is important to collectors.

## Brand new

The brand name also affects an item's value, particularly if displayed in a style characteristic of that brand. Some brands changed their look over time, and collectors can trace these changes. Familiar, long-standing names, such as Oxo and Ovaltine already fetch good prices. Lesser-known brands are generally cheaper, but their vast range and often excellent artwork provides plenty of scope for collecting. Brand loyalty was vital to many manufacturers and they often used

**A Trumans plastic advertising figure, 'Brewers of Good Beer'.**
*1960s, 20cm (8in) high.*
**£40–60**

**A 'Marquise Slumber & Setting Net' card sign.**
*1930s, 32cm (12½in) high.*
**£30–35**

celebrities to promote a product. Their identity not only helps to date an object but can tell us who was famous at the time.

Advertising materials featuring celebrities are often more valuable, as they appeal equally to fans of the celebrity. Some manufacturers also used fictitious characters to personify their brand, such as the Fairy Liquid baby, or Kellogg's Frosties' 'Tony The Tiger', or their Cornflakes' cockerel: a 1960s advertising card for 'Cornflakes' can be worth around £10–15 today.

## Signs of the times

Lithographed tin and enamelled metal signs are highly collectable and were popular from the late 19th century

**A Player's embossed tin advertising sign.**
*c.1910, 39cm (15¼in)* diam.
**£300–400**

**Two tin advertising whistles for Nugget boot polish,** made in England and colour lithographed. *1920s, 4cm (1½in) high.*

**£20–25 each**

until about 1950, when plastic signs and the promotional media of TV and radio began to take over. They fetch from around £80 to more than £800. A 1920s enamelled metal sign for Craven A cigarettes can cost around £150–200, and a 1910 Player's Navy Cut tobacco sign around £350.

Counter displays, known as 'point of sale material', were a popular form of advertising in shops. Card signs, known as 'standees', were usually made of thick cardboard with a stand or hanging device on the back. They carried the brand name and were sometimes also dispensers for small items. They used similar artwork to posters, but are less expensive and can be found for around £5–100 or more, depending on the date, brand name, product, and artwork. A 1920s card sign for Dubonnet, the French aperitif, can fetch around £40–60.

Manufacturers also advertised products with counter-top objects, ranging from dispensers to novelty figurines, often based on characters used in advertising campaigns. A large 1950s counter-top Cerebos Salt tin in good condition can be worth £30–50. From the 19th century to the 1940s, many small items were sold in glazed wooden counter-top display cabinets with gilt or coloured transfers showing the objects or naming the brand. These are usually valuable, costing £100–500 upwards. A glazed oak cabinet for Waterman pens in good condition can fetch more than £200.

Look out for novelty pieces, as these add variety to a collection. Plastic models of dinners and desserts used to tempt people into a café may come into their own. Although not yet widely collected, they are kitsch, colourful, and can be found in car-boot sales or junk shops for about £3–20.

The popularity of smoking spawned many advertising ashtrays promoting cigarettes or drinks. Those produced from the 1920s–60s can be worth £30 to £50, depending on the brand and artwork. Cigarette advertising itself may soon rise in value. A Craven A advertising calendar currently fetches around £30. If you do decide to collect cigarette memorabilia, the best-known brands are the most popular because of their innovative packaging designs and constantly changing advertising campaigns.

## Cataloguing the past

Product catalogues are also popular and are useful for reference. A Dinky Toys or Meccano catalogue from the mid-1950s may fetch around £8–12. Other makers' catalogues can fetch more, especially if scarce or from the 19th century. Small promotional objects, such as tin 'clickers' and whistles given to children from the 1910s to 1930s, are generally worth £10–40. Other novelty items include rulers and games, such as dominos, which usually fetch well under £100.

**An OXO double-sided tin advertising sign.** *1930s, 33cm (13in) high.*

**£70–100**

## Top Tips

- Visit museums and study books on advertising ephemera so you can learn to recognise the genuine article and the styles of different periods.
- Examine the surface of a supposedly old item carefully. If it is too clean, has no signs of wear, and is brightly coloured, it is probably a reproduction.
- Check the paintwork on tin signs and advertising figurines to make sure that they haven't been repainted, repaired, or damaged, as this reduces value.
- Look for objects that display the brand name and known slogans or characters associated with the brand.

## BUY

*Many manufacturers produce items to commemorate landmark or historic events, as this can be an excellent opportunity for publicity. Such pieces will often interest several groups of people, causing prices to remain consistent, and perhaps to rise for some events.*

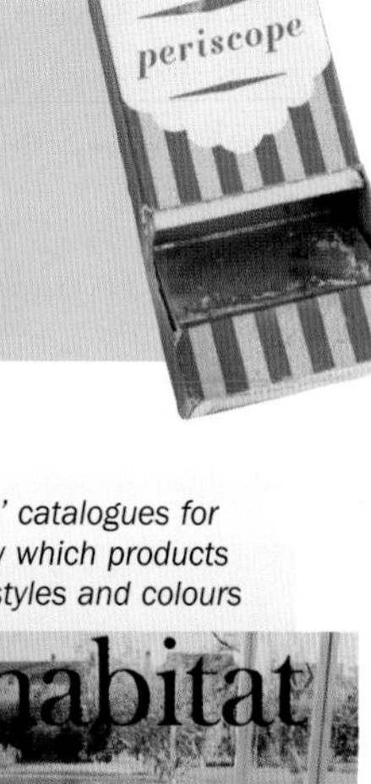


**A Hovis coronation periscope,** to commemorate Elizabeth II's coronation. This piece would interest royal-memorabilia collectors as well as those of the Hovis brand. *1953, 32cm (12½in) wide.*

**£30–40**

## KEEP

*Retailers' or manufacturers' catalogues for furniture and interiors show which products were being sold and what styles and colours they were in. This helps collectors to date items, see what was being sold to accompany their pieces, and find out what was in fashion. Catalogues from the 1950s onwards should rise in value.*

**A 1973 Habitat catalogue.** Habitat has always brought good design to the popular market, enabling people to buy stylish furniture at reasonable prices. If the 1950s and 1960s are anything to go by, the 1970s may well become the next design fad. *1973, 30cm (11¾in) high.*

**£15–20**

# Vintage posters capture the aspirations of past consumers. Their popularity is fuelled by nostalgia and, judging by the way their appeal is growing, collectors will soon be pining for the era when they were less expensive.

Notices advertising products, sales, and events have existed for centuries, but they were largely unillustrated. The modern advertising poster was born in the 1860s when the French artist Jules Chéret exploited developments in colour lithographic printing, which made the mass-production of attractive designs and eye-catching images possible for the first time. Chéret's fame grew, and his Art Nouveau designs advertising the Moulin Rouge and Folies-Bergère music halls in Paris in the 1890s are now legendary.

## All in a brand name

Progressive firms soon recognised the power of this new promotional tool to fix a brand image in the minds of consumers. Pioneering designers such as Chéret and Leonetto Cappiello were skilled in using striking artwork to convey a sales message. Cappiello's 'L'Apéritif' for Campari (1921) captures the product's appeal – a bitter-sweet slice of sophistication – by using the image of a clown inside a twist of lemon. Such posters are beyond most people's pocket, but there are plenty of others that can be found for £50–200. For example, an early 20th-century poster for Monis Cognac Champagne can be worth £150–200.

Although France led the way, other countries followed. Posters for Coca-Cola and Guinness first appeared in the 1920s. Early posters for these and other enduring brands are desirable and fetch high prices. For example, a colourful 1940s Oxo poster can fetch around £300. Although posters for many well-known brand names may be expensive as they have a strong following, a great many inexpensive examples of beautifully styled posters from all periods can still be found.

## Saving the nation

Governments were also quick to spot the potential of the poster. During World Wars I and II, posters were used extensively: for example, to recruit soldiers and to seek National Savings contributions to support the war effort. Examples can be found for £50–100 or less, but those by notable names such as Norman Wilkinson and Abram Games can fetch £200–400 or more.

**'Health and Vigour Thanks to Oxo',** by an unknown designer, published by Oxo Ltd; folds are visible. *c.1930s–40s, 153cm (60¼in) wide.*

**£250–350**

**'Convoy Your Country to Victory – Buy National Savings Certificates',** designed by Rowland Hilder and printed by J. Weiner Ltd for His Majesty's Stationery Office. *c.1940, 76cm (30in) high.*

**£150–200**

## Period details

Vintage advertising posters have both an aesthetic and a nostalgic value. Those with strong, colourful artwork tend to be the most desirable, particularly if they evoke the styles or trends of their period. A 1950s Du Maurier cigarettes poster showing an elegant woman in a foreign seaside location reflects the glamour and sophistication attached to overseas travel at a time when it was just beginning to become popular.

The typography of the poster is important too. It should complement the artwork and reflect the style of the time, such as the swirling lines of Art Nouveau or the angular, linear lettering used during the Art Deco period.

## Sizing it up

Posters can vary greatly in size. Some were made for large billboards, but smaller ones were made for shops. Larger posters are more valuable, often fetching £800–1,000 or more. They

## A closer look at... two Art Nouveau posters

The Art Nouveau period was the first 'golden age' of poster design. Examples from this era usually fetch high prices, although the overall appearance and style of a poster can be important in determining value, as this comparison shows.

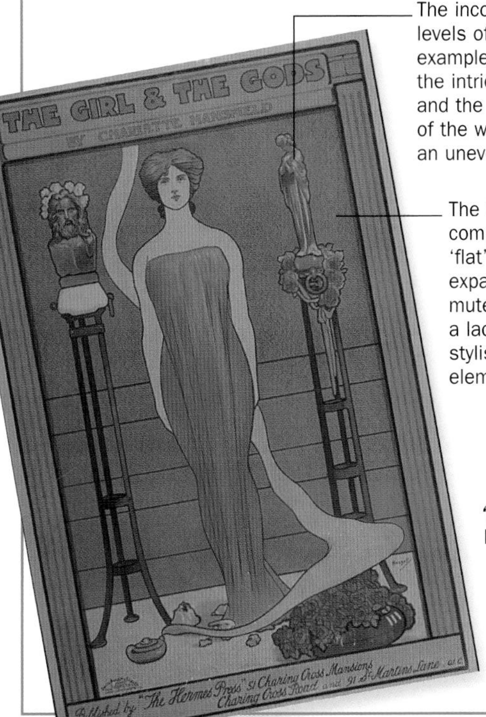


The inconsistent levels of detail (for example, between the intricate statues and the simple figure of the woman) give an uneven effect

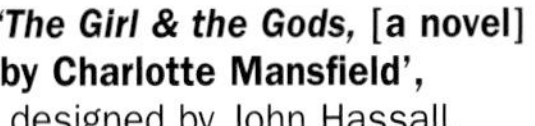

The layout is comparatively 'flat', with large expanses of plain, muted colour and a lack of typically stylish Art Nouveau elements

**'The Girl & the Gods, [a novel] by Charlotte Mansfield',** designed by John Hassall, printed by David Allen. *c.1910s, 76cm (30in) high.*

**£300–400**

The design is intricate and well composed, with strong Art Nouveau elements such as the flowing hair and clouds

The name of the brand of ink is boldly displayed in Art Nouveau-style lettering which fits onto the table – a seamless component of the design

**'Encre L. Marquet',** designed by Eugène Grasset, published by Galérie de Malherbe, Paris. *1892, 120.5cm (47½in) high.*

**£800–1,000**

usually come in two or more parts. Smaller examples – 75cm (30in) or less in height or width – can be found for £50–500. They provide an ideal opportunity to own fine pieces of period artwork that are easy to display.

### The cost of specialising

People often focus on one theme, such as automobile advertising – a potentially expensive niche. One of the most sought-after posters in this genre is 'A Votre Santé Le Pneu Michelin Boit L'Obstacle' ('Michelin tyres wish you good health by swallowing obstacles'), designed by Marius Rossillon in 1898. It can fetch £10,000–15,000, mainly because it marks the debut of the Michelin Man. Posters that have local interest are also worth looking out for, as are those with temporary appeal, such as posters advertising a product with a limited run, or those publicising key one-off events.

While some enthusiasts look for brand-name posters, which command top prices, others choose named artists, such as those known for Art Nouveau or Art Deco styles, including fine artists such as Chéret or Alphonse Mucha. These, too, can be expensive, often fetching thousands of pounds.

### Lucky finds

The best places to look for vintage posters are general house clearance auctions and provincial auction houses, where the audience may not be experts in this area. Richer, but usually more expensive, sources include collectors' fairs and specialised advertising memorabilia and poster dealers. Prices at general auctions tend to start at £50. A good way to start a collection is to buy 'group lots' of posters, rather than individual items. Those found will probably be rolled up or more often folded. Open them with care to check for damage.

### All aboard

Rail and London Underground posters are a popular collecting area. The 1920s and 30s are often seen as the halcyon days of British train travel:

**'Du Maurier: The Most Widely Smoked Filter Cigarette in the World'.** *c.1950s, 76cm (30in) high.*

**£100–150**

rail posters from this period are particularly sought after. But the supply of well-preserved examples is drying up, so prices are rocketing. A 1930s poster by Fortunino Matania for the London Midland & Scottish Railway Company (LMS) called 'Southport, for a Holiday in Wintertime', showing a scene of smartly dressed patrons outside a theatre, might have fetched £300–500 in 1990; today it is probably worth up to 10 times that amount.

## The new day-tripper

The railways, and in particular the London Underground, were among the first organisations in Britain to recognise posters as an art form. In 1907 London Transport began a poster campaign illustrating locations that could be reached by tube. Regional railway companies picked up on the concept and encouraged people to take day trips to the seaside or to the country. Eye-catching and brightly coloured images of calming activities – golf, fishing, relaxing on the beach – in beautiful scenery were designed to appeal to tired city workers in need of a break.

## A closer look at... a Cassandre travel poster

When collecting posters, always consider the artist. The work of the most renowned can fetch high prices. Most artists worked in a particular style and those that are highly representative of a period will always be popular. Using the pseudonym 'Cassandre', Adolphe Mouron is one of the most respected poster artists of the 20th century, with much of his work in the Art Deco style.

The image of the train steaming across Europe is immensely powerful, and strongly suggests speed

The clear shapes, exaggerated perspective, and restrained use of colour are typical of Cassandre's work

**'Nord Express',** designed by Cassandre, printed by Hachard & Cie, Paris. It is mounted on Japanese paper; there is a repaired tear at the top margin and slight fading. In near mint conditon, this poster can make £20,000. *1927, 105cm (41¼in) high.*

**£8,000–12,000**

## Iconic images

London Transport often commissioned posters by high-profile avant-garde artists, such as Edward McKnight Kauffer, Horace Taylor, and Man Ray. Prices for McKnight Kauffer's posters start at about £800, although some experts consider them undervalued.

Of the regional railway company posters, many of the best were produced for London and North Eastern Railway (LNER), Great Western Railway (GWR), London Midland & Scottish Railway (LMS), and Southern Railway (SR). These come in two standard sizes: 102 x 64cm (40 x 25in), in portrait format, and 102 x 127cm (40 x 50in), in landscape format. Look out for examples by known artists such as Frank Mason and Charles Shepherd (who signed his work 'Shep'), as they tend to be among the most eye-catching.

Many of the works by the leading artists are already in collections or change hands for thousands of pounds, but there are plenty of other striking posters to choose from for between £100 and £500. Invest in those that show styles of the period, and those that you find appealing: if you like them, other collectors probably will too. Look for bright, fresh colours and evocative depictions of popular resorts. Many of the more affordable posters were produced for lesser-known and smaller railway lines. They are usually in portrait format and slightly smaller than the larger, more valuable versions produced for renowned railways such as the GWR.

**'Victoria Line: Cut Travelling Time',** designed by Tom Eckersley of Eckersley Studio and published by London Transport; in mint condition. *c.1968, 101.5cm (40in) high.*

**£800–1,000**

## Changing tastes

Rail posters from the 1950s are likely to become more sought after, given the growth in interest in this decade. These can be found for £100–800 or more, depending on the artwork, designer, and company. A good

**'Dolgoch Station on the Talyllyn Railway'**, designed by Terence Cuneo, printed by Waterlow, and published by the Talyllyn Railway. *c.1930s, 102cm (40¼in) high.*

**£600–700**

example is works by Abram Games (designer of the Festival of Britain logo), which have a strong design and may well rise in value. Designs from the 1950s that fetch high prices today include Alan Durman's 'Bognor Regis' poster (1955), in which a woman in a yellow bathing costume holds a beach ball; and Jack Merriott's 'Newquay' poster (1954), showing a girl surfing through breaking waves.

## Cruising in luxury

The romance associated with foreign travel began in the early 20th century with luxury cruise liners such as the *Mauretania*, the *Olympic*, the ill-fated *Titanic*, and the *Normandie*. Posters that show the ships themselves are popular, especially if they feature period design – most notably the Art Deco style. Perhaps the most famous example is the 1935 poster for the *Normandie* by Adolphe Mouron ('Cassandre'). Using his typical bold colours, simple lines, and clean design with large, flat forms, he depicts the mighty ship powering through the sea. Although this poster can fetch £5,000–10,000, its design and stylistic hallmarks are worth bearing in mind when looking at other examples. Less expensive liner and ship posters can be found by lesser-known artists. For example, a stylised Nelson Steam Navigation Company poster from the 1930s depicting a line-up of ships, perhaps imitating Cassandre, can fetch around £600.

Brand names also count. Partly owing to the immense public interest in the *Titanic*, owned by the White Star Line, prices for their posters will generally be high, as will those for other giants such as P&O and Cunard, particularly if the artwork is note-worthy. But such was the popularity of travel by liner that many other companies operated overseas. These smaller lines offer a more accessible option, with prices often ranging between £150 and £500.

## Journey's end

Part of the attraction of ocean travel was the exotic destination. Look for alluring images of foreign destinations. Colours are usually bright and saturated, calling people away from

### Did You Know?

*The highest price at auction in the United Kingdom for a travel poster is still the £26,400 paid at Christie's in May 1994 for a poster by Man Ray for London Transport entitled 'Keeps London Going' from 1939. A renowned photographer and artist, Man Ray was deeply involved in Surrealism – the 1930s artistic movement which took its inspiration from the bizarre world of dreams. His poster plays on the similarity of the London Transport logo to a ringed planet, such as Saturn.*

grey, rainy Britain. These posters can be found from around £150. For example, a Blue Star Line poster for Mediterranean cruises showing a North African view with a man riding a camel amid Moorish buildings can fetch around £200.

## The end of an era

Later posters for liners in the 1950s and 60s, when sea travel began to fall out of fashion, are often less valuable than those from the 1920s and 30s and can fetch £50–250 or more for known brand names, those by notable designers, or those with superb designs in period styles. As the best posters become too expensive for most collectors, these later posters may make a good investment.

## Plane sailing

Air travel offered a swifter alternative to journeys by sea. The slogan, 'Africa in days instead of weeks', on an Imperial Airways poster of 1937 neatly makes this point. Until Pan American (Pan Am) and Imperial Airways had planes with the range to make the trip across the Atlantic, flying boats provided the competition for liners. This was perhaps the most glamorous way to travel from Southampton to New York. An Imperial Airways poster from the 1930s shows a passenger reclining in comfort attended by a waiter carrying cocktails on a tray. Many of these 1930s posters can be valuable, fetching £200–600 or more, as they often have striking Art Deco artwork. As before, those by lesser-known or unidentified designers generally fetch less.

## Come fly with me

After World War II, passengers grew to expect the convenience of a plane flying from a nearby airport. In the 1950s, foreign holidays by air

**'Blue Star Line: Mediterranean Cruises'**, designed by Maurice Randall and printed by Philip Reid, London; there are small areas missing and folds. *c.1920s, 102cm (40¼in) wide.*

**£500–700**

## Some airline posters to look for:

▪ Air France ▪ British European Airways ▪ BOAC ▪

**'Air France: Flying Holidays this Year!'.** Air France posters are highly sought after. *1930s, 100cm (39¼in) high.*

**£1,000–1,500**

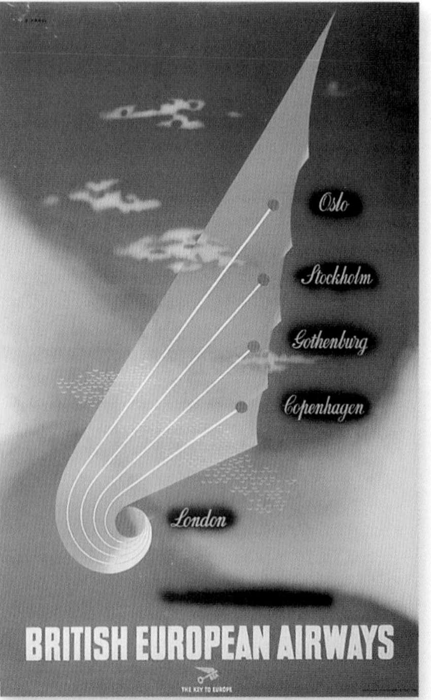


**'British European Airways: The Key to Europe'.** Notable designers, such as Abram Games, are in great demand. *1946, 101cm (39¾in) high.*

**£500–600**

**'BOAC: It's a Small World by Speedbird'.** Bold, recognisable logos, such as this one for BOAC, are likely to appeal. *c.1947, 99cm (39in) high.*

**£200–300**

became cheaper and services expanded. Planes became less luxurious and emphasis was placed on speed. Posters with images of speeding planes are desirable, and many have their stylistic origins in the 1930s, with clean lines, flat areas of bold colour, and angular shapes. Those showing a multitude of foreign destinations, all conveniently served by the featured airline, are popular. If by a leading designer such as Abram Games, they are usually valuable and can fetch £200–600 or more.

Posters for well-known airlines such as Pan Am, British Overseas Airways Corporation (BOAC), and Air France have loyal followings and can fetch £500–1,000 or more. Less expensive posters in the style of the period can sometimes be found.

## Supersonic luxury

Concorde represented the ultimate in luxury travel, and poster prices are probably yet to reach their peak. The withdrawal of Concorde from service in 2003 may cause values to rise. A Concorde poster from 1977 (the year in which the plane first took paying passengers) can fetch £30–50. As Concorde was operated by only two airlines, Air France and British Airways, examples are rare compared to posters for the more widespread Boeing 747, for example, and could prove to be a wise investment.

### Top Tips

- Store posters flat between sheets of acid-free tissue. Never roll them, as you can crease and crack the poster.
- Make sure your hands are clean before touching a poster; keep handling to a minimum.
- Avoid posters that are extensively faded or damaged, especially if a tear extends into the image.
- Frame your poster using acid-free museum mounts and hang it away from direct light and heat to protect its colours from fading.
- Do not undertake conservation work yourself – this is a job for an expert.
- Learn to spot a reproduction: the image will be made up of pixels (dots) and the paper will often be glossier and thicker than on an original.



**BUY**

*Posters with striking graphics and that adhere to period style and design are likely to have lasting appeal and should rise in value.*

**'International Industries Fair Brussels 1939',** by an anonymous designer, printed by Créations Brussels. The strong colours, clean lines, and integration of lettering into the artwork are typical of the late 1930s and make this poster collectable; there are a few tears and folds. *1939, 101cm (40¼in) wide.*

**£150–200**

**KEEP**

*Bright colours, an attractive design, and an idyllic evocation of sea bathing are the marks of a good poster by a notable artist. These factors should mean that such a poster will at least hold its value, if not increase.*

**'Weston-super-Mare',** designed by Tom Purvis, printed by Jordison, and published by Railway Executive. The charming scene of the mother and child add to the appeal of this poster. *1949, 102cm (40¼in) high.*

**£800–1,000**

**KEEP**

*Hold on to airline posters from the the 1950s: the age of expansion for air travel. Posters with strong period-style artwork, by notable artists, for a well-known airline are most likely to retain their value, and may even appreciate.*

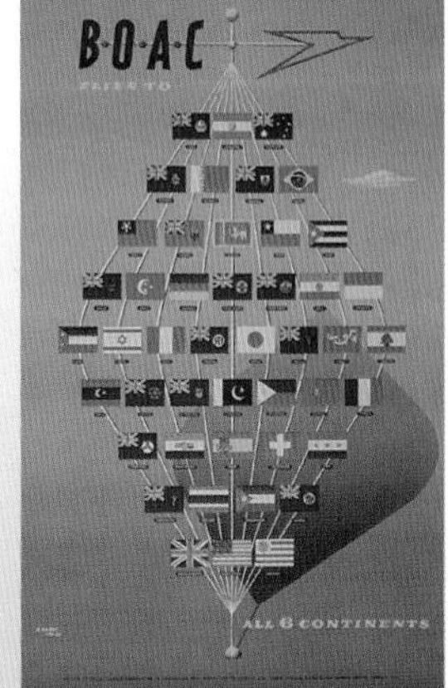


**'BOAC Flies to all 6 Continents',** designed by Abram Games and printed by Baynard. BOAC (forerunner of British Airways) is a popular name and the strong design of this poster makes it desirable. *1953, 101cm (39¾in) high.*

**£500–600**

**KEEP**

*Well-known brand names are popular, especially if combined with a familiar theme or character. Attractive, brightly coloured imagery adds to the appeal of a poster.*

**'Give 'em all Kodaks',** designed by John Hassall and printed by Menpes Ltd, London. The Christmas theme makes it desirable. *c.1920s, 76cm (30in) high.*

**£500–800**

**SELL**

*Travel posters showing less popular destinations, such as Guildford, are not as sought after as those for coastal resorts or beautiful areas of countryside, especially if the artist is not one of the most notable.*

**'Guildford',** by Walter Spradbery and published by Southern Railway, shows Abbot's Hospital, in Guildford. Sell to someone with connections to the town who will appreciate its historic relevance. *1931, 101cm (39¾in) high.*

**£100–150**

**SELL**

*Most posters were stored folded, leaving fold marks and creases. Tears that affect the image are more serious and lower value. Unless extremely rare, these posters are unlikely to rise in price.*

**'Messageries Maritimes',** by an anonymous designer. This poster is by an unknown artist, and is missing a substantial area at the bottom of the poster, which cannot be repaired. *c.1920s, 102cm (40¼in) high.*

**£25–35**

LIFT HAND-MICRO & LISTEN FOR
DIAL TONE
HORNCHURCH
BEFORE DIALLING.
TELECON

# Technology and Travel

From the first radios to TVs, early calculators to sophisticated personal organisers, the romance of early cruise liners to the speed of Concorde, no century has seen so much technological change. Objects representing each of these advances are available to own.

Cylinder music box, p.334

Horn gramophone, p.334

Bakelite radio p.336

# The changing face........

**No one would have thought in 1900 that cars would come to dominate our roads, that leisure time would be centred on the TV, or that it would be possible to travel faster than the speed of sound. Objects that reflect technological change can be surprisingly valuable.**

Up until about 1900, clockwork or wind-up music boxes (1) and wind-up gramophones (2) were the only way in which people could enjoy recorded music. Thirty years later human voices were being transmitted to radio receivers in homes across the country. Early gramophones, with their distinctive horns, are popular as decorative items, but beware of modern reproductions.

## On the radio

Radiograms – large wooden-cased radios – are not particularly valuable today, although many people like them as interesting period pieces of furniture. Radios from the 1920s (3) to the 50s are much more popular, particularly those with colourful Bakelite or shaped cases.

The first televisions appeared in 1936. Sets from the 1930s and 40s are rare, so many enthusiasts prefer to look out for sets from the 1960s and 70s. Examples such as the JVC Videosphere (4) are truly space age in design.

Royal Bar-Lock typewriter, p.340

BBC Micro computer, p.340

Motorola mobile phone, p.346

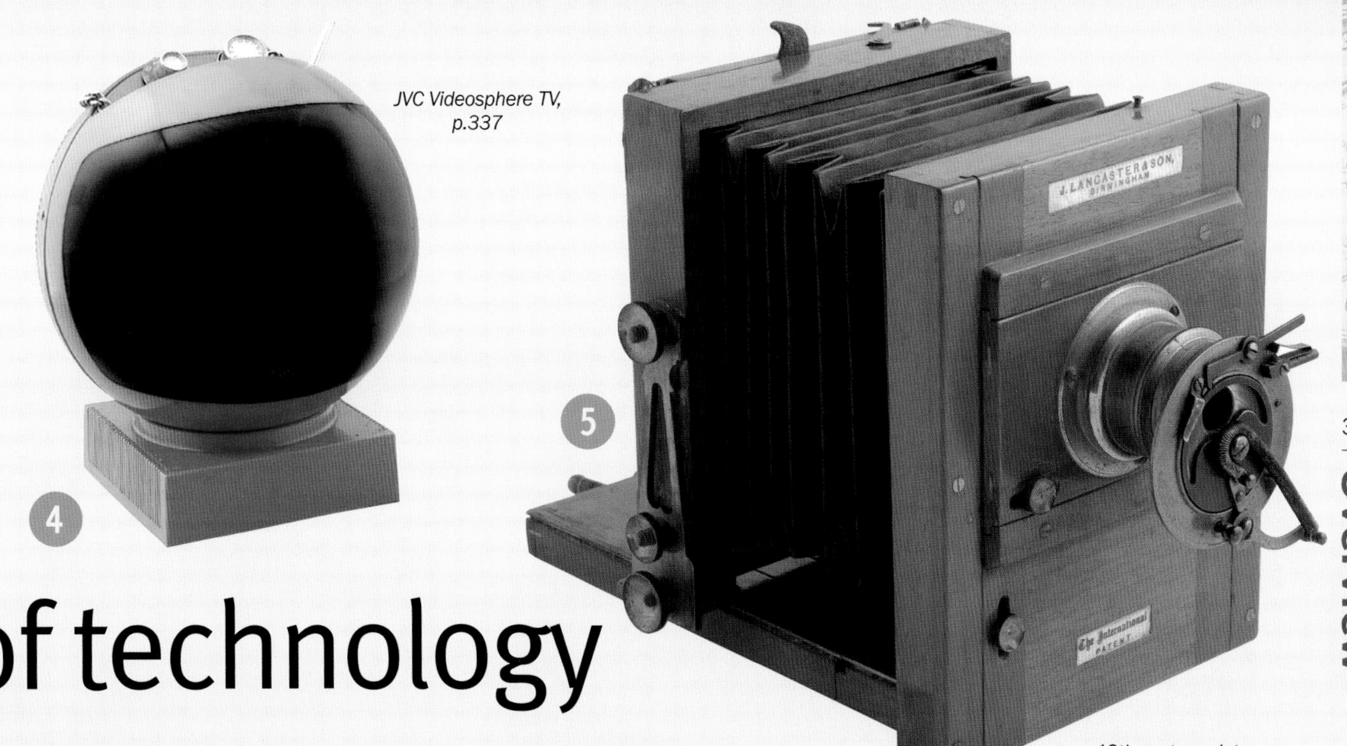

JVC Videosphere TV, p.337

4

5

19th-century plate camera, p.339

# ...of technology

## Snap shot

From early plate cameras (5), with their brass bound wood cases and bellows, to the first Leicas and the Kodak Box Brownie, there are plenty of cameras to look out for. High quality Leicas are especially popular as so many different types were made. The opposite is the case with the Box Brownie – mass production has meant that values are low for vintage examples.

The typewriter (6) revolutionised office life in the early 20th century. At first, people thought that computers (7) would only ever be used in offices, but by the late 1970s the first home computers were being made. Both vintage typewriters and early computers are collected today as people are fascinated by how they have changed over the years.

## On call

Another area where technology has leaped ahead is mobile phones (8). Early models are becoming sought after as the mobile has now become such an intrinsic part of our daily life.

Travel has moved on from steam trains, cruise liners, and erratic early cars to the supersonic flights of Concorde and beyond. Memorabilia from all these modes of transport is highly desirable today, including car mascots (9), railway signs (10), and *Titanic* memorabilia (11). If you were lucky enough to fly on Concorde it's worth keeping any souvenirs as they are likely to rise in value in future.

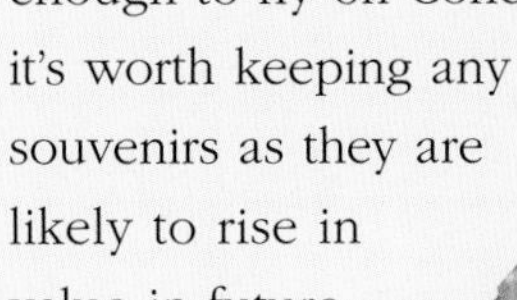

*Titanic* picture, p.352

11

9

Rolls-Royce car mascot, p.350

10

Railway warning sign, p.348

# Mechanical music

From delicately crafted Victorian musical boxes to the portable record players of the 1960s, music machines have captured people's imagination and played an important role in home entertainment.

The first cylinder musical boxes date from about 1810. Most of them were made in Switzerland and have a clockwork mechanism which turns the cylinder. Boxes with longer cylinders play more notes, so are sought after.

## Striking tunes

A cylinder music box plays six to 12 tunes, often displayed on a song sheet inside the lid. Large and early boxes and those by well-known makers such as Nicole Frères, Paillard, and B.A. Bremond often fetch £1,000–4,000 or more. Boxes with features such as bells and drums, miniature wind organs, or automated figures are also desirable. Smaller 19th-century boxes, unmarked or by less-known makers, usually fetch from £400 to £1,000.

Prices for musical boxes have remained fairly constant and have even risen a little. Specialist dealers or auction houses are the best places to start looking. Before buying, check that the tune is clear and regular and examine the steel comb for missing or replaced teeth.

The revolving-disc musical box came about in the 1880s. Current value depends on the maker and the size of disc. Smaller tabletop 'Polyphon' boxes, of about 1900, can fetch around £200–700. Large, decoratively carved examples, often coin-operated, can fetch £2,000–5,000 or more.

## From cylinder to disc

In the late 1870s, Thomas Edison developed the phonograph, which

**An Apollo tabletop horn gramophone** in a mahogany case. It is fitted with an Apollo 'Grand Prix Milan 1906' sound box and mahogany horn. *1920s, 35.5cm (14in) wide.*

**£600–800**

## A closer look at... a mechanical music box

Always inspect the mechanism and the case when buying a cylinder mechanical music box. Extra features, makers' names, and a decorative box that is in its original condition are always more desirable.

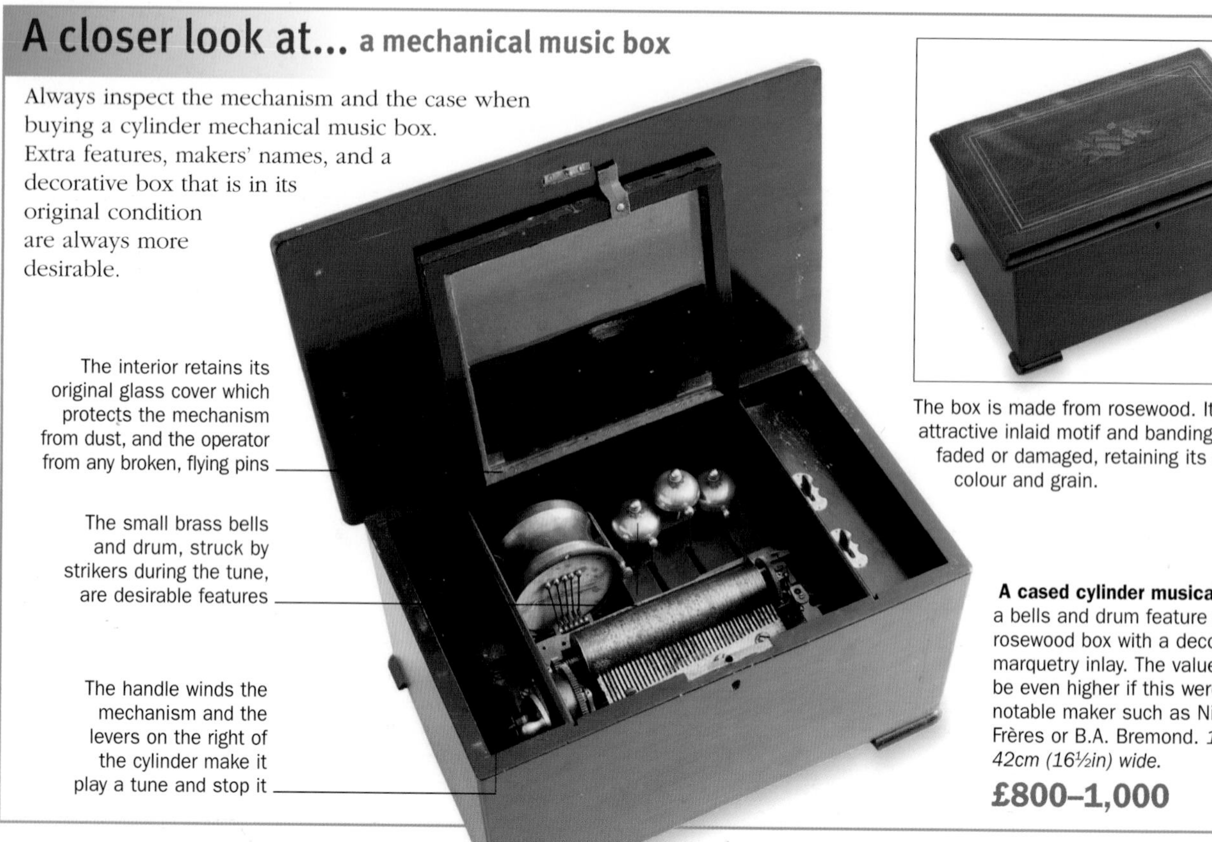


The box is made from rosewood. It has an attractive inlaid motif and banding and is not faded or damaged, retaining its appealing colour and grain.

**A cased cylinder musical box,** with a bells and drum feature and a rosewood box with a decorative marquetry inlay. The value would be even higher if this were by a notable maker such as Nicole Frères or B.A. Bremond. *1880s, 42cm (16½in) wide.*

**£800–1,000**

could both record and play sound. Small phonographs such as the Edison Gem are usually worth £200–400, or more for large or early examples.

## Sound the horn

Developed in 1887 by Emile Berliner, the gramophone was the precursor of the record player and became popular around the turn of the century. Tabletop gramophones with large horns made from brass, wood, or decorated tin by HMV, Victor, Columbia, or the Gramophone Company are the most sought after. Values start at £300–500 and rise to more than £3,000–£5,000.

Large cabinet-style gramophones with internal horns, dating from the 1910s–30s, are more common and less popular than the tabletop versions with external horns; they usually fetch £150–500. Smaller tabletop examples with internal horns are similarly valued. Small portable gramophones from the 1930s, which resemble small suitcases when closed, are also less expensive. They can fetch £70–200, especially if in an unusual or coloured case and by a noted maker such as HMV. There are even smaller portable examples: the Swiss Mikiphone of the 1920s–30s folds up into a pocket watch-shaped case that only measures 12.5cm (5in) in diameter and can fetch £300–500. Others, which look like the slim Kodak folding cameras of the 1920s and 30s, can fetch £80–250.

Radiograms from the 1930s–50s are a combination radio-and-record player set into a sideboard-style cabinet. Their size has limited their appeal, so values remain under £100–200.

## Portable pop

One of the most commonly owned machines during the 1950s was the colourful Dansette record player. Developed by Samuel Margolin and released around 1952, it revolutionised the way people listened to music, mainly because it was electric, portable, and had an internal speaker.

With the new rock'n'roll and pop singles of the era, the Dansette was a must-have for teenagers and although it was relatively expensive – it was often bought on hire purchase – over a million were sold between the 1950s and the 1970s. Current prices vary from £50 to 200 or more, depending on the model and its condition. Red and blue were the most popular colours, and legs were available to create a free-standing version.

**An Italian 'Penny' 45rpm 'handbag' record player.** *1970s, 20cm (8in) wide.*

**£60–100**

### Top Tips

- Look for key-wound music boxes of the mid- to late 19th century, and those with interchangeable cylinders; they are usually extremely valuable.
- Never try to wind up a cylinder music box without asking; mechanisms are often jammed and damage is costly.
- Don't stop a cylinder music box halfway through a tune as this places undue stress on the pins and teeth.
- Watch out for fake gramophones. They often have dark HMV transfers, yellow brass horns, and poorly carved cases.

### BUY

*Gramophones made for children are highly collectable. Look for those in tinplate, preferably by notable makers, that still have their transfer-applied decoration and are in working order. These should retain their value.*

**A children's tinplate 'Pigmyphone' by Gebrüder Bing of Nuremberg.** *c.1930, 25cm (9in) wide.*

**£100–200**

### KEEP

*Portable record players provide an accessible way to listen to period music. Although they are common and usually inexpensive, those with decorative cases in excellent condition make a good investment.*

**A Decca wind-up children's portable record player,** decorated with nursery rhyme scenes based on Dora Roderick's illustrations. *c.1951, 34.5cm (12¾in) wide.*

**£120–180**

# Radios and TVs are reminders of an era when families sat together to enjoy their favourite programmes. Their attractive cases and the immense variety available makes them highly collectable today – even if not in working order.

**A Bush mottled-brown Bakelite DAC90 radio.** *1940s–50s, 24cm (9½in) high.*

**£30–40**

The phenomenon of radio began to take hold after 1910. Valve radio receivers were expensive, so many enthusiasts built their own more affordable 'crystal sets' to pick up radio waves. A 1923 Marconiphone V2A valve radio receiver can fetch around £500–800 or more, but a more common, home-made crystal set often sells for less than £20–50. Finer-made crystal sets, by noted makers such as Ericsson, can cost about £300–400.

## Fine tuning

During the 1920s and 30s, radios became simpler to use and more affordable. The 'superhet' (Supersonic Heterodyne) was introduced in the mid-1920s, enabling the user to tune the radio by turning a knob.

In the 1930s, Bakelite and Catalin, plastics that were simple to produce and less costly than other materials, were used to make radios. Those in bright colours (like yellow or blue) such as a FADA 'Bullet' or Emerson 'Tombstone' can fetch £500–800 or more. Brown and black Bakelite radios, made in large numbers, can be inexpensive – many models cost around £20–100 and often no more than £200–400 for more desirable ones.

Look out for radios with the clean lines associated with the Art Deco period, from the 1930s and late 40s. Radios produced in the 1950s in a modified Art Deco style are popular. Stylish wooden radios of the period are also desirable. The Phillips 'SuperInductance' range, made from plastic-laminated boards that resemble rosewood, can often be found for around £300–600.

## Exceptional finds

The 'round' EKCO radio was designed by Wells Coates for the E.K. Cole Company (hence the name EKCO) in the 1930s. Today its archetypal Art Deco form is considered a style classic. It was produced in a range of designs mostly in brown, mottled brown, or black Bakelite. The stunning AD65 of 1934 featured an illuminated semicircular tuning window, and provided superb sound quality and accurate tuning. These radios can cost about £700–1,000 or more. Brighter colours, such as green, can command up to £10,000. Also look for other EKCO models, such as the M23.

One of the most commonly found radios is the boxy Bush DAC90 of the 1950s, with its circular speaker grille; it may sell for around £50–80. Other makers to look out for include Tesla,

## Some radios to look for:

■ EKCO ■ K.B. ■ Panasonic ■ Tomy ■

**A brown Bakelite EKCO A22.** The A22 combined form and function – it has a circular Perspex dial and a travelling cursor that moves as you tune it to the required station. *c.1945, 37cm (14½in) high.*

**£500–800**

**A Kolster Brandes FB10.** This K.B. 'Toaster' radio ca in a range of colours, both solid (taking its colour fro the plastic, as above) and spray-painted, which is usu less valuable. *c.1955, 30.5cm (12in) wide.*

**£70–100**

Philco, and Cossor. Radios by these makers can often be found for up to £150.

## Set styles

The first domestic, wooden-cased TV sets appeared in 1936. These pre-war sets are rare and can command high prices (as much as £5,000 or more). By 1948, about 50,000 sets were in use, both floor-standing and tabletop models. Pye tabletop TVs with brown Bakelite casings are common. The TV62 model from the 1950s can fetch £100–150 if the case is undamaged.

TV sets from the 1960s and 70s can cost from £50–200 for portable models to £300–800 or more for larger, floor-standing types. Look out for sets that represent technological advances, such as the first portable TV, or those with strong design elements.

## 'Futuristic' TVs

The JVC Videosphere or 'Sputnik' set from the late 1960s, was shaped like a space helmet and could be suspended from the ceiling. Some sets had a radio and alarm clock in the base, too, although these models are less common. Values range from about £200 to £500.

The larger floor-standing 'Keracolour' TV from around 1970, shaped like a globe on a tapered circular plinth, is desirable. The starkly modern black, white, or orange versions can sell for around £500–700, with the rarer 'teak' finish being even more costly.

**An orange JVC Videosphere TV.** *1970s, 33cm (13in) high.*

**£400–500**

**A Panasonic 'Tootaloop' R-72 bangle radio.** When closed, this radio could be worn around the wrist. Design classics like this are always popular. *1970s, closed 15cm (6in) diam.*

**£50–80**

**A Japanese Tomy 'Mr DJ' Robot radio.** The trend for robot toys in the 1980s was dominated by Tomy. These radios are now highly sought after. *1980s, 18cm (7in) high.*

**£50–80**

## Top Tips

- Consult a specialist before you decide to restore a valve radio.
- Ask an electrician to inspect vintage radios or TVs before plugging them in.
- Look for a radio with its original speaker cloth; make sure that it isn't torn – replacements can be too bright.
- Chips and cracks on Bakelite radios lower value, so run your finger over the surface to feel for imperfections.
- Consider collecting transistors – they are inexpensive and need less space.

## BUY

*Sinclair's electrical products were often groundbreaking. Many pieces can still be found for less than £100, but they may appreciate as interest grows and recognition of their importance increases.*

**A Sinclair flat-screen black-and-white pocket TV.** The second of its portable TVs, this one was much smaller than the first and truly portable. *c.1981, 14cm (5½in) wide.*

**£55–65**

## KEEP

*Transistor radios, introduced in the late 1950s, are growing in popularity. Early Japanese models can be rare. Good condition is vital, especially for later models. If they were innovative designs of their time, they should hold their value or appreciate.*

**A National Panasonic 'PanaPet' R-70 radio.** The 'Panapet' was one of the most popular transistor radios of the 1970s. Without its original box the value would be at least halved. *1970s, box 14cm (5½in) high.*

**£70–100**

# Cameras have come a long way since the first unwieldy wet-plate models of the 19th century. From Brownies to SLRs, and from Instamatics to spy cameras, the changing technology can make for a fascinating collection.



The first photograph was taken in 1826 by a Frenchman, Joseph Niépce, and the photographic plate was invented 12 years later by Louis Daguerre. In 1880 George Eastman set up the 'Eastman Dry Plate Company', later renamed Kodak, and its full developing and printing service first brought photography to a wide market. Kodak produced the Brownie camera between 1900 and 1930, but so many were made that they are not worth much today.

That's not the case with the Leica camera. Produced in Germany since 1925, it was one of the first really practical, compact 35mm film cameras. Some Leicas are now worth £3,000 or more, so inspect any engraving and the serial number on the top, as it can be used to help date the camera.

Generally, though, many vintage cameras are affordable. A 1930s folding camera can be bought for just £15–20, and late 19th-century mahogany and brass cameras can fetch from £100 to £350, so check out specialist camera fairs as well as all the usual places, such as car-boot sales, provincial auctions, and junk shops.

At present, the market for modern cameras such as digital and disposable models is small, but they may prove to be a worthwhile investment in time.

▲ **A Franke & Heidecke Rolleiflex 2.8f,** in working order. Twin reflex cameras such as this example allowed the photographer to look at the image through one lens, while the second lens took the picture. Classic Rolleiflexes are highly collectable. *1950s, 17.5cm (7in) high.*

**£150–200**

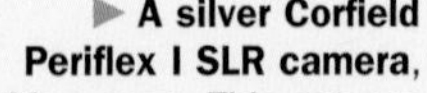

► **A brown Bakelite Coronet 'Midget' subminiature camera,** with case. This camera came in five colours including brown, mottled green, and blue. Bright colours fetch higher prices than the black or brown versions. *c.1936, 7.5cm (3in) high.*

**£70–100**

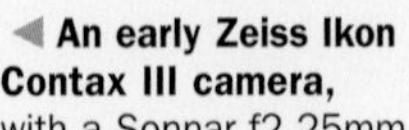

► **A silver Corfield Periflex I SLR camera,** with a case. This camera has a moveable periscope, which allows the user to examine a shot for fine focus before pressing the shutter. *1955, 16.5cm (6½in) long.*

**£120–180**

◄ **An early Zeiss Ikon Contax III camera,** with a Sonnar f2 25mm lens. The Contax was a sophisticated camera and used fine quality Zeiss lenses and optical equipment. *c.1936, 17.5cm (6¾in).*

**£200–250**

◄ **A Leica IIIa, with a Summar f2 50mm lens and case.** Although one of the more common Leicas, it is in excellent condition – a real plus to collectors. *1939, 16.5cm (6½in) long.*

**£300–400**

◀ **A Bakelite Kodak Baby Box Brownie camera,** with box. A huge number of Brownies was produced for the young and those who wanted to take inexpensive photos. This one is worth more because it has its original box. *c.1935, 11.5cm (4½in) high.*

**£15–20**

◀ **A Kodak Disc 4000,** in near mint condition and boxed. Disc- format cameras came to the fore in the mid-1980s, spurred on by this, Kodak's first model. It was not successful and the format did not last, making it scarce and desirable today. Potentially, a good investment. *c.1985, 10cm (4in) wide.*

**£15–20**

## Collectors' Tips

- Look for accessories, such as extra lenses, carrying cases and light meters, as they add value to a camera
- Examine a Leica for military markings for the British or German armies or air forces, as these are desirable
- Seek out cameras with their original packaging and instruction booklets

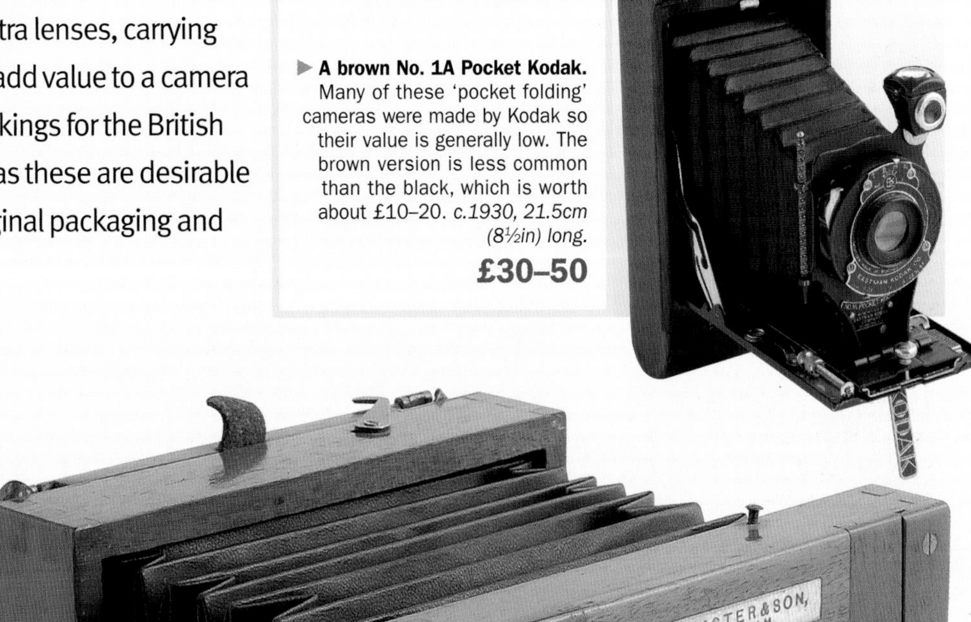


▶ **A brown No. 1A Pocket Kodak.** Many of these 'pocket folding' cameras were made by Kodak so their value is generally low. The brown version is less common than the black, which is worth about £10–20. *c.1930, 21.5cm (8½in) long.*

**£30–50**

▼ **A Russian spy camera,** disguised as a packet of John Player cigarettes. It has a metal body with a box and a Russian-language information sheet. Hidden or disguised cameras – often called 'detective cameras' – can command high prices. *1970s, 12cm (4¾in) high.*

**£200–300**

▶ **A 19th-century mahogany Lancaster International** quarter plate camera, with rare blue bellows and a rotary shutter. Folding dry-plate cameras often come in leather cases, with many different accessories. *c.1880.*

**£300–400**

# Typewriters and computers

can be good investments. Typewriters are attractive, well-engineered pieces of machinery. Many early mass-produced computers (and calculators) have achieved cult status and are still inexpensive.

**A Royal Bar-Lock typewriter,** mounted on the original box base and with the original wooden hood (not shown). *c.1902, 40.5cm (16in) wide.*

**£150–200**

In the 1870s the first commercially available typewriters in the USA used an 'understroke' method, whereby type bars were struck upwards onto the ribbon and paper. Early 1880s typewriters by Remington, Caligraph, and Smith Premier can cost about £80. Other firms also made understroke machines until about 1915, and these can be found for around £30–40.

The single-element typewriter, with characters on a single drum or ball that rotated when a key was pressed, was also made in the late 19th century. Machines by Hammond can be picked up for around £50, but early models may cost more – an 1893 Hammond No.12 can be worth about £280–320.

The standard front-stroke typewriter, with type bars that swing forward onto a roller, was first mass-produced by Underwood in 1895. Underwoods from the early 20th century often fetch well under £50, but the first models (which carry a label that reads 'Wagner Typewriter Co.') usually cost at least £100. Other firms include Franklin, Corona, and Oliver, but aside from their earliest models, such large numbers were made that many can be bought for as little as around £10–30.

## Portables and electrics

Generally, post-World War II manual typewriters are worth very little (£15–20). However, portables, which were made from the 1920s onwards, may rise in value, especially those in pristine condition with carry cases. Examples from companies such as Corona, Remington, Hermes, and Olympia are worth seeking out. Rare models such as a 1925 German Urania-Piccola with Gothic type can cost about £200.

Blickensderfer made the first electric typewriter in 1902 (now extremely rare), but it wasn't until about 20 years later that electric typewriters became widely available. Expect to pay around £20–30 for an early model. In 1961 IBM released the Selectric, with a rotating 'golfball'-type element that contained the machine's characters. An original

## Some early computers to look for:

- BBC Micro
- Sinclair Spectrum ZX

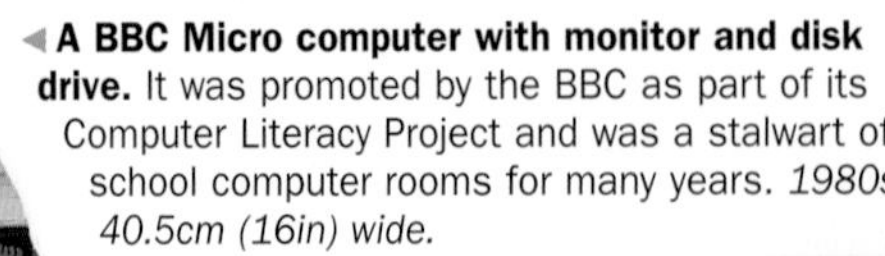

◀ **A BBC Micro computer with monitor and disk drive.** It was promoted by the BBC as part of its Computer Literacy Project and was a stalwart of school computer rooms for many years. *1980s, 40.5cm (16in) wide.*

**£30–50**

▶ **A Sinclair Spectrum 48K ZX personal computer** in its original carrying case. This was one of the first affordable home computers. The rare 16K version often fetches more than the 48K, and sets including accessories such as cables, power pack, manual, and carrying case also attract a premium. *1982–88, 21.5cm (8½in) wide.*

**£100–150**

Selectric I can be bought for about £20, but examples are becoming harder to find, and values may rise.

## The whole spectrum

Personal computers entered the market in the late 1970s, and rare machines from IBM and Apple can command high prices if in mint condition. Only 200 of Apple's first model – the Apple I – were made, and these can be worth £30,000. Computers from the 1980s by makers such as Amstrad can be found for about £100–300 or less. Look out for Sinclair's ZX81 and Spectrum, both of which can be worth about £30–80; Atari's 1040, which can cost £70–90, and 800XL, worth up to about £50–80; and the Commodore C64, which sell for around £20–30.

In the late 1990s, computer design moved away from the traditional 'grey box' look. Apple's Imac, launched in 1998 and featuring a range of brightly coloured translucent plastic casings, was a huge hit, although it is too early to say how it will fare as a collectable.

## To sum up

Calculating machines first appeared in the 19th century. One notable manual calculator is the Fuller slide rule, produced in wood and then Bakelite from the 1890s until the 1950s, and now worth about £50–100. Another classic is the German Curta calculator, made for 20 years from the late 1940s; it fetches about £100–400 depending on model, date, and condition.

The electric calculator was introduced in the 1960s. Sharp's CS10A was one of the first desk models and can now fetch around £100. Calculators from the early 1970s can be picked up for a few pounds, though milestone models such as Hewlett Packard's 1974 HP-65 – the first hand-held programmable calculator – can cost £100–400.

**A Curta calculator type 2,** serial no. 501613, with slides, black metal canister, and instruction leaflet. *c.1950s, 15.5cm (6in) high.*

**£200–250**

### Top Tips

- Look for desirable early typewriters, particularly those with unusual shapes or made for short periods of time.
- If buying an IBM Selectric, consider a below-average example, as replacement parts are easy to find.
- If you own an original 'Bondi Blue' Apple Imac, keep it (with its box, if possible). Already a design classic, early Imacs may become collectable.
- Ensure all hand-held electronics come complete with an undamaged battery cover, as values fall if this is missing.
- Look out for calculator watches, as they can be worth high sums. For example, Hewlett Packard's seminal HP-01 can fetch £500 or more.

### BUY

*Sinclair is one of the most collectable names in late 20th-century technology. Consider buying early examples (if in good condition), as they were the 'must haves' of the day and are increasingly becoming so again among today's collectors.*

**A Sinclair Cambridge calculator.** This model – Sinclair's second calculator – should increase in value. *c.1973, 15.5cm (6in) high.*

**£60–80**

### KEEP

*British company Psion revolutionised the hand-held computer market during the 1990s with its brick-shaped Psion II, and later the Psion 3. Examples in mint condition, with their boxes and accessories, are most likely to rise in value if interest grows.*

**A Psion Series 3C organiser.** Released in 1997, this continues to be a popular machine. The clam-shell design and large screen are major enhancements of previous models. *c.1997, 16.5cm (6½in) wide.*

**£30–40**

## ▪ Commodore C64 ▪ Amstrad Pen Pad ▪

**A Commodore C64 home computer.** The model was originally designed to work inside an arcade machine, so had good sound and graphics. *1982–93, 41cm (16¼in) wide.*

**£20–30**

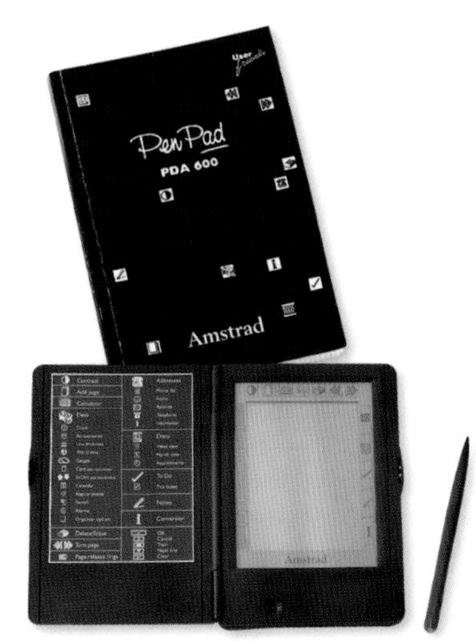


**An Amstrad Pen Pad PDA 600.** This was one of the first Personal Digital Assistants, the forerunner of today's ubiquitous Palm Pilot and Ipaq. *c.1993, 16cm (6¼in) high.*

**£30–50**

# Fountain pens and other writing instruments from the 20th century are always stylish and can be an expression of their owner's personality. Leading makers include Parker, Waterman, and Montblanc.

The mass-market fountain pen is a late 19th-century invention, introduced when two Americans, Lewis Edson Waterman and George S. Parker, separately patented reliable ink-feed systems. Within a few years the industry was booming and many different ink-filling mechanisms were introduced, as well as a variety of barrel shapes, colours, and sizes.

## A splash of colour

Although early pens do attract interest, most had barrels made from hard black rubber, so later, more attractive coloured pens are often preferred. In the 1920s, Waterman released a range of 'ripple' pens in bold colours. Today, they may fetch £30–300, depending on size, colour, and condition.

Parker's Duofold, introduced in the early 1920s, was a landmark design, initially offered in a red-orange colour, earning it the nickname 'Big Red'. From the mid-1920s, the Duofold was sold in Senior and Junior sizes in blue, jade green, and the prized 'mandarin yellow'. While a standard 'Big Red' may be worth around £100–150 today, a Duofold Senior in yellow may cost as much as £800–1,000.

Produced between 1941 and 1972, the Parker 51, with its futuristic rocket shape and hooded nib, was snapped up by the public – total sales ran to more than 20 million units over 30 years. It came in various colours and cap finishes. Used 51s, with a standard cap, can be bought for around £10–30, while an early American 51, or one in a rare colour or with an unusual cap, can sell for up to £800. Prices rise for pens in mint condition and those with a precious metal overlay.

## British schooldays

In the early 1940s Parker set up a factory in England, but it is also worth

1 2 3

**1 A Waterman Filigree,** hard black rubber eyedropper filler, overlaid with Sterling silver 'three leaf' decorated filigree with a fine Waterman No.4 nib; in good condition with some wear. *1915–20, 14cm (5½in) long.*

**£250–300**

**2 A limited-edition Montblanc 'Oscar Wilde' 13300/20000,** with a pearl and black resin barrel, a vermeil clip, and a medium 18K (18 carat gold) Montblanc nib, complete with box and papers; in mint condition. *1994, 14cm (5½in) long.*

**£500–600**

**3 A Parker 51 Custom,** black plastic aerometric filler, with a medium nib; in mint condition with original shop chalk rubbing over the name-stamp on the barrel. *1950s, 13.5cm (5¼in) long.*

**£100–150**

## A closer look at... a Dunhill Namiki maki-e 'Balance'

During the 1930s, the British company Alfred Dunhill and Japan's Namiki Mfg Co. Ltd collaborated on a series of pens, employing various artists to decorate them. The designs, painted in lacquer, are works of art. Those by Kohkyo are highly sought after and valuable.

**A Dunhill Namiki maki-e 'Balance'** by Kohkyo, decorated with an exotic bird on a black *roiro-nuri* lacquer background, with a Pilot 14K nib. The pen is signed with a red-lacquered signature on the reverse side (below the lever) in Japanese by the artist, using his 'art name' Kohkyo. *1930s, 13cm (5in) long.*

**£3,000–5,000**

The lacquerwork is unworn and the pen is in mint condition

The whole composition is skilfully contrived to draw the eye to the flying bird

The maki-e lacquerwork decoration is painstakingly applied by hand over many weeks, using different coloured lacquers, shell fragments, and gold dust

**4 A Conway Stewart Dinkie 540,** 'grey jazz' multicoloured celluloid ring-top lever filler, with a broad Conway Stewart nib; boxed, in fine condition. *1920s, 8cm (3¼in) long.*

**£100–200**

**5 A Mabie Todd & Co. 44 ETN,** jade green celluloid lever filler, with a No.4 Eternal nib; in very good condition with a little discoloration. *c.1928, 14cm (5½in) long.*

**£80–120**

**6 A Montblanc 144 Meisterstück,** black celluloid piston filler with a two-colour 4810 nib; in good condition. *1949–60, 14cm (5½in) long.*

**£150–200**

looking for classics by other British makers. Popular names include Conway Stewart, Swan, and Onoto. Look for bright or unusual colours, such as Conway Stewart's 'Cracked Ice' (produced from the 1930s to the 50s). This was made from black plastic shot through with silvery-white 'lightning strikes'. Examples with good patterning can fetch around £100 or more.

## Size matters

Size is a key factor in the value of a pen. Small 'lady' pens fitted easily into a handbag and often had rings on their caps to take a ribbon, but larger pens, with their impressive size and showy nibs, are more sought after. The name of a former owner engraved on the pen can lower its value, unless the owner was famous, but a presentation box usually makes a piece more desirable. A pen with its original nib is worth more than one with a replacement. The nib's value alone is not high, unless it is large or rare.

## Writing in style

Dip pens, pencil holders, and propelling pencils from the 19th century and earlier are all desirable. Usually found in solid or plated gold or silver, propelling pencils may also have inlaid or enamelled decoration.

Look for makers such as Sampson Mordan, who produced a range of novelty-shaped pencils in the late 19th century. Values vary, but expect to pay from £20 upwards. A good example of Mordan's novelty pencils can fetch around £300 or more.

## Modern editions

Collecting modern limited editions by major makers is a new phenomenon. Many are high-priced luxury goods and collectors keep them unopened in the hope of increasing their value. The German-made Montblanc 'Lorenzo de Medici' retailed at about £800 in 1992; now rare and desirable, it can fetch up to £2,000. But later editions, such as the 'Oscar Wilde', still sell for less than their original price.

The size of the edition, the maker, and the look of the pen are important. Small editions of elegant pens by the best makers are likely to appreciate.

## Top Tips

- Do not dismiss pens with perished ink sacs as these can easily be restored to working order by a professional.
- Avoid plastic pens with cracks, burn marks, or scratches, and metal-overlaid pens with dents or splits – all will devalue a pen.
- Make sure that a pen and pencil sold as a set really do match.



## BUY

*High-quality rolled-gold pens were luxury items during the 1920s. Any mint-condition, plated, or precious metal pen with fine details such as engravings will make an excellent investment, as it should at least hold its value and is likely to appreciate.*

**A Waterman 0552 'Pansy Panel',** black hard-rubber lever filler, with a yellow rolled-gold overlay, decorated with panels of pansy flowers, with a fine Waterman Ideal No.2 nib, in near-mint condition. *1924–27, 14cm (5½in) long.*

**£200–250**

## KEEP

*Many schoolchildren used Conway Stewart pens from the 1930s to the 70s (although quality began to decline in the late 60s). Examples from the 1930s–50s are of good quality, are easy to repair, and are still usable. They are also beginning to be appreciated by international collectors, so prices should rise.*

**A Conway Stewart 58** green and black line-marbled celluloid lever filler, with a fine Conway Stewart Duro nib, in very good condition. *c.1949, 14cm (5½in) long.*

**£100–150**

## SELL

*The 'Big Red' Parker Duofold from the 1920s and 30s is a classic vintage pen, but prices have remained static for years. Sell now and speculate elsewhere as values are unlikely to rise substantially in the near future.*

**A Parker 'Lucky Curve' Duofold Senior** in red Permanite with a button filler, with a Parker Duofold nib, box, and leaflet; in excellent condition. *c.1927, 14cm (5½in) long.*

**£200–250**

# Telephones have undergone numerous design changes in the past 120 years, from wall-mounted to touch-tone versions. Not only are they fascinating, but most period models can be updated for use today.

The evolution of the telephone has been so rapid that we look back at models we used just a decade or so ago with nostalgia. Telephone technology was developed in the USA in the late 19th century, and the British Post Office began installing wall-mounted phones in the 1880s. These early models are rare, which is reflected in their prices. A complete wooden phone with brass fittings from around 1900 can be worth up to £300–500 or more, while scarcer wall phones can command £2,000 or more if the cases are decoratively carved and in good condition.

**An English white-painted metal candlestick telephone.** *1920s, 30.5cm (12in) high.*

**£100–150**

## Off the wall

Smaller, tabletop telephones were introduced towards the end of the 19th century. Designed by the Swedish Ericsson company, the 'skeleton' phone had exposed workings and was made from 1895 to 1931. It also featured gilt transfers and a black base. Early examples in good condition can command from £500 to £800 or more.

The first enclosed table phone was made in the early 1900s. Prices range from £50–100 for an Ericsson model from 1910, to £300 or more for rarer, decorative continental examples. Another design, the candlestick phone, was popular in the USA and Britain from about 1900 to the 1920s. Expect to pay about £80–150 for a phone in good condition, but if it has Bakelite fittings, or is made in mahogany and brass, it can be worth £150–300.

**A black Bakelite 200 Series telephone.** *1930s, 20cm (8in) wide.*

**£200–300**

## Modern Bakelite

By the early 1930s, telephones with bells in the base rather than in a separate unit were available. Coupled with the use of Bakelite in their construction, they introduced a style of 'modern' phone that remained in production for more than 50 years.

Seminal models include the Tele 232, part of the 200 Series. Although this model did not have the bell in its base, it had a pull-out drawer for storing telephone numbers. As well as the standard black Bakelite version, the Tele 232 came in green, red, and ivory. These variations are highly sought after: an original green phone (the rarest of the colours) can sell for around £400–500 or more. Other notable Bakelite phones from the decade include the Gecophone by GEC and AT&E's Strowgerphone.

## A closer look at... a 1970s telephone

The range of telephones available expanded greatly after World War II, but some were more innovative – and are therefore more collectable – than others. When building a collection or investing in a single piece for use, consider features such as the form, colour, and positioning of the elements.

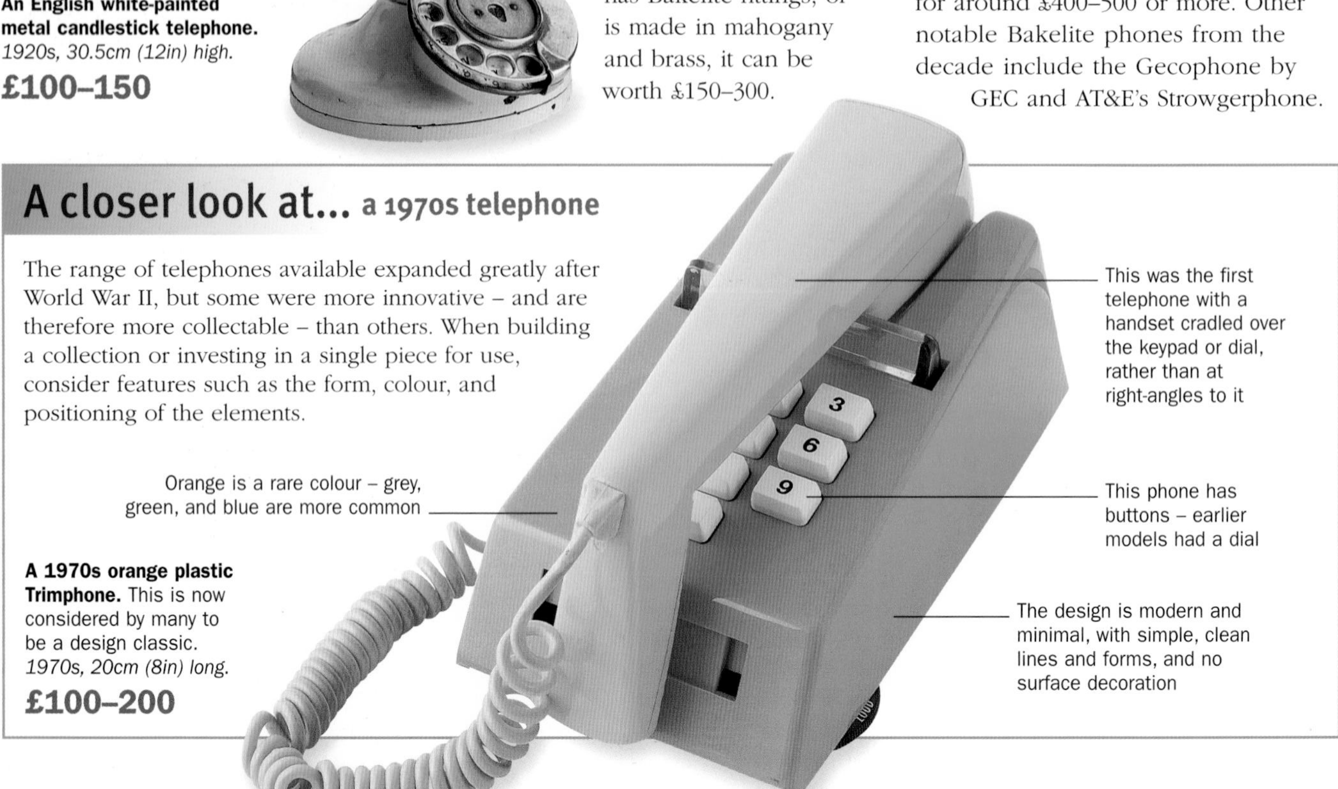


**A 1970s orange plastic Trimphone.** This is now considered by many to be a design classic. *1970s, 20cm (8in) long.*

**£100–200**

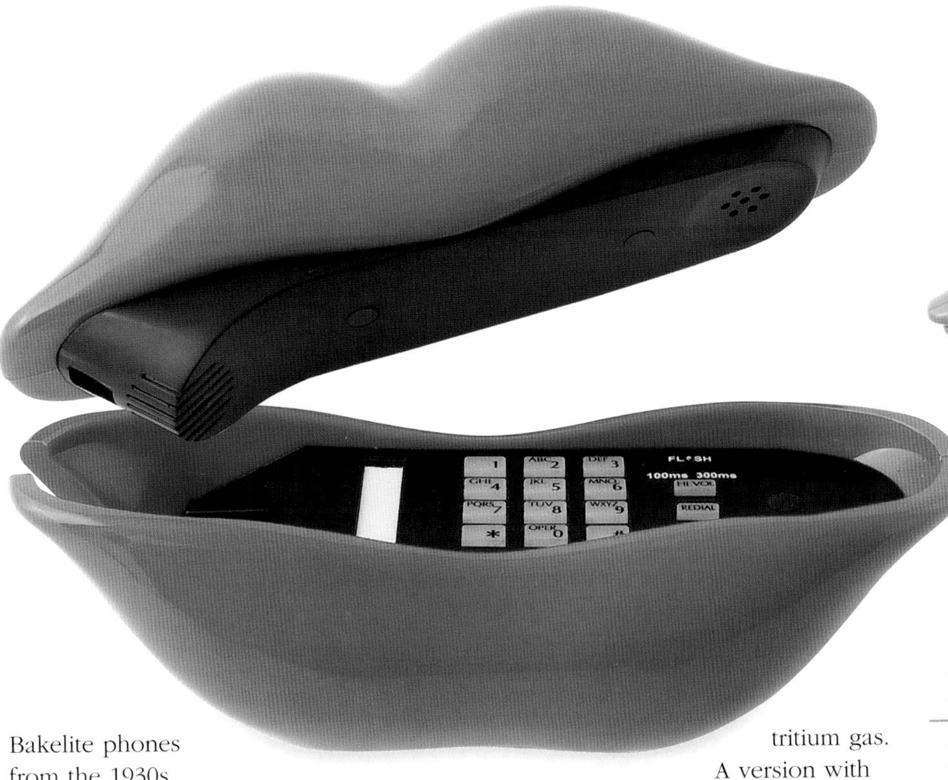

Bakelite phones from the 1930s generally sell for £80–150, but classic models such as the 200 Series and the later 300 Series (in production until the 1950s) can often fetch more.

## Pushing the right buttons

The Post Office's 700 Series was introduced in 1959. These were the first phones available in a wide range of colours (and also the first to come with a curly cord). Early rotary-dial versions such as the see-through 706 are much sought after, but push-button models from the mid-1960s are the most collectable. Rotary-dial 700s are worth about £25–35; rare push-button models often fetch £50–70 or more.

## Design classics

Based on a 1940s design, Ericsson's Ericofon (also known as the 'Cobra') was one of the first successful single-piece phones. Launched for domestic use in 1956, the phone's dial was housed in the base of the unit. About 2.5 million were made before it was discontinued in 1972, but prices still range from about £50–100 for a standard phone to around £100–150 for a special reprise edition to mark the company's centenary in 1976.

The Trimphone was produced from the 1960s to the early 1980s. Its distinguishing features include an electronic ringer that gets louder with each ring, and a dial illuminated by tritium gas. A version with a keypad was introduced in 1973, and a touch-tone dial became available two years later. Rotary-dial Trimphones can be found for about £35–45, with keypad models selling for around £50–100. Other designer phones of note include the Grillo, a 1960s Italian model with a body that flips open, worth around £150–200; Dawn, the last rotary-dial BT phone, worth about £20–30; and the 1970s Genie, worth about the same.

## Engaging novelties

Many novelty phones were made in the USA. Examples include the R2-D2 Star Wars phone, valued at about £30–50; a teddy bear phone worth about £40–60; and phones from the 1970s and 80s featuring Snoopy, Mickey Mouse, and Kermit the Frog, which can fetch £50–200. Specialist phones, including models for cruise liners or hotels, and early speaker-phones, are also popular.

### *Top Tips*

- Be wary of fake Bakelite phones. Look out for uneven mouldings and models over-painted in rarer colours.
- Feel the numbers on the handset of a Bakelite phone: those on a copy are not as 'raised' as ones on an original.
- When buying a Trimphone, do not expect the illuminated dial to work, as the gas will probably have seeped out.

**A red plastic 'Hot Lips' telephone.** *1980s, 21.5cm (8½in) wide.*

**£100–200**

## BUY

*Recent telephones by important and influential designers are likely to have lasting appeal and interest and should at least hold their current values.*

**A blue plastic 'Ola' T1000GD telephone by Thomson.** This telephone was designed by the noted French designer Philippe Starck. Starck is also famous for his interiors, furniture, and bath and kitchenwares. *c.1996, 28cm (11in) long.*

**£100–200**

## KEEP

*Key designs from the second half of the 20th century are most likely to hold their value, as they represent period design trends and can usually be converted for modern use. Visit design museums so you can identify those that are considered important, as these are more likely to hold, or even increase, their value.*

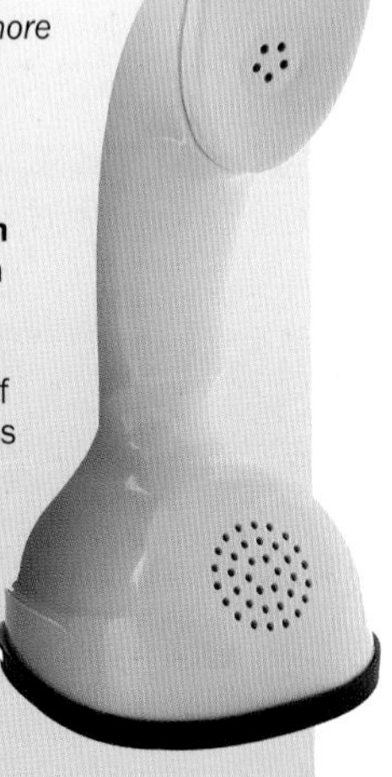

**A cream plastic Ericsson Ericofon telephone,** with dialling buttons on the underside of the base. The New York Museum of Modern Art described this telephone – nicknamed the 'Cobra' – as one of the best industrial designs of the 20th century. *1970s, 21cm (8¼in) high.*

**£100–150**

# Mobile phones can be a lifeline, a fashion accessory, or a collectable evoking technology's recent past. Since the first mobiles appeared in the early 1980s, there have been many variations, each one smaller and with more enhancements than the last.

Dr Martin Cooper of Motorola was credited with inventing the first mobile handset in 1973. Cellular phones were only approved for public use in 1982 in the USA, and a few years later in Europe. Various analogue systems, including ETACS (Extended Total Access Communication System), were tried but found wanting. A more secure digital global standard – GSM (Global System for Mobile Communications) – was introduced from 1982.

Now, mobile phones are 'upgraded' as soon as technology or, arguably, fashion advances, so there is a rapid turnover in handsets. Early mobiles can easily be recognised by their bulk and weight: examples in good condition are now becoming desirable. Interest is growing, particularly in models from the late 1980s and early 90s. But it is not possible to tell accurately how many handsets have survived overall, or what condition most are in, which means that prices are still unpredictable.

Market leaders such as Nokia and Motorola are likely to be most collected. Mobile phones produced to promote events or films (such as *Tomb Raider*) are likely to create a lively niche market.

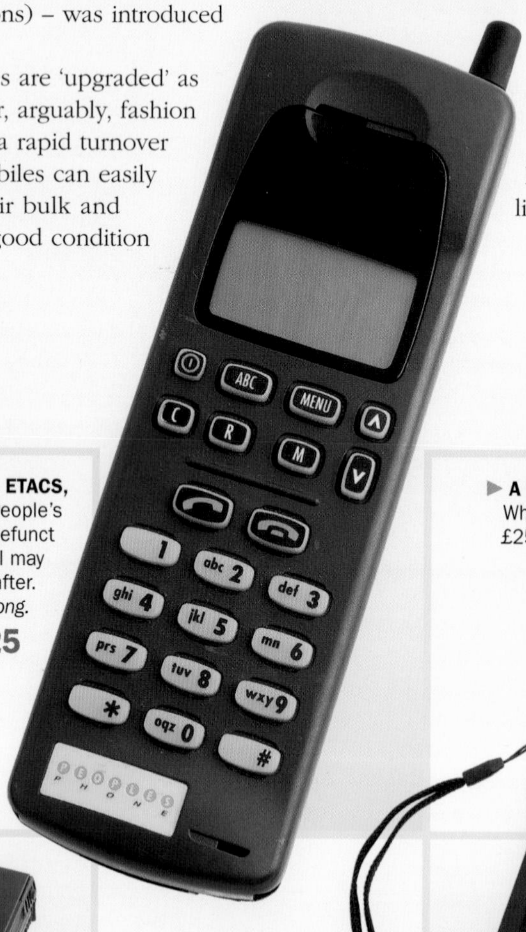

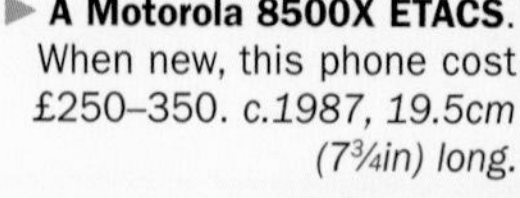

► **A blue Nokia 101 ETACS,** produced for 'People's Phone', a now-defunct retailer. This model may become sought after. *c.1992, 17cm (6¾in) long.*

**£20–25**

► **A Motorola 8500X ETACS.** When new, this phone cost £250–350. *c.1987, 19.5cm (7¾in) long.*

**£75–85**

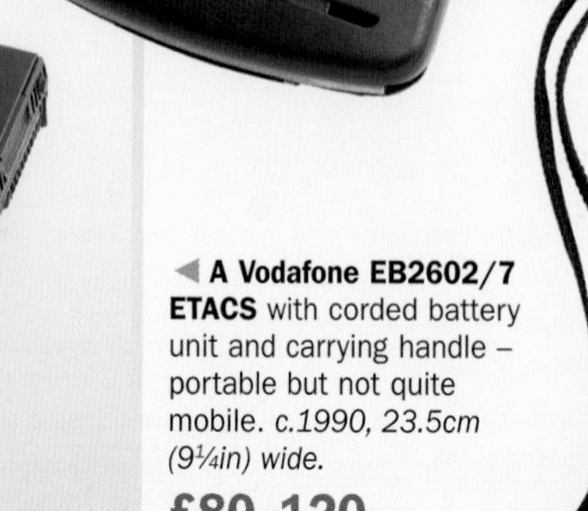

◄ **A Vodafone EB2602/7 ETACS** with corded battery unit and carrying handle – portable but not quite mobile. *c.1990, 23.5cm (9¼in) wide.*

**£80–120**

◄ **An angular NEC P4 ETACS,** with retractable aerial, made for Mercury Communications. This model originally cost £400 and had only eight hours of standby time. *c.1992, 17.5cm (7in) long.*

**£20–25**

◀ **A Motorola 'Personal Phone' ETACS.** This model cost £249 when released in the early 1990s, and is unusual in that it has no LCD or digital display. *c.1992, 16cm (6¼in) long.*

**£25–35**

◀ **A Nokia 100 analogue mobile phone.** Produced for market leader Vodafone, this model has an extending aerial. *c.1993, 17cm (6¾in) long.*

**£30–40**

▶ **A mock walnut Nokia 2110 GSM.** Nokia mobiles, known for their ease of use and reliability, may become one of the most popular names for vintage phones, particularly non-standard models. *c.1994, 17cm (6½in) long.*

**£50–60**

## Collectors' Tips

- Look for landmark models that were the first to use a new technology, such as the first GSM phone, or the first digital handset
- Always check that the battery cover is present and that the aerial remains intact

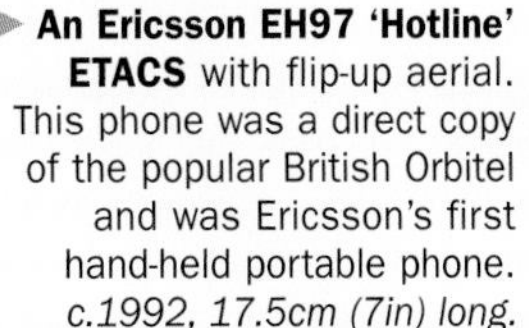

◀ **A Motorola 8800X ETACS,** complete with its original Motorola fitted leather case and a sleeve (not shown here) for the spare battery. *c.1990, 20cm (8in) long.*

**£100–150**

▶ **An Ericsson EH97 'Hotline' ETACS** with flip-up aerial. This phone was a direct copy of the popular British Orbitel and was Ericsson's first hand-held portable phone. *c.1992, 17.5cm (7in) long.*

**£15–25**

◀ **A Siemens S6 'Classic' GSM.** This phone has a Hi-Fi loudspeaker earpiece. *c.1996, 19cm (7½in) long.*

**£20–30**

◀ **A Motorola 'Startac' GSM.** 'Clamshell' phones, in which the earpiece folds over the keyboard, have proved to be more popular abroad than in Britain but, even so, this is a landmark design. *c.1998, 9.5cm (3¾in) long.*

**£30–50**

# Railway memorabilia

dates back to the start of steam travel in the 1800s. In addition to locomotive nameplates and station signs, there are many evocative railway-related items around – and some are quite affordable.

**A Somerset & Dorset three-aspect hand lamp,** unrestored and complete with a reservoir for oil and an unmarked burner. *c.1920s, 33cm (13in) high.*

**£100–150**

By the early 20th century, there were more than 100 district railway companies operating in Britain. In 1923 these were amalgamated into four groups: the London, Midland & Scottish (LMS); London & North-Eastern Railways (LNER); the Southern Railway (SR); and the Great Western Railway (GWR). The most popular memorabilia dates from the early 1920s until nationalisation in 1948. The Beeching Report on the British railway network, published in 1963, led to the closure of many lines and stations, yielding more collectables.

## Popular names

Nameplates, especially those from steam locomotives that operated on mainline routes, are prized. The class of locomotive, condition of the metal plate (often cast iron or brass), and even the name itself affect prices. The record for a nameplate is £54,000, paid in 2002 for 'Sir William A. Stainer FRS'. As demand is high and the supply is limited, steam loco nameplates are rarely found for less than £10,000. Even more recent electric or diesel plates can fetch high prices: a 'Queen Elizabeth I' nameplate from a 1991 Class 91 electric loco can cost £6,000–7,000.

## The numbers game

Locomotives also incorporated number plates ('cab side' and 'smokebox') and works plates. Cab-side plates are valuable, with rare brass examples commanding around £10,000–15,000 or more. More common examples can cost less than £1,000. Values have levelled out, so keep an eye on price trends before investing.

Smokebox plates are smaller in size and less expensive than cab-side plates, although rarer examples can command high prices: a 1948 plate from the 'Duchess of Sutherland' is valued at about £6,000–7,000. Prices for smokebox plates generally start at around £200, but values are starting to rise.

## Totems and trespassers

Station signs – known as 'totems' – have increased in value over the past few years. When the railways were nationalised in 1948, British Railways set up a colour-coding system for each region, and this is reflected in the colours of the enamel. For example, the Eastern Region had dark blue totems, and the North Eastern region's totems were orange. A common Southern Region totem can be bought for less than £300, but a rare North Eastern or Scottish Region example can be worth up to £3,000.

Station information notices, trackside signs, including 'Beware of the Trains'

## Some railway signs to look for:

▪ Totems ▪ Warnings ▪ Signals ▪ Building Signs ▪

**A British Rail (Midland region) totem station sign for Ambergate.** Totems were displayed at railway stations and make evocative and recognisable display pieces. This example is finished in Midland Railway burgundy and was for an ex-Midland Railway mainline station between Derby and Chesterfield. *c.1950s, 150cm (59¼in) wide.*

**£1,000–2,000**

**An alloy 'Crossing No Gates' warning sign,** depicting a smoking 0-6-0 locomotive, with original paint and a clear post mark on the rear. Many of these signs, such as this one, are made of cast iron and simply painted with bold warnings. *1920s–30s, 53.5cm (21in) high.*

**£250–350**

**A postcard of Highbridge station,** Somerset, which closed in 1966. *c.1905, 14cm (5½in) wide.*

**£20–30**

notices, and signal box name-boards are less expensive, with prices starting at around £50 and rising to more than £2,000 for unusual or pristine pieces. Other collectables include ticket boxes and the 'key tokens' exchanged by train crews to prevent two trains from travelling in opposite directions on single-track lines.

## Light and sound

Rare 19th-century signalling lamps can be worth thousands of pounds, but early 20th-century lamps can sell for about £30–50. Luxury carriage fittings are sought after, and Pullman table lamps can cost around £1,500–2,000. Brass whistles can be a good buy: a pair of GWR whistles can cost less than £300.

## Printed matter

Railway posters can be pricey, but postcards are more affordable at less than £2, up to around £50. Those showing stations before nationalisation are the most desirable. Vintage timetables are also popular and can cost less than £10. Jigsaws made by Chad Valley for the GWR between 1923 and 1939 are also collected: complete sets can fetch more than £40.

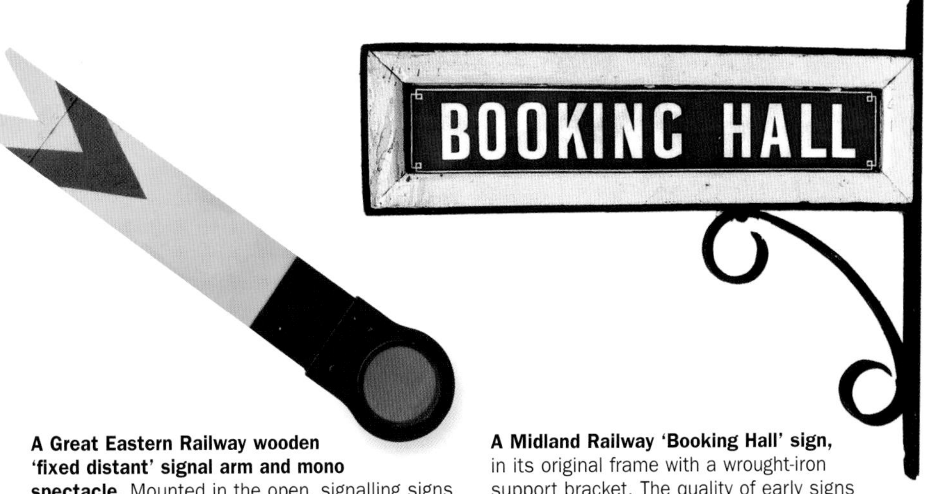


**A Great Eastern Railway wooden 'fixed distant' signal arm and mono spectacle.** Mounted in the open, signalling signs were prone to weather damage, so examples in good condition can be hard to find. This signal for the GER is rare. *c.1930s, 85cm (33in) long.*

**£100–150**

**A Midland Railway 'Booking Hall' sign,** in its original frame with a wrought-iron support bracket. The quality of early signs such as this reflects the high standards of Britain's proud railway heritage. *c.1930s, 53.5cm (21in) wide.*

**£200–300**

## Top Tips

- Take care when handling cast-iron railway signs – they are often brittle and damage easily.
- Look for pieces with original fittings and finishes, as these can add value.
- Snap up any piece of railway memorabilia that comes with an original British Railways receipt – it will add value to the item.
- Look for railway company stampings on lamps and ensure that all the internal pieces are present.

## BUY

*Uniforms from the great age of the railways, before nationalisation, add variety to a collection and are generally of fine quality. Look for items from the four major companies. Demand should mean that values remain consistent, at the very least.*

**A London, Midland & Scottish peaked cap,** in top condition. This rare cap is likely to have enduring appeal to LMS fans, as well as offering an inexpensive way to start a collection. *c.1930s, 28cm (11in) long.*

**£30–50**

## KEEP

*Games or jigsaws connected to the great age of steam can command high prices. Look for those endorsed by one of the four railway companies. Complete items with striking images and a box are likely to rise in value.*

**A Chad Valley Great Western Railway jigsaw puzzle 'Royal Route to the West'.** The superb image, the connection with the GWR, and the notable British toymaker make this a collectable item. It is complete and in good condition. *c.1930, 46cm (18in) wide.*

**£60–100**

# Automobilia represents a bygone age of handmade signs, crafted bonnet mascots, and ephemera full of period character. It covers a wide range of items connected with cars, trucks, motorbikes, and other motorised vehicles.

There are markets for everything automotive, including toolkits, hubcaps, and spark plugs, and prices to suit most budgets – from enamel petrol cans from the 1930s–50s, worth about £5–30, up to the most valuable bonnet mascots: a Mr Bibendum (Michelin Man) mascot by Ets Generes of Paris can fetch £5,000 or more.

## Appreciating mascots

Car mascots, placed on top of the radiator cap, are often expensive, but early examples from the 1920s can sell for less than £200–400, especially if they are small or for a lesser-known make. Common themes are goddesses and lucky horseshoes. A mascot marked with a high-quality maker's name, such as F. Bazin, Lejeune, Red Ashay, or Lalique, is highly prized. A 1920s silver-plated bronze mascot by Bazin can go for more than £2,000.

Factors affecting price include condition and rarity, with the highest prices paid for hard-to-find mascots from 1900–30. Glass mascots from this period are sought after. Lalique made the best quality, although pristine examples by period imitators Sabino of Paris and Red Ashay in Britain can also cost at least £2,000–3,000. Smaller or newer mascots from the 1940s onwards can be more reasonably priced, but are starting to attract interest. A 7.5cm (3in) high Bentley 'B' mascot with outstretched wings from the 1950s–60s can often be found for less than £200.

**A Rolls-Royce chrome-plated 'Silver Wraith' car mascot, 'The Spirit of Ecstasy'.** *1930s–40s, 12cm (4½in) high.*

**£700–1,000**

## Lighting the way

Older lamps generally command the highest prices. A pair of brass side-lamps from 1910 can be worth about £1,000–1,500. Lamps from the 1950s onwards are less expensive, and can be bought for around £30–100; a 1960s Lumax car lamp with its original box is worth about £30–40. The German

## Some grille badges to look for:

- BARC
- Bugatti Owners Club
- British Racing & Sports Car Club

**A Bugatti Owners Club enamelled and chromed motor badge.** Badges from clubs for owners of prestigious motor cars such as Bugatti and Ferrari are sought after – this one is in the shape of a classic Bugatti radiator, which adds to its appeal. *1930s–40s, 10cm (4in) high.*

**£80–120**

**A British Automobile Racing Club badge.** Memorabilia for historic and important racing clubs such as the BARC, founded in 1912 and still in existence, consistently attract attention. *c.1980s, 9.5cm (3¾in) high.*

**£80–120**

company Carl Zeiss made headlamps from the 1920s onwards and these are particularly sought after, especially the rare fork-mounted examples.

## Adorning the grille

Grille badges issued by motoring organisations, such as the AA and RAC, and car clubs are eagerly collected. High-quality badges are made from chromed brass, embellished with coloured vitreous enamels. Badges from the 1950s onwards can be found for around £30–100 or less, but examples from the 1920s and 30s can be worth more than £200. Badges for members of owners' clubs or racing clubs made from the 1950s onwards tend to sell for about £50–150.

## On the forecourt

Original signs from garage forecourts and sales material from showrooms are popular. A 1920s Vacuum Motor Car Oils enamel sign can be worth about £200 and a rare enamel Golden Shell Motorcycle Oil sign can cost double. Porcelain signs from the 1920s and 30s made by companies such as Esso and Mobiloil can cost more than £400–500. If you have space, petrol pumps are also desirable, especially those from the late 1950s and 60s with illuminated globes. Expect to pay £700–800 or more for a 1958 Shell pump with a functioning globe.

**A Desmo brass motor vehicle horn.** *c.1920s, 37cm (14½in) long.*

**£80–120**

## Top Tips

- Check the quality and weight of grille badges: fakes are made of painted steel, rather than vitreous enamel on chrome-plated brass, so are lighter.
- Aim to buy pairs of car lamps rather than single examples, as a single lamp is worth about 25 per cent of the value of a pair.
- With prestige makers, such as Bugatti, look for smaller pieces. These will often be more affordable.
- Hunt for items related to lesser names or common models such as the Mini, as they are often less expensive.

## BUY

*Keyrings make a colourful and varied collection and can be found for as little as £3-5. Look out for unusual or obscure clubs, or marques that are no longer in existence, as these will be more likely to appreciate in value.*

**An ERA ringed logo leather key fob.** This rare fob was made for a 1989–91 'Mini ERA Turbo' of which only around 500 were produced. It used a marque (English Racing Automobiles) associated with Brooklands race track and dating back to the 1930s. *c.1989, 3.75cm (1½in) wide.*

**£30–40**

## National Motorists Association

**An enamelled British Racing & Sports Car Club badge,** which dates from the club's first few decades. Its large size and impressive artwork make it highly collectable. *1950s–60s, 11.5cm (4½in) high.*

**£100–150**

**An enamelled and chrome-plated National Motorists Association badge.** This historic and decorative badge is highly desirable. The NMA was eventually superseded by clubs such as the AA and RAC. *1930s–40s, 14cm (5½in) high.*

**£150–200**

## KEEP

*Items produced for regional clubs, usually in small production runs of 50–100, are worth keeping. They will appeal to current members of the society and to more general automobilia collectors, so should retain their value, or even go up in price, owing to their comparative rarity.*

**An enamelled and chrome-plated Brighton & Hove Motor Club member's radiator top fitting.** This example has attractive imagery that would be desirable to a collector, and it could easily be mounted on a plinth and displayed as a desk accessory. *1960s, 9cm (3½in) high.*

**£150–200**

# Ocean liner memorabilia

reminds us of a more glamorous era when the only way to travel the world was by ship, usually in some style. Nostalgia and the chance to own a tiny slice of liner luxury spurs on the modern collector.

At the beginning of the 20th century, the giant luxury liners of shipping companies such as Cunard and White Star plied the transatlantic passenger trade. Notable ships included the *Olympic,* the *Britannic,* and the *Mauretania*, but the market for ocean- and cruise-liner collectables is dominated by the ill-fated *Titanic*.

## The tip of the iceberg

*Titanic* artefacts and memorabilia have increased in price since the 1997 film. Items produced after the sinking of the *Titanic* in 1912 are generally of less value. Top prices of £3,000–10,000 or more are paid for rare memorabilia owned or used by survivors or rescuers, such as watches, spoons, menus, and plates.

Postcards and photographs are more reasonably priced, as so many were made. They can fetch around £50–100 each, often less. Handwritten postcards that mention the *Titanic* are valuable, depending on the message, date, and sender. Cards sent from the ship when it docked at Cherbourg or Queenstown attract premium prices. A small framed photograph of the liner can fetch around £100–150.

## Art Deco opulence

In the 1920s and 30s, ships such as the French *Normandie*, launched in 1932, set new standards of luxury, speed, and safety. Her first-class dining room was an extraordinarily lavish Art Deco creation of bronze, hammered glass, and Lalique fixtures. She was in New York when World War II broke out in Europe and was commandeered. Unfortunately, an accidental fire caused her to capsize, and she was scrapped in 1942.

## Sister ships

Memorabilia from the Queen Mary is commonly found, and usually fetches less than £100. Launched in 1934, she is now a tourist attraction in California. Commemorative ceramics, now often sold in the on-board souvenir shop, can cost £50–150, while a souvenir tin can fetch around £50–70.

**A *Titanic* in memoriam picture,** in a shell frame. *1912, 15cm (6in) diam.*

**£200–300**

### *Did You Know?*

*Memorabilia from passengers who escaped from the 'Titanic' are in the top league and have shot up in value. In 1999 an original painted cast-iron plaque from one of the lifeboats fetched more than £20,000 at auction, and in 2002 a rare first-class dinner menu dated 10 April 1912 (the day she sailed), made a world record price of £27,000.*

**A *Queen Mary* souvenir cup and saucer,** made by Aynsley to commemorate her maiden voyage in May 1936. *c.1936, saucer 14cm (5½in) diam.*

**£30–40**

Cunard's *Queen Elizabeth* entered passenger service in 1946. Like her sister ship, she had luxurious Art Deco-inspired interiors. Memorabilia related to her tends to be less expensive than *Queen Mary* souvenirs. A menu from her last voyage can cost less than £20 and a 1964 course book, enabling passengers to follow her route, can fetch around £30–50.

The growth in air travel brought to an end the era of the great liners. The *Queen Mary* was withdrawn from service in 1967 and the *Queen Elizabeth* the following year.

## Ship stock and souvenirs

In general, collectors focus on the best-known liners and shipping companies – Cunard, the White Star Line, Union Castle, P&O, Canadian Pacific, and Compagnie Générale Transatlantique. Memorabilia associated with lesser-known foreign lines, and those not operating the transatlantic route, are usually less costly. Objects showing the ship or boldly displaying the company logo are the most prized.

Items taken from the liners themselves can fetch high prices, depending on the type of object, with pieces related to first-class travel being the most desirable. Official souvenirs are popular too, but are often confused with ship stock – the former usually show an image of the ship while the latter have a more discreet logo or wording. Many official souvenirs (as opposed to items that were taken from the ship and kept as

## Essential ocean liner memorabilia

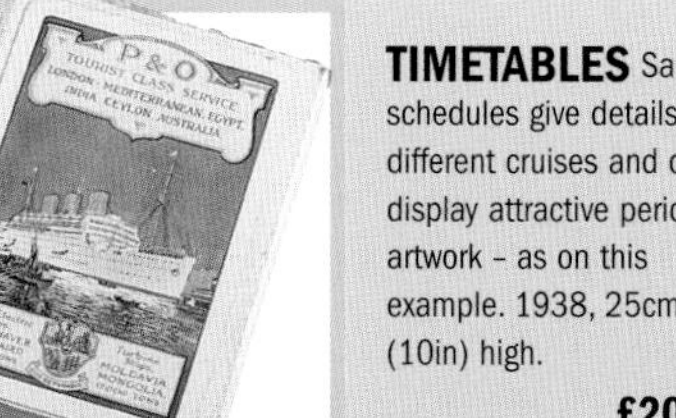

**PLAYING CARDS** Card games were a favourite pastime on cruises. Cards showing the liner or the company's logo, such as these, are popular. 1930s, 9cm (3½in) high.

**£20–25**

**TIMETABLES** Sailing schedules give details of different cruises and often display attractive period artwork – as on this example. 1938, 25cm (10in) high.

**£20–30**

**FIXTURES AND FITTINGS** Original fixtures and fittings, such as this *Queen Mary* brass oil lamp, are rare and often valuable. 1936, 64cm (25¼in) high.

**£400–450**

**BROCHURES** In later brochures, companies (such as P&O) focused on the glamour of cruises, but early brochures are more desirable and valuable. *c.*1976, 30cm (12in) high.

**£10–20**

**SOUVENIRS** Giftware from on-board shops is sought after, especially if well made, attractive, or early – like this rare pin cushion. *c.*1900, 13.5cm (5¼in) wide.

**£80–100**

**MENUS** Standard menus are easy to find, but first-class or special-occasion examples, such as this QEII 'Coronation' gala dinner menu, are more desirable. 1953, 28cm (11in) high.

**£20–30**

mementoes) were bought and saved, so prices are usually lower than for pieces from the ship itself.

Items from the ocean liners' 'golden ages' (1900–10 and the 1930s) usually fetch the highest prices, while a brochure for the P&O *Canberra* from 1965 may fetch less than £10. Brochures often feature period artwork and show how companies attempted to draw passengers in an age when faster modes of travel were preferred.

As well as the more obvious mementoes – menus, deck plans, and brochures – often kept by passengers as keepsakes, look out for items such as packaging, luggage tags, and magazines or newspapers. Prices remain low (usually under £10–30), but these items exist in finite numbers and form the backbone of many collections. They may rise in value.

**A P&O Orient Line paper carrier bag,** with an image of the *Chusan* on one side and the *Arcadia* on the other. *c.1960s, 40cm (16in) high.*

**£10–15**

### *Top Tips*

- Keep *Titanic* memorabilia: the centenary in 2012 is likely to make prices rise.
- Hunt for postcards, particularly in Art Deco style, and sepia photographs from original negatives.
- Favour items from before World War II – pre-war travel had the 'glamour' factor.

### BUY

*Items from notable ships from the 'golden age' have huge appeal. Paper items are often damaged, so any in good condition are a worthwhile investment.*

**A *Normandie* deck plan.** The stunning artwork makes this deckplan both attractive and useful as a historical record. *c.1936, 33cm (12¾in) high.*

**£150–200**

### SELL

*Although post-war items are slowly rising in value, it is unlikely that this trend will extend to ferries, which are not known for either luxury or glamour. Sell and invest in a piece from a luxury liner.*

**A P&O Ferries souvenir plate, by Poole Pottery.** The artwork on this plate showing two ferries is attractive and realistic, making it a good display piece for a collector of Poole pottery. *1970s, 15cm (6in) diam.*

**£5–10**

# Aeronautica has been sought after ever since man first rose into the sky, taking the world's imagination with him. From manned balloon flights to Concorde, the souvenirs and artefacts are legion – and some are quite affordable, although many prices soar.

After the first manned balloon flight in 1783, ballooning became popular and various themed items, such as rings and fans, were made. Memorabilia from the 18th and 19th centuries is scarce: items can fetch £500–1,500 or more. Pieces from the late 19th and early 20th centuries are less expensive.

## A lot of hot air

From 1928 onwards, the Zeppelin company used large hydrogen-filled airships for commercial transatlantic flights to the USA and Brazil. In 1937 the largest Zeppelin ever built – the *Hindenburg* – burst into flames in New Jersey, killing 35 people. Memorabilia from any Zeppelin, but especially the *Hindenburg*, is collectable. Items from the dinner service are the most sought after, but even menus can sell for up to £300. Promotional merchandise is less costly: many items, such as match books and photographs, raise less than £50–100.

## Solo endeavours

The great aviators are avidly collected. These include the Wright brothers, Louis Blériot, Charles Lindbergh, Amy Johnson, and Amelia Earhart, the first woman to fly solo across both the Atlantic and the Pacific. Ephemera recording their feats can be found for less than £100, but an Amy Johnson signature can fetch £100–300. A 14ct-gold Waterman pen presented to Johnson sold for £2,800 in 1997.

**The first issue of *Aviation Stories and Mechanics* from July 1927,** devoted to Charles Lindbergh's transatlantic flight. *1927, 30cm (12in) high.*

**£20–30**

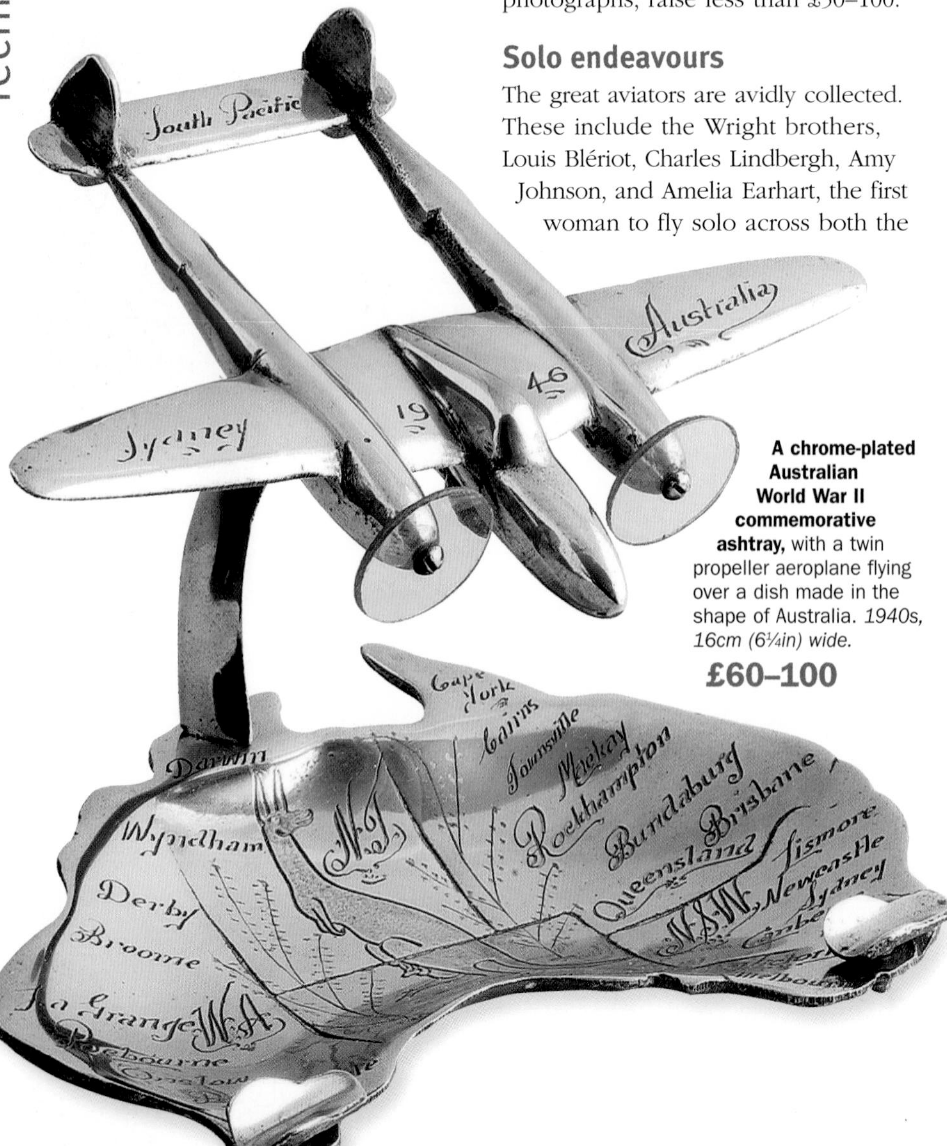


**A chrome-plated Australian World War II commemorative ashtray,** with a twin propeller aeroplane flying over a dish made in the shape of Australia. *1940s, 16cm (6¼in) wide.*

**£60–100**

## Lining up

Much airline memorabilia is accessibly priced at less than £100. Collectables include china, menus, and playing cards from the cabin. A silver-plated cream jug engraved 'British Airways' from the late 1970s is worth about £15–20. Woollen lap blankets from the 1960s–70s can fetch £40–60, depending on condition. Sick bags, which can show excellent artwork, usually sell for less than £10–15. Look for items from air terminals such as postcards,

### Did You Know?

*When Joseph and Etienne Montgolfier announced that they were building a balloon that could carry passengers, Louis XVI decreed that the first travellers be 'expendable' criminals. Chemist Jean-François Pilâtre de Rozier, incensed that felons were to be offered the glory of being the first men into the air, offered himself for the experiment. In November 1783 he flew 900 metres in a balloon kept aloft by burning straw.*

## A closer look at... a ballooning jug

Ballooning memorabilia from the 18th and 19th centuries is desirable, but this popularity means that a large number of reproductions can be found, particularly prints and ceramics. Examine a piece closely to look for interesting historical details, and to ensure that it is authentic.

Minor damage, which hints at age, helps to distinguish a genuine item from a reproduction

The figures exclaiming in speech bubbles are an attractive period touch – seeing a balloon was an astounding, and often disconcerting, event

The coppery lustre finish and freehand pink decoration are typical of early Sunderland ceramics

**An early 19th-century Sunderland pink lustre-ware jug,** printed with 'The Ascent of the Aerial Balloon' on one side and the iron bridge over the Wear on the other. This piece has been damaged and repaired. *c.1820s, 22cm (8¾in) high.*

**£800–1,000**

ashtrays, and cases. BOAC tote bags from the 1960s can fetch £20 or more.

### Take your time

Early airline timetables are collectable and offer a chance to see some of the best graphic design of the time. Some people limit themselves to airline posters, stickers, or tickets. A KLM sticker, commemorating its 30th anniversary in 1949, and BEA and Air France airline tickets from the 1960s can often be found for £5–10.

### End of an era

Concorde memorabilia reached high prices at auctions in 2003: a mach-meter fetched £28,000. Items at more accessible prices included stationery sets, lambswool blankets, luggage tags, and duty-free catalogues.

**A German *Graf Zeppelin's Weltreise* ('World Tour') board game, by Klee.** *c.1928, box 30cm (12in) wide.*

**£180–220**

### Top Tips

- Research the early history of aeronautics so that you can recognise key names.
- Be careful when checking the condition and provenance of any material relating to balloons and airships: it tends to be in short supply.
- If you are looking for affordable items of Concorde memorabilia, consider original Concorde postcards, which can usually be found for less than £20.
- Look for original airline memorabilia from the better-known airlines, especially if they are now defunct – their value is more likely to rise.

### BUY

*Look for objects used on modern airlines. Pieces from the 1950s to the 70s are rising in value, as interest in the now-forgotten romance and glamour of air travel grows.*

**A BOAC ceramic cup and saucer, by Copeland Spode.** As well as clearly showing the logo of a known airline, the maker is notable, and the stylised shape is typical of the period. *1960s, saucer 14cm (5½in) diam.*

**£10–20**

### KEEP

*Keep anything relating to a trip on Concorde, especially if it is well made and has a logo. Since the aircraft's retirement in 2003, values have been rising, but it will be interesting to see if they remain high in the long term.*

**A silver souvenir wine bottle label reading 'Port', with its original gift box, presented to Concorde passengers.** As it is made from solid silver and has a branded box, the value should rise. *1999, 7.5cm (3in) wide.*

**£40–60**

# Modern Design

Most of our homes accumulate an eclectic mix of the styles of the past 70 years. From the sleek lines of Art Deco to the flamboyant optimism of post-war kitsch, and the cool looks of the 1960s to the clean lines of Scandinavian design, there is something we all remember from every era of our lives.

1930s teapot, p.361

The 1930s were the years when plastic came into its own, whether Bakelite, celluloid, or Catalin.

# Stylish designs in a……

**Modern design, which took off in the 1930s, is increasing in desirability as people look to the past for inspiration. While some are content with modern copies of old favourites, others demand the real thing. And, thanks to mass production, they are still able to buy it.**

The stylised lines of Art Deco can be found in household items as simple as a 1930s teapot (1) or a clock. The style's bright colours are also in evidence in the contemporary posters for the London Underground. The 1930s were the years when plastic came into its own, whether Bakelite (2), celluloid, or Catalin. Clocks, radios, napkin rings and picnic sets made from any form of early plastic are an inexpensive way to achieve the Deco look but prices are rising.

## Brave new world

After the austerity of World War II, the public embraced the colourful, 'New Look' pieces of the late 1940s and 50s. As new types of materials were developed, the rationing of other materials ended and a new optimism took hold. Key 1950s designs to look out for include ceramics by Midwinter (who commissioned talented designers including

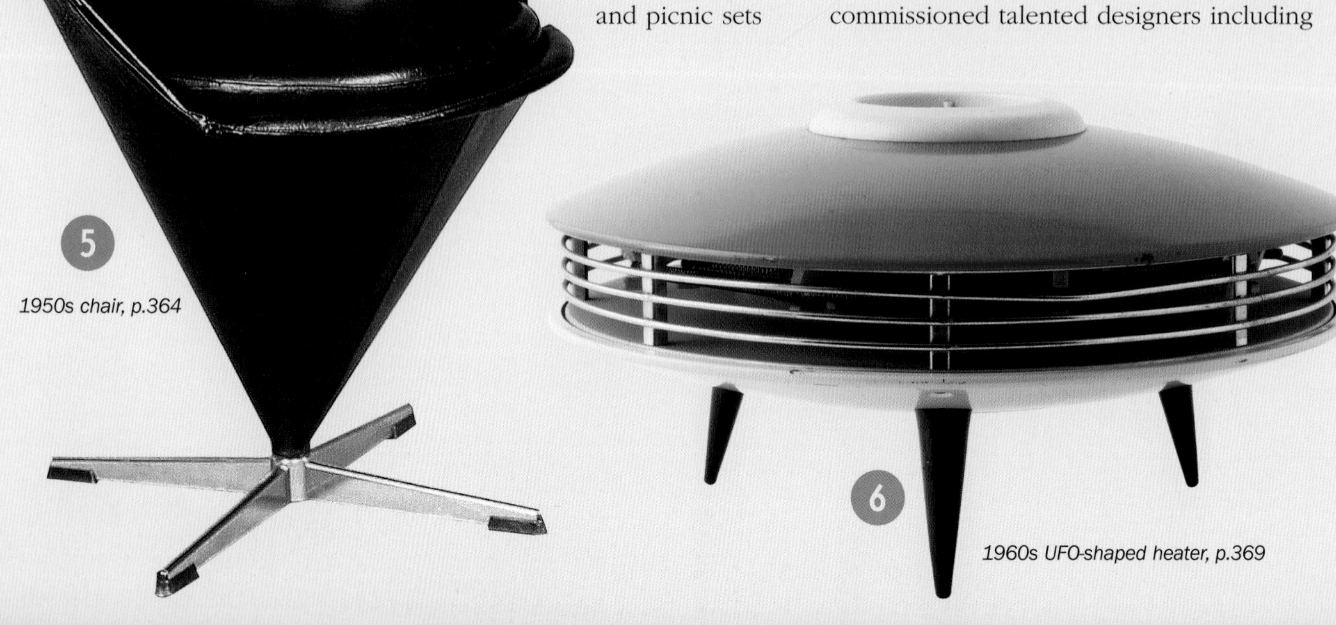
1950s chair, p.364

1960s UFO-shaped heater, p.369

1930s Bakelite clock, p.362

1950s glass, p.365

1950s chair, p.365



# .modern world

Sir Terence Conran), Ridgway's 'Homemaker' range, and Midwinter's 'Zambesi' range *(see also 1950s ceramics, pp44–5)*. These featured innovative modern design, gaudy colours, and stylised shapes. Calendars, drinking glasses, and ashtrays featured pin-up girls (3) and furniture (4) was often rounded (5) with tubular metal legs.

## Future fantastic

During the 1960s the modern look was taken even further with flower power and psychedelia. UFO-shaped heaters (6), lava lamps, and the swirling patterns of Poole Pottery's 'Delphis' range (7) all show the 1960s look at its most extreme.

## So Seventies

During the 1970s some designers continued to develop the funky look of the previous 20 years, while others went back to basics, using earthy colours on sturdy ceramics (8). Potteries such as Troika, Hornsea, and Briglin are names to look out for. Plastics harked back to the 1930s with items like brightly coloured storage units (9). And the space age theme was still in evidence in TV and radio design. Pin-up girls continued to decorate men's accessories – thanks in part to the run-away success of *Playboy*.

1960s plate, p.370

1970s jug, p.374

1970s storage unit, p.375

# The 1930s are epitomised by Art Deco, a distinctive style based on clean lines, geometric shapes, and architectural influences. As many objects in this style suit a modern home and are often inexpensive, they remain popular today.

**A Czechoslovakian ceramic jug,** with the handle modelled as a stylised saxophone player. *1930s, 24cm (9½in) high.*

**£100–200**

Art Deco takes its name from the 1925 Paris exhibition of modern decorative arts – the Exposition Internationale des Arts Décoratifs et Industriels Modernes – where this distinctive, between-the-wars style first gained widespread exposure. The flowing lines of Art Nouveau and the sober tones of wartime Europe gave way to the strikingly modern objects exhibited by French and Swiss designers.

## An instant success

The exhibition featured items in many new materials, such as plastics and laminates, made with new industrial processes. Objects were brightly coloured and decorated with geometric lines and angular shapes. The look was hugely popular and mass-production techniques enabled many people to buy these glamorous and fashionable objects at affordable prices for their own homes.

## The shape of things

Early Art Deco items are often rounded, and feature Art Nouveau-inspired decoration, such as flowers, deer, and pearls. Later Deco objects frequently carry stylised motifs with modern angular forms, including sunbursts, spirals, and chevrons. Popular objects decorated with this look include vases, lamps, and clocks. Items can be found from around £30–50 or more, depending on the style and maker, with items by leading names, such as Clarice Cliff or Susie Cooper, or which exhibit key designs fetching upwards of £200–800.

## Worldly influences

Designs of the period were influenced by changes in the world at large. Jazz, athletics, and travel were in vogue and had an impact on many 1930s objects. Bronze and spelter (a zinc-based metal) figures were made in large numbers. Unmarked painted plaster or spelter pieces can be found for up to £100–300, while signed ivory or bronze figures will cost around £400–10,000 or more.

Decorative objects of the period sometimes reflected the bold, abstract patterns of African art, Egyptian and oriental styles, and Cubism.

▼ **The interior of a house** used as a film set for MGM in the jazz age comedy *Our Modern Maidens*. Typical of the look of the period are the sweeping curves of the armchair and the clean lines of the stylish fireplace with its elegant marble slip, hearth, and firedogs. *c.1929.*

► **A walnut-veneered display cabinet,** in a circular shape, raised on a panelled base, with twin glazed doors enclosing two glass shelves. *1930s, 187cm (73½in) high.*

**£500–800**

## A closer look at... a pair of Royal Lancastrian ceramic bookends

Geometric or angular patterns and bright colours are typical of the Art Deco style, and still look good in today's interiors. Consider both the form and the decoration. Objects in original condition that are quintessentially 1930s should maintain their price and may even rise in value.

Bright colours were typical of the 1930s

The form of the antelope is stylised, with no surface decoration

Leaping wild animals, particularly deer and antelopes, were a common Art Deco theme

The foliage is simplified into clean, curved lines, echoing the shape of the bookend

**A pair of Royal Lancastrian ceramic bookends,** modelled as antelopes, with impressed factory marks. Royal Lancastrian is a collectable name, adding to the value. *c.1930s, 16cm (6½in) high.*

**£400–600**

The glamour of early Hollywood led to a rise in luxury materials such as shagreen (a mottled, often green, shark skin), mirrored objects, and cocktail and smoking accessories. In the USA, designers began to 'streamline' objects, with lines becoming cleaner and more curved. Chrome and Bakelite were used to mass-produce items of style, such as radios.

### The best – and the rest, for less

Ceramics by Clarice Cliff and Susie Cooper, opalescent glass by René Lalique, and furniture by Eileen Grey and Betty Joel are all collectable. Prices can be high (often £2,000– 10,000 or more) but smaller items or less popular designs tend to be more affordable. The best designs were often copied – a 1930s Lalique bowl with shells or a geometric design may cost £600–1,000 or more, but a similar bowl by Etling may fetch £200–300.

Items do not need to be by major names to be valuable, but they should be representative of the style of the period and in excellent condition. Bronze figures are expensive, so look for attractive spelter figures, such as elegant ladies with outstretched arms – but beware of fakes or poor quality.

### Stylish living

Art Deco furniture from lesser-known designers can be bought for similar prices to new furniture. A dressing table with a column-shaped chest of drawers, large mirror, and curving top can be found for around £200–300. Look out for circular display cabinets on rectangular bases as these are typical of the period – they can cost upwards of £300–600. Deco-styled leather armchairs may command around £1,000 or more for a pair, but many wood-framed examples can usually be found for about £300–500 or less.

### Top Tips

- Visit architectural salvage merchants if you are looking for Art Deco fixtures.
- Beware of fake or reproduction spelter and bronze Art Deco figures – if pieces have resin or plastic parts or the metal detailing is poor, they are unlikely to be original.
- Look for chrome items, such as picture frames, that have no pitting. If you really like a piece, though, you may have to accept a *little* pitting.

### BUY

*The 1930s saw many Art Deco style wooden mantel clocks being made, and today these add affordable and functional Art Deco style to a room. Prices are generally low, and are unlikely to drop any further.*

**A 1930s Art Deco walnut veneered clock,** the geometric form and stepped sides are typically Art Deco, and the walnut veneer is appealing. *1930s, 35.5cm (14in) wide.*

**£40–50**

### KEEP

*Even functional household items were given a colourful Art Deco make-over. Those that display the hallmarks of the style and that are visually stunning are always worth keeping as their desirability is unlikely to fall considerably.*

**The colourful geometric pattern** on this chrome and glass teatray shows the front or back bumper of a car. Speeding forms of transport was another strong Art Deco theme. *1930s, 45.5cm (18in) wide.*

**£250–350**

# Plastics and Bakelite

epitomise the energy of modern design between the wars. Their bright colours, exciting styling, and new, affordable materials caught people's imagination. Now their appeal has been discovered anew.



Bakelite, the first synthetic plastic, was developed in 1907 by a Belgian, Dr Leo Baekeland. In its heyday in the 1920s and 30s, it was known as the 'material of 1,000 uses'. Bakelite and its imitations ushered in a new age of colourful and stylish, yet inexpensive, household goods.

Bakelite can be identified by the strong carbolic smell it gives off when it is rubbed. It was made in mottled and plain browns, black, green, red, and blue. Other early plastics that are also keenly collected include Lucite, which is usually either clear or translucent, and cast phenolic resins such as Catalin, which are often brightly coloured.

Colours other than browns and black make any plastic object more desirable. Styling is equally important. Pieces that reflect the Art Deco style of the 1930s – typified by stepped forms, streamlining, and clean lines – are especially collectable.

Plastics from the 1950s onwards tend to be less desirable and valuable as styling is not as strong and quality generally poorer than plastics from around 1910 to the 30s. Later plastics are also usually lighter and less robust.

Classic radios can sell for many hundreds of pounds or more, so most collectors concentrate on other themes.

▲ **Two polythene duck-shaped clothes brushes in their holders.** These quirky animal brushes with their holders are easily found and still usable. *1950s, 28.5cm (11¼in) high.*

**grey duck £10–15**
**blue duck £15–20**

▲ **A Bakelite mantel clock by Blangy.** The distinctive Art Deco styling of this clock, with its stepped form and clean lines, makes it desirable. *1930s, 13cm (5¼in) high.*

**£100–150**

► **Three novelty animal-shaped cast phenolic napkin rings** in different colours. Napkin rings mounted on tiny wheels are more valuable than these plain ones. *1930s, squirrel 7cm (2¾in) high.*

**£20–30 each**

◄ **A blue urea-formaldehyde lemon squeezer.** Plastics were used for a huge array of kitchen items in the 1930s, and many are still inexpensive today. Look for bright colours (especially the comparatively rare blue) and good condition. *1930s, 13.5cm (5¼in) diam.*

**£30–40**

◀ **A pair of Lucite 'pineapple' buttons.** Lucite was particularly popular in the 1950s, and it was made in a variety of colours. *1950s, 4cm (1½in) diam.*

**£2–3 each**

◀ **A Carvacraft double pen holder by Dickinson Products.** In a move away from the typical dark colours of early Bakelite, these streamlined items were made in three bright colours – amber, yellow, and green. The green is rare and more valuable. *c.1948, 16.5cm (6½in) wide.*

**£60–80**

▶ **A Bakelite toast rack.** The design incorporates the strong, angular lines of Art Deco. The brown and red mottling is typical of Bakelite. *1930s, 14cm (5½in) wide.*

**£15–20**

▶ **A Catalin magnifying glass** with a folding handle. As well as being brightly coloured, this piece is also moulded and carved, which makes it more desirable. *1930s, 11cm (4¼in) long.*

**£15–25**

## Collectors' Tips

- Avoid chipped or cracked objects, unless rare – damage devalues a piece
- For cohesion, focus your collection on items from a specific room or area such as the kitchen, or dressing table
- Look in particular for large objects made of Bakelite, as these are rare and therefore valuable

▼ **A Bandalasta ware plate, cup, and saucer.** Bandalasta ware was a urea-formaldehyde, often marked with the name 'Beatl' or 'Beetleware'. It was extensively used for 1930s picnic sets. *1930s, saucer 13cm (5in) diam.*

**£20–30**

◀ **A Bakelite ashtray with folding cigarette rests** (shown closed and open). This design was made in several colour combinations for Dunlop. *c.1930, 12cm (4¾in) diam.*

**£100–150**

◀ **A urea-formaldehyde egg cup.** Egg cups were produced in many styles and colours and can form a varied collection. The most desirable examples are those with good period styling and attractive colours, such as this mottled red and yellow. *1940s, 4.5cm (1¾in) diam.*

**£5–10**

# The 1950s was a time for people to make a fresh start. Post-war optimism and hope were reflected by an enthusiasm for new products, materials, and designs – from sofa beds to kidney-shaped tables and tulip chairs.

**A cream Bakelite Goblin Teasmade,** combining an alarm clock and tea maker, with a heart-shaped tray. *1950s, 26.5cm (10½in) wide.*

**£80–100**

In 1950, few families had a TV, car, or telephone. As manufacturing resources were channelled away from the war effort, technological innovations appeared in the home, along with materials such as plastic, glass fibre, and nylon. Objects were designed in abstract shapes and patterns, breaking away from the austerity of wartime. Today, there is a renewed interest in objects from this era.

## Practical living

Small new houses called for more compact furniture, and the decade saw the popularisation of trolleys, ironing boards, and sofa beds. Practical stacking furniture made its first appearance, as did flat-packed furniture. Tiered stands for plants were popular and can fetch around £50–100.

Kitchen tables were made from easy-to-clean Formica. Look out for 'dinette' sets – a matching table and four chairs for the kitchen. Plain, white versions, or those with flecked designs in the laminated surfaces, cost about £70–150. Those with abstract patterns often fetch about £100–150 or more.

Rectangular coffee tables printed with plain designs can sell for £20–30, but those with abstract patterns or stars can fetch around £80. Kidney-shaped tables are usually worth less than £50, but the more popular 'artist's palette'-shaped and three-tiered tables may cost from around £50 up to £150–200.

In 1950, there were 350,000 TV sets in Britain; by 1952, 2.5 million were in use. Manufacturers spotted a market and created TV lamps and chairs. The ceramics company Midwinter even launched compartmentalised TV-dinner plates as part of its Stylecraft range.

## Designer furniture

Many designers used materials such as bent plywood and moulded plastic or glass fibre combined with metal tubular frames to create strong, simple designs. Look out for pieces by Charles and Ray Eames, Arne Jacobsen, and Eero

## Some 1950s chairs to look for:

▪ RAR ▪ Cone ▪ Tulip ▪ Ant ▪

**An 'RAR' rocking chair,** designed by Charles and Ray Eames and produced by Herman Miller. The RAR chair – Rocking Armchair Rod – was designed in 1950 with a glass fibre shell on a wire and wood frame. This chair was produced around 1980 – original 1950s examples can fetch twice this price. *c.1980, 90cm (35½in) high.*

**£600–800**

**A swivelling 'Cone' chair,** designed by Verner Panton. Panton moved away from preconceived ideas of how a chair should be shaped in developing the 'Cone'. The frame was made from wire with an upholstered seat and back pad. *1950s–70s, 59cm (23¼in) wide.*

**£350–450**

**Two late 1950s West German Schmider 'Tigris' range cat-shaped vases,** designed by Anneliese Beckh in 1956. *10cm (4in) high.*

**£30–60 each**

◀ **A family clusters around a TV** in the 1950s to enjoy *Watch With Mother.*

Saarinen. Values can range from less than £100 for a stacking chair, up to £1,500–2,000 or more for one of their larger or more classic designs.

## From atoms to abstraction

Atoms, molecules, and boomerangs dominated surface design, and abstract patterns appeared on everything from curtains to plates. Parisian-style street scenes, palettes, poodles, and Siamese cat designs were also fashionable. Patterns on textiles became brighter, bolder, and more abstract. Designs by Lucienne Day, Marion Mahler, and Hilda Durkin are popular. A pair of curtains by Day can fetch £200–500. Likewise, ceramics by Wade, Poole, and others took on a 1950s look.

## The homemaker's terrain

Electrical gadgets aimed at helping the housewife, such as the Goblin Teasmade, can cost around £100–300. Collectors value them for their period styling rather than as functional pieces.

**One of a pair of 'Tulip' chairs,** designed by Eero Saarinen, comprising one armchair and one side chair (not shown). By attaching the moulded white glass-fibre chair to an enamelled metal base, Saarinen removed 'troublesome' legs in this iconic design. The red woven slip seats are original. *c.1956, 81cm (32in) high.*

**£200–400 each**

**An 'Ant' chair,** designed by Arne Jacobsen and manufactured by Fritz Hansen, design 3105, comprising a one-piece plywood back and seat on tubular supports. Released in a series from 1951, each with slightly different back shapes, these successful stacking chairs are still in production today. *1950s, 81cm (32in) high.*

**£100–200**

## Top Tips

- Look for the key motifs of the period – playing cards, glamour girls, and 'atomic' abstract designs – in bright colours or strong pastels.
- Choose eccentric shapes – kidney, palette, and asymmetrical, curving forms – and materials such as bent plywood, glass fibre, and plastics.
- Check for wear in any drinking glasses bearing painted transfers. Do not scrub a transfer – it may wear off.
- Buy small pieces of furniture if you wish to add a 1950s touch to a room quickly.
- Look for original upholstery fabric as this adds value to a chair.

## BUY

*When buying furniture look for pieces that exhibit the typical themes, materials, and shapes of the period, as these are more likely to at least hold their value in the long term. Space-saving objects were popular in the 1950s.*

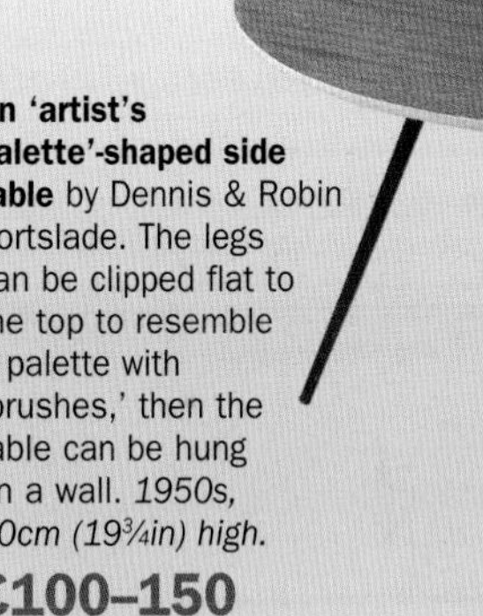

**An 'artist's palette'-shaped side table** by Dennis & Robin Portslade. The legs can be clipped flat to the top to resemble a palette with 'brushes,' then the table can be hung on a wall. *1950s, 50cm (19¾in) high.*

**£100–150**

## BUY

*Typical 1950s motifs range from gambling to glamorous girls. Even small objects from the period are desirable, as values have risen, but only choose pieces in excellent condition.*

**A pin-up girl glass,** with a double-sided transfer of a dancing girl. Unusually for a utilitarian piece, this is in top condition – the front-and-back transfer is an attractive and desirable feature. *1950s, 11cm (4¼in) high.*

**£20–30**

# The Festival of Britain

symbolised the nation's recovery after the war and was a milestone of our social history. Demand is increasing for memorabilia from this event as part of the recent upsurge of interest in 1950s styles and achievements.

In 1951, after years of austerity, the Festival of Britain was mounted to celebrate all that was good about Britain and to promote the arts and sciences and their impact on modern design. Although the Festival was countrywide, its heart was London's South Bank, where the enormous Dome of Discovery, the rocket-shaped Skylon, and the Royal Festival Hall (which is still used today) embodied a new view of modernity. More than 10 million people visited the Festival over a period of five months.

The designer and typographer Abram Games created the official emblem for this landmark event: a profile of Minerva, the Roman goddess of wisdom and crafts, surmounting a four-pointed compass. Games also designed much of the printed literature.

A vast number of commemorative objects was produced, most items now costing well under £100. Look out for less common pieces, such as glassware, ties, or car badges bearing the Festival logo or images of any of the key buildings. Badges, programmes, and postcards are easy to find and cost anything from £2 upwards.

▲ **A chrome tea caddy spoon,** with the emblem of the Festival on the handle. *c.1951, 7.5cm (3in) long.*

**£10–20**

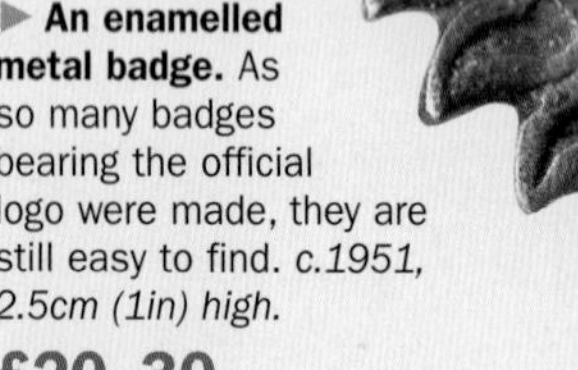

► **An enamelled metal badge.** As so many badges bearing the official logo were made, they are still easy to find. *c.1951, 2.5cm (1in) high.*

**£20–30**

► **A Paragon bone-china commemorative mug.** The fine quality and notable manufacturer make this a valuable piece. It would have been comparatively expensive in its day. *c.1951, 10cm (4in) high.*

**£120–180**

◄ **A French decanter and six glasses,** in amber-tinted glass, each item carrying the Festival emblem. The modernity of the design echoes a key theme of the Festival. *c.1951, decanter 19cm (7½in) high.*

**£50–70 for the set**

◄ **A programme for a children's concert at the Royal Albert Hall,** London. Items related to events beyond the South Bank are still of interest to collectors. *c.1951, 25.5cm (10in) high.*

**£3–5**

◀ **A commemorative tin.** Tins are popular with collectors but must be in good condition. This one has a design and colour typical of the period. *c.1951, 11.5cm (4½in) wide.*

**£20–30**

◀ **A leather purse, by Arden Forest** in mint condition. If the gilt were worn and the stitching broken, the value would be halved. *c.1951, 7.5cm (3in) wide.*

**£25–35**

## Collectors' Tips

Look out for these desirable features:

- Look for finely made items carrying the Festival emblem, as these tend to fetch good prices
- Favour pieces whose design and colours typify the period

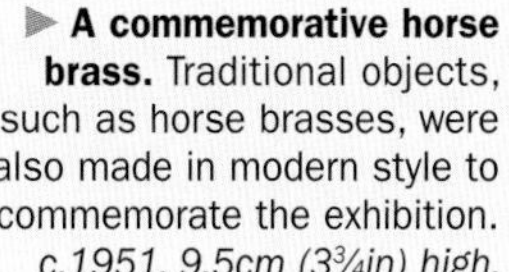

▶ **A commemorative horse brass.** Traditional objects, such as horse brasses, were also made in modern style to commemorate the exhibition. *c.1951, 9.5cm (3¾in) high.*

**£10–15**

◀ **An Ingersoll pocket watch** (both sides shown), one of a vast range of everyday objects that were engraved with the Festival emblem and sold as souvenirs. *c.1951, 5cm (2in) diam.*

**£80–100**

▼ **A copper egg cup,** with an applied enamel emblem. Many domestic objects were made, but few survive in good condition, as most have become worn through use. *c.1951, 3.75cm (1½in) high.*

**£15–20**

▶ **A cotton bale label.** Items showing major Festival buildings were probably designed by Abram Games and are much sought after. *c.1951, 20.5cm (8in) high.*

**£30–40**

# The 1960s brought a mix of colourful, modern, space-age, and anti-traditional styles with a dash of nostalgia. The current trend for retro styles has renewed interest in the fun and optimism of 60s design.

**A set of four Ravenhead glass tumblers,** in their original box, produced from 1964. *1960s, 12cm (4¾in) high.*

**£30–40**

The 1960s was the decade that brought psychedelia, free love, and flower power. Objects with the distinctive look of the period – from designer chairs to everyday homeware such as kettles and pen holders – are eagerly sought after. The current interest in revisiting styles from past decades and the popularity of an eclectic look in interior design have led many people to choose at least one 1960s-style piece for their homes.

## A wealth of materials

'Swinging London' was at its peak in the late 1960s. Everyone wanted to share in the lifestyle by furnishing their homes and dressing like the 'dedicated followers of fashion' they saw on TV and in magazines. Homes became more open-plan, and materials found in them included plastic, upholstered foam, bright – even clashing – colours, and the exoticism of foreign lands such as India and Morocco. Kitchens gained inexpensive 'mod cons' such as refrigerators and washing machines, and oven-to-tableware dishes that matched the crockery were extremely popular. Items made of stainless steel also found their way onto fashionable dining tables.

The 1950s had moved away from traditional tastes and historical influences, but the 60s promiscuously ransacked the past, adopting styles from the late 19th and early 20th centuries, and updating them with a splash of vibrant colour. An excellent example is the revival of Art Nouveau's sinuous, 'whiplash' lines and stylised flower motifs – transformed by bold, bright psychedelic colours such as purple, orange, acid green, and yellow.

## Look to the stars

Not all 1960s design looked backwards – much looked forwards too. The mysteries of outer space fascinated the public, from the UFO and sci-fi films of the 1950s up to 1969 when Neil

**A Paul Cadovius '291–00' chair,** manufactured by Cado. The fabric seat can be detached from the white glass fibre shell. *c.1969, 76cm (30in) high.*

**£100–200**

▼ **The 'Futuro' House** was a portable home made entirely of glass-filled polyester resin by Oy Polykem AB, Helsinki. Shaped like a UFO and featuring futuristic furnishings, it reflected the general interest in outer space in the 1960s. Only 20 were made before the early-1970s oil crisis rendered the design uneconomical. *c.1969.*

*Did You Know?*

*When Terence Conran's first Habitat store opened in 1964 on the Fulham Road in London, the staff outfits were designed by Mary Quant and early customers included John Lennon and George Harrison.*

Armstrong set foot on the moon. Androgynous clothes designed in futuristic materials such as plastic by cutting-edge designers such as André Courrèges, or mini-skirts and high boots were the look to acquire. In the home, furniture designed to resemble space pods, such as the 'Garden Egg' chair, typifies this style and can be found from around £300 upwards.

## Top tables

Tables also followed the decade's general trends, with many smaller examples being produced in brightly coloured plastic and larger items made in a combination of wood and metal tubing. The smaller pieces are often desirable, as they fit in modern homes. Depending on the designer, size, and condition, values range from about £100 to more than £1,000–2,000.

## Sitting pretty

Geometric shapes, including spheres, circles, and symmetrical curves, were popular. Plastic and upholstered foam overtook the use of laminated woods and could be easily formed into futuristic shapes. Foam furniture by the Danish designer Verner Panton or the Frenchmen Olivier Mourgue and Pierre Paulin can command about £600–£1,000 or more, although plastic examples can be less expensive. Moulded plastic stacking chairs by Joe Columbo and Panton's curving one-piece stacking chair, introduced in 1960, can cost up to £100–400 or more.

Other space-age forms include Eero Aarnio's 'Ball' chair, introduced in 1966 and featured in the cult 1960s TV show *The Prisoner* and the film *The Italian Job* (1969). The chair was shaped like a giant sphere with a cut-out section that allowed access to the upholstered interior, and stood on a swivelling base. Its film and TV links make this chair desirable and valuable, fetching around £2,000 or more. Stacking 'Polyprop' chairs designed by Robin Day are less expensive, often selling for about £15–20 or less. More than 15 million of these chairs have

## A closer look at... a Reuter Produkts 'Garden Egg' chair

Consider the material, shape, and colour, as well as the design, of 1960s chairs. Ideally all these factors should be in keeping with the trends and styles of the decade.

**A Reuter Produkts 'Garden Egg' chair, with a hinged lid enclosing a blue upholstered seat.** It was designed by the German Peter Ghyczy in 1968 and has been in production ever since. *c.1968, 82cm (32¼in) long.*

**£400–600**

The hinged cover has a seal to prevent water from damaging the fabric seat

The casing is made from fibreglass, allowing it to be used both indoors and out

The clean-lined space-age pod shape is typical of the 1960s

**A metal UFO-shaped floor heater made by ITHO.** *1960s, 35cm (13¾in) diam.*

**£100–200**

**A Robin Day 'Polyprop' chair, with a moulded-plastic shell on tubular steel supports,** designed in 1962–63 and made by Hille. *c.1960s, 85cm (33½in) high.*

**£30–50**

*Did You Know?*

*The most notable name in lava lamps still producing today is Mathmos. The company took its current name from the gloopy substance that sucked away the life-force and lived under the inhabitants of the futuristic city of Sogo, in the cult 1960s sci-fi film 'Barbarella'.*

## A closer look at... a pair of Piero Fornasetti pen holders

The Italian designer Piero Fornasetti was largely ignored by the Modern design movement in the 1950s and 60s, although he was popular with the public. His ceramics and furniture with opulent and intricate surface decoration are uncharacteristic of the period. His more individual pieces have the most appeal, and show consistent or rising values.

**A pair of ceramic pen holders, designed by Piero Fornasetti.** Fornasetti's unique designs have undergone a revival in popularity since the 1980s, and continue to be sought after today. *c.1960s, each 7cm (2¾in) high.*

**£50–100 each**

been made since the design was first seen in 1963.

Inflatable chairs were also popular in the 1960s – they were part of the 'Pop Art' movement championed by Andy Warhol, which highlighted the growing trend towards ephemeral objects which were thrown away once they went out of fashion. New materials such as plastic made the disposable society possible, and much was produced in bright, primary colours.

### Lighting the way

One of the most innovative objects of the 1960s was the lava lamp, designed by Edward Craven Walker and launched in 1963. It was shaped like a clear plastic rocket, filled with a brilliantly coloured, illuminated 'lava' of oil and wax which rose and fell in water. The lamp came in many different sizes and was widely imitated. New lamps cost around £50, but vintage pieces from the 1960s and 70s may sell for around £70–150 or more, depending on shape, size, and condition.

**A Poole Pottery plate from the Delphis range.** *1960s, 20cm (8in) diam.*

**£80–100**

Lighting also became more exciting. The variety was enormous, from plastic chandeliers to table lamps, floor lamps, up-lighters, and spotlights. Many were made in plastic or metal and had a space-age look. The spherical 'Moon light' shade by Verner Panton is an excellent example. Made up of layers of curving strips of coloured aluminium, it can be moved to reveal more or less of the bulb and so adjust the brightness. Examples can be found for about £100–300. Other shades that copied this idea, and were made of cut plastic strips that were assembled at home, can fetch about £20–50. The plastic 'Shattaline' table lamps, retailed by British Home Stores from 1968, are also typical of the period – examples can be found for less than £50.

### Soft furnishings

Fabrics followed either the flowing lines of Art Nouveau or the startling optical illusions of 'Op Art', best seen in the work of Bridget Riley. As a result, many fabrics had bold, geometrical, or abstract patterns in a palette that included oranges, browns, and creams, as well as the brighter colours associated with the decade. Look out for patterns produced by David Whitehead, or those designed by Verner Panton, Barbara Brown, and Peter McCulloch for the London retailer Heals. Value is determined by the size of the piece of fabric as well as by the designer and pattern. Pieces large enough to make a standard-sized pair of curtains usually cost around £100–200 or more. Smaller pieces – suitable mainly for cushion covers – will generally cost less than £30–50.

## On the table

Decorative objects were brightly coloured, with clean, space-age lines. Orange was a key colour, particularly in Poole Pottery's ceramic designs, such as the Delphis range, which can cost about £70–200 or more, depending on pattern and size. Carlton Ware, Midwinter, and Portmeirion adopted the space-age look, using cylinder and cone shapes combined with modern, bright patterns – many pieces can be found for about £50–100 or less. Brightly-coloured flower patterns were also common: 'Gaytime' by the Lord Nelson Pottery of Staffordshire is a notable example. Smaller items, such as milk jugs, plates, and jam pots, decorated with bold, multi-coloured flowers, can be found for around £20 or less.

Art pottery – decorative ceramic objects, handmade in limited numbers in small factories – also grew in popularity, with Troika, founded in 1963 in Cornwall, being one of the best-known names. Geometric-shaped pieces with hand-decorated, coloured surfaces featuring angular or primitive patterns can range from as little as £30–50 up to £500 or more.

**A 'Shattaline' turquoise plastic resin lamp base with a yellow spun glass fibre shade.** The lamp base also came in amber and green. *c.1968, base 18cm (7in) high.*

**£40–60**

## Geometric glass

Scandinavian design continued to have a major impact on ceramics, and also on glassware. Geometric forms and textured surfaces became the most notable styles: brightly coloured vases can be found for around £30–100 or less. Murano glass was still popular, as was the British Whitefriars factory.

Domestic glassware can be found for less than £50. Choose items in bright colours, with designs that are typical of the period. Values vary from about £3–5 for a glass up to around £20–30 for a set of four in their original box.

### Top Tips

- Choose original pieces where possible – many 1960s furniture designs are still produced today, but originals or limited editions are more desirable.
- To learn about 1960s themes and designers, study magazines and catalogues of the period. They are often inexpensive, at less than £5–15.
- If you want an item by a top designer, look for smaller or more common pieces, as they can be found more easily and are usually less expensive than bigger pieces.
- To date a Verner Panton chair, look for marks, including the name of the maker, on the underside of the piece.
- Look for marks on the base of the 'Ball' chair to identify the date it was made; those marked 'Adelta' date from after 1992.

### BUY

*The post-war decades saw many innovations in design and use of materials. These often become icons of the decade - and of modern design - and their popularity is likely to last.*

**An inflatable PVC 'Blow' chair,** made by Zanotta. PVC can discolour, so this still-clear example is desirable. *c.1967, 85cm (33½in) wide.*

**£50–70**

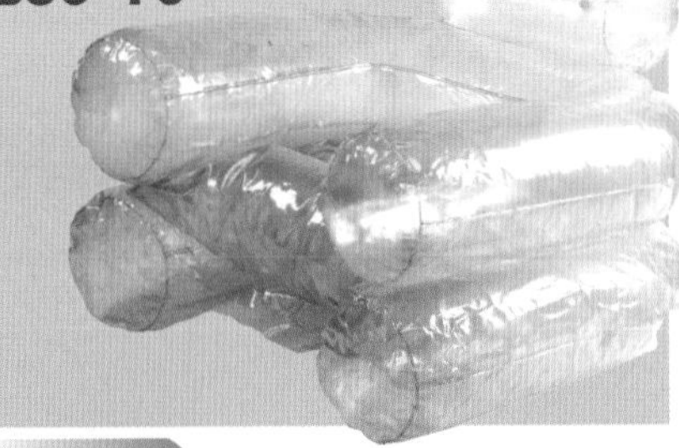

### BUY

*Lighting can be a relatively inexpensive way to add a 1960s touch to your home. The best investments will both sum up the style of the era and display the materials used.*

**A pair of Italian Artemide 'Dalu' plastic table lamps,** designed by Vico Magistretti. The curving design and bright plastic are typical. *c.1969, 26.5cm (10½in) high.*

**£200–300**

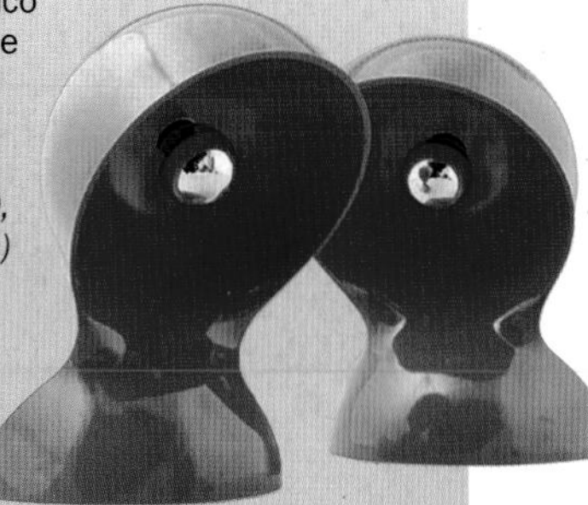

### KEEP

*Look out for even the most mundane homewares that represent the style of the period. Many sellers consider them to be less valuable as they are not furniture, lighting, ceramics or glass. Buy and cash in, as prices paid can be surprisingly high.*

**A 1960s printed plastic coathanger.** The psychedelic face and mirrored sunglasses capture so much of the style, fun, and colour of 1960s design. *34cm (13½in) wide.*

**£100–200**

### KEEP

*Hold on to pieces made by the most notable factories, as they already have a following and so are good prospects for value increases.*

**A Troika wheel vase,** with each side decorated with an abstract design. The wheel-shape of the vase and the geometric pattern, both typical of Troika, make this vase worth keeping. *c.1960s, 20cm (8in) diam.*

**£100–150**

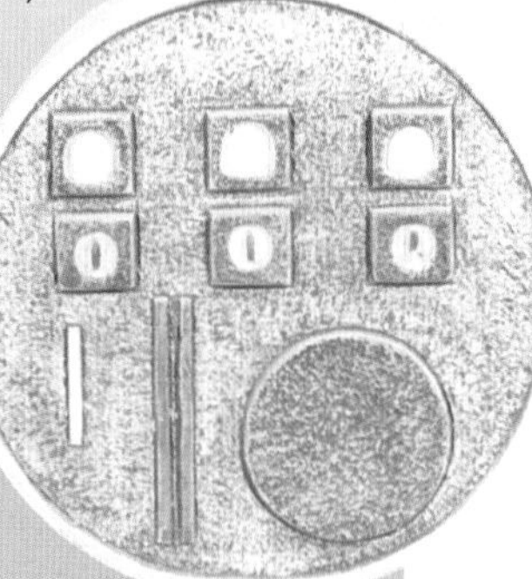

# Lamps from the 1930s to the 60s, often idiosyncratic, were beacons of contemporary style. As they fell out of favour, they were consigned to lofts and attics, but now they are being hunted out again, in great demand once more.

The styles that enthralled a public eager for the latest fashions in past decades are casting a bright light in today's homes, where retro fashions are back in vogue.

Lamps of the 1930s often have the sharp angular lines, architectural styling, and chrome features typical of the Art Deco period. In the 1940s, lamp designs emulated the 'streamlining' of speeding cars and trains.

After wartime austerity, designs became stunningly innovative in the 1950s and 60s. Brass and painted plaster was used a great deal, often in exotic or kitsch forms. Look for typical 1950s examples featuring glamour girls, playing-card motifs, and polka dots. The Italian Castiglioni brothers dominated the designer end of the market.

Psychedelic colours – orange, purple, and lime green – were the hallmarks of the 1960s. Lamps of the period still look fresh today and are rising in value. Those by admired designers such as Verner Panton can fetch up to £200–800 or more, but less expensive 'look-a-likes', often fetch under £100. Look for shapes inspired by outer space, such as rocket-shaped 'lava' lamps, and disc-shaped UFOs.

▲ **A 'dancer' lamp.** The body is of plaster and the fabric skirt forms the shade. Such fine condition is rare in figural lamps like this, as plaster is fragile. *1950s, 94cm (37in) high.*

**£800–1,000**

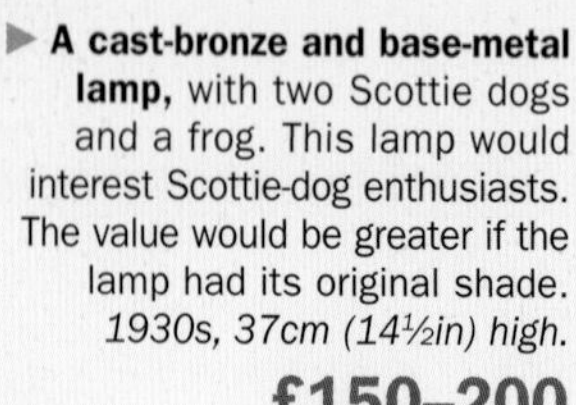

► **A cast-bronze and base-metal lamp,** with two Scottie dogs and a frog. This lamp would interest Scottie-dog enthusiasts. The value would be greater if the lamp had its original shade. *1930s, 37cm (14½in) high.*

**£150–200**

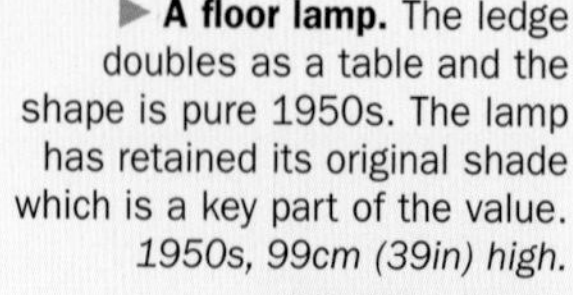

► **A floor lamp.** The ledge doubles as a table and the shape is pure 1950s. The lamp has retained its original shade which is a key part of the value. *1950s, 99cm (39in) high.*

**£200–250**

◄ **A pair of chrome 'face' Art Deco table lamps,** which are modern reproductions of 1930s Revere lamps, as they have metal, not black, bases. They were possibly designed by Doris Marks Dreyfuss. *c.1990s, 25.5cm (10in) high.*

**£100–200**

◄ **A brown Bakelite French 'Jumo' table lamp.** The streamlined form of this folding table lamp makes it a design classic. Look out for the rarer versions in white Bakelite. *c.1945, 50cm (19½in) high.*

**£300–500**

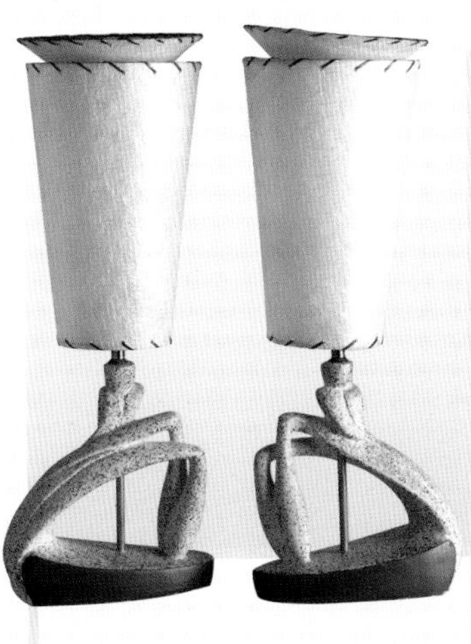

◀ **A pair of speckled black-and-gold plaster table lamps,** typical of 'Modernist' design. The original shades add to the value. *1950s, 61cm (24in) high.*

**£200–300**

◀ **A Bakelite and chrome 'aeroplane' lamp,** with a clock, by Sessions. The propellers on this example are Lucite replacements; they were originally chrome. *c.1948, 52cm (20½in) wide.*

**£250–350**

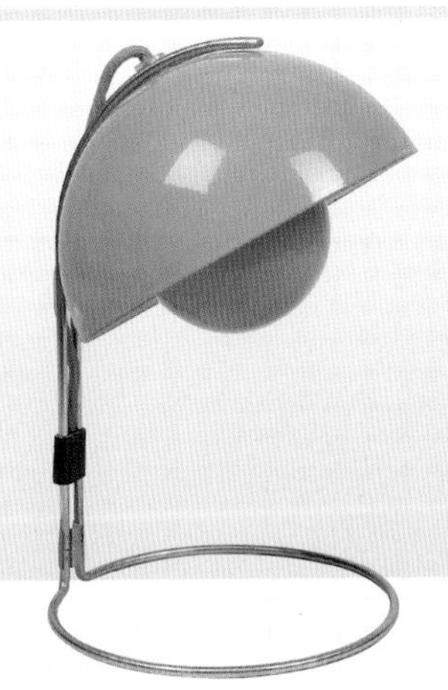

▶ **A 'Flower Pot' table lamp,** designed by Verner Panton. The bright orange colour and mushroom shape of the shade show the vigour and playfulness of 1960s design. *c.1968, 34cm (13½in) high.*

**£200–300**

## Collectors' Tips

- Look for lamps with the original shade
- Before using a lamp, have it checked by an electrician to ensure that the wiring is safe
- Buy pairs of lamps when you can – they are worth more than single items

▶ **A pair of Art Deco table lamps,** with chromed gazelles and black vitriolite glass bases. The stepped bases, figures, and frosted glass shades mimicking the work of René Lalique, are quintessential Art Deco. *1930s, 22cm (8¾in) high.*

**£300–400**

▶ **A Cosmo Designs chrome table lamp,** with a four-piece revolving shade. The shape and colour of the shade embody 1960s psychedelia. *1960s, 33cm (13in) high.*

**£50–100**

◀ **A painted plaster backlit TV lamp.** In the 1950s, these lamps were set on the TV to even the contrast between the screen and the room. *1950s, 45cm (17¾in) wide.*

**£80–120**

◀ **A pair of plaster 'fairy' lamps,** with their original shades. The complex shapes and kitsch figures make these lamps sought after. *1950s, 86cm (33¾in) high.*

**£600–700**

# The 1970s were characterised by two distinct home-interior styles: the back-to-nature rustic look and the bolder and more colourful influences of Pop and Op Art.

**A chrome and wire 'bubble' sculpture** with blue and green balls. *1970s, 45.5cm (18in) high.*

**£20–30**

The 1970s was the era of glam rock, disco, and punk, as well as flared trousers and boob tubes. Pop Art was popular for home-interior styles, but so was the rural look epitomised by *The Good Life* TV series.

## Brown is beautiful

'Natural' wood panelling, cork tiles, and hessian wall covering – in colours described as 'beautiful brown' – were in vogue. Shag-pile carpets were popular, as was vinyl wallpaper. Those who did not like brown could choose from deep red, orange, tomato-red, and purple, inspired by fashionable interiors such as Biba's London department store. The shop sold 'far out' clothes, fabrics, and household accessories, including Biba paint and distinctive wallpapers.

## Fantastic plastic

The craze for plastic furniture continued into the early 1970s. Although still retaining a curving shape, many pieces gained a slight angularity. A green plastic 'Vicario' chair by Vico Magistretti may cost around £100–150.

The oil crisis of the 1970s led to a decrease in plastic furniture. Wood and wood substitutes took over – their tones were also better suited to contemporary colour schemes.

Modular seating was all the rage. Its graduated sections could be arranged to fit any space. Such multi-purpose, furniture, designed for ultra-modern open-plan living, is now among the most collectable of 1970s pieces.

Smoked-glass topped tables were popular. A large table by William Plunkett can command around £600–1,000, but smaller unmarked pieces may be worth about £200–500.

## Making light of it

Lighting became part of a home's décor – as personal to taste as wall-paper or paint. The Italians were supreme in the field, producing designs helped by 1970s technological advances. Values start around £30–50 for an unmarked plastic mushroom-shaped table lamp, rising to around £1,000–2,000 for larger ceiling- or wall-mounted pieces by designers

## Some 1970s ceramics to look for:

▪ Langley ▪ Hornsea ▪ Jersey ▪ Briglin ▪

◄ **A Langley Pottery jug** from Lovatt & Lovatt, and designed by Glyn Colledge, who is better known for producing designs for Denby. This jug has hand-painted, inverted heart-shaped and foliate patterns. In the 1970s, Lovatt & Lovatt produced hand-painted decorative and functional wares. *1970s, 20cm (8in) high.*

**£30–50**

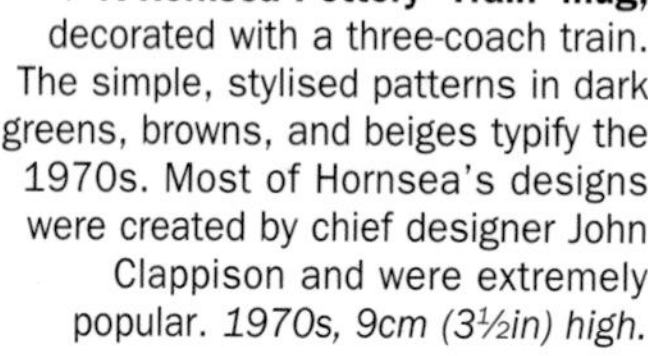

► **A Hornsea Pottery 'Train' mug,** decorated with a three-coach train. The simple, stylised patterns in dark greens, browns, and beiges typify the 1970s. Most of Hornsea's designs were created by chief designer John Clappison and were extremely popular. *1970s, 9cm (3½in) high.*

**£10–15**

▼ A 1970s rustic-style living-dining room with natural pine decoration and grass-green floor covering.

such as Verner Panton (Denmark) and Walter Pichler (Austria).

## Colour range

Textile colours ranged from hot yellow, orange, or cherry, to more earthy, abstract, natural browns. Patterns were flowing and made up of blocks of colour covering the entire surface of the fabric. Look for textiles sold by Heals of London.

## Setting the table

The 1970s trend for oven-to-table ware was called 'dining co-ordination'. Inspired by the idea of self-sufficiency, pottery firms like Denby, Midwinter, and Portmeirion created new country-style shapes and patterns. Sets can cost from about £5 to around £100.

Glassmakers created naturalistic textures, such as bark. Carafes by firms such as Whitefriars and Iittala were in vogue. Stainless steel was also popular – look for 'Old Hall' items, which usually sell for around £10 up to £100.

**A Vico Magistretti 'Vicario' chair** with a green moulded plastic body. *c.1970, 100cm (39½in) high.*

**£150–200**

## Top Tips

- Look out for boxes and labels identifying the maker, as these can add value to an object.
- Look for the decade's cutting-edge designs, produced in small numbers, by innovators such as Joe Colombo (creator of the 'Boby' unit, below).
- Consult original retailers' catalogues and fashion magazines to familiarise yourself with key designers whose works may not be signed or marked.

## BUY

*Plastic was a defining material used for homeware in the 1970s. Plastic objects were often brighter and more angular than 1960s pieces. If an item is by a notable designer and still useful, it should increase in value.*

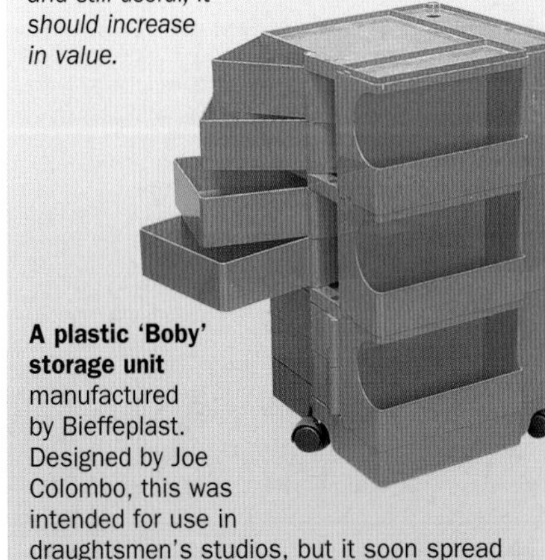

**A plastic 'Boby' storage unit** manufactured by Bieffeplast. Designed by Joe Colombo, this was intended for use in draughtsmen's studios, but it soon spread to the home. It was available in red, yellow, black, and white. *1970, 53cm (21in) high.*

**£100–200**

## KEEP

*Soft furnishings, from cushions to curtains, can be an excellent way to add a period touch to the home. Many are collectable, so check any old curtains before throwing them away. Look out for colours of the period and bold geometric patterns, as interest is growing.*

**A piece of Heals 'Omega' pattern fabric,** designed by Barbara Brown. Many of her designs combine colours and geometrical shapes to create a three-dimensional pattern on a flat surface. Her popularity makes her designs worth keeping. *1970s, 1m (39½in) wide.*

**£30–60**

**A pair of Jersey Pottery flower vases** with a hand-painted design. Founded in 1946, the Jersey Pottery prided itself on handmade, hand-painted pottery that adapted to the decorative styles of the period. *c.1970, 16cm (6¼in) wide.*

**£10–15 each**

**A Briglin Pottery vase** with a cow-parsley design. The Briglin pottery made affordable yet functional and decorative ceramics for modern homes in browns, blues, and creams, often with natural motifs scored into the surface. *1970s, 26.5cm (10½in) high.*

**£30–50**

# Glossary

**almandine** A deep violet-red garnet, used as a gemstone.

**anodisation** The process of coating a metal object, often aluminium, with a thin protective film.

**applied** Denotes a separate part that has been added to an object, such as a handle or decoration to a ceramic body.

**Art Deco** A style known for its geometric shapes, bright, bold colours, and architectural inspirations that was popular from c.1918 to 1940. The name is derived from the 1925 *Exposition Internationale des Arts Décoratifs et Industriels Modernes in Paris. See Paris Exhibition of 1925.*

**Art Nouveau** Popular from the 1890s to c.1910, a style based on sinuous curves, flowing lines, asymmetry, and organic forms. Flower and leaf motifs were often incorporated into the designs.

**Arts and Crafts Movement** A late 19th-century movement, led by the British designer William Morris, advocating a return to simple design and quality craftsmanship.

**aurora borealis stone** A type of rhinestone that has surfaces coated with a metallic sheen to create an iridescence reminiscent of the shimmering green and blue lights seen in northern skies.

**aventurine** A type of translucent glass with metallic – usually copper – specks; the term also applies to other finishes with a similarly shiny appearance such as lacquer and glaze.

**backstamp** The mark printed on the base of a ceramic object that identifies the manufacturer, the model name and/or number, and sometimes the designer.

**baguette** A gemstone cut in a long, rectangular shape.

**Bakelite** A type of plastic made of phenolic resin and formaldehyde, patented by Dr Leo Baekeland in 1907. When rubbed, it gives off a benzene-like smell. Mottled brown and black are the most common colours, but green and blue can also be found.

**baluster** A double-curved form with a slender neck and bulbous body.

**base metal** Any nonprecious metal such as brass, bronze, iron, and steel or an alloy. It may be coated with a precious metal such as gold or silver. Often known in the USA as 'pot metal'.

**bisque** A type of unglazed porcelain used for making dolls from c.1860 to c.1925.

**black basalt** A fine-grained volcanic rock. Basalt ware, made in imitation of this stone, is a hard, unglazed black stoneware produced by Staffordshire potteries, particularly Wedgwood.

**bone china** A durable porcelain made of kaolin (china clay), petuntse (china stone), and dried, powdered bone. It was developed as a way to compete with Chinese imports made of hard-paste porcelain. The Spode factory began producing it in England in 1794, and it is still manufactured today.

**bright-cutting** A type of engraving or cutting used on metal, gems, or glass where the surface is cut at an angle to form facets that reflect the light.

**cabinet ware** Porcelain wares, such as plates, cups, and saucers, that are made for display rather than for practical purposes.

**cabochon** A large, domed stone with a polished, unfaceted surface.

**cameo** A hardstone, gem, glass object, or shell with a carved design in relief, usually contrasting with the background. Commonly depicted subjects include portraits, classical groups, and landscapes.

**cane** A stick of glass that is made by fusing together a bundle of glass rods, or lengths. The rods may be coloured to form a multicoloured cane.

**carded** A term used when referring to toy figures and other merchandise still in its original packaging, comprising a card backing with a plastic cover that allows the enclosed objects to be seen. 'Loose' refers to an object no longer in its packaging.

**cartouche** A framed area, often in the shape of a paper scroll or shield, which can be inscribed. It is often found on furniture or small boxes.

**cased glass** Glassware consisting of two or more layers of glass in different colours. The thick outer layer is the first to be blown; subsequent layers are blown into the first layer.

**Catalin** A type of cast phenolic plastic made in bright colours. It was used from c.1938 to c.1946 to produce radio cabinets, costume jewellery, and other small, simply shaped items.

**celadon** Used in China for more than 2,000 years, this distinct greyish-green or bluish-green glaze serves to imitate jade. It can also be found on wares from Japan and South Korea.

**ceramics** From the Greek word for 'clay', a term that refers to clay-based products – including bone china, earthenware, porcelain, and stoneware – that have been hardened by heating at high temperatures.

**chalcedony** A usually greyish quartz used as a gemstone.

**chinoiserie** A style popular in Europe during the late 17th and 18th centuries, in which oriental-style figures and motifs – including pagodas, birds, dragons, and lotus flowers – were used to decorate Western-style wares.

**chromolithography** An early form of colour printing that uses limestone slabs. Each slab is carved with a pattern and prints one colour. By imposing one slab exactly over another, a multicoloured image is made.

**chronograph** Any precision watch that can measure time accurately to the nearest second or fraction of a second, often to determine elapsed time in sporting events or to record speed.

**citrine** A type of quartz used as a gemstone. Usually a pale yellow, it can also be a reddish-brown or reddish-orange. It is sometimes mistaken for topaz.

**Classical style** Decoration based on the shapes and ornamentation of ancient Greece and Rome, featuring motifs such as palmettes, husks, garlands of flowers, urns, and mythical creatures. *See neoclassicism.*

**clockwork mechanism** A motor powered by a spiral spring that is wound up with a key; it is sometimes found in a mechanical toy or music device.

**cloisonné** An enamelling technique where fine metal wire is attached to a body to form connecting compartments or cells; these are filled with coloured enamel paste before the object is fired in a kiln to harden the enamel. *See enamel.*

**comport** A dish, often supported by a stem or foot, used during the dessert course to hold fruit.

**composition** A plaster-like substance consisting of whiting (chalk), resin, and size (glue) or other substances. It is used for producing dolls and other toys.

**couturier** A person who designs, manufactures, and sells high-fashion clothes for women.

**cranberry glass** Also known as ruby glass, a type of 19th-century glass with copper oxide or gold chloride added to create a pink hue; it was made both in Britain and the USA.

**crazing** A network of fine cracks in a ceramic glaze – caused by uneven shrinking when the object was fired in the kiln. The term can also apply to cracks on a painted surface.

**creamware** A type of durable earthenware with a cream-coloured body and lead glaze, first produced c.1720. Wedgwood referred to it as Queen's ware.

**cut glass** Glass that has been decorated by cutting patterns – such as blazes, combs, diamonds, flutes, stars, steps, and swags – into the surface of the glass.

**diamanté** A sparkling artificial crystal, also often called a rhinestone. *See rhinestone.*

**die-cast** Metal items, such as toy cars or figures, made inexpensively from metal alloys cast in a reusable mould.

**earthenware** Pottery that is fired in a kiln at a low temperature to a porous state. It then requires a glaze and a second firing to make it waterproof.

**Edwardian** Relating to the styles popular in Britain when Edward VII reigned, between 1901 and 1910.

**Elastolin** A generic term for early 20th-century toy soldiers made from a mixture of sawdust, casein, kaolin, and glue which was moulded around a wire figure. The firm O. & M. Hausser of Neustadt, Germany, was the first to use the term.

**embossed** A large-scale relief design on metal (or leather) created by hammering or pressing on the reverse side of the material; other techniques using hammers and punches are then used to add any fine details.

**enamel** A hard decorative or protective coating, such as a glaze on a ceramic object.

**ephemera** A term for all printed matter originally intended for immediate use and disposal, including packaging and wrappers, tickets, cards (such as cigarette, greetings, post, and trade cards), labels, and postage stamps.

**escapement** The part of a watch that governs the delivery of power to its movement, determining the speed at which the hands turn. The verge escapement was the first widely used method. By the 19th century, the cylinder escapement and lever escapement were the two most popular mechanisms, the latter of which was more efficient and has dominated since the 1830s.

**fazzoletto** A style of vase, shaped to resemble a scrunched-up handkerchief falling to the ground, made by Murano glassmakers, particularly Venini, from the 1950s.

**filigree** An open ornamental work of fine gold or silver wire or plate that has been twisted or formed into a decorative shape.

**finial** A decorative knob on a lid or as the terminal of a piece, such as the decorative form at the end of a handle on a spoon.

**first edition** A copy of a book from the original, first printing of the publication. Any subsequent print runs produce other editions, which may or may not have revisions.

**fixed distant** A railway signal which is fixed in the 'on' position to indicate a permanent speed restriction or other need for caution further along the line.

**flambé** A type of glaze produced to mimic the ancient *sang de boeuf* glaze. Introduced by Royal Doulton in 1902, the copper oxide formula creates a lustrous, crimson-red glaze with hints of a bright blue – hence its name, which is French for 'flamed'.

**flange** The projecting disc-like rim of a glass object, such as a vase.

**floriform** In the shape of a flower.

**fluting** A pattern of parallel grooves that run vertically along a surface, forming concave columns.

**foliate** Leaf and vine decoration.

**foot** The supportive base of a vase or drinking glass, found in a variety of styles, including conical, domed, firing, flanged, lemon squeezer, pedestal, and stepped square.

**frieze** Originally an architectural term, it refers to the horizontal band found below the cornice on a piece of case furniture such as a cabinet or bookcase; a frieze rail is the wooden support below the top of a desk or table.

**gadrooning** Found on silver, ceramics, and furniture, a continuous pattern of vertical or spiralling curves in a convex profile.

**gauge** The distance between the rails of a railway track. Toy trains are often classified according to the gauge of the tracks they are designed to ride on. 0-gauge, commonly used for early models, is 3.2cm (1¼in) wide; 00-gauge, introduced in 1938 for Meccano train sets, is 1.6cm (⅝in) wide.

**gemstone** A stone cut and polished for use in jewellery. The commercial value of a gem determines its category: diamonds, emeralds, pearls, rubies, and sapphires are examples of precious gems; amethyst, aquamarine, peridot, and tourmaline are semi-precious gems; and agate, lapis lazuli, and onyx are ornamental gems.

**gilt** The gold finish applied to a silver or electroplated object or to a ceramic, wood, or glass item by one of several techniques.

**glacé** A French word describing a smooth, glossy, or glazed surface found on silks or leathers.

**glaze** A glassy material applied to ceramics that forms a smooth, shiny, decorative, and protective surface when fired in a kiln. Tin and celadon glazes are opaque, while a lead glaze is transparent.

**gold filled** Jewellery made with a thin outer surface of solid gold bonded to another less expensive metal. It has many of the same physical characteristics as solid gold, such as beauty, strength, and durability.

**good condition** A term used to refer to an item that is complete but shows some sign of age or use, perhaps with slight wear and tear, but nothing that dramatically affects its overall appearance and attraction. Some dealers might differentiate between 'good' and 'very good' condition.

**gramophone** The precursor to the record player, a mechanical device for reproducing sound using a flat disc, stylus, and diaphragm; the sound is amplified through a horn, which may be built in or external.

**ground** The background or base colour of an object. Decoration is often applied on top of it.

**group** A ceramic object consisting of more than one figure.

**guilloche** A continuous pattern consisting of a pair of bands that twist to form interlacing plaits; these are sometimes filled with rosettes or other floral motifs and are often covered with coloured enamel.

**gutta-percha** Developed in the late 19th century, a hard, dark, rubbery material produced from the resin of several Malaysian trees and used to make dolls' heads, golf balls, and other small objects.

**hallmark** The official series of marks found on a British silver or gold item, attesting to its purity and identifying its maker, date of manufacture, and the city in which it was assayed (tested for quality).

**hardstone** A term used to describe any semi-precious stone, such as agate or malachite.

**hollow-casting** A cost-effective method of casting a figure that saves metal. A molten metal alloy is poured into a mould. Once the outer layer has set, the interior, still molten metal is poured out from the centre of the figure.

**Imari porcelain** Japanese porcelain made at Arita from the late 17th century onwards; it was shipped from the port of Imari, hence the name. It is recognisable by its underglaze blue, iron red, and gilt palette.

**impressed marks** Marks that have been made in the surface of a ceramic, glass, or metal body, usually on the base of the piece. They may provide information such as the manufacturer, designer, pattern, or range.

**incised decoration** A pattern or inscription scratched into a ceramic, metal, or glass body by using a sharp tool such as a metal point.

**intaglio** An Italian term for incised decoration, where the design is cut into the surface of a glass, ceramic, metalwork, or hardstone object. Unlike a cameo, where the design protrudes, the design in intaglio is recessed.

**jet** A type of black fossilised wood, or coal, that was carved and polished by the Victorians to create mourning jewellery and buttons. It was usually sourced from the Whitby area, in Yorkshire.

**Kakiemon** Used to decorate Japanese porcelain from c.1660, a distinctive palette of colours, including dark blue, turquoise, iron red, yellow, black, and sometimes brown. The term is taken from the name of a Japanese potter. European factories copied the style in the early 18th century.

**kapok** A heavy fibre similar to cottonwool used as a stuffing for teddy bears and other soft toys.

**knop** A rounded, bulbous part on the stem of a drinking glass, or a rounded, bulbous handle on a lid.

**lace paper** A type of paper that is embossed, cut, and perforated to create an open design that imitates lace. It was used by the Victorians to make Valentine cards.

**lapis lazuli** A semi-precious opaque blue gemstone; it has flecks of pyrite ('fool's gold').

**latticinio** From the Italian *latte* (milk), a type of white glass often in the form of woven threads in clear glass.

**lithography** The technique for making a print by taking an absorbent stone block and drawing on it with a special greasy crayon. When ink is applied to the block, it sticks only to the greasy areas; by lightly pressing paper on top of the block, the ink is transferred to the paper. It was developed in Germany by Aloys Senefelder in 1798, and spread to the rest of Europe and the USA over the following 20 years.

**lithophane** A panel or plaque made of thin, translucent, unglazed porcelain with a three-dimensional picture or design pressed into it. Lithophanes were used in lamp shades, hung in windows, and sometimes formed the base of a cup or plate. Thinner sections created the illusion of light, while thicker sections created shadows.

**Lucite** Also known as Plexiglass and later, Perspex, a transparent plastic first produced commercially in the 1930s. It sometimes yellows or cracks with age.

**lustre ware** Ceramics with an iridescent, metallic finish, created by adding or applying one of several metal oxides to the glaze.

**maki-e** A Japanese decorative technique for lacquerwork, in which gold or coloured dust is sprinkled onto wet lacquer to form a design – maki-e is Japanese for 'sprinkled illustration'. The background is usually black, gold, or red, and the technique can be found on boxes and inro, small containers that hang from a belt and were commonly used to carry a seal.

**marquetry** Veneer and inlays of other materials such as bone, ivory, mother-of-pearl, and metals that form various patterns in wood, including geometric shapes and floral designs.

**Mauchline ware** Souvenir wooden boxes and small household goods in a distinctive style from the town of Mauchline in Scotland, although the term refers to all similar items from Scotland. The wood is usually sycamore, and the wares often have a transfer print showing a scenic or historical view.

**millefiori** The Italian term for 'thousand flowers', a glassmaking technique in which different-coloured glass canes are cut into sections and embedded into a glass body so that their cross-section forms a pattern. The technique is often associated with glass paperweights made since the 19th century.

**mint condition** A term used to describe an item that is pristine, as if brand new, unused, and complete, showing no signs of age, wear and tear, or any other damage. This is the most desirable condition for an object and can enhance value considerably.

**Modern style** A term embracing a number of different decorative art styles from *c.*1920 to the 1950s, all of which featured clean lines without adornments. Geometry, new materials, and mass-production were key to these styles, as was the principle that form should follow function.

**mohair** Hair from the Angora goat, used in the 19th century for dolls' hair and for fur on pre-World War II teddy bears. It has long, lustrous fibres that are easy to dye.

**mon** The badge of a Japanese family, most commonly circular and in the form of a 16-petalled chrysanthemum, but also seen depicting birds, flowers, and other natural motifs.

**mother-of-pearl** An easily carved, iridescent material from the interior of certain seashells, such as the nautilus shell. It is used in jewellery and as an inlay material in marquetry.

**mould-blown** Molten glass that is blown into a mould to form a shape. The mould may be full size, or it may be a smaller 'dip' mould, which forms a shape that is then re-blown to a larger size.

**moulding** Strips of wood, metal, or other material applied to a surface to form a decorative geometric profile, often based on architectural features, or to hide a joint.

**murrine** A type of Murano glassware in which short lengths or slices of coloured glass canes (*murrine*) are used to form a mosaic pattern on the surface of an object.

**neoclassicism** An 18th-century revival of the Classical style, which was based on the ornamentation and forms of ancient Greece and Rome found during the excavations of Pompeii and Herculaneum. *See Classical style.*

**novelty shape** An item made in a decorative, unusual, or amusing and witty shape, such as a teapot in the shape of a cottage or a salt shaker in the shape of a snowman.

**one-sheet poster** A portrait format film poster commonly used in the USA, sized at 68.5cm x 104cm (27in x 41in).

**Op Art** The popular abbreviation for Optical Art, a 1960s art movement that created an illusion of space, movement, and volume by using abstract compositions of spirals, grids, undulating lines, stripes, and spots.

**overglaze decoration** Enamel colours that are applied by hand, or by a transfer print, onto a glazed ceramic object, which is then fired a second time at a low temperature.

**Paris Exhibition of 1925** The Anglicised name for the *Exposition Internationale des Arts Décoratifs et Industriels Modernes,* which was held in Paris in 1925. Several million visitors viewed more than 150 exhibition stands and pavilions dedicated to works that displayed 'new inspiration and real originality'. Many objects were in the style now referred to as Art Deco. *See Art Deco.*

**paste** A hard, versatile glass compound, which can have many of the properties of gemstones when certain minerals and oxides are added to it. Pastes have been used in a wide range of colours to make jewellery since the 18th century.

**pastille burner** A ceramic object used to hold a pastille – a small perfumed tablet – which was lit to scent a room. They were popular during the 18th and 19th centuries.

**pastoral** An object or decoration that is characteristic of, or depicts, rural life or scenery.

**pâte de verre** From the French, meaning 'glass paste', a type of translucent glass produced by making a paste of powdered glass mixed with paint or enamels. The technique was used by the French in the 19th century to create small, elaborate objects.

**pillar-cutting** A method of cutting glass that leaves a pattern of deeply cut vertical flutes.

**plate** A term referring to items made of gold, silver, or another metal, often for domestic purposes, but also for ceremonial use, especially in churches. It is also sometimes used as an abbreviation for Sheffield plate.

**plique à jour** A type of unbacked, translucent enamel, reminiscent of a stained-glass window when light shines through it. It was popular in Art Nouveau jewellery.

**pontil mark** Found on the base of a blown-glass object, a disc or irregular-shaped mark created where the object was held by a pontil rod while it was being blown.

**poor condition** A term used to refer to an item that shows considerable signs of wear and damage, possibly with missing parts.

**Pop Art** A style where everyday and mass-produced items – such as advertisements, packaging, and comic strips – were seen as possible forms of art. The style emerged in Britain in the mid-1950s and peaked in New York in the 1960s.

**porcelain** A hard, white, translucent ceramic made from kaolin (china clay) and petuntse (china stone). It should ring when struck.

**porringer** A cylindrical silver, pewter, or ceramic cup for holding soup; it has two handles and a cover.

**Potteries, the** An area in Staffordshire known for its ceramics factories. It comprises the 'Six Towns' of Burslem, Fenton, Hanley, Longton, Tunstall, and Stoke-on-Trent.

**provenance** Documentation or a verifiable account that is supplied with an object to identify its origins or history, or both. The provenance of an object can increase its value, especially if it is interesting, or links the object to a renowned maker, owner, event, or location.

**pulled rim** The rim of a glass object that has been pulled to form an extended, abstract shape.

**quad poster** A landscape format film poster used in Britain, sized at 76cm x 101.5cm (30in x 40in).

**Queen's ware** Creamware made by Wedgwood from *c.*1765 – named after Queen Charlotte, who had visited the factory.

**reeding** A type of decorative relief moulding formed of thin, parallel, convex rods, or reeds; it is most commonly found on furniture and silver. The effect is similar to fluting. *See fluting.*

**Regency** A generic term for the decorative arts style found in Britain between *c.*1800 and 1830, towards the end of neoclassicism. Forms were heavier, larger, and more richly decorated, especially in furniture. The style was named after the Prince Regent, who became George IV.

**reign mark** Used on ceramics and works of art in China from the beginning of the Ming dynasty (1368–1644), an Imperial Chinese mark written as either four or six characters in script or seal form to provide the name of the emperor and usually the dynasty. The marks were often made for an earlier emperor, either out of respect or to avoid punishment for using the reign mark of a current emperor on wares not intended for his use.

**relief decoration** Ornamentation that is made by a mould, stamped, or carved so that it is raised above the background surface; the depth of the decoration is referred to as high, medium, or bas (low) relief.

**repeating mechanism** Also known as a repeater, a mechanism found in clocks and watches that repeats the strike of the previous hour – and sometimes quarter hour and last five minutes – when a cord or button is touched. It allows the user to know the time without having to look at the face.

**resist** In ceramic decoration, an area or sections on the body covered with wax or paper to resist, or block, a lustre solution applied to the rest of the piece. Once the solution has been applied, the resist is removed.

**rhinestone** This term originally referred to a type of clear quartz used in costume jewellery, but it now includes any colourless paste or rock crystal used in costume jewellery to imitate diamonds. *See diamanté.*

**rock crystal** A common mineral consisting of pure silica that has been used as a decorative ornament for centuries. It is polished or faceted to be used in jewellery and was used for cameos and seals in the 19th and 20th centuries.

**roiro-nuri** A Japanese lacquer finish with a waxy black or highly reflective, brilliant black appearance. It is used as a ground. *See ground.*

**rolled gold** A type of imitation solid gold used in the 19th and 20th centuries to produce inexpensive jewellery and small decorative items. A thin layer of gold was fused to a base metal, such as copper, then rolled into a sheet for use.

**salt glaze** A type of glaze applied to stoneware, which is created by throwing salt into the kiln during firing. It vaporises, leaving behind a thin, clear glaze.

**samovar** A large, usually decorative urn for tea or hot water, often with a tap at the front to pour the tea into a cup or a smaller, more portable teapot.

**sandwich set** A serving tray and matching plates for serving sandwiches during afternoon tea. These were popular during the first half of the 20th century.

**sang de boeuf** From the French, literally meaning 'beef's blood', a bright plum-red glaze used to decorate ceramics; it was developed in China in the early 18th century.

**Satsuma** A general term for potteries on the island of Kyushu, Japan, which made simple wares for export to the West. These had a cream-coloured body and a clear yellowish glaze that was often crackled. The wares were often decorated with figures and flowers in coloured enamel and with gilding.

**scrap** A small novelty piece of paper or thin card colour-printed and shaped in the form of an animal, flowers, people, or other popular motifs. Fashionable during the Victorian period, they were collected in albums or glued to small pieces of furniture, among other uses.

**Secessionist style** A pure, abstract art style advocated by a group of Viennese avant-garde designers, artists, and architects; the group was established in 1897 and led by Josef Hoffman and Koloman Moser.

**seconds** Pottery items in which the body or the glaze is damaged or becomes imperfect in some way during manufacture.

**seed pearl** A tiny, imperfectly formed pearl.

**self-winding** A mechanism that winds itself automatically, usually using the constant movement of a hand.

**sgrafitto** A decorative effect created by scratching or scoring through the surface of unfired slip applied to a ceramic object. *See slip.*

**shagreen** A rough shark or ray skin, usually dyed green, with raised 'scales' in a circular or lozenge shape, used as an inlay or to cover boxes and other small objects. The term is also sometimes used to refer to roughened animal skins.

**shibayama** A type of Japanese inlay, using various materials, including glass, ivory, shell, and tortoiseshell, set into a lacquered or ivory ground. *See ground.*

**sleeping eyes** A type of doll's eyes, weighted internally so that they remain open while the doll is upright but close when the doll is lying down.

**slip** A term meaning liquid clay; slip is often applied to a ceramic body as a finish, as decoration, or to bond two pieces together.

**slip-cast ware** Pottery that has been made by pouring slip, or liquid clay, into a mould.

**SLR** The abbreviation for a single lens reflex camera. When the button is pressed, light enters through the lens and continues to the film as the viewfinder mirror is retracted.

**smoker's companion** Any object with accessories for a smoker.

**snuff mull** A small tobacco box with a ridged interior against which a plug of tobacco is ground to create snuff. Early mulls were made from horn; later examples in precious metals and tortoiseshell.

**sommerso** From the Italian for 'submerged', a glassmaking technique where one or more layers of differently coloured glass are encased in a thick layer of clear glass. Up to around four different layers of coloured glass may be used under the clear layer.

**stoneware** A hard, dense non-porous type of ceramic that is often decorated with a salt or lead glaze. It was first produced in China during the Shang dynasty (*c.*1500–1028 BC) and rediscovered during the Middle Ages in Germany. It eventually spread to Britain in the late 17th century.

**sucrier** The French word for a sugar bowl.

**Supermarionation** A term coined by Gerry Anderson combining the words 'super', 'marionette', and 'animation'. It refers to his series of TV programmes based on puppet characters, such as *Thunderbirds.*

**Surrealism** A 1920s movement in art and literature, characterised by the juxtaposition of incongruous images, in an attempt to create the effect of unconscious thoughts and elements of dreams.

**tessuto** An Italian glassmaking technique in which finely striped canes decorate the body in a criss-crossing pattern to resemble woven fabric.

**tin plate** A coating of tin or a tin alloy applied to steel, then decorated with hand painting or a transfer. Tinplate was used for toys between the mid-19th and mid-20th centuries.

**trail** A type of decoration found on glass in which strands of plain or coloured glass are trailed, or wound, around or onto the handle, foot, or body of a vessel to form a linear pattern.

**transfer print** A ceramic decorating technique which involves printing paper with a copper-plate engraving and then transferring the design to the object by pressing the paper on to it while the ink is still wet. The design is made permanent when the object is glazed and fired.

**treen** An old English word meaning 'of the tree', which is used to denote small wooden items (usually for domestic use) that have been turned on a lathe or carved. They were made in a variety of woods, such as fruitwood and holly.

**trio** A ceramic set comprising a plate, cup, and saucer.

**trompe l'oeil** From the French, meaning 'trick the eye', a type of decoration that imitates another surface or texture such as wood, marbling, or a realistic scene.

**tube lining** Decoration formed by piping or trailing thick slip clay onto the surface of a ceramic piece.

**Tunbridge ware** Souvenir wooden boxes and small household goods from Tunbridge Wells in Kent.

**underglaze** Decoration applied to a ceramic object before it is glazed and fired in the kiln.

**vermeil** Derived from the French word for 'rosy', meaning silver that has been plated, or covered, with a thin layer, or 'wash', of gold.

**Victorian era** The period during the reign of Queen Victoria, from 1837 until 1901. This era was dominated by the Industrial Revolution, which led to the growth of mass-produced objects for the increasingly prosperous middle classes. A general fascination for a range of historical and exotic styles meant that there was no one definable style that characterised the period. Revival styles were also popular.

**vignette** Derived from the French word for 'vine', a carved ornament with a continuous design of grapevine leaves and tendrils. The word is also used when referring to a photograph or a drawing in which the edges fade away, or to a small room setting.

**wall pocket** A ceramic flower vase that has a flat back and is pierced so that it can be hung on the wall.

**wheel engraving** A technique for making incised decoration in glass, using a small rotating wheel fitted with a stone or copper disc and an abrasive paste.

**white ware** Ceramic pieces in their unglazed state.

# Find out more

## CERAMICS

### 20–23 Clarice Cliff
- *Clarice Cliff: The Art of Bizarre,* Leonard Griffin. Pavilion, 2001
- *Taking Tea with Clarice Cliff: A Celebration of Her Art Deco Teaware,* Leonard Griffin. Pavilion, 1998
- The Potteries Museum and Art Gallery, Bethesda Street, Hanley, Stoke-on-Trent, Staffordshire ST1 3DW. Tel: 01782 232 323 www.stoke.gov.uk

### 24–25 Susie Cooper
- *Susie Cooper: A Pioneer of Modern Design,* Andrew Casey and Ann Eatwell. Antique Collectors Club, 2002

### 26–27 1930s ceramics
- *Burleigh Ware,* Julie McKeown. Richard Dennis, 2003
- *Carlton Ware,* Julie McKeown. Francis Joseph, 1994
- *The Carlton Ware Collectors' Handbook,* David Serpell. Francis Joseph, 2003

### 30–31 Lustre ware
- *19th-Century Lustreware,* Michael Gibson. Antique Collectors Club, 1999
- Royal Ontario Museum, 100 Queen's Park, Toronto, Ontario M5S 2C6 Canada. Tel: 001 416 586 8000, www.rom.on.ca

### 32–35 Floral ceramics
- *Moorcroft: A Guide to Moorcroft Pottery 1897–1993,* Paul Atterbury and Beatrice Moorcroft. Richard Dennis, 1993

### 36–37 Keith Murray
- *20th-Century Ceramic Designers in Britain,* Andrew Casey. Antique Collectors Club, 2001

### 38–39 Oriental ceramics
- *Marks and Monograms on European and Oriental Pottery and Porcelain,* William Chaffers. Reeves, 1965
- *Japanese & Oriental Ceramics,* Hazel Gorham. Simon & Schuster, 1991
- *Imari, Satsuma and Other Japanese Export Ceramics,* Nancy N. Schiffer. Schiffer, 1977
- *Collecting Noritake A to Z: Art Deco & More,* David Spain. Schiffer, 2001
- *Guide to Oriental Ceramics,* Elizabeth Wilson. Tuttle, 1995

### 40–41 Traditional ceramic ware
- *The Doulton Burslem Wares,* Desmond Eyles. Barrie & Jenkins, 1987
- *An Illustrated Encyclopaedia of British Pottery and Porcelain,* Geoffrey Godden. Herbert Jenkins, 1966

### 42–43 Cups and saucers
- *Collector's Encyclopedia of English China: Identification and Values,* Mary Frank Gaston. Collector Books, 2002
- *British Tea and Coffee Cups,* Steven Goss. Shire, 2000
- *Collectible Cups and Saucers,* Jim and Susan Harran. Collector Books, 2000

### 44–45 1950s ceramics and 46–49 1960s tableware
- *20th-Century Ceramic Designers in Britain,* Andrew Casey. Antique Collectors Club, 2001
- *Poole Pottery: Carter & Company and Their Successors 1873–1995,* L. Hayward. Richard Dennis, 1995
- *Ceramics of the 50s and 60s: A Collectors Guide,* Steven Jenkins. Miller's, 2001
- *Portmeirion Pottery,* S. Jenkins and S. Mackay. Richard Dennis, 2000
- *Ceramics of the 1950s,* Graham McClaren. Shire, 1997
- *Homemaker: A 1950s Design Classic,* Simon Moss. Cameron and Hollis, 1997

### 50–51 Cottage ware
- *Cottage Ware: Ceramic Tableware Shaped as Buildings 1920s–1990s,* Eileen Rose Busby. Schiffer, 1997
- *The Royal Winton Collector's Handbook: From 1925,* Muriel M. Miller. Krause Publications, 1999
- *Lilliput Lane Cottages,* Annette and Tom Power. Charlton Press, 2000

### 52–53 Toby and character jugs
- *Royal Doulton Jugs,* Jean Dale. Charlton Press, 2003
- *Toby and Character Jugs of the 20th Century and Their Makers,* David Fastenau and Stephen Mullins. Kevin James, 1999

### 54–55 Nursery ware
- *Gifts for Good Children: The History of Children's China 1890–1990,* Maureen Batkin. Richard Dennis, 1996
- *The Shelley Style,* Susan Hill. Jazz Publications, 1990

### 56–57 Staffordshire and fairings
- *Victorian Fairings,* Margaret Anderson. Lyle Publications, 1975
- *Victorian China Fairings: The Collectors' Guide,* Derek H Jordan. Antique Collectors Club, 2003
- *Staffordshire Portrait Figures and Allied Objects of the Victorian Era,* P.D. Gordon Pugh. Barrie & Jenkins, 1971

### 58–59 Royal Doulton figures
- *Royal Doulton Figurines* (7th Edition), Jean Dale. Charlton Press, 2000
- *Royal Doulton Figures: Produced at Burslem Staffordshire 1892–1994,* Desmond Eyles and Louise Irvine. Richard Dennis, 1994

### 60–61 Ceramic figures
- *Luckey's Hummel Figurines and Plates,* Carl F Luckey. Krause Publications, 2003
- *Royal Worcester Porcelain, from 1862 to the Present Day,* Henry Sandon. Barrie and Jenkins, 1979
- *Collecting Lladró: Identification and Price Guide,* Peggy Whiteneck. Krause Publications, 2001

### 62–67 Ceramic animals
- *Collecting SylvaC Pottery,* Stella Ashbrook. Francis Joseph, 2000
- *The Pendelfin Collector's Handbook,* Stella Ashbrook and Frank Salmon. F&W Publications, 2003
- *Collecting SylvaC,* Mick and Derry Collins. The SylvaC Collector's Circle, 1998
- *Royal Doulton Animals (3rd Edition),* Jean Dale. Charlton Press, 2002
- *Collecting Doulton Animals: A Collector's List,* Jocelyn Lukins. Venta Books, 1991
- *Doulton Flambé Animals,* Jocelyn Lukins. Venta Books, 1981
- *The Beswick Price Guide (4th Edition),* Harvey May. Francis Joseph, 1997
- *Royal Worcester Porcelain, from 1862 to the Present Day,* Henry Sandon. Barrie & Jenkins, 1979
- *The SylvaC Story,* Susan Jean Veerbeek. Pottery Publications, 2002

## HISTORICAL MEMORABILIA

### 72–73 Early royal commemorative ware and 74–75 Elizabeth II
- *British Royalty Commemoratives,* Douglas H. Flynn and Alan H. Bolton. Schiffer, 1999

### 76–77 Later royal commemorative ware
- *Diana – an Illustrated Collection and Price Guide: Porcelain Plates,* Mary McMaster and Jose P. Torres. First Books Library, 2003
- *Diana: Collecting on a Princess,* Charles Nobles. Hobby House Press, 1999

### 80–81 Sir Winston Churchill
- *Churchill: A Life,* Martin Gilbert. Pimlico, 2000
- Chartwell (Churchill's home), Mapleton Road, Westerham, Kent TN16 1PS. Tel: 01732 868 381 www.nationaltrust.org.uk

### 82–83 Goss and crested ware
- *Let's Collect Goss China,* A.A.C. Hedges. Jarrold Publishing, 1980
- *Goss and Other Crested China,* Nicholas J. Pine. Shire, 1998
- *William Henry Goss: The Story of the Staffordshire Family of Potters Who Invented Heraldic Porcelain,* Nicholas and Lynda Pine. Seven Hills Book Distributors, 1987

### 84–85 Wooden souvenir ware
- *Tunbridge Ware and Related European Decorative Woodwares,* Brian Austen. Foulsham, 2001
- *Mauchline Ware and Associated Scottish Souvenir Ware,* John Baker. Shire, 1999
- *Tartanware,* Princess Ira von Furstenberg. Pavilion, 1996
- *Tunbridge Ware,* Margaret A.V. Gill. Shire, 1999
- *The Collector's Guide to Mauchline Ware,* David Trachtenberg. Antique Collectors Club, 2002

### 86–87 Stanhopes
- *Stanhopes – A Closer View,* Jean Scott. Greenlight, 2002

### 88–89 British medals
- *Ribbons and Medals,* H. Taprell Dorling with L.F. Guille. George Philip, 1963
- *British Campaign Medals 1815–1914,* Peter Duckers. Shire, 2000
- *British Campaign Medals 1914–2000,* Peter Duckers. Shire, 2001
- *British Gallantry Awards,* Peter Duckers. Shire, 2001
- *British Battles and Medals,* Major L.L. Gordon. Spink, 1988
- *The Medal Yearbook.* Token Publishing (annually)

### 90–91 Philately
- *Stamp Collecting for Dummies,* Richard Sine. Hungry Minds, 2001

### 92–93 Coins and paper money
- *Standard Catalogue of World Paper Money volume 1 – General Issues,* Colin Bruce II and Neil Shafer. Krause Publications
- *Standard Catalogue of World Coins vols 1–4,* Chester L. Krause and Clifford Mishler. Krause Publications

## HOUSEHOLD AND KITCHENALIA

### 98–99 Old brass and copper and 100–101 Wooden objects
- *Collecting Kitchenware,* Christina Bishop. Octopus, 2000
- *Antique Brass and Copper – An Identification and Value Guide,* Mary Frank Gaston. Collector Books, 1992
- *Kitchen Antiques,* Mary Norwak. Ward Lock, 1975
- The Geffrye Museum, Kingsland Road, London E2 8EA Tel: 020 7739 9893 www.geffrye-museum.org.uk

### 102–103 Jelly moulds
- *Jelly Moulds,* Sally Kevill-Davies. Lutterworth Press, 1999

### 104–105 Cornishware
- *Cornishware and Domestic Pottery by T.G. Green,* Paul Atterbury. Richard Dennis, 2001

### 106–109 Blue-and-white ware
- *Transfer Printed Pottery,* Robert Copeland. Shire, 1999
- *The Dictionary of Blue and White Printed Pottery: Vols I & II,* A.W. Coysh and R.K. Henrywood. Antique Collectors Club, 2001
- *Blue and White Pottery: A Collector's Guide,* Gillian Neale. Miller's, 2000

### 110–111 Vintage household packaging
- Opie's Museum of Memories, The Wigan Pier Experience, Trencherfield Mill, Wigan WN3 4EF www.robertopiecollection.com

### 112–113 Scottie dogs
- *A Treasury of Scottie Dog Collectables,* Candace Sten Davies and Patricia Baugh. Collector Books, 1999

- *Scottie Showcase: A Pictorial Introduction to Scottie Dog Collectibles,* Donna Newton. Country Scottie, 1988

**114–117 Tins**
- *Biscuit Tins,* Tracy Dolphin. Shire, 1999
- *British Biscuit Tins 1868–1939: An Aspect of Decorative Packaging,* M.J. Franklin. New Cavendish Books, 1992
- *Decorative Printed Tins: The Golden Age of Printed Tin Packaging,* David Griffith. Studio Vista, 1979
- Museum of Reading, The Town Hall, Blagrave Street, Reading, Berkshire RG1 1QH. Tel: 0118 939 9800. www.readingmuseum.org.uk

**118–119 Kitchen tools**
- *Collecting Kitchenware,* Christina Bishop. Octopus, 2000
- *300 years of Kitchen Collectibles (3rd Edition),* Linda Campbell Franklin. Books Americana, 1991
- *Price Guide to Collectible Kitchen Appliances – from Aerators to Waffle Irons 1900–1950,* Gary Miller and K.M. Scotty Mitchell. Wallace-Homestead, 1991
- *Kitchen Antiques,* Mary Norwak. Ward Lock, 1975
- *Kitchen Collectibles – The Essential Buyer's Guide,* Diane Stoneback. Wallace-Homestead, 1994
- The Science Museum, Exhibition Road, South Kensington, London SW7 2DD. Tel: 0870 870 4868. www.sciencemuseum.org.uk

**120–121 Vintage sewing tools**
- *Sewing Accessories – A Collector's Guide,* Elaine Gaussen. Octopus, 2001
- *The Collector's Guide to Thimbles,* Bridget McConnel. Bracken Books, 1995
- *Needlework Tools and Accessories – A Collector's Guide,* Molly Proctor. The Bath Press, 1990
- *Antique Needlework Tools & Embroideries,* Nerylla Taunton. Antique Collectors Club, 1997

**122–123 Salt and pepper shakers**
- *The Complete Salt and Pepper Shaker Book,* Mike Schneider. Schiffer, 1997
- *Collecting Salt & Pepper Shaker Series,* Irene Thornburg. Schiffer, 1995

**124–125 Stainless steel tableware**
- *Hand and Machine,* Robert Welch. Robert Welch, 1986

**126–127 Corkscrews**
- *The Ultimate Corkscrew Book,* Donald Bull. Schiffer, 1999
- *A Guide to Corkscrew Collecting,* Peter Coldicott. BAS Printers, 1993
- *Corkscrews and Bottle Openers,* Evan Perry. Shire, 1999

**128–129 Decanters and cocktail shakers**
- *The Cocktail Shaker,* Simon Khachadourian. Philip Wilson, 2000

## GLASS

**134–135 Carnival glass**
- *A Century of Carnival Glass,* Glen Thistlewood. Schiffer, 2001
- *Collector's Companion to Carnival Glass: Identification and Values,* Bill Edwards and Mike Carwile. Collector Books, 2003
- *Collecting Carnival Glass,* Marion Quintin-Baxendale. Francis Joseph, 2002

**136–137 Perfume bottles**
- *The Art of Perfume: Discovering and Collecting Perfume Bottles,* Christie Mayer Lefkowith. Thames & Hudson, 1998
- *Miller's Perfume Bottles: A Collector's Guide,* Madeleine Marsh. Miller's, 1999

**138–139 Coloured glass**
- *British Glass 1800–1914,* Charles Hadjamach. Antique Collectors Club, 1991
- *20th-Century Factory Glass,* Lesley Jackson. Mitchell Beazley, 2000
- Broadfield House Glass Museum, Compton Drive, Kingswinford, West Midlands DY6 9NS. Tel: 01384 812 745. www.dudley.gov.uk

**140–141 Bottles**
- *Bottles and Pot Lids: A Collector's Guide,* Alan Blakeman. Miller's, 2002
- *Antique Glass Bottles – A Comprehensive Illustrated Guide,* Willy Van den Bossche. Antique Collectors Club, 2001
- The National Bottle Museum, Elsecar Heritage Centre, nr Barnsley, South Yorkshire S74 8AJ

**142–143 Vintage drinking glasses**
- *Eighteenth-Century Drinking Glasses: An Illustrated Guide,* L.M. Bickerton. Woodbridge, 1986
- Broadfield House Glass Museum, Compton Drive, Kingswinford, West Midlands DY6 9NS. Tel: 01384 812 745. www.dudley.gov.uk
- Museum of London, London Wall, London EC2Y 5HN. Tel: 020 7001 9844. www.museumoflondon.org.uk
- The Victoria & Albert Museum, Cromwell Road, London SW7 2RL Tel: 0207 942 2000. www.vam.ac.uk

**144–147 Glass of the 1930s and 40s and 150–153 Scandinavian glass**
- *20th-Century Glass,* Judith Miller, Dorling Kindersley, 2004
- *Glass of the '50s & '60s,* Nigel Benson. Miller's, 2002
- *20th-Century Factory Glass,* Lesley Jackson. Mitchell Beazley, 2000
- *Miller's Collector's Guide: Popular Glass of the 19th and 20th Centuries,* Raymond Notley. Miller's, 2000
- *Scandinavia: Ceramics and Glass in the 20th Century,* Jennifer Opie. V&A Publications, 1989
- *Nineteenth-Century British Glass,* Hugh Wakefield. Faber and Faber, 1982
- *English Cameo Glass in the Corning Museum of Glass,* David Whitehouse. Corning Museum of Glass, 1994
- *Miller's Collecting Glass: The Facts at Your Fingertips,* Sarah Yates. Miller's, 2000
- The Victoria & Albert Museum, Cromwell Road, London SW7 2RL Tel: 0207 942 2000 www.vam.ac.uk

**148–149 Paperweights**
- *The Encyclopaedia of Glass Paperweights,* Paul Hollister. Paperweight Press, 1986
- *All About Paperweights,* Lawrence H. Selman. Paperweight Press, 1992
- Bristol City Museum & Art Gallery, Queen's Road, Bristol BS8 1RL Tel: 0117 922 3571 www.bristolmuseums.org.uk

**150–153 Scandinavian glass**
*See 144–147 Glass of the 1930s and 40s*

**154–157 Post-war Whitefriars**
- *Glass of the '50s & '60s,* Nigel Benson. Mitchell Beazley, 2002
- *20th-Century Factory Glass,* Lesley Jackson. Mitchell Beazley, 2000
- *Circa Fifties Glass from Europe & America,* Lesley Pina. Schiffer, 1997

**158–165 Studio and factory glass**
- *Glass of the '50s & '60s,* Nigel Benson. Mitchell Beazley, 2002
- *Austerity to Affluence – British Design 1945–1972,* Rayner and Stapleton Chamberlain. Merrell Holberton, 1997
- *20th-Century Factory Glass,* Lesley Jackson. Mitchell Beazley, 2000
- *Studio Glass Since 1945 – The Dan Klein Collection,* Dan Klein. Pavilion, 1984
- *Modern Glass,* Ronald Stennett-Willson. Studio Vista, 1975

**166–169 Murano glass**
- *Murano Glass (1910–1970): Theme and Variations,* Marc Heiremans. Arnoldsche Art Publishers, 2003
- *Venetian Glass 1890–1990,* Rosa Barovier Mentasti. Arsenale Editrice, 1997
- *Murano Glass: A History of Glass,* Gianfranco Toso. Arsenale Editrice, 2001

## BEAUTY AND FASHION

**174–175 Vintage fashions**
- *Art Deco Fashion,* Suzanne Lussier. V&A Publications, 2003
- *Twentieth-Century Development in Fashion and Costume: Performing Arts,* Alycen Mitchell. Mason Crest, 2002
- *Chanel: Her Style and Her Life,* Janet Wallach. Bantam Doubleday Dell, 1998
- Fashion Museum, Assembly Rooms, Bennett Street, Bath, Avon BA1 2QH. Tel: 01225 477 789 www.fashionmuseum.co.uk

**176–177 1940s and 50s fashions**
- *Christian Dior,* Richard Martin and Harold Koday. Metropolitan Museum of Art, 2000
- *Forties Fashion and the New Look,* Colin McDowell. Bloomsbury, 1997
- *Reconstructing Italian Fashion,* Nicola White. Berg, 2000

**178–179 Hats**
- *The Century of Hats,* Susie Hopkins. Aurum, 1999
- *Hats: Status, Style and Glamour,* Colin McDowell. Thames & Hudson, 1997
- *Women's Hats of the 20th Century: For Designers and Collectors,* Maureen Reilly and Mary Beth Detrich. Schiffer, 1997

**180–181 1960s fashions**
- *Emilio Pucci,* Katel Le Bourhis, Stefania Ricci and Luigi Settembrini (eds). Skira Editore, 1997
- *Boutique: A '60s Cultural Icon,* Marnie Fogg. Mitchell Beazley, 2003
- *Pierre Cardin: Past, Present, Future,* Valerie Mendes. Dirk Nishen, 1990
- *Ossie Clark: 1965–74,* Judith Watt. V&A Publications, 2003

**182–183 Post-1960s fashions**
- *Vintage Style: The Art of Dressing Up,* Tracey Tolkien. Pavilion, 2000

**184–185 Sunglasses**
- *Spectacles: Utility Article and Cult Object,* B. Michael Andressen. Arnoldsche Art Publishers, 1998
- *Spectacles, Lorgnettes and Monocles,* D.C. Davidson and R.J.S. MacGregor. Shire, 2002
- *Sunglasses,* Mike Evans (ed). Hamlyn, 1996
- *Specs Appeal: Extravagant 1950s and 1960s Eyewear,* Leslie Pina and Donald-Brian Johnson. Schiffer, 2001

**186–187 Handbags**
- *Plastic Handbags: Sculpture to Wear,* Kate E. Dooner. Schiffer, 1993
- *Handbags,* Anna Johnson. Workman, 2002
- *Whiting & Davis Purses: The Perfect Mesh,* Leslie Pina. Schiffer, 2002

**188–189 Shoes**
- *Salvatore Ferragamo: The Art of the Shoe, 1898–1960,* Salvatore Ferragamo, Stefania Ricci and Edward Maeder. Rizzoli International, 1993
- *Shoes: Fashion and Fantasy,* Colin McDowell. Thames & Hudson, 1994
- *Shoes: A Celebration of Footwear,* Linda O'Keeffe. Workman, 1997

**190–191 Fans**
- *Fans,* Hélène Alexander. Shire, 1994
- *Fans,* Avril Hart and Emma Taylor. V&A Publications, 1998
- *Fans: Ornaments of Language and Fashion,* James Mackay. Parkgate Books, 2000
- The Fan Museum, 12 Crooms Hill, Greenwich, London SE10 8ER Tel: 020 8305 1441

**192–193 Gentlemen's accessories**
- *Fit to be Tied: Vintage Ties of the Forties and Early Fifties,* Rod Dyer and Ron Spark. Abbeville Press, 1991
- *Fashion Accessory Series: Ties,* Avril Hart. V&A Publications, 1998
- Cufflinks, Bertrand Pizzin and Jean-Noel Liaut. Editions Assouline, 2002

**194–195 Smoking accessories**
- *Collector's Guide to Cigarette Lighters,* James Flanagan. Collector Books, 1997
- *Collectible Lighters,* Juan Manuel Clark. Flammarion, 2003
- *Matchsafes,* Deborah Sampson Shinn. Scala, 2001
- *The Legend of the Lighter,* Ad Van Weert. The Abbeville Press, 1995

**196–197 Powder compacts**
- *Vintage and Vogue Ladies' Compacts,* Roselyn Gerson. Collectors Books, 2001
- *Collector's Encyclopedia of Compacts, Carryalls and Face Powder Boxes (Volumes 1 & 2),* Laura M. Mueller. Collectors Books, 1994 & 1997

- *Vintage Compacts and Beauty Accessories,* Lynell Schwartz. Schiffer, 1997

**198–201 Costume jewellery**
- *The Jewels of Miriam Haskell.* Antique Collectors Club, 1997
- *Amazing Gems: An Illustrated Guide to the World's Most Dazzling Costume Jewellery,* Denna Farneti Cera. Harry N. Abrams, 1997
- *Kenneth Jay Lane: Faking It,* Kenneth Jay Lane and Harrice Simons Miller. Harry N. Abrams Inc., 1996
- *Jewelry by Chanel,* Patrick Mauries. Thames & Hudson, 2000
- *DK's Collector's Guide: Costume Jewellery,* Judith Miller. Dorling Kindersley, 2003
- *Hollywood Jewels: Movies, Jewelry, Stars,* Penny Proddow, Debra Healy, and Marion Fasel. Harry N. Abrams Inc., 1996
- *A Collector's Guide to Costume Jewellery,* Tracy Tolkien and Henrietta Wilkinson. Thames & Hudson, 1997

**202–203 Jewellery**
- *Art Nouveau Jewellery.* Thames & Hudson, 1998
- *Antique and 20th-Century Jewellery,* Vivienne Becker. N.A.G. Press, 1990
- *Earrings,* Daniela Mascetti and Amanda Triossi. Thames & Hudson, 1999
- *An Illustrated Dictionary of Antique Jewelry,* Harold Newman. Thames & Hudson, 1987
- *Art Deco Jewelry,* Sylvie Raulet. Thames & Hudson, 2002

**204–205 Watches**
- *The Wristwatch Almanac,* Michael Balfour. Eric Dobby, 1994
- *Watches: Time on Your Wrist,* G.L. Brunner and Christian Pfeiffer. Konemann, 1999
- *The History of The Modern Wristwatch,* Pieter Doensen. Snoeck-Ducaju & Zoon, 1998
- *Wristwatches – A Connoisseur's* Guide, Frank Edwards. Apple Press, 1997
- *The New Collector's Guide to Pocket* Watches. Barry S. Goldberg
- *Collectible Wristwatches,* René Pannier. Flammarion, 2001
- *Complete Price Guide to Watches,* Cooksey Shugart, Tome Engle, and Richard E. Gilbert. Cooksey Shugart, 2003

**206–207 Digital watches**
- *History of the Modern Wrist Watch,* Pieter Doensen. Snoeck-Ducaju & Zoon, 1994

**TOYS, DOLLS, AND TEDDIES**

**212–213 Tinplate toys**
- *The Book of Penny Toys.* New Cavendish Books, 1999
- *Tinplate Toys: From Schuco, Bing & Other Companies,* Jurgen Franzke. Schiffer, 1997
- *Tin Toys 'The Collector's Corner',* R. Kingsley. Grange Books, 1999
- *The Art of the Tin Toy,* David Pressland. New Cavendish Books, 1990
- Museum of London, London Wall, London EC2Y 5HN. Tel: 020 7001 9844. www.museumoflondon.org.uk

**214–215 Dinky toys**
- *Dinky Toys,* Edward Force. Schiffer, 1996
- *Ramsay's British Die-Cast Model Toys Catalogue (9th Edition),* John Ramsay. Swapmeet Publications, 2001
- *The Great Book of Dinky Toys,* Mike and Sue Richardson. New Cavendish Books, 2000

**216–217 Corgi toys**
- *The Great Book of Corgi 1956–1983,* Marcel Van Cleemput. New Cavendish Books, 1989
- *Corgi Toys,* Edward Force. Schiffer, 1996
- *Ramsay's British Die-Cast Model Toys Catalogue (9th Edition),* John Ramsay. Swapmeet Publications, 2001

**218–219 Matchbox and other die-cast makers**
- *Encyclopedia of Matchbox Toys (3rd Edition),* C. Mack. Schiffer, 2002
- *Ramsay's British Die-Cast Model Toys Catalogue (9th Edition),* John Ramsay. Swapmeet Publications, 2001

**220–221 Toy trains**
- *Ramsay's British Model Trains Catalogue,* Pat Hammond (ed). Swapmeet Publications, 2002
- *Christie's Toy Trains,* Hugo Marsh and Pierce Carlson. Watson-Guptill Publications, 2002

**222–223 Marbles**
- *Marbles – Identification & Price Guide,* Robert Block. Schiffer, 1999

**224–225 Toy figures**
- *The Great Book of Hollow-Cast Figures,* Norman Joplin. New Cavendish Books, 2000
- *Britains Civilian Toy Figures,* Norman Joplin. Schiffer, 2002
- *Collecting Foreign-Made Soldiers: Identification and Value Guide,* Richard O'Brien. Krause Publications, 1997

**226–227 Puppets**
- *Collecting Pelham Puppets,* David Leech. Dwallem Marketing, 1999

**228–231 Teddy bears**
- *The Teddy Bear Encyclopaedia,* Pauline Cockrill. Dorling Kindersley, 2001
- *Bears,* Sue Pearson. De Agostini Editions, 1995

**232–233 Soft toys**
- *Soft Toys: A Collector's Guide,* Frankie Leibe. Miller's, 2000
- *Steiff Identification and Price* Guide, Linda Mullins. Hobby House Press, 2001

**234–235 Snow domes**
- *Collectible Snowdomes,* Lélie Carnot. Flammarion, 2002
- *Snow Globes: The Collector's Guide to Selecting, Displaying, and Restoring Snow Globes,* Connie A. Moore and Harry L. Rinker. Courage Books, 1993

**236–237 Bisque dolls, 240–241 Fabric dolls, and 242–243 Plastic dolls**
- *The Collector's Encyclopaedia of Dolls: Volumes 1 & 2,* Elizabeth A. Coleman, Dorothy S. Coleman, and Evelyn J. Coleman. Crown, 1976
- *The 14th Blue Book: Dolls & Values,* Jan Foulke. Hobby House Press, 1999
- *Doll Registry: A Guide to the Description and Value of Antique and Collectible Dolls,* Florence Thériault. Doll Masters, 1988

**238–239 Half dolls**
- *Half-Dolls Price Guide,* Sally Van Luven and Susan Graham. Hobby House Press, 2004
- *The Collector's Encyclopedia of Half-Dolls,* Frieda Marion and Norman Werner. Crown, 1979

**240–241 Fabric dolls and 242–243 Plastic dolls**

*See 236–237 Bisque dolls*

**244–245 Barbie**
- *Identifying Barbie Dolls: The New Compact Study Guide and Identifier,* Janine Fennick. Chartwell, 1999
- *Barbie Doll Collector's Handbook,* A. Glenn Mandeville. Hobby House Press, 1997
- *The Barbie Doll Years (Comprehensive Listing & Value Guide of Dolls & Accessories),* Patrick C. Olds and Joyce L. Olds. Collector Books, 2002

**246–247 Dolls' houses**
- *Collecting Dolls' Houses and Miniatures,* Nora Earnshaw. New Cavendish Books, 1999
- *Collector's History of Dolls' Houses: Doll House Dolls and Miniatures,* Constance Eileen King. Smithmark Publishing, 1987

**248–249 Nursery playthings**
- *Rocking Horses: The Collector's Guide to Selecting, Restoring, and Enjoying New and Vintage Rocking Horses,* Tony Stevenson and Eva Marsden. Courage Books, 1993
- *Jigsaw Puzzles: An Illustrated History and Price Guide,* Anne D. Williams, Chilton Books, 1990

**250–251 Games**
- *Victorian Board Games,* Olivia Bristol. St Martins Press, 1995
- *Board Games,* Desi Scarpone. Schiffer, 1995

**ENTERTAINMENT AND SPORTS**

**256–257 Star Wars**
- *Tomart's Price Guide to Worldwide Star Wars Collectibles,* Stephen Sansweet. Tomart Publications, 1997
- *A Universe of Star Wars Collectibles: Identification and Price Guide (2nd Edition),* Stuart W. Wells III. Krause Publications, 2002

**258–259 Cult TV**
- *A Collector's Guide to TV Toys and Memorabilia: 60 & 70s (22nd Edition),* Bill Morgan. Collector Books, 1998

**260–261 Sci-Fi TV memorabilia**
- *Star Trek Collectibles,* Sue Cornwell and Mike Kott. House of Collectibles, 1997
- *The Unauthorized Handbook and Price Guide to Star Trek Toys by Playmates,* Kelly Hoffman. Schiffer, 2000
- *Trekkies' Guide to Collectibles,* Jeffrey B. Snyder. Schiffer, 1999

**262–263 Doctor Who**
- *Doctor Who: The Television Companion,* David J. Howe and Stephen James Walker. BBC, 1998
- *Doctor Who: The Greatest Show in the Galaxy,* Stephen Wyatt. Target, 1991

**268–271 Animation**
- *Animation Art: Buyer's Guide & Price Guide,* Jim Korkis and John Crawley. Malibu Graphics, 1992
- *Animation Art at Auction: Since 1994,* Jeff Lotman. Schiffer, 1998
- *Animation Art: The Later Years 1954–1993,* Jeff Lotman. Schiffer, 1996
- *Animation Art: The Early Years 1911–1953,* Jeff Lotman and Jonathan Smith. Schiffer, 1995
- *Disney Dolls: Identification & Value Guide,* Margo Rana. Hobby House Press, 2000
- *Stern's Guide to Disney Collectibles,* Michael Stern. Collector Books, 1995

**272–273 Computer games**
- *Electronic Plastic,* Jaro Gielens (ed). Die Gestalte Verlag, 2001
- *The Ultimate History of Video Games: From Pong to Pokemon – The Story Behind the Craze that Touched Our Lives,* Steve L. Kent. Prima Publishing, 2001

**274–275 Elvis Presley**
- *The Official Price Guide to Elvis Presley Records & Memorabilia,* Jerry Osborne. House of Collectibles, 1994

**276–277 The Beatles**
- *The Official Price Guide to The Beatles' Records and Memorabilia,* Perry Cox. Random House, 1999
- The Beatles Story, Britannia Vaults, Albert Dock, Liverpool, Merseyside L3 4AA. Tel: 0151 709 1963

**278–283 Rock and pop music**
- Rare Record Price Guide: 2004. Omnibus Press, 2002
- *Christie's Rock and Pop Memorabilia,* Sarah Hodgson and Peter Doggett. Pavilion Books, 2003
- Miller's Rock and Pop Memorabilia, Sarah Hodgson and Peter Doggett. Mitchell Beazley, 1994
- *Miller's Collecting Vinyl,* John Stanley. Miller's, 2002
- *A Music Lover's Guide to Record Collecting,* Dave Thompson. Backbeat UK, 2002

**284–287 Football memorabilia**
- *Soccer Memorabilia: A Collector's* Guide, Graham Budd. Philip Wilson, 2000
- *Famous Football Programmes,* John Litster, Tempus, 2002
- *The Supporters' Guide to Football Programmes 2004,* John Robinson (ed). Soccer Books, 2003

**288–289 Golf**
- *Beyond the Links: Golfing Stories, Collectibles and Ephemera,* Sarah Fabian. Studio Editions, 1992
- *Miller's Golf Memorabilia,* Sarah Fabian-Baddiel. Miller's, 1994
- *Vintage Golf Club Collectibles: Identification & Value Guide,* Ronald John. Collector Books, 2001

**290–291 Fishing gear**
- *Classic and Antique Fly-fishing Tackle,* A.J. Campbell. The Lyons Press, 1997
- *Collecting Fishing Tackle: A Beginner's Guide,* Tom Quinn. The Sportsman's Press, 1994

- *Classic Fishing Lures and Tackle,* Eric L. Sorenson and Howard Lambert. Voyageur Press, 2003

**292–293 Other sports**
- *An Index to Wisden Cricketers' Almanack, 1864–1984.* Queen Anne Press, 1985
- *Coykendall's Complete Guide to Sporting Collectibles,* Ralph Coykendall. Taunton Press, 1996
- *Sports Memorabilia for Dummies,* Pete Williams and Gary Carter. DG Books, 1998

## THE WRITTEN WORD AND EPHEMERA

**298–299 Modern first editions**
- *Book Collecting 2000: A Comprehensive Guide,* Allen and Patricia Ahearn. Putnam Publishing Group, 2000
- *Annual Register of Book Values: Modern First Editions,* M. Cole (ed). The Clique Ltd
- *Guide to First Edition Prices,* R.B. Russell (ed). Tartarus Press, 2001

**300–301 Children's books**
- *Collecting Children's Books,* Crispin Jackson (ed). Diamond Publishing Group Ltd, 2001

**302–303 Cookery and other books**
- *A Guide to Collecting Cookbooks,* Bob Allen. Collector Books, 1994
- *Cookbooks Worth Collecting,* Mary Barile. B.T. Batsford, 1994
- *Book Finds: How to Find, Buy, and Sell Used and Rare Books,* Ian C. Ellis. Perigee Books, 2001
- *Miller's Collecting Modern Books,* Catherine Porter. Miller's, 2003

**304–305 Children's comics**
- *Happy Days: A Century of Comics,* Denis Gifford. Bloomsbury, 1998
- *The Complete Catalogue of British Comics,* Denis Gifford. Webb & Bower, 1985

**308–309 Printed ephemera**
- *Collecting Cigarette and Trade Cards,* Gordon Howsden. New Cavendish Books, 1995
- *The Story of Cigarette Cards,* Martin Murray. Murray Cards, 1987

**312–313 Postcards**
- *Miller's Postcards: A Collector's Guide,* Chris Connor. Miller's, 2000
- *Collecting Picture Postcards,* Geoffrey A. Godden. Phillimore & Co., 1996
- *Picture Postcards: Introduction to the Hobby,* C.W. Hill. Shire, 1999

**314–315 Christmas memorabilia**
- *Christmas Cards for the Collector,* Arthur Blair. B.T. Batsford, 1986
- *Christmas 1940–1959: A Collector's Guide to Decorations and Customs,* Robert Brenner. Schiffer, 2002
- *Christmas Cards,* Michelle Higgs. Shire, 1999

**316–317 Autographs**
- *Autograph Collector: Celebrity Autograph Authentication Guide.* Odyssey Publications, 1999
- *The Standard Guide to Collecting Autographs: A Reference and Value Guide,* Mark Allen Baker. Krause, 1999
- *Autographs: Identification and Price Guide,* George S Lowry. Harpercollins, 2003

**318–319 Guinness advertising**
- *The Book of Guinness Advertising,* Jim Davies. Guinness Publishing Ltd, 1998

**320–321 Coca-Cola**
- *Petretti's Coca-Cola Collectibles Price Guide (11th Edition),* Allan Petretti. Antique Trader, 2001
- *Identifying Coca-Cola Collectibles,* Randy Schaffer and Bill Bateman. Courage Books, 1997

**322–323 Vintage advertising**
- *Advertising Collectables,* Keith Gretton. BBR Books, 1989
- *The Art of the Label,* Robert Opie. Chartwell, 2001
- *Remember When: A Nostalgic Trip Through the Consumer Era,* Robert Opie. Mitchell Beazley, 2002

**324–325 Vintage posters**
- *The Posters of Jules Chéret: 46 Full-colour Illustrations and an Illustrated Catalogue Raisonné,* Jules Broido and Lucy Chéret. Dover, 1992
- *Miller's Collecting Prints & Posters,* Janet Gleason, Richard Barclay, Louise Martin, Stephen Maycock, and Caroline Wiseman. Miller's, 1997
- *Power of the Poster,* Margaret Timmers. V&A Publications, 1999

**326–327 Vintage posters**
- *Railway Posters 1923–1947,* Beverley Cole and Richard Durack. Laurence King, 1992
- *Underground Art,* Oliver Green. Laurence King, 2001
- *Happy Holidays: The Golden Age of Railway Posters,* Michael Palin. Pavilion Books, 1998

**328–329 Vintage posters**
- *The Art of the Airways,* Geza Szurovy. Motorbooks International, 2002
- *Looping the Loop: Posters of Flight,* Henry Serrano Villard Jr and Willis M. Allen. Kales, 2003
- *Bon Voyage! Travel Posters of the Edwardian Era,* Julia Wigg. HMSO, 1996

## TECHNOLOGY AND TRAVEL

**334–335 Mechanical music**
- *Old Gramophones and Other Talking Machines,* Benet Bergonzi. Shire, 1999
- *The Musical Box: A Guide for Collectors, Including a Guide to Values,* William W.J.G. Ord-Hume. Schiffer, 1994
- *Collecting Phonographs and Gramophones,* Christopher Proudfoot. Smithmark Publications, 1984

**336–337 Radio and TV**
- *TV is King,* Michael Bennett-Levy. MBL Publications (for an exhibition at Sotheby's), 1994
- *Collector's Guide to Transistor Radios,* Marty and Sue Bunis. Collector Books, 1993
- *Radio! Radio!,* Jonathan Hill. Sunrise Press, 1986

**338–339 Cameras**
- *Leica Camera and Lens Pocket Book,* Dennis Laney. Hove Collectors Books, 1996
- *McKeown's Price Guide to Antique and Classic Cameras,* James M. McKeown and Joan C. McKeown (ed). Centennial Photo, (biennially)
- *The First Time Collector's Guide to Classic Cameras,* Kate Rouse. Apple Press, 1994
- *Collector's Guide to Classic Cameras: 1945–1985,* John Wade. Hove Books, 1998

**340–341 Typewriters and computers**
- *The Complete Collector's Guide to Pocket Calculators,* Guy Ball and Bruce Flamm. Wilson/Barnett, 1997
- *Collector's Guide to Personal Computers and Pocket Calculators,* Thomas F. Haddock. Books Americana, 1993
- *Collectible Microcomputers,* Michael Nadeau. Schiffer, 2002
- *Antique Typewriters and Office Collectibles: Identification and Value Guide,* Darryl Rehr. American Quilters Society, 1997

**342–343 Fountain pens**
- *Victorian Pencils: Tools to Jewels,* Deborah Crosby. Schiffer Publishing, 1998
- *The Fountain Pen – A Collector's Companion,* Alexander Crum Ewing. Running Press, 1997
- *Fountain Pens of the World,* Andreas Lambrou. Philip Wilson Publishers, 1995
- *Fountain Pens: United States of America & United Kingdom,* Andreas Lambrou. Philip Wilson, 2000

**344–345 Telephones**
- *Telephones, Antique to Modern,* Kate Dooner. Schiffer, 1992
- *Telephone Collecting,* Kate Dooner. Schiffer, 1993
- *Old Telephones,* Andrew Emmerson. Shire, 2000

**348–349 Railway memorabilia**
- *The Book of British Railway Station Totems,* Dave Brennand and Richard Furness. Sutton Publishing Ltd, 2002
- *British Locomotive Builders' Plates,* Keith Buckle and David Love. Midland, 1994
- *A Collector's Guide to Railwayana,* Handel Kardas (ed). Ian Allan Publishing Limited, 2001

**350–351 Automobilia**
- *The Official Price Guide to Automobilia,* David Bausch. Random House, 1996
- *Mascots Passion,* Michel Legrand. Antic Show, 1999
- *Car Badges of the World,* T.R. Nicholson. Cassell, 1970

**352–353 Ocean liner memorabilia**
- *The White Star Line: An Illustrated History 1869–1934,* Paul Louden-Brown. Titanic Historical Society, 2001

**354–355 Aeronautica**
- *Flight,* R.G. Grant. Dorling Kindersley, 2002
- *Airline: Identity, Design and Culture,* Keith Lovegrove. Laurence King, 2000
- *Vintage Flying Helmets and Aviation Headgear Before the Jet Age,* Mick J. Prodger. Schiffer, 1995

## MODERN DESIGN

**360–361 The 1930s**
- *Art Deco Interiors: Decoration & Design Classics of the 1920s and 30s,* Patricia Bayer. Thames & Hudson, 1998
- *Art Deco 1910–1939,* Charlotte Benton (ed). V&A Publications, 2003

**362–363 Plastics and Bakelite**
- *Bakelite Style,* Tessa Clark and Gad Sassower. Chartwell, 1997
- *Classic Plastic,* Sylvia Katz. Thames & Hudson, 1984

**364–365 The 1950s**
- *The Fifties and Sixties: A Lifestyle Revolution,* Miriam Akhtar and Steve Humphries. Boxtree, 2002
- *Living with Mid-century Style: Modern Retro,* Neal Bingham and Andrew Weaving. Ryland Peters and Small, 2000
- *Fifties Homestyle,* Mark Burns and Louis Di Bonis. Thames & Hudson, 1998
- *Modern Furniture Classics: Postwar to Post-modernism,* Charlotte and Peter Fiell. Thames & Hudson, 2001
- *Collecting the 1950s,* Madeleine Marsh. Miller's, 1997
- *The 1950s Scrapbook,* Robert Opie. New Cavendish Books, 1998
- *Fifties Source Book,* Christopher Pearce. Grange Books, 1999

**368–371 The 1960s**
- *Op to Pop: Furniture of the 1960s,* Cara Greenberg. Little, Brown & Company, 1999
- *The 1960s Scrapbook,* Robert Opie. New Cavendish Books, 2001
- *Remember When: A Nostalgic Trip Through the Consumer Era,* Robert Opie. Mitchell Beazley, 2002

**372–373 Lamps**
- *Lamps of the '50s & '60s,* Jan Lindenberger. Schiffer, 1997
- *Art Deco Lighting,* Herb Millman and John Dwyer. Schiffer, 2001

**374–375 The 1970s**
- *Collecting the 1970s,* Katherine Higgins. Miller's, 2001
- *A Century of Design: Design Pioneers of the 20th Century,* Penny Sparke. Mitchell Beazley, 1998
- *An Introduction to Design and Culture in the 20th Century,* Penny Sparke. Routledge, 1986
- *Retro Home,* Suzanne Trocme. Mitchell Beazley, 2000
- *20th-Century Design,* Jonathan M. Woodman. Oxford Paperbacks, 1997

# Clubs and societies



## ADVERTISING

**The Crunch Newsletter**
John Cahill, 9 Weald Rise, Tilehurst,
Reading, Berkshire RG3 6XB

**The Guinness® Collectors Club**
8 Hartley Road,
North End, Portsmouth,
Hampshire PO2 9HU
www.guinntiques.com

**The UK Sucrologists Club**
14 Marisfield Place,
Selsey, Chichester,
West Sussex PO20 0PD
ukscsugar@hotmail.co.uk
www.uksucrologistclub.org.uk

## BOOKS

**The Enid Blyton Society**
93 Milford Hill, Salisbury,
Wiltshire SP1 2QL
tony@enidblytonsociety.co.uk
www.enidblytonsociety.co.uk

**The Followers of Rupert Bear**
John Beck, 29 Mill Road, Lewes,
East Sussex BN7 2RU
Tel: 01273 477 555
www.rupertbear.co.uk

**The Lewis Carroll Society**
www.lewiscarrollsociety.org.uk

## BOTTLES

**The Mini Bottle Club**
membership@theminibottleclub.uk
www.theminibottleclub.uk

**The World of Bottles and Bygones**
30 Brabant Road,
Cheadle Hulme,
Cheadle, Cheshire SK8 7AU
Tel: 0161 486 0927
mike@bygones.demon.co.uk
www.mikesheridan.tripod.com

## CAMERAS

**Photographic Collectors Club of Great Britain**
5 Buntingford Road, Puckeridge,
Ware SG11 1RT
www.pccgb.net

## CARTOONS

**The Political Cartoon Society**
16 Lower Richmond Road, Putney,
London SW15 1JP
Tel: 0208 789 0111
info@politicalcartoon.co.uk
www.original-political-cartoon.com

## CERAMICS

**Belleek Collectors Group**
chairman@belleek.org.uk
www.belleek.org.uk

**The Beswick Collectors Club**
Collecting Doulton, 5 Southbrook Mews,
Southbrook Road, London SE12 8LG
Tel: 020 8318 9580
frank.salmon@carltonware.co.uk

**Chintz World International**
Tel: 01525 220 272
chintz4u@aol.com

**Clarice Cliff Collectors Club**
Fantasque House,
Tennis Drive, The Park,
Nottingham NG7 1AE
www.claricecliff.com

**Fieldings Crown Devon Collectors Club**
PO Box 462,
Manvers, Rotherham,
South Yorkshire S63 7WT
Tel: 01709 874 433
www.fieldingscrowndevclub.co.uk

**Friends of Blue (British Blue-and-White Pottery)**
PO Box 996, Cheltenham,
Gloucestershire GL50 9FX
www.fob.org.uk

**Goss Collectors Club**
24 Mansfield Hill,
London E4 TJT
Tel: 0788 987 4929
www.gosscollectorsclub.org

**Hornsea Pottery Collectors & Research Society**
128 Devonshire Street, Keighly,
West Yorkshire BD21 2QJ
hornsea@pdtennant.fsnet.co.uk
www.hornseapottery.co.uk

**Lilliput Lane Collectors Club**
Brunthill Road, Kingstown,
Carlisle, Cumbria CA3 0EN
Tel: 01228 404 022
enquiries@lilliputlane.co.uk
www.lilliputlane.co.uk

**Mabel Lucie Attwell**
Abbey Antiques, 63 Great Whyte,
Ramsey, Huntingdon,
Cambridgeshire PE26 1HL
Tel: 01487 814 753
www.mabellucieattwellclub.com

**Moorcroft Collectors Club**
Sandbach Road, Burslem,
Stoke-on-Trent, Staffordshire
ST6 2DQ
Tel: 01782 820 500
enquiries@moorcroft.com
www.moorcroft.com

**Myott Collectors Club**
Tel: 07986 437 904
martin@myottcollectorsclub.com
www.myottcollectorsclub.com

**Noritake Collectors Club (UK) Ltd**
13 Station Road, Ilkeston,
Derbyshire DE7 5LY
Tel: 01159 440 424

**Official International Wade Collectors Club**
Victorian Business Centre,
Ford Lane, Arundel, West Sussex,
England, BN18 0EF
Tel: 01243 555 371
club@wadecollectorsclub.co.uk
www.wadecollectorsclub.co.uk

**Pendelfin Family Circle**
Cameron Mill, Howsin Street, Burnley,
Lancashire BB10 1PP
boswell@pendelfin.co.uk
www.pendelfin.biz

**Poole Pottery Collectors Club**
The Quay, Poole, Dorset BH15 1HJ
Tel: 08454 632 209
admin@poolepotterycollectorsclub.net
www.poolepotterycollectorsclub.uk

**Portmeirion Collectors Club**
143-145 Commercial Road,
Paddock Wood, Kent TN12 6DS
Tel: 0189 283 5098
www.houseofportmeirion.co.uk

**The Shelley Group**
'Kingsleigh' 4 Ashlyn's Road,
Frinton-on-Sea, Essex CO13 9ED
information@shelley.co.uk
www.shelley.co.uk

**Susie Cooper Collectors Group**
mark@susiecooper.net
www.susiecooper.net

## CIGARETTE CARDS

**Cartophilic Society of Great Britain**
membership@card-world.co.uk
www.card-world.co.uk

**M.I.C.E. Free Card Guild**
John W. Townsend, 4 Stiles Avenue,
Marple, Stockport,
Cheshire SK6 6LR
Tel: 004 0161 427 103

## CLOCKS AND WATCHES

**The Antiquarian Horological Society**
New House, High Street, Ticehurst,
East Sussex TN5 7AL
Tel: 01580 200 155
secretary@ahsoc.org
www.ahsoc.org

## COINS AND MEDALS

**British Art Medal Society**
c/o Department of Coins and Medals,
British Museum,
London WC1B 3DG
Tel: 01713 238 171
pattwood@thebritishmuseum.ac.uk
www.bams.org.uk

**British Numismatic Society**
c/o The Warburg Institute,
Woburn Square,
London WC1H 0AB
www.britnumsoc.org

**International Bank Note Society**
www.theibns.org

## COMMEMORATIVE WARE

**Commemorative Collectors Society**
Steven Jackson, Lumless House,
77 Gainsborough Road,
Winthorpe, nr Newark-on-Trent,
Nottinghamshire NG24 2NR
Tel: 01636 671 377
commemorativecollectorssociety@hotmail.com
www.commemorativescollecting.co.uk

## COSTUME AND ACCESSORIES

**British Compact Collectors Society**
B.C.C.S.,
PO Box 1969,
Newport NP19 1BU
bccs.uk@virginmedia.com
www.compactcollectors.co.uk

**Costume Society**
150 Aldersgate Street,
London EC1A 4AB
info@costumesociety.org.uk
www.costumesociety.org.uk

**Fan Circle International**
www.fancircleinternational.org

**The UK Perfume Bottle Collectors Club**
Assembly Antiques Centre,
5–8 Saville Row, Bath,
Avon BA1 2QP
Tel: 01225 448 488

## DOLLS

**Doll Club of Great Britain**
dollclubgb@yahoo.co.uk
www.dollclubgb.com

**The Fashion Doll Collectors Club of GB**
www.fashiondollcollectorsclubgb.co.uk

## EPHEMERA

**The Ephemera Society**
PO Box 112,
Northwood,
Middlesex HA6 2WT
Tel: 01923 829 079
www.ephemera-society.org.uk

## FILM, TV, AND ENTERTAINMENT

**Battlestar Galactica Club**
www.battlestargalactica.com

**Fanderson – The Official Gerry Anderson Appreciation Society**
24 Bluebell Rise,
Midsomer Norton,
Radstock, Somerset BA3 2RR
query@fanderson.org.uk
www.fanderson.org.uk

**The James Bond International Fan Club**
PO Box 21,
York YO41 1WX,
Tel: 01347 878837
davidblack@007.info
www.007.info

**Starfleet – The International Star Trek Fan Association**
www.sfi.org

## GLASS

**Caithness Glass Paperweight Collectors Society**
Dartington Crystal (Torrington) Ltd,
Torrington, Devon EX38 7AN
Tel: 01805 626 262
info@caithnessglass.co.uk
www.caithnessglass.co.uk

**The Carnival Glass Society (UK)**
PO Box 14, Hayes,
Middlesex UB3 5NU
pmphyllis@aol.com
www.thecgs.co.uk

**The Glass Association**
membership@glassassociation.org.uk
www.glassassociation.org.uk

**Pressed Glass Collectors Club**
4 Bowshot Close, Castle Bromwich,
West Midlands B36 9UH
Tel: 0121 681 4872

## KITCHENALIA

**British Iron Collectors**
t.gilchrist11@btinternet.com

**Tools and Trades History Society**
92 Marine Parade,
Leigh On Sea, Essex SS9 2NL
www.taths.org.uk

## MECHANICAL MUSIC

**The City of London Phonograph and Gramophone Society**
Tel: 01440 821 308
kharrison@clpgs.org.uk
www.clpgs.org.uk

**Musical Box Society of Great Britain**
c/o Grange Musical Collection,
Old Bury Road, Palgrave,
DISS, Norfolk IP22 1AZ
info@mbsgb.org.uk
www.mbsgb.org.uk

## METALWARE

**Antique Metalware Society**
www.antiquemetalwaresociety.org.uk

**National Horse Brass Society**
dickbradshaw1960@yahoo.co.uk
www.nationalhorsebrasssociety.org.uk/core/horse-brass/pages/default.aspx

## MILITARIA

**Arms and Armour Society**
PO Box 10232, London SW19 2ZD
Tel: 01323 844 278
armsandarmour.soc@fireflyuk.net
http://www.condottiero.com/ep675p9oyht9/armsandarmoursociety/home.html

**Military Historical Society**
38 Hawthorn Way, Shipston on Stour,
Warwickshire, CV36 4FD
troopers.mt@btinternet.com
www.themilitaryhistoricalsociety.co.uk

**Orders & Medals Research Society**
PO Box 6195,
Royal Leamington Spa, CV31 9JU
Tel: 01926 312176
www.omrs.org.uk

**Victorian Military Society**
20 Priory Road, Newbury RG14 7QN
www.victorianmilitarysociety.org.uk

## ORIENTAL

**The Oriental Ceramic Society**
Balsham, Cambridge CB21 5BE
Tel: 01223 881 328
ocs.london@btinternet.com
www.ocs-london.com

## PENS AND WRITING

**The Writing Equipment Society**
membership@wesonline.org.uk
www.wesonline.org.uk

## POSTCARDS

**The Postcard Club of Great Britain**
34 Harper House, St James' Crescent,
London SW9 7LW
Tel: 0171 771 9404

## POSTERS

**International Vintage Poster Dealer Association**
PO Box 501, Old Chelsea Station,
New York, NY, USA 10113
www.ivpda.com

## RADIOS AND TVS

**The British Vintage Wireless Society**
membership@bvws.org.uk
www.bvws.org.uk

## RAILWAYANA

**British Titanic Society**
PO Box 401, Hope Carr Way, Leigh,
Lancashire WN7 3WW
info@britishtitanicsociety.com
www.britishtitanicsociety.com

## SCIENTIFIC, TECHNICAL, AND MEDICAL INSTRUMENTS

**Ophthalmic Antiques International Collectors Club**
The College of Optometrists,
42 Craven Street,
London WC2N 5NG
www.college-optometrists.org/en/college/museyeum/aperture/oaicc.cfm

**Scientific Instrument Society**
The Old School House, Stadhampton,
Oxfordshire OX44 7TR
www.scientificinstrumentsociety.org

## SCRIPOPHILY

**International Bank Note Society**
Spink & Son, 69 Southampton Row,
Bloomsbury, London WC1B 4ET
www.ibnslondon.org.uk

**The International Bond & Share Society**
Philip Atkinson, 167 Barnett Wood Lane,
Ashtead, Surrey KT21 2LP
Tel: 01372 276 787
secretary@scripophily.org
www.scripophily.org

## SEWING

**The Thimble Society**
141-147 Portobello Road,
London W11 2DY
Tel: 07941 455 259
antiques@thimblesociety.com
www.thimblesociety.com

## SMOKING

**Cigarette Packet Collectors Club of GB**
Barry Russell, 9 Regent Place,
Heathfield, East Sussex TN21 8TJ
Tel: 01435 865 427
www.cigarettepacket.com

**Lighter Club of Great Britain**
richard@lighter.co.uk
www.lighterclub.co.uk

## SPORTING

**Cricket Memorabilia Society**
4 Stoke Park Court, Stoke Road,
Bishop's Cleeve, Cheltenham,
Gloucestershire GL25 8US
Tel: 07929 967 653
cms87@btinternet.com
www.cricketmemorabilia.org

**International Philatelic Golf Society**
50 Pine Valley, Cwmavon, Port Talbot,
West Glamorgan SA12 9NF

## STAINLESS STEEL

**The Old Hall Stainless Steel Tableware Club**
Sandford House, Levedale,
Staffordshire ST18 9AH
Tel: 01785 780 376
oht@gnwiggin.freeserve.co.uk
www.oldhallclub.co.uk

## STAMPS AND PHILATELY

**British Postmark Society**
26 Redhall Crescent,
Edinburgh EH14 2HU
british.postmarks@which.net
www.britishpostmarksociety.org.uk

**Postal History Society**
www.postalhistory.org.uk

## STANHOPES

**The Stanhope Collectors Club**
Tel: 01202 768 768
jean@stanhopes.info
www.stanhopes.info

## TEDDY BEARS AND SOFT TOYS

**Merrythought International Collectors Club**
Ironbridge, Telford, Shropshire TF8 7NJ
Tel: 01952 432 054
www.merrythought.co.uk/about-us/club

**Steiff Club Office**
Margarete Steiff GmbH,
Richard-Steiff Strasse 4,
D-89537 Giengen/Brenz, Germany
info@steiff-club.de
www.steiff.com

## TELECOMMUNICATIONS AND TELEPHONES

**Telecommunications Heritage Group**
Dalton House, 60 Windsor Avenue,
London SW19 2RR
Tel: 0330 321 1844
www.thg.org.uk

## TEXTILES

**Embroiderers' Guild**
County Museum, Church Street,
Aylesbury, Bucks HP20 2QP
Tel: 07455 597 039
administrator@embroiderersguild.com
www.embroiderersguild.com

## TOYS

**The Bassett-Lowke Society**
Tracy Haydon-White (Membership Secretary),
51, Causey Farm Road,
Halesowen, B63 1EQ
info@bassettlowkesociety.org.uk
www.bassettlowkesociety.org.uk

**Benevolent Confraternity of Dissectologists (Jigsaws)**
info@thebcd.co.uk
www.thebcd.co.uk

**The British Model Soldier Society**
www.bmssonline.com

**Corgi Collectors Club**
www.corgi.co.uk/club

**The English Playing Card Society**
11 Pierrepont Street, Bath,
England BA1 1LA
Tel: 01225 465 218
robertwelsh32@talktalk.net
www.epcs.org

**Historical Model Railway Society**
HMRS Museum & Study Centre,
Midland Railway Centre,
Butterley Railway Station,
Ripley, DE5 3QZ
Tel: 01773 745 959
www.hmrs.org.uk

**Hornby Collectors Club**
3rd Floor,
The Gateway Innovation Way,
Discovery Park,
Sandwich, Kent CT13 9FF
Tel: 01843 233 512
newclubs@hornby.com
www.hornby.com

**Hornby Railway Collectors Association**
John Harwood,
PO Box 3443,
YEOVIL,
Somerset BA21 4XR
Tel: 01935 474830
www.hrca.net

**The International Society of Meccanomen**
www.internationalmeccanomen.org.uk

**Matchbox International Collectors Association**
5 Village Road, Oxton,
Wirral CH43 5SR
www.matchboxclub.com

**The Model Railway Club**
Keen House,
4 Calshot Street,
London N1 9DA
www.themodelrailwayclub.org

**Muffin the Mule Collectors Club**
www.muffin-the-mule.com

**The Train Collectors Society**
PO Box 290,
Winsford, CW7 9GS
traincolsoc-subscribe@yahoogroups.com
www.traincollectors.co.uk

**William Britain Collectors Club**
10420 Geiser Road Holland,
Ohio 43528
Tel: 419 865 5077
www.wbritain.com

**Wrenn Railways Collectors Club**
Barry Fentiman, "Southern Drift",
Heathfield Road, High Wycombe,
Bucks HP12 4DQ
Tel: 07947 612 459
barry@wrennrailways.co.uk
www.wrennrailways.co.uk

## TREEN AND BOXES

**The Mauchline Ware Collectors Club**
contact@mauchlineware.com
www.mauchlineware.com

# Internet resources



Over the past decade or so, the Internet has revolutionised the buying and selling of collectables. Many millions of items are offered for sale and traded daily, with sites varying from global online marketplaces, such as eBay, to specialist dealers' websites. Most collectables are easily defined, described, and photographed. Shipping is also comparatively easy, as most items are relatively small and light. Prices are generally more affordable and accessible than for many antiques and the Internet can provide a cost-effective way of buying and selling, avoiding the overheads of shops and auction rooms – particularly for collectables valued at less than £50. Nevertheless, you should be aware that all of the administration, including describing, photographing, packing, and shipping the item, as well as dealing with payment, is your responsibility.

When searching online, remember that some sellers may not know how to describe their item accurately – if in doubt, always ask questions politely. General category searches, even though more time-consuming, can yield otherwise hidden results, as can deliberately misspelling a name – this can reveal interesting items that have been incorrectly described. If something looks too good to be true, it probably is. On eBay, always look at a seller's feedback rating – this shows how many items they have sold and how happy buyers are with their service. If a seller has a couple of negative ratings, take the time to read about the reasons why – a third party problem (such as a postal strike) may be to blame.

As you will understand from using this book, colour photography is vital – look for online listings that include as many images as possible and check them carefully. Be aware that colours may not be reproduced accurately, and can vary even from one computer screen to another.

It is crucial to ask the vendor questions about the object, particularly regarding condition. If there is no image, or you want to see another aspect of it – ask. Most sellers (private or trade) will want to realise the best price for their items so will be happy to help if approached sensibly.

On top of the 'e-hammer' price, you will have to pay additional fees such as packing, shipping, and possibly regional or national import or sales taxes. It is best to ask for an estimate of these transactional costs before bidding. This will also help you to tailor your bid, as you will have an idea of the maximum price the item will cost if you are successful.

Beyond well-known names such as eBay, the Internet has a host of useful online auction resources for buying and selling, including sites which publish date listings for fairs and auctions.

**The Antiques Trade Gazette**
www.antiquestradegazette.com
The online version of the UK trade newspaper, containing British auction and fair listings, news, and events.

**AuctionBytes**
www.ecommercebytes.com
An auction resource with community forum, news, events, tips, and a regular newsletter.

**Auctionnet.com**
www.auction-net.co.uk
A simple online resource listing more than 500 websites related to auctions online.

**eBay**
www.ebay.com
The largest and most diverse of the online auction sites, based in the USA, allowing users to buy and sell in an online marketplace with more than 62 million registered users. There is a UK version (www.ebay.co.uk). Collectors should also view eBay Live Auctions (www.ebayliveauctions.com) where traditional auctions are combined with real-time online bidding, allowing users to place real-time bids over the Internet as the auction takes place.

**La Gazette Drouot**
www.gazette-drouot.com/en/
The online home of the magazine, La Gazette de l'Hôtel Drouot, listing all auctions to be held in France at the Hôtel Drouot in Paris and beyond. An online subscription enables you to download the magazine online.

**GoAntiques/WorthPoint.com**
www.goantiques.com
www.worthpoint.com
An online global aggregator, bringing together art, antiques, and collectables dealers who showcase their stock online, allowing users to browse and buy.

**Invaluable**
www.invaluable.com
customercare@invaluable.com
A subscription service which allows users to search selected auction house catalogues from Britain and Europe. The site also offers an extensive archive for appraisal uses.

**Live Auctioneers**
www.new.liveauctioneers.com
A free service that allows users to search catalogues from selected auction houses in Britain, Europe, and the USA. Through its connection with eBay, users can bid live via the Internet into salerooms as auctions happen. Registered users can also search through an archive of past catalogues and receive a free newsletter by email.

**Maine Antiques Digest**
www.maineantiquedigest.com
The online version of America's trade newspaper including news, articles, fair and auction listings, and more.

# Specialist dealers



## ANIMATION ART

**Art You Grew Up With**
Selfridges, Trafford Centre
Manchester M17 8DA
www.artyougrewupwith.com

## ART DECO

**Art Deco Etc**
73 Upper Gloucester Road,
Brighton, East Sussex BN1 3LQ
Tel: 01273 202 937
decojohn@hotmail.com

**The Design Gallery**
5 The Green, Westerham,
Kent TN16 1AS
Tel: 01959 561 234
www.designgallery.co.uk

## AUTOGRAPHS

**Fraser's Autographs**
399 Strand,
London WC2R 0LX
Tel: 020 7836 9325
sales@frasersautographs.co.uk
www.frasersautographs.com

**Lights, Camera, Action**
6 Western Gardens,
Western Boulevard, Aspley,
Nottingham NG8 5GP
Tel: 0115 913 1116
nickjstraw@gmail.com

## AUTOMOBILIA

**Finesse Fine Art**
Empool Cottage, West Knighton,
Dorset DT2 8PE
Tel: 07973 886 937
tony@finesse-fine-art.com
www.finesse-fine-art.com

## BOOKS

**Biblion**
Gray's Mews Antiques
Market, 1-7 Davies Mews,
London W1K 5AB
Tel: 020 7629 1374
www.biblion.co.uk

## CAMERAS

**Collectors Cameras**
PO Box 16, Pinner,
Middlesex HA5 4HN
Tel: 020 8421 3537

## CERAMICS

**Beth Adams**
Alfies Antique Market,
13-25 Church Street,
Marylebone,
London NW8 8DT
Tel: 020 7723 6066
info@alfiesantiques.com
www.alfiesantiques.com

**Chinasearch**
4 Princes Drive, Kenilworth,
Warwickshire CV8 2FD
Tel: 01926 512 402
info@chinasearch.uk.com
www.chinasearch.uk.com

**Feljoy Antiques**
Tudor House,
Sheep Street,
Stow-on-the-Wold,
Gloucester, GL54 1AA
Tel: 077710 169 811
mail@feljoy-antiques.co.uk
www.feljoy-antiques.co.uk

**Gallery 1930 – Susie Cooper Gallery**
18 Church Street,
London NW8 8EP
Tel: 020 7723 1555
gallery1930@aol.com

**Gentry's Antiques and Collectables**
Number One Little Green,
Polperro PL13 2RF
Tel: 01503 272789

**Gillian Neale Antiques**
PO Box 247, Aylesbury,
Buckinghamshire HP20 1JZ
Tel: 01296 423 754
gillianneale@aol.com

**Sue Norman**
The Bourbon Hanby Arcade,
151 Sydney Street, Chelsea,
London SW3 6NT
Tel: 07747 654 354
www.suenormanblueandwhitechina.co.uk

**Vintage Living and Lifestyle**
Unit 61, Cirencester Antiques
Centre, 25 Market Place,
Cirencester, Gloucestershire
GL7 2NX
Tel: 07767 267 607
www.vintage-lifestyle.co.uk

## CIGARETTE CARDS AND POSTCARDS

**Carlton Antiques**
43 Worcester Road, Malvern,
Worcestershire WR14 4RB
Tel: 01684 573 092

## COMICS

**Book & Comic Exchange**
30 & 32,
Pembridge Road,
London W11 3HN
Tel: 020 7598 2233
www.mgeshops.com/book-comic-exchange

**The Book Palace**
Jubilee House,
Bedwardine Road,
Crystal Palace,
London SE19 3AP
Tel: 020 8768 0022
webenquiry@bookpalace.com
www.bookpalace.com

## COMMEMORATIVE WARE

**Hope & Glory**
131a Kensington Church Street,
London W8 7LP
Tel: 020 7727 8424

## CORKSCREWS

**Christopher Sykes Antiques**
The Old Parsonage,
Woburn, Milton Keynes,
Buckinghamshire MK17 9QL
Tel: 01525 290 259

## COSTUME

**Beyond Retro**
23-28 Penn Street,
London N1 5DL
Tel: 020 7729 9001
customercare@beyondretro.com
www.beyondretro.com

**Cloud Cuckoo Land**
6 Charlton Place, Camden
Passage, London N1 8AJ
Tel: 020 7354 3141

**Linda Bee**
Gray's Mews Antiques
Market, Stand L18-L20,
1-7 Davies Mews,
London W1K 5AB
Tel: 020 7629 5921

**Vintage to Vogue**
28 Milsom Street,
Avon, Bath BA1 1DG
Tel: 01225 337 323
contact@vintagetovoguebath.co.uk
www.vintagetovoguebath.co.uk

## COSTUME JEWELLERY

**Cristobal**
26 Church Street,
London NW8 8EP
Tel: 020 7724 7230
Mob: 07900 880 909
sminers@aol.com
www.cristobal.co.uk

## CULT TV

**Toy Heroes**
51 Stanley Road Carshalton,
Surrey SM5 4LE
Tel: 020 8668 0312
toyheroesltd@aol.com
www.toyheroes.co.uk

## DOLLS

**Victoriana Dolls**
101 Portobello Road,
London W11 2BQ
Tel: 01737 249 525
heather.bond@homecall.co.uk

## EPHEMERA

**All Our Yesterdays**
6 Park Road, Kelvin Bridge,
Glasgow G4 9JG
Tel: 0141 334 7788

**Quadrille**
Valerie Jackson-Harris,
Quadrille, PO Box 327,
Northwood HA6 9ES
Tel: 01923 829 079
ephemeraquadrille@btinternet.com
www.quadrille-ephemera.com

## GLASS

**Andrew Lineham Fine Glass**
Tel: 01243 576 241
Mob: 07767 702 722
www.antiquecolouredglass.com

**Frank Dux Antiques**
Trilogie Antiques,
45 Long Street,
Tetbury, Gloucestershire
Tel: 01225 312 367
m.hopkins@antique-glass.co.uk
www.antique-glass.co.uk

**The Studio Glass Merchant**
Tel: 07843 022591
info@thestudioglassmerchant.co.uk
www.thestudioglassmerchant.co.uk

**Jeanette Hayhurst Fine Glass**
PO Box 83, Tetbury,
Gloucestershire, GL8 0AL
Tel: 07831 209 814

**Nigel Benson 20th-Century Glass**
Tel: 07971 859 848
nigel@20thcentury-glass.com
www.20thcentury-glass.org.uk

## HOUSEHOLD AND KITCHENALIA

**Below Stairs of Hungerford**
103 High Street,
Hungerford,
Berkshire RG17 0NB
Tel: 01488 682 317
hofgartner@belowstairs.co.uk
www.belowstairs.co.uk

## JEWELLERY

**Joseph Bonnar**
72 Thistle Street,
Edinburgh EH2 1EN
Tel: 0131 226 2811
enquiries@josephbonnar.com
www.josephbonnar.com

**Sylvie Spectrum**
Gray's Mews Antiques
Market, Stand 371-372,
58 Davies Street &
1-7 Davies Mews,
London W1K 5AB
Tel: 020 7629 3501

## MARINE AND CRUISE LINER

**Cobwebs**
78 Old Northam Road,
Southampton SO14 0PB
Tel: 02380 227 458
www.cobwebs.uk.com

## MECHANICAL MUSIC

**The Talking Machine**
30 Watford Way,
London NW4 3AL
Tel: 020 8202 3473

## MILITARIA

**Christopher Seidler**
PO Box 59979,
London SW16 9AZ
Tel: 0845 644 3674
chris@antique-militaria.co.uk
www.antique-militaria.co.uk

**Q&C Militaria**
22 Suffolk Road,
Cheltenham,
Gloucestershire GL50 2AQ
Tel: 01242 519 815
qcmilitaria@btconnect.com
www.qcmilitaria.com

## ORIENTAL CERAMICS

**Guest & Gray**
Gray's Mews Antiques Market,
1-7 Davies Mews,
London W1K 5AB
Tel: 020 7408 1252
info@chinese-porcelain-art.com
www.chinese-porcelain-art.com

**Justin Garrard**
Dolphin Arcade,
155 Portobello Road,
London W11
Tel: 07766 601315
garrardjustin@hotmail.com

**Roger Bradbury**
Skeyton Lodge,
Long Rd, Skeyton,
Norwich NR10 5ED
Tel: 01692 538 293
roger.bradbury@btinternet.com

## PENS AND WRITING

**Battersea Pen Home**
PO Box 6128,
Epping, Essex CM16 4CG
Tel: 01992 578 885
orders@penhome.co.uk
www.penhome.co.uk

## PHILATELY

**Bath Stamp & Coin Shop**
12–13 Pulteney Bridge,
Bath, Avon BA2 4AY
Tel: 01225 431 918
info@bathstampandcoinshop-bath.co.uk
www.bathstampandcoinshop-bath.co.uk

**Intercol London**
43 Templars Crescent,
London N3 3QR
Tel: 020 8349 2207
www.intercol.co.uk

**Stanley Gibbons Ltd**
399 Strand,
London WC2R 0LX
Tel: 020 7836 8444
help@stanleygibbons.com
www.stanleygibbons.com

## POSTERS

**At The Movies**
18 Thayer Street,
Marylebone,
London W1U 3JY
Tel: 0207 486 9464
info@atthemovies.co.uk
www.atthemovies.co.uk

**DODO**
Stand F071-73,
Alfie's Antique Market,
13-25 Church Street,
Marylebone, London, NW8 8DT
Tel: 020 7706 1545
Liz@dodoposters.co.uk
www.dodoposters.com

**Rennies**
Rennies Seaside Modern,
47 The Old High Street,
Folkestone, Kent CT20 1RN
Tel: 01303 242 427
info@rennart.co.uk
www.rennart.co.uk

## RADIOS

**On the Air Ltd**
The Vintage Technology Centre,
The Highway, Hawarden,
Deeside CH5 3DN
Tel: 01244 530 300
info@vintageradio.co.uk
www.vintageradio.co.uk

## ROCK AND POP

**More Than Music**
PO Box 2809,
Eastbourne,
Sussex BN21 2EA
Tel: 01323 649 778
morethnmus@aol.com

**Tracks**
PO Box 117, Chorley,
Lancashire PR6 0UU
Tel: 01257 269 726
sales@tracks.co.uk
www.tracks.co.uk

## SCIENTIFIC AND TECHNICAL, INCLUDING OFFICE, MEDICAL, OPTICAL

**Branksome Antiques**
370 Poole Road, Branksome,
Dorset BH12 1AW
Tel: 01202 763 324
info@branksomeantiques.co.uk
www.branksomeantiques.co.uk

**Early Technology**
Monkton House,
Old Craighall Musselburgh,
Midlothian EH21 8SF
Tel: 0131 665 5753
earlytech27@gmail.com
www.earlytech.com

## SMOKING

**Richard Ball**
richard.ball@lighter.co.uk
www.lighterclub.co.uk

## SPORTING MEMORABILIA

**Manfred Schotten**
109 High Street, Burford,
Oxfordshire OX18 4RG
Tel: 01993 822 302
admin@schotten.com
www.sportantiques.co.uk

**Sporting Antiques**
9 Church Street, St Ives,
Cambridgeshire PE27 6DG
Tel: 01480 463 891
johnlambden@sportingantiques.co.uk
www.sportingantiques.co.uk

## TELEPHONES

**Telephone Lines Ltd**
Higher Tippacott Farm,
Brendon, Devon EX35 6PU
Tel: 01598 741 343
www.telephonelines.net

## TEXTILES

**Mendes Antiques Textiles & Lace**
Tel: 02920 252 745 or 07813 014 065
joachim@mendes.co.uk
www.mendes.co.uk

## TOYS AND GAMES

**Collectors Old Toy Shop & Antiques**
89, Northgate, Halifax,
North Yorkshire HX1 1XF
Tel: 01422 360 434
collectorsoldtoy@aol.com
www.collectorsoldtoyshop.com

**Donay Traditional Games & Pastimes**
Tel: 01444 416 412
info@donaygames.com
www.donaygames.com

**Sue Pearson**
42 Cliffe High St, Lewes,
East Sussex BN7 2AN
Tel: 01273 595 734
sales@suepearson.co.uk
www.suepearson.co.uk

**Wheels of Steel**
Shepherdswell,
Kent CT15 7PT
Tel: 01304 449 517
Mob: 07583 175 774
jeff@wheels-of-steel.org
www.wheels-of-steel.org

## TREEN AND BOXES

**Mostly Boxes**
93 High Street,
Eton, Windsor,
Berkshire SL4 6AF
Tel: 01753 865 447
customerservice@mostlyboxesantiques.com
www.mostlyboxesantiques.com

**Rogers de Rin**
76 Royal Hospital Road,
Paradise Walk, Chelsea,
London SW3 4HN
Tel: 020 7720 3898
rogersderin@rogersderin.co.uk
www.rogersderin.co.uk

## WATCHES

**70s Watches**
Tel: 01603 741 222
graham@70s-watches.com
www.70s-watches.com

**Kleanthous Antiques**
144 Portobello Road,
London W11 2DZ
Tel: 020 7727 3649
antiques@kleanthous.com
www.kleanthous.com

# Specialist auction houses



### BEDFORDSHIRE

**W. & H. Peacock**
The Auction Centre,
26 Newnham Street,
Bedford MK40 3JR
Tel: 01234 266 366
info@peacockauction.co.uk
www.peacockauction.co.uk

### BERKSHIRE

**Dreweatts**
Donnington Priory,
Donnington, nr Newbury,
Berkshire RG14 2JE
Tel: 01635 553 553
info@dnfa.com
www.dreweatts.com

**Special Auction Services**
81 Greenham Business Park,
Newbury, Berkshire
Tel: 01635 580 595
www.specialauctionservices.com

### BUCKINGHAMSHIRE

**Amersham Auction Rooms**
125 Station Road, Amersham,
Buckinghamshire HP7 0AH
Tel: 01494 729 292
info@amershamauctionrooms.co.uk
www.amershamauctionrooms.co.uk

**Dickins Auctioneers**
Claydon Saleroom,
Calvert Court,
Middle Claydon,
Buckinghamshire MK18 2EZ
Tel: 01296 714 434
info@dickinsauctioneers.com
www.dickinsauctioneers.com

### CAMBRIDGESHIRE

**Cheffins**
Clifton House,
1&2 Clifton Road, Cambridge,
Cambridgeshire CB1 7EA
Tel: 01223 213 343
cambridge@cheffins.co.uk
www.cheffins.co.uk

### CHANNEL ISLANDS

**Martel Maides**
Martel Maides Auctions,
Cornet Street,
St. Peter Port,
Guernsey, GY1 1LF
Tel: 01481 722 700
auctions@martelmaides.co.uk
www.martelmaidesauctions.com

### CHESHIRE

**Bonhams (Chester)**
2 St. John's Court,
Vicars Lane,
Chester CH1 1QE
Tel: 01244 313 936
chester@bonhams.com
www.bonhams.com/locations/CHE

### CLEVELAND

**Vectis Auctions Ltd**
Fleck Way, Thornaby,
Stockton-on-Tees,
Cleveland TS17 9JZ
Tel: 01642 750 616
admin@vectis.co.uk
www.vectis.co.uk

### CORNWALL

**David Lay**
The Penzance Auction House,
Alverton, Penzance,
Cornwall TR18 4RE
Tel: 01736 361 414
enquiries@davidlay.co.uk
www.davidlay.co.uk

**W.H. Lane & Son**
Jubilee House,
Queen Street, Penzance,
Cornwall TR18 4DF
Tel: 01736 361 447
info@whlane.auction
www.whlane.auction

### CUMBRIA

**Penrith Farmers & Kidds PLC**
Skirsgill, Penrith,
Cumbria CA11 0DN
Tel: 01768 890 781
info@pfkauctions.co.uk
www.pfkauctions.co.uk

### DEVON

**Bearnes, Hampton and Littlewood**
St Edmund's Court,
Okehampton Street,
Exeter, Devon EX4 1LX
Tel: 01392 413 100
info@bhandl.co.uk
www.bhandl.co.uk

**Bonhams: Exeter**
The Lodge,
Southernhay West,
Exeter EX1 1JG
Tel: 1392 425 264
exeter@bonhams.com
www.bonhams.com/locations/EXE

**Onslows**
The Coach House,
Manor Road, Stourpaine,
Dorset DT11 8TQ
Tel: 01258 488 838
onslow.auctions@btinternet.com
www.onslows.co.uk

### ESSEX

**G.E. Sworder & Sons**
14 Cambridge Road,
Stansted Mountfitchet,
Essex CM24 8GE
Tel: 01279 817 778
auctions@sworder.co.uk
www.sworder.co.uk

### GLOUCESTERSHIRE

**Mallams (Cheltenham)**
26 Grosvenor Street, Cheltenham,
Gloucestershire GL52 2SG
Tel: 01242 235 712
cheltenham@mallams.co.uk
www.mallams.co.uk

### HAMPSHIRE

**Andrew Smith & Sons**
Winchester Auction Rooms,
Manor Farm, Itchen Stoke,
Nr Winchester,
Hampshire SO24 0QT
Tel: 01962 735 988
auctions@andrewsmithandson.com
www.andrewsmithandson.com

### HEREFORDSHIRE

**Brightwells**
Easters Court,
Leominster,
Herefordshire, HR6 0DE
Tel: 01568 611 166
info@brightwells.com
www.brightwells.com

### KENT

**Westenhanger Auctioneers**
Westenanger Auction Galleries,
Station House,
Stone Street, Westenhager,
Hythe CT21 4HX
Tel: 01303 813 545
thehogbens@btinternet.com
www.westenhangerauctioneers.com

### LANCASHIRE

**Capes Dunn**
13 Queen Street, Lytham,
Lancashire, FY8 5LQ
Tel: 01253 796 245
capesdunn.lytham@gmail.com
www.capesdunn.com

### LEICESTERSHIRE

**Gilding's**
The Mill, Great Bowden Road,
Market Harborough,
Leicestershire LE16 7DE
Tel: 01858 410 414
sales@gildings.co.uk
www.gildings.co.uk

### LONDON

**Bonhams**
101 New Bond Street,
London W1S 1SR
Tel: 020 7447 7447
info@bonhams.com
www.bonhams.com/locations/BS

**Christie's**
85 Old Brompton Road,
London SW7 3LD
Tel: 020 7930 6074
info@christies.com
www.christies.com

**Dreweatts & Bloomsbury Auctions**
Bloomsbury House (London),
Bloomsbury House, 24 Maddox
Street, London W1S 1PP
Tel: 020 7495 9494
info@bloomsburyauctions.com
www.dreweatts.com

**Rosebery's**
70-76 Knights Hill,
London SE27 0JD
Tel: 020 8761 2522
clientservices@roseberys.co.uk
www.roseberys.co.uk

**Sotheby's**
34–35 New Bond Street,
London W1A 2AA
Tel: 020 7293 5000
www.sothebys.com

### MERSEYSIDE

**Cato, Crane & Co.**
6 Stanhope Street,
Liverpool L8 5RE
Tel: 0151 709 5559
info@catocrane.co.uk
www.catocrane.co.uk

### NORFOLK

**Keys**
Aylsham Salerooms,
Off Palmers Lane, Aylsham,
Norwich, Norfolk NR11 6JA
Tel: 01263 733 195
salerooms@keysauctions.co.uk
www.keysauctions.co.uk

**T.W. Gaze & Son**
Diss Auction Rooms,
Roydon Road, Diss,
Norfolk IP22 4LN
Tel: 01379 650 306
auctions@twgaze.co.uk
www.twgaze.co.uk

### OXFORDSHIRE

**Mallams (Oxford)**
Bocardo House,
St Michaels Street,
Oxford OX1 2EB
Tel: 01865 241 358
oxford@mallams.co.uk
www.mallams.co.uk

### SHROPSHIRE

**Halls Fine Art (Shrewsbury)**
Halls Holdings House,
Battlefield, Shrewsbury SY4 3DR
Tel: 01743 450 700
fineart@hallsgb.com
www.hallsgb.com

**Mullocks**
The Old Shippon,
Wall-under-Heywood,
Church Stretton,
Shropshire SY6 7DS
Tel: 01694 771 771
auctions@mullocksauctions.co.uk
www.mullocksauctions.co.uk

### SOMERSET

**Clevedon Salerooms**
Kenn Road,
Kenn, Clevedon,
Bristol BS21 6TT
Tel: 01934 830 111
info@clevedon-salerooms.com
www.clevedon-salerooms.com

**Gardiner Houlgate**
9 Leafield Way, Corsham,
Wiltshire SN13 9SW
Tel: 01225 812 912
auctions@gardinerhoulgate.co.uk
www.gardinerhoulgate.co.uk

**Lawrence's Fine Art Auctioneers Ltd**
The Linen Yard, South Street,
Crewkerne,
Somerset TA18 8AB
Tel: 01460 73041
enquiries@lawrences.co.uk
www.lawrences.co.uk

### STAFFORDSHIRE

**Potteries Specialist Auctions**
Potteries Auctions,
Silverdale Salerooms, Unit 4A
Silverdale Enterprise Park,
Newcastle under Lyme,
Staffordshire ST5 6SS
Tel: 01782 638 100
enquiries@potteriesauctions.com
www.potteriesauctions.com

**Richard Winterton Auctioneers Ltd**
Wood End Lane,
Fradley Park,
Staffordshire WS13 8NF
Tel: 01543 251 081
office@richardwinterton.co.uk
www.richardwinterton.co.uk

### SUFFOLK

**Diamond Mills**
117 Hamilton Road,
Felixstowe,
Suffolk IP11 7BL
Tel: 01394 282 281
diamondmills@btconnect.com
www.diamondmills.com

**Neal Sons & Fletcher**
26 Church Street, Woodbridge,
Suffolk IP12 1DP
Tel: 01394 382 263
enquiries@nsf.co.uk
www.nsf.co.uk

### SURREY

**Ewbank Auctioneers**
Ewbank's,
Burnt Common Auction Rooms,
London Road, Woking,
Surrey GU23 7LN
Tel: 01483 223 101
antiques@ewbankauctions.co.uk
www.ewbankauctions.co.uk

### EAST SUSSEX

**Gorringes**
15 North Street, Lewes,
East Sussex BN7 2PE
Tel: 01273 472 503
clientservices@gorringes.co.uk
www.gorringes.co.uk

**Wallis & Wallis**
West Street Auction Galleries,
Lewes, East Sussex BN7 2NJ
Tel: 01273 480 208
auctions@wallisandwallis.org
www.wallisandwallis.co.uk

### WEST SUSSEX

**Bellmans Auctioneers & Valuers**
Bellmans Auctioneers
& Valuers, Newpound,
Wisborough Green,
West Sussex RH14 0AZ
Tel: 01403 700 858
enquiries@bellmans.co.uk
www.bellmans.co.uk

**Denhams**
Dorking Road,
Warnham, Nr. Horsham,
West Sussex RH12 3RZ
Tel: 01403 255 699
enquiries@denhams.com
www.denhams.com

### TYNE & WEAR

**Anderson & Garland**
Anderson House, Crispin Court,
Newbiggin Lane, Westerhope,
Newcastle upon Tyne NE5 1BF
Tel: 0191 430 3000
info@andersonandgarland.com
www.andersonandgarland.com

### WARWICKSHIRE

**Locke & England**
12 Guy Street,
Leamington Spa CV32 4RT
Tel: 01926 889 100
info@leauction.co.uk
www.leauction.co.uk

### WEST MIDLANDS

**Bonhams (Knowle)**
The Old House, Station Road,
Knowle, Solihull,
West Midlands B93 0HT
Tel: 01564 776 151
knowle@bonhams.com
www.bonhams.com/locations/KNO

**Fellows & Sons**
Augusta House, 19 Augusta Street,
Hockley, Birmingham,
West Midlands B18 6JA
Tel: 0121 212 2131
info@fellows.co.uk
www.fellows.co.uk

### WILTSHIRE

**Woolley & Wallis**
51–61 Castle Street,
Salisbury, Wiltshire SP1 3SU
Tel: 01722 424 500
enquiries@woolleyandwallis.co.uk
www.woolleyandwallis.co.uk

### WORCESTERSHIRE

**Gloucestershire Worcestershire Railwayana Auctions**
The Willows,
Badsey Road, Evesham,
Worcestershire WR11 7PA
Tel: 01386 760 109
simont@gwra.co.uk
www.gwra.co.uk

**Phillip Serrell**
The Malvern Saleroom,
Barnards Green Road, Malvern,
Worcestershire WR14 3LW
Tel: 01684 892 314
auctions@serrell.co.uk
www.serrell.com

### EAST YORKSHIRE

**Dee, Atkinson & Harrison**
The Exchange Saleroom, Driffield,
East Yorkshire YO25 6LD
Tel: 01377 253 151
andrews@dahauctions.com
www.dee-atkinson-harrison.co.uk

### NORTH YORKSHIRE

**Tennants**
The Auction Centre,
Harmby Road, Leyburn,
North Yorkshire DL8 5SG
Tel: 01969 623 780
enquiry@tennants-ltd.co.uk
www.tennants.co.uk

### SOUTH YORKSHIRE

**A.E. Dowse & Sons**
Sheffield Auction Gallery,
Windsor Road,
Heeley, Sheffield,
South Yorkshire S8 8UB
Tel: 0114 281 6161
enquire@sheffieldauctiongallery.com
www.sheffieldauctiongallery.com

**BBR Auctions**
Elsecar Heritage Centre,
5 Ironworks Row, Wath Road,
Elsecar, Barnsley,
South Yorkshire S74 8HJ
Tel: 01226 745 156
www.onlinebbr.com

### WEST YORKSHIRE

**Andrew Hartley Fine Arts**
Victoria Hall Salerooms,
Little Lane, Ilkley,
West Yorkshire LS29 8EA
Tel: 01943 816 363
info@hartleysauctions.co.uk
www.andrewhartleyfinearts.co.uk

### IRELAND

**Mealy's**
Kilkenny Road,
Castlecomer,
Co. Kilkenny,
Ireland
Tel: 00 353 56 4400942
info@mealys.ie
www.mealys.ie

### SCOTLAND

**Bonhams (Edinburgh)**
22 Queen St,
Edinburgh EH2 1JX
Tel: 0131 225 2266
edinburgh@bonhams.com
www.bonhams.com/locations/EDI

**Lyon & Turnbull**
33 Broughton Place,
Edinburgh EH1 3RR
Tel: 0131 557 8844
www.lyonandturnbull.com

**McTears**
Meiklewood Gate,
31 Meiklewood Road,
Glasgow G51 4EU
Tel: 0141 810 2880
enquiries@mctears.co.uk
www.mctears.co.uk

**Thomson Roddick Scottish Auctions**
The Auction Centre,
118 Carnethie Street,
Rosewell, Edinburgh EH24 9AL
Tel: 0131 440 2448
edinburgh@thomsonroddick.com
www.thomsonroddick.com

### WALES

**Peter Francis**
Towyside Salerooms,
Old Station Road,
Carmarthen SA31 1JN
Tel: 01267 233 456
enquiries@peterfrancis.co.uk
www.peterfrancis.co.uk

# Index

References to picture captions are in *italics*

# N



# O



# P



# Q



# R

## S



## T

## U



## V



## W



## X



## Y



## Z

# Acknowledgements



The following images, photographed with permission from the sources itemised below, are copyright © Judith Miller & Dorling Kindersley. Abbreviations: t=top, b=bottom, r=right, l=left, c=centre, R=row (eg, R3r=third row right).

**10th Planet Limited,** Unit 36 Vicarage Field Shopping Centre, Ripple Road, Barking, Essex IG11 8DQ. Tel: 020 8591 5357. www.10thplanet.co.uk. 260bl, 262br, 262cr, 262tr, 263bl, 263R3l, 263t, 263br, 263R2r, 263R2c. **Beth Adams**, Unit G043/044, Alfies Antique Market, 13–25 Church Street, London NW8 8DT. Tel: 0207 723 5613. 39bl, 44b, 122b, 123tr. **All Our Yesterdays**, 6 Park Road, Kelvinbridge, Glasgow G4 9JG. Tel: 0141 334 7788. antiques@allouryesterdays.fsnet.co.uk. 34bl, 42cl, 43R2r, 79bc, 250bc, 250br, 308br, 308bl, 309bl, 309cl, 335bl. **Andrew Lineham Fine Glass**, The Mall, Camden Passage, London N1 8ED. Tel: 020 7704 0195 or 07767 702 722. www.andrewlineham.co.uk. 42br. **Animation Art Gallery**, 13–14 Great Castle Street, London W1W 8LS. Tel: 0207 255 1456. www.animaart.com. 270tl, 271bl, 271br, 271r, 271tr. **Antique Glass at Frank Dux**, 33 Belvedere, Lansdown Road, Bath, Avon BA1 5HR. Tel/Fax: 01225 312 367. www.antique-glass.co.uk. 142bl, 143R2l. **Antique Textiles and Lighting**, 34 Belvedere, Lansdowne Road, Bath, Avon BA1 5HR. Tel: 01225 310 795. joannaproops@aol.co.uk. 191tl. **Art Deco Etc**, 73 Upper Gloucester Road, Brighton, East Sussex BN1 3NQ. Tel: 01273 329 268. johnclarke@artdecoetc.co.uk. 33t, 370bl. **At the Movies**, 17 Fouberts Place, Carnaby Street, London W1F 7QD. Tel: 020 7439 6336. www.atthemovies.co.uk. 264bl, 264br, 264tr, 265bl. **Atomic Age**, 318 E. Virginia Road, Fullerton, CA 92831, USA. Tel: 001 714 446 0736. atomage100@aol.com. 244cr, 245tc, 320tr, 320bl, 321tl, 321R2l, 321br. **Auction Blocks**, PO Box 2321, Huntington Station, CT 06484, USA. Tel: 001 203 924 2802. www.auctionblocks.com. 222cl, 222bl, 222br, 222cr, 222tr, 223bl, 223R2r, 223tl, 223tr, 223R3l. **Auction Team Köln**, Postfach 50 11 19, Bonner Str. 528–530, D-50971 Köln, Germany. Tel: 00 49 (0)221 38 70 49. www.breker.com. 118bl, 119tr, 121br, 262bl, 269t 'Money banks', 281tr, 315bl(&R4l), 335cr, 336bl, 338tr, 338cl, 338bl, 338br, 338cr, 339bl, 340tr. **Auktionshaus W.G. Herr**, Friesenwall 35, D-50672, Köln, Germany. Tel: 00 49 (0)221 25 45 48. www.herr-auktionen.de. 166bl, 166bc, 166br, 167bc, 167br, 169tl, 375cr. **Aurora Galleries International**, 30 Hackamore Lane, Suite 2, Bell Canyon, CA 91307, USA. Tel: 001 818 884 6468. www.auroragalleriesonline.com. 354tr. **Colin Baddiel**, Stand B25, Stand 351–3, Grays Antique Market, South Molten Lane, London W1Y 2LP. Tel: 020 7408 1239. 216bl. **Baubles**, South Street Antiques Center, 615 South 6th Street, Philadelphia, PA 19147, USA. Tel: 001 215 592 0256. Tel: 001 215 487 0207. 196cr, 196tr. **Bauman Rare Books**, 4535 Madison Avenue, between 54th & 55th Streets, New York, NY 100022, USA. Tel: 001 212 751 0011. www.baumanrarebooks.com. 299bc, 299br. **BBR Auctions**, Elsecar Heritage Centre, nr Barnsley, South Yorkshire S74 8AA. Tel: 01226 745 156. www.bbrauctions.co.uk. 140bl, 140tr, 141cr, 141tl. **Bébés & Jouets**, c/o Post Office, 165 Restalris Road, Edinburgh EH7 6HW. Tel: 0131 332 5650. bebesetjouets@u.genie.co.uk. 227r, 229br, 231tr, 232bcr, 232tr, 237l. **Linda Bee**, Grays in The Mews, Antiques Market, 1–7 Davies Mews, London W1K 5AB. Tel/Fax: 020 7629 5921 or tel: 07956 276 384. 136br, 137tl, 137tr, 137R2r, 137bl, 137br. **Below Stairs of Hungerford**, 103 High Street, Hungerford, Berkshire RG17 0NB. Tel: 01488 682 317. www.belowstairs.co.uk. 98bl, 99tl, 99bl, 99br, 101cr, 118br, 119br, 291br. **Nigel Benson**, 20th-Century Glass, 58–60 Kensington Church Street, London W8 4DB. Tel: 020 7938 1137. 144tr, 145t 'Streaky', 145t 'Ribbon-trailed', 154tr, 155bl. **Beverley**, 30 Church Street, London NW8 8EP. Tel: 0207 262 1576. 26bl, 27bl, 28bcl, 28br, 29tl, 29R2r, 29R3l, 29bl, 33tr, 34t, 35bl, 35br, 45cr, 49c, 54b, 123R3r, 318bl, 319tl. **Beyond Retro**, 110–112 Cheshire Street, London E2 6EJ. Tel: 020 7613 3636. www.beyondretro.com. 180cl. **Biblion**, 1–7 Davies Mews, London W1K 5AB. Tel: 020 7629 1374. www.biblion.com. 298bl, 298bc, 299bl, 299cr, 300bl, 300br, 300tr, 301bc, 301bl, 301bc, 301br, 302bl, 302tr, 303bc, 303br, 303cr, 303tr, 303tl. **Bonhams**, 101 New Bond Street, London W1S 1SR. Tel: 020 7629 6602. www.bonhams.com. 20tr, 54tr, 62tr, 88c. **Bonhams Bayswater**, 10 Salam Road, London W2 4DL. Tel: 020 7313 2727 www.bonhams.com. 147br, 153bc, 153tr, 364bl, 375c. **Bonhams Edinburgh**, 65 George Street, Edinburgh EH2 2JL. Tel: 0131 225 2266. www.bonhams.com. 61br, 149bl, 149R3r, 365bc, 368bl, 369br, 371c. **Bonhams Knightsbridge**, Montpelier Street, London SW7 1HH. www.bonhams.com. 221tl, 226br, 228bl, 228br, 229bl, 229tr, 230t 'Gadget bears', 230t 'Coloured bears', 232bl, 232bcl, 241tl, 248br, 249tl, 301cr. **Bonhams Knowle**, The Old House, Station Road, Solihull, West Midlands B93 0HT. Tel: 01564 776 151. www.bonhams.com. 190bl, 191br. **Bonhams Sevenoaks**. No longer trading. *See Bonhams*. 39cr, 40br. **Joseph Bonnar**, 72 Thistle Street, Edinburgh EH2 1EN. Tel: 0131 226 2811. 203br, 203cr. **The Book Palace**, Jubilee House, Bedwardine Road, Crystal Palace, London SE19 3AP. Tel: 020 8768 0022. www.bookpalace.com. 304bl, 304br, 304bc, 304tr, 305t, 305bc, 305br, 305cr. **Roger Bradbury**, Church Street, Coltishall, Norwich, Norfolk NR12 7DJ. Tel: 01603 737 444. 39tl 'Nanking', 39tl 'Diana', 39tl 'Tek Sing'. **Bracketts Fine Art Auctioneers**, Auction Hall, The Pantiles, Tunbridge Wells, Kent TN2 5QL. Tel: 01892 544 500. www.bfaa.co.uk. 85tr, 85tl. **Branksome Antiques**, 370 Poole Road, Branksome, Poole, Dorset BH12 1AW. Tel: 01202 763 324. 134bl, 134bc, 134br, 134tr, 135t, 135bc, 135r, 135br, 344cl. **Bristol Auction Rooms**, (Collectors' Saleroom), Baynton Road, Ashton, Bristol BS3 2EB. (Main Saleroom), St John's Place, Apsley Road, Clifton, Bristol BS8 2ST. Tel: 0117 973 7201. www.bristolauctionrooms.co.uk. 21tr, 23br, 31t, 31bl. **Bucks County Antique Center**, Route 202, Lahaska PA 18931, USA. Tel: 001 215 794 9180. 268tr, 269br. **Cad van Swankster at The Girl Can't Help It**, Alfies Antique Market, Shop G115, Ground Floor, 13–25 Church Street, London NW8 8DT. Tel: 020 7723 0564. 185tr, 193tl, 193cr, 258tr, 306tr, 365br. **Carlton Antiques**, 43 Worcester Road, Malvern, Worcestershire WR14 4RB. Tel: 01684 573 092. www. carlton-antiques.com. 309t, 312tr, 313bl, 313bc, 313br, 313cr, 349tl. **C.A.R.S. of Brighton**, 4–4a Chapel Terrace Mews, Kemptown, Brighton, East Sussex BN2 1HU. Tel: 01273 601 960. 350bl, 350tr, 351bl, 351bc, 351br, 351cr. **Cheffins**, The Cambridge Saleroom, 2 Clifton Road, Cambridge CB1 4BW. Tel: 01223 213 343. www.cheffins.co.uk. 31r, 63bl, 63bc, 64b 'Peter Rabbit', 64b 'Pigling Bland', 149tl, 214b, 217b, 218bl, 259t, 259bc, 261bl, 276bl. **Chiswick Auctions**, 1–5 Colville Road, London W3 8BL. Tel: 020 8992 4442. 135bl, 141bl, 311tr. **Christine Bertrand Collection**. 120b 'Iles', 120b 'Fenton', 120b 'Horner', 120b 'Dorcas', 120b 'Bros', 121bl. **Christopher Sykes Antiques**, The Old Parsonage, Woburn, Milton Keynes MK17 9QL. Tel: 01525 290 259/467. www.sykes-corkscrews.co.uk. 126tr, 126b, 126c, 127t, 127bl, 127bc, 127br, 127r, 128tr, 193tr. **Clevedon Salerooms**, The Auction Centre, Kenn Road, Clevedon, Bristol BS21 6TT. Tel: 01934 830 111. www.clevedon-salerooms.com. 43bl, 59r, 59bl, 60tr. **Cloud Cuckoo Land**, 6 Charlton Place, Camden Passage, London N1. Tel: 020 7354 3141. 177br, 180r, 184cr, 188tr. **Cobwebs**, 78 Old Northam Road, Southampton SO14 0PB. Tel: 02380 227 458. www.cobwebs.uk.com. 219bl, 352c, 352tr, 353cr, 353br, 353bl, 353t 'Fixtures and fittings', 353t 'Playing cards', 353t 'Brochures', 353t 'Souvenirs', 353t 'Timetables', 353t 'Menus', 355cr. **Collectors Cameras**, PO Box 16, Pinner, Middlesex HA5 4HN. Tel: 020 8421 3537. 339R2r, 339tr, 339br. **Sheila Cook**, 283 Westbourne Grove, London W11 2QA. Tel: 020 7792 8001. www.sheilacook.co.uk. 175tl, 175cr, 188b '1900s', 188b '1920s'. **Cowan's Historic Americana Auctions**, 673 Wilmer Avenue, Cincinnati, OH 45226, USA. Tel: 001 513 871 1670. www.historicamericana.com. 192bl, 192br. **Cristobal**, 26 Church Street, London NW8 8EP. Tel/Fax: 020 7724 7230. www.cristobal.co.uk. 186b, 198bl(&bc), 199bc, 199br, 199bl, 200tr, 201c. **David Lloyd Collection**. 284bl, 284bc, 284br, 285bl, 285bc, 285br. **David Rago Auctions**, 333 North Main Street, Lambertville, NJ 08530, USA. Tel: 001 609 397 9374. www.ragoarts.com. 277bl 'Records'. **Dawson's Auctioneers & Appraisers**, 128 American Road, Morris Plains, NJ 07950, USA. Tel: 001 973 984 6900. www.dawsons.org. 55bl, 231cr. **Deco Etc**, 122 West 25th Street, (between 6th & 7th Avenues), New York, NY 10010, USA. Tel: 001 212 675 3327. deco_etc@msn.com. 129cr, 372bl, 372tr, 373tl, 373R4l, 373bl, 373br, 373tr. **Dee Carlton Collection**. qnoscots@aol.com. 112cl, 112bl, 112cr, 112tr, 113tl, 113cl, 113cr, 196bl. **The Design Gallery**, 5 The Green, Westerham, Kent TN16 1AS. Tel: 01959 561 234 or 07974 322 858. www.thedesigngallery.uk.com. 361br. **Design Twentieth Century**. www.design20c.com. 49cr, 337bl, 337t, 337br, 368tr, 371bl, 371cr, 374br, 374tr. **Dickins Auctioneers**, The Claydon Saleroom, Calvert Road, Middle Claydon, Buckinghamshire MK18 2EZ. Tel: 01296 714 434. www.dickins-auctioneers.com. 58bc, 63t, 101br, 119bl. **DODO**, Alfies Antique Market, 1st floor (F073, 83 & 84), 13–25 Church Street, London NW8 8DT. Tel: 020 7706 1545. dodoposters@yahoo.com. 313cl, 322tr, 325br. **Doll Express**, 2222 N. Reading Road, Denver, PA 17517, USA. Tel: 001 717 335 3300. www.thedollexpress.com. 233cr, 233bl, 236br, 241bc, 241cr, 242r, 243tl(&tc), 243cr, 243br, 244cl, 244bl, 244br, 244tr, 245tl, 245bl, 245r, 245bc. **Donay Games & Pastimes**, 3 Pierrepont Row, Camden Passage, London N1 8EF. Tel: 01444 416 412. donaygames@btconnect.com. 249cr, 250bl, 250tr, 251bc, 251br. **Dorotheum**, A–1010 Vienna, Dorotheergasse 17, Austria. Tel: +43 1 515 60 - 0. www.dorotheum.com. 372br, 373R2l. **Dreweatts & Bloomsbury Auctions**, Donnington Priory Salerooms, Donnington, Newbury, Berkshire RG14 2JE. Tel: 01635 553 553. www.dreweatts.com 33cr, 35tl 'Recent pieces', 38b, 40tr, 41r, 50bl, 52b, 55br, 55r, 57tc, 57tl, 58tr, 68bl, 78bl, 82bl, 82br, 83t, 83bl, 83cr, 109tl, 114tr, 115b, 118tr, 123tl, 129br, 145t 'Wavy', 145t 'Cloudy', 147cr, 148bl, 152tr, 165br, 165bl, 168bl, 169bc, 221br, 226bl, 226tr, 227br, 229tl, 229bc, 231tl, 240bl, 248tr, 269r, 285tr, 286br, 334tr, 349br, 361t, 371br. **Early Technology**, Monkton House, Old Craighall, Edinburgh, Scotland. Tel: 0131 665 5753. www.earlytech.com. 119t, 231br. **Feljoy Antiques**, Shop 3, Angel Arcade, Camden Passage, London N1 8EA. Tel: 020 7354 5336. www.chintznet.com/feljoy. 32cl, 32b, 32tr, 35tr. **Sandra Fellner**, Stand 125/B14, Grays Mews Antiques Market, Davies Mews, South Molton Lane, London W1Y 5AB. Tel: 020 8946 5613. fellner-sellers@grays.clara.net. 228tr, 246tr, 247bc, 247br. **Fellow's & Sons**, Augusta House, 19 Augusta Street, Hockley, Birmingham B18 6JA. Tel: 0121 212 2131. www.fellows.co.uk. 122cl, 192cl, 202br, 205t, 205cr, 238bl, 238cl, 238cr, 238br, 238tr, 239tl, 239tr, 239R3r, 239bl, 239br, 239R2l, 249bl, 268c, 269t 'Die-cast', 350br, 351cl. **Jill Fenichell**, 305 East 61st Street, New York, NY, USA. Tel: 001 212 980 9346. jfenichell@yahoo.com. 50tr 'Coffee pots', 50tr 'Jugs', 50tr 'Cheese dishes', 50tr 'Jam pots', 51br. **Festival**, 136 South Ealing Road, London W5 4QJ. Tel: 020 8840 9333. info@festival1951.co.uk. 24b 'Late style', 44tr, 45br, 45t 'Fifties flowers', 45t 'Black and white', 45t 'Polka dots', 45t 'Youth appeal', 46tr, 47tr, 47cl, 47b 'Talisman', 47b 'Totem', 47b 'Monte Sol', 47b 'Magic City', 48bl, 48br, 49br, 49bc. **France Antique Toys**. Tel: 001 631 754 1399. 276tr. **Fraser's Autographs**, 399 The Strand, London WC2 R0LX. Tel: 020 7836 9325. www.frasersautographs.com. 316br, 316tr, 317tl, 317bl, 317br. **Freeman's**, 1808 Chestnut Street, Philadelphia, PA 19103, USA. Tel: 001 215 563 9275. www. freemansauction. com. 20b, 26tr, 30br, 56tr, 137R2l, 195bc, 274tr, 365bl. **Gallery 1930 Susie Cooper Ceramics Art Deco**, 18 Church Street, London NW8 8EP. Tel: 020 7723 1555. www.susiecooperceramics.com. 20br, 22br, 24b 'Nursery ware', 24b 'Early work', 24b 'Restrained design', 24b 'Towards Art Deco', 24b 'Art Deco', 25t, 25bl, 25r, 25br, 27br, 27bc, 28bl, 28b, 29br, 29tr, 36bl, 36tr 'Tableware', 36tr 'Slip-cast', 36tr 'Accessories', 37tc, 37tr, 37cr, 37b, 55cl, 55cr, 55t. **Gentry Antiques**, c/o Rod & Line Shop, Little Green, Polperro, Cornwall PL13 2RF. Tel: 07974 221 343. www.cornishwarecollector.co.uk. 104b, 104tr, 105br, 105cr, 105t, 105bl. **Richard Gibbon**, 34/34a Islington Green, London N1 8DU. Tel: 020 7354 2852. neljeweluk@aol.com. 198tr, 201tl. **Gillian Neale Antiques**, PO Box 247, Aylesbury, Buckinghamshire HP20 1JZ. Tel: 01296 423754 or 07860 638700. www.gilliannealeantiques.co.uk. 106br, 107tr, 107cl, 108bl, 109tr. **The Glass Merchant**. Tel: 07775 683 961. as@titan98.freeserve.co.uk. 150tr, 151bc, 153br, 165cr, 165t, 168r, 169bl, 169tr. **Goodwins Antiques Ltd**, 15 & 16 Queensferry Street, Edinburgh EH2 4QW. Tel: 0131 225 4717. 194tr. **Gorringes**, 15 North Street, Lewes, East Sussex BN7 2PD. Tel: 01273 472 503. www.gorringes.co.uk. 21r, 23bl, 23r, 23t, 31bc, 35tl 'Florian ware', 36tr 'Simple shapes', 37br, 37tl, 41br, 148cl, 149R3l, 292br, 342bl. **Graham Cooley Collection**. Tel: 07968 722269. grahamcooley_ffc@hotmail.com. 124bl, 124br, 124tr, 125bl, 125br, 125cr, 125cl, 142cr, 144bl, 145t 'Optic', 146bl, 147tr, 147bl, 148tr, 152bl, 153bl, 155tl, 155tr, 156br, 157tr, 157cr, 157br, 157tl, 157bl, 158tr, 158bl, 159br, 159tl, 161br, 161bl, 163bl, 334bc(&cr), 348cl, 348bl, 348bc, 348cr, 349tl, 349R3l, 349R4l, 349bl, 349br, 349R2r, 349tr, 374bl, 375bc. **Gary Grant**, 18 Arlington Way, London EC1R 1UY. Tel: 020 7713 1122. 45t 'Rare shapes', 45t 'Atomic design', 46bl, 47b 'Tivoli', 47b 'Magic Garden'. **Ken Grant**, F109–111, Alfies Antique Market, 13 Church Street, London NW8 8DT. 98tr, 99cr. **Great Western Railway Auctions**, The Willows, Badsey Road, Evesham, Worcestershire WR11 7PA. Tel: 01684 773 487. www.gwra.co.uk. 348bl, 348br, 348tr, 349bl, 349bc, 349cr.

**Griffin & Cooper Antiques**, South Street Antiques Center, 615 South 6th Street, Philadelphia, PA 19147, USA. Tel: 001 215 582 0418/3594. 61bl. **Guernsey's Auctions**, 108 East 73rd Street, New York, NY 10021, USA. Tel: 001 212 794 2280. www.guernseys.com. 274cr, 275tl. **Halcyon Days**, 14 Brook Street, London W1S 1BD. Tel: 020 7629 8811. www.halcyondays.co.uk. 275cr. **Hamptons**, Baverstock House, 93 High Street, Godalming, Surrey GU7 1AL. Tel: 01483 423 567. www.hamptons.co.uk. 21bl, 78tr. **Harper General Store**, 10482 Jonestown Road, Annville, PA, 17003, USA. Tel: 001 717 865 3456. www.harpergeneralstore.com. 228bc, 230t 'Berlin bears', 230t 'Pandas', 230t 'Novelty bears', 269t 'Badges'. **Hope and Glory**, 131A Kensington Church Street, London W8 7LP. Tel: 020 7727 8424. 72bl, 72br, 72tr, 73t, 73bl, 73br, 74bl, 74tr, 74br, 75bl, 75tr, 75cr, 76br, 76bc, 76tr, 77tl, 77bl, 77bc, 77br, 77tr, 78br, 79tl, 79cr, 79br, 80tr, 80cl, 80cr, 80bl, 80br, 81tr, 81tl, 81R2l, 81bl, 366cr, 367tl. **Hunt Auctions**, 75 E. Uwchlan Avenue, Suite 130, Exton, PA 19341, USA. Tel: 001 610 524 0822. www.huntsauctions.com. 189cr. **Huxtins**, 11 & 12 The Lipka Arcade, 288 Westbourne Grove, London W11. Tel: 07710 132 200. www.huxtins.com. 110tr, 110bl, 110br, 111bl, 111bc, 111br, 111cr, 111cl, 114bl, 115tl, 115tc, 116tl, 116tr, 116b, 117br, 117t, 241br, 269t 'Tins', 288tr, 318tr, 319bl, 319tr, 322bl, 322br, 323tl, 323cr, 323bc, 355bl, 366cl, 366bl, 366br, 366tr, 367tr, 367R2r, 367cl, 367bl, 367br. **InterCol**, 114 Islington High Street, London W1X 3HB. Tel: 020 7354 2599. www.intercol.co.uk. 92tr, 92bl, 93bc, 93tc, 93cr, 93br, 251bl. **Jacobs & Hunt Fine Art Auctioneers**, 26 Lavant Street, Petersfield, Hampshire GU32 3EF. Tel: 01730 233 933. www.jacobsandhunt.com. 123R2r. **James Bridges Collection**. 336tr, 361bc, 362cr, 362b, 362tr, 363br, 363tl. **Jean Scott Collection**, Stanhope Collectors' Club, 42 Frankland Crescent, Parkstone, Poole, Dorset BH14 9PX. www.stanhopes.info. 85br, 86l, 86br, 86tr, 87tl, 87l, 87bl, 87tr, 87br, 120tr, 121tl, 121tr, 141br. **Jeanette Hayhurst Fine Glass**, 32A Kensington Church Street, London W8 4HA. Tel: 020 7938 1539. 128br, 128bc, 142cl, 142br, 142tr, 143bl, 143br, 143tl, 145t 'Cut', 146tl, 146tr, 154bl. **Karl Flaherty Collectables**. Tel: 02476 445 627. kfckarl@aol.com. 256b, 256tr, 257bcl, 257bl, 257bcr. **Kitsch-N-Kaboodle**, South Street Antiques Center, 615 South 6th Street, Philadelphia, PA 19147-2128, USA. Tel: 001 215 382 1354. 257tl. **Bill and Rick Kozlowski**. Tel: 001 215 997 2486. 192tr. **Law Fine Art Ltd**, Firs Cottage, Church Lane, Brimpton, Berkshire RG7 4TJ. Tel: 0118 971 0353. www.lawfineart.co.uk. 41t, 53br. **Lawrence's Fine Art Auctioneers**, South Street, Crewkerne, Somerset TA18 8AB. Tel: 01460 73041. www.lawrences.co.uk. 57bl, 57br, 57tr, 88b, 136R2l, 195br, 230t 'Unknown bears', 236bl, 336br, 341c. **Legacy**, G50/51 Alfies Antique Market, 13–25 Church Street, London NW8 8DT. Tel: 020 7723 0449. legacy@alfies.clara.net. 81br, 82tr, 83br, 312bl, 312br, 315R2l, 319br. **Hugo Lee-Jones**. Tel: 01227 375 375 or 07941 187 2027. electroniccollectables@hotmail.com. 257br, 272tr, 272cr, 272br, 272bl, 272cl, 273tl, 273R2l, 273R3l, 273R3r, 273tr, 273br, 273bl, 341cr. **L.H. Selman Ltd**, 123 Locust Street, Santa Cruz, CA 95060, USA. Tel: 001 800 538 0766. www.selman.com/pwauction. 148cr, 148br, 149R2r, 149tr. **Lights, Camera, Action**, 6 Western Gardens, Western Boulevard, Aspley, Nottingham NG8 5GP. Tel: 0115 913 1116 or 07970 342 363. www.lca-autographs.co.uk. 265t. **Lilliput Lane**, Enesco Ltd. www.lilliputlane.co.uk. 51tl, 51tr. **Lucy's Hats**, South Street Antiques Center, 615 South 6th Street, Philadelphia, PA 19147, USA. Tel: 001 215 592 0256. shak06@aol.com. 178cl, 178bl, 178br, 178cr, 179tl. **Luna**, 323 George Street, Nottingham NG1 3BH. Tel: 0115 924 3267. www.luna-online.co.uk. 122tr, 122cr, 125bc, 337bc, 337cr, 344b, 344tr, 345br, 345cr, 345t, 364tr, 369tr, 369bl, 375br.

**Lyon and Turnbull Ltd**, 33 Broughton Place, Edinburgh EH1 3RR. Tel: 0131 557 8844. www.lyonandturnbull.com. 31br, 35tl 'Art Nouveau', 35tl 'Native flowers', 40bl, 40bc, 59t, 74cl, 145bl, 145cr, 289tc, 360br, 361br, 364br. **Mad Hatter Antiques**, Unit 82, Admiral Vernon Antique Market, 141–149 Portobello Rd, London W11. Tel: 020 7262 0487 or 07931 956 705. madhatter.portobello@virgin.net. 42bl, 42cr, 42tr, 43tl, 43tr, 43R3l, 43R3r, 43br. **Manic Attic**, Stand S011, Alfies Antique Market, 13 Church Street, London NW8 8DT. Tel: 020 7723 6105. manicattic@alfies.clara.net. 28tr, 29R2l, 334br, 365tl, 365cr, 372cr. **Mark Hill Collection**. Tel: 07798 915 474. stylophile@btopenworld.com. 162bl, 162tc, 163tr, 164l, 164tr, 169br, 324tr, 362l, 363bl, 363R4r, 363R2r, 363R2l, 363tr. **Mark Slavinsky Collection**. 270b. **Francesca Martire**, Stand f. 131–137, First Floor, Alfies Antique Market, 13–25 Church Street, London NW8 0RH. Tel: 020 7724 4802. martire@alfies.clara.net. 167t, 370tr. **Mary Ann's Collectibles**, South Street Antiques Center, 615 South 6th Street, Philadelphia, PA 19147, USA. Tel: 001 215 592 0256/923 3247. 60bl, 179cr, 185R3r, 197R2r, 314bl. **Mary Wise and Grosvenor Antiques**, 27 Holland Street, London W8 4NA. Tel: 020 7937 8649. 52l. **Mendes Antique Lace and Textiles**, Flat 2, Wilbury Lawn, 44 Wilbury Road, Hove, East Sussex BN3 3PA. Tel: 01273 203 317. www.mendes.co.uk. 190tr, 190cl, 190cr, 190br, 191c, 191bl, 191tr. **Mick Collins Collection**. admin@sylvacclub.com. 53bl, 61cr, 65br, 66tl, 66tr, 67cr. **Mod-Girl**, South Street Antiques Center, 615 South 6th Street, Philadelphia, PA 19147, USA. Tel: 001 215 592 0256/413 0434. 178tr. **Mostly Boxes**, 93 High Street, Eton, Windsor, Berkshire SL4 6AF. Tel: 01753 858 470. 84tr. **Mullock Madeley**, The Old Shippon, Wall-under-Heywood, Church Stretton, Shropshire SY6 7DS. Tel: 01694 771 771. www.mullock-madeley.co.uk. 284tr, 286cr, 287br, 287cr, 287tl, 289cr, 290bl, 290bc, 290br, 290tr, 291bl, 291bc, 291cr, 291cl, 292bl, 292bc, 293tl, 293bl, 293br, 293cr. **Mum Had That**. www.mumhadthat.com. 150bl, 150br, 151bl, 151br, 151tr, 159bl, 159tc, 160bl, 161tr, 161t, 162tr, 375bl. **Nigel Wright Collection**. xab@dircon.co.uk. 123R3l, 234cl, 234bl, 234br, 234cr, 234tr, 235tl, 235R2r, 235cl, 235bl, 235tr, 235br. **Noel Barrett Antiques & Auctions Ltd**, PO Box 300, Carversville, Pennsylvania, 18913, USA. Tel: 001 215 297 5109. www.noelbarrett.com. 212bl, 213cr, 213bl(&bc), 269bl, 269t 'Early designs', 270tr. **Onslows**, The Coach House, Manor Road, Stourpaine, Dorset DT11 8TQ. Tel/Fax: 01258 488 838. www.onslows.co.uk. 324bl, 325tl, 325tr, 326tr, 327tr, 328tr, 328bl, 328bc, 328br, 329cl, 329c, 329cr, 329bl, 329bc, 329br. **Otford Antiques and Collectors Centre**, 26–28 High Street, Otford, Kent TN15 9DF. Tel: 01959 522 025. www.otfordantiques.co.uk. 39br, 60bcl, 60bcr, 60br, 76bl, 85bc, 85bl, 138tr, 138bl, 139bl, 143R4l, 143tr, 242bc, 339tl, 354bl. **Cooper Owen**, 10 Denmark Street, London WC2H 8LS. Tel: 020 7240 4132. www.cooperowen.com. 251tr, 264bc, 266br, 266tr, 267br, 267cr, 267cl, 274bl, 275br, 277tl, 277cr, 277bl 'Merchandise', 277bl 'Signatures', 277bl 'Personal items', 279tr, 280cl, 281tc, 281bl 'Albums', 281bl 'Posters', 282bl, 282bc, 282br, 283bc, 283br, 283cl, 283c, 283cr, 317bc, 317tr, 342tl, 342tc, 342tr, 343tr, 343cr, 343br, 343tl 'Dinkie', 343tl 'ETN', 343tl 'Meisterstuck'. **Petersham Books**, Unit 67, 56 Gloucester Road, Kensington, London SW7 4UB. Tel/Fax: 020 7581 9147. www.modernfirsts.co.uk. 298br, 298tr, 301tl. **Posteritati**, 239 Center Street, New York, NY 10013, USA. Tel: 001 212 226 2207. www.posteritati.com. 266bc, 266bl, 267bl, 267bc. **Potteries Specialist Auctions**, 271 Waterloo Road, Cobridge, Stoke-on-Trent, Staffordshire ST6 3HR. Tel: 01782 286 622. www.potteriesauctions.com. 51bc, 51bl, 52tr, 53r, 56br, 58l, 58br, 59bc, 59br, 62bl, 62br, 63br, 64t, 64b 'Flopsy, Mopsy, and Cottontail', 64b 'Mr Benjamin Bunny', 64b 'Simpkin', 64b 'Mrs Tiggywinkle', 65tl, 66br, 67t, 67cl, 67bl, 67bc, 67c, 73bc, 77cr, 278tr, 310br, 311R3r. **Private Collection**. 30tr, 39tl 'Hatcher', 75br, 84bl, 139br, 159cr, 169c, 174tr, 197tl , 201br, 203bc, 232br, 249br, 308tr, 309cr, 309br, 310cl, 310bl, 310cr, 310tr, 311b, 311R3l, 311R2r, 311tl, 314br, 314cr, 315R1l, 315R1r, 315br, 340br, 340bl, 341bl, 341bc, 341br. **Quittenbaum Kunstauktionen München**, Hohenstaufenstraße 1, D-80801, München, Germany. Tel: 089 33 00 75 6. 166tr, 167bl. **R. & G. McPherson Antiques**, 40 Kensington Church Street, London W8 4BX. Tel: 020 7937 0812 or 07768 432 630. www.orientalceramics.com. 39tl 'Hoi An hoard', 39tl 'Vung Tao'. **Rennies**, 13 Rugby Street, London WC1 3QT. Tel: 020 7405 0220. info@rennart.co.uk. 177cr, 179bl, 326bl. **Richard Ball Lighters**. richard@lighter.co.uk. 195tr. **Rick Hubbard Art Deco**, 3 Tee Court, Bell Street, Romsey, Hampshire S051 8GY. Tel/Fax: 01794 513 133. www.rickhubbard-artdeco.co.uk. 22tr, 26bc, 26br, 27cr, 27c, 33b, 42tr. **Ritchie's Auctioneers & Appraisers**, 288 King Street East, Toronto, Ontario, Canada M5A 1KA. Tel: 001 416 364 1864. www.ritchies.com. 181bc. **Rogers de Rin**, 76 Royal Hospital Road, Paradise Walk, Chelsea, London SW3 4HN. Tel: 020 7352 9007. www.rogersderin.co.uk. 35cr. **Sanford Alderfer Auction Company**, 501 Fairgrounds Road, Hatfield, PA 19440, USA. Tel: 001 215 393 3000. www.alderferauction.com. 174l, 176bl. **Sara Covelli Collection**. 174br, 187cr. **Seaside Toy Center**, 179 Main Street, Westerly, Rhode Island 02891, USA. Tel: 001 401 596 0962. 257cr. **Seventies Watches**. Tel: 020 7274 4342. www.70s-watches.com. 204bl, 204bc, 204br, 205bl, 205bcl, 205bcr, 206bl, 206bc, 206br, 206tr, 207R2l, 207tl, 207R3l, 207br, 207tr. **Sign of the Tymes**, 2 Morris Farm Road, Lafayette, NJ 07848, USA. Tel: 001 973 383 6028. www.millantiques.com. 314cl, 314tr, 315r, 320cl, 320br, 320cr, 321R4l, 321tr. **Simon Dunlavey Collection**. 90bl, 90bc, 90br, 90tr, 91cr, 91br, 91bc, 91bl, 91c. **Sloans**. No longer trading. 230br. **Sparkle Moore at The Girl Can't Help It**, Alfies Antique Market, Shop G100 & G116, Ground Floor, 13–25 Church Street, London NW8 8DT. Tel: 020 7724 8984 or 07958 515 614. www.sparklemoore.com. 123R4r, 176tr, 184br, 188b '1950s', 189bl, 189br, 196br, 196cl, 197tr, 197R3l, 197bl, 197br. **Sylvie Spectrum**, Grays Antique Market, Stand 372, 58 Davies Street, London W1Y 2LB. Tel: 020 7629 3501. 193br, 202tr. **Steinberg and Tolkien**, 193 King's Road, Chelsea, London SW3 5ED. Tel: 020 7376 3660. 175br, 179br, 180bl, 181tr, 181br, 181cr, 181tc, 182bl, 182br, 182bc, 182tr, 183cr, 183bc, 183br, 183tl, 186tr, 187tl, 187br, 188b '1940s', 188b '1960s', 188b '1970s', 189tc. **Roxanne Stuart**. Tel: 001 888 750 8869/215 750 8868. 112br, 113b, 113tr, 123b, 198br, 200bc(&br), 201bc, 372cl. **Sue Norman at Antiquarius**, Stand L4, Antiquarius, 135 King's Road, Chelsea, London SW3 4PW. Tel: 020 7352 7217. www.sue-norman.demon.co.uk. 106tr, 106bl, 106c, 107bc, 107cr, 109bl, 109br. **Sue Scrivens Collection**. 100bl, 100br, 100tr, 101tr, 101bc, 101bl, 102cl, 102bl, 102br, 102cr, 102tr, 103tl, 103tr, 103R2r, 103R3r, 103bl, 103br. **T.W. Conroy**, 36 Oswego Street, Baldwinsville, NY 13027, USA. Tel: 001 315 638 6434. www.twconroy.com. 140br. **T.W. Gaze & Sons**, Diss Auction Rooms, Roydon Road, Diss, Norfolk IP22 4LN. Tel: 01379 650 306. www.twgaze.co.uk. 49bl, 259br, 277br, 278bl(&c), 278br, 278bc, 279bl, 280tr, 281bl 'Instruments', 281bl 'Magazines', 282tr, 283bl, 373cr. **Tagore Ltd**, Stand 302, Grays Antique Market, 58 Davies Street, London W1Y 2LP. Tel: 020 7499 0158. tagore@grays.clara.net. 129bl. **Take-A-Boo Emporium**, 1927 Avenue Road, Toronto, Ontario M5M 4A2 Canada. Tel/Fax: 001 416 785 4555. www.takeaboo.com. 79bl, 202bl, 203tl, 204tr, 205br. **Tennants Auctioneers**, The Auction Centre, Leyburn, North Yorkshire DL8 5SG. Tel: 01969 623780. www.tennants.co.uk. 286c, 288bl, 289cl, 289br, 292tr. **Terry Rodgers & Melody**, 30 & 31 Manhattan Art and Antique Center, 1050 2nd Avenue, New York, NY 10022, USA. Tel: 001 212 758 3164. melodyjewelnyc@aol.com. 201cr. **Toy Heroes**, 42 Westway, Caterham-on-the-Hill, Surrey CR3 5TP. Tel: 01883 348 001. www.toyheroes.co.uk. 258bl, 259bl, 259cr, 260tr, 261br, 261cr. **Toy Road Antiques**, 2200 Highland Street, Canal Winchester, OH 43110, USA. Tel: 001 614 834 1786. toyroad@aol.com. 117cr. **Trio**, Stand L24, Grays Antique Market, 1–7 Davies Mews, London W1Y 2LP. Tel: 020 7493 2736. www.trio-london.fsnet.co.uk. 136bl, 136bc, 136tr. **Vectis Auctions Limited**, Fleck Way, Thornaby, Stockton-on-Tees, Cleveland TS17 9JZ. Tel: 01642 750 616. www.vectis.co.uk. 215br, 216br, 217br, 217r, 218r, 219br, 224br, 225cl, 225tr, 225t, 225bl, 225cr, 225br, 225cl, 258br. **Ventisemo**, 4 Unit S001, Alfies Antique Market, 13–25 Church Street, London NW8 8DT. Tel: 07767 498 766. 194bl, 215bl, 261tl. **Victoriana Dolls**, 101 Portobello Rd, London W11 2BQ. Tel: 01737 249 525. heather.bond@total-serve.co.uk. 203tr, 236bcl, 236bcr, 237cr. **VinMag**, 39/43 Brewer Street, London W1R 9UD. Tel: 020 7439 8525. www.vinmag.com. 265cr, 306bl, 306br, 307bl, 307bc, 307br, 307cr, 323br. **Vintage Eyeware**. Tel: 001 917 721 6546. www.vintage-eyeware.com. 184cl, 184bl, 184tr, 185tl, 185R2r, 185b, 185R3l. **Vintage to Vogue**, 28 Milsom Street, Bath, Avon BA1 1DG. Tel: 01225 337 323. www.vintagetovoguebath.com. 177bl. **W. & H. Peacock**, 26 Newnham Street, Bedford MK40 3JR. Tel: 01234 266 366. www.peacockauction.co.uk. 48tr, 233br, 236tr, 237br, 240tr, 268br, 269t 'Pottery figures'. **Wallis and Wallis West Steet Auction Galleries**, Lewes, East Sussex BN7 2NJ. Tel: 01273 480 208. www.wallisandwallis.co.uk. 88t, 89t, 89bl, 89br, 89r, 139tr, 149br, 213br, 213tl, 214tr, 215cr, 215c, 216b, 216tr, 217t, 218tr, 219tl, 219tr, 220tr, 220br, 221cr, 227t, 246b, 247tl, 247tr, 265br. **Mike Weedon**, 7 Camden Passage, Islington, London N1 8EA. Tel: 020 7226 5319. www.mikeweedonantiques.co.uk. 139tl. **Woolley and Wallis**, 51–61 Castle Street, Salisbury, Wiltshire SP1 3SU. Tel: 01722 424 500. www.woolleyandwallis.co.uk. 24tr, 30bl, 38tr 41bl, 67br, 128bl, 215tl, 355br, 355tl, 360tr, 361tr. **Bonny Yankauer**. bonnyy@aol.com. 199tr.

**JACKET IMAGES**

Front: **Auction Team Köln**, fcra. **Cheffins**, ca; **Cristobal**, cla. **Fellow's & Sons**, fcla. **Woolley and Wallis**, cra. Back: **Design Twentieth Century**, b. **Gallery 1930 Susie Cooper Ceramics Art Deco**, bl. **Harper General Store**, cr. **Hope and Glory**, c. **Wallis and Wallis West Street Auction Galleries**, cl.

**ARCHIVE PICTURE ACKNOWLEDGEMENTS**

The publisher would like to thank the following people, museums, and photographic libraries for permission to reproduce their material. Every care has been taken to trace copyright holders. However, if we have omitted anyone we apologise and will, if informed, make corrections to any future edition.

**Alamy Images/Janine Wiedel Photolibrary**, 12bl. **Camera Press**, London/Heilemann. 280b. **Elizabeth Whiting Associates**, London. 375tl. **Hulton Archive/Getty Images**, London. 34br, 92br, 129bc, 316bl, 360bl, 365tc, 368br. **Mary Evans Picture Library**, London. 230bl. **The Museum of London**. 156bl. **Rex Features/Nils Jorgensen**. 10bc. **Stoke-on-Trent City Archives**. 22bl.

**PUBLISHER'S ACKNOWLEDGEMENTS**

Dorling Kindersley would like to thank Angela Wilkes, Paula Regan, and Caroline Hunt for editorial assistance, Sarah Duncan for picture research, and Joanna Walker and Anna Plucinska for design assistance.